JOSHUA

THE NIV
APPLICATION
COMMENTARY

From biblical text . . . to contemporary life

JOSHUA

THE NIV APPLICATION COMMENTARY

From biblical text . . . to contemporary life

ROBERT L. HUBBARD JR.

ZONDERVAN®

ZONDERVAN.com/
AUTHORTRACKER
follow your favorite authors

ZONDERVAN

The NIV Application Commentary: Joshua
Copyright © 2009 by Robert L. Hubbard Jr.

Zondervan, *Grand Rapids, Michigan 49530*

Library of Congress Cataloging-in-Publication Data

Hubbard, Robert L., Jr., 1943-
    Joshua / Robert L. Hubbard Jr..
        p. cm. (The NIV application commentary)
    Includes bibliographical references and index.
    ISBN 978-0-310-20934-8 (hardcover)
    1. Bible. O.T. Joshua—Commentaries. I. Title.
  BS1295.53.H83 2009
  222'.207—dc22
                                              2009007655

Printed in the United States of America

11 12 13 14 15 • 25 24 23 22 21 20 19 18 17 16 15 14 13 12 11 10 9 8 7 6 5 4

For Pam
wife, lover, friend

The NIV Application Commentary Series

When complete, the NIV Application Commentary
will include the following volumes:

Old Testament Volumes

Genesis, John H. Walton

Exodus, Peter Enns

Leviticus/Numbers, Roy Gane

Deuteronomy, Daniel I. Block

Joshua, Robert L. Hubbard Jr.

Judges/Ruth, K. Lawson Younger

1-2 Samuel, Bill T. Arnold

1-2 Kings, August H. Konkel

1-2 Chronicles, Andrew E. Hill

Ezra/Nehemiah, Douglas J. Green

Esther, Karen H. Jobes

Job, Dennis R. Magary

Psalms Volume 1, Gerald H. Wilson

Psalms Volume 2, Jamie A. Grant

Proverbs, Paul Koptak

Ecclesiastes/Song of Songs, Iain Provan

Isaiah, John N. Oswalt

Jeremiah/Lamentations, J. Andrew Dearman

Ezekiel, Iain M. Duguid

Daniel, Tremper Longman III

Hosea/Amos/Micah, Gary V. Smith

Jonah/Nahum/Habakkuk/Zephaniah,
   James Bruckner

Joel/Obadiah/Malachi, David W. Baker

Haggai/Zechariah, Mark J. Boda

New Testament Volumes

Matthew, Michael J. Wilkins

Mark, David E. Garland

Luke, Darrell L. Bock

John, Gary M. Burge

Acts, Ajith Fernando

Romans, Douglas J. Moo

1 Corinthians, Craig Blomberg

2 Corinthians, Scott Hafemann

Galatians, Scot McKnight

Ephesians, Klyne Snodgrass

Philippians, Frank Thielman

Colossians/Philemon, David E. Garland

1-2 Thessalonians, Michael W. Holmes

1-2 Timothy/Titus, Walter L. Liefeld

Hebrews, George H. Guthrie

James, David P. Nystrom

1 Peter, Scot McKnight

2 Peter/Jude, Douglas J. Moo

Letters of John, Gary M. Burge

Revelation, Craig S. Keener

To see which titles are available,
visit our web site at www.zondervan.com

Contents

NIV Application Commentary
Series Introduction

THE NIV APPLICATION COMMENTARY Series is unique. Most commentaries help us make the journey from our world back to the world of the Bible. They enable us to cross the barriers of time, culture, language, and geography that separate us from the biblical world. Yet they only offer a one-way ticket to the past and assume that we can somehow make the return journey on our own. Once they have explained the *original meaning* of a book or passage, these commentaries give us little or no help in exploring its *contemporary significance.* The information they offer is valuable, but the job is only half done.

Recently, a few commentaries have included some contemporary application as *one* of their goals. Yet that application is often sketchy or moralistic, and some volumes sound more like printed sermons than commentaries.

The primary goal of the NIV Application Commentary Series is to help you with the difficult but vital task of bringing an ancient message into a modern context. The series not only focuses on application as a finished product but also helps you think through the *process* of moving from the original meaning of a passage to its contemporary significance. These are commentaries, not popular expositions. They are works of reference, not devotional literature.

The format of the series is designed to achieve the goals of the series. Each passage is treated in three sections: *Original Meaning, Bridging Contexts,* and *Contemporary Significance.*

THIS SECTION HELPS YOU understand the meaning of the biblical text in its original context. All of the elements of traditional exegesis—in concise form—are discussed here. These include the historical, literary, and cultural context of the passage. The authors discuss matters related to grammar and syntax and the meaning of biblical words.[1] They also seek to explore the main ideas of the passage and how the biblical author develops those ideas.

---

1. Please note that in general, when the authors discuss words in the original biblical languages, the series uses a general rather than a scholarly method of transliteration.

After reading this section, you will understand the problems, questions, and concerns of the *original audience* and how the biblical author addressed those issues. This understanding is foundational to any legitimate application of the text today.

THIS SECTION BUILDS A bridge between the world of the Bible and the world of today, between the original context and the contemporary context, by focusing on both the timely and timeless aspects of the text.

God's Word is *timely*. The authors of Scripture spoke to specific situations, problems, and questions. The author of Joshua encouraged the faith of his original readers by narrating the destruction of Jericho, a seemingly impregnable city, at the hands of an angry warrior God (Josh. 6). Paul warned the Galatians about the consequences of circumcision and the dangers of trying to be justified by law (Gal. 5:2–5). The author of Hebrews tried to convince his readers that Christ is superior to Moses, the Aaronic priests, and the Old Testament sacrifices. John urged his readers to "test the spirits" of those who taught a form of incipient Gnosticism (1 John 4:1–6). In each of these cases, the timely nature of Scripture enables us to hear God's Word in situations that were *concrete* rather than abstract.

Yet the timely nature of Scripture also creates problems. Our situations, difficulties, and questions are not always directly related to those faced by the people in the Bible. Therefore, God's word to them does not always seem relevant to us. For example, when was the last time someone urged you to be circumcised, claiming that it was a necessary part of justification? How many people today care whether Christ is superior to the Aaronic priests? And how can a "test" designed to expose incipient Gnosticism be of any value in a modern culture?

Fortunately, Scripture is not only timely but *timeless*. Just as God spoke to the original audience, so he still speaks to us through the pages of Scripture. Because we share a common humanity with the people of the Bible, we discover a *universal dimension* in the problems they faced and the solutions God gave them. The timeless nature of Scripture enables it to speak with power in every time and in every culture.

Those who fail to recognize that Scripture is both timely and timeless run into a host of problems. For example, those who are intimidated by timely books such as Hebrews, Galatians, or Deuteronomy might avoid reading them because they seem meaningless today. At the other extreme, those who are convinced of the timeless nature of Scripture, but who fail to discern its timely element, may "wax eloquent" about the Melchizedekian priesthood to a sleeping congregation, or worse still, try to apply the holy wars of the Old Testament in a physical way to God's enemies today.

The purpose of this section, therefore, is to help you discern what is timeless in the timely pages of the Bible—and what is not. For example, how do the holy wars of the Old Testament relate to the spiritual warfare of the New? If Paul's primary concern is not circumcision (as he tells us in Gal. 5:6), what *is* he concerned about? If discussions about the Aaronic priesthood or Melchizedek seem irrelevant today, what is of abiding value in these passages? If people try to "test the spirits" today with a test designed for a specific first-century heresy, what other biblical test might be more appropriate?

Yet this section does not merely uncover that which is timeless in a passage but also helps you to see *how* it is uncovered. The authors of the commentaries seek to take what is implicit in the text and make it explicit, to take a process that normally is intuitive and explain it in a logical, orderly fashion. How do we know that circumcision is not Paul's primary concern? What clues in the text or its context help us realize that Paul's real concern is at a deeper level?

Of course, those passages in which the historical distance between us and the original readers is greatest require a longer treatment. Conversely, those passages in which the historical distance is smaller or seemingly nonexistent require less attention.

One final clarification. Because this section prepares the way for discussing the contemporary significance of the passage, there is not always a sharp distinction or a clear break between this section and the one that follows. Yet when both sections are read together, you should have a strong sense of moving from the world of the Bible to the world of today.

THIS SECTION ALLOWS THE biblical message to speak with as much power today as it did when it was first written. How can you apply what you learned about Jerusalem, Ephesus, or Corinth to our present-day needs in Chicago, Los Angeles, or London? How can you take a message originally spoken in Greek, Hebrew, and Aramaic and communicate it clearly in our own language? How can you take the eternal truths originally spoken in a different time and culture and apply them to the similar-yet-different needs of our culture?

In order to achieve these goals, this section gives you help in several key areas.

(1) It helps you identify contemporary situations, problems, or questions that are truly comparable to those faced by the original audience. Because contemporary situations are seldom identical to those faced by the original audience, you must seek situations that are analogous if your applications are to be relevant.

(2) This section explores a variety of contexts in which the passage might be applied today. You will look at personal applications, but you will also be encouraged to think beyond private concerns to the society and culture at large.

(3) This section will alert you to any problems or difficulties you might encounter in seeking to apply the passage. And if there are several legitimate ways to apply a passage (areas in which Christians disagree), the author will bring these to your attention and help you think through the issues involved.

In seeking to achieve these goals, the contributors to this series attempt to avoid two extremes. They avoid making such specific applications that the commentary might quickly become dated. They also avoid discussing the significance of the passage in such a general way that it fails to engage contemporary life and culture.

Above all, contributors to this series have made a diligent effort not to sound moralistic or preachy. The NIV Application Commentary Series does not seek to provide ready-made sermon materials but rather tools, ideas, and insights that will help you communicate God's Word with power. If we help you to achieve that goal, then we have fulfilled the purpose for this series.

The Editors

General Editor's Preface

IN HIS BOOK *Liquid Modernity*, British sociologist Zygmunt Bauman describes the first decade of the twenty-first century as a time of unparalleled fluidity. Nothing is permanent. Even the solidity our parents counted on in terms of jobs, relationships, and social structures have all become as ephemeral as lace. Concrete has turned to gelatin, rock into shifting sand.

People are terrified. The great promise of globalization—freedom—not so long ago touted as an unparalleled blessing, has turned to ashes in the mouths of its beneficiaries. Blessed freedom, freedom beyond their wildest dreams, seems to produce nothing but anxiety. Religious terrorism doesn't help. Leave it to the religions to use their freedom to press irreligious agendas.

The same nation states that have slowly but surely lost their centrality and power with the coming of new technologies and worldwide trading markets sense their chance to become important again. Nations begin to promise security. Freedom from fear, whether economic or military, becomes a mantra. In exchange for just a little of that freedom—that freedom that after all has caused much of the anxiety—we will give you back peace of mind.

It is a world gone mad. The religions and the nation-states, in the past our Rocks of Gibraltar, have turned into the agents of fluidity and anxiety.

IN THE BIBLICAL BOOK of Joshua, the author describes a time of great flux. The children of God are poised to enter the land long promised to them. Their assignment is to take the land by force. The inhabitants of the land are, according to rumor, gigantic, fierce, and ready to fight to defend their turf. Slavery in Egypt was bad. Forty years of wandering in the wilderness caused great suffering. But all-out war?

The Israelites are terrified. The promise of a new land filled with milk and honey not so long ago seemed like a dream come true. Now who can think it is possibly worth the anguish and fear that the prospects facing them will undoubtedly cause? It doesn't help that they have had a leadership change, that the man who led them for forty plus years is gone and in his place a new, untested leader.

There were no nation-states to give Middle Eastern people of this era security. This was a tribal culture. Each tribe (extended family really) had its god. It was this family god that provided security. The god, through sign and wonder, told the people when to fight and when to flee, when to hunker down and when to move on. Security came from obeying the family god—and trusting that their family god was more powerful than their neighbor's god.

It was a world gone mad.

TWO WORLDS, SEPARATED by up to 3,500 years and enormous social changes, faced with the same problem. Human anxiety caused by relying overmuch on our own technology, on our war-making ability, on false gods. Interestingly, the two worlds with the same problem have available to them the same, fail-safe solution:

> Be strong and very courageous. Be careful to obey all the law my servant Moses gave you; do not turn from it to the right or to the left, that you may be successful wherever you go. Do not let this Book of the Law depart from your mouth; meditate on it day and night, so that you may be careful to do everything written on it. Then you will be prosperous and successful. Have I not commanded you? Be strong and courageous. Do not be terrified; do not be discouraged, for the LORD your God will be with you wherever you go. (Joshua 1:7–9)

The inhabitants of both worlds—liquid modernity and biblical tribalism—tend to make two fundamental errors that give free rein to uncontrolled angst.

The first error mistakes the source of freedom. The error is to mistakenly think that freedom comes from not having to obey anyone. *Freedom is not the absence of obedience but the result of it.* Anxiety, as we have seen, comes from the absence of obedience. True freedom comes after we choose to obey God and God's law.

The second mistake is to think that we are strong and courageous because we somehow find these two virtues inside ourselves. Unfortunately we don't—they are not there. *Strength and valor come not from inside us but from God.* When God speaks to Joshua, he does not tell him to look deep inside himself and somehow release the strong and courageous being that resides there. No, God commands him to be strong and courageous. Obeying this command produces the desired emotions.

What has come in our day and age as existential angst is cured by the 3,500-year-old words recorded in the first chapter of Joshua. Read and obey.

Terry C. Muck

Author's Preface

IT IS A PLEASURE to offer this commentary in the service of serious Bible readers in worshiping communities. Were the book not part of this series, I would be tempted to title it *Surprised by Joshua* since its preparation involved many surprises, most of them pleasant. The book of Joshua itself came wondrously alive for me, and the series' requirement to combine typical exegesis with application proved to be a stretching experience both intellectually and spiritually. At one point, the process confronted me personally with a question: did I love God or not? (After honest reflection, I concluded that I did). In the end, the book leaves me humbled and ashamed of how far short my life falls from its ideals, but also uplifted at the powerful, loving presence at work in and through me. My hope is that the book will in some small measure facilitate similar spiritual awareness in readers.

As with any project, there are plenty of people to thank for their contributions behind the scenes. I am grateful for the invitation to contribute to this series, and especially to Professor John Walton for kindly and expertly improving the manuscript. The men in my small accountability group (Paul, Steve, Don, and Max) supported and encouraged me as I navigated my way along. Thanks for expert and long-suffering help go to my recent teaching assistants at North Park Theological Seminary: David Mortimer, Dr. Liang her-Wu, Paul Corner, and Andrew Freeman. Andrew completed most of the indexes. I also happily say thanks to friends and colleagues who generously commented on select portions of the book: Dr. Timothy S. Laniak, Dr. William W. Wells, and the Rev. Andy Sebanc. The manuscript was completed during an enjoyable sabbatical in residence at Regent College, Vancouver, B.C. It is pleasure to thank North Park Theological Seminary for granting the sabbatical and Regent College for its warm hospitality and fine library resources.

My wife, Pam, read and commented on the entire manuscript and helped with the bibliography. She gave me what she called "the view from the pews" and helped keep the book grounded in the realities of daily Christian living. It is a joy to dedicate this book to her, not only because she helped in its production, but especially because of her love, encouragement, prayers, and wisdom throughout our long life of love and adventure together.

Author's Preface

Permit me two small authorial comments. First, at several key points I have included liturgies through which congregations might respond to given texts of Joshua. Second, parts of the book of Joshua resemble a telephone book or grocery list, and readers may be tempted to skip them. But, in fact, they mark some of the most important parts of the book. To miss them will be to miss one of the richest surprises in the book of Joshua.

Robert L. Hubbard Jr.
North Park Theological Seminary

Abbreviations

AB	Anchor Bible
ABD	*Anchor Bible Dictionary*
AEHL	A. Negev and S. Gibson, *Archaeological Encyclopedia of the Holy Land*, revised and updated edition, 2001
Ai I or II	Israel's first or second battle at the city of Ai
ANET	J. B. Pritchard, ed., *Ancient Near Eastern Texts Relating to the Old Testament*, 3rd edition
ASOR	American Schools of Oriental Research
BAR	*Biblical Archaeology Review*
BASOR	*Bulletin of the American Schools of Oriental Research*
b. B. Bat.	Babylonian Talmud: Tractate Baba Bathra
BBB	Bonner Biblische Beiträge
BBR	*Bulletin of Biblical Research*
BDAG	W. Bauer, F. W. Danker, W. F. Arndt, and F. W. Gingrich, *Greek-English Lexicon of the New Testament and Other Early Christian Literature*, 3rd edition
BETL	Bibliotheca Ephemeridum Theologicarum Lovaniensium
BHS	*Biblia Hebraica Stuttgartensia*
Bib	*Biblica*
BJS	Brown Judaic Studies
BRS	The Biblical Resource Series
BZ	*Biblische Zeitschrift*
ca.	Lat. *circa* ("approximately")
CANE	J. M. Sasson, ed., *Civilizations of the Ancient Near East*
CBA	Y. Aharoni, M. Avi-Yonah, A. F. Rainey, and Z. Safrai, *The Carta Bible Atlas*, 4th edition
CBOT	Coniectanea Biblica, Old Testament
CBQ	*Catholic Biblical Quarterly*
CBR	*Currents in Biblical Research*
cent.	century
CHANE	*Culture and History of the Ancient Near East*
COS	W. W. Hallo and K. L. Younger, Jr., eds. *The Context of Scripture*, 3 vols.
CTJ	*Calvin Theological Journal*
DCH	D. J. A. Clines, ed., *Dictionary of Classical Hebrew*

Abbreviations

DDD	*Dictionary of Deities and Demons in the Bible*, ed. Karel van der Toorn
DH	Deuteronomistic History
DOTHB	B. T. Arnold and H. G. M. Williamson, ed., *Dictionary of the Old Testament Historical Books*
EA	El-Amarna Letters
EDB	*Eerdmans Dictionary of the Bible*
esp.	especially
ExpTim	*Expository Times*
GKC	Gesenius, Kautzsch, Cowley, *Gesenius' Hebrew Grammar*
HAR	*Hebrew Annual Review*
HAT	Handbuch zum Alten Testament
Heb.	Hebrew
hi.	Hiphil
hithp.	Hithpael
idem	Latin for "the same author just cited"
IEJ	*Israel Exploration Journal*
ITC	International Theological Commentary
JAOS	*Journal of the American Oriental Society*
JANES	*Journal of the Ancient Near Eastern Society*
JBL	*Journal of Biblical Literature*
JM	P. Joüon and T. Muraoka, *A Grammar of Biblical Hebrew*
JNSL	*Journal of Northwest Semitic Languages*
JQR	*Jewish Quarterly Review*
JSOT	*Journal for the Study of the Old Testament*
JSOTSup	Journal for the Study of the Old Testament Supplement Series
JSS	*Journal of Semitic Studies*
KB	L. Koehler and W. Baumgartner, *Hebräisches und Aramäisches Lexikon*, 3rd edition
KJV	King James Version
LXX	Septuagint
mi.	miles
MT	Masoretic Text
Naʾaman	N. Naʾaman, *Borders and Districts in Biblical Historiography*
NAC	New American Commentary
NDBT	T. D. Alexander and B. S. Rosner, eds., *The New Dictionary of Biblical Theology*
NEAEHL	E. Stern, ed., *New Encyclopedia of Archaeological Excavations in the Holy Land*
NICOT	New International Commentary on the Old Testament

NIDB	K. D. Sakenfeld, ed., *New Interpreter's Dictionary of the Bible*
NIDNTT	C. Brown, ed., *New International Dictionary of New Testament Theology*
NIDOTTE	W. VanGemeren, ed., *New International Dictionary of Old Testament Theology and Exegesis*
NIGTC	New International Greek Testament Commentary
NRSV	New Revised Standard Version
OEANE	E. M. Meyers, *The Oxford Encyclopedia of Archaeology in the Near East*
OTG	Old Testament Guides
OTL	Old Testament Library
OTS	Oudtestamentische Studiën
pi.	Piel
REB	Revised English Bible
RevExp	*Review and Expositor*
RTR	*Reformed Theological Review*
SBJT	*The Southern Baptist Journal of Theology*
SBLDS	Society of Biblical Literature Dissertation Series
SEÅ	*Svensk Exegetisk Årsbok*
SJOT	*Scandanavian Journal of the Old Testament*
TDNT	*Theological Dictionary of the New Testament*
TDOT	*Theological Dictionary of the Old Testament*
THAT	*Theologisiches Handwörterbuch zum Alten Testament*
TNIV	Today's New International Version
TNK	Jewish TANAKH
TOTC	Tyndale Old Testament Commentary
TrinJ	*Trinity Journal*
v.	verse
vv.	verses
VT	*Vetus Testamentum*
VTSup	Supplements to *Vetus Testamentum*
WBC	Word Biblical Commentary
Williams	R. J. Williams, *Hebrew Syntax: An Outline*
WO	B. K. Waltke and M. O'Connor, *An Introduction to Biblical Hebrew Syntax*
ZAW	*Zeitscrift für die Alttestamentliche Wissenschaft*
ZDPV	*Zeitschrift des Deutschen Palästina-Vereins*
//	parallels, is parallel to

Introduction

BAM! THAT IS THE mental sound I imagine readers hear when they encounter the book of Joshua for the first time. Reading it can be, frankly, a jarring experience, especially if one's first exposure to the Bible comes through hearing the gospel from friends and through immersion in the New Testament. The New Testament does not prepare readers for the world of military violence and ethnic cleansing in Joshua's pages. Serious, troubling questions about God's attitude toward his created peoples arise, questions with no easy answer. But the book of Joshua presents itself, warts (and wars!) and all, and asks readers to let it tell its story from its point of view and out of its ancient context. It asks them to give it the benefit of the doubt and permit it to speak to them.

This commentary aims to give its voice a clear hearing—to translate its ancient cultural form in such a way that it freely speaks about the life of faith today. Basically, the book of Joshua tells how biblical Israel navigated a major historical transition early in its national life. For ancient Israel, the transition concerns a change of leadership from Moses to Joshua and a change of lifestyle—from life as wandering clans of herdsmen to life as a settled nation of farmers on its own land. The book shows that guiding these changes is Israel's God, Yahweh, through his chosen servant, Joshua. The introductory sections to follow set the scene for entering the book of Joshua and the ancient world about which it reports.

Getting Started

TITLE AND CANON. Jewish tradition claims that "Joshua wrote the book that bears his name,"[1] but few affirm that today. More likely, the book of Joshua is named for its main character whose exploits as Israel's leader after Moses dominate its contents. The book is the sixth book in the Hebrew Biblej24, following the five books of its first canonical section, the Torah. Joshua also marks the first book of the canon's second section, the Prophets—more specifically, the subsection known as the Former (i.e., "earlier") Prophets, books often designated as "historical books" (Joshua, Judges, 1–2 Samuel,

---

1. See *b. B. Bat.* 14b.

1 – 2 Kings). The Latter Prophets comprise the second subsection and include books familiar to most readers as prophetic (e.g., Isaiah, Jeremiah, Ezekiel, and the twelve minor prophets). Thus, the compilers of the canon regarded Joshua as a "prophetic book," either because they traced its origin to a prophet (or prophets), or because they believed it proclaimed God's word. At the end of the book, Joshua invokes the messenger formula like a typical prophet ("This is what the LORD, the God of Israel, says") and proclaims Yahweh's word in the first person (Josh. 24:2 – 13). This may have influenced their thinking.

Text. Compared to other biblical books, the Hebrew text (MT) of Joshua is in relatively good condition, so scholars rarely need to propose emendations for it to make sense. It provides the textual basis for the present commentary. The situation with the ancient Greek translation of the Old Testament (the Septuagint or LXX), however, is more problematic. It is preserved in several versions (or recensions) with the Old Greek being the most important.[2] Its overall length is about five per cent shorter than the MT, even lacking a few verses present in the latter (6:4; 8:13, 26; 10:15; 20:4 – 6). Scholars have wondered how to account for the LXX. Does it imply that the translators used a Hebrew text different from MT, or did they simply abbreviate the MT while rendering it into Greek? The two fragments of Joshua among the Dead Sea Scrolls seem to confirm the former assumption and suggest that the Qumran scribes also made use of a third Hebrew text, one that even differed from MT.[3]

The Contents of the Book of Joshua

THE BOOK OF JOSHUA tells the story of how Joshua led the Israelites to conquer and settle in Canaan, the land of promise. The book proceeds through three main sections: reports about the conquest (chs. 1 – 12), reports about Joshua's distribution of tribal inheritances (chs. 13 – 21), and reports during the early years of settlement (chs. 22 – 24).

The conquest section opens with Yahweh's affirmation of Joshua as Moses' successor after the latter's death. Joshua has his officers prepare the people to enter the land while he himself reconfirms an earlier promise by the Transjordanian tribes to help the other tribes conquer land west of the Jordan (ch. 1). As his first strategic move, Joshua dispatches spies to

---

2. Cf. L. J. Greenspoon, "The Book of Joshua — Part I: Texts and Versions," *CBR* 3.2 (2005): 229 – 61; idem, *Textual Studies in the Book of Joshua* (HSM 28; Chico, Calif.: Scholars Press, 1983).

3. A. H. W. Curtis, *Joshua* (OTG; Sheffield: Sheffield Academic Press, 1994), 12 – 14.

Jericho, where a Canaanite prostitute named Rahab shelters them, reveals Canaanite terror of Yahweh and Israel, and receives an oath of safety from the spies (ch. 2). On Yahweh's orders, the ark of the covenant leads Israel's dramatic, ceremonial crossing of the Jordan. When it reaches the river, the Jordan stops flowing and Israel crosses on dry land, a miracle whose meaning Israel is to teach future generations (chs. 3–4). On Joshua's orders, a prechosen representative from each tribe also carries a stone from the dry riverbed, and Joshua arranges the twelve into a stone memorial at Gilgal.

At Gilgal, Israel's first campsite inside the land, Joshua circumcises all uncircumcised males and leads Israel in celebrating the Passover (ch. 5). These acts ritually sanctify Israel for doing Yahweh war and celebrate their long-awaited arrival in the Promised Land. Further, Israel's daily wilderness staple, manna, stops, so produce of Canaan will now feed them. Empowered by a surprise, mysterious meeting with the commander of Yahweh's heavenly army (5:13–15), Joshua leads a seven-day ceremonial conquest and fiery destruction of Jericho—sparing Rahab, of course—and curses the city (ch. 6).

Advised by a second spy mission, Joshua sends a small military force inland to capture the city of Ai, but they are unexpectedly routed. The defeat upsets Joshua but also reveals the secret sin of a Judahite named Achan at Jericho. Lot-casting unmasks him as the criminal responsible for the rout, and Joshua and Israel take him to Trouble Valley, where they stone and burn him and his family. They pile rocks over him to mark his gravesite, and the name "Trouble" Valley forever recalls the terrible "trouble" he caused Israel (ch. 7). On Yahweh's orders, Joshua and the whole army again attack Ai, this time toppling it by a clever ambush. Joshua burns the city and executes its king, piling stones over his body to mark his burial place (ch. 8).

The implications of Ai's fall to Israel so frightens kings in Canaan that they gather to prepare for war. But one threatened ethnic group, the Gibeonites, visits Gilgal pretending to be foreigners on a long trip to make peace with Israel. Their ruse succeeds and Israel swears an oath by Yahweh to seal the treaty. When their deception comes to light, Israel lets the Gibeonites live but assigns them permanently to supply Yahweh's sanctuary with wood and water (ch. 9). Learning of the treaty, the king of Jerusalem rallies Canaanite allies to lay siege to Gibeon, but with Yahweh's assurance of victory, Israel breaks the siege and destroys the fleeing army. The day's highpoint is that Yahweh answers Joshua's petition to have the sun "stand still," and the battle has amazing results. Israel not only captures and executes the original five royal conspirators but, more importantly, ends up capturing all of southern Canaan (ch. 10).

Next, a northern campaign wins Israel all of northern Canaan and includes the burning of Hazor, its most prominent city. A long closing summary (ch. 11) celebrates the totality of Joshua's conquests—all of Canaan and even the dreaded Anakites—and its resulting rest from war. Joshua 12 tallies up Israel's victories: thirty-one kings defeated on both sides of the Jordan.

The book's second section opens with a survey of areas of Canaan not yet in Israel's hands and of lands in Transjordan previously distributed by Moses to Reuben, Gad, and East Manasseh (ch. 13). Then Joshua and Eleazar the priest distribute inheritances among the tribes, the first allotments going to the hero Caleb, Judah (chs. 14–15), Ephraim (ch. 16), and West Manasseh (ch. 17). But for the first time the Bible writer also sounds an ominous note, the inability of these tribes to dislodge the Canaanites from their inheritances (15:63; 16:10; 17:12–18). Next, after surveying the areas still available, the remaining seven tribes cast lots at Shiloh to distribute land to Benjamin (ch. 18), Simeon, Zebulun, Issachar, Asher, Naphtali, and Dan (ch. 19). The people of Israel also give Joshua his inheritance—the town of Timnath Serah in Ephraim (19:49–50)—and a concluding summary draws the distribution of tribal inheritances to a close (19:51). But the book's settlement section also reports two special land provisions: the naming of cities of refuge throughout the land (ch. 20) and the assignment of towns and pastures within every tribe's inheritance for the Levites (ch. 21). To conclude, the writer emphatically affirms that Yahweh has kept every promise, including his ancient promise of land and rest (21:43–45).

Finally, three dramatic scenes comprise the last section (chs. 22–24). Joshua dismisses the Transjordanian tribes to their inheritances east of the Jordan, the end of an important theme from ch. 1. The discovery of a huge, suspicious altar built by them on the west bank, however, leads a west-bank delegation to visit the Transjordanians and to accuse them of idolatry. But the east-bank tribes explain that the altar is not for idolatrous sacrifices but a witness to their worship of Yahweh and membership in Israel. Their persuasive explanation ends the threat of civil war (ch. 22).

About this time, Joshua gives a passionate farewell speech before an all-Israelite assembly, probably at Shiloh. He urgently warns Israel to keep their distance from the remaining Canaanites lest the latter ensnare them in religious compromise (ch. 23). At another national assembly at Shechem, Joshua leads Israel to renounce other gods and willingly to covenant together to serve only Yahweh. The book ends where it began—with death—specifically, with three burial notices of key Israelite leaders (Joshua, Joseph, and Eleazar). The author applauds Joshua and his generation of leaders for keeping Israel faithful to Yahweh during their tenure (ch. 24).

Who Is Joshua?

JOSHUA IS BEST KNOWN as the hero of the book that bears his name. He assumes the helm of Israel after Moses' death, leads the conquest and settlement of the land, and prepares Israel for life with Yahweh in Canaan after his death. Often overlooked, however, is his long, notable career prior to his succession of Moses. He makes his narrative debut rather suddenly in Exodus 17 when Moses abruptly tasks him — canonically, unheard-of before but certainly well known to Moses — with leading Israel's defense against Amalekite raiders (17:9–10).[4] Joshua's victory — fledgling Israel's first — early confirms his leadership abilities later put on display in Canaan. More telling, after the battle Yahweh orders Moses to make sure that Joshua hears God's promise to wipe out Amalek (v. 14). Implicitly, this comment hints that Joshua will eventually succeed Moses, although Israel has not yet even reached Sinai (v. 14).

Joshua next appears as Moses' aide during the period at Mount Sinai when Yahweh issues his instructions (Ex. 24:13; 33:11). Joshua's first reported words may reveal something of his military instincts. As he and Moses descend Mount Sinai, Joshua immediately interprets the shouting coming from the direction of Israel's camp as "the sound of war" (32:17). In reality, the ruckus is the sound of Israel worshiping the golden calf.

Joshua seems to emerge as a leader during Israel's itinerary through the wilderness toward Canaan. His second-reported words are a short, passionate plea that Moses stop two Israelite men from prophesying, a plea Moses rejects (Num. 11:28). More importantly, Joshua makes a fateful choice in connection with Moses' dispatch of twelve spies to reconnoiter Canaan. A man named Hoshea son of Nun represents the tribe of Ephraim among the spies (Num. 13:8), and a later parenthetical comment explains that Joshua was the name that Moses used for Hoshea (v. 16).[5] Moses' preference for Joshua (Heb. *yehošuaͨ*, "Yahweh is salvation") over Hoshea ("salvation") certainly highlights Joshua's relationship with Yahweh and perhaps even attests his life of loyal obedience.[6] Among the returning spies, only Joshua

---

4. Numbers 11:28 says that Joshua "had been Moses' aide since youth," so Exodus 17 may assume him to be in that position already despite the absence of the term "aide." For the Hebrew term, see below.

5. So NLT. If so, Hoshea probably was simply a shortened form of Joshua. Alternatively, Numbers 13:16 may claim that Moses actually changed Hoshea's name to Joshua; cf. NIV; NRSV; TNK.

6. Cf. D. A. Howard Jr., *Joshua* (NAC; Nashville: Broadman, 1998), 73. According to Howard, Joshua is the first personal name in the Bible to incorporate God's personal name, "Yahweh." Interestingly, the LXX renders "Joshua" as *Iesous*, the New Testament name for Jesus. For the thesis that biblical narratives purposely delayed Joshua's emergence until

and Caleb favor moving ahead with the invasion of Canaan. Their fateful choice places them among the few from the exodus generation whom Yahweh permits to enter the land (Num. 14:6, 30, 38; 26:65).[7]

Several important scenes prepare Israel for the leadership transition from Moses to Joshua. First, Yahweh has Moses publicly commission Joshua, his long-time "aide" (Heb. *mešaret*; Ex. 24:13; 33:11; Num. 11:28), as his successor. This step is necessary because Yahweh had already declared that Moses himself would not lead Israel into the land (Num. 20:12). In a dramatic scene played out before Eleazar the priest and all Israel, Moses lays his hands on Joshua, symbolically effecting Joshua's appointment (Num. 27:18–23).

Next, Joshua's subsequent narrative appearances in the Pentateuch also concern the coming transition from Moses to Joshua. Moses briefs his successor-designate (and Eleazar) on his special agreement with the Transjordanian tribes to ensure that Joshua and Eleazar hold them accountable, a duty Joshua in fact later carries out (Num. 32:28; cf. Josh. 1:12–18; 22:1–9). Further, through Mosaic appointment, Yahweh publicly names Joshua and Eleazar to oversee the distribution of inheritances among the tribes once Israel possesses the land (Num. 34:17; cf. Josh. 14:1; 19:51). Later, as assembled Israel watches, Moses publicly affirms Joshua as the one to lead Israel into the land and charges him to be "strong and courageous" (Deut. 31:3, 7).

In another dramatic scene, Yahweh orders Moses and Joshua to appear together at the Tent of Meeting so that Yahweh himself may commission Joshua (Deut. 31:14). Yahweh reiterates Moses' charge to Joshua ("be strong and courageous") and promises Joshua success and Yahweh's own presence with him in the future (v. 23). Later, Joshua accompanies Moses while the latter sings his lengthy song before all Israel (32:44). After Moses' death, Yahweh formally puts the long-expected plan into effect in a long personal address (Josh. 1:1–9). Israel readily accepts Joshua's leadership because Moses had conveyed to him "the spirit of wisdom" (Deut. 34:9), and the book of Joshua traces its hero's rise in popular stature during the conquest and settlement.[8] At his own death, Joshua receives a closing tribute similar to that accorded Moses (Josh. 24:31; Judg. 2:8). In retrospect,

---

Joshua 1, see G. C. Chirichigno, "The Use of the Epithet in the Characterization of Joshua," *TrinJ* 8 (1987): 72–79.

7. The others would include at least the high priest Eleazar and his son, Phinehas (Ex. 6:25; Num. 25:7; Josh. 14:1; 17:4; 22:13).

8. For an illuminating study of Joshua as a character, see P. J. Kissling, *Reliable Characters in the Primary History: Profiles of Moses, Joshua, Elijah, and Elisha* (JSOTSup 224; Sheffield: Sheffield Academic Press, 1996), 69–95.

what sets Joshua apart are two essential spiritual qualifications for leadership: he has God's spirit (Num. 27:18 ["a man in whom is the spirit"]) and shows a consistent pattern of obedience (32:12 ["followed the LORD wholeheartedly"]).

Finally, memories of Joshua surface in other biblical texts. First Kings 16:34 recalls Joshua's cursing of Jericho (cf. Josh. 6:26). About 450 B.C. Nehemiah observes that the Feast of Booths had not been observed in Israel since Joshua's days (Neh. 8:17), and ca. 400 B.C. the Chronicler records his genealogy (1 Chron. 7:27). Four centuries later, the soon-to-be-martyred Stephen mentions Joshua (Acts 7:45) and the writer of Hebrews contrasts the "rest" that Joshua did not give with the "rest" available to believers today (Heb. 4:8).

The Historical Setting of Joshua

THE GEOGRAPHICAL ARENA IN which the book of Joshua plays out is the Levant, including Canaan, Transjordan, Lebanon, and southern Syria. The time period assumed, however, depends on which of the two possible dates one prefers for the exodus from Egypt.[9] According to 1 Kings 6:1, 480 years intervened between the Exodus and Solomon's fourth year (966 B.C.), data that yield the so-called early date for the Exodus (1446 B.C.).[10] Those who hold to a late date, however, interpret the 480 years as a round, symbolic figure rather than a chronological one (i.e., 12 generations of 40 years each). Further, they argue that Rameses (Ex. 1:11; 12:37) is probably the royal city Pi-Rameses founded by Pharaoh Rameses II (1290–1224 B.C.), and so the Exodus must be dated to his reign (ca. 1250 B.C.). The present writer favors the latter view, but the discussion to follow will describe the situation in Canaan relevant to both dates (ca. 1500–1100 B.C.).[11]

---

9. For further details and bibliography on this discussion, cf. I. Provan, V. P. Long, and T. Longman III, *A Biblical History of Israel* (Louisville: Westminster John Knox, 2003), 131–32, 140; and T. Longman III and R. B. Dillard, *An Introduction to the Old Testament* (2nd ed.; Grand Rapids: Zondervan, 2006), 124–25.

10. The figure of 300 years prior to Jephthah that Israel had controlled Transjordan (Judg. 11:26) is also often cited as support.

11. Recently, Chavalas and Adamthwaite have argued the untenability of both the conventional "early" and "late" dates and the superiority of a fourteenth-century date for the Exodus-Conquest events. Whether their view will gather a consensus remains to be seen; cf. M. W. Chavalas and M. R. Adamthwaite, "Archaeological Light on the Old Testament," in D. W. Baker and B. T. Arnold, eds., *The Face of Old Testament Studies* (Grand Rapids: Baker, 1999), 78–90.

Introduction

Egypt dominates the politics of Syria-Palestine during this period, a hegemonic grip hard won in a century of wars (sixteenth to fifteenth cent. B.C.) that later loosens in the late twelfth-century B.C.[12] Canaan forms a key part of an Egyptian empire that extends north and east of Canaan and over which authorities posted by the pharaoh preside. The pharaonic representatives supervised the local princes, each of whom ruled a central fortified city and the small villages in the surrounding countryside. Some megacities like Hazor and Shechem even held sway over other cities within their geographical reach (cf. Josh. 10:1–5).

Most cities lay along the Mediterranean coast, the land's few rivers, and roads leading inland, but a few also were in the hill country (i.e., Shechem, Jerusalem). Ancient sources also mention a more mobile population in the region, pastoral peoples like the much-discussed *habiru*, who migrated seasonally in the land.[13] The late fifteenth century saw a decrease in the number of Canaanite cities and in the population in the hill country and the Negev. The number of Egyptian military forts and administrative centers, however, increased to maintain control and to raise revenues for the pharaoh.[14] Canaan sent him an impressive list of "profits": grain, wine, oil, horses, copper, timber, furniture, pottery, garments, and slaves. Pharaoh shared in the dynamic, prosperous "world economy" of international trade that at the time linked and enriched peoples of the entire eastern Mediterranean.[15]

The Amarna Letters offer brief, illuminating snapshots of life in Canaan in the following century (fourteenth cent. B.C.). To promote better Egyptian-Canaanite relations, Canaanite princes were taken to Egypt and raised there, and their daughters became part of the imperial court. Despite the strong Egyptian presence, local Canaanite rulers still jockeyed for political power with each other. The Egyptians often had to intervene in such conflicts, but they also played them to their own advantage. In the thirteenth to twelfth centuries, events on the edges of the empire — the Hittites' conquest of southern Syria and increasing incursions of herders into southern

---

12. For what follows, cf. A. Kuhrt, *The Ancient Near East c. 3000–330 B.C.* (New York; London: Routledge, 1995), 1:317–29; and A. E. Killebrew, *Biblical Peoples and Ethnicity* (Atlanta: Society of Biblical Literature, 2005), 24–28, who also summarizes the archaeological evidence (51–92).

13. Despite the linguistic similarities, the *habiru* cannot be equated with "Hebrews," but the latter may have formed part of them. The term is a catchall word for a diverse group living on the margins of ancient society ("runaway slaves, political exiles, brigands, and landless peasants"); cf. Kuhrt, *The Ancient Near East*, 1:320.

14. Ibid., 1:324.

15. The term and concept come from Killebrew, *Biblical Peoples and Ethnicity*, 21.

Canaan—spawned an increase in pharaonic campaigns, fortresses, and governor's palaces to tighten Egypt's grip.

About 1200 B.C., however, great changes swept lands in and along the Aegean Sea as well as countries along the eastern Mediterranean. A widespread political and economic crisis gripped the formerly stable and prosperous region.[16] The once-great Hittite empire disintegrated, and important cities like Ugarit (south Lebanon) and Emar (north Syria) suffered destruction and went unoccupied. In Greece, the once-important Mycenaean cities lost influence and were either destroyed or left vacant. By the mid-twelfth century, Egypt had completely retreated from Canaan.

As a result, a kind of "dark age" descends on the region until signs of recovery dawn in the tenth century.[17] At the same time (and perhaps because of the crisis), migrations of large people groups like the mysterious "sea peoples" known from Egyptian sources reshape the region's ethnic landscape.[18] The later biblical Philistines, probably a subgroup among them, apparently arrived in Canaan as mercenaries manning strategic Egyptian garrisons like Gaza, Beth Shean, and Dor.[19] But Egypt's withdrawal from Canaan apparently left those troops to fend for themselves, so each garrison reconstituted itself as an independent city. By ca. 1000 B.C., five such cities comprised a confederation of Philistines, each with its own ruler (Josh. 13:3; 1 Sam. 6:4, 18).[20] Meanwhile, the demise of the international "superpowers" and their ancient networks left Canaan fragmented among smaller, more regionalized cultures and economic centers during Iron Age I (post–1200 B.C.).[21]

In short, the lay of the land of Canaan that Israel would have navigated upon entrance depends on the century of that entry. On arrival ca. 1400 B.C. the Israelites would have found a Canaan presided over by local kings ruling city-states but accountable to the Egyptian empire. Geographically, population centers lay along the coast, the Sharon Plain, the Jordan and Jezreel Valleys, and along main roads. Important Canaanite cities included Shechem, Taanach, Megiddo, Bethel, Gezer, and Beth Shean (Judg. 1:22,

---

16. Cf. Kuhrt, *The Ancient Near East*, 2:385–86; Killebrew, *Biblical Peoples and Ethnicity*, 32–33.

17. For the reasons behind the widespread upheaval, see Kuhrt, *The Ancient Near East*, 2:385–86, 392–93; Killebrew, *Biblical Peoples and Ethnicity*, 33–42.

18. This otherwise complex story receives a good, nuanced treatment by Kuhrt, *The Ancient Near East*, 2:386–93.

19. Kuhrt, *The Ancient Near East*, 389–90, 425. Killebrew, *Biblical Peoples and Ethnicity*, 197–245, provides a detailed description of Philistine material culture.

20. Heb. *seren* ("ruler") is thought to originate from a Philistine word.

21. Killebrew, *Biblical Peoples and Ethnicity*, 27–28, 42.

27, 29), but the hill country was relatively unpopulated. Canaan's share in international trade graced the region with material prosperity.

The geographical situation greeting an Israelite entry a few decades before 1200 B.C. would not have markedly differed from the situation just noted (cf. Num. 13:29). Canaan's major cities included Dor along the coast, Taanach and Megiddo along the Jezreel Valley, Beth Shean in the Jordan Valley, Bethel in the hill country, and Gezer in the western lowlands (Judg. 1:22, 27, 29). There was also an enclave of Amorites entrenched in the Aijalon Valley (Judg. 1:34). Politically, the same major city-states still existed but were in decline, and the Egyptians were either gone or on their way out. Economically, regional connections between ethnic groups had replaced the former world economy. Prosperity was not reigning as in the past, Canaan's material culture was in decline, and the entire region was in the process of redefining itself. In sum, this was an unsettled time of great transition but one fraught with great possibilities.

How and When We Got the Book of Joshua

UNLIKE JEWISH TRADITION, THE Old Testament nowhere explains how the book of Joshua came to be, so internal clues offer the only illumination on the matter. Thankfully, the clues are plentiful, but to tease out their significance requires careful nuancing.

The remarkable variety of materials within the book offers the first clue. Joshua has a spy story (ch. 2), battle reports (8:1–29; ch. 11), annalistic reports (10:28–39), and reports of dramatic religious ceremonies (chs. 3–4; 5; 6; 8:30–35; 24:1–28). Toward the end of the book, speeches play a prominent role (ch. 22; 23 [Joshua]; 24:2–13 [Yahweh]), as does the long report of the land distribution among the tribes (chs. 13–19). The latter is particularly interesting in two respects. First, the kind and depth of information varies strikingly from tribe to tribe (see the table below). For example, Judah and Benjamin receive very detailed treatments (ch. 15; 18:11–28) compared to the sketchy pictures of Issachar and Dan (19:17–23, 40–48). Also, the description of Ephraim, one of Israel's two largest tribes (with Judah) and the heart of the later northern kingdom, is startling in its complete omission of a list of towns (16:1–10). Second, several town lists include the same town—e.g., Kiriath Jearim by Judah and Benjamin (15:60; 18:28), and Eshtaol by Judah and Dan (15:33; 19:41). These minor discrepancies probably reflect small, unexplained shifts in tribal boundaries and, more importantly, imply that the lists derive from diverse sources, even chronologically. All the above phenomena suggest that Joshua comprises an edited compilation of source materials.

The second important clue is the strong influence of the book of Deuteronomy on Joshua. The book often stresses how the actions of Joshua and/or Israel line up with Moses' commands in Deuteronomy. This is supremely true of his mandate that Israel annihilate Canaan's seven peoples (Deut. 7:1–2; 20:16–18; cf. Josh. 9:24; 11:12) and that Joshua distribute the land of Canaan among the tribes (Deut. 31:7; cf. Josh. 14:2, 5).[22] Key terms in Joshua also echo the language of Moses in Deuteronomy — e.g., the theme of Canaan as divinely given "rest [from enemies]" (Josh. 1:13; 21:44; 22:4; 23:1; cf. Deut. 3:20; 25:19), and the demand that Israel "love" and "serve" only Yahweh (Josh. 22:5; cf. Deut. 10:12; 11:13).

The same deuteronomic influence is evident in Judges, 1–2 Samuel, and 1–2 Kings, and that important observation led M. Noth to argue that Joshua and the latter books originated as a single, long history, the Deuteronomistic History (DH), with Deuteronomy as its preface.[23] According to Noth, an editor (the "Deuteronomist") compiled the entire history during the Exile (ca. 550 B.C.), shaping it in light of Deuteronomy's theology of history. Noth's thesis has spawned more than a half century of lively scholarly discussion that has considerably modified the theory.[24] For example, many scholars now believe that the DH actually appeared in two successive editions, the first during the reign of Josiah (seventh cent. B.C.) and the second during the Exile (ca. 550 B.C.). The first edition recounted the history from Joshua to Josiah, while the second continued it down to the release of King Jehoiachin from prison in Babylon (2 Kings 25:27–30). But as Hess has noted, many themes that constitute deuteronomic theology are also attested elsewhere in the ancient Near East and prior to the seventh century B.C.[25]

Furthermore, acceptance of a Deuteronomistic historian does not deny the antiquity of the contents of much of Deuteronomy, nor does it preclude the possibility that the DH, or at least parts of it, may have found written form as early as the early monarchy.[26] Moreover, if one holds that the book flowered in Josiah's day, it probably had roots much earlier in Israel. The implication for the question of how the book of Joshua came to be is

---

22. Other examples include the remaining obligation of the Transjordanian tribes (Josh. 1:13 [Deut. 3:20]) and the altar building on Mount Ebal (Josh. 8:30–31 [Deut. 27:4–6]).

23. The translation of his German original from 1943 is M. Noth, *The Deuteronomistic History* (JSOTSup 15; Sheffield: Sheffield Academic Press, 1981).

24. Longman and Dillard, *Introduction*, 123–24. For the current state of the discussion, see T. Römer, *The So-Called Deuteronomistic History* (London; New York: T & T Clark, 2007); cf. Curtis, *Joshua*, 17–21, 32–35.

25. R. S. Hess, *Joshua* (TOTC; Downers Grove, Ill.: InterVarsity Press, 1996), 33.

26. Cf. the judicious assessment of A. E. Hill and J. H. Walton, *A Survey of the Old Testament* (2nd ed.; Grand Rapids: Zondervan, 2000), 169–71.

this: one may tentatively regard the Deuteronomist as its author, whatever date one assigns him, since that person in effect wrote it drawing on earlier sources. His is the voice that often wraps up a verse or episode by noting something just reported from the past that still exists "until this day" (ʿad hayyom hazzeh).[27] The remark reveals that time has intervened between the event(s) reported and his own day.

The present book still shows evidence of the earlier sources on which the Deuteronomist drew. In Joshua 10:12–13, he explicitly cites the Book of Jashar, usually thought to be a collection of ancient poetry (cf. 2 Sam. 1:18), in connection with Joshua's poetic prayer.[28] Also, in my view, the instruction to explain the Jordan crossing to later generations seems to imply an ongoing tradition of family pilgrimages to Gilgal (4:6, 21–24). This (and other texts) has led many scholars to theorize that the ancient sanctuary at Gilgal may have been the source of many of the cultic ceremonies that the present book reports (e.g., chs. 3–4; ch. 5).[29] Many scholars also believe that the Deuteronomist's treatment of the Conquest incorporated and expanded a much earlier account (Josh. 1–11).[30] Younger's influential study certainly shows that Joshua 9–12 compares closely to ancient Near Eastern conquest accounts (1300–600 B.C.).[31]

But the lengthy report of the land allotments (Josh. 13–19) marks the most obvious use of sources by the Deuteronomist and has elicited considerable scholarly discussion concerning their source and date. The narrator awards pride of place to Judah, an indication perhaps of the writer's Judahite perspective and sources.[32] That the writer lumps Ephraim and Manasseh with Judah probably reflects their historical importance in his eyes. Judah and Joseph comprise the core of the Israelite heartland between Hebron and Shechem.[33]

The lists of cities/towns and boundaries probably were compiled at least as early as the era of David and Solomon (tenth cent. B.C.) and represent the

---

27. Josh. 4:9; 5:9; 6:25; 7:26; 8:28–29; 9:27; 13:13; 14:14; 15:63; 16:10; cf. 22:3, 17; 23:9.

28. For further comment, see the appropriate section of the commentary on Josh. 9–10.

29. Since Israel's early conquests (Jericho, Ai, Bethel, and Gibeon) all fell within the later territory of Benjamin, many scholars also suggest that Benjaminite sources may underlie some of the Conquest narratives.

30. E.g., R. D. Nelson, *Joshua* (OTL; Louisville: Westminster John Knox, 1997), 7–8.

31. K. L. Younger Jr., *Ancient Conquest Accounts: A Study in Ancient Near Eastern and Biblical History Writing* (JSOTSup 98; Sheffield: Sheffield Academic Press, 1990). Indeed, the accounts compare so closely as to undermine scholarly claims of later assertions in Josh. 9–12.

32. Nelson, *Joshua*, 185, 207.

33. Ephraim and Manasseh are the two sons of Joseph, each of whom founded a tribe among the twelve; cf. Gen. 48.

historical reality of that day.[34] That the Canaanites pose the prime threat to Israel in Joshua possibly confirms an early monarchical date for those portions of Joshua, since the Canaanites (but not their religion) virtually slip from the biblical radar screen after Solomon's subjection of them (see 1 Kings 9:20–21).[35] But, as Hess plausibly argues, an origin for the materials that comprise Joshua 13–19 in the premonarchical period also remains possible.[36] The land divisions in those chapters correspond most closely to the picture of Canaan's regions in the Amarna letters (fourteenth cent. B.C.), the only time in Israel's history that such a correspondence would be the case. Furthermore, early Israel's agricultural economy would certainly have needed some system of land boundaries in order to function. Whatever the case, it seems likely that in Joshua 13–19 the Deuteronomist has incorporated ancient materials to round out his portrait of Israel's settlement. The boundary descriptions in Cisjordan may, in fact, actually follow ancient Iron Age roads.[37]

Finally, some scholars propose that priests edited and supplemented the book of Joshua in the Persian period (fifth cent B.C.).[38] The introduction of the priest Eleazar to preside with Joshua over the land distribution (14:1; 17:4; 19:51; 21:1; 24:33) strikes them as literarily abrupt, and they credit the land allotment narrative (chs. 13–19) and certain cultic texts (e.g., 5:2–12; 8:30–35) to late priestly editorial activity. Though possible, this thesis remains a matter of dispute, mainly because the observations that underlie it bear other equally plausible explanations. Also, even to accept them as priestly need not require the Persian period date often proposed.

---

34. The definitive study remains Z. Kallai, *Historical Geography of the Bible: The Tribal Territories of Israel* (Jerusalem: Magnes, 1986), 99–444. Both Kallai (279) and Na'aman (75–117) date the lists to the early monarchy under David and Solomon.

35. G. Mitchell, *Together in the Land: A Reading of the Book of Joshua* (JSOTSup 134; Sheffield: JSOT Press, 1993), 127. References to the Jebusites (Josh. 15:63) and to Jerusalem as "the Jebusite city" (15:8; 18:16, 28) also point to an early, if not Solomonic, date for the materials within 13–19 (cf. 2 Sam. 5:6–9, the Jebusites' defeat by David).

36. R. S. Hess, "Asking Historical Questions of Joshua 13–19: Recent Discussion Concerning the Date of the Boundary Lists," in *Faith, Tradition, and History: Old Testament Historiography in Its Ancient Near Eastern Context*, ed. A. R. Millard et al. (Winona Lake, Ind.: Eisenbrauns, 1994), 196–204; cf. idem, "Late Bronze Age and Biblical Boundary Descriptions of the West Semitic World," in *Ugarit and the Bible*, ed. G. J. Brooke et al. (Münster: Ugarit-Vorlag, 1994), 123–38.

37. M. G. Seleznev, "The Origin of the Tribal Boundaries in Joshua: Administrative Documents or Sacral Geography?" in L. G. Kogan et al., eds., *Memoriae Igor M. Diakonoff: Babel und Babel 2* (Winona Lake, Ind.: Eisenbrauns, 2005), 330–61.

38. Cf. Römer, *The So-Called Deuteronomistic History*, 179–80; R. Albertz, "The Canonical Alignment of the Book of Joshua," in O. Lipschits, G. N. Knoppers, and R. Albertz, eds., *Judah and the Judeans in the Fourth Century B.C.E.* (Winona Lake, Ind: Eisenbrauns, 2007), 288–90.

Genres in Joshua 13–19

Text	Genre	Tribe
13:1–7	Report: Commission to Joshua	
13:8–33	Retrospect	Transjordanian tribes
13:8–14	Summary report	
13:15–23	Boundary description List of towns	Reuben
13:24–28	Boundary description List of towns	Gad
13:29–31	Boundary description List of towns	East Manasseh
14:1–5	Summary report	
14:6–14	Flashback	Caleb's inheritance: Hebron
15:1–12	Boundary description	Judah
15:13–19	Flashback	Caleb's inheritance distributed
15:20–63	List of towns and villages	Judah
16:1–4	Boundary description	Joseph
16:5–10	Boundary description	Ephraim
17:1–13	Boundary description	West Manasseh
17:14–18	Report: extra allotment	Ephraim and West Manasseh
18:1–11	Report: land survey and distribution by lots	Seven tribes
18:12–20	Boundary description	Benjamin
18:21–28	List of towns	Benjamin
19:1–9	List of towns (within Judah)	Simeon
19:10–16	Boundary description List of towns	Zebulun
19:17–23	Boundary description List of towns	Issachar
19:24–31	Boundary description List of towns	Asher
19:32–39	Boundary description List of towns	Naphtali
19:40–48	List of towns (and comment)	Dan
19:49–50	Report: city given to Joshua	Joshua
19:51	Conclusion formula	

Did the Conquest Really Happen?

SCHOLARS HAVE LONG OBSERVED that the Bible seems to offer two different portraits of the conquest of Canaan. The portrait in Joshua 1–12 affirms that "Joshua took the entire land" (Josh. 11:16, 23), but the second pictures the conquest as a long process carried out locally by individual tribes.[39] The contrasting pictures have led many scholars to doubt the historical accuracy of this book. Indeed, a third portrait—the emerging archaeological portrait of Canaan's history—has further intensified that skepticism among them. It has, further, led them to propose several new, alternative scenarios concerning how the conquest of Canaan happened (or did not). Some scenarios also imply an understanding of how the people of Israel itself came into being that differs from the biblical portrait. The proposals surveyed below range across a spectrum from "minimalist" (i.e., Israel originated no earlier than the Persian period) and "maximalist" (Israel originated pretty much as the Bible says).[40]

Exogenous Models

SEVERAL CONQUEST MODELS TRACE Israel's origins to somewhere (or somehow) outside of Canaan. The *military conquest model* concedes that the process of arrival and settlement may have been complex but accepts the biblical account as historically reliable. In the past, archaeological evidence—especially the widespread destruction in Canaan ca. 1200 B.C.—played a key evidentiary role.[41] But that approach faces three difficulties. First, only two of nineteen sites that Joshua mentions suffered destruction; second, it is unclear exactly who (Israel or others) destroyed the two sites; and, third, the appeal to widespread destruction conflicts with biblical statements that Israel burned only three cities—Jericho, Ai, and Hazor (Josh. 6:24; 8:28; 11:13). Today, advocates of this view, the present writer included, accept that Joshua 6–11 offers a repetitive, stereotyped account marked by occasional hyperbole, yet affirm its historical value.

---

39. E.g., Josh. 15:13–19; 16:10; 17:11–13; 19:47; Judg. 1.

40. See conveniently, Longman and Dillard, *Introduction*, 126–27 (with bibliography). For more detailed treatments, cf. Provan, Long, and Longman, *A Biblical History of Israel*, 139–47; Killebrew, *Biblical Peoples and Ethnicity*, 181–85, who proposes her own synthesis, "the mixed multitude theory" (184–85; see below); K. L. Younger Jr., "Early Israel in Recent Biblical Scholarship," in D. W. Baker and B. T. Arnold, eds., *The Face of Old Testament Studies* (Grand Rapids: Baker, 1999), 178–200.

41. Younger, "Early Israel," 178–79. Many students meet this view in J. Bright, *A History of Israel* (3rd ed.; Philadelphia: Westminster, 1981).

Introduction

The *peaceful infiltration model* first proposed a half-century ago by A. Alt and M. Noth suggests that Israel, formerly nomads or seminomads for centuries, peacefully infiltrated Canaan.[42] They settled in the sparsely populated hill country, thus avoiding military conflicts, and gradually came to dominate the land. The worship of Yahweh and a loose political organization called an amphictyony united them. Recent scholars, however, have abandoned the amphictyony concept as an accurate description of Israel's situation. Also, they understand the relationship between nomadic herders and settled peoples to be an ongoing, symbiotic one rather than assume (as Alt and Noth did) an inherent conflict between nomads and nonnomads. Finally, some scholars question the necessity of the skeptical stance that led Alt and Noth to deny the historical reliability of the biblical record.

The *peasants' revolt model*, the theory of G. Mendenhall and N. Gottwald, proposes a sociopolitical scenario for the conquest.[43] Mendenhall's view traces it to an alliance of rural, marginalized Canaanite peoples with a newly arrived group of slaves treasuring a myth of rescue from slavery by their God Yahweh and bound to him by a covenant. (The role that Mendenhall assigns this external group stamps his view as exogenous.) As simple farmers and herdsmen living in rural areas, both groups found themselves at the bottom of Canaanite society oppressed by the kings of powerful city-states. According to Mendenhall, the emergence in Canaan of the *hapiru* (in his view, the Hebrews) as an alienated group lit the match of revolt among aggrieved peasant farmers. Gottwald's unique contribution is to interpret this revolt through Marxist ideology — that is, as the revolutionary attempt of a proletariat peasantry to overthrow their feudal overlords.

Several criticisms stand against the peasants' revolt model. First, it seems to assume (wrongly, in the view of many) that nomads favor an egalitarian approach to leadership rather than a hierarchical one. Second, it fails to reckon with the now well-attested symbiotic relationship between city-dwellers and rural folk noted above. Put differently, to presume that a transition from a nomadic lifestyle to a sedentary one somehow marks a form of cultural advance is questionable. Finally, as noted above, the present consensus no longer reads the term *hapiru* as an ethnic term that equates to "Hebrews."

---

42. A. Alt, "The Settlement of the Israelites in Canaan," *Essays on Old Testament History and Religion* (trans. R. A. Wilson; Sheffield: JSOT Press, 1989), 135–69; M. Noth, *The History of Israel* (2nd ed.; London: A & C Black, 1960), 53–84; cf. Younger, "Early Israel," 179–81.

43. G. E. Mendenhall, *The Tenth Generation: The Origins of the Biblical Tradition* (Baltimore: Johns Hopkins Univ. Press, 1973), 174–97; N. K. Gottwald, *The Tribes of Yahweh: A Sociology of the Religion of Liberated Israel, 1250–1050 B.C.E.* (Maryknoll, N.Y.: Orbis, 1979), 210–33; cf. Younger, "Early Israel," 181–82.

Indigenous Models

MOST RECENT MODELS PROPOSE scenarios in which Israel originates within Canaan rather than outside it. They appeal to archaeological evidence for Iron Age I, especially the sudden population surge evident in the central hill country. Specific proposals vary, but they all share two common questions: who are the people that suddenly settle in the central hill country in such great numbers and from where do they come?

Archaeologist W. Dever recently proposed a *collapse model* for Israel's origins within Canaan.[44] In his view, these "proto-Israelites" (his term) originally were long-settled rural farmers from the fringes of Canaanite society. When major Canaanite coastal cities collapsed in the Late Bronze Age (1570–1200 B.C.), Israel emerged from the people who moved inland to the hill country as pioneers. They both brought with them pottery styles from the lowlands and used technological advances appropriate to the highlands (e.g., terraced farming, hewn water cisterns, stone grain silos, etc.). They built unique four-room houses with courtyards, tended small herds (but not pigs), and used unique collar-rim jars for storage. In his view, the continuity between these ethnic markers and later monarchical Israel confirms the continuity between proto- and later-Israel. In short, Dever's understanding excludes any idea of an Israelite conquest of Canaan and also, in effect, disconnects Israel's origins from the biblical claims of the Exodus. Many find his minimal use of the biblical story problematic.[45]

Interpreting the same data as Dever, fellow archaeologist I. Finkelstein proposes a *cyclic model* that traces Israel's origins to pastoral nomads who settled permanently in the highlands.[46] Nomads are always elusive to track, but Finkelstein claims that archaeological evidence from sanctuaries and cemeteries points to their presence—in his view, the *shasu* of ancient Egyptian (and other) texts. Behind Finkelstein's proposal is his observation that during the third and second millennia B.C. Canaan saw three waves or cycles of settlement and two intervals of decline, all driven by socioeconomic factors. He argues that the new Iron Age developments in the central hill country simply comprise the third part of that larger cycle in which nomadic peoples give up migration for settlement. It is these newly settled

---

44. The most recent statement of his long-evolving view is W. G. Dever, *Who Were the Early Israelites and Where Did They Come From?* (Grand Rapids: Eerdmans, 2003); cf. conveniently, the summary in Younger, "Early Israel," 183–85.

45. At length (223–37) he attempts to "salvage" (his metaphor) the biblical traditions, in my view, unsuccessfully.

46. I. Finkelstein and A. Mazar, *The Quest for the Historical Israel: Debating Archaeology and the History of Early Israel* (Atlanta: Society of Biblical Literature, 2007), 9–20, 41–55, 73–83; cf. Younger, "Early Israel," 185–87.

nomads who populate the new hill country, not refugees from collapsed coastal cities (against Dever), and they form the Israel that later becomes a nation. In short, like Dever, Finkelstein's view includes no Israelite conquest in it. Against Finkelstein, however, scholars wonder whether the limited data about the region's ancient history can sustain his alleged pattern of cycles. Further, some critics fault him for explaining historical developments exclusively through environmental changes—a kind of "environmental determinism."[47]

Finally, on the extreme "minimalist" side of the spectrum are scholars like P. R. Davies and W. Lemke, whose model marks a *rejection of the conquest.*[48] In general, they exclude biblical reports as useless for any reconstruction of Israel's early history. They reckon them as legendary, too theologically tainted, too dependent on unreliable oral tradition, and too chronologically late to contribute to any discussion of history. In their view, the history of Israel that the Bible recounts is simply a literary and theological creation of people in the postexilic period. Instead, scholars sharing this view lean primarily on archaeology and anthropology to support their individual theses concerning the history of Canaan.[49] Discussion of an Israelite conquest is not an option, and some scholars hold that Israel as a distinct people did not actually emerge until the Persian period, if not later.

Needless to say, scholarly response to these so-called minimalists has been spirited and the criticisms many. Even scholars one might call "higher critics" criticize their dismissal of biblical traditions to irrelevancy as needlessly extreme. By far the most thorough recent assessment and alternative proposal comes from J. B. Kofoed.[50] He argues persuasively that the skepticism of the minimalists is unsustainable and shows that the time lag between written biblical texts and the events they report does not disqualify the texts as historical sources.[51] He, thus, aligns himself with many scholars who accept the antiquity of biblical traditions at least in oral tradition if not in written form.

If this view holds, then the one unique contention of the minimalists—the extremely late date they assign to the origin of Israel as a

---

47. Younger, "Early Israel," 187. In addition, Finkelstein tends to regard biblical historical claims more skeptically than does Dever.

48. Cf. P. R. Davies, *In Search of Ancient Israel* (Sheffield: JSOT Press, 1992); W. Lemke, *The Israelites in History and Tradition* (Louisville: Westminster John Knox, 1998).

49. For the unique views of specific scholars, cf. conveniently Younger, "Early Israel," 187–91.

50. J. B. Kofoed, *Text and History: Historiography and the Study of the Biblical Text* (Winona Lake, Ind.: Eisenbrauns, 2005).

51. Cf. ibid., 30 ("the texts of the Hebrew Bible contain reliable information for a reconstruction of the period it purports to describe").

people—would become questionable.[52] Also, discussion of the Conquest in Joshua as in some sense historical regains its place in scholarship.[53]

An Alternate Approach

THE APPROACH TO THE Conquest in the present commentary both departs from and draws on the above discussion. It aims at a more comprehensive model of the Conquest than those reviewed above and, hence, includes both biblical and archaeological evidence.[54] Its point of departure is an understanding of the literary nature of the book of Joshua.

First, it recognizes that literary devices of hyperbole, ideology, and legitimation play important roles in the book. It accepts that Joshua simply invokes features typical of history writing in the ancient Near East.[55] By implication, the presence of such traditional devices should caution readers against an overly literal interpretation of texts in Joshua.

Second, it accepts both the valuable contribution of Joshua to historical reconstruction and the limits of the book's information (e.g., its selective content, its highly-structured narratives).

Third, unlike some scholars, the present approach refuses to pit biblical texts against each other (e.g., Josh. 10 versus Josh. 13 or Judg. 1) and decide that one is "historical" and the other "theologized." In my view, it is preferable to accept potentially or apparently conflicting texts as reflecting either the literary genres in play (each demanding the appropriate reading strategy), the complex reality behind the text, or both.

To speak of that "complex reality" implies recognition of something crucial. Joshua pictures the conquest process as more complex than a simple,

---

52. An additional scholarly criticism centers on the inherent limitations of the philosophy of history on which some minimalists depend, e.g., the French school of *Les Annales* and especially the views of L. Braudel. They prefer an approach to understanding history broader than the French school's focus on enduring political structures (called *longue durée*), a focus that excludes the study of actual events and political changes; cf. Younger, "Early Israel," 192 ("there are certainly more contributions in the arena of the philosophy of history than simply the *Annales* movement!").

53. Recently, Killebrew (*Biblical Peoples and Ethnicity*, 184–85) proposed a *mixed multitude model.* ("Mixed multitude" is a term from the KJV of Ex. 12:38). In her view, Israel emerged when, after the crisis of ca. 1200 B.C., a "multitude" of loosely-organized, disparate groups from "mixed" backgrounds (rural Canaanites, nomads, displaced farmers, runaway Semitic slaves, the lawless *hapiru* and *Shasu*, etc.) coalesced around the shared saga of their relationship with Yahweh as his chosen people. Killebrew promises to develop her thesis in a future publication.

54. It draws on the model suggested by Younger, "Early Israel," 203–6.

55. In other words, to read biblical texts properly requires familiarity with comparable ancient Near Eastern literature, especially ancient conquest accounts. This comparative approach clarifies how ancient peoples wrote and suggests how best to read similar biblical texts (so Younger, "Early Israel," 204).

short military blitzkrieg. Instead, the picture is of "a long process of infiltration, fighting (including infighting), and transformation and realignment."[56] What took decades to accomplish, the book of Joshua has telescoped into a simplified, selective, focused glimpse. Certainly, the fall of the Egyptian empire, the presence of the Sea Peoples and nomadic stockbreeders, and the crisis of 1200 B.C. played important roles. One may allow that natural disasters like droughts and plagues also intervened.

Such a comprehensive, nuanced understanding helps explain the mysterious case of Shechem that figures prominently in the thinking of some scholars. According to Joshua, Israel twice convenes at that major, ancient city (Josh. 8:30–35; 24:1–28), but the book nowhere reports its conquest. Assuming a complex conquest and looking at Israel's ancestral ties with the city, one may rightly speculate that Shechem came to Israel through some unusual means (e.g., peaceful infiltration, surrender, etc.). In addition, the cases of Rahab and the Gibeonites may represent a sample of other non-Israelite peoples that contributed to the process and formed part of early Israel in Canaan. In short, the biblical record follows the stereotypical conventions and telescoping of events typical of ancient conquest accounts. One must first understand it as literature before one can glean history from it. Its basic outline is historical but highly simplified; the conquest probably involved a long, drawn-out process accomplished over decades.

Early Israel and Archaeology

WHAT MAY ONE GLEAN about Israel from the archaeological record? The short answer is: very little about the Conquest but a good deal about the settlement. According to Joshua, the Israelites only destroyed three cities—Jericho, Ai, and Hazor—leaving the rest intact and ready for Israelites to occupy later. Thus, the frequent citation of destroyed cities other than that trio as evidence for the Israelite conquest is in reality biblically unnecessary.

A more important piece of evidence is the victory stele (1209 B.C.) of the Egyptian pharaoh Merneptah found at Thebes. It marks the earliest extrabiblical reference to Israel in the ancient world and clearly establishes the presence of an "Israel" at least ca. 1210 B.C. in the area of Canaan.[57] The stele commemorates the pharaoh's victories during his campaign into Canaan and lists "Israel" among his conquests:

---

56. Younger, "Early Israel," 203.

57. L. E. Stager, "Forging an Identity: The Emergence of Ancient Israel," in *The Oxford History of the Biblical World*, ed. M. D. Coogan (New York; Oxford: Oxford Univ. Press, 1998), 124–27; Dever, *Who Were the Israelites?* 201–8; M. G. Hasel, "Israel in the Merneptah Stela," *BASOR* 296 (1994): 45–61.

The Canaan has been plundered into every sort of woe;
Ashkelon has been overcome;
Gezer has been captured;
Yanoam is made nonexistent;
Israel is laid waste and his seed is not;
Hurru is become a widow because of Egypt.[58]

What is striking is that the hieroglyphs linguistically distinguish between Israel and the other adversaries (Ashkelon, Gezer, Yanoam). They define the latter as city-states or kingdoms headquartered at those cities but Israel as a "people" — as loosely connected, rural herders or farmers organized by tribes. But the context also implies them to be "a political-ethnic entity of sufficient importance to the Egyptians to warrant mention alongside the three Canaanite city-states."[59] Further, four battle reliefs at Karnak visually depict what the stele celebrates in words. Notably, it portrays Israel, not as nomads like the Shasu, but with the same hairstyles and clothing as the Canaanite city-states. The implication is that the Egyptians regarded Israel as an established socioethnic component of Canaan at the time of the battle.[60] Finally, it implicitly locates Israel, so to speak, "in the open places," which at the time would most likely be the hill country.[61]

Now if we factor in both archaeological and biblical data, several other lines of evidence point to the presence of Israel ca. 1200 B.C. in the sparsely populated central highlands. (1) The hill country shows clear evidence of numerical growth between the Late Bronze Age (thirteenth cent. B.C.) and the Iron Age (eleventh cent. B.C.). The number of village or hamlet sites increased from 29 to 254 with an estimated population rise from ca. 12,000 to ca. 42,000.[62] It is especially telling that most of the sites are completely new ones, not ones built on the ruins of preexisting sites.

(2) The new settlements feature a new type of dwelling, the four-room, pillared house surrounding a small open courtyard. Further, the settlements cluster two or three such houses together with shared walls to form a kind of "family compound."[63]

---

58. Cited from Stager, "Forging an Identity," 124. For a map of the campaign, see Dever, *Who Were the Israelites?* 205.

59. Stager, "Forging an Identity," 125; cf. Hasel, "*Israel* in the Merneptah Stela," 54, 56, n.12.

60. Stager ("Forging an Identity," 125–27) compares the Israel of these Egyptian sources with the picture of Israel's tribes in Judges 5.

61. Dever, *Who Were the Israelites?* 206.

62. Cf. ibid., 97–99; Stager, "Forging an Identity," 134–35 (with statistical table). During the same period, the population increase for Canaan as a whole was from 50,000 to 150,000.

63. Dever, *Who Were the Israelites?* 103–6 (quote 105 and drawings 104 and 106). For Stager's proposed alignment of the family compound architecture with Hebrew socioeconomic terms, see 107.

(3) Food remains and animal bones suggest that the settlers farmed and herded primarily sheep and goats but also donkeys and cattle. One anomaly is striking, however: compared to Iron I coastal sites, pig bones are virtually absent from these hill country villages, a possible telling ethnic mark for the settlers' Israelite identity.[64]

(4) Several technological advances, again probably adaptations to the terrain, are evident.[65] The hilly terrain proved the mother of invention among the settlers, specifically, the development of terrace-farming around their villages. Otherwise, for the most part hill country agriculture compares to that known for Canaanites, and that is not a surprise. Israel and the Canaanites shared common roots in West Semitic culture and had a history of contacts at least in the patriarchal past if not during the transition to settlement.[66] Other technological innovations include unique means of storage — plastered water cisterns and grain silos.

However, iron implements appear to have replaced bronze only very slowly in the central highlands, a situation the Bible itself explains (1 Sam. 13:19–23). Similarly, there is little evidence of an indigenous, flourishing artistic tradition, perhaps because the settlers had priorities elsewhere or because the aesthetics of their neighbors was poor. In short, biblical and archaeological data open some windows through which to glimpse the pioneers who built up the hill country. The Mereneptah stele places Israel as a significant socioethnic entity in Canaan at least by 1210 B.C. Granted, no ancient writing identifies the new hill country arrivals as Israelites, but the population increase and technological innovations fit well the biblical picture of the arrival of Israel from elsewhere and its gradual settlement there.

Now, about All That Killing...

SOME YEARS AGO, HISTORIAN John Bright half-facetiously said about Joshua, "You simply cannot preach from this book, and you ought not to teach it to children. Shield our gentle ears from violence such as this!"[67] What does one do with the wholesale killing of the Canaanites mandated in Deuteronomy

---

64. Ibid., 108; but cf. Younger's caution concerning this datum ("Early Israel," 195–96).

65. Dever, *Who Were the Israelites?* 113–25. For the controversy surrounding whether collar-rim jars are Israelite or not, see 118–25.

66. Cf. Younger, "Early Israel," 196.

67. J. Bright, *The Authority of the Old Testament* (Grand Rapids: Baker, 1975), 243. Cf. L. D. Hawk, "The Problem with Pagans," in T. K. Beal and D. M. Gunn, eds., *Reading Bibles, Writing Bodies: Identity and the Book* (London and New York: Routledge, 1996), 153: "For many readers in an age haunted by violence ... this is an ugly, repugnant story that scarcely deserves retelling."

and carried out in Joshua?[68] What are Christian readers to make of the God whom Joshua portrays, much less the book by that name?

Basic Ideas

TO BEGIN, IT IS important to clarify the basic ideas that strike readers as offensive and problematic. The book of Joshua concerns "Yahweh war," a well-attested biblical theme about the military victories God wins over his enemies, victories in which Israel participates.[69] In Joshua, Yahweh war drives the defeats of Jericho, Ai, Gibeon, and southern and northern campaigns. Such war is a sacred act and, hence, requires ritual purity in Israel's war camp and among its soldiers (Deut. 23:9–14; cf. Josh. 3:5; 1 Sam. 7:9–10). Theologically, this concept assumes that Yahweh has his enemies, that he alone (not Israel) wins the victory, and that Israel must simply rely on his power.[70] The idea of *ḥerem* (including its prohibition of plunder) along with a cluster of other literary and theological themes show God's role in the conquest stories and affirm that it is God's work.

A second basic concept concerns the practice of *ḥerem*. In Joshua, the Hebrew word designates a religious act—"to devote to destruction" or "ban" (e.g., Josh. 6:21)—by which Israel consecrates objects to Yahweh for his exclusive possession and use. The prominence of *ḥerem* in Joshua, however, should not obscure the severe limitations of the practice. Only Yahweh himself has the authority to impose *ḥerem* on a city or people; no Israelite leader can do so. It is Yahweh, not Moses, Joshua, or anyone else, who decrees that Israel apply *ḥerem* to Canaan's inhabitants (Deut. 20:16–18).

Further, in a specific instance of Yahweh war God does not automatically involve the imposition of *ḥerem*. On the contrary, Yahweh may fight and defeat enemies without the destruction being an act of *ḥerem*.

Finally, the primary application of the idea is to the conquest of Canaan rather than a broad policy with wide applicability and a long record of use. In the case of Canaan, it serves a specific, limited purpose, to protect the Israelites from idolatry by ridding the land of idol worshipers (Deut. 20:18). That protection is necessary lest Israel's unfaithfulness hamper the advance of God's salvation plan. In short, the concepts of Yahweh war and

---

68. For a more in-depth discussion (with bibliography), see the *Bridging Contexts* sections of chs. 5–6 and 7–8.

69. Cf. the valuable overview by G. H. Jones, "The Concept of Holy War," in R. E. Clements, ed., *The World of Ancient Israel: Sociological, Anthropological, and Political Perspectives* (Cambridge: Cambridge Univ. Press, 1989), 299–321.

70. Cf. also the discussion of the theme of Yahweh the warrior in the section below on theological themes.

sacred destruction (*ḥerem*) comprise the violent, offensive reality that readers confront in Joshua, a reality that sparks questions about the character of God. My response to the problem begins with a challenge for readers squarely to face three unappealing, if not harsh, realities.

Three Unappealling Realities

THE FIRST UNAPPEALING REALITY is perhaps the most unpalatable to many: If there is any justice in the world, there still are people who do deserve destruction. This is the assumption that both the Old Testament and the New Testament share. Many psalms speak of "evildoers" worthy of divine destruction (Ps. 14:6; 125:5), and the prophets foresee destruction both for other nations and for Israel (Isa. 13:11; Jer. 7:12–15). Jesus condemned the Pharisees to future disaster for being "You snakes! You brood of vipers!" (Matt. 23:33). The scene of the Great White Throne judgment certainly assumes a final day of reckoning with eternal destruction a certain outcome for some (Rev. 20:11–15).

Most Bible readers know this, and that knowledge helps explain why they seem to have no qualms about the extermination of Sodom and Gomorrah (Gen. 18–19), even though the destruction of Jericho and Hazor also are acts of God. That the Bible pictures the former as depraved may ease their qualms, but it is also of interest that the peoples Canaan initiated hostilities against Israel, not the other way around (Josh. 9:1–2; 10:1–5; 11:1–5; cf. 2:2–3). Israel's northern and southern campaigns (Josh. 10, 11) were in response to those hostile initiatives, not preemptive strikes. Even though the peoples knew the power of God (according to Rahab and the Gibeonites), they choose to stand against him. This fact should caution us against viewing the peoples of ancient Canaan simply as victims of some sort of injustice. At least some of them were God's opponents.

The second unappealing reality is that ultimately a solution to the problem of the violence in Joshua may be elusive—at least, that is my conclusion after many years of wrestling with it. Emotionally, I do not see myself ever feeling completely comfortable with what transpires in Joshua. By that I do not mean that the book of Joshua, including its violence, has nothing to teach us or that it should never be read. Notwithstanding Bright's comment above, I affirm that the book deserves to be preached and taught to children. After all, like it or not, it is part of the biblical canon. The commentary to follow will surely rebut any thoughts of blacklisting Joshua. I mean simply that people today read Joshua through modern lenses tinted by modern culture's abhorrence of war and violence and—in the case of Christians—by Jesus' ethical teachings.

The world of Joshua jars modern readers because it lies so distant from and sounds so discordant with theirs. The reality is that the ancient and modern worlds are truly different, with a gaping chasm of three thousand years and vast cultural distance between them. But, in a sense, readers' discomfort with Joshua is a good sign: it shows the depth with which the gospel has transformed them. Few of us would rest easy with a Christian whose response to the destruction of Jericho was, "Hurray! That's exactly what some people I know deserve!"

In fact, this second unappealing reality leads to my first two major points. (1) It is a fact that our situation today is totally different from that in Joshua's day. There is no possible way to imitate the Conquest today. None of us lives as a covenant people entering a promised covenant land where the inhabitants stand under God's judgment. In short, there is no biblical basis to apply the Conquest literally today.

(2) More importantly, the teachings of Jesus, so to speak, permanently eliminate the "Joshua option" of violence done in Jesus' name. It is simply out of the question for Christians to resort to violence in the Christian cause. The world's governments may treat Christians within their borders shabbily if not with extreme cruelty. Decisions by city councils, zoning authorities, or enforcers of building codes may occasionally make life difficult for a local church. In some situations, outright opposition to the gospel may in fact drive their deeds. But, in my view, one may not appeal to the book of Joshua to justify burning down city hall as Israel did Ai or stoning uncooperative local officials as Israel did Achan. Such actions would contradict everything that Jesus teaches and would also give the gospel a black eye in the public's view. In short, Jesus' teaching sets aside Joshua's *ḥerem* and models a far different way of relating to outsiders. The book of Joshua in no way authorizes Christians today to "go and do likewise" to perceived enemies regardless of how unjust, outrageous, or insane the treatment received. It simply shows us what God did (it is descriptive), not what we should do (it is not prescriptive).

Further, L. Stone has rightly argued that texts within Joshua itself seem aimed to soften the book's violent tone and subtly shift its focus elsewhere. They suggest that even the book's editors felt discomfort with the idea of holy war and the annihilation of the Canaanites.[71] A subtle downplaying of the martial and territorial motifs of Yahweh war is evident. For example, the book starkly contrasts the acceptance of Yahweh's plan for Canaan by Rahab and the Gibeonites (2:9–11; 9–10) with the resistance to it by Canaanite kings (5:1; 9:1–2; 10:1–5; 11:1–5). Further, the contrast

---

71. L. G. Stone, "Ethical and Apologetic Tendencies in the Redaction of the Book of Joshua," *CBQ* 53 (1991): 25–36.

intentionally makes the case that the Canaanites perished for resisting Yahweh, not for religious decadence or economic oppression of peasants. The book's message promotes responsiveness to Yahweh's actions and warns against resistance to them.[72] Its main theme is that holy war (Stone's term) is ultimately more about "uncompromising obedience to Yahweh's law" than about "territory or warfare."[73] Similarly, I would argue that Joshua 7–10 affirms actual divine acceptance of foreigners like Rahab and the Gibeonites within Israel.[74] Catastrophe surrounds them, but they alone receive compassion—indeed, *salvation*—and their very survival implies that Yahweh permits exceptions to the *ḥerem* mandate. Those who acknowledge his greatness seem eligible for a waiver.

In short, the book of Joshua teaches two things: first, those who honor Yahweh's greatness and do not teach Israel idolatry may remain in the land (e.g., Rahab, the Gibeonites); and, second, Yahweh expects of everyone in the land rigorous obedience to his instruction (e.g., references to it and Moses).[75] Thus, Joshua's openness to non-Israelites parallels the Old Testament's inclusive themes and compares to the New Testament's emphasis on the international ethnic inclusivity of the gospel (e.g., Acts 1:8; Rev. 5:9; 14:6).[76] More importantly, Joshua displays the same mercy and compassion that Christians experience through Jesus Christ.

The rest of the Old Testament further confirms the point made above concerning the limited focus of the *ḥerem* policy on late second millennium Canaan. After Judges 2:23 the hero Joshua receives no mention at all until 1 Kings 16:34 recalls his oath over Jericho, after which he reappears only twice—in his family genealogy (1 Chron. 7:27) and in Nehemiah 8:17.[77] Reviews of Israel's early history by Samuel (1 Sam. 12:9–11), Yahweh (Mic. 6:5; Jer. 2:7), and the psalmist (Ps. 105:43–45) completely skip the

---

72. Ibid., 34, 35. Stone specifically argues (34–36) that the Deuteronomist reshaped the book to introduce the law as the object of Israel's acceptance or resistance (e.g., Josh. 1:1–9; 8:30–35; ch. 23).

73. Ibid., 36.

74. I argue this case in R. L. Hubbard Jr., "'What Do These Stones Mean?': Biblical Theology and a Motif in Joshua," *BBR* 11 (2001): 25–49. The contrasting fates of Achan (an insider rejected) and Rahab (an outsider included) also support this theme.

75. See Josh. 1:7, 8, 17; 4:10, 12; 8:30–35; 9:24; 11:12, 15; 20:2; 21:2, 8; 22:2, 5; 23:6; 24:6, 26. The call to obedience to the law fits well with the larger biblical stress on the duty of believers to obey Scripture as God's Word (e.g., Deut. 8:3; Ps. 1:2; Prov. 30:5; Matt. 4:4; John 2:22; 1 Tim. 4:13; 2 Tim. 3:15–16; James 2:8).

76. For the Bible's treatment of Ruth the Moabite as an example, see R. L. Hubbard Jr., *The Book of Ruth* (NICOT; Grand Rapids: Eerdmans, 1988), 64–65, 116–21.

77. Cf. R. L. Hubbard Jr., "Only a Distant Memory: Old Testament Allusions to Joshua's Days," *Ex Auditu* 16 (2000): 131–48.

conquest, as does Ezekiel's vision of restoration (Ezek. 40–48). Other texts feature broad statements by Yahweh recalling how he "drove out" (*garaš*) the Canaanites (Judg. 6:9; Ps. 78:55; 80:8 [Heb. 9]) or brought Israel into the land (Ezek. 20:28). To my knowledge, only three texts, two featuring the verb *yaraš* ("take possession, destroy"), describe violent dispossession in war (Neh. 9:23–25; Ps. 44:2–3; Amos 2:10).[78] Instead, other more inclusivist themes come to dominate the Old Testament: Yahweh's beneficent rule over all nations and their worship of him in the present and future.[79]

In sum, the Old Testament rarely recalls the violent conquest, never glories in its goriness, and never promotes it as policy for the future. All references to it concern the display of Yahweh's great power and generosity in giving Israel the land of promise. Clearly, they assume that only Yahweh has authority to take such actions, and he chose to do so in a specific time and place for specific purposes. In my view, the implication is that after Joshua the Old Testament, so to speak, "moved on" to more internationalist priorities. In that sense, the Old Testament even compares to Jesus' teachings on violence.

The third unappealing reality is the fact that a theological truth accepted by readers probably undergirds biblical violence—the sovereignty of God. In Joshua 6–8, Yahweh applies *ḥerem* to Jericho and Ai differently. All of Jericho is *ḥerem* ("devoted to destruction") so no plunder may be taken, but at Ai Israel may keep objects or animals for themselves.[80] In my view, the latter displays God's gracious concern to take care of his people's needs. But behind both applications of *ḥerem* stands the important theological truth that God, as part of his universal sovereignty, owns everything. As owner, he has the authority to decide who may enjoy the use of his property. Psalm 24:1–2 almost echoes a deed of ownership when it says:

> The earth is the LORD's, and everything in it,
>   the world, and all who live in it;
> for he founded it upon the seas
>   and established it upon the waters.

The Lord owns . . . , well, everything, including humans and all that they create from his created raw materials. Earth has no areas marked "Property

---

78. Of these, Neh. 9:23–25 has striking linguistic ties to Joshua, using *yaraš* three times, as well as *natan beyad* ("to hand over to") and *lakad* ("to capture"; v. 25). For further discussion of *yaraš* and its violent connotation, see the Bridging Contexts section of Josh. 13–19.

79. For detailed discussion, see R. P. Knierim, "Israel and the Nations in the Land of Palestine in the Old Testament," in *The Task of Old Testament Theology*, ed. R. Knierim (Grand Rapids: Eerdmans, 1995), 309–21.

80. He did, however, exempt silver and gold and objects of bronze and iron from destruction at Jericho, ordering them saved and deposited in his treasury (Josh. 6:19, 26).

of X" or "Belonging to Y"; everything is marked "Property of God" with no footnotes or exception clauses. Because he created everything, he owns everything, and humans own nothing—not even their own lives. The unappealing (to us) truth is that God can do whatever he wishes with what belongs to him—even take human lives. This leads to my third major point: the *ḥerem* policy is simply one way—from a human standpoint, a frightening one, to be sure—in which God, for whatever reason, chooses to exercise his sovereignty.

Finally, recall that the lone explanation in the book of Joshua for the annihilation of the Canaanites is that Yahweh decided to "harden their hearts" so that they would attack Israel and be destroyed by Yahweh (Josh. 11:20). The motive for his action may be finally to punish "the sin of the Amorites"—whatever that is—mentioned in Genesis 15:16. The timing certainly seems right: Their "sin" was to run its course, and then Israel—four generations after Abraham—would return to Canaan from slavery in Egypt. But the context of Joshua 11 instead simply contrasts their military aggression with the peace-seeking approach of the people of Gibeon (v. 19; cf. Josh. 9). As I noted above, the implication is that, had other Canaanites taken the latter approach, they, too, would have survived—that the Canaanites themselves bear responsibility for what happened to them.[81] These comments voice the biblical writer's perspective on Yahweh's actions.

Ultimately, however, in reckoning with the violence in Joshua, we find ourselves entering the dark, foggy realm of God's mysterious nature with little clear illumination. In the end, however dissatisfying the above discussion may strike readers, one does well to remember that God is on record as stating his preference for life and blessing over death and destruction (e.g., Ezek. 18:23; 33:11). To accept personally that preference as ancient and ongoing one need think no farther than the cross of Christ.

Who Owns the Land Today?

DOES THE BOOK OF JOSHUA explain who owns the land of Canaan today?[82] Many readers might answer, "Yes, it shows that God gave the land to Israel, and that gift is still valid." Some might also supplement evidence from Joshua by citing texts about Israel's future from Old Testament prophets. This

---

81. Cf. the in-depth discussion of this view (with bibliography) in the Bridging Contexts section of Josh. 13–19.

82. For more extensive discussion of this question, see the Bridging Contexts section of Josh. 13–19.

---

approach underlies the political support that Israel has traditionally enjoyed in North America, especially among evangelicals and fundamentalists.

In my view, however, two weaknesses undermine such an approach. (1) It fails to reckon adequately with the implications of an idea that most Christians accept—progressive revelation. Progressive revelation affirms that God has chosen to reveal his truth through Bible writers over time, and that means that later biblical books may modify the ideas of earlier ones. This is most obvious in moving from Old Testament to New Testament, where Christians believe, for example, that the death of Jesus ended the need to follow the Israelite sacrificial system.

(2) The second weakness of this approach is that it simply jumps from the Old Testament to today, entirely skipping the New Testament. It misses the modifications the New Testament may have made on the subject. The question is, Did the New Testament reaffirm God's promise of land for Israel or in any way modify its understanding of it? In reply, the New Testament says little theologically about land compared to the Old Testament.[83] It recalls past and present events that take place there (e.g., Matt. 2:20; Acts 7:3–5, 45; James 5:17), but to my knowledge only Hebrews 11:9 interprets it theologically (see below). The New Testament seems to concur with the Old Testament's view: The land is theologically important, but Israel's relationship to God transcended "that realm and was not permanently or exclusively bound to it."[84]

For example, the father-son metaphor for Yahweh's relationship with Israel (e.g., Ex. 4:22; Hos. 11:1) predates the Exodus and (by implication) the gift of land. It also anchors the later restoration when Israel is landless (i.e., in exile) and explains why Israel can still have a relationship with Yahweh without land.[85] Further, Wright observes in later Israelite prophecy "a 'loosening' of—almost a dispensing with" the ancient connection of land with Israel's relationship with God. He has in mind texts that anticipate the future inclusion of types of foreigners whose membership in Israel, if based upon the traditional family-land connection, would otherwise be uncertain or unclear.[86]

---

83. Cf. J. G. Millar, "Land," *NDBT*, 623–27.

84. C. J. H. Wright, *God's People in God's Land* (Grand Rapids: Eerdmans, 1990), 110. For a lengthy survey of the Old Testament's view of the land with implications for the contemporary political situation, see G. M. Burge, *Whose Land? Whose Promises?* (Cleveland, Ohio: Pilgrim, 2003), 67–111. Burge also treats the New Testament's view (167–89) from a perspective similar to the present one.

85. Wright, *God's People in God's Land*, 15–16, 21–22.

86. E.g., unmarried, childless Israelite women (Isa. 54:1), foreigners and eunuchs (Isa. 56:3–7), and resident aliens (Ezek. 47:22).

Introduction

The New Testament also reflects this "loosening" in a telling way. The land-promise is noticeably absent in its interpretation of the Abrahamic promises. Paul reckons all believers in Jesus as descendants of Abraham regardless of their ethnic background (Gal. 3:7). He teaches that their faith fulfills the patriarchal theme of blessing to the nations (vv. 8, 29, 36; cf. Eph. 3:3). But Paul makes no mention of the patriarchal promise of land, presumably because it plays no role in that blessing.

The reference to Abraham in Hebrews 11 shows the land's decreased importance even more clearly. It says that Abraham sojourned in Canaan to await, not settlement there, but "the [future] city with foundations, whose architect and builder is God" (vv. 9–10). He saw clearly that God's plan "transcended security and prosperity in a parcel of real estate on the eastern shore of the Mediterranean."[87] In short, the New Testament accepts the land of Israel as the homeland of Jews, but its prime concern lies elsewhere—with Jewish and Gentile believers throughout the Roman world whose faith in Jesus fulfills the Abrahamic promise.

The New Testament interprets the Old Testament *typologically*. Since God's way of working in history never changes, "NT persons consciously considered their experiences to match the patterns of God's redemptive history that began with Israel."[88] They read the Old Testament through the lenses of promise-fulfillment: Old Testament events were "promise" and corresponding New Testament ones "fulfillment." For example, Jesus not only fulfills Old Testament messianic expectations, but also embodies Israel at its God-pleasing best.[89] He is the Savior of both Jews and non-Jews (Luke 2:30–32) and the temple—the place (or person) to offer prayers and to deal with sin (John 2:19–32). He is the good shepherd (10:11–16) who gathers all kinds of sheep into a new Israel.

Typology also underlies the foundational New Testament conviction that the church is the new Israel, the new community founded by the Messiah.[90] Apostolic writers apply to early Christian congregations, with both Jewish and Gentile members, covenant concepts and terms previously associated with Israel (Gal. 6:16; 1 Peter 2:9–10). Churches are "the elect" (1 Thess. 1:4–5), the "redeemed" (Rom. 3:24; Eph. 1:7), and the "children of God" (Rom. 8:14; cf. Ex. 4:22). God's covenant faithfulness reassures

---

87. D. A. Hagner, *Hebrews* (Peabody, MA: Hendrickson, 1990), 190. Undoubtedly, the eschatological heavenly Jerusalem is in view (cf. v. 16; 12:22; 13:14; Rev. 21:2).
88. W. W. Klein, C. L. Blomberg, and R. L. Hubbard Jr., *Introduction to Biblical Interpretation* (Nashville: Nelson, 2004), 182–84 (quote 184).
89. S. Motyer, "Israel (Nation)," *NDBT*, 584–85.
90. Wright, *God's People in God's Land*, xvii–xviii.

them of safety in the face of all dangers (Rom. 8:31–39) and will reward them with "an inheritance" for faithful service (Col. 3:23–24).

In short, the apostles teach that the church, a mixture of Jews and Gentiles, is the new Israel—the ultimate offspring of Abraham by faith. It is international in scope, and its temple is not a building in Jerusalem but a dispersed temple, the collective body of Christian believers—both Jews and Gentiles—spread throughout the world (1 Cor. 3:16–17; cf. Eph. 2:21). Wherever located, the physical body of every believer also comprises a temple where the Holy Spirit dwells (1 Cor. 6:19).[91] The unexpected fall of the Holy Spirit on non-Jews after they believed in Jesus convinced the apostles to welcome them as fellow believers without joining Israel first (Acts 11:15–18; 15:7–11).

The New Testament also views the land typologically. The land continues in the church but not in a geographical sense (i.e., location is unimportant). To explain the Gentiles' new status as Christians, Paul invokes two Old Testament motifs, sonship and inheritance (Eph. 2–3). Previously, the Gentiles were "excluded from citizenship and foreigners to the covenant," but Christ tore down the "wall of hostility" between Jews and Gentiles to give those "excluded" access (Eph. 2:13–16).[92] Now they are "fellow citizens with God's people" rather than "foreigners and aliens" (2:19). In the Old Testament language of inheritance, Paul declares them "heirs together with Israel," the two cosharing "the promise in Christ Jesus" (Eph. 3:6).[93] What the prophets expected is now true: God's people includes the Gentiles, God's "son" entitled to their "inheritance" and full citizens of God's new Israel (cf. 1 Peter 1:3–5). As Millar writes, "the inheritance in Christ is no doubt different from the land received and lost by Israel, but it is greater, not less, than that land."[94]

Finally, what is Israel's status today? This controversial matter requires careful, gentle discussion since the subtle, sinister specter of anti-Semitism always haunts such conversations. Paul provides the key scriptural exposition in Romans 9–11. First, by "Israel" Paul means neither the physical land, nor a political state, nor Jews as an ethnic group (Rom. 9:6–7). He has in mind the "children of promise" (v. 8)—the "remnant" (both Jews and Gentiles) who have received salvation by faith (vv. 23–27; 10:6–13).

Second, Paul denies that God has completely rejected Israel as a whole, rebutting the mistaken idea that God's covenant with Israel has

---

91. Cf. Millar, "Land," 623.

92. Cf. Wright, *God's People in God's Land*, 111.

93. Cf. ibid., 111: "The inheritance language ... evokes the triangular pattern of relationships between God, Israel, and the land."

94. Cf. Millar, "Land," 627.

ended (11:1). Rather, Paul cites himself—an Israelite but also a believer in Jesus—as evidence that God has sovereignly preserved from Israel a "remnant chosen by grace" (11:1, 5). To explain the big picture, the apostle invokes an Old Testament metaphor for Israel, an olive tree (Hos. 14:6; Jer. 11:16). Because Israel rejected the gospel, God pruned them from the root tree as unsatisfactory branches (Rom. 11:17, 20), a sad fact with a happy outcome. It opened the way for Gentiles to be saved—i.e., to be grafted into the original root (vv. 12, 15, 17).

But Paul quickly trashes potential Gentile pretentions of spiritual superiority based on that grafting. In so doing, he strongly nips the basis for anti-Semitism in the bud (vv. 17–20). Israel was a fine, cultured olive tree—a high compliment—while the Gentiles are by nature "wild shoots"—not a compliment! His grafting of them into the superior root tree was "contrary to nature" (vv. 17, 24)—an unnatural mixing of cultured and wild. Gentile arrogance is utter nonsense since, without the superior root (Israel), the far inferior branch (Gentiles) would have no support at all (v. 18). If they nurse spiritual pride, the Gentiles also run the risk of being pruned by God as was Israel (v. 21).

But God has a future in mind for Israel—another one of his mysteries (v. 25). He will show Israel the same mercy as he has the Gentiles (vv. 31–32). In the end, Israel's election, covenant, and patriarchal promises—all of them "irrevocable" (v. 29)—still count. God will mysteriously save "all Israel" (vv. 26–28), a reference neither to the church as a whole nor to every individual Jewish person alive at the time. The condition for this salvation is their faith in Jesus the Messiah.[95] Now, the existence of the modern state of Israel might anticipate that fulfillment, but nothing is said here (or elsewhere in the New Testament, for that matter) about the involvement of a "nation" of Israel in it. In my view, the reference is to some future recognition among Jews of Jesus as Messiah without reference to a political state presiding over national boundaries.

In summary, the whole tenor of New Testament teaching points Christians away from a Holy-Land-based perspective toward an international one—from Jerusalem to the uttermost parts of the earth. Its concern is with Jews *and* Gentiles worldwide—and this would include Palestinians—and not simply with modern Israel, itself a secular state. In my view, the demands of the gospel support a just, even-handed approach toward the question of the land.[96]

---

95. Klein, Blomberg, and Hubbard, *Introduction to Biblical Interpretation*, 497, with full bibliography. The quotation from Isaiah 59:20–21 (LXX) in Rom. 11:26–27 clearly stipulates that faith in Jesus the Messiah is the condition for the prophecy to be fulfilled.

96. For further discussion, see Burge, *Whose Land?* 190–204.

Theological Themes

THEMATIC THREADS WEAVE THE patchwork of sources behind the book of Joshua into the striking literary tapestry in our Bibles. This section surveys the most important of those threads.

Yahweh the Promise Keeper

FROM BEGINNING TO END, the book of Joshua identifies Yahweh's commitment to fulfill his promises to Israel as the driving force behind its narratives. The primary promise is his gift of *the land* of Canaan, a promise that goes back to the patriarchs Abraham (Gen. 12:7; 15:18–21), Isaac (26:3–4), and Jacob (28:4; 35:12). Yahweh cites it twice during his commissioning of Joshua (Josh. 1:2, 6) and reviews its broad territorial extent (v. 4), signaling that the entire book concerns its fulfillment. In the last chapter, Yahweh reminds the people of the land-gift they now possess, highlighting its cities ready for occupancy and its soil ready for cultivation (24:13). The land promise theme echoes throughout the book (e.g., 1:11; 18:3); even the Canaanite Rahab and the crafty Gibeonites speak of it (2:9; 9:24). In fact, the prostitute's comment excites the spies to believe that the promise is about to happen (2:24; cf. v. 14). It echoes in the evocative word "inheritance" (*naḥalah*), which debuts in an authorial comment bridging the conquest and land allocation narratives (11:23) and which thematically weaves the book's two halves together (e.g., 12:7; 13:6–8; 14:1).

Promised long ago (Ex. 32:13; Deut. 12:10), inheritance implies permanent possession and family roots in soil to be passed down over generations in perpetuity. It assures the once-landless Israelites of two basics, a place to live and a steady food supply. The divine land-gift to Israel is what the land distribution narrative is all about (chs. 13–19)—and why that narrative ranks among the most important in the book. That explains the authorial caption that draws the curtain down on the settlement story: "So the LORD gave Israel all the land he had sworn to give their forefathers, and they took possession of it and settled there" (21:43; cf. 19:51).

Within the land theme also fall several special allotments of property within the book. Specific divine promises drive the land received by West Manasseh (17:4) and by the aged Caleb, the latter as the reward for his faithful service in the wilderness (14:6–15; 15:13–19). The Levites also receive from Yahweh a special, land-related provision. The book stresses that, unlike the other tribes, they are to receive *no* inheritance in Canaan (13:14, 33; 14:3; 18:17) because they are the one tribe set aside for Yahweh's personal service. But once the other tribes settle, the Levites receive what Yahweh promised them—towns and pasturelands throughout Canaan (ch. 21).

Besides land, a second promise whose fulfillment the book of Joshua features is Yahweh's promised gift of *rest* (*nuaḥ* hi.) for Israel. The roots of this theological idea lie in the phrase "to give rest from (one's) enemies" (e.g., Deut. 12:10; 25:19; Josh. 21:44; 23:1). It describes the state of calm, quiet, peace, security, and safety that follows the end of war — the time when enemies, now vanquished, no longer threaten.

Joshua himself first voices this theme. He tells the eastern tribes that once the west-bank tribes receive Yahweh's rest in owning land, they themselves may settle in rest in their lands along the Jordan's east bank (Josh. 1:13, 15). Later, the author especially highlights two moments that finally usher in "rest from war" for Israel: the conquest of all of Canaan (11:23) and the defeat of the Anakites (14:15). It is that rest — the fears of sudden, hostile attacks swept away — that frees Israel to pursue land distribution and settlement without worry or continuing vigilance. Anyone who has lived through war or whose vulnerability to unexpected violence requires a life on constant alert can understand the huge relief the word "rest" connotes.

Further, a brief comment by the narrator that closes the land allocation story celebrates the wonder of Yahweh's gift of rest (21:44). The rest permits the eastern tribes to return home and settle down (22:4) and sets the scene for Joshua's farewell speech (23:1). Finally, the author emphatically states the outcome of the promise theme: at the end of the day, *not one single promise* remained undone; Yahweh has made them all come true (21:45).

Yahweh the Warrior

AN EARLY BIBLICAL POEM, the Song of the Sea, celebrates that "the LORD is a warrior; the LORD is his name" (Ex. 15:3). In several formulas, the book of Joshua sounds the same theme of Yahweh as a warrior who pursues Yahweh war. At key points the narrator invokes the phrase "the LORD fights/fought for Israel" to express wonder over Yahweh's listening to Joshua at Gibeon (10:14) and to explain how outnumbered Israel trounced the five southern kings (10:42). Similar awe colors Joshua's recollection of what Israel had seen Yahweh do since they first crossed the Jordan (23:3). Like the narrator, Joshua explains how a single Israelite soldier can rout a thousand enemy ones: it is because Yahweh fights for his people, just as he promised (23:10). The literary juxtaposition of the phrase twice in the report of the southern campaign (10:14, 42) implies that Yahweh the warrior provides the margin of victory in all the victories in between.

Further, before battles Yahweh typically calms Joshua or Israel ("do not be afraid") and/or promises victory ("I have/will give [the enemy] into your hands"). This is true before Jericho (6:2; cf. v. 16), Ai II (8:1; cf. v. 7), Gibeon (10:8), and the northern campaign (11:6). Twice during the southern campaign, Joshua exhorts his officers along the same line and for the same reason (10:17, 25). Promises of victory, in turn, shape the language of retrospective summary reports of victory (10:12, 30, 32; 11:8; 24:8, 11). By the same token, bitter irony echoes in Joshua's lament after Israel's defeat at Ai I because it invokes the promise formula, with Israel as the enemy on the receiving end ("deliver us into the hands of the Amorite" [7:7]).

Two theological subthemes, Yahweh's overwhelming power and his personal presence, undergird the theme of Yahweh as warrior. The book abounds with images of Yahweh's unbelievable power. A simple, gilded, wooden box—the ark of Yahweh—overwhelms the waters of the Jordan (even at flood stage), stops their flow, and amazingly lets Israel cross on dry land (chs. 3–4). A simple seven-day ritual siege—six days of silent circling broken by trumpet blasts and a lusty war cry on the seventh—topples the walls of ancient Jericho (ch. 6). Divinely sent panic on the ground and hailstones from heaven pull off victory for Israel at Gibeon (10:10, 11).

At the same time, Yahweh's warrior-might also empowers the clever ambush—on the surface, a purely human maneuver—that brings down Ai (ch. 8). It also drives the defeat of the northern alliance, including the metropolis of Hazor, again through the human stratagem of surprise (ch. 11). Yahweh's overwhelming power backs up his repeated reassurance that no one will be able to put a stop to (or withstand) Israel's advance (1:5; 10:8; 23:9; cf. 7:12–13). Indeed, Yahweh's role in the conquest so outshines Israel's that Yahweh can rightly claim in retrospect—in my paraphrase—that it all happened without Israel so much as lifting a finger (24:12).

As for the reality of Yahweh's presence, that subtheme emerges both in Yahweh's reassurances of being "with" Joshua (1:5, 9; 3:7) and in one comment by the narrator (6:27; cf. 1:17). The starring roles that the ark plays in the Jordan crossing, in Jericho's fall, and in the covenant ceremony at Mount Ebal (chs. 3–4; ch. 6; 8:33) also symbolize Yahweh's personal presence with Israel at key points. Theologically, the book everywhere assumes that Yahweh, Israel's God, personally accompanies them from the Plains of Moab (ch. 1) to the closing scene at Shechem (ch. 24). Yahweh's blunt, irritated riposte of Joshua's accusatory lament over the disaster of Ai I displays an intense personal presence (7:6–15). The same passionate presence also marks the assembly at Shechem, the only time in Joshua that Israel hears Yahweh addressing them directly in the first person (24:1–13). On that occasion, Yahweh offers Israel irrefutable evidence of his presence—the sound of his voice.

The subtheme of divine presence also surfaces in Joshua's surprise encounter with the commander of Yahweh's army near Jericho (5:13–15). An eerie sense of wonder and mystery surrounds the scene because, though

Joshua meets a visible "man," the terminology implicitly identifies him as a member of Yahweh's heavenly entourage.[97] Elsewhere Yahweh's army is invisible (e.g., 2 Kings 6:15–17), so the presence of the commander implies the presence of those unseen "hosts" ready to do battle at Jericho as Israel's ally. Further, the commander's order that Joshua remove his sandals because of holy ground obviously echoes the scene of Moses and the burning bush (Ex. 3:5). The parallel seems to imply the very presence of Yahweh himself, a presence that sanctifies (or sets aside) Jericho for Yahweh himself. The implied presence reassures Joshua that the victory there is certain.

In conclusion, modern readers may find the idea of Yahweh the warrior offensive, but in fact opponents of the gospel of Christ abound today and will continue to do so until defeated at Christ's second coming. The absence of persecution among most readers today should not blind any thoughtful believer to the larger cosmic struggle playing itself out between now and the end of time.

Joshua the Successor

THE CONTINUITY BETWEEN MOSES and Joshua is an obvious concern of the book of Joshua. At stake is Israel's confidence in Joshua's leadership, a confidence that hinges on Yahweh's presence with him. While commissioning Joshua, Yahweh himself first sounds this theme in his promise to be with Joshua just he was with Moses (1:5). The Transjordanian tribes, however, soon voice the theme as a wish (*"may* the LORD ... be with you" [my italics]), perhaps a subtle glimpse of popular anxiety over the risky transition (1:17). Apparently, from the people's perspective, whether Yahweh backs Joshua as he did Moses is no sure thing.

The ambiguities of the Rahab episode also perhaps stir doubts in some Israelites concerning Joshua's spiritual and military leadership mettle. Yahweh seems to have them in mind when, on the day that Israel dramatically crosses the Jordan, he promises to "begin to exalt [Joshua] in the eyes of all Israel" (3:7). The miraculous stopping of the Jordan so persuades Israel that Yahweh is with Joshua that they "revere him all the days of his life, just as they had revered Moses" (4:14). The decisive defeat of Jericho further verifies Yahweh's powerful presence with Joshua and even spreads Joshua's fame throughout the land of Canaan (6:27).

In addition, the biblical writer has woven into the narrative life of Joshua echoes of episodes from the life of Moses. The following table summarizes these echoes:

---

97. KB, 934.

Echoes of Moses' Life in Joshua's

Moses	Joshua
Commissioning (Ex. 3–4)	Commissioning (Josh. 1:1–9)
Red Sea crossing (Ex. 14–15)	Jordan crossing (Josh. 3–4)
Uplifted rod during battle (Ex. 17:8–16)	Uplifted scimitar during battle (Josh. 8:18, 26)
Proclamation of the Instruction (Deut. 27–28)	Proclamation of the Instruction (Josh. 8:30–35)
Farewell speeches (Deut. 31–33)	Farewell speech (Josh. 23)
Covenant ceremony (Deut. 29–30; cf. Ex. 24:3–8)	Covenant ceremony (Josh. 24:1–28)
Burial report (Deut. 34:5–8)	Burial report (Josh. 24:29–31)
Editor's eulogy (Deut. 34:10–12)	Editor's eulogy (Josh. 24:31)

These parallels both reinforce the sense that Joshua is the worthy successor of Moses and strongly suggest that Joshua is in fact Moses' peer.[98]

But the book of Joshua also portrays Joshua as far more than a Mosaic clone. Granted, obedience to Moses' commands guides many of his actions, as the narrator points out: "As the LORD commanded his servant Moses, so Moses commanded Joshua, and Joshua did it; he left nothing undone of all that the LORD commanded Moses" (11:15; cf. 4:10; 8:33, 35; 11:12; 17:4). Granted, also, that the Instruction of Moses plays a foundational, formative role throughout Joshua's career (1:7, 8; 8:31, 32, 34; 23:6; 24:26). But authorial comments at key literary junctures also underscore that Joshua exceeds Moses in two crucial respects. (1) Only Joshua conquers all of Canaan, including its kings and population, as God commanded (10:40–43; 11:16–17, 23). That is no small accomplishment, notwithstanding Yahweh's decisive role in Israel's string of victories. (2) Further, only Joshua receives an inheritance in the land as a gift of the Israelites, the town of Timnath Serah in the hill country of Ephraim (19:49–50). Thus, unlike Moses, he resides in death among his clan and kin within the Promised Land, a reward that recognizes his long years of faithful service rendered for Yahweh and for Israel.[99]

---

98. Also, the book of Joshua itself shows one Moses-Joshua parallel that supports Joshua's peer status with Moses: it reports that both leaders give inheritances; for Moses, cf. 12:6; 13:8, 15, 24, 29; 14:3; 17:4; 18:7; for Joshua, cf. 12:7; 14:13 and 15:13–19 (Caleb); 22:7 (West Manasseh).

99. By contrast, Moses lies buried in Moab, his gravesite unknown since God himself buried him (Deut. 34:6).

In addition, two texts portray Joshua as creatively applying Moses' instruction to Israel's new situation in Canaan. At Mount Ebal (8:30–35), Joshua leads Israel in a special covenant ceremony by innovatively weaving together elements of Moses' teaching to give the ritual its unique meaning for Joshua's Israelite audience. Also, in dealing with the Gibeonites (ch. 9), in my view Joshua seems to base his actions on two Mosaic teachings: how to make treaties with foreign countries and how to treat aliens residing within Israel.[100] In the end, the narrator affirms the Moses-like stature that Joshua achieves by posthumously awarding him the same prestigious title that Moses, "servant of the LORD" (24:29), bore. He also writes what amounts to Joshua's epitaph—that "Israel served the LORD throughout the lifetime of Joshua" (24:31). What Yahweh began at the Jordan—the elevation of Joshua in Israel's eyes—did indeed succeed remarkably.

The People of God

PREOCCUPATION WITH THE BOOK'S HEROES, Yahweh and Joshua, should not obscure the themes it echoes concerning the people of God. They form the all-important supporting cast in the drama of this book. They are the recipients and executers of the orders that Joshua gives from Israel's campsite in the Plains of Moab to the book's final assembly at Shechem. Two youths among them stumble upon and strike a deal with Rahab at Jericho (ch. 2), and Israelite feet feel the crunch of the Jordan's dry riverbed during the crossing. Twelve of them carry stones from the bed that end up in Joshua's monument to the crossing at Gilgal (ch. 3–4). It is Israelite males whom Joshua circumcises there, and the Israelites comprise the crowd celebrating the Passover (ch. 5).

The Israelites perform the week-long ritual conquest of Jericho and carry out the killing and burning that follows (ch. 6). One anonymous Israelite secretly cheats Yahweh out of *ḥerem* at Jericho, so all Israel shares in the shameful, unnerving defeat of Ai I. But they also share in the lot-casting that unmasks Achan, hurl the stones that effect his execution, realize the special triumph of Ai II, pile up the rocks over the grave of Ai's executed king, and happily carry off Ai's plunder and livestock. They witness Joshua's altar-building on Mount Ebal and offer sacrifices on it, then listen below the mount as he reads them the Instruction from the summit (chs. 7–8).

Israelite leaders make a treaty with the crafty Hivites (ch. 9), and their troops rescue Gibeon and sweep the southern and northern areas of the country into Israel's possession (chs. 10–12). They are the people who,

---

100. For further details, see the commentary on 8:30–35 and chs. 9–10.

obeying Moses, distribute the land among the tribes (14:5), each of their families receiving a land-gift from Yahweh (chs. 13–19; cf. 1:2). Some Israelites struggle with leftover Canaanites nearby (e.g., 16:10; 17:13), and one tribe (Dan) even has to relocate elsewhere in the land because of indigenous resistance (19:47). It is the Israelite people who set aside seven cities nationwide as cities where a killer may find refuge from avengers and have his case dispassionately adjudicated (ch. 20). It is the Israelites who sacrificially surrender their own towns and fields so the Levites may have places to live and pastures to herd their animals (ch. 21). They are the ones who settle the altar dispute (ch. 22), hear Joshua's passionate farewell (ch. 23), and take upon themselves the covenant with Yahweh (ch. 24).

Several subthemes thread their way through the book. One subtheme concerns the very geography of the entity called "Israel." The book stresses that Israel comprises people enjoying inheritances along both sides of the Jordan, not just on the west bank. The book occasionally seems to reflect a western bias, especially among some who regard the Jordan as a national boundary (e.g., chs. 14–17, 22), but for the most part it carefully includes the eastern tribes (e.g., 1:12–18; 4:12; 12:1–6; 13:8–33; 18:7; ch. 22).

Another subtheme speaks of the complex makeup of Israel. At first glance, Israel seems an uncomplicated, fairly homogenous people, but the book shows that the term "people of Israel" embraces a complex mix of "myriad elements."[101] The narrator occasionally passes before us a brief snapshot of the diversity of "all Israel"—e.g., "aliens and citizens alike, with their elders, officials and judges ... the priests, who were Levites" and "women and children" (8:33, 35).

The book's mind-numbing, detailed administrative chapters (chs. 13–21)—the ones that many readers may skip as they would a phonebook—in reality spread a metaphor for this multifaceted Israel. Countless tribal and clan groups make up the Israelites, strewn across every corner of the land. Many reside in major cities of well-known historical pedigrees, but most inhabit obscure, small towns or hamlets way off the beaten track and totally unknown elsewhere. Among the people live many non-Israelites like Rahab and her family, the Hivites centered around Gibeon, nameless resident aliens, as well as enclaves of surviving Canaanites. The boring details betray a challenge for Israel—"to translate those lists and allotments into an actual community in actual possession of the Promised Land."[102]

---

101. Cf. the appreciations of these chapters in D. M. Gunn, "Joshua and Judges," in R. Alter and F. Kermode, eds., *The Literary Guide to the Bible* (Cambridge, Mass.: Belknap, 1987), 102–3 (quote 103); and Curtis, *Joshua*, 26.

102. Gunn, "Joshua and Judges," 103.

But the most important theme pertaining to Israel concerns the absolute necessity for the Israelites to maintain their unique identity as God's special people. Holiness is part of that identity, so circumcision sanctifies Israelite soldiers, making them fit for service in Yahweh war (ch. 5). Covenant ceremonies demand that Israel reaffirm its exclusive commitment to Yahweh alone as their God (8:30–35; 24:1–28)—indeed, a "holy" and "jealous" God (24:19).

But by far the strongest voice proclaiming this theme is that of Joshua himself. In his farewell speech (ch. 23), he passionately warns Israel to avoid too cozy relationships with their Canaanite neighbors. He discourages casual contacts and condemns intermarriage, strongly branding them as "snares and traps ... whips on your backs and thorns in your eyes" (23:13). He forbids them to serve any other gods but Yahweh and threatens that a furious Yahweh will annihilate them if they abandon him and worship other gods (23:15–16). Their very identity is on the line, Joshua says, and he strings together phrases that sum up what Yahweh demands. Israel must "obey" Moses' law (v. 6), "hold fast to the LORD" (v. 8), and "love" him (v. 11). In chapter 24 Joshua invokes as the key word the need to "serve the LORD" (24:14–16, 18, 19–22, 24).

In both chapters, Joshua lays it on the line in the strongest terms: Yahweh will assuredly bring on Israel "all the evil he has threatened" just as he surely has fulfilled his every "good promise" (23:15–16). In short, Israel is God's people or it is no people. Its reason for existence is to serve Yahweh, and the logical outcome of failure to do so is total destruction.

Israel and the Peoples

IN THE DISCUSSION ABOVE concerning violence in Joshua, an important theme emerged that bears repetition in conclusion.[103] We pointed out that despite the deadly shadow of ethnic cleansing that haunts the book, it also reflects a surprisingly inclusive stance toward non-Israelites. This theme first surfaces in two narrative motifs: the conciliatory treatment of Rahab and the Gibeonites, and the contrast between their nonresistance to Yahweh and Israel and the militant resistance of Canaan's kings (cf. 11:18–20).

Above, following L. Stone, we suggested that the book promotes obedience to the Instruction of Moses as the basis for anyone, Israelite or non-Israelite, to remain in the land. Here I wish simply cite the contrasting fates of Rahab and Achan as a further example of that point. Rahab typifies the ultimate outsider—a Canaanite, female, prostitute on the *ḥerem*

---

103. Cf. the "Now, About All That Killing ..." section above.

hit-list—while Achan typifies the ultimate insider—an Israelite, male, and from the prestigious tribe of Judah. Rahab survives and lives in Israel, while Achan dies and is remembered with shame. The difference is that Achan has violated the covenant (i.e., resisted Yahweh's will), while Rahab humbly submits to Yahweh and his will. The implication is that openness and submission count for more than ethnicity.

But what about the book's references to conflicts between Israel and Canaan's peoples (e.g., 15:63; 16:10; 17:13)? Do they imply a serious failure by Israel to carry out ḥerem as Yahweh commanded? That is a possibility, but several observations suggest that the Israelite-Canaanite conflicts be read less critically. In my view, taken at face value, the biblical statements in question simply state the facts rather than voice criticism of the Israelites. Ideally, Israel is in violation of Deuteronomy 20, but the book of Joshua seems not to press the point. Instead, it appears simply to accept the Canaanite presence as a given to be worked around. Further, in his farewell speech Joshua notes that Yahweh himself will "drive out" the remaining Canaanites (23:5; cf. 13:6). Yahweh's promise seems aimed genuinely to compensate for Israel's weakness in the ethnic standoff rather than to demonstrate Israel's lack of faith.

Even more to the point, Joshua's main plea is that Israel must vigilantly guard against corrupting Canaanite influences rather than totally get rid of them. Indeed, it strikes me as particularly telling that Joshua passes up the opportunity to urge his audience finally to complete the conquest by implementing ḥerem as Yahweh intended. In short, these observations seem of a piece with the more inclusive stance toward non-Israelites that Rahab and the Gibeonites reflect. To be sure, the Canaanites pose a deadly danger to Israel's loyalty to Yahweh, and Yahweh holds Israel accountable to its covenant commitment. But the book of Joshua seems to leave the final solution to Yahweh—and perhaps also to leave the door open to other Rahabs and Gibeonites from among the Canaanite enclaves who might choose submission over resistance.

Outline

---

104. For an alternative outline, see M. A. Sweeney, *King Josiah of Judah: The Lord Messiah of Israel* (Oxford/New York: Oxford Univ. Press, 2001), 131.

A Select Bibliography on Joshua

Commentaries

Boling, Robert G. *Joshua*. AB 6. Garden City: Doubleday, 1982.

Butler, Trent C. *Joshua*. WBC 7. Waco: Word, 1983.

Creach, J. F. D. *Joshua*. Louisville: John Knox, 2003.

Fritz, V. *Das Buch Josua*. HAT 7. Tübingen: J. C. B. Mohr [Siebeck], 1994.

Hamlin, E. J. *Inheriting the Land: A Commentary on the Book of Joshua*. ITC. Grand Rapids: Eerdmans, 1983.

Hawk, L. D. *Joshua*. Berit Olam; Collegeville, MN: Liturgical, 2000.

Hertzberg, H. W. *Die Bücher Josua, Richter, Rut*. Göttingen: Vandenhoeck & Ruprecht, 1969.

Hess, Richard S. *Joshua*. TOTC. Downers Grove, Ill.: InterVarsity Press, 1996.

Howard, David M. *Joshua*. NAC. Nashville: Broadman & Homan, 1998.

Kaufmann, Y. *The Biblical Account of the Conquest of Canaan*. 2nd ed. Jerusalem: Magnes, 1985.

Nelson, Richard D. *Joshua*. OTL. Louisville: Westminster/John Knox, 1997.

Woudstra, Martin H. *Joshua*. NICOT. Grand Rapids: Eerdmans, 1981.

Related Works

Albertz, R. "The Canonical Alignment of the Book of Joshua." Pp. 288–90 in *Judah and the Judeans in the Fourth Century B.C.E.* Eds. O. Lipschits, G. N. Knoppers, and R. Albertz. Winona Lake, Ind.: Eisenbrauns, 2007.

Assis, E. "The Choice to Serve God and Assist His People: Rahab and Yael." *Bib* 85/1 (2004): 82–90.

_____. "'For It Shall Be A Witness Between Us': A Literary Reading of Josh 22." *SJOT* 18/2 (2004): 208–31.

_____. "'How Long Are You Slack to Go to Possess the Land?' (Jos. 18:3): Ideal and Reality in the Distribution Descriptions in Joshua 13–19." *VT* 53 (2003): 1–25.

Barmash, P. *Homicide in the Biblical World*. Cambridge: Cambridge University Press, 2005.

Barnes, B. "Was Rahab's Lie a Sin?" *RTR* 54 (1995): 1–9.

Barr, J. "Migrash in the Old Testament." *JSS* 29 (1984): 15–31.

Barstad, H. M. "The Old Testament Feminine Personal Name *raḥab*. An Onomastic Note." *SEÅ* 54 (1989): 43–49.

Ben-Ami, D. "Early Iron Cult Places—New Evidences from Tel Hazor." *Tel Aviv* 33/2 (2006): 121–33.

_____. "The Iron Age I at Hazor in Light of the Renewed Excavations." *IEJ* 51/2 (2001): 148–70.

_____. "Mysterious Standing Stones: What Do These Ubiquitous Things Mean?" *BAR* 33/2 (March–April 2006): 38–45.

Ben-Tor, A., and Rubiato, T. "Excavating Hazor I: Solomon's City Rises from the Ashes." *BAR* 25 (March–April 1999): 26–37, 60.

_____. "Excavating Hazor II: Did the Israelites Destroy the Canaanite City?" *BAR* 25 (May–June 1999): 22–39.

Ben Zvi, E. "The List of Levitical Cities." *JSOT* 54 (1992): 77–106.

Bienkowski, P. *Jericho in the Middle Bronze Age.* Warminster: Aris & Phillips, 1986.

_____. "Jericho Was Destroyed in the Middle Bronze Age, Not the Late Bronze Age." *BAR* 16/5 (September–October 1990): 45–49, 68–69.

Bird, P. "The Harlot as Heroine: Narrative Art and Social Presuppositions in Three Old Testament Texts." *Semeia* 46 (1989): 119–39.

Brekelmans, C. "חרם." *THAT*, 1:635–39.

_____. "Joshua v 10–12: Another Approach." *OTS* 25 (1989): 89–95.

Brueggemann, W. "Revelation and Violence: A Study in Contextualization." Pp. 285–318 in *A Social Reading of the Old Testament: Prophetic Approaches to Israel's Communal Life.* Ed. P. D. Miller. Minneapolis: Fortress, 1994.

Bruins, H. J., and J. van der Plicht. "Tell Es-Sultan (Jericho): Radiocarbon Results of Short-Lived Cereal and Multiyear Charcoal Samples from the End of the Middle Bronze Age." *Radiocarbon* 37/2 (1995): 213–20.

Campbell, A. F., and M. A. O'Brien. *Unfolding the Deuteronomistic History.* Minneapolis: Fortress, 2000.

Chavalas, M. W. and M. R. Adamthwaite, "Archaeological Light on the Old Testament." Pp. 59–96 in *The Face of Old Testament Studies.* Eds. D. W. Baker and B. T. Arnold. Grand Rapids: Baker, 1999.

Chirichigno, G. C. "The Use of the Epithet in the Characterization of Joshua." *TrinJ* 8 (1987): 72–79.

Clements, R. E. "Achan's Sin: Warfare and Holiness." Pp. 113–26 in *Shall Not the Judge of All the Earth Do What Is Right?* Eds. D. Penchansky and P. L. Redditt. Winona Lake, Ind: Eisenbrauns, 2000.

Coats, G. "The Ark of the Covenant in Joshua: A Probe into the History of a Tradition." *HAR* 9 (1985): 137–57.

Culley, R. C. "Stories of the Conquest: Joshua 2, 6, 7, and 8." *HAR* 8 (1984): 25–44.

Curtis, A. H. W. *Joshua*. OTG. Sheffield: Sheffield Academic Press, 1994.

Del Monte, G. F. "The Hittite Herem." Pp. 21–45 in *Memoriae Igor M. Diakonoff*. Eds. L. Kogan et al. Winona Lake, Ind.: Eisenbrauns, 2005.

Dever, W. G. *Who Were the Early Israelites and Where Did They Come From?* Grand Rapids: Eerdmans, 2003.

Dorsey, D. A. *The Roads and Highways of Ancient Israel.* Baltimore; London: Johns Hopkins University Press, 1991.

Dus, J. "Die Analyse zweier Ladeerzählungen des Josuabuches (Jos 3–4 und 6)." *ZAW* 72 (1960): 107–34.

Fleming, D. E. "The Seven-Day Siege of Jericho in Holy War." Pp. 211–28 in *Ki Baruch Hu*. Eds. R. Chazan, W. W. Hallo, and L. H. Schiffman. B. A. Levine Festschrift. Winona Lake, Ind.: Eisenbrauns, 1999.

Fuhs, H. F. "יָרֵא." *TDOT*, 6:290–315.

Garstang, J., and J. B. E. Garstang. *The Story of Jericho.* 2nd ed. London: Marshall, Morgan, & Scott, 1948.

George, D. B. "Yahweh's Speech at Jos 1:2–6 and Deut 11: Semantics, Intertextuality, and Meaning." *ZAW* 112 (2000): 356–64.

Gilmour, G. "Foreign Burials in Late Bronze Age Palestine." *Near Eastern Archaeology* 65/2 (2002): 112–19.

Gottwald, N. *The Tribes of Yahweh.* Maryknoll, N.Y.: Orbis, 1979.

Greenspoon, L. J. "The Book of Joshua—Part I: Texts and Versions." *CBR* 3.2 (2005): 229–61.

_____. *Textual Studies in the Book of Joshua*. HSM 28. Chico, Calif.: Scholars Press, 1983.

Grintz, J. M. "The Treaty of Joshua with the Gibeonites." *JAOS* 86 (1966): 113–26.

Gunn, D. M. "Joshua and Judges." Pp. 102–21 in *The Literary Guide to the Bible*. Eds. R. Alter and F. Kermode. Cambridge, Mass.: Belknap, 1987.

Hasel, M. G. "*Israel* in the Merneptah Stela." *BASOR* 296 (1994): 45–61.

Hawk, L. D. *Every Promise Fulfilled: Contesting Plots in Joshua*. Louisville: Westminster/John Knox, 1991.

_____. "The Problem with Pagans." Pp. 153–63 in *Reading Bibles, Writing Bodies: Identity and the Book*. Eds. T. K. Beal and D. M. Gunn. London and New York: Routledge, 1996.

_____. "Strange Houseguests: Rahab, Lot, and the Dynamics of Deliverance." Pp. 89–97 in *Reading between the Texts: Intertextuality and the Hebrew Bible*. Ed. D. N. Fewell. Louisville: Westminster John Knox, 1992.

Hess, R. S. "Achan and Achor: Names and Wordplay in Joshua 7." *HAR* 14 (1994): 89–98.

_____. "Asking Historical Questions of Joshua 13–19: Recent Discussion concerning the Date of the Boundary Lists." Pp. 106–204 in *Faith, Tradition, and History: Old Testament Historiography in Its Ancient Near Eastern Context.* Eds. A. R. Millard, J. K. Hoffmeier, and D. W. Baker. Winona Lake, Ind.: Eisenbrauns, 1994.

_____. "Late Bronze Age and Biblical Boundary Descriptions of the West Semitic World." Pp. 123–38 in *Ugarit and the Bible.* Eds. G. J. Brooke et al. Münster: Ugarit-Vorlag, 1994.

_____. "Non-Israelite Personal Names in the Book of Joshua." *CBQ* 58 (1996): 205–14.

_____. "The Book of Joshua as a Land Grant." *Bib* 83 (2002): 493–506.

Hesse, F. "חָזַק." *TDOT,* 4:301–8.

Holland, T. A., and E. Netzer, "Jericho." *ABD,* 3:723–40.

Holloway, J. "The Ethical Dilemma of Holy War." *Southwestern Journal of Theology* 41 (1998): 44–69.

Hom, M. K. "A Day Like No Other: A Discussion of Joshua 10:12–14." *ExpTim* 115/7 (2004): 217–23.

Horn, P. H. "Josua 2, 1–24 im Milieu einer 'dimorphic society'." *BZ* 31 (1987): 264–70.

House, P. R. "Examining the Narratives of the Old Testament Narrative: An Exploration in Biblical Theology." *WTJ* 67 (2005): 229–45.

_____. "The God Who Gives Rest in the Land: Joshua." *SBJT* 2 (1998): 12–33.

Howard, D. M., Jr. "All Israel's Response to Joshua: A Note on the Narrative Framework of Joshua 1." Pp. 81–91 in *Fortunate the Eyes That See.* Ed. A. B. Beck et al. Grand Rapids: Eerdmans, 1995.

Hubbard, R. L., Jr. "Caleb, Calebites," *DOTHB,* 120–22.

_____. "Gilgal." *DOTHB,* 334–36.

_____. "Only a Distant Memory: Old Testament Allusions to Joshua's Days." *Ex Auditu* 16 (2000): 131–48.

_____. "The Go'el in Ancient Israel: Theological Reflections on an Israelite Institution." *BBR* 1 (1991): 3–19.

_____. " 'What Do These Stones Mean?': Biblical Theology and a Motif in Joshua." *BBR* 11.1 (2001): 25–49.

Hulse, E. V. "Joshua's Curse and the Abandonment of Ancient Jericho: Schistosomiasis as a Possible Medical Explanation." *Medical History* 15 (1971): 376–86.

Jenson, P. P. "אֶלֶף." *NIDOTTE,* 1:416–18.

Jones, G. H. "The Concept of Holy War." Pp. 299–321 in *The World of Ancient Israel: Sociological, Anthropological, and Political Perspectives.* Ed. R. E. Clements. Cambridge: Cambridge University Press, 1989.

Kallai, Z. *Historical Geography of the Bible.* Leiden: Brill, 1986.

Kaminsky, J. S. "Joshua 7: A Reassessment of Israelite Conceptions of Corporate Punishment." Pp. 315–46 in *The Pitcher Is Broken: Memorial Essays for Gösta Ahlström.* Eds. S. W. Holloway and L. K. Handy. JSOTSup 190; Sheffield: Sheffield Academic Press, 1995.

Kempinski, A. "Joshua's Altar: An Iron Age I Watchtower." *BAR* 12/1 (January–February 1986): 42, 44–49.

Kenyon, K. M. *Archaeology in the Holy Land.* 5th ed. Nashville: Nelson, 1985.

———. "Jericho." *NEAEHL*, 2:674–81.

Killebrew, A. E. *Biblical Peoples and Ethnicity.* Atlanta: Society of Biblical Literature, 2005.

Kissling, P. J. *Reliable Characters in the Primary History: Profiles of Moses, Joshua, Elijah, and Elisha.* JSOTSup 224; Sheffield: Sheffield Academic Press, 1996.

Kitchen, K. A. *On the Reliability of the Old Testament.* Grand Rapids: Eerdmans, 2003.

Kitz, A. M. "The Hebrew Terminology of Lot Casting and Its Ancient Near Eastern Context." *CBQ* 62 (2000): 207–14

———. "Undivided Inheritance and Lot Casting in the Book of Joshua." *JBL* 119 (2000): 601–18.

Kloppenberg, J. S. "Joshua 22: The Priestly Editing of An Ancient Tradition." *Bib* 62/3 (1981): 347–71.

Knierim, R. P. "Israel and the Nations in the Land of Palestine in the Old Testament." Pp. 309–21 in *The Task of Old Testament Theology.* Ed. R. P. Knierim. Grand Rapids: Eerdmans, 1995.

Koopmans, W. T. "Vengeance and the Fair Trial Venue: A Sermon on Joshua 20." *CTJ* 37/1 (2002): 95–98.

Kotter, W. "Gilgal." *ABD*, 2:1022–24.

Kruger, H. "Sun and Moon Marking Time: A Cursory Survey of Exegetical Possibilities in Joshua 10:9–14." *JNSL* 26/1 (2000): 137–52.

Kuhrt, A. *The Ancient Near East c. 3000–330 B.C.* 2 Vols. London: Routledge, 1995.

Kurz, W. S. "Luke 22:14–38 and Greco-Roman and Biblical Farewell Addresses." *JBL* 104/2 (1985): 251–68.

Lipiński, E. "'Anaq-Kiryat ᵓArbaᶜ-Hébron et Ses Sanctuaires Tribaux." *VT* 24 (1974): 41–55.

———. "נָחַל." *TDOT*, 9:319–35.

Lohfink, N. "חָרַם." *TDOT*, 2:180–99.

———. "יָרַשׁ." *TDOT*, 6:368–96.

Longman, T., III, and D. G. Reid. *God Is a Warrior*. Grand Rapids: Zondervan, 1995.

MacLaurin, E. C. B. "Anak/Anaks." *VT* 15 (1965): 468–74.

Malamat, A. "Israelite Conduct of War in the Conquest of Canaan according to the Biblical Tradition." Pp. 35–55 in *Symposia Celebrating the 75ᵗʰ Anniversary of the American Schools of Oriental Research (1900–1975)*. Ed. F. M. Cross. Cambridge, Mass.: ASOR, 1979.

McConville, J. G. *Grace in the End: A Study in Deuteronomic Theology*. Grand Rapids: Zondervan, 1993.

Millar, J. G. "Land." *NDBT*, 623–27.

Mitchell, G. *Together in the Land*. JSOTSup 134. Sheffield: Sheffield Academic Press, 1993.

Naʾaman, N. *Borders and Districts in Biblical Historiography: Seven Studies in Biblical Geographic Lists*. Jerusalem: Simor, 1986.

Nelson, R.D. "*Ḥerem* and the Deuteronomic Social Conscience." Pp. 39–54 in *Deuteronomy and Deuteronomic Literature*. Eds. M. Vervenne and J. Lust. Leuven: Leuven University Press, 1997.

_____. "Josiah in the Book of Joshua." *JBL* 100 (1981): 531–40.

Niditch, S. *War in the Hebrew Bible: A Study in the Ethics of Violence*. New York: Oxford University Press, 1993.

Noort, E. "The Disgrace of Egypt: Joshua 5:9a and Its Context." Pp. 3–19 in *The Wisdom of Egypt*. Eds. A. Hilhorst and G. H. van Kooten. Leiden: Brill, 2005.

_____. "The Traditions of Ebal and Mount Gerizim: Theological Positions in the Book of Joshua." Pp. 161–80 in *Deuteronomy and Deuteronomic Literature*. Ed. M. Vervenne and J. Lust. BETL 133. Leuven: Uitgeverij Peeters, 1997.

Noth, M. *The Deuteronomic History*. JSOTSup 15. Sheffield: Sheffield Academic Press, 1981.

Organ, B. E. "Pursuing Phinehas: A Synchronic Reading." *CBQ* 63 (2001): 203–18.

Oswalt, J. N. "Rest." *NIDOTTE*, 4:1132–36.

Ottosson, M. "Rahab and the Spies." Pp. 419–27 in *Dumu-e₂-dub-ba-a: Studies in Honor of Åke W. Sjöberg*. Eds. H. Behrens et al. Philadelphia: Samuel Noah Kramer Fund, 1989.

Peckham, B. "The Composition of Joshua 3–4." *CBQ* 46 (1984): 413–31.

Polzin, R. *Moses and the Deuteronomist*. New York: Seabury, 1980.

Porter, J. R. "The Background of Joshua 3–5." *SEÅ* 36 (1971): 5–23.

Preuss, H. D. "נוּחַ." *TDOT*, 9:277–86.

Provan, I., V. P. Long, and T. Longman III. *A Biblical History of Israel*. Louisville: Westminster John Knox, 2003.

Rehm, M. D. "Levites and Priests." *ABD*, 4:297–310.

Ringgren, H. "מָעַל." *TDOT*, 8:460–63.

Robinson, G. "The Idea of Rest in the OT and the Search for the Basic Character of the Sabbath." *ZAW* 92 (1980): 32–42.

Robinson, R. B. "The Coherence of the Jericho Narrative: A Literary Reading of Joshua 6." Pp. 311–35 in *Konsequente Traditionsgeschichte*. Eds. R. Bartelmus et al. Göttingen: Vandenhoeck & Ruprecht, 1993.

Rofé, A. "The Piety of the Torah-Disciples at the Winding-Up of the Hebrew Bible: Josh 1:8; Ps 1:2; Isa 59:21." Pp. 78–85 in *Bibel in jüdischer und christlicher Tradition*. Ed. M. Köckert. BBB 88. Frankfurt am Main: A. Hain, 1993.

Römer, T. *The So-Called Deuteronomistic History*. London; New York: T & T Clark, 2007.

Rowlett, L. "Inclusion, Exclusion and Marginality in the Book of Joshua." *JSOT* 55 (1992): 19–23.

_____. *Joshua and the Rhetoric of Violence*. JSOTSup 226; Sheffield: Sheffield Academic Press, 1996.

Saydon, P. "The Crossing of the Jordan, Jos. Chaps. 3 and 4." *CBQ* 12 (1950): 194–207.

Schäfer-Lichtenberger, C. "Hazor—A City State between the Major Powers." *SJOT* 15 (2001): 104–22.

Scharbert, J. "אָרַר." *TDOT*, 1:405–18.

_____. "בָּרַךְ." *TDOT*, 2:279–308.

Schmidt, L. "Leviten- und Asylstädte in Num. XXXV und Jos. XX; XXI 1–42." *VT* 52/1 (2002): 103–21.

Schreiner, J. "אָמַץ." *TDOT*, 1:323–27.

Seleznev, M. G. "The Origin of the Tribal Boundaries in Joshua: Administrative Documents or Sacral Geography?" Pp. 330–61 in *Memoriae Igor M. Diakonoff: Babel und Babel* 2. Eds. L. G. Kogan et al. Winona Lake, Ind: Eisenbrauns, 2005.

Sherwood, A. "A Leader's Misleading and a Prostitute's Profession: A Re-examination of Joshua 2." *JSOT* 31/1 (2006): 43–61.

Smend, R. *Yahweh War and Tribal Confederation*. Nashville: Abingdon, 1970.

Snaith, N. H. "The Altar at Gilgal: Joshua 22:23–29." *VT* 28/3 (1978): 330–35.

Spina, F. A. *The Faith of the Outsider: Exclusion and Inclusion in the Biblical Story*. Grand Rapids: Eerdmans, 2005.

Stackert, J. "Why Does Deuteronomy Legislate Cities of Refuge? Asylum in the Covenant Collection (Exodus 21:12–14) and Deuteronomy (19:1–13)." *JBL* 125 (2006): 23–49.

Stager, L. E. "Forging an Identity: The Emergence of Ancient Israel." Pp. 123–76 in *The Oxford History of the Biblical World*. Ed. M. D. Coogan. New York; Oxford: Oxford University Press, 1998.

Stec, D. M. "The Mantle Hidden by Achan," *VT* 41 (1991): 356–59.

Stek, J. H. "Rahab of Canaan and Israel: The Meaning of Joshua 2." *CTJ* 37 (2002): 24–48.

Stern, P. D. *The Biblical Herem: A Window on Israel's Religious Experience*. BJS 211. Atlanta: Scholars Press, 1991.

Stone, L. G. "Ethical and Apologetic Tendencies in the Redaction of the Book of Joshua." *CBQ* 53 (1991): 25–35.

Sutherland, R. "Israelite Political Theory in Joshua 9." *JSOT* 53 (1992): 65–74.

Svensson, J. *Towns and Toponyms in the Old Testament*. CBOT 38. Stockholm: Almqvist & Wiksell, 1994.

Van der Meer, M. N. *Formation and Reformulation: The Redaction of the Book of Joshua in the Light of the Oldest Textual Witnesses*. VTSup 102; Leiden: Brill, 2001.

Von Rad, G. *Holy War in Ancient Israel*. Grand Rapids: Eerdmans, 1991.

_____. "There Still Remains a Rest for the People of God." Pp. 82–88 in *From Genesis to Chronicles: Explorations in Old Testament Theology*. Ed. K. C. Hanson. Minneapolis: Fortress, 2005.

Wagenaar, J. A. "The Cessation of Manna. Editorial Frames for the Wilderness Wandering in Exodus 16,35 and Joshua 5,10–12." *ZAW* 112 (2000): 192–209.

_____. "Crossing the Sea of Reeds (Exod 13–14) and the Jordan (Josh 3–4)." Pp. 461–70 in *Studies in the Book of Exodus*. Ed. M. Vervenne. Leuven: Leuven University Press, 1996.

Wallis, G. "אָהַב." *TDOT*, 1:101–18.

Walton, J. H. "Joshua 10:12–15 and Mesopotamian Celestial Omen Texts." Pp. 181–90 in *Faith, Tradition, and History*. Eds. A. R. Millard, J. K. Hoffmeier, and D. W. Baker. Winona Lake, Ind.: Eisenbrauns, 1994.

Weinfeld, M. "בְּרִית." *TDOT*, 2:253–79.

_____. *The Promise of the Land*. Berkeley: University of California Press, 1993.

Wilcoxsen, J. "Narrative Structure and Cult Legend: A Study of Joshua 1–6." Pp. 43–70 in *Transitions in Biblical Scholarship*. Ed. J. Rylaarsdam. Chicago: University of Chicago Press, 1968.

Wood, B. G. "Dating Jericho's Destruction: Bienkowski Is Wrong on All Counts." *BAR* 16/5 (September–October 1990): 45, 47–49, 68–69.

_____. "Did the Israelites Conquer Jericho? A New Look at the Archaeological Evidence." *BAR* 16/2 (March–April 1990): 44–58.

Wright, C. J. H. "נָחַל." *NIDOTTE*, 3:77–81.

_____. *God's People in God's Land.* Grand Rapids: Eerdmans, 1990.

Yadin, Y. *Hazor.* London: Oxford University Press, 1972.

Younger, K. L. *Ancient Conquest Accounts: A Study in Ancient Near Eastern and Biblical History Writing.* JSOTSup 98. Sheffield: Sheffield Academic Press, 1990.

_____. "Early Israel in Recent Biblical Scholarship." Pp. 178–200 in *The Face of Old Testament Studies.* Eds. D. W. Baker and B. T. Arnold. Grand Rapids: Baker, 1999.

_____. "The 'Conquest' of the South (Jos. 10:28–39)." *BZ* 39 (1995): 255–64.

Zakovitch, Y. "Humor and Theology or the Successful Failure of Israelite Intelligence: A Literary-Folkloric Approach to Joshua 2." Pp. 75–98 in *Text and Tradition: The Hebrew Bible and Folklore.* Ed. S. Niditch. Atlanta: Scholars Press, 1990.

Zevit, Z. "Archaeological and Literary Stratigraphy in Joshua 7–8." *BASOR* 251 (1983): 23–35.

Zertal, A. "Has Joshua's Altar Been Found on Mt Ebal?" BAR 11/1 (January–February 1985): 26–43.

_____. "How Can Kempinski Be So Wrong?" *BAR* 12/1 (January–February 1986): 43, 49–53.

Zuckerman, S. "Where Is the Hazor Archive Buried?" *BAR* 32/2 (March–April 2006): 34.

Other Works Cited

Balmer, R. *Mine Eyes Have Seen the Glory.* New York: Oxford University Press, 1989.

_____. *Grant Us Courage.* New York: Oxford University Press, 1996.

Barton, W. *Safed and Keturah.* Atlanta: John Knox, 1978.

Benner, D. G. *Desiring God's Will.* Downers Grove, Ill.: InterVarsity Press, 2005.

Custis James, C. *The Gospel of Ruth.* Grand Rapids: Zondervan, 2008.

Eller, V. *King Jesus' Manual of Arms for the 'Armless.* Nashville: Abingdon, 1973.

Gladwell, M. *Blink: The Power of Thinking without Thinking.* New York: Back Bay Books, 2005.

Hunter III, G. G. *The Celtic Way of Evangelism: How Christianity Can Win the West—Again.* Nashville: Abingdon, 2000.

Lanham, R. *The Sinner's Guide to the Evangelical Right.* New York: Penguin, 2006.

A Select Bibliography on Joshua

McNeal, R. *The Present Future: Six Tough Questions for the Church*. San Francisco: Jossey-Bass, 2003.

Oates, S. B. *Let the Trumpet Sound*. New York: Mentor, 1982.

Peterson, E. H. *A Long Obedience in the Same Direction*. 2nd ed. Downers Grove, Ill.: InterVarsity Press, 2000.

Robinson, M. *Gilead*. New York: Farrar, Straus and Giroux, 2004.

Yancey, P. *The Jesus I Never Knew*. Grand Rapids: Zondervan, 1995.

Joshua 1:1–18

❧

AFTER THE DEATH of Moses the servant of the LORD, the LORD said to Joshua son of Nun, Moses' aide: ²"Moses my servant is dead. Now then, you and all these people, get ready to cross the Jordan River into the land I am about to give to them—to the Israelites. ³I will give you every place where you set your foot, as I promised Moses. ⁴Your territory will extend from the desert to Lebanon, and from the great river, the Euphrates—all the Hittite country—to the Great Sea on the west. ⁵No one will be able to stand up against you all the days of your life. As I was with Moses, so I will be with you; I will never leave you nor forsake you.

⁶"Be strong and courageous, because you will lead these people to inherit the land I swore to their forefathers to give them. ⁷Be strong and very courageous. Be careful to obey all the law my servant Moses gave you; do not turn from it to the right or to the left, that you may be successful wherever you go. ⁸Do not let this Book of the Law depart from your mouth; meditate on it day and night, so that you may be careful to do everything written in it. Then you will be prosperous and successful. ⁹Have I not commanded you? Be strong and courageous. Do not be terrified; do not be discouraged, for the LORD your God will be with you wherever you go."

¹⁰So Joshua ordered the officers of the people: ¹¹"Go through the camp and tell the people, 'Get your supplies ready. Three days from now you will cross the Jordan here to go in and take possession of the land the LORD your God is giving you for your own.'"

¹²But to the Reubenites, the Gadites and the half-tribe of Manasseh, Joshua said, ¹³"Remember the command that Moses the servant of the LORD gave you: 'The LORD your God is giving you rest and has granted you this land.' ¹⁴Your wives, your children and your livestock may stay in the land that Moses gave you east of the Jordan, but all your fighting men, fully armed, must cross over ahead of your brothers. You are to help your brothers ¹⁵until the LORD gives them rest, as he has done for you, and until they too have taken

possession of the land that the LORD your God is giving them. After that, you may go back and occupy your own land, which Moses the servant of the LORD gave you east of the Jordan toward the sunrise."

¹⁶Then they answered Joshua, "Whatever you have commanded us we will do, and wherever you send us we will go. ¹⁷Just as we fully obeyed Moses, so we will obey you. Only may the LORD your God be with you as he was with Moses. ¹⁸Whoever rebels against your word and does not obey your words, whatever you may command them, will be put to death. Only be strong and courageous!"

WITH TWO EPISODES OF preparation, the narrator launches this important story. The present chapter features three short scenes at Israel's camp on the Plains of Moab, while the next tracks a spy mission across the Jordan. The first episode prepares Israel for the coming invasion, while the second probes the enemy's internal situation. Both stories anticipate the dramatic river crossing in which Israel finally enters the Promised Land for the first time (3:1 – 5:1). In the background stand the long centuries since Yahweh first gave the promise of the land (Gen. 12:7). Those centuries saw the sojourning of the patriarchs, Israel's harsh slavery in Egypt, the miraculous Exodus, the covenant-making at Mount Sinai, and the wilderness wandering.

With Joshua 1, however, a new day dawns for Israel. Structurally, three scenes make up Joshua 1: Yahweh's dramatic commissioning of Joshua (vv. 1 – 9), Joshua's brief instructions to his officers (vv. 10 – 11), and a dialogue between Joshua and the two-and-a-half Transjordanian tribes (vv. 12 – 18). Several themes thread their way through these three scenes, in reality the central themes of the entire book. The first concerns the transfer of authority from Moses to Joshua (see v. 18). Long ago, Moses had designated Joshua as his successor (Deut. 31:1 – 8), and now his commissioning by Yahweh makes it official (vv. 2 – 9). His command that Joshua prepare Israel to cross the Jordan confirms Joshua as Israel's new leader (v. 2).

The second theme concerns the fulfillment of Yahweh's promise of land. Both the commissioning and the command serve a single aim, to deliver on Yahweh's promise to give Israel the land (vv. 2, 3, 11, 15). The narrator anticipates the two phases through which the fulfillment will become reality. He hints at the military defeat of Canaan's current occupants (vv. 5a, 9, 14), the story of Joshua 1 – 12. The threefold call for Joshua to be "strong and courageous" has the coming battles in mind (vv. 6, 7, 9; cf. v. 18). Two remarks foreshadow the distribution of land portions as Israel's "inheritance" (vv. 6, 11), the story of Joshua 13–24.

The third theme offers Joshua reassurance that Yahweh will support Joshua just as wholeheartedly as he did Moses (vv. 5, 17; cf. 3:7). There is no point in Israel's moving forward if Yahweh's support were only luke-warm. To verify this, Yahweh assures Joshua of complete military success (vv. 3–5a) and promises never to abandon him (v. 5b).

A fourth theme stresses that the adventure about to unfold involves Israel as a unified people. The dialogue with the Transjordanian tribes sounds this theme, one that will echo in later references to "all Israel" (3:7, 17; 4:14; 7:24; 8:33; 10:29; 23:2; 24:1). Moses had granted the two-and-a-half tribes land east of the Jordan provided they help the other tribes conquer Canaan (cf. Num. 32). The book makes special efforts to track their faithful promise-keeping and to explain their unique inheritance (cf. 4:12; 13:8–33; 18:7; 22:1–8). A later episode (ch. 22) will show some of the strains threatening that unity.

Finally, the author introduces the absolute centrality of obedience to the Instruction (*torah*) of Moses.[1] Joshua's success hangs totally on his unswerv-ing obedience to it (1:7–8), as does Israel's continued blessing by Yahweh in the future (22:5; 23:6; cf. 24:26). The book carefully traces how Joshua and Israel carry out things that Moses had commanded (1:13; 4:10; 8:31, 33, 35; 11:12; 14:2; 22:2).[2]

Joshua's Marching Orders (1:1 – 9)

THIS IS HOW A new day dawns for Israel, camped east of the Jordan but with all eyes aimed west toward Canaan and Israel's future there.

The introduction (v. 1a). The brief opening report formula, "after the death of Moses," signals that Joshua 1 picks up where Deuteronomy 34 left off and pushes the story forward.[3] Readers are to regard everything to follow as the continuation of events in Moses' life. Indeed, although we presume a major canonical break between the books of Deuteronomy and Joshua, the narrative does not.[4] Further, it reiterates that the chapter's

---

1. I read Heb. *torat mošeh* (lit., "law of Moses") as a technical term and prefer the rendering "instruction of Moses" or (in some cases) simply "the instruction" (instead of "the law").

2. Several texts also recall "as the LORD commanded Moses" or "the command of the LORD through Moses" (11:15; 14:5; 17:4; 21:2, 8).

3. The phrase *wayehi ʾaḥare mot X* (lit. "It was after the death of [proper name]") introduces other significant transitions in Israel's history (Judg. 1:1 [death of Joshua]; 2 Sam. 1:1 [death of Saul]) and may reflect the literary style of the DH; cf. also Gen. 25:11.

4. For a discussion of canonical issues, see B. S. Childs, *Introduction to the Old Testament as Scripture* (Philadelphia: Fortress, 1979), 113–14.

geographical setting remains that of Deuteronomy, the Israelite camp in the plains of Moab east of the Jordan River.

The death of Moses leaves a leadership vacuum in Israel, so it is no surprise that the book immediately turns to a speech by Yahweh (v.1b). The compiler of Joshua to 2 Kings (DH) often includes speeches, especially farewell speeches by historic leaders, to sound important themes (e.g., Samuel to Israel [1 Sam. 12]; David to Solomon [1 Kings 2:1–9]). The book of Joshua itself ends with three speeches by Joshua to various Israelite assemblies (22:2–5; ch. 23; 24:1–15). Joshua 1:1–9 marks the first of many occasions on which Yahweh will address Joshua (3:7; 4:1, 15; 5:9; 6:2; 7:10; 8:1, 18; 10:8; 11:6). But on only two occasions does the address amount to a speech—concerning ridding Israel of Achan's sin (7:10–15) and concerning Yahweh's past great deeds for Israel (24:2–13).

That Yahweh addresses Joshua son of Nun also is not a surprise. Joshua's long career of leadership precedes this moment.[5] He was the hero of Israel's first military victory, the defeat of Amalek (Ex. 17:9, 13). A comment in Numbers 13:16 implies that Moses either changed the future leader's name from Hosea ("salvation") to Joshua (Heb. *yehošuaˁ*, "Yahweh is salvation") or (more likely) preferred the latter. Moses' intention was perhaps to identify him as an Israelite who consistently obeyed Yahweh.[6] The LXX renders "Joshua" as *Iesous*, the New Testament name for Jesus, an apt name for one who brought "salvation" both to Israel and to the whole world.

In Numbers 14, Joshua and Caleb were the only spies who favored invading Canaan. Hence, only they of the generation that had escaped Egyptian slavery were permitted to enter the land (vv. 6, 30, 38; 26:65). His long career as Moses' "aide" (Heb. *mešaret*; Ex. 24:13; 33:11; Num. 11:28) culminated in God's command that Moses publically commission Joshua as his successor (Num. 27:18–23; 32:28; Deut. 31:3). Yahweh recognized in him two spiritual qualifications for leadership, the indwelling of Yahweh's spirit (Num. 27:18 ["a man in whom is the spirit"]) and a consistent pattern of obedience (32:12 ["followed the LORD wholeheartedly"]).

When Moses died, Israel readily accepted Joshua's leadership because Moses' hands had given him "the spirit of wisdom" (Deut. 34:9). Nevertheless, with Moses gone, Yahweh's address here establishes his personal

---

5. For a more in-depth treatment of his life and career, see "Who Is Joshua?" in the Introduction.

6. Cf. D. M. Howard Jr. *Joshua* (Nashville: Broadman and Holman, 1998), 73, who notes that Joshua is the first personal name in the Bible to incorporate God's personal name, "Yahweh." For the thesis that biblical narratives purposely delayed Joshua's emergence until Joshua 1, see G. C. Chirichigno, "The Use of the Epithet in the Characterization of Joshua," *TrinJ* 8 (1987): 72–79.

relationship with Joshua and confirms the validity of his prior commission. No leadership vacuum will trouble Israel, and Israel will know whom God has now put in charge. The drumbeat of God's plan for Israel moves on. But as we will see, though Moses is dead, his words and decisions mark the blueprint that shadow and guide most of what follows. Joshua may erect a new nation on the promised soil, but its architect remains Moses.

Joshua's commissioning (vv. 2 – 9). Yahweh immediately tells Joshua what to do now that Moses is gone. Literarily, the commissioning speech sounds like a king issuing battle plans to his field general, and its language compares with other biblical passages (Deut. 11:24 – 25; 31:6, 8; 1 Chron. 28:20).[7] The speaker, of course, is Yahweh, Israel's Savior from slavery and covenant partner. Ordinarily, the words "Moses my servant is dead" (v. 2a) might launch a period of Israelite mourning. Certainly, the phrase "my servant" makes Moses worthy of a spectacular state funeral and of the unique posthumous title "servant of Yahweh" (Deut. 34:5; Josh. 1:13, 15; et al.).[8] But Israel has already mourned Moses for thirty days (Deut. 34:8), so "Now then . . ." announces the moment for new action. The glorious Mosaic era is over, but Israel must move forward with God's help.

Specifically, Joshua and Israel are to "cross the Jordan" into the land which Yahweh will give them (v. 2b). The command assumes that the river has a separating rather than a uniting function.[9] A quick glance backward underscores how momentous this command is. The realization of the ancient promise of land made to Abram six centuries earlier—the very same land into which Israel will cross—is to begin (Gen. 12:7; 15:18). The text betrays no excitement or wonder at the thought of ancient hopes-come-true, but readers know how significant this day is. Rather, "I am about to give" stresses the land as the generous gift of Yahweh, Israel's mighty Savior from slavery and gracious covenant partner. In sum, the command to cross creates reader expectation of eventual conquest, an expectation toward which subsequent events mark progress and whose completion Joshua 11:23 declares officially.[10]

The gift includes the *whole* Promised Land. Yahweh quotes Moses' own words in a slightly expanded form (Deut. 11:24) to reiterate the promise

---

7. According to Robert Polzin, *Moses and the Deuteronomist* (New York: Seabury, 1980), 75 – 76, the narrator is the successor to Moses because he quotes divine speech in what follows. T. Butler, *Joshua* (WBC 7; Waco: Word, 1983), 5 – 6, provides detailed discussion, critique, and bibliography of recent scholarly discussion of this scene.

8. Joshua receives this approbation after his death (Josh. 24:29). David is the primary recipient of this accolade (e.g., 2 Sam. 7:5, 8//1 Chron. 17:4, 7; 1 Kings 11:13; Ps. 89:3; Isa. 37:35). For Moses as "my servant," see also Num. 12:7, 8; Josh. 1:7; 2 Kings 21:8; Mal. 4:4.

9. Cf. M. Woudstra, *Joshua* (NICOT; Grand Rapids: Eerdmans, 1981), 58.

10. R. C. Culley, "Stories of the Conquest: Joshua 2, 6, 7 and 8," *HAR* 8 (1984): 25 – 26.

spoken through him (vv. 3–4).[11] The quotation dramatically highlights that the ancient promise of land is about to be fulfilled. It also implies that, though off scene at the moment, Israel also participates in it through Joshua. "Every place where you set your foot" (v. 3) stresses that Israel's new territory is so vast that wherever he walks, Joshua will never leave it. Furthermore, earlier Yahweh had directed this exact same phrase to the people (Deut. 11:24), but here he addresses it to Joshua. The subtle change underscores that Joshua truly is Israel's new leader. He enjoys the same relationship with Yahweh as Moses did, and he is the one through whom the promise will become a reality. "Now Joshua no longer listens to Moses report Yahweh's commands. He has become the recipient of Yahweh's messages for the people."[12]

The traditional boundary markers (v. 4) trace Israel's borders in a crisscross pattern: south ("the desert) to north ("Lebanon"), then east ("the Euphrates") to west ("the Great Sea" [the Mediterranean]).[13] Slight embellishments of Moses' original words give the description added flourish. "Lebanon" here is (lit.) "this Lebanon," the Euphrates is "the great river," and the Mediterranean Sea is (lit.) "the great sea of the sunset." Also, the phrase "all the Hittite country" between Lebanon and the Euphrates probably evokes memories of that ancient superpower.[14] In short, the embellished picture paints Israel's new land as huge and fabled.

But for Joshua the crucial question is not the extent of the terrain but its conquerability. Perhaps for a moment Joshua recalls a mob scene a generation ago, the panicked voices of his fellow ten spies despairing of the conquest dream (see Num. 13). They reckoned Canaan's inhabitants as too "powerful," too gargantuan, and their cities too heavily fortified, to be conquered (13:28, 31–34). A popular proverb taught that no combatant could hold his ground against the storied sons of Anak (Deut. 9:2). Surely,

---

11. The present quotation retains the plural pronouns "you" and "your" from Deuteronomy, even though the rest of the context implies that Yahweh only addresses Joshua ("you" sing.). For full discussion of the intertextuality between Josh. 1 and Deut. 11, cf. D. B. George, "Yahweh's Speech at Jos 1:2–6 and Deut 11: Semantics, Intertextuality, and Meaning," *ZAW* 112 (2000): 356–64. For other interpretations of the use of "you" plural (vv. 3–4) see Butler, *Joshua*, 7–8.

12. George, "Yahweh's Speech," 358–59, 364 (quote).

13. S. Talmon, "מִדְבָּר," *TDOT*, 8:100; cf. M. Saebo, "Grenzbeschreibung und Landideal im AT mit besonderer Berücksichtigung der min-ʿad Formel," *ZDPV* 90 (1974): 14–37; cf. R. D. Nelson, *Joshua* (OTL; Louisville: Westminster John Knox, 1997), 33.

14. Cf. R. S. Hess, *Joshua* (TOTC; Downers Grove, Ill.: InterVarsity Press, 1996), 70. Present-day Turkey was the heartland of the ancient Hittite Empire. But cf. LXX, which lacks the phrase and much of the MT's verbal elaborations.

Israel feared, those giants would trample Israel like so many tiny grasshoppers. On this day, those voices—all Joshua's contemporaries and fellow leaders—lay forever silent in desert graves.

But perhaps a nagging grain of truth distilled from their hyperbole still stirred up Joshua's own doubts (Num. 13–14). Perhaps he wondered what tough human foes awaited him. No matter. A divine promise applying to Joshua words that Moses spoke to Israel accompanies the divine command to cross. It reassures the new leader that no human enemy can "stand up against you [Joshua]" (i.e., hold his position and thwart the onslaught), no matter how long he lived (v. 5; cf. Deut. 11:25). This astonishing invincibility derives not from raw human strength, superior technology, or strategic stealth. Rather, it comes from the presence of Almighty God with Joshua—the very presence that won Moses' stunning victories. The presence is not only invincible but irrevocable. In a word pair, Yahweh promises never to "leave" (i.e., "relax efforts") or "forsake" (i.e., "desert") Joshua.[15] Yahweh's efforts on his behalf will always be vigorous, his presence always constant.

For his part, Joshua receives Yahweh's command to "be strong and courageous" (Heb. *ḥazaq weʾemaṣ*), a formula of encouragement reiterated three times (vv. 6, 7, 9; cf. v. 18; 10:25). In my view, the formula may form a hendiadys to be rendered "unshakeably (or doggedly) courageous." Structurally, the formula (vv. 6 and 9) forms a thematic inclusio around vv. 7–8. The former sounds the speech's key theme—i.e., "be strong and courageous"—while the latter highlights its key arena of implementation ("follow the Instruction").[16]

Elsewhere *ḥazaq weʾemaṣ* appears in contexts where a king commissions subordinates to undertake specific actions. For example, David commissions Solomon to build the temple (1 Chron. 22:13; 28:20) and Hezekiah appoints military officers to lead the fight against the invading Assyrians (2 Chron. 32:7). The present context, however, directly parallels the wording of Deuteronomy 31, where both Moses (v. 7) and Yahweh (v. 23) invoke it in appointing Joshua as Moses' successor.[17] Indeed, the word repetition verbally links the two contexts, implying that here Yahweh formally installs

---

15. The same negated verb pair occurs in Deut. 31:6, 8; 1 Chron. 28:20; cf. Ps. 37:8. Cf. R. Wakely, "רָפָה," *NIDOTTE*, 3:1181–82.

16. For a colometric analysis of Josh. 1:6–9 and literary discussion of Deut. 10–12, see George, "Yahweh's Speech," 359–63.

17. Cf. Butler, *Joshua*, 8: "Indeed, Deuteronomy never explicitly uses the formula to express the divine presence with Moses, but it is typical of Deuteronomistic argument to refer back to the divine presence with the fathers or with predecessor(s)."

Joshua in the office to which he had appointed him in Deuteronomy 31.[18] Indeed, for Israel this installation marks Joshua as the chosen leader whom Yahweh expects them to follow. His specific task is to lead them to inherit the Promised Land (v. 6b; cf. Deut. 31:7).

Further illumination concerning his task emerges from an understanding of the possible legal status of that land in light of Ancient Near Eastern law. According to Kitz, the legal principle of residual rights and the institution of undivided inheritance supply the background.[19] Yahweh owns the land of Canaan (Deut. 12:10) but has transferred ownership to the patriarchs (Abraham, Isaac, and Jacob) while still retaining residual rights (i.e., the right to rescind that ownership). As the "sons of Israel," Jacob's descendants have inherited Canaan but as undivided land — land held in common as a whole by coheirs. Once the land is divided and distributed among them, the coheirship and collective ancestral "house" will end and each tribe will own its own inheritance.[20]

In the interim, the coheirs will appoint an administrator to manage their property until the division takes place. Given this background, when Yahweh tells Joshua that "you will lead these people to inherit [*tanḥil*] the land" (Josh. 1:6), Yahweh may actually appoint him as estate administrator on behalf of the Israelites.[21] If so, to execute this duty Joshua must make the situation in Canaan conducive to the legal allocation of land. He must lead the coheirs to remove the squatters currently inhabiting it (i.e., the Conquest [chs. 1 – 12]) and divide and distribute it among the heirs so they may take possession of it (i.e., the settlement [chs. 13 – 24]). In essence, the first duty removes the legal barrier for the accomplishment of the second. Clearly, the appointment implies that the Israelites have a legal right to take possession of the land because they own it. In short, by Yahweh's

---

18. Alternatively, the original life setting of the formula of encouragement may be the rituals of Yahweh war (so F. Hesse, "חָזַק," *TDOT*, 4:306 – 7) or royal ideology (so J. Schreiner, "אָמַץ," *TDOT*, 1:325 – 26). Many scholars follow Nelson, who argues that, given the phrase's use elsewhere by royal figures, the writer here pictures Joshua as a royal figure anticipating Josiah; cf. R. D. Nelson, "Josiah in the Book of Joshua," *JBL* 100 (1981): 531 – 40.

19. A. M. Kitz, "Undivided Inheritance and Lot Casting in the Book of Joshua," *JBL* 119 (2000): 601 – 18.

20. Kitz (ibid., 609 – 10) draws the further implication — a plausible one, in my view — that the estate division marks a decisive legal turning point for Israel — the legal dissolution of one legal entity (the house of Israel) with its collective management of legal rights. In its place emerge the independent tribal houses, each responsible for the management of matters within their limited tribal boundaries.

21. According to Kitz (ibid., 608), *tanḥil* "could refer to the inherited rights of ownership, which, under these circumstances, could not be fully enjoyed until the Israelites dwelt in the land as independent tribal units."

---

appointment Joshua is probably to wear two hats—that of military commander and that of estate administrator.[22]

As for Yahweh's command, the negated word pairs "do not be terrified; do not be discouraged" often parallel *ḥazaq weʾemaṣ* (see v. 9) and further illumine its meaning.[23] The persons addressed always face a momentous, risky, humanly impossible task. To human eyes, to build a magnificent temple, to defeat the mighty Assyrians, and to conquer Canaan pose mountains too lofty to scale. The danger is that fears, feelings of inadequacy, and doubts may cripple the leader's resolve, muddle his mind, and shake his confidence. The resulting confusion, wavering, and tentativeness sow despair, if not dissent, among the followers and endanger the mission. The temptation, then, is to back off from risks, to strike compromises, or to retreat altogether. To "be strong and courageous" means to be steady, resolute, bold, and unafraid.

Undergirding Joshua's confidence is the simple fact that he is not alone. Yahweh All-Powerful leads the way and surrounds him with his presence.[24] That is why vv. 7 – 8 detail the single proviso that Joshua must observe.[25] Joshua's actions must carefully conform to what Moses taught (Heb. *torah*, "instruction"; v. 7a; cf. Num. 31:21; Josh. 22:5; 2 Kings 21:8). Indeed, the very success of his future endeavors hangs upon his never wavering from Moses' teachings (v. 7b). For the first time in the Bible the "obey-Moses" principle emerges, and we will soon see how thoroughly Moses shapes all that Joshua does. Though dead and buried, Moses remains the gold standard to guide Joshua and all later leaders of Israel. And all future generations of Israel will likewise live or die by that same standard. More important, for the present generation it is Joshua's unique task as Israel's new leader to enforce their obedience.[26]

How can Joshua align his conduct with Moses' teaching and thereby assure its successful outcome? The key is "this Book of the Law" (v. 8), an allusion to a document that, according to Deuteronomy, Moses wrote shortly before his death (Deut. 28:58; 29:21; 30:10; 31:26). Scholarly

---

22. In accepting two roles, my view differs from that of Kitz (ibid., 607 – 9), who subordinates the military role to what she deems to be Joshua's "primary function" as estate administrator.

23. The negated parallel verbal pairs combine the roots *yareʾ* ("to fear"), *ʿaraṣ* ("be awestruck"), and *ḥatat* ("to be dismayed"); cf. Deut. 31:6; Josh. 1:9; 10:25; 1 Chron. 22:13; 28:20; 2 Chron. 32:7.

24. R. Wakely, "אָמַץ," *NIDOTTE*, 1:436 – 37; idem, "חָזַק," *NIDOTTE*, 2:66 – 67.

25. Syntactically, the particle *raq* ("only") signals that they summarize v. 6 and highlight its most important implications (see also vv. 17b, 18b); cf. WO §39.3.5a.

26. George, "Yahweh's Speech," 364.

speculation about this book abounds, but it probably contained at least the legal portions of Deuteronomy (i.e., Deut. 12 – 26).[27] Moses instructed the Levites to place it beside the ark of the covenant as a "witness" against Israel. From sad personal experience, the great lawgiver anticipated that inevitably the people would reject his teaching and reap bitter divine judgment (31:26 – 29). As if dramatically pointing a finger at "this book," Yahweh urges Joshua, so to speak, to prove Moses wrong by engaging rather than ignoring it. To "not depart from your mouth" (Josh. 1:8a) means that the book is always to be in his mouth — to be read aloud, at least, and perhaps, by implication, talked about constantly or shaping all of one's words.

The metaphor implies that Joshua should treat the book's contents as something to read in the hearing of others — to be shared with the community rather than hoarded to oneself.[28] Most important, success will follow Joshua only if he "meditate(s) on [the law] day and night." To "meditate on" the law (Heb. *hagah be*) probably means "to murmur audibly" while reading it.[29] Perhaps we are to imagine soft oral recitation or a quiet reading so intense as to produce audible whispering. "Day and night" is a Hebrew expression for "always."

In any case, the phrase implies eager, focused study free of distractions. The reader's posture pictures the text's importance: the reader hunches over it, eyes riveted on every syllable in order not to miss any detail. The posture also mirrors how critical is the law's guidance; only rigorous reflection can mine its depths. To "skim" the law is to imperil one's future by missing something crucial. Indeed, it is not enough simply to read it, think about it,

---

27. This is not the place to rehearse views concerning the composition of the Pentateuch. The reader may find convenient discussions and alternative views in R. N. Whybray, *Introduction to the Pentateuch* (Grand Rapids: Eerdmans, 1995), 12 – 28; D. A. Garrett, *Rethinking Genesis: The Sources and Authorship of the First Book of the Pentateuch* (Grand Rapids: Baker, 1991); L. R. Bailey, *The Pentateuch* (Nashville: Abingdon, 1981). For a new approach to the problem of Mosaic authorship, see J.-P. Sonnet, *The Book within the Book* (Leiden: Brill, 1997).

28. The mandate may be to establish a practice of regular public reading of the Instruction, notwithstanding the following verb ("murmur"); cf. K. van der Toorn, *Scribal Culture and the Making of the Hebrew Bible* (Cambridge, Mass.: Harvard Univ. Press, 2007), who cites this phrase (11 – 12) to make his case that in the ancient world all reading was aloud (even "muttered" reading), not silent. I am grateful to Professor John Walton for referring me to this source. Elsewhere the phrase occurs only in Isa. 59:21; cf. Job 23:12.

29. A. Negoitá and H. Ringgren, "הָגָה," *TDOT*, 3:321 – 24; cf. Ps. 1:2; 63:6; 77:12; 115:7; 143:5; Isa. 27:8); and the LXX rendering *meletao* ("to study, think about"). For a comparison of Josh. 1:8 with two parallel texts, see A. Rofé, "The Piety of the Torah-Disciples at the Winding-Up of the Hebrew Bible: Josh 1:8; Ps 1:2; Isa 59:21," in *Bibel in jüdischer und christlicher Tradition* (Frankfurt am Main: A. Hain, 1993), 80 – 85.

or even talk about it. Joshua must "be careful to act" on it—to put Moses' instructions into practice, live it out, and give it feet in the real world. Only "doing" the law will give Joshua success, a point rhetorically hammered home by the two parallel sentences (lit., "only then ... and only then ...") which conclude v. 8b.

Yahweh's speech ends by sounding again its main theme ("Be strong and courageous"). The preceding rhetorical question gives the scene a climactic rhetorical flourish. Given Hebrew style, the question "Have I not commanded you?" actually expresses a strong declaration (so NRSV, "I hereby command you ...").[30] In other words, rather than look back to vv. 6 and 7, v. 9 simply reiterates the key pair of commands, appending a negative pair ("Do not be terrified; do not be discouraged") for emphasis.

Literarily, the two parallel, contrasting pairs again drive home the speech's main point: Joshua must maintain firm faith and fixed focus, leaving fear and despair no quarter. The basis for his faith and focus also reiterates a theme in v. 5b—God's constant, never-ending presence with him ("the LORD ... will be with you"). And the twofold repetition of "wherever you go" (vv. 7, 9) underscores that his presence knows no territorial boundaries. Joshua need never wonder whether he may unwittingly wander into realms where Yahweh cannot go and is powerless to conquer. On the contrary, wherever Joshua's mandate takes him, no human can stop him (v. 5a), and his obedience to the law guarantees success (vv. 7b, 8b). With God he is unstoppable.[31]

Thus, with a dramatic speech, Yahweh orders Israel to cross into Canaan and officially installs Joshua as Moses' successor. The plan of God for Israel did not die with Moses, although Moses' shadow will follow Joshua everywhere. On several later occasions, Joshua will carry out specific instructions that Moses gave prior to his death. But for now, Joshua is Yahweh's on-scene commander, and the stage is set for his relationships with both Yahweh and Israel to grow or decline. For Israel, the long-awaited moment to realize a long-cherished dream has begun.

Joshua Passes the Word (1:10–18)

TO THE OFFICERS (VV. 10–11). Joshua puts in motion the divine commander's marching orders. First, he orders his officers to prepare the people for crossing (vv. 10–11), then he addresses the Transjordanian tribes

---

30. GKC, §150e; cf. Gen. 27:36; Judg. 4:6; Ruth 2:8, 9; 3:1, 2; 2 Sam. 13:28; 2 Kings 19:25; et al.

31. For a useful discussion of the connection between obedience and prosperity, including the words *ṣalaḥ* ("to prosper") and and *śakal* ("to succeed"), see Howard, *Joshua*, 87–90.

(vv. 12–18).[32] The "officers" probably are civilian administrators supporting Joshua rather than military officers.[33] In lists of Israelite leaders, the term is often paired with "elders" (Num. 11:16; Deut. 29:9; 31:28) or "judges" (Deut. 16:18; Josh. 23:2; 24:1; 1 Chron. 23:4; 26:29; cf. Josh. 8:33) rather than with "(military) officers" or "soldiers." The officers comprise the secular counterpart of the priests, both of whom Joshua addresses.[34] They are to fan out through the Israelite camp and command the people to prepare provisions for a departure in three days (v. 11).

The term "supplies" (*ṣēdāh*) commonly refers to food carried along to sustain one on a journey (Gen. 42:25; 45:21; Josh. 9:1; Judg. 20:10; 1 Sam. 22:10). This would include, for example, bread (Ps. 132:15), grain to be cooked later, and fruits like figs, dates, or raisins (cf. Gen. 44:23; Ex. 12:39).[35] In biblical narratives, "three days" seems to have a symbolic rather than a chronological sense.[36] It denotes the stylized biblical time period to mark momentous events (Ex. 10:22, 23) or important transitions (Gen. 30:36; Josh 2:16, 22; 9:16; 1 Kings 12:5//2 Chron. 10:5). It also marks important journeys (Ex. 3:18; 5:3), especially into the wilderness (8:27; 15:22; Num. 10:33; 33:8).

Strikingly, Joshua's instructions to the people focus on food, not weapons of war.[37] They may reflect his great confidence in Yahweh and also anticipate Israel's coming transition to dependence on the food of Canaan rather than on divinely sent manna (cf. Josh. 5:12). In other words, Israel will only need a three-day food supply—roughly enough for the transition.

Finally, repeated words in the last half of v. 11 signal the significance of events about to unfold. Israel is (lit.) to "enter" Canaan, the land that

---

32. Yahweh had commanded him (*ṣāwah* pi., v. 9), so Joshua issues implementing orders (*ṣāwah* pi., vv. 10, 11, 16, 18) to subordinates. David Howard argues that both the officers (v. 10) and the Transjordanian tribes (vv. 12–15) articulate the response of vv. 16–18 representing the entire nation and as part of a single event. In my view, however, that response seems an awkward, if not senseless, reply to v. 11, so it seems better to read vv. 10–11 and 12–18 as separate events; cf. D. M. Howard Jr., "All Israel's Response to Joshua: A Note on the Narrative Framework of Joshua 1," in A. B. Beck et al., eds., *Fortunate the Eyes That See* (Grand Rapids: Eerdmans, 1995), 81–91.

33. Cf. Deut. 1:15; 20:9; 1 Chron 27:1; 2 Chron. 19:11; 26:11; 34:13); Howard, "All Israel," 90. The term also describes Israel's Egyptian labor supervisors (Ex. 5:6, 10, 14, 15, 19).

34. Hess, *Joshua*, 75.

35. It also designates hunted game (Gen. 27:3) and manna (Ps. 78:25).

36. For a more chronological understanding, see Howard, *Joshua*, 91; idem, "Three Days in Joshua 1–3: Resolving a Chronological Conundrum," *JETS* 41 (1998): 539–50; cf. Josh. 3:2.

37. So H. W. Hertzberg, *Die Bücher Josua, Richter, Ruth* (Göttingen: Vandenhoeck & Ruprecht, 1969), 16.

Yahweh (lit.) "is giving you" in order to "take possession" of it "for your own." This is, indeed, a historic moment. After nearly eight centuries as vulnerable resident aliens in Canaan and oppressed slaves in Egypt, Israel is about to receive the long-awaited gift of land.[38] Three days later the officers again will fan out through the camp to issue orders concerning Israel's next move (3:2–4).

To the eastern tribes (vv. 12–18). Second, Joshua deals specially with the Transjordanian tribes—Reuben, Gad, and half of Manasseh (vv. 12–18). Literarily, the sudden, startling focus on them pricks the reader's curiosity.[39] The narrator probably singles them out for several reasons. He wants to confirm that, from the very first day, Joshua obeys Moses as Yahweh has commanded him (vv. 7–8). Here Joshua passes his first test, implementing Moses' earlier instructions concerning these tribes (Num. 32:28–30).

Also, the writer is aware that special circumstances distinguished these two-and-a-half tribes from the others. They have already received their inheritance from Moses, land along the east banks of the Dead Sea and Jordan River. Numbers 32 even implies that they have already conquered it, rebuilt its cities, and lived in houses (see vv. 24, 26, 33–42). If so, they have already begun to taste the long-awaited "rest." They have also probably joined the other tribes at this time from scattered locations and from a settled lifestyle. Finally, the author may wish to affirm that Joshua's authority extends to the soldiers of the eastern tribes.[40] This background may explain why Joshua addresses them specifically. Verses 12–18 may actually present a scene geographically separate from that of vv. 10–11 but narratively closely connected to it.

"Remember the command that Moses gave you" (v. 13) recalls Moses' decrees in Numbers 32. He gave them land on one condition—that they first fight to win land for the other tribes west of the Jordan (Num. 32:20–30). Joshua's brief quotation of Moses (Josh. 1:13b, "The LORD your God is giving you rest . . .") actually seems to paraphrase Deuteronomy 3:18 and 20 where Moses reviewed the same episode. "Quoting" Moses, Joshua reminds them of Yahweh's promise that they will eventually enjoy "rest" since he has already given them "this land" (i.e., the territory north and

---

38. Cf. Woudstra, *Joshua*, 65: the key words "cross" and "take possession" signal concern not with military aspects but with entrance and taking possession, an emphasis reminiscent of Deut. 3:18.

39. R. G. Boling, *Joshua* (AB; Garden City, N.Y.: Doubleday, 1982), 136, who also discusses the population explosion in Transjordan in the Late Bronze Age (136–38). The disjunctive word order—i.e., indirect object(s) + verb rather than vice versa—which opens v. 12 signals that these tribes are a new topic; cf. Nelson, *Joshua*, 35.

40. Hess, *Joshua*, 77.

south of where they stand). The repetition of key terms — "Moses," "give," "land" — drives home the key points.[41]

The language of "rest" evokes for the Transjordanian tribes the hope that all the tribes cherished and which Deuteronomy nourished (i.e., Deut. 12:30; 25:19). To "enjoy rest" (Heb. *nuaḥ* hi.) means finally to settle in peace and security — truly to be serenely "home" at last — after years of migration, struggle, and war.[42] Only after the west-bank tribes finally have "rest" (Josh. 21:44; 23:1) will Joshua dismiss the east-bank tribes to enjoy theirs (22:4).[43] For now, their wives, children, and livestock are to remain on the east-bank inheritance that Moses gave them (v. 14a).[44]

Meanwhile, the men are to augment the invasion force, but not merely as support troops in the rear. All of them are gutsy soldiers — "fighting men," "fully armed" (cf. 4:12) and ready to "help them" fight (v. 14b).[45] More important, they form the tip of the Israelite spear — the vanguard troops who lead the way ("ahead of your brothers"). They have apparently volunteered for the assignment (Num. 32:17; LXX *prophylake* "guard out front"), probably to silence suspicions about their willingness to take risks.

Again nearly quoting Moses verbatim (cf. Deut. 3:20), Joshua reiterates the two conditions that must prevail before they can go home: when Yahweh finally has given their fellow Israelites the same "rest" they themselves have already sampled, and when their west-bank kin also possess their inheritance (v. 15).[46] The military venture about to begin is not the exclusive duty only of the west-bank tribes but an all-Israelite operation. All Israel will bear its burdens, suffer its losses, pay its prices, and share in it victories.

The chapter concludes with the reply of the two-and-a-half tribes (vv. 16–18). Though speaking of themselves, literarily they articulate the

---

41. Butler, *Joshua*, 21.

42. Cf. J. N. Oswalt, "נוח," *NIDOTTE*, 3:58; idem, "Rest," *NIDOTTE*, 4:1132–36; cf. G. Braulik, "Zur deuteronomistischen Konzeption von Freiheit und Frieden," in J. Emerton, ed., *Congress Volume: Salamanca, 1983* (Leiden: Brill, 1985), 35–38. The classic study by G. von Rad, "There Still Remains a Rest for the People of God," in K. C. Hanson, ed., *From Genesis to Chronicles: Explorations in Old Testament Theology* (Minneapolis: Fortress, 2005), 82–88, still offers much insight on this topic.

43. Woudstra, *Joshua*, 66.

44. Here Joshua's very words seem to echo the language of Num. 32:26 and Deut. 3:19.

45. "Fighting men" (*gibborey ḥaḥayil*, lit., "mighty men of power") is the common Hebrew phrase for "soldiers" (Josh. 6:2; 8:3; 10:7; 2 Kings 24:14), but in some contexts it implies an unusually fine warrior or "battle hero" (Judg. 6:12; 11:1; 2 Kings 5:1; 1 Chron. 5:24; 7:2; cf. Gen. 6:4; 1 Sam. 14:52; 2 Sam. 17:10; 23:8–39). For its sense "wealthy man," see Ruth 2:1; 1 Sam. 9:1; 2 Kings 15:20.

46. Three key Hebrew roots rhetorically drive the point home to both groups. Yahweh will give both groups rest (*nuaḥ* hi., vv. 13, 15) in land that he (or Moses) has given or will give (*natan*, vv. 13, 14, 15 [2x]) and of which they will take possession (*yaraš*, v. 15).

loyalty expected of all tribes from here on.[47] A subtle argument undergirds their words: If the Transjordanian tribes with no personal interest in west-bank land affirm what follows, how much more so the others. Structurally, v. 16 offers their summary statement, while vv. 17–18 comprise two parallel statements verbally linked by repetition of the word "all," the root "to hear" or "obey," and final sentences prefaced by the restrictive particle "only ...." Emphatically the tribes agree to do whatever Joshua commands and to go wherever he sends them (v. 16).

The pairing of "command" (ṣawah pi.) and "send" (šalaḥ) highlights the wide authority they recognize in Joshua. They accord him authority reminiscent of Pharaoh over his servants (Gen. 12:20) and of God himself over his word (2 Kings 17:13), natural disasters (2 Chron. 7:13), the nation of Assyria (Isa. 10:6), and his prophets (Jer. 14:14; 23:32). The east-bank tribes promise Joshua the same obedience they gave Moses (v. 17).

It is one thing for Yahweh to commission Joshua as leader and another for the people to follow him, so given the context, this last affirmation is especially significant. It signals the successful transfer of tribal allegiance from Moses to Joshua (vv. 16–17a).[48] As they obeyed Moses, they will obey Joshua, doing what he commands and going where he sends them, all without question or dispute.[49]

The restrictive clause in v. 17b ("only may the LORD be with you"), however, seems to stipulate a condition for their continued loyalty, as if they meant, "We're with you as long as Yahweh is, otherwise we're gone!" In reality, v. 17b clarifies their affirmation by a simple heartfelt wish that Joshua will enjoy the same power-giving divine presence as Moses (v. 17b).[50] They wish for continuity of God's powerful presence with their new leader. The mention of Moses here gives the chapter a nice thematic inclusio, a literary device that further underscores the continuity between Moses and Joshua. The day began with reference to Moses' death (v. 1) and ends with a wish for divine presence on par with that enjoyed by Moses (v. 17b).

---

47. Nelson (*Joshua*, 35) compares the conversation between Joshua and the eastern tribes to a chorus in a Greek drama, which voices the thinking of the whole people.

48. Cf. Hess, *Joshua*, 68, for whom the point of chapter 1 is the role of Joshua as Moses' successor.

49. Thus, their loyalty far exceeds that of the tribes whom the Song of Deborah later faults for failing to aid Deborah and Barak in their victory over the Canaanites (Judg. 5:15–17); cf. Woudstra, *Joshua*, 66.

50. Grammatically, the restrictive particle *raq* (vv. 7, 18) here provides for clarification of v. 16; cf. WO §39.3.5c. Alternatively, its double use here may reflect slightly dampened enthusiasm and introduce some tension into the plot; cf. Nelson, *Joshua*, 36; Howard, *Joshua*, 95.

As if to underscore their allegiance, the Transjordanians propose the penalty for disobedience. Indeed, "whoever rebels ... will be put to death" sounds like legal sentences found in the law, although the grammar here differs significantly.[51] The pairing of "rebel" and "not hear" may echo terms from Moses' report of Israel's wilderness rebellions (Deut. 9:23, 24). If so, v. 18a probably articulates a quasi-legal principle applicable to the tenure of Joshua based on Moses' words.[52] Certainly, it aims to curb the one thing that might derail the Israelite juggernaut—rebellion in the ranks. As Moses said, Israel had displayed such refractoriness on more than one occasion (Deut. 9:23–24), so the concern to restrain it here is justified.

The speakers, however, carefully specify what kind of rebellion they have in mind. To rebel is to "not obey your [Joshua's] word," that is, to *not* do "whatever you may command them," or, to use their own promise as an example (v. 16), to *not* go where Joshua sends them. And the proposed penalty for such disobedience is death—an indicator of how important they reckon Israelite obedience to be. The assumption is that rebellion is a capital crime, ranking alongside murder (Ex. 21:12), desecration of the Sabbath (Ex. 31:14, 15; 35:2), adultery (20:14), and blasphemy of the Lord's name (Lev. 24:16).

The death penalty reckons rebellion to be the most outrageous kind of conduct. Undoubtedly, it is outrageous because it destabilizes Israelite unity, undermines their morale, and weakens their resolve. Clearly, the concern of the Tranjordanian tribes is to buttress the authority of Joshua and to motivate their fellows to obey him. In so doing, they anticipate the later episode in which the tribes actually impose the penalty here decreed on the disobedient Achan (Josh. 7).

Finally, after affirming Joshua's authority they address him personally. They themselves reiterate Yahweh's command that Joshua "be strong and courageous" (v. 18b). Paraphrased, their point is this: "We're with you—and anyone who rebels will be executed. Your job, Joshua, is to be brave and firmly resolved." In short, as Joshua must obey Moses' commands (vv. 7–8), so must Israel obey Joshua's. The fulfillment of the patriarchal promise and the realization of all their own hopes and dreams hang on both leader and people doing their parts well.

---

51. Cf. legal sentences comprising a participle describing an offense (i.e., "the one who does such-and-such ...") followed by the penalty formula (" ... shall surely be put to death" [*mot yumat*]); Gen. 26:11; Ex. 19:12; 21:12, 15, 16, 17; 22:19; et al. The grammar here ("everyone who rebels ... shall be put to death" [*kol ʾîš ʾašer yamreh*]) comes closest to laws in Lev. 20:2, 9, 10, 15, 16, 17; 24:17.

52. For the phrase *marah* hi. + *peh* (lit. "show rebelliousness against the mouth of"), see also Deut. 1:26, 43; 1 Sam. 12:14.

JOSHUA 1 RECOUNTS HOW Joshua succeeded Moses as Israel's leader. The dramatic voice of Yahweh addressing Joshua dominates the main scene (vv. 1–9). The speech interweaves promises, both national (vv. 2b, 3–4) and personal (vv. 5, 6b, 9b), with exhortations to Joshua (vv. 6a, 7–8, 9a). Its total effect is formally to commission Joshua as Moses' successor, assure him of success, and exhort him faithfully to exercise his duties. With the commission, Yahweh also grants Joshua the same authority over Israel that Moses had. In vv. 10–18, Joshua begins to exercise that authority by issuing orders to officers and tribal leaders. By obeying him, they signal their acceptance of it, and the episode marks the successful transition of leadership from Moses to Joshua.

Yahweh's exhortations, however, assume that dark shadows of fear and failure haunt Israel's thoughts about the coming conquest venture. (1) Israel undoubtedly worries about its ability to conquer the land set before them. From a human standpoint, it is a huge, if not impossible, undertaking. The land is vast in size and varied in terrain. The raw physical demands on Israel's infantry just to maneuver it are daunting. Israel lacks the military technology of the opponents they are about to face, especially the normal means of toppling heavily-fortified cities. They are, after all, basically a group of nomadic herders. While aimed to encourage, descriptions of the land (vv. 3–4) might also raise Israel's anxiety level a notch.

(2) There is uncertainty concerning how well Joshua will handle the huge challenges ahead. Indeed, those challenges may outstrip the ones that Moses himself faced. Will Joshua be able to fill Moses' sandals? Will he enjoy the same relationship with Yahweh as Joshua?

(3) There is uncertainty concerning Israel's courage under fire. Thus far her national history offers a mixed bag. On the one hand, she has won important victories—for example, over the two Transjordanian kings Sihon and Og (Num. 21:21–35). On the other hand, a sorry history of failure haunts her past. Granted, the sour, rebellious generation is gone, leaving the future to their children. But it remains to be seen what bad effects their poor example may have left on their offspring. For example, notwithstanding their reaffirmation (vv. 12–18), doubts may remain as to how long the Transjordanian tribes will stay. Finally, the question remains as to whether Israel's tribes will hang together over the long haul.

The commissioning: its main themes. In the context of fear and potential failure, Joshua 1 sounds several themes that lay a bridge from the ancient text to our contemporary scene. Though not prominent, the book's main theme, *the fulfillment of the patriarchal promise of land*, earns some mention. To be specific, the spotlight falls on the land as a *gift* of Yahweh. It is the land that Yahweh "is about to give" Israel (v. 2) and which Joshua will lead them to inherit just as Yahweh had sworn to their ancestors (v. 6). The land includes every place their feet take them (v. 3), and as its giver, Yahweh proves himself a generous God to his people. He also shows himself a God who keeps his promises, sticking with his people despite their failures and rebellions. Were Yahweh not faithful, Israel would not be poised to realize its ancient hopes for land. Without divine protection, the nation would have starved to death or been massacred by its enemies enroute. This theme will gain prominence in later chapters, so additional comment must await that occasion.

The second theme, however, is more prominent—*Joshua's need for courage* against the dark backdrop of fear. As noted above, three times Yahweh exhorts Joshua to be "doggedly courageous" (vv. 6, 7, 9)—to be resolute and brave. He is to control his human fears in the face of imminent danger in order to execute fully the mission entrusted to him. Just prior to combat, other biblical military leaders urge their followers to show courage under fire (2 Sam. 10:12//1 Chron. 19:10; 2 Chron. 32:7). Absalom issues the command to his servants afraid of killing Amnon (2 Sam. 13:28). But the prophet Azariah also calls King Asa to be courageous in initiating needed religious reform (2 Chron. 15:7). In his farewell speech, David admonishes Solomon to bravery by obeying Yahweh's law (1 Kings 2:2), especially in building the temple (1 Chron. 22:13; 28:10, 28).

Yahweh also calls for courage among the returnees from exile, dispirited by the crudeness of the temple they have just rebuilt (Hag. 2:4). Two besieged psalmists conclude their poems with calls for patient, resolute waiting for Yahweh's intervention (Ps. 27:14; 31:24). A vision terrified Daniel, but his visionary visitor's call for courage eased his terror (Dan. 10:19). But Joshua 1 calls for more than just fearlessness. It enjoins the application of strength and bravery to ensure *obedience to Moses' teaching* (vv. 7–8; cf. 1 Kings 2:2). Indeed, the absolute necessity of obeying the Instruction of Moses marks the chapter's third and most fundamental theme. As noted above, the text probably has in mind at least the legal portions of Deuteronomy (chs. 12–26), Moses' last will and testament.

Here two issues arise that need comment. The first concerns the contrast between the obvious delight Joshua is to have in the law and the aversion to law typical of modern readers. Modern Christians commonly think of "law" and "grace" as antonyms, assuming that Christ somehow replaced law with grace (John 1:17) and that therefore Christians are "not under law, but under grace" (Rom. 6:14; cf. Gal. 5:4). They would happily sing that old hymn from my childhood, "Free from the law, O happy condition!"

They find law a bitter taste to be spit out as old and rancid, rather than a sweet treat to be rolled around the mouth and savored. To them "law" evokes images of harsh, rigid Pharisees, coldly coercing common people to "toe the line." Their minds equate "law" with "legal code" and "legalism," a sinister heresy that teaches that good deeds earn the doer increased favor with God.

Contrast this aversion to the relish that OT writers have toward the Instruction.[53] The psalmists regard it as a delight (Ps. 1:2; 119:70, 77, 92, 174), a source of wonder and grace (119:18, 29), and a precious treasure (119:72) that is true (119:142). Israel reveres it as an object of devotion (2 Chron 31:4) worthy of careful study and observance (Deut 6:25; 31:11 – 13; Josh. 1:8; Neh 8:3, 13) as well as love (Ps. 119:97, 113, 163, 165). Rather than protect children from it, Israel is to teach it to them (Deut. 31:33; cf. 11:19–21). Jeremiah even predicts a day when the Instruction will be inscribed on Israel's heart (Jer. 31:33). It will form part of their inner make-up, exerting its influence on their will more directly than its externally read Mosaic form could.

Two key ideas explain this startling delight in the Instruction. (1) Unlike modern readers, when ancient Israel heard the Hebrew word *torah*, they thought of "teaching" or "instruction," not "law" or "legal code." They call the Pentateuch *torah* because its main contents—ancestral lives and Mosaic teaching—instruct Israel on how to live in ways that please God. (2) The context of the Instruction is not the law court but the covenant relationship between God and Israel. Divine promise gave that relationship birth (Gen. 12:1 – 3), divine deliverance from slavery confirmed God's commitment to it (Ex. 20:2), and divine teaching laid down the ground rules for its continuation. The Instruction teaches Israel about the character of God, his loving devotion to his people, and his beneficent expectations of them. In short, Israel regards the Instruction with the same high reverence and warm affection that Christians feel for "Scripture." The challenge for Christians is to permit Israel's attitude to soften their aversion to law so that its instruction might illumine their lives and demonstrate how surprisingly delicious it really is.[54]

The second issue that Joshua 1 raises concerns the connection between intense study of the Instruction and Joshua's effectiveness. How will study

53. Cf. P. Enns, "Law of God," *NIDOTTE*, 4:896–97; cf. W. VanGemeren, "The Law Is Righteousness in Jesus Christ—A Reformed Perspective," in W. VanGemeren, ed., *The Law, The Gospel, and the Modern Christian* (Grand Rapids: Zondervan, 1993), 24–35.

54. For further discussion see my article "Law is Grace: Theological Reflections on OT Laws of Redemption," *Covenant Quarterly* (February 1999): 2–14.

produce success in Joshua's efforts, and how does it relieve, if not banish, human fears of weakness and failure? Given the nature of the Instruction, several reflections come to mind. (1) To study the law will remind Joshua of crucial tasks commanded by Moses to be finished. For example, Moses ordered Israel to establish cities of refuge once they are settled in the land (Num. 35), an order whose completion Joshua 20 reports. Joshua's careful study of Moses' teaching will ensure that he completes the great leader's unfinished agenda.

(2) The very quantity and complexity of Moses' teaching requires ongoing study to learn it. Humanly speaking, the frailties of human memory pose a danger. Joshua (and Israel) will do the things they remember and leave undone the things they forget. Further, the human tendency is to remember the law selectively — to recall readily its easier provisions but conveniently to "forget" its unpleasant ones. Certainly, some commands demand things one may prefer not to do, and some prohibitions outlaw one's favorite things. That is why Moses often urged Israel to "remember" their experience of Yahweh and what he had taught them (e.g., Num. 15:39 – 40; Deut. 8:18; 9:7; 24:18; 32:7; et al.).[55]

In sum, constant study of Moses' Instruction jogs the memory of items forgotten and confronts one afresh with provisions missed (or consciously ignored) before. It keeps one from forgetting too much of God's expectations and leads to their inculcation into daily life. Consistent meditation on the teaching shapes one's conduct in ways that please God.

By whose authority? Joshua's order to his officers and his conversation with the east-bank tribes (vv. 10 – 18) sound the theme of *leadership authority*. Both groups willingly accept and follow Joshua's leadership. Theologically, Israel's view of human authority and leadership undergird it. All authority in Israel derives from Yahweh himself. That is, humans in themselves only have authority because Yahweh gives it for them to exercise on his behalf.

Two family lines dominated Israel through much of the Old Testament period. The priestly line of Aaron led Israel's religious life and the royal line of David the nation's political life. At times, both families exercised power as if they were accountable to no one. Early on, Moses' own siblings, Aaron and Miriam, stirred up trouble against him because of his marriage to an Ethiopian (Num. 12). Many generations later, Eli's priestly sons "were scoundrels" with "no regard for the LORD or for the duties of the priests to the people" (1 Sam. 2:12 – 13 NRSV). They improperly demanded portions of offerings (vv. 13 – 17) and committed adultery with women who worked

---

55. For discussion of this larger topic, see H. Eising, "זָכַר," *TDOT*, 4:64 – 82; L.C. Allen, "זָכַר," *NIDOTTE*, 1:1100 – 1106.

at the sanctuary (v. 22). Centuries later, the prophets indict the priests for contributing to Israel's defection from Yahweh (e.g., Jer. 14:18; 23:11; Hos. 4:4–6; Mic. 3:11; Zeph. 3:4).[56] The royal track record was no better. The book of Kings repeatedly charges the kings of both northern and southern kingdoms with either outright apostasy or religious compromise (e.g., 1 Kings 11:6; 15:26, 34; 2 Kings 8:18, 27; 21:2, 20; 23:32, 37; 24:9, 19). Their poor performance notwithstanding, all served simply because Yahweh had appointed their family line as priests (Ex. 28, 29; Lev. 8) or kings (2 Sam. 7).[57]

Further, theologically any Israelite leader is simply a human stand-in for God. The violent clash between divine holiness and human sinfulness requires such mediators. The Old Testament teems with examples of this fundamental fact of reality. That clash underlies the expulsion of Adam and Eve from the Garden of Eden and the posting of an angelic sentry to bar their return (Gen. 3:22–24). It explains Israel's retreat in terror from the foot of Mount Sinai when Yahweh descended—and why they pushed Moses up front to mediate (Ex. 19:16; Deut. 5:5, 23–27). It stands behind the strictly regulated access to God's presence in the Most Holy Place, whether in tabernacle or temple (Ex. 30:10; Lev. 16:2, 34; Heb. 9:7; cf. 3 Macc. 1:11). It underlies the sudden death of Uzzah simply for touching the ark of the covenant to stabilize it (2 Sam. 6:6–7) and David's despair over its proper care (v. 9).

God must graciously, so to speak, "keep his distance"—to work through mediatorial leaders—since direct contact with humans might destroy them. For a holy God to converse with sinful humans requires a go-between—for example, a Moses, a Joshua, and priests and prophets over the centuries. Israelite leaders fill the gap created by human sinfulness between God and his people. In the present case, Joshua serves as the mediator between Yahweh the warrior ready for battle and Israel encamped east of the Jordan.

And, though borrowed from Yahweh, their authority is virtually absolute.[58] The semilegal declaration by the Tranjordanian tribes (v. 18)

56. Two priestly heroes, however, are Jehoiada (ninth cent. B.C.), whose brave efforts removed the usurper, Queen Athaliah, and placed the child-king Joash on Judah's throne (2 Kings 11); and Hilkiah (seventh cent. B.C.), who apparently aided the reform movement of King Josiah (2 Kings 22–23; 2 Chron. 34–35).

57. The principle of divine appointment underlies Yahweh's complaint that "they set up kings without my consent" (Hos. 8:4); cf. also Elisha's anointing of Jehu to be king (2 Kings 9). By the same token, the authority of the prophets also derives from divine discretion (e.g., Jer. 1:5, 7; 23:21, 32; Amos 7:14).

58. For a thorough discussion, see R. Hutton, *Charisma and Authority in Israelite Society* (Minneapolis: Fortress, 1994).

assumes this. Joshua can make decisions and issue orders, and the people are expected to follow them without hesitation or questioning. To disobey him is to "rebel" (*marah* hi.), a crime so serious that it merits the death penalty. The text might imply that rebellion against Joshua is tantamount to rebellion against Yahweh himself. Such absolute authority may leave modern readers, accustomed to more democratic processes, uneasy if not alarmed. They ask, "Does God bestow on them the same authority? Does he expect me to obey my leaders—my pastor, church elders, small group leader—similarly? Am I never to ask any questions? Am I forbidden ever to disagree? If I oppose them, am I to be dismissed from the church? In fact, is it wrong even to vote on church actions rather than to follow leadership?"

Further, while some leaders may relish such authority, many pastors balk at it because of their own self-understanding. They may see themselves more as the player-coach of a congregation, someone who, besides giving direction, is also just another player. They have no aspirations to be Vince Lombardi!

The difference-maker: God's presence. Reassurance of God's presence with Joshua is another important theme in Joshua 1. The words "I will be with you" literally bracket the heart of Yahweh's commission (vv. 5, 9). That powerful presence guarantees that Joshua is unstoppable (v. 5) and Israel's inheritance of Canaan under his leadership is inevitable (v. 6). It is that presence that backs up the commands to "be doggedly courageous" (vv. 6, 7, 9) and to "not be afraid" (v. 9). Without the presence, Joshua has everything to fear—stiff Canaanite resistance, a humiliating retreat or defeat, lost confidence in his leadership, and rebellions within Israel's ranks. Such fears sap strength, weaken courage, and soften resolve. But with it Joshua need fear nothing. The presence empowers him to lead Israel with boldness, conviction, and confidence.

The reality of God's presence—the reassuring formula "I am/will be with you"—undergirds much of the Bible. It reassured Jacob of safety and success as he fled frightened from Esau's vengeance to seek a wife in Haran (Gen. 28:15). It also reassured him that he need not fear the perils of a return to Canaan (31:3). At the burning bush, "I will be with you" encouraged a nervous Moses to return to Egypt and lead Israel out of slavery. It countered Gideon's terror of the marauding Midianites and gave him the courage to defeat them against humanly impossible odds (Judg. 6:16). Its power to rescue God's imperiled servants emboldened Jeremiah to proclaim coming divine judgment without fear (Jer. 1:8, 19; 15:20). The power of that presence gave downcast Israel the courage to dream of returning home from exile (Isa. 41:10; 43:5) and the spirit to rebuild the temple when they got there (Hag. 1:3; 2:4).

Exodus 33 – 34 illustrates how crucial Israel regarded the presence of God. The golden calf episode had shown Israel to be stiff-necked and rebellious (Ex. 32). Yahweh announced that he would decide what to do with Israel (Ex. 33:5), a comment that suddenly casts grave doubt on Israel's national future. But Moses interces for the people, pleading:

> If your Presence does not go with us, do not send us up from here. How will anyone know that you are pleased with me and with your people unless you go with us? What else will distinguish me and your people from all the other people on the face of the earth? (Ex. 33:15 – 16; cf. 34:9)

Moses' argument is simple but bold: "No presence, no go." Without God's presence with Israel, there is no point in leaving the Sinai desert for the Promised Land. Alone, Israel would face certain annihilation from its inhabitants. Israel's chance of survival is far better in the desert where they might face only an occasional skirmish with other nomads. More important, Moses says, that presence marks Israel as God's special people. No other people enjoy that distinction and the special favor it brings. Other peoples might know about Yahweh, respect him, and perhaps even worship him. But Israel's distinguishing mark is that he lives only among them. It is the divine presence, and access to God's power, which makes any Israelite undertaking viable. It alone banishes Israel's fear.

Above all: "Hang together, people!" The text's final theme concerns the unity of Israel as a people. This issue emerges from the fact that Reuben, Gad, and half of Manasseh already have their inheritance east of the Jordan. Humanly speaking, there seems to be no compelling reason for them to leave their families and risk their lives across the river. Yahweh has enough personal firepower to overwhelm any opponent. Victory does not depend on the size of the Israelite invasion force. Logically, why should they cross over to fight rather than to solidify Israel's foothold on the east bank? Why not secure the rear for the west-bank venture?

However, is it fair for the west-bank tribes to let the Transjordanians get off so easy? Granted, from a human perspective, Yahweh's will may not always be "fair." For reasons known only to him, some people *do* suffer greater hardships in his service than others. But the point is to accept one's lot, to trust in God's wisdom and goodness, and to obey Yahweh whatever the circumstances. Here as elsewhere, however, human logic must give way to biblical theology. Theologically, Israel is not just a loose association of tribes but a single people. As Eissfeldt observed long ago, "To Israelite thought ... unity is prior to diversity, the community is prior to the individual; the real entity is the community, and the individuals belonging to it have their origin therein."[59]

Collective biblical terms reflect this profound sense of metaphysical unity that binds the tribes into one nation. Yahweh identifies Israel as his "firstborn son," whom Pharaoh must free (Ex. 4:22–23; cf. Hos. 11:1), and frequently the name "Jacob" parallels "Israel."[60] The effect is to personify the whole people in a single person—Jacob, the ancestor from whom the people have descended.[61] That sense of national solidarity undergirds the conviction that no tribe (Judg. 21:3, 6, 17) or city (2 Sam. 20:19–20) be cut off from Israel.

That underlying metaphysical unity also explains Moses' demand of the Transjordanian tribes that the present context reiterates. No tribe may enjoy its long-awaited "rest" until every tribe does, and no tribe may fully possess its inheritance until every tribe does (Josh. 1:15).[62] Israel does not really possess the Promised Land—that is, the patriarchal promise is not in fact fulfilled—until every tribe possesses its allotted share. The implied message of Joshua 1 is, "Hey, people, hang together no matter what!"

Further, potential divisions necessitate Joshua's conversation with the Transjordanian tribes (vv. 12–18). They might have simply refused to cross the river, notwithstanding their prior promise. With the actual invasion of Canaan imminent, it is crucial that Israel unite behind the common enterprise of conquest. However minor, any discord, division, or dissent within the ranks poses a grave threat to Israel's ability to subdue the land. At this crucial juncture, too much is at stake to tolerate tribal jealousies or personal vendettas. Most important, as never before, Israel must wholeheartedly trust the wisdom and judgment of their leader, Yahweh, and his on-site commander, Joshua. The Transjordanians' declaration that anyone disobeying Joshua will face the death penalty (v. 18) hints at the possibility of future rebellions against Joshua. From a military viewpoint, fractious discus-

---

59. O. Eissfeldt, "The *Ebed-Jahwe* in Isaiah xl.-lv: In the Light of the Israelite Conception of the Community and the Individual, the Ideal and the Real," *ExpTim* 44 (1933): 264; cf. also H.-J. Zobel, "יִשְׂרָאֵל," *TDOT*, 6:412–19. For a fine discussion of the corporate nature of Israel's election by Yahweh, see W. W. Klein, *The New Chosen People* (Eugene, Ore.: Wipf & Stock, 2001), 25–44.

60. Cf. Gen. 49:7; Num. 24:5; Deut. 33:10; 1 Chron. 16:17; Ps. 14:7; Isa. 9:8; et al.

61. Observe also the parallelism between "Israel," "daughter of Zion," and "daughter Jerusalem" (Zeph. 3:14).

62. This sense of corporate unity seems all the more remarkable since, besides its ethnic core descended from Jacob's twelve sons, Israel also apparently included other ethnic groups (Ex. 12:38; Lev. 24:10; Num. 11:4; Neh. 13:3; Ruth 2:12). The early history of Israel remains a controversial topic; for a convenient summary of some of the issues see Zobel, "יִשְׂרָאֵל," 6:406–12.

sions about strategy or tactics will only halt forward movement, squander momentum, and undermine troop morale. Thus, Israel's unity becomes of paramount importance.

Israel's abysmal track record justifies the text's concern for internal unity. Indeed, one suspects that the biblical writer writes with that sorry history in mind. Talk about a "dysfunctional family"—refractoriness seems to be a family trait! The book of Genesis narrates the family troubles among Israel's ancestors. Recall the favoritism shown by Isaac and Rebekah toward Esau and Jacob, respectively (Gen. 25:28; 26:35), and the animosity that alienated the two brothers (chs. 27 – 28; 32 – 33). The jealous squabbling between Jacob's twelve sons that fomented their crimes against Joseph (Gen. 37) betrays similar familial headstrongness (cf. also the portraits of tribes in Jacob's blessings, Gen. 49).

Things do not improve later under Moses. No sooner had Yahweh liberated Israel from cruel Egyptian slavery than they complain against Moses over bitter water (Ex. 15:22 – 25) and shortages of food and water (ch. 16; 17:1 – 7). While Moses is away on Mount Sinai, they worship a golden calf in a wild, idolatrous incident that angers Yahweh (ch. 33). Later they question Moses' leadership (Num. 11) and eventually, in response to the spies' report, try to overthrow him and return to Egypt (Num. 13 – 14). One is not surprised by Moses' assessment of Israel's future conduct: "I know how rebellious and stiff-necked you are. If you have been rebellious against the LORD while I am still alive and with you, how much more will you rebel after I die!" (Deut. 31:27; cf. v. 29). One is also not surprised that, after Solomon's death, once-united Israel split into separate countries (1 Kings 12).[63]

This is why the Bible stresses the unity of God's people so strongly. Rebellions thwart the progress of God's plan. They also squander the blessings that God desires his people to enjoy.

ONE SUMMER NIGHT DURING a severe thunderstorm a mother was tucking her small son into bed. She was about to turn the light off when, in a trembling voice, he asked, "Mommy, will you stay with me all night?" The mother smiled, gave him a warm, reassuring hug, and said tenderly, "I can't dear. I have to sleep in Daddy's room."

---

63. For details and background on this historic schism, see conveniently Provan, Long, Longman, 259 – 63; and J. M. Miller and J. H. Hayes, *A History of Israel and Judah* (Philadelphia: Westminster, 1986), 94 – 98, 103 – 6, 229 – 33.

A long silence followed as she moved toward the door. At last it was broken by a shaky voice saying, "The big sissy!"

Fear lurks in the background of Joshua 1. Fear of danger and fear of failure haunt the three scenes. Fear is an experience that all humans share. Since 9/11, I sense an intensification of fear among some people I know. They seem more wary of other people, especially foreigners, and they favor leadership that is tough or courageous. They speak openly of "the Evil One" (i.e., Satan) as a real presence—a spiritual terrorist plotting the spiritual ruin of themselves and their Christian friends. Joshua 1, however, points to four truths as the antidote to such fears: our unique identity as God's people, our dependence on God's word, our bond of unity with other believers, and God's powerful presence with us.[64]

Our unique identity: a mission people. The scene in which God commissions Joshua closely parallels the scene in which Jesus issues the Great Commission to his disciples (Matt. 28:16–20). As Moses' departure left Joshua in charge of Israel, so the Lord's ascension to heaven left the church in the hands of the apostles (Acts 1:1–9). Both texts also feature a major geographical transition for God's people. As Joshua's commission launched Israel's crossing into Canaan, Jesus' Great Commission launched the exodus of God's people from Canaan "to the ends of the earth" (Acts 1:8). In that sense, as Christians take the gospel everywhere, they extend God's commission of Joshua outward from the land of Israel to the rest of the world. Thus, execution of the Great Commission further carries out the commission given Joshua but pushes its horizons out to the earth's limits. Certainly, the Great Commission echoes some provisions of Joshua's mandate.

The commission first given to the apostles applies to all believers:

> Therefore go and make disciples of all nations, baptizing them in the name of the Father and of the Son and of the Holy Spirit, and teaching them to obey everything I have commanded you. And surely I am with you always, to the very end of the age. (Matt. 28:19–20)

As with Joshua ("Cross!"), Jesus the Commander-in-Chief commands Christians to move forward ("Go!"). Fearful of the future, many Israelites might secretly have preferred to admire the Promised Land from the safety of Transjordan rather than risk actually entering Canaan. Harsh as nomadic life was, at least it was familiar, its dangers well known. It offered Israel a "comfort zone" to which they were long accustomed. The temptation to

---

64. For other helpful expositions of Joshua 1:1–9, see J. Nogalski, "Preaching from Joshua in Canonical Contexts," *RevExp* 95 (1998): 263–65; and M. Nogalski, "Only Be Strong and Very Courageous," *RevExp* 95 (1998): 427–33.

remain safely within a "comfort zone" also seduces Christians. At church we tend to arrive about the same time, park in the same parking space, sit in the same pew, and hang with the same people. Church activities with church people tend to clog our calendars, leaving little or no time for contacts with non-church people. We obey the command to "Go!"—we go to church!

Someone has suggested that there are four types of churches.[65] The *museum church* resembles those found in Europe. They are old, beautiful, and empty. No one goes there for weekly worship. They are nothing but show-pieces of the past. No spiritual vitality throbs within their ancient walls.

The *maintenance church* does a little better. It is almost empty but hanging on. Its mission is simply to survive—to maintain itself against the spiritual and social changes swirling around it. It survives by slavish devotion to its creed, The Seven Last Words of the Church: "We never did it that way before." But as its stalwart members inevitably die off, it will soon become a museum church.

The *ministry church*, by contrast, pursues genuine Christian ministry but only to people already within the church. Its offers a full calendar of activities—Sunday worship with coffee and donuts afterward, Bible studies and prayer meetings galore, a good youth group, weekly choir rehearsal, special annual holiday services, summer camps for all ages, and monthly potluck dinners for fellowship. A fine staff of loving pastors and devoted members administer its full-service program, and it generously supports many missionaries around the globe. But it lacks only one thing—ministry contact with people outside the church. It would rather stay securely across the Jordan than to cross into their territory to engage them in conversation.

It is the *mission church* that offers truly "full-service" ministry.[66] It cares for its own members *and* reaches out to serve its community and to win the lost. It takes Jesus' command to "Go!" seriously. It goes out the church door into the neighborhood. It understands that its purpose is to "make disciples" (Gk. *matheteusate*) of those who are *not* already followers of Jesus.[67] Our contacts and conversations with them aim to draw them into his circle of

---

65. For intriguing ethnographic studies of various American churches, see R. Balmer, *Mine Eyes Have Seen the Glory* (New York: Oxford Univ. Press, 1989), and *Grant Us Courage* (New York: Oxford Univ. Press, 1996), which treat evangelicalism and mainline Protestant churches, respectively. His works have no connection, however, with the popular typology of churches offered here.

66. For one such exemplary church, see Balmer, *Grant Us Courage*, 57–66.

67. Originally, this verb meant "to be a disciple," but Hellenistic influences transformed intransitive active verbs like this one into causatives ("to make a disciple of"); cf. F. Blass, A. Debrunner, and R. W. Funk, *A Greek Grammar* (Chicago: University of Chicago Press, 1961), §148 (3).

friends. In a sense, our evangelism follows up several episodes in the book of Joshua. Chapters 2 and 6 tell us how the prostitute Rahab came to survive Israel's first military victory and to become part of Israel. Her remarkable confession about Israel's God saved her life and earned her membership in Israel (see the commentary at ch. 2). Chapters 9–10 add another slightly different precedent, the sparing of the people of Gibeon. They, too, confess the greatness of Yahweh and end up serving at the temple, albeit doing menial tasks.

The point is that Christians always keep the doorway into the people of God open to outsiders. Indeed, our unique identity in Christ compels us regularly to cross from the safe sanctuary of church life to rub shoulders with neighbors, to listen to their thoughts, and to show our love for Christ in practical ways. Under God's good hand, such "crossing/going" will open the way for mutual sharing—how they see their lives and how Jesus enriches ours. Hopefully, over time—and after many honest, low-key exchanges—some will surrender to the call of Jesus and become his followers.

When that happens, our commission requires two further steps.[68] First, we baptize them. This familiar ritual of initiation symbolizes their identification with Jesus' death and resurrection (cf. Rom. 6). Through baptism they publically declare their commitment to be Jesus' disciples. We who have witnessed baptisms know how joyous those ceremonies are! (For more on this see the Contemporary Significance section of Josh. 8:30–35.)

But baptism marks only the first step of discipleship. Jesus' second requirement is that we "[teach] them to obey everything I have commanded you" (v. 20). Here, too, our commission echoes that of Joshua. His success hangs on his study and obedience of the teaching of Moses. The same is true of new Christian disciples: We must teach them to do (i.e., to obey) "everything I have commanded you." Strikingly, we are not to teach them just to "know" what Jesus commanded—to be able to summarize his main ideas or to paraphrase his key statements. It is not enough for them simply to learn to recite catechisms or creeds about him. Such practices serve all disciples well, but they do not quite meet Jesus' expectations. His demand is that we teach them to "do" his commands—to put them into daily practice. Disciples are to do them on the job site, in the office, in the supermarket, in the classroom, at the gas pump, at the bus stop, across the back fence, and in the living room.

---

68. The two following present active participles, *baptizontes* ("baptizing") and *didaskontes* ("teaching"), are modal ("by means of . . ."); cf. D. B. Wallace, *Greek Grammar beyond the Basics* (Grand Rapids: Zondervan, 1996), 630, 645.

Our manual for success: God's Word. Most organizations have a manual of some kind that details their policies and procedures. That was true when I joined the Navy in 1970 and when I joined the faculty of North Park Theological Seminary in 1995. Life in the Navy is governed by a huge document, *Navy Regulations*, that covers every imaginable topic. Also, major Navy commands write specific instructions that govern their specific areas of responsibility. For example, one instruction promulgates Navy policy concerning the duties of chaplains, another the rules for handling religious offerings. North Park has two handbooks, one for faculty and another for students.

The purpose of all these manuals is to clarify procedures and expectations of members of the communities they govern. They detail the pathways to function properly within the organization. People who consult the manual get along fine, but people who ignore it soon run afoul of the organization's leaders or members. But such manuals do more than lay down rules. They also cultivate a culture of cooperation and fairness—a community, as it were—within the membership. They also voice the values that members share. In short, they show members how to be successful within the organization.

God gave Joshua such a manual to guide his service for God. God stressed how crucial Moses' Instruction would be for Joshua's success. It told him what to do and not do to enjoy God's full favor. Our study of Scripture takes on a similar urgency if we are to be successful followers of Jesus. If Jesus' example is to shape our lives, we need constant immersion in his life and teachings for success. Only as we see Jesus in action with real people and "meditate day and night" on his words will they "not depart from our mouth." Only then—and certainly over much time—will our actions take on the character of true Christlikeness.

Bear in mind, too, that according to Jesus, the test of Christian discipleship is not how fellow believers see us but how the outside world does. For example, he calls us to obey the two great commandments (Matt. 22:37−39). The first is: "Love the Lord your God with all your heart and with all your soul and with all your mind" (quoting Deut. 6:5). The second says, "Love your neighbor as yourself" (quoting Lev. 19:18). Jesus orders us to pour our all into loving God and loving our neighbor with the same level of love that we give to ourselves. He leaves us no wiggle room for negotiation on these. No disciple can truly love God only with his or her mind because purely intellectual love is only partial love. Neither can a disciple love God only with his or her heart because purely emotional love is only partial love, too. No, true love of God invests the whole self in actions that demonstrate genuine commitment to a personal relationship with God.

Jesus also allows no exceptions in the love of neighbor. Someone once replied, "Oh, I love my fellow humans, alright; it's just the people next door I can't stand!" Such hairsplitting is unworthy of a follower of Jesus, who lovingly forgave even those responsible for his death (Luke 23:34). As the new Moses, Jesus also issued a new commandment of his own: "Love one another. As I have loved you, so you must love one another. By this all men will know that you are my disciples, if you love one another" (John 13:34–35).

Jesus commands his followers to love each other. Of course, one wonders what it means to "love one another." Jesus explains that such love is "as I have loved you." Jesus' love for us is the standard by which we gauge whether our treatment of each other qualifies as truly Christlike. Jesus did not merely "tolerate" us but genuinely "loved" us. He gave his own life on the cross so that we might escape eternal death and enjoy eternal life. We were first drawn to him by his love, and our love for others is to draw others to his love, too.

A poignant scene in *The Lord of the Rings: The Return of the King* illustrates this biblical dynamic of love. Pippin comforts Denethor, the last ruling Steward of Gondor, after the death of his eldest son, Boromir. Boromir's warrior skills had won him the rank of Captain of the White Tower. At a secret meeting in the Elf-city of Rivendell, Boromir, the hobbits Frodo, Pippin, Merry, and Aragorn (another human) had formed the Fellowship of the Ring. The mission of this elite Fellowship was to destroy the ring and its magical powers by delivering it to the fires of Mount Doom. Destruction of the ring would finally defeat the evil Sauron.

Together the Fellowship set off for the Mount on their important mission. En route, however, the defenseless Pippen and Merry suddenly find themselves alone and facing an oncoming attack by the wizard Saruman's Uruk-hai. Boromir soon comes to their rescue and valiantly keeps the attackers at bay until mortally wounded by three arrows in the chest. Later, Pippin visits Denethor, who is deeply grieving his son Boromir's death. Sensitive to Denethor's grief and owning his own debt to Boromir's bravery, Pippin offers his life in service to the Steward—his life for Boromir's life. He does so because Boromir died while saving his life from the attacking Uruk-hai.

Similarly, Jesus' sacrifice of his own life dramatically put on public display his tremendous love for us. That sacrifice spared us eternal death and opened the way for us to experience eternal life. We commit ourselves to follow the risen Jesus because he first loved us (cf. 1 John 4:19). By displaying the same sacrificial love to others, we give people a glimpse of Jesus' love and draw them to salvation in him. But we will only understand what that sacrificial love looks like by meditating on the Jesus Manual—the Scriptures.

"Hang together, people!" The ringing phone some years ago surprised me. The caller was my pastor asking me to meet with him and the assistant pastor. I agreed, although my hunch was that the appointment had to do with recent church troubles. In my view, a pastoral transition several years earlier had gone poorly. Many of my closest friends had already migrated to other congregations, and my wife and I increasingly lost confidence in the pastor's leadership. Occasionally, I privately vented my frustrations to Christian friends and publically opposed new pastoral initiatives that I deemed unwise in light of the ongoing congregational exodus. Thus, I was not surprised at the meeting when the pastors confronted me with Hebrews 13:17:

> Obey your leaders and submit to their authority. They keep watch over you as men who must give an account. Obey them so that their work will be a joy, not a burden, for that would be of no advantage to you.

They asked me how my actions related to that instruction. More than a decade later, guilt over my conduct throughout that experience still pains me. I still wonder if I contributed to the division that was rending that congregation. Theologically, I affirm the priority of church unity and abominate those who sow division. For several years my wife and I struggled against a growing spiritual malaise as people continued to leave the church. Attempts to rouse the elder board to action met with sympathetic but unyielding resistance. It amounted to a classic church split in slow motion. Attendance numbers dwindled, giving declined, and even support of missionaries suffered from the budget shortfall. Only when the pastor's marital infidelity came to light—a surprise to everyone, I might add—did the board act to remove him from leadership.

Sadly, many of us have suffered through such splits, some even more acrimonious than my example. Despite the spiritual warfare raging all around, wars often break out inside churches. Members fall out with each other over the color of the sanctuary's new carpet or whether the service should begin at 10:30 or 11:00. A recent flashpoint in some congregations has been controversy over the style of worship—contemporary, traditional, or blended. The feelings on all sides run so high and the conflict so sharp that "worship wars" may erupt.

But our study of Israel's unity reminds us of the importance of congregational unity. In fact, the same corporate assumption that bound Israel as one people underlies this later comment of Paul: "If one part suffers, all suffer together with it; if one part is honored, all rejoice together with it"

(1 Cor. 12:26). Indeed, Paul's theology of the church as the body of Christ (1 Cor. 12) derives its corporate assumption from the Old Testament idea of Israel. In his view, the one communion loaf that Christians share symbolizes that "we, who are many, are one body" (10:17).

Paul articulates several principles that bear review in light of the ever-present danger of church disunity. (1) He stresses that as many members comprise the human body (i.e., eyes, ears, hands, feet, etc.) and yet it remains a single living organism, so it is with the church (1 Cor. 12:12, 20). In other words, when a local church meets for worship, it meets as only one body with many parts, not as a collection of bodies sitting in the same building.

(2) Paul says that that unity even transcends the church's ethnic ("Jews or Greeks") and economic ("slave or free") diversity (1 Cor. 12:13; cf. Eph. 2:16; 3:6). The diversity of members, he says, makes the church a complete, healthy organism. It has all its "members"—hands to handle objects and feet to maneuver. But its unity affirms that each member, however lowly in human eyes, is indispensable to the functioning of the whole (1 Cor. 12:16–19; cf. Eph. 4:16). I think Paul would applaud the diversity of some contemporary churches that provide worship services in various languages. The "Jews or Greeks" of Paul's day compare to the Koreans and Hispanics of today. It must warm God's heart each week to hear his praises echo from the same building in many tongues!

And such multiethnicity is not limited only to large cities. I have seen signs announcing ethnic services in smaller towns, too. But I think Paul would ask whether that building houses one church body or several. I think he would challenge us to build bridges across congregations, to strive to support each other, and ideally to function truly as a single body with members speaking several tongues. Paul would push us beyond the dominance of one congregation, usually the English-speaking one, over the non-English ones. Whether about offerings, office space, or office hours, I believe that Paul would desire each multiethnic body to function truly as a single body, sharing its resources equitably regardless of whose contributions fund most of the budget.

(3) Paul says that the church's unity prohibits one member from denigrating another as unnecessary to the body's work (1 Cor. 12:21–22). Indeed, Paul pushes the metaphor one further, even more radical, step. Within the body of Christ, God gives greater honor to its weakest members than to its strongest ones (v. 24). In other words, people whom society dishonors—for example, the poor, the indigent, the diseased, the mentally ill, the physically disabled—God honors more within the body than those humanly deemed "more important." This is a radical demand, indeed! Imagine a worship service in which a smelly, unkept beggar reads the Scripture

while a man in a pin-striped suit is ushered to a back row. Picture a service in which the church awards a "certificate of merit" to several members. One goes to the hard-working single parent who succeeds simply by getting the family through the week, the other to a naturally-gifted leader who led a wonderful missions trip. That is the kind of body Paul has in mind.

Sadly, the roles are more likely to be reversed in most churches. I have several Christian friends whose cerebral palsy has left them physically disabled and unable to speak clearly. They even joke about talking a foreign language called "C-P-ese" ("C-P" for cerebral palsy). I am appalled at the dishonorable treatment they sometimes receive from churches. Ushers routinely seat them either out of sight, so they cannot be noticed and upset anyone, or in the aisle, where people have to go around them to enter or exit. Such treatment implies that my friends' attendance is an unwelcome bother because their physical disabilities make other members uncomfortable.

It is no wonder that, according to a denominational report I read some years ago, people with disabilities is one of the least evangelized populations in America today. Paul, by contrast, would urge our congregations to depart from the norm of the larger society by honoring those whom society ignores. The upshot of Paul's teaching is that Christian unity outlaws divisions and promotes mutual concern of Christians for each other (1 Cor. 12:25). Because the church is an integral body, the pain of one member pains the whole body and the joy of one member makes the whole body rejoice (v. 26). In short, just as Israel with its various tribes was one people, so the church today with its diverse membership is one unified people of God.[69]

(4) Finally, Israel's history of refractoriness should alert contemporary Christians to the danger that similar conduct today poses to the church. Indeed, disunity is not the exclusive province of Israel. Fault lines of division also threatened the New Testament church. Members in the church at Corinth, for example, quarreled over the person who had baptized them. Apparently, they thought that being baptized by Apollos should enhance their status in the church (1 Cor. 1:10 – 16). They also disputed Paul's rights as an apostle (ch. 9) as did Jewish Christians in the region of Galatia (Gal. 1:11 – 12). They also insisted that new Gentile converts be circumcised and obey pharisaic law (Gal. 2:15 – 16; 5:2 – 6). In each case, Paul rebutted their errors and pled for unity — sadly, a plea that needs to be heard today, too.

In reality, the theological roots of refractoriness run back to the Garden of Eden. God told Adam and Eve, "You are free to eat from any tree in the garden" (Gen. 2:16). He generously granted the first human pair free access to the surrounding bounty. Sadly, what preoccupied them was the one tree

---

69. For the role of Christ in nourishing the body, see also Eph. 5:29; Col. 2:19.

declared off-limits, the "tree of the knowledge of good and evil" (2:17; 3:2 – 3). They cared little that to eat of it would mean death. They rebelled, ate, and doomed humanity, including Israel and the church, to a sad history of jealousy, violence, and death. Israel's rebellions and Christian divisions are nothing less than symptoms of sinful human corruption.

In the epic novel *The Brothers Karamazov*, Dostoyevsky aptly diagnoses the underlying disease:

> All mankind in our age have split up into units. Man keeps apart, each in his own groove; each one holds aloof, hides himself and hides what he has, from the rest. He ends by being repelled by others and repelling him. He heaps up riches by himself and thinks, "How strong I am now and how secure." And in his madness he does not understand that the more he heaps up, the more he sinks into self-destructive impotence. For he is accustomed to rely upon himself alone and to cut himself off from the whole; he has trained himself not to believe in the help of others, in men and in humanity, and only trembles for fear he should lose his money and the privileges that he has won for himself. Everywhere in these days men have ceased to understand that the true security is to be found in social solidarity rather than in isolated individual effort.[70]

That portrait fits Western culture today. But it is precisely here that Jesus calls the church to counter that cultural decadence with a healthy, thriving corporate model. As Christians, we need not follow Joshua 1:18 literally. We need not execute fellow Christians who sow dissension and disunity, to say nothing of division, in the church. But we do need at least to treat such refractoriness with the same seriousness. The unity of the body—and its very effectiveness as God's instrument in the world—are at stake.

That was the point of Joshua's talk with the Transjordanian tribes. It reminds us that God's people comprise a single body whose diverse parts live to support and enrich all the others. The warfare in which we are engaged may be spiritual rather than physical, but it is no less threatening. Only a healthy congregation—one whose members egg each other on and hold each other up—will win any battles. That is why Jesus asks us to make unity—warm, genuine, mutual commitment to our fellow believers—our top priority. Only when we enjoy that quality of harmony will our churches enjoy "rest"—a level of wholesome life together that outsiders will find appealing. Only that kind of unity will compel the watching world to stop and take us seriously.

---

70. F. Dostoyevsky, *The Brothers Karamazov* (New York: Penguin, 1957 [1880]), 279.

The second act of the musical Monty Python's *Spamalot* features a song called "I'm All Alone." By this point in the plot, King Arthur has reached a point of despair: The Holy Grail is out of reach, and he feels all alone. The stage grows dark, but in the spotlight King Arthur begins in song to lament his desperate loneliness. The audience, however, begins to laugh because, while the king decries being alone, King Arthur's servant, Patsy, stands beside him with an exasperated look on his face. King Arthur is not alone! Patsy has faithfully remained at his side during the whole play. As Arthur again sings the chorus "I'm all alone," Patsy echoes, "He's all alone," reminding the king of his presence. But Arthur's blindness persists. As he sings "all by myself," Patsy responds, "except for me." Through the rest of the song, Arthur and Patsy humorously go back-and-forth: "I'm all alone" (Arthur) ... "although I'm here" (Patsy) ... "So all alone" (Arthur) ... "so very near" (Patsy). Soon, all of King Arthur's knights have joined the pair and joined in the song. At the end, everyone is singing the chorus, "*We're* all alone." The humorous irony of the scene is not lost on the audience. They see a stage full of people ridiculously claiming that they are all alone.[71]

Unlike poor King Arthur, we Christians are not alone. We are surrounded by sisters and brothers, all part of the body of Christ. They pick up our spirits when we are down, lift us up when we fall, walk with us through our dark valleys, and celebrate our triumphs. Our task is to look up from our isolated self-preoccupation and recognize that they are there—and that they care, too.

The powerful presence. Finally, like Joshua, we also have the assurance of Jesus' presence with us as part of the Great Commission: "And surely I am with you always, to the very end of the age" (Matt. 28:20b). Joshua led Israel across the Jordan to face the Canaanites because God promised to be with him. Like Israel under Joshua, we Christians are an army engaged in warfare—a *spiritual* army fighting a *spiritual* war against a powerful *spiritual* enemy. Like Joshua and Israel, we face many dangers and live with many fears. But we are not alone—Jesus promised to be with us every moment. As that reassurance banished Joshua's fears, so it should ours as well.

Some time ago, I heard a fascinating story that brings home this truth about Jesus' presence with us. A mother had agreed to drive her son's car from Michigan to California as part of his move there. It was Christmastime, so the plan called for her to drive the car out, for her husband to fly there for the holiday, and for the two of them to fly home from California together. The day before her departure, however, the woman fell and

---

71. I am grateful to my former student, the Rev. Joseph Stackwell, for sharing this example with me.

broke her left wrist. Despite the cumbersome cast from wrist to elbow, she decided to go anyway and carefully planned the long trip.

About the fourth day out, she felt so tired that she pulled off the road for a short nap, then drove to a restaurant for coffee and a few phone calls to friends who lived nearby. As she stepped outside the restaurant, things got interesting. A man approached and asked if she was driving a Ford Explorer with Michigan plates, and whether she had pulled off the road somewhere earlier. The woman was understandably apprehensive about being questioned by a stranger, but he assured her that he meant no harm. Once she answered his questions, he asked her to wait while he made a phone call and then promised to explain.

When he returned, he told her that truck drivers had been following her since Indiana. One of them had noticed this little white-haired lady, with a cast on her left arm, driving a stick-shift across the country. They had taken it upon themselves to watch over her. Unbeknownst to her, they carefully tracked her to the motels she stayed each evening. Each morning another trucker would pick up her trail and shadow her progress. If a trucker had to exit, he would radio another rig-driver to take his place. When she pulled off for that nap, they had lost track of her and were about to alert the State Police. They were still seriously searching for her when one of them spotted her car at the restaurant. The woman had no idea that somebody cared enough about her to initiate such a protection plan. Until that moment, she had been totally unaware that, across all the miles, someone was looking after her day and night.

The presence of Jesus with us is no less watchful and faithful. Armed with his simple assurance ("I am with you"), we Christian soldiers can daily march into war. The spiritual battlefield may be our own homes, neighborhoods, job sites—perhaps even our own souls. Our lives seek to mirror the model of our Lord—or, at least, that is our dream. Like him, we bring good news to a broken, hurting, lost world. And we do so with fear offset, if not banished, by the wonderful reality that, come what may, we are "never alone." As recent writers put it,

> The truly good news is that God is not a distant God, a God to be feared and avoided, a God of revenge, but a God who is moved by our pains and participates in the fullness of the human struggle. The miraculous cures in the Gospels are hopeful and joyful reminders of this good news, which is our true consolation and comfort.[72]

---

72. H. J. M. Nouwen, D. P. McNeill, and D. A. Morrison, *Compassion* (New York: Image, 1982), 18.

Joshua 2:1–24

THEN JOSHUA SON of Nun secretly sent two spies from Shittim. "Go, look over the land," he said, "especially Jericho." So they went and entered the house of a prostitute named Rahab and stayed there.

²The king of Jericho was told, "Look! Some of the Israelites have come here tonight to spy out the land." ³So the king of Jericho sent this message to Rahab: "Bring out the men who came to you and entered your house, because they have come to spy out the whole land."

⁴But the woman had taken the two men and hidden them. She said, "Yes, the men came to me, but I did not know where they had come from. ⁵At dusk, when it was time to close the city gate, the men left. I don't know which way they went. Go after them quickly. You may catch up with them." ⁶(But she had taken them up to the roof and hidden them under the stalks of flax she had laid out on the roof.) ⁷So the men set out in pursuit of the spies on the road that leads to the fords of the Jordan, and as soon as the pursuers had gone out, the gate was shut.

⁸Before the spies lay down for the night, she went up on the roof ⁹and said to them, "I know that the LORD has given this land to you and that a great fear of you has fallen on us, so that all who live in this country are melting in fear because of you. ¹⁰We have heard how the LORD dried up the water of the Red Sea for you when you came out of Egypt, and what you did to Sihon and Og, the two kings of the Amorites east of the Jordan, whom you completely destroyed. ¹¹When we heard of it, our hearts melted and everyone's courage failed because of you, for the LORD your God is God in heaven above and on the earth below. ¹²Now then, please swear to me by the LORD that you will show kindness to my family, because I have shown kindness to you. Give me a sure sign ¹³that you will spare the lives of my father and mother, my brothers and sisters, and all who belong to them, and that you will save us from death."

¹⁴"Our lives for your lives!" the men assured her. "If you don't tell what we are doing, we will treat you kindly and faithfully when the LORD gives us the land."

¹⁵So she let them down by a rope through the window, for the house she lived in was part of the city wall. ¹⁶Now she had said to them, "Go to the hills so the pursuers will not find you. Hide yourselves there three days until they return, and then go on your way."

¹⁷The men said to her, "This oath you made us swear will not be binding on us ¹⁸unless, when we enter the land, you have tied this scarlet cord in the window through which you let us down, and unless you have brought your father and mother, your brothers and all your family into your house. ¹⁹If anyone goes outside your house into the street, his blood will be on his own head; we will not be responsible. As for anyone who is in the house with you, his blood will be on our head if a hand is laid on him. ²⁰But if you tell what we are doing, we will be released from the oath you made us swear."

²¹"Agreed," she replied. "Let it be as you say." So she sent them away and they departed. And she tied the scarlet cord in the window.

²²When they left, they went into the hills and stayed there three days, until the pursuers had searched all along the road and returned without finding them. ²³Then the two men started back. They went down out of the hills, forded the river and came to Joshua son of Nun and told him everything that had happened to them. ²⁴They said to Joshua, "The LORD has surely given the whole land into our hands; all the people are melting in fear because of us."

THIS IS ONE OF the Bible's best-known stories, the report of a secret reconnaissance mission to Jericho by a pair of young Israelites. Their task is to ascertain the terrain and conditions Israel may expect when they cross into Canaan. The story also introduces one of the Bible's more colorful characters, the prostitute Rahab, and marks the second step in Joshua's preparation of Israel for entrance into Canaan.

From one angle, the story of Rahab offers an odd, surprising follow-up to chapter 1. One would expect the Jordan crossing to follow next, but inexplicably chapter 2 postpones that event until chapters 3–4. Also, whereas chapter 1 features Joshua at center stage in the leading role, chapter 2 stars the Canaanite Rahab while Joshua plays a minor supporting role. With Zakovitch, some readers may wonder, "Why does the Jericho prostitute get such a prominent place … on the very opening pages … of the Former Prophets?"[1] Further, the mercy accorded Rahab in chapter 2 clearly contradicts the expectation that all Canaanites are to be killed. These and other observations lead some scholars to view the chapter as a later addition, but Sherwood presents a persuasive interpretation of its literary and thematic role in its present context.[2]

Literarily, the Rahab episode comprises a spy story with the distinct feel of a cloak-and-dagger affair.[3] Except for Rahab and Joshua (2:1, 2, 4, 24), anonymity prevails among the characters—the spies ("the men" [vv. 4b, 5a]), the "king of Jericho" (vv. 2, 3), and his own "men" (v. 7; cf. v. 2). It is as if the author were intentionally hiding their identities. Structurally, Joshua's commission of the spies (v. 1) and their report to him of their findings (vv. 23–24) bracket the lengthy report concerning the spy mission itself (vv. 2–22). Clearly, dialogue rather than action dominates that report: the king and king's men talk with Rahab (vv. 3–7), and Rahab talks with the spies (vv. 8–21). The latter conversation forms the chapter's literary highpoint.

Several narrative ambiguities, however, leave the reader wondering how to assess the performance of Joshua and the two spies. Joshua dispatches the spies secretly, and his orders seem vague and general (see below).[4] Hence, one can read them either as presupposing more complete, unreported instructions or as simple poor planning. The connection between those orders and the spies' entrance into the city and dealings with Rahab likewise yield alternative readings. Do their actions faithfully execute what Joshua

---

1. Y. Zakovitch, "Humor and Theology or the Successful Failure of Israelite Intelligence: A Literary-Folkloric Approach to Joshua 2," in *Text and Tradition: The Hebrew Bible and Folklore*, ed. S. Niditch (Atlanta: Scholars Press, 1990), 71–72.

2. A. Sherwood, "A Leader's Misleading and a Prostitute's Profession: A Re-examination of Joshua 2," *JSOT* 31/1 (2006): 43–61. Butler (*Joshua*, 27–32), by contrast, represents scholars who read the chapter as a later addition.

3. The Bible shows three other examples: the disastrous mission of the twelve spies (Num. 13–14), the clever conquest of Bethel by the tribes of Joseph (Judg. 1:22–26), and the conquest of Laish by the tribe of Dan (18:1–26). The latter two parallel Joshua 2 in that cities are the spies' targets, but of these the episode in Judges 1 may offer the closest parallel. Bethel falls because of inside information provided the spies by a local resident whose life the conquerors spare for his cooperation.

4. The LXX and Syriac versions omit "secretly" in v. 1, perhaps because the translators no longer understood this word (it only occurs here in the MT); so Boling, *Joshua*, 141.

wants, or are the spies freelancing on their own—and perhaps bungling the job? Chapter 2 marks Joshua's debut as commander-in-chief—his "first opportunity to prove himself" after succeeding Moses (see below).[5] The narrative seems to leave open the question as to how well he comes off. But if, as some contend, Joshua's actions constitute a "false start" in the race to victory, the happy outcome is that Yahweh graciously rescues him through Rahab.[6]

The clever story is more than simply literary fun. It sounds important theological themes and advances the plot of the book of Joshua. The conversational sparring between the king and his men, Rahab, and the spies foreshadows the impending, titanic struggle for control of Canaan, the subject of Joshua 3–11. Also, as Spina notes, the Rahab/spies encounter sharply contrasts the Israelites' encounter (God's chosen "insiders" now outside the land) with Rahab, the "virtual *representative*" of the Canaanites (the "outsiders" in God's eyes who still occupy it).[7] The fate of Rahab herself also anticipates the story of other outsiders, the Gibeonites (chs. 9–10), and provides a literary foil for the unexpected, contrasting fate that befalls the consummate insider, Achan (ch. 7).[8] And if Joshua's debut marks a misstep (certainly a possibility), that motif would alert the reader to one of the book's important themes, the rise of Joshua's reputation in Israel during the Conquest.

Finally, though present behind the scenes, Yahweh's providential work through Rahab proves him to be a gracious and hands-on divine warrior. Whatever one's assessment of Joshua and the spies, Yahweh clearly follows up his commitments from chapter 1, a harbinger of many victories to come.[9] Dramatically, the chapter ends with the spies' excited interpretation of their findings, quoting—of all people!—Rahab herself (v. 24).

---

5. I owe this phrase to Sherwood, ibid., 46.

6. See Sherwood, ibid., 60, who may be right (43, 60−61) in arguing that ch. 2 criticizes Joshua's actions.

7. F. A. Spina, *The Faith of the Outsider: Exclusion and Inclusion in the Biblical Story* (Grand Rapids: Eerdmans, 2005), 53. As Spina notes (54), "She is as Canaanite as they get!" I am grateful to my friend and colleague, Professor R. K. Johnston, for pointing me to this source.

8. J. H. Stek, "Rahab of Canaan and Israel: The Meaning of Joshua 2," *CTJ* 37 (2002): 48.

9. The Rahab story probably originated in an oral tale, perhaps passed down by her descendants who continued to live in Israel (see 6:25), and reached written form during the early monarchy long before its later incorporation by the Deuteronomist into his history. For literary-critical discussion, see V. Fritz, *Das Buch Josua* (Tübingen: Mohr [Siebeck], 1994), 33–35. Slightly different scenarios are proposed by M. Ottosson, "Rahab and the Spies," in *Dumu-e₂-dub-ba-a: Studies in Honor of Åke W. Sjöberg*, ed. H. Behrens et al. (Philadelphia: Samuel Noah Kramer Fund, 1989), 427; and H. M. Barstad, "The Old Testament Feminine Personal Name *raḥab*. An Onomastic Note," *SEÅ* 54 (1989): 44.

The Spy Mission (2:1–21)

Joshua's commission (v. 1). Joshua secretly commissions two unnamed men as spies to (lit.) "go, see the land, Jericho" (v. 1). In so doing, Joshua continues Moses' well-known practice (cf. Num. 14:3, 31; Deut. 1:39), a step he will also take later with Ai (Josh. 7:2 – 3). But his approach differs from his mentor's pattern in several ways. Moses dispatched spies at Yahweh's direction (Num. 13), but here Joshua takes the initiative without divine direction.[10] Unlike Moses, he sends two spies rather than twelve—and "secretly," too, to minimize risk. Further, Yahweh had specified that the spies be tribal leaders, but Joshua selects two ordinary Israelite young men (see 6:23).

Joshua's terse, general orders ("Go, look over the land" [2:1]) sharply contrast the lengthy instructions of Moses (Num. 13:17 – 20). The ambiguity of Joshua's words is striking, but the differences between the two missions might explain the contrasts with Moses. The latter sent the twelve spies on a broad reconnoitering of Canaan, while Joshua's young pair conducts a covert military reconnaissance. Certainly, a pair of spies—and young ones, at that—might arouse less suspicion in Jericho than would a team of twelve.[11] Further, one might read Joshua's initiation of the spy mission as simply indicative of a wise, trusted, conscientious commander at work, not someone whom Yahweh must micromanage.

But some readers may read Joshua's simple orders as an odd follow-up to Yahweh's more visionary command ("[you and Israel] cross the Jordan" [1:2]). Yahweh has assured Joshua of certain victory (see 1:2 – 5, 10 – 11, 15), so why send the spies at all? What else does Joshua need to know? More importantly, readers may wonder about Joshua's leadership and the depth of his faith. Despite receiving God's emphatic reassurance and promise of victory (1:3 – 9), he opts for a cautious rather than a bold first step forward. Has he forgotten the terror of Israel that Yahweh promised would precede them in Canaan (Deut. 11:25)? Is it wise not to consult with God (cf. Josh. 9:14)? Does the mission suggest, as Spina alleges, "at least a failure of nerve, if not of faith, on Joshua's part?"[12]

Inside Jericho (vv. 2–8). The young pair's first move is to lodge in the house of a prostitute named Rahab. As noted earlier, the reader wonders

---

10. His initiative here also contrasts with Josh. 1 in which Joshua carries out Yahweh's initiative.

11. Ottosson ("Rahab and the Spies," 420) suggests that the use of two may depend on the treaty later made with Rahab, perhaps giving the transaction two required witnesses (cf. Deut. 17:6; 19:15; 1 Kings 21:10).

12. Spina, *The Faith of the Outsider,* 57.

whether it violates or executes Joshua's orders—whether the spies are being cunning or bumbling.[13] There is no explanation as to how or why they link up with Rahab. Perhaps they think her house offers them the safety of anonymity or the best spot to gather information. Clearly, Rahab, not the spies, is the star here—and the only fully human character, too. Aside from Joshua, she is the only one known by name.[14]

In itself, to visit a prostitute creates an unusual, if not amusing, situation.[15] But some scholars suggest that the storyteller may intentionally weave in sexually suggestive language, as if playfully titilating the reader's imagination. The writer uses "enter (into)" (*boʾ*) and "stay" (*šakab*, "to lie down, lodge"), verbs that elsewhere also describe sexual intercourse, often in morally problematic circumstances.[16] Borne by a prostitute, the name Rahab ("wide, broad") may aim to sound risqué, much as the modern slang word "broad" describes a woman of notoriously loose morals.[17] If so, "house of the prostitute named Rahab" might mean "brothel," with Rahab its madam (cf. Isa. 57:8; Ezek. 16:24, 31).[18]

A reader might wonder with some amusement whether the two Israelite GIs may have combined "pleasure" with "business" by enjoying Rahab's sexual services.[19] Hawk finds it strange that Israel's first act upon entering

---

13. Command/fulfillment forms a common pattern in the book of Joshua. The spies' actions offer a startling break in the pattern—in Sherwood's terms ("A Leader's Misleading," 49), "command/*failed* fulfillment" (italics, mine). He also interprets (50) the spies as "pawns in Joshua's struggle against the king" and suggests that, by a tactical overextension, Joshua "has placed his men in danger."

14. Nelson, *Joshua*, 46.

15. For "prostitute" (Heb. *ʾiššah zonah*, lit. "a whoring woman"), cf. Judg. 11:1; 16:1; Prov. 6:26; Jer. 3:3; Ezek. 16:30; 23:44; S. Erlandsson, "זָנָה," *TDOT*, 4:100–101. It also speaks against the view that she was a sacred prostitute (normally *qedešah*).

16. Cf. Sherwood, "A Leader's Misleading," 50–51. For *šakab*, cf. Gen. 19:32, 35; 39:12, 14; 2 Sam 13:11; for *boʾ* ("to enter" [Josh. 2:1b, 2b, 4b]) and *boʾ ʾel* ("go into" [vv. 3b, 4b]), cf. Gen. 16:4; Judg. 16:1; Ezek. 23:44). For a similar, sexually suggestive use of double entendre, see Ruth 3:4, 7, 8; cf. Hubbard, *Ruth*, 204, n.33. Against this suggestion, see Hess, *Joshua*, 83–84.

17. Spina, *The Faith of the Outsider*, 54–55; Sherwood, "A Leader's Misleading," 47–48.

18. Nelson, *Joshua*, 43; P. Bird, "The Harlot as Heroine: Narrative Art and Social Presuppositions in Three Old Testament Texts," *Semeia* 46 (1989): 127–28. On the other hand, Horn's thesis that Rahab was an Israelite woman working in Jericho as an innkeeper presupposes a social situation for which Josh. 2 offers little evidence and contradicts the text's clear portrait of her as a Canaanite; cf. P. H. Horn, "Josua 2, 1–24 im Milieu einer 'dimorphic society'," *BZ* 31 (1987): 264–70. She may have been, however, both prostitute and innkeeper (so Hess, *Joshua*, 83–84).

19. Cf. Spina, *The Faith of the Outsider*, 54: "Thus the phrase 'the spies lodged there' at the house of a prostitute likely is a *double-entendre*: one can't be sure whether they simply 'lodged' there or whether they—ahem—'lodged' there."

the land is to engage "in forbidden activity with the very people who are to be destroyed."[20] The above literary features are ambiguous, however, and an extreme sexual reading does run the risk of being anachronistic—of wrongly reading a modern perspective into an ancient text. The words "enter" and "lie down" may simply describe those actions without sexual innuendo. And the name *raḥab* may play on *reḥob* ("public square"), thus invoking the narrative type scene "hospitality to strangers in danger" evident in Genesis 19 (at Sodom) and Judges 19 (at Gibeah).[21] In any case, whether as prostitute, innkeeper, or both, Rahab's house is where the spies stay in Jericho.

Alas, whatever her "establishment," it fails to provide the spies with adequate cover. Someone notices their arrival and informs the king (v. 2), who sends word demanding that Rahab hand them over (v. 3). At first glance, the Hebrew of verse 3 reads clumsily (unlike the more tidy versions), but the clumsiness may in fact convey a coarse, crude double entendre: "Send out the men who entered you ... er, who entered your house."[22] Undoubtedly, the narrative assumes that Israel's large encampment east of the Jordan will not go unnoticed in Jericho. Observation of Israel's comings and goings by Canaanite scouts seems likely and may partly explain how the king knows the two spies' whereabouts.

But two things bear mention here. First, Rahab's actions presume upon the ancient Semitic custom of hospitality. This practice accorded visiting guests, otherwise vulnerable to abuse as social outsiders, protection.[23] The king's envoys also seem to respect it, otherwise they would have forced their way in and dragged the spies out.[24] Second, the king interprets the coming of the Israelite pair specifically as something sinister (vv. 2b, 3b). Joshua's mandate was merely (lit.) to "see" the land and Jericho (v. 1). But the king and his men believe their intent is more serious—"to gather information" (*ḥapar*, lit., "to dig [in the ground]") about it (vv. 2, 3).

---

20. L. D. Hawk, *Every Promise Fulfilled: Contesting Plots in Joshua* (Louisville: Westminster/ John Knox, 1991), 62.

21. Cf. Nelson, *Joshua*, 43; L. D. Hawk, "Strange Houseguests: Rahab, Lot, and the Dynamics of Deliverance," in *Reading between the Texts: Intertextuality and the Hebrew Bible*, ed. D. N. Fewell (Louisville: Westminster John Knox, 1992), 89–97.

22. The rendering of Spina, *The Faith of the Outsider*, 55. According to Assis, the messengers offer Rahab two possibilities, i.e., that the Israelites "came" for sexual relations or simply to "lodge" there (but not with Rahab); cf. E. Assis, "The Choice to Serve God and Assist His People," *Bib* 85 (2004): 83.

23. It is the violation of that custom that makes the mistreatment of guests in Sodom and Gomorrah (Gen. 19) and Israelite Gibeah (Judg. 19:22–30) especially outrageous; cf. Fritz, *Josua*, 37; Nelson, *Joshua*, 43.

24. Against Spina (*The Faith of the Outsider*, 57–58), for whom this failure signals that the king's men are as incompetent as Joshua's spies.

If the spies sought safe anonymity with Rahab, the contrasting words literarily imply that the Israelite pair has, so to speak, lost their "cover." Suddenly, the mission has turned sour. The spies have barely arrived ("tonight," v. 2b), but enemy intelligence threatens to imperil their mission and their lives. They find themselves at the mercy of a total stranger, Rahab the Canaanite prostitute. Their survival and the accomplishment of their mission lie completely in her hands. Cleverly, the narrator sounds what Sherwood calls a "calamity motif"—a foreboding sense of imminent disaster.[25]

Rahab's life probably hangs in the balance, too. Socially, she already has one strike against her—her profession. As Bird observes, it marks her as "a marginal figure in the society, tolerated but despised."[26] By harboring enemies, she presumably faces execution by the king for treason. But, for reasons yet to be explained, Rahab risks her life and cunningly protects her two guests. She first hides them from the messengers at her door (v. 4a) and then, on the spot, spins a scheme to throw the king off their trail (vv. 4b–5).[27] The reader wonders how Rahab hid the men without the messengers' knowledge, but we are not told—at least, not now.[28]

Withholding that information leaves two literary effects. It portrays Rahab as a smooth operator, as if she has covered for customers before. And it makes the reader wonder (and worry!) about what game she is playing. Is she out for profit, angling for revenge, or bent on betrayal? In reply, she concedes that the men "came to me" but denies knowing from where (v. 4). If Assis is right, the phrase aims to deceive the king by implying that the Israelites have had sex with Rahab and left satisfied. Her strategy would be to dispel any suspicions that she has cooperated with them and to head off the need to pump her for information.[29] The less the king thinks she knows, the greater her chances of surviving suspicions of treason. As verses

---

25. Sherwood, "A Leader's Misleading," 50–52.

26. Bird, "The Harlot as Heroine," 119.

27. The verbs of v. 4 suggest sequential action (so NRSV, "But the woman took ... and hid.... Then she said....") rather than either a retrospective report followed by a sequential action (against NIV, "But the woman had taken and hidden.... She said....") or two separate contacts between the king and Rahab (against Hess, *Joshua*, 85). Alternatively, the taking and hiding might be contemporaneous to her speaking to the king's messengers. For a linguistic defense of a pluperfect (so NIV), see Howard, *Joshua*, 100, n.11.

28. According to Fritz (*Josua*, 37), the spies are still in the house. In my view, however, v. 6 will detail in retrospect their actual location and how they came to be there.

29. Assis, "The Choice to Serve God," 83. But, in his view, the narrator had already signaled that they merely spent the night (cf. "lodged" [v. 1]). By contrast, had she claimed that they came only to get some sleep, her questioners would not have believed her statement that the visitors had already left.

9−11 reveal, however, this is a bald-faced lie. She knows exactly where they are from.[30]

Next, Rahab lies about their present whereabouts (v. 5). She explains that the men left before the city closed its gate for the night. This is important: It places their whereabouts outside the city, probably hurrying toward the river and the safety of the Israelite camp. If the king believes her, she and her hidden guests will escape scrutiny, at least for a while. Playing for time, she urges the king's emissaries immediately to chase after the fleeing spies. The sooner they start the search, the sooner they will overtake them. This may be the cleverest move of all. It compels the messengers either to seize the moment, without thinking or even consulting the king, or to squander any hope of catching them. In sum, Rahab's lies buy her time to talk with her visitors, redirect royal attention eastward, and open up a way for the spies to escape Jericho safely.

A shift to subject-first syntax (v. 6) and an inclusio set off verses 6−8 from what precedes. In my view, the change signals a literary transition to the chapter's central scene (vv. 9−21).[31] Initial pronouns or nouns emphatically position all the key players—Rahab ("she," vv. 6a, 8b), the pursuit team ("the men," v. 7), and the spies ("they," v. 8a)—for what follows. Verse 6 explains the truth behind Rahab's daring lies (vv. 4b−5)—and to the reader's great relief. She had hid her guests on the roof under piles of flax stalks.[32]

Flax is an agricultural product well attested earlier in Egypt and Mesopotamia. The Gezer Calendar (tenth cent. B.C.) lists it among Canaan's annual crops. In the ancient world, flax provided fibers for linen, a lighter, more comfortable cloth than wool.[33] Some evidence confirms its cultivation in pre-Israelite Canaan, but the reference here may simply be to wild flax that Rahab harvested and laid out on the roof to dry.[34] Wild flax is

---

30. Inexplicably, LXX lacks her denial of an Israelite connection (v. 4b).

31. The pronoun *hîʾ* (= Rahab) plus the root *ʿalah* ("to go up") comprise the inclusio (vv. 6a, 8b).

32. Nelson, *Joshua*, 49; Howard, *Joshua*, 100, although he views v. 6 as "a parenthetical aside." I render *heʿelatam* "she had (i.e., caused) them go up," not "she had taken/brought them up" (so NRSV; NIV; et al.). My rendering leaves ambiguous her means of hiding them in conformity to the apparent ambiguity of the narrative.

33. Cf. I. Jacob and W. Jacob, "Flora," *ABD*, 2:815; J. Hoffmeier, "פֵּשֶׁת," *NIDOTTE*, 3:711−12.

34. According to Jacob and Jacob (ibid., 815), flax seeds were found in Early Bronze Stratum IV at Tel el-Areini in the Shephelah; cf. also M. Zohary, *Plants of the Bible* (New York: Cambridge Univ. Press, 1982), 72, 78. But Howard (*Joshua*, 100, n.114) and Boling (*Joshua*, 146) prefer wild flax, following the case against flax cultivation by S. Talmon, "The Gezer Calendar and the Seasonal Cycle of Ancient Canaan," *JAOS* 83 (1963): 177−87.

typically scarce, so its availability as a hiding place here suggests a providential stroke of good luck.[35] The piles happen to be there just when they are needed.

Meanwhile, swallowing Rahab's lie, the king's "men" hotly pursue the allegedly fleeing Israelite "men" down the road to the river. They prove to be putty in her cunning hands—and gullible and incompetent, too.[36] The city's gates immediately close behind them (v. 7), ironically damning them to an all-night wild goose chase. They presume the Israelites are hightailing it for home, so the trackers head eastward, straight for the nearest crossing point. Probably, the "fords of the Jordan" is the silt sandbar known today as Al-Maghtas, eight miles southeast of Jericho.[37]

For the spies, these mark ominous developments. The locked gates trap them inside Jericho, while the search outside cuts off their escape route back to Joshua. They, too, have fallen into Rahab's hands. Rahab joins the pair, snugly hidden on her roof, before they retire for the night (v. 8).[38] The "roof" is probably the floor of the top storey of Rahab's house—the place where its occupants slept and, hence, "the most private and secret part of the house."[39] Out of earshot of people below, it offers the ideal spot for the frank, revealing conversation that follows.

The reader still wonders, however, what game the prostitute is playing. From one angle, the scene is almost humorous. The spies came to "dig up" (*ḥapar*) information (vv. 2, 3) but end up "buried" (*ṭaman*, NIV "hid") under piles of flax. They sought obscurity in Rahab's house but end up in a highly visible hiding place.[40] And it is difficult to "see" the land (cf. v. 1) hiding under a rooftop pile of flax! Like it or not, their fate rests in the wily prostitute's hands. Clearly, she is no "dumb broad" or garden-variety madam. On the contrary, she seems the most competent character in the story, with quick wits and decisive action.[41] Indeed, her intervention surprisingly

---

35. So Boling, *Joshua*, 146 ("the relative scarcity ... would heighten the sense of escape 'by the skin of your teeth'").

36. Assis, "The Choice to Serve God," 84.

37. H. O. Thompson, "Jordan River," *ABD*, 3:957; cf. Boling, *Joshua*, 137 (an excellent map), 170. When silt from surrounding hills piles up in a river bottom, a sandbar or "ford" forms, providing a shallow crossing point for foot traffic.

38. Nelson (*Joshua*, 49, n.21) provides a simple solution to the oft-discussed discrepancy between the report (v. 1) that the spies "lay down" or "went to sleep" (*šakab*) and the claim that they had not yet done so (*šakab*, v. 8). They did lie down (v. 1), were relocated by Rahab (vv. 4, 6 [a flashback of details]), but had not lain down again (v. 8).

39. Hess, *Joshua*, 87. For further comments on her house, see below.

40. Nelson, *Joshua*, 49 ("a place of dubious safety and undignified discomfort"); cf. 2 Sam. 11:2; 16:22.

41. Spina, *The Faith of the Outsider*, 58.

transforms the calamity motif into a "deliverance motif."[42] The scene is set for the highpoint of the story, Rahab's speech and negotiations. The reader will soon learn why this Canaanite prostitute has risked her own life to protect two total strangers.

Rahab strikes a deal (vv. 9–21). On the roof, alone with the spies and temporarily free of royal scrutiny, Rahab finally explains herself (vv. 9–11). In truth, she proves to be a shrewd observer of the emerging historical reality about to engulf the land. Certainly, she is more in tune with it than Jericho's defiant king. She acknowledges ("I know that …") three crucial things.

(1) She knows that Yahweh has given Canaan into Israel's hands (v. 9). The perfect "has given" states that truth as a "done deal"—an already established fact soon to become reality. This unexpected statement probably startles the reader as much as it undoubtedly does the two trapped spies. Who would have dreamed that this Canaanite woman knew Israel's God by name ("Yahweh") and that she knew anything about his intended future for her homeland? What Israelite would have ever considered the fall of Canaan as inevitable? Spina may be right: At this moment, she seems "more confident that YHWH will deliver as promised than Joshua is."[43] Soon we will learn why she has drawn this conclusion about Canaan's loss to Israel.

(2) She reveals the popular mood in Canaan. A terrible dread of Israel now grips the land.[44] If Yahweh has given the land to Israel, then Israel must be unstoppable—and a Canaanite massacre inescapable. The phrase "great fear of you" invokes the Old Testament tradition of Yahweh the mighty warrior who fights for his people (e.g., Ex. 15:16; 23:27; Job 9:34; 20:25). Such "great fear" is precisely what the warrior Yahweh promised to spread among Israel's enemies (Deut. 11:25).[45] Theologically, Israel's imminent victory derives from their alliance with Yahweh, not their own strength or cunning. The Canaanites also had warrior gods, but according to Rahab those gods are no match for Yahweh.

---

42. Sherwood, "A Leader's Misleading," 53, 54.

43. Spina, *The Faith of the Outsider*, 59; cf. Sherwood, "A Leader's Misleading," 54 ("the spies' lives are ironically safer in the hands of a Jericho native than in Joshua's").

44. The LXX makes this statement the reason (Gk. *gar*) for the preceding one (i.e., "Yahweh has given the land *because* fear of you has fallen on us") and omits the rest of the verse. Hess (*Joshua*, 89–90) suggests that a chiastic or concentric structure underlies all of vv. 9–11.

45. H.-J. Zobel, "אֵימָה," *TDOT*, 1:220–21. For in-depth discussion, see the Bridging Contexts section. The fundamental study on Yahweh as warrior remains G. von Rad, *Holy War in Ancient Israel* (Grand Rapids: Eerdmans, 1991), but see also conveniently T. Longman III and D. G. Reid, *God Is a Warrior* (Grand Rapids: Zondervan, 1995).

(3) The same tradition also underlies her third revelation, the terrible toll taken by this fear on Canaanite resolve. Plainly, whatever firm determination the inhabitants once had has become terrified panic like hard ground reduced by rain to mushy mud (cf. Ex. 15:15).[46] Keeping company with Yahweh the warrior gives Israel a terrible aura, too. But what caused this panic and fatalism? According to Rahab, they have "heard" (Heb. *šamaᶜ*, vv. 10, 11) that Yahweh "dried up" the Red Sea and that Israel "completely destroyed" the two Transjordanian kings, Sihon and Og (Num. 21:21 – 35; cf. 32:33; 1 Kings 4:19; Ps. 136:19 – 20). These two events — the Exodus and the conquest of Transjordan — mark the beginning and end of Israel's wilderness period. Hence, Rahab may be invoking a kind of historical merismus for all Yahweh's wonderful deeds during that era.[47]

Canaan's inhabitants dread the prospect of similar divine miracles on their soil, and they are right. Indeed, by invoking two causative verbs (*yabaš* ["to dry up"] and *ḥaram* ["to exterminate" (ritually)]), Rahab anticipates two of the book's main themes, Israel's dramatic crossing of the Jordan on dry land (Josh. 4:23; 5:1) and the elimination of Canaan's inhabitants (e.g., 6:21 [Jericho]; 8:26 [Ai]; 11:12 [northern Canaanite cities]).[48] In so doing, Rahab either draws on some form of ancient "common knowledge" or shows remarkable familiarity with two Israelite theological terms and the central concept of *ḥerem*.[49]

For now, Rahab again underscores the panicked reaction in Canaan to the news from Egypt and Transjordan (v. 11). Besides sparking terror (v. 9), it has plunged the land into utter despair. Sensing imminent doom, the people no longer have either the courage ("heart") or the physical strength ("spirit") to resist.[50] In short, according to Rahab, Canaan is rife with popular panic and despair over Israel, and Rahab herself has already accepted the

---

46. Cf. A. Baumann, "מוג," *TDOT*, 8:149–52, invoking one of the root's concrete meanings "to melt, dissolve"; cf. Amos 9:13; Ps. 75:3.

47. Similarly, Hess, *Joshua*, 88–89. Spina (*The Faith of the Outsider*, 59) contrasts the detailed accuracy of her geographical knowledge of these key events with the erroneous understanding of the Philistines in 1 Sam. 4:8.

48. *Ḥaram* hi. "to devote to the 'ban'" is central to the Deuteronomistic theory of holy war, which guides Israel's treatment of the Canaanites (see Deut. 7:2; 20:15 – 18); cf. Butler, *Joshua*, 33; Hess, *Joshua*, 89. See Josh. 6:17, 21; 8:26; 10:1; 11:11; for the noun *ḥerem*, cf. 6:18; 7:1, 11, 12, 13, 15; 22:20.

49. Spina, *The Faith of the Outsider*, 60, favors the latter, although the former is also possible. For definition and discussion of this term, see comments on Josh. 5 – 6. For discussion of the larger problem of violence in Joshua, see the Introduction ("Now, About All That Killing …").

50. For the phrase "our hearts melted," see also Deut. 20:8; Josh. 7:5; Isa. 13:7; 19:1; H. Ringgren, "מסס," *TDOT*, 8:438–39. To my knowledge, its parallel ("everyone's courage failed") only occurs here. Joshua 5:1b repeats verbatim both phrases from 2:11a.

loss of the land to Israel. Compared to Moses' twelve spies, what a different story this pair will tell Joshua if they can only get back to him safely!

To conclude her explanation, Rahab returns to Yahweh, the cause of the current disarray in Canaan. She affirms that "the LORD your God is God in heaven above and on the earth below" (v. 11b).[51] The phraseology is plainly deuteronomistic, occurring elsewhere only on the lips of Moses and Solomon (Deut. 4:39; 1 Kings 8:23).[52] Not bad theological company for a Canaanite prostitute!

But a careful appreciation of her words sifts out what they say and what they do not say. The reference to "heaven . . . and . . . earth" forms a merismus affirming God's sovereign power and right to exercise it throughout the whole universe. Clearly, Rahab pays the God of Israel high honor as a powerful deity everywhere—by implication, a deity worthy of her recognition, obedient response, and perhaps even worship. By honoring Yahweh's victories at the Red Sea and over Sihon and Og (v. 10), she tacitly affirms the superiority of his power at least to that of some of the gods of Egypt and of the Amorites east of the Jordan. Further, the fear of Yahweh in Canaan implies an expectation that he may also prove superior to some of the gods of Canaan. But she stops short—just short, perhaps—of saying that Yahweh is the *sole* sovereign of the universe and the only God rightfully entitled to worship.[53]

The limits of her statement become even clearer when she refers to Yahweh as "your [the spies'] God." Yahweh is not yet her God; she has not yet made him her most important, much less her only, God as an Israelite would. The Canaanites worshiped a pantheon of gods headed by the parental pair, El and his consort Athirat. They presided over Baal (the storm god), Yam (the sea), and Mot (the underworld) in the council of gods.[54] In my view, Rahab may simply have added Israel's God to that pantheon, albeit with exalted rank. The most important point is that her words signal the crossing of one significant line. She has sided with Israel against the king of Jericho at the risk of her life and with Yahweh against the gods of Canaan. She also seems to concede the superiority of Yahweh's power over theirs.

---

51. In the ancient world, religion was the choice of the tribe or clan rather the individual. Thus, here Rahab speaks on behalf of her entire family—and anyone else in Jericho who may have joined them in making an accommodation with Israel.

52. For the phrase "heavens above and earth below" cf. Ex. 20:4 and Deut. 5:8.

53. Her statement refers to "God" rather than, say, "the only God" or "God alone" (cf. Deut. 6:13; Ps. 86:10). In my view, if read carefully, the theological affirmations of Nebuchadnezzar similarly seem to stop short of recognizing Yahweh's exclusive sovereignty (Dan. 4:2–3, 34–37).

54. Cf. conveniently, J. Day, "Canaan, Religion of," *ABD*, 1:831–32. For more on Canaanites gods, see the Bridging Contexts section in Josh. 24.

In short, Rahab's words mark a step in the direction of a more complete, if not exclusive, commitment to Yahweh and toward the other missing pieces in her statement—the renunciation of all other gods and the use of idols. They mark a step of faith based on what she knows about Yahweh and Israel, not the mere acceptance of biblical ideas about them. Thus, it seems unwise to portray her as theologically an Israelite—at least, not yet—but she seems on the way there.[55] Further, her words imply support of Yahweh's right to cede Israel the land and subtly promote her worthiness to remain alive in the land.[56]

At least she falls among a distinguished line of foreigners who acknowledge Yahweh's power and sovereignty: the seer Balaam (Num. 22–24), the Moabitess Ruth (1:16–17), the Syrian general Naaman (2 Kings 5), King Nebuchadnezzar of Babylon (Dan. 4), and King Darius of Persia (Ezra 6; Dan. 6).[57] They symbolize a prominent Old Testament theme, the worship of Yahweh by other nations.[58] Canonically, that theme reaches its consummation with the eschatological gathering of "saints from every tribe and language and people and nation" (Rev. 5:9; cf. 14:6). At the same time, her affirmations may betray a subtle literary irony: It is a Canaanite, not an Israelite, who first introduces Yahweh into the narrative. On this occasion, *she* may be the one with the highest regard for Yahweh's power as divine warrior. She implies that Yahweh will deliver the spies from their current difficulty—and through *her*, of all things. Certainly, when the story began, no reader expected anything like that![59]

Now Rahab makes the request for which her statement paves the way (vv. 12–13).[60] She asks them to swear an oath in the name of Yahweh, the God whose greatness she has just affirmed. The oath obligates Israel

---

55. Cf. Spina, *The Faith of the Outsider*, 61 ("the narration seems clearly and boldly to present her as a confessing Israelite"). In his view, Rahab's confession arguably ranks as the best one in the book of Joshua, surpassing anything spoken by Joshua himself.

56. On the latter, cf. Assis, "The Choice to Serve God," 87–88; and Nelson (*Joshua*, 50), who also argues that her statement (vv. 9–11) and the subsequent survival in Israel of Rahab's family (6:25) support Israel's claim to the land. In my view, her words—certainly remarkable—stop short of being a full confession of faith in Israel's God; against Howard, *Joshua*, 103–4.

57. Nelson, *Joshua*, 50. The Contemporary Significance section below discusses several of these examples in more depth.

58. E.g., 1 Kings 8:41–43; Ps. 22:27–28; 86:9; 102:15; Isa. 2:3//Mic. 4:2; Jer. 3:17; Amos 9:12; Zeph. 2:11; Zech. 2:11; 8:22–23; 14:16; Mal. 1:11, 14.

59. Cf. Bird, "The Harlot as Heroine," 131; Sherwood ("A Leader's Misleading," 54, 55), who notes that Rahab is responsible for all occurrences of the name Yahweh in ch. 2.

60. Syntactically, "Now then" (*weʿattah*) signals the logical outcome from what precedes (e.g., "Given these facts, now swear ..."); cf. WO §39.3.4f; Isa. 5:3, 5; Ruth 3:11–12.

to spare the lives of her whole family when they take Jericho (v. 13).[61] Elsewhere, people inferior in power seek to offset their vulnerability by asking a superior power to swear an oath to accept certain obligations (see Gen. 21:23; 1 Sam. 24:21). By conceding that Yahweh has handed the land to Israel (v. 9), Rahab concedes her powerlessness to Israel. By getting the oath, however, she hopes to overcome it in order to survive.

Moreover, notice the nature of the agreement in play here. Israel is not offering the Canaanite Rahab a covenant and thereby violating its obligation to impose *ḥerem*. Rather, it is Rahab who affirms the sovereignty of Yahweh and accepts his purposes—a basic confession of her faith—and who, on that basis, asks Israel (and, implicitly, Yahweh) to promise to spare her life.[62] But why should the spies bother? Her persuasive leverage is her kindness (*ḥesed*) in protecting them (v. 12; cf. vv. 4–5). Her kindness in sparing their lives obligates them to reciprocate with equivalent kindness, the sparing of her and her family's lives.[63]

This request, of course, puts the reader (and perhaps the spies) in an awkward bind. Granted, Rahab's high respect for Yahweh and the risking of her life are worth something. By usual standards, some sort of reciprocation is in order. But do they justify waiving the demands of the *ḥerem* mandate in her case (Deut. 20:16–18)? Nevertheless, the spies readily grant her request (v. 14). If Sherwood is right, their decision implies that Yahweh as divine warrior will deliver "not just the spies through Rahab, but also Rahab herself."[64]

But the reader still wonders whether, trapped in Jericho and surviving at Rahab's mercy, the spies have simply taken the easy way out. Their initial, unconditional "Our lives for your lives!" (v. 14) betrays awareness of their precarious predicament. On the surface, their decision seems to violate Moses' prohibition against making covenants with any people in Canaan (Deut. 7:1–5). If so, it marks their fateful choice "as one of the most radical

---

61. The use of two parallel, synonymous statements ("cause to live" and "save from death") make this plea for survival all the more emphatic. The phrase "all who belong to them" would include servants and possibly domestic animals.

62. Sherwood, "A Leader's Misleading," 54, n.46. I depart from Sherwood in reading Rahab's request as a request for a covenant.

63. For the formula "to do kindness to," see Judg. 8:35; Ruth 1:8; 1 Sam. 15:6; 2 Sam. 2:6; 3:8; 10:2; 1 Chron. 19:2; 2 Chron. 24:22. According to Nelson (*Joshua*, 50), her kindness here derives specifically from the assumed host-guest relationship, but I trace it to her intervention with the king (vv. 4–5). On the subject of *ḥesed*, see K. Sakenfeld, *The Meaning of Ḥesed in the Hebrew Bible* (Missoula, MT: Scholars Press, 1978), esp. 64–70.

64. Sherwood, "A Leader's Misleading," 55–56.

features of the story."[65] But while accepting a simple swap of "lives," the spies also make it conditional on Rahab's silence about the agreement. Only then will they keep their oath once they return to claim the land that Yahweh has given them (v. 14b).

Apparently, Rahab accepted that proviso, for immediately we learn that she lowers the pair by a rope dropped from her window (v. 15). To explain this, the author reveals something surprising: Rahab's house, the place where she lives, is in the city wall and has an outside window.[66] "In part of the city wall" literally reads "in the wall (*qir*) of the wall (*ḥomah*)," a problematic phrase that requires brief discussion. Some scholars suggest that it designates the city's casemate wall, a type of fortification consisting of two parallel walls with intervening cross-walls.[67] Filled with rubble, its series of compartments gave the city a defensive perimeter able to blunt invaders' battering rams. But left empty, they served as storage rooms or residences (as possibly with Rahab).

Archaeological evidence, however, shows that casemates come into use later, in Iron Age Israel (tenth cent. B.C.), so it is unlikely that Rahab lives in one of that type. By contrast, Late Bronze Age (LBA) cities in the Levant basically neglected the fortification systems inherited from earlier generations. Most were small in size (on average, one to nine acres)—more "hamlets" or "towns" than "cities."[68] Basically, they consisted of residences encircled by "a belt of houses with no city wall at all" other than the contiguous walls of the homes.[69] Thus, what "in part of the city wall" means is uncertain.

That she "let … down" the spies by rope through a window implies a location above ground level "in" (or possibly "atop") a wall of some sort and a window facing outside the city. Joshua 6 also says that the city's "wall" (sing.) collapsed (vv. 5, 20), yet Israelite troops were able to fetch Rahab and her family from her house, the latter apparently still intact (v. 22). Some LBA cities do reutilize older fortifications, and perhaps one such wall somehow

---

65. Spina, *The Faith of the Outsider*, 57.

66. Interestingly, LXX lacks both the rope (v. 15a) and the explanation concerning the house's location (v. 15b). Since haplography seems an unlikely explanation here, both are probably additions in MT to clarify details implicit in the narrative.

67. Boling, *Joshua*, 148, 213 (an excellent drawing of Jericho's excavated walls); cf. Nelson, *Joshua*, 39. Woudstra (*Joshua*, 74) compares Rahab's house to houses built on dikes in the Netherlands.

68. R. Gonen, "Urban Canaan in the Late Bronze Period," *BASOR* 253 (1984): 61–73.

69. Jericho itself shows this same unwalled design. Interestingly, during the LBA both the average population of these unwalled towns and their total number declined sharply; cf. Z. Herzog, "Cities in the Levant," *ABD*, 1:1036–37 (quote 1036); Gonen, "Urban Canaan," 63–69; but cf. Hess, *Joshua*, 87, n.2.

protected Jericho and accommodated Rahab's house.[70] For the moment, as Howard remarks, "the exact nature of Rahab's house is unclear."[71]

Some readers may suddenly wonder, however, when the two young spies first learned of this window escape route. If earlier, then they made their agreement with Rahab with full knowledge. If only now, then they immediately know that their harlot host has cunningly played them for suckers—and rued their foolish naiveté. In any case, though the men are no longer trapped in Jericho, Rahab still has charge of them. To avoid meeting the pursuit team, she instructs them to go west into the hills (the latter word is emphatic) and hide there three days. By then their pursuers would have returned to Jericho—empty-handed, of course!—leaving the Israelites a safe route home (v. 16).

Given the dicey circumstances, however, the reader finds it odd, if not amusing, that Rahab and the spies still continue to talk within earshot of Jericho with the city already on alert. The NIV pluperfect ("she had said") avoids the oddity, making vv. 16–21 a flashback, but the Hebrew syntax seems to portray them as following v. 15 sequentially.[72] There is no indication of a prior conversation or that they have all whispered to maintain secrecy. So their conversation must either presume safety—i.e., an isolated location along the wall, city guards occupied elsewhere, a safe distance from the pursuers, etc.—or intend to inject a little humor into the story.[73]

Whatever the case, once free of Rahab's trap (but not of Jericho's listening ears?), the young spies regain the initiative and prolong the conversation rather than silently vanish into the hills (vv. 17–20). At first glance, their opening line seems to undo the deal just made ("This oath ... is not binding") because it was done under duress ("you made us swear"). Indeed, the same phrase forms an inclusio around vv. 17–20, a clue as to why the spies risk discovery to do further business. They attach two new stipulations to the oath they have just taken for it to be valid (vv. 18–19).[74]

---

70. Were the wall with her house somewhat detached from the city itself, her window would not compromise the city's defensive posture against would-be invaders.

71. Howard, *Joshua*, 113. For other escapes through windows, see 1 Sam. 19:12; Acts 9:25. In addition, Nelson (*Joshua*, 51) regards conversations involving women in windows or on walls as possibly "another stereotypical narrative situation"; cf. 2 Sam. 20:16–21; 2 Kings 9:30–31.

72. Attempts to identify this as another example of "dischronologized narrative" strike me as a form of special pleading; against Howard, *Joshua*, 114, 115; Hess, *Joshua*, 93.

73. For alternative explanations, see Howard, *Joshua*, 114.

74. Previously, the only condition was that Rahab keep their business a secret (v. 14). Syntactically, *binneh* (v. 18a) introduces the condition (NIV "unless"; NRSV, Vulgate "if") for vv. 18b–19; cf. WO §40.2.1d.

Certainly, the wording betrays their preoccupation with avoiding bloodguilt later on.[75]

First, Rahab must display "this scarlet cord" (lit. "this cord of scarlet thread") in the window through which they have just escaped (v. 18). The context does not clarify whether the crimson cord is the one that just lowered them or one that the spies hand her (i.e., "*this* cord"). The latter seems unlikely (would the spies have it with them?), but a crimson cord also sounds a little luxurious for a normal means of escape.[76] That the Hebrew words for "rope" (*ḥebel*, v. 15) and "cord" (*tiqwah*, v. 18) differ may also suggest two different objects. Some scholars speculate that the red cord already hung out her window to identify Jericho's "red rope district."[77] But evidence for such a practice is lacking and may not quite fit if the proposal concerning her house offered above holds. Whatever the case, since the wall probably has other houses, the attacking Israelites will need something readily visible to find hers. Without it they might let the wrong family live and wrongly kill Rahab's.

Second, Rahab must assemble her family in her house when Israel conquers Jericho (v. 18b). To give their demand legal weight, the spies invoke two legal terms, the so-called "bloodguilt formula" ("blood on [his/our] head"; cf. 2 Sam. 2:16; 1 Kings 2:32, 33, 37; Ezek. 18:13; 33:4) and the word "innocent" (*naqi*) common in legal declarations (cf. Gen. 44:10; Ex. 21:28; 2 Sam. 3:28).[78] Relatives found outside the house will bear the bloodguilt for their own death, the spies' bloodguilt for any who die in her house (v. 19). Each pays the penalty (or enjoys the innocence) for disobeying (or obeying) the terms agreed upon.

Finally, the spies reiterate that if Rahab reveals their business, the spies will be free of the oath that Rahab got them to swear (v. 20; cf. v. 17). Perhaps not wanting to prolong the chancy conversation further, Rahab accepts the new conditions and sends them on their way (v. 21a). In tying the crimson cord in the window (v. 21b), she fulfills the first of the spies' two stipulations. She is half-ready for Israel's siege of Jericho. Indeed, here

---

75. Cf. Sherwood, "A Leader's Misleading," 56–57 ("not a renegotiation but a 'cover-our-backside' clause").

76. E.g., Spina, *The Faith of the Outsider*, 62–63 ("Rahab's business calling card"). Nelson (*Joshua*, 51) speculates that the cord may be a humorous touch (e.g., a "very feminine and sexy" thread).

77. So Bird, "The Harlot as Heroine," 130, n.34; cf. Nelson, *Joshua*, 51–52. For a discussion of the scarlet cord as typology, see Woudstra, *Joshua*, 75, and Howard, *Joshua*, 115–17. The latter associates the cord with the crimson cord tied on one of Tamar's newborns (Gen. 38:28, 30) and the blood on the doorposts at Passover (Ex. 12).

78. Cf. K. Koch, "Der Spruch 'Sein Blut bleibe auf seinem Haupt' und die israelitische Auffassung vom vergossenen Blut," *VT* 12 (1962): 396–416.

the word "cord" (*tiqwah*) may play on the same-sounding word "hope" (*tiqwah*), as if—besides guiding Israel to her house—the dangling rope symbolizes Rahab's expectant hope of survival.[79]

The Spies Debrief Joshua (2:22–24)

HAVING PAUSED FOR A long conversation, the story now hurries to its conclusion. While Rahab obeys the two spies, the two spies obey her. They hide in the hills for three days, watching for the return of the search party (v. 22a). Meanwhile, east of the Jordan, Israel spends the same period preparing to enter that very land (1:11; cf. 3:2). As expected, the search party's thorough search of the road finds (Heb. *maṣaʾ*) nothing and they reenter Jericho empty-handed (v. 22b). Their escape route now free of scrutiny, the two fugitives descend the eastern slope, cross the Jordan, and reach Joshua (v. 23a).

Rather than replay everything, the narrator simply reports that the spies tell Joshua "everything that had happened to [*maṣaʾ*, lit. "find"] them" (v. 23b). By punning on the root *maṣaʾ*, the storyteller hints at an important irony—that while their pursuers failed to "find" them, incredible events did indeed "find [i.e., happen to] them."[80] But the reader is left to wonder about Joshua's reaction either to their perilous modus operandi or to the oath they had sworn. Does he applaud them for pluck or reprimand them for bungling? How does he assess their dealings with the cunning Rahab? How does he view the oath by which the two soldiers, invoking Yahweh's name, have obligated Israel to spare Canaanites in violation of Yahweh's orders? Does he read their story as a replay of Israel's sorry, unfaithful past or as evidence of divine providence at work?[81]

Instead, to conclude the story, the author has the spies basically borrow two of Rahab's lines (v. 24). Emphatically ("surely") they affirm their faith that Yahweh has given Israel the whole land (cf. v. 9a). They revel in their discovery that all its inhabitants "are melting in fear" because of Israel (cf. v. 9b). This positive report sharply contrasts that of Moses' infamous

---

79. Nelson, *Joshua*, 52; Sherwood, "A Leader's Misleading," 57.

80. Nelson, *Joshua*, 52. Their discoveries confirm God's assurance of victory (ch. 1) and may, thereby, imply the narrator's criticism of Joshua for initiating the spy mission rather than invading Canaan immediately; cf. Sherwood, "A Leader's Misleading," 57–58.

81. Note, of course, that the spies' agreement with Rahab may not have actually "violated" any prior command and put Israel at risk. If the main concern of *ḥerem* is to wipe out Canaanites in order to stave off syncretism in Israel, then sparing Rahab poses no threat since she shows an interest in Yahweh, allegiance to Israel, and a willingness to join them. Also, the agreement does not compromise the prohibition against taking plunder since Rahab and her family would likely bring their goods with them rather than leave them in their homes.

twelve spies (Num. 13), much to the relief of readers who fear a sad reprise of that disaster. Israel now has the inside information that the troubled king of Jericho tried to deny them. It is as if the fall of Jericho's wall of secrecy anticipates the later fall of her physical walls.[82]

Certainly, such powerful intelligence will boost spirits in the Israelite camp and build momentum for the coming invasion.[83] Enemy fear of Yahweh and Israel runs as a thematic thread through the book (see 5:1; 6:1; 9:1–3; 10:1–2; 11:1–5). But for Israel the essential thing is confidence in Yahweh, the divine warrior. That Israel embraces the reality of his awesome power from the words of a Canaanite prostitute, Rahab, adds one last irony to the story. Through her, Israel learns that a terrified Jericho predestines Israel for inevitable victory. Through her, Yahweh brings good out of Joshua's perhaps less than sterling debut as commander-in-chief. Soon, the book will take great pains to trace Joshua's long career of exemplary leadership. Here, Yahweh deserves praise: He providentially delivers the imperiled spies from death and also graciously spares Rahab and her family. He is indeed positioning Israel to conquer the land—finally!

RAHAB IS TRULY ONE of the Bible's more fascinating characters—but an ambiguous one as well. Her profession does not commend her to most readers, nor does her lying under pressure.[84] And what is her relationship to Israel? Is she truly a friend, or merely an opportunist who schemes successfully to save her own skin? Her confession seems to stop short of full conversion (e.g., "Yahweh is my God"), and though her descendants continued to live in Israel for centuries (Josh. 6:25), the Old Testament says nothing more about her.[85] Some readers may even wonder whether the spies biblically erred in sparing her life.

Rhetorical strategy. But the most important question is this one: What do her character and confession contribute to the rhetorical strategy of

---

82. Nelson, *Joshua*, 52.

83. The dream that Gideon would secretly hear in the Midianite camp decades later will have that effect (Judg. 7:13–15; see below). Whether the Rahab episode implies the existence of other secret allies and Canaanite sympathizers is possible but speculative; cf. Hess, *Joshua*, 96.

84. Concerning Rahab's deceit, cf. B. Barnes, "Was Rahab's Lie a Sin?" *RTR* 54 (1995): 1–9. Barnes concludes (8–9) that since the king of Jericho aims to murder the spies, Rahab has the right, if not the obligation, to deceive him; hence, her lie is no sin.

85. Readers should not confuse her with Rahab the mythical sea monster (Job 9:23; 26:12; Ps. 87:4; 89:10; Isa. 30:7; 51:9), whose name has a different middle letter (*he* [ה] instead of *beth* [ב]) in Hebrew.

the book of Joshua? Obviously, the Rahab episode anticipates the events in chapter 6 concerning the fall of Jericho. Her agreement with the spies leaves the reader eager to see whether it holds—and whether her picture of Jericho's vulnerability proves true. Further, her confession demonstrates that God is at work to give Israel the Promised Land. Her reassuring words buoy Israel's confidence as they prepare to leave the safety of Transjordan, head toward their first target (Jericho), and launch the invasion of Canaan. It also leads the reader to expect a series of victories (chs. 6–11) and, more importantly, the actual allocation of lands among the Israelites in the end (chs. 13–21).

At the same time, the optimism of Rahab's confession cleverly pulls a set-up on the reader. It creates positive expectations that clash with the unexpected surprises to come—the shocking defeat at Ai, the execution of Achan (ch. 7), the clever Gibeonite initiative (ch. 9), and the altar controversy (ch. 22). Literarily, these reversals of expectation force the reader to engage the important questions that those surprises present.

Moreover, Rahab the character for the first time sounds the important theme of Israel's relationship with the Canaanites given the *ḥerem* mandate. As the book's main Canaanite character, she foreshadows the later treaty with the book's other prominent non-Israelites, the Gibeonites, and later references to conflicts between Canaanites and Israelite tribes (e.g., 15:63; 16:10). Also, her acceptance into Israel subtly anticipates the author's later theological explanation for why Yahweh's imposition of *ḥerem* in Canaan became inevitable (11:19–20). She wins that acceptance because she responds to what she knows about Yahweh and Israel by surrendering herself. Her choice serves sharply to contrast the response of the kings of the land, who have similar knowledge yet refuse to submit. The reader understands that they suffer appropriate punishment (*ḥerem*) for not responding in a similar manner to what they, too, undoubtedly know.

A final, related theme concerns another surprising reversal, the contrasting fates of Rahab and Achan (ch. 7). The reader expects Rahab the Canaanite to die, but she escapes *ḥerem* by identifying with Yahweh and Israel. The reader expects Achan, an Israelite from the prominent tribe of Judah, to live, but he dies as *ḥerem* because he stole *ḥerem* that belonged to Yahweh. Thus, early in the book (chs. 2, 6–7) the juxtaposition of Rahab with Achan underscores that what truly counts with God is submission to his will, not ethnic identity. A trusting Canaanite may join Israel, but a rebellious native son must be excluded. The juxtaposition of the two memorable characters, therefore, sheds further light on the thorny question of genocide against the Canaanites. It underscores that the underlying issue concerns submission to or rebellion against Yahweh.

The issue of unswerving obedience later echoes in the covenant ceremony on Mount Ebal (8:30–35) and in Joshua 22–24. The latter three chapters treat the early post-settlement period and anticipate the following era of the judges. The altar controversy (ch. 22), Joshua's farewell speech (ch. 23), and the concluding covenant ceremony (24:1–28) all feature the theme of obedience to Yahweh. The imminence of Joshua's death makes it critical that Israel embrace that truth, for only complete loyalty to Yahweh will enable Israel successfully to navigate their long future in the land. In short, though an intriguing, complex character, the Canaanite Rahab casts a long, narrative shadow over the rhetorical shape of the entire book of Joshua.

Yahweh war. To understand the book of Joshua as a whole also requires readers to understand the background of a specific theme that Rahab sounds—Israel's practice of Yahweh's war.[86] From early days, Israel knew Yahweh to be the divine warrior who routed his (and Israel's) enemies (Ex. 17:16; Deut. 4:34; Ps. 24:8; Isa. 42:13).[87] Numbers 21:14 briefly quotes the "Book of the Wars of the LORD," apparently a volume recounting divine battles and victories. The historically early Song of the Sea (Ex. 15) celebrates the decisive victory over Pharaoh at the Red Sea that freed enslaved Israel. It particularly revels in the awesome power, especially mastery of wind and sea, that Yahweh's wonders displayed (vv. 6–10, 19; cf. 2 Sam. 22:15//Ps. 18:14). It also highlights one stunning result of Yahweh's victory, the terror and panic that paralyzes the surrounding nations. News of the victory signals that they may be next-in-line for his wrath (vv. 13–16).

Later Yahweh promised to send that same terrible, confusing dread ahead of Israel's army whenever it went to war (Ex. 23:27), a debilitating phenomenon to which Rahab herself testifies (Josh. 2:9, 11; cf. Ex. 14:24; Josh. 10:10; Judg. 4:14; 1 Sam. 7:10). For their part, Israel goes to battle without fear because of God's presence with the army (Deut. 20:1). Even when biblical narratives feature human combat without direct divine action, they affirm that such combat actually fights the Lord's battles (1 Sam. 18:17; 25:28).

Biblical battle reports show that Yahweh's war wields a variety of elements rather than follows a rigid schema. I will limit myself to those parallel to Joshua 2, deferring until later treatment of elements particularly relevant

---

86. I prefer this term to the more common but too modern and misleading "Holy War." The latter denotes war waged by humans for religious reasons, while in the Old Testament religious wars are always waged by Yahweh, the divine warrior, albeit occasionally through human means (hence, "Yahweh's war"); cf. R. Smend, *Yahweh War and Tribal Confederation* (Nashville: Abingdon, 1970).

87. For a convenient overview, see T. Longman III, "Divine Warrior," *NIDOTTE*, 4:545–49; Longman and Reid, *God Is a Warrior*, 31–47.

to later chapters of Joshua. In some reports Israel seeks and receives Yahweh's instructions concerning when and how to fight.[88] In such instructions Yahweh commonly invokes the formula of reassurance, "I have given X [an enemy] into Y's [Israel or an Israelite leader's] hands" (Josh. 2:9, 24).[89] Occasionally, the formula supports the command "do not fear" (Num. 21:34; Deut. 3:2; Josh. 8:1; 10:8).

Two narratives parallel Joshua 2 in offering Israel the assurance of victory from the mouths of the enemy itself. Creeping through the Midianite camp at night, Gideon just "happens" to overhear an enemy soldier's dream predicting Israel's defeat of Midian (Judg. 7). The dream reassures Gideon of Yahweh's victory (v. 15) and signals him to launch the attack. On a later occasion, the words of Philistine sentries similarly give Jonathan and his armor bearer the "go-ahead" and offer divine reassurance (1 Sam. 14:6–12, 23; cf. 2 Chron. 20:15).

Theologically, holy war musters a mysterious synergy of divine and human actions. Parallel lines from another early Israelite poem, the Song of Deborah (Judg. 5), voice this assumption:

> . . . consider the voice of the singers at the watering places.
>> They recite the righteous acts of the LORD,
>> the righteous acts of his warriors in Israel. (Judg. 5:10b–11)

According to Israel's singers, "the righteous acts" both of Yahweh and of "his warriors in Israel" won the victory over the Canaanite Sisera. To the combined effort, Yahweh contributes the awesome forces of his creation—deep sea waters, wind, river torrents, and the opened-mouth earth (Ex. 14:21; 15:5, 10, 12; Judg. 5:21). He also dispatches his heavenly army (the "hosts of heaven"), including "the angel of the LORD" (Ex. 14:19; cf. Josh. 5:13–15; 2 Kings 6:18) and even the stars of heaven (Judg. 15:20). Given Yahweh's spectacular firepower, one might assume Israel's role to be a passive one—to mop up on the ground when the fireworks end. But Israel's army marches into battle just like any other army (Judg. 5:11, 13–15), and tribes who fail to participate earn severe censure (vv. 16–18, 23). Indeed, Judges 5 highlights the irony that Sisera finally fell, not to the might of Yahweh or Israel's army, but to the simple hammer of a cunning woman named Jael (Judg. 5:26–27).[90]

---

88. E.g., Judg. 1:2; 20:18, 21, 28; 1 Sam. 23:4; 2 Sam. 5:19; 1 Kings 20:13–14, 28; 22:15.

89. Num. 21:34; Deut. 3:2; Josh. 6:2; 8:1, 18; 10:8; Judg. 1:2; 7:9, 15; et al.; cf. Judg. 4:14.

90. For a comparison of Rahab and Jael, see E. Assis, "The Choice to Serve God," 82–90.

This brings us back to the clever Rahab, whom Bird rightly describes as "both savior and oracle."[91] She is "savior" in that she protects the two hunted spies and facilitates their safe return home. More importantly, in Yahweh's war a priest or prophet customarily gives Israel the assurance of victory before the battle may commence. In this case, Rahab, the worldly wise prostitute, is the "oracle" who plays the role of priest or prophet (Josh. 2:9 – 11). By virtually quoting her (v. 24), the spies accept her words to be as true as any oracle, and her reassurance paves the way for Israel's movement the next morning toward the Jordan (3:1). Her words — and the high view of God that underpins them theologically — encourage Israel that Yahweh is, indeed, on their side and that victory is certain.

Subsequent history. But, what happened to Rahab after Jericho fell and Joshua honored the spies' oath (see Josh. 6:23, 25)? Despite her important role in Joshua, the Old Testament never mentions her again. Beyond the general report that "she lives among the Israelites to this day" (6:25), readers learn nothing more about her until she reappears in the New Testament. The genealogy of Jesus informs us that she became the wife of the Judahite Salmon and the mother of Boaz (Matt. 1:5; cf. Ruth 4:21). That would make her the paternal mother-in-law of another remarkable foreigner, Ruth, whom Matthew also mentions (Matt. 1:5). It would also imply a remarkable reversal of fortune for her. The once crafty Canaanite prostitute condemned under *ḥerem* ends up a member of the prestigious royal line of David and an ancestress of the Messiah. The consummate outsider becomes the consummate insider in Israel.

She and Ruth, therefore, share company with two other notable women in the royal Davidic line — Tamar, wife of Judah (Matt. 1:3), and Bathsheba, wife of David (1:6 ["Uriah's wife"]). Even more remarkable, Hebrews 11 lists Rahab in its "Hall of Faith." The writer apparently takes his cue from Joshua 6:25, which explains that Joshua spared her life "because she hid the men Joshua had sent." Hebrews 11:31 interprets her welcome of the spies specifically as an act of faith on par with that of the other honorees in the "Hall." His comment that she escaped the fate of the "disobedient" also paints the welcome as an act of obedience, presumably to God's will.

Finally, James 2:25 goes even further. In the apostle's view, people commonly consider her "righteous" — in right standing with God — because she models James's ideal combination of faith and works (v. 26).[92] In short,

---

91. Bird, "The Harlot as Heroine," 127.
92. As "works" he cites her offer of hospitality ("she gave lodging to the spies") and her clever strategy ("[she] sent them off in a different direction").

Matthew 1 honors her genealogically (her rise to prominence in Israel), Hebrews 11 and James 2 theologically (an example of faith, obedience, good works, and righteousness). A condemned non-Israelite has become a card-carrying full Israelite.

The above New Testament writers all read Rahab from a specifically Jewish-Christian perspective as a type of the ideal, righteous Israelite. But, in my view, her transition from religious outsider to religious insider also marks her as a type of the believing Gentiles who flooded into the early church in great numbers. It is this outsider-insider motif that shapes the meaning of her story for today.

BOTH RAHAB AND THE two young spies understand that spying is a dangerous business. But Aldrich H. Ames also knew its potentially lucrative financial payoff. The movie *Traitor Within* chronicles his now-famous spying, treachery, and eventual discovery. Ames was a mid-level bureaucrat in the Central Intelligence Agency who yielded to temptation—the easy money of espionage. The Russian KGB paid him $2.5 million over nine years, and apparently no one at the CIA questioned how he could drive a Jaguar and own a half-million-dollar home on his $70,000 salary.

But for the KGB it was money well spent. A thirty-year CIA veteran, Ames gave them precious, highly sensitive American military secrets, especially about intelligence moles within the KGB's own ranks. Compromised by Ames' espionage, hundreds of such double-agents went to prison in Russia or were executed. On February 21, 1994, however, Ames' secret world collapsed when the FBI arrested him and his wife, and a federal court subsequently sent both to prison terms for spying. Today she has completed her prison time and resides in South America. Ames himself is serving a life sentence in the high-security federal prison at Allenwood, Pennsylvania.

Why does espionage pay so well? Because warring enemies crave inside information to gain strategic advantage over their foes. The more one knows about the enemy—his location, troop strength, supply lines, strategic philosophy, and current plans—the greater the chance of victory. By the same token, effective *dis*information (i.e., the dissemination of false data) is also money well spent. In junior high, I read a book called *The Man Who Never Was*.[93] It told how during World War II the British created a fictitious intelligence agent, including an actual cadaver strategically released

---

93. E. Montagu, *The Man Who Never Was* (Philadelphia: Lippincott, 1954).

into the Mediterranean from a submarine for the Germans to recover. A very detailed scheme of fake identity cards and prior fictitious secret communications convinced Berlin that the cadaver carried real Allied war plans.

That discovery actually led the Germans to redeploy troops from Sicily prior to the Allied invasion. In warfare, good inside information and good disinformation serve to win one side in a conflict the advantage. But espionage is not limited to warfare. Some modern corporations have paid industrial spies top dollar for the secrets of their competitors. In response, new companies specializing in the prevention of such thievery have recently done a brisk business with corporate clientele.[94]

Biblical Rahab also parlays her insider status in Jericho—and intimate knowledge of its workings—to preserve the life of her family. Some modern Bible readers may still suspect that she "gamed" two naïve Israelite GIs—that she is a Canaanite Aldrich Ames. But conniver though she be, she is probably best understood as a biblical character-type whom Frank Spina calls "the outsider." She may have wangled a deal for herself, but her meaning for today derives from that unique status.

Remarkably (and perhaps ironically), God used her, a woman slated for destruction under *ḥerem*, to encourage Israel that victory at Jericho was in the offing before they had even crossed the Jordan. Her description of terror in Canaan confirmed that God had kept his promise to do just that as part of Yahweh war. Her faith, however shallow and rudimentary, even won for her and her family survival and an entrée into the people of Israel. The shadow of divine providence that stalks her story seems to imply that God cares for her, a condemned outsider though she be. Rahab, thus, has much to teach us. Our own Jerichos (whether towns or churches) teem with such folk, and the God who apparently cared for Rahab cares about them, too. Indeed, she reminds us of an important truth that applies to everyone.

Who is the "outsider"? Biblically, an "outsider" is someone who stands outside Israel (in the Old Testament) or the kingdom of God (in the New). They do not belong to God's inner circle of special relationship—his chosen people—and hence are not party to what he is doing with the latter. Even worse, like Rahab they stand condemned—not under *ḥerem* for being Canaanite, of course, but under God's eternal judgment for their sin and rebellion. The distant relationship of outsiders to God and his people appears in Paul's comments about the former life of some early Christians. For example, he writes to the Ephesians:

---

94. C. Warren, "I Spy," *American Way* (November 15, 2007), 58–64.

Therefore, remember that formerly you who are Gentiles by birth and called "uncircumcised" by those who call themselves "the circumcision" (that done in the body by the hands of men)—remember that at that time you were separate from Christ, excluded from citizenship in Israel and foreigners to the covenants of the promise, without hope and without God in the world. But now in Christ Jesus you who once were far away have been brought near through the blood of Christ. (Eph. 2:11 – 13)

Formerly, these believers had many strikes against them. They were "Gentiles by birth"—they stood outside the in-group, God's elect people Israel. The pejorative label "the uncircumcision" further underscored their nonmembership in that covenant community: They lacked the physical sign of membership. Paul piles up terms to hammer home their distance from God: they were *"separate* from Christ, *excluded* from citizenship in Israel and *foreigners* to the covenants of the promise" (italics, mine). A frightening destiny awaited them, though they did not know it. They were "without hope and without God"—a recipe for misery and doom if there ever was one. The fact that the blood of Christ had to "bring [them] near" confirms just how far away they were! In short, insuperable barriers and huge distances barred their entry into the kingdom of God.

The day the spies entered her house, similar (if not worse!) big disqualifications separated Rahab from the kingdom. She was, of course, a native-born Canaanite—in Paul's terms, "a Gentile by birth" and "a foreigner to the covenant." Her ethnicity doomed her and her relatives to certain death under Israel's policy of *ḥerem.* Her religious background posed a grave threat to Israel's loyalty to Yahweh (see Josh. 23). That was why she and everyone like her had to be killed.

Rahab also had the social disadvantage in the ancient world of being a woman—and apparently unmarried and childless. Her description of her family ("father and mother, my brothers and sisters, and all who belong to them" [2:13]) mentions neither husband nor children of her own. She inhabited a world presided over by men—politically, the king of Jericho and, commercially, her male customers. Worse yet, she was a prostitute, and possibly even a madam running her own bordello. Her singleness, thus, may not be surprising. What self-respecting man would marry a prostitute or tolerate his wife practicing such a profession? Only a divine call to prophesy compelled Hosea to do so (Hos. 1:2 – 3).

In addition, her profession probably meant that she had few female friends, especially married ones. In short, it marked the third disqualifier—the third strike that declared her "out." Ancient society apparently accommodated her profession (see Gen. 38), but she still lived on its margins — literally. There is nothing more marginal in an ancient city than a house set in the city's outer wall!

But she is not alone in the Bible. The common impression is that Israel kept aloof from non-Israelites and excluded outsiders from God's people. Several outsiders figure prominently in Israel's history, however. Ruth, the central character in the biblical book that bears her name, is one of the best known.[95] She was a Moabitess who married into an Israelite family during their temporary stay in her country. Tragically, death claimed her husband, but rather than remain and remarry in Moab, she moved to Judah with her widowed mother-in-law, Naomi. There she experienced life as an outsider — a foreigner from one of Israel's competitor countries, a woman in a man's world, and a childless widow in a world of married couples with children.

The biblical author several times calls her "Ruth the Moabitess" (e.g., Ruth 1:22; 2:21), a subtle reminder that she is "not from around here." Her vulnerability as an outsider comes into sharp relief when Boaz, her family benefactor (and eventual husband), twice instructs his male workers not to mistreat her (2:15, 16).[96] But her loyalty to Naomi ushers in a remarkable reversal of fate. The childless, widowed foreigner becomes the wife of Boaz, a leading citizen of Bethlehem (4:9–12), and bears Obed, grandfather of the great King David. In short, through God's providence and her own stunning commitment (1:16–17), she moves from outside Judah to inside one of its prominent families. She becomes a full-fledged Israelite spiritually by her faith and sociologically by her marriage.

The Syrian general Naaman also transitions from Israelite outsider to insider (2 Kings 5).[97] But in one surprising way, his story departs significantly from Ruth's. As head of the Syrian army, royal confidant, and popular war hero, he was part of his country's upper crust. But a terrible skin disease plagues him. Providentially, a young Israelite woman captured during a raid works for his wife. She advises him to seek healing from Elisha the prophet in Israel. Initially, he angrily rejects the prophet's prescription — to immerse

---

95. For an excellent exposition of this book and its implications for women, see C. Custis James, *The Gospel of Ruth* (Grand Rapids: Zondervan, 2008). Cf. also Spina, *The Faith of the Outsider*, 117–36.

96. Naomi reflects a similar concern for her safety when she instructs Ruth to work beside Boaz's female workers, not his male ones, to avoid harm (Ruth 2:22).

97. Cf. the illuminating discussion in Spina, *The Faith of the Outsider*, 72–93. He notes how, like Achan, the sin of the insider, Gehazi (Elisha's servant), demotes him to the status of cursed insider (my term). This shows that ethnicity, geography, religious background, etc., are not the only determiners of membership in Israel.

himself seven times in the Jordan—as offensive. At his staff's urging, however, he obeys and pops up the seventh time healed. The experience proves to him that Yahweh is God, and he is converted (v. 15).

But now comes the surprise: Naaman the convert has to return to his life in Syria where he faces a more complex future as an Israelite than Ruth does in Bethlehem. In a poignant gesture, he requests a two-mule load of Israelite soil to build a dirt altar to Yahweh back home (v. 17). Further, his job requires him ceremonially to bow before the god, Rimmon, so he asks Elisha in advance for Yahweh's forgiveness for that apparent idolatry (v. 18). Amazingly, Elisha sends him home with a reassuring word—in essence, "Not to worry" (v. 19). The reassurance dispenses a startling moment of divine grace: Yahweh accommodates his demands for exclusive worship in light of Naaman's evident sincerity and unique circumstances. In theology and religious devotion, both Ruth and Naaman belong to Israel, but in national identity and geographical homeland Naaman remains a Syrian.[98] Naaman signals that one can be an Israelite insider in belief but an outsider in geography—in one sense, the beginning of the Israelite diaspora.[99]

Finally, King Nebuchadnezzar marks an outsider who, I would argue, comes close to the kingdom but does not quite acquire Israelite status. He personally recounts the astounding story of God's dealings with him in Daniel 4. He dreams of a gigantic, lusciously leafy fruit tree—a typical biblical symbol for a thriving kingdom (cf. Dan. 5:22 – 23; Ezek. 17:23; 31:6; Matt. 13:32). Alas, divine judgment dooms this tree to be cut down and stripped of its many branches and delicious fruit (Dan. 4:14). Daniel explains that the dream decrees the king's own fate—a double dose of humiliation. He is to lose not only his grip on royal power but also on reality itself; his mind is to become utterly deranged (vv. 25, 33). Driven from human society, the once mighty monarch will live for a long while among cattle, grazing on grass and drenched with dew.

But, the king reports, when he came to his senses—when he humbly bowed before the sovereignty of God and praised his greatness—God restored both his mind and his monarchy (vv. 34 – 36). His report ends where it began, with a personal testimony acknowledging the supremacy of God's kingdom over all human ones (v. 37; cf. vv. 1 – 3). But notice that Nebuchadnezzar simply refers to "God" but never invokes God's personal

---

98. Cf. Spina, *The Faith of the Outsider*, 88.

99. The "Israelite diaspora" designates the scattering of many Israelites from the Promised Land to permanent settlement in other nations. This phenomenon probably began with the falls of the Northern and Southern Kingdoms (722 and 587 B.C., respectively) and underlies the encounters of the apostles with Jews around the Mediterranean in the book of Acts.

name ("Yahweh"), unlike Ruth and Naaman. In modern terms, he sounds more like a deist—someone who accepts the existence and sovereign working of God in his or her life but who lacks an ongoing, personal relationship with God. His experience of humble submission is genuine and his affirmations about God's sovereignty are true. But, in my view, his relationship with God lacks the same closeness of true Israelites like the Moabite and the Syrian general. At least, not yet.

Lessons for insiders. The above outsiders represent an intriguing cross-section of personal traits. One is a prostitute, another a military hero of one of Israel's enemies, and the other an emperor with a huge ego who had also destroyed Jerusalem. From an insider's perspective, each is in some way problematic for a typical Israelite. Imagine, for example, the conversations that followed the news that the spies had promised a prostitute named Rahab that she and her family would live. Ridicule or praise might shadow the young GIs—ridicule for being snookered by the worldly wise Rahab, praise for cleverly escaping Jericho alive. Religious purists would scorn the spies' deal as a violation of God's plain mandate to kill every Canaanite. They would fret that Yahweh might punish the whole camp for what they regarded as the spies' foolish naiveté.

Others would simply wonder whether Rahab would remain in Israel or migrate to another country once Israel settled. She did not belong to any existing tribe, so where would she fit if she stayed? Would she be entitled to share in any tribal territory? Others would joke about what the notorious prostitute would do for a living in settled Israel! Parents might even agonize over what Rahab's presence might do to the morals of their sons—and wives, the morals of their husbands. A common thread links these thoughts: This woman is not like us!

This marks the first lesson for insiders: We must confess that outsiders are "not like us." They know little or nothing about life inside the average church. They do not speak "churchese" and are clueless as to the unique subculture that constitutes the average church. Do they understand why the first name of some churches is "First," "Bethany," "Calvary," "Immanuel," or "Ebenezer"? Where else would they encounter a "foyer," "narthex," "nave," or "fellowship hall"? Where else would they meet a "deaconess," "elder," "trustee," "liturgist," or "sexton"? Where else would they sit in pews surrounded by stained-glass windows and sing music led by an organ? (Most would probably experience organ music only at funerals). Where else would they drop money into plates or felt pouches passed down rows by nicely-dressed "ushers"? Where else would they be handed a "bulletin" or asked to fill out a "record of attendance"? Where else would they see someone receive "the right hand of fellowship" or witness an "invitation"?

How would they know what the "Dorcas Circle" and "Sunday School" are? How would they know which class to attend—the "Kingdom Builders," "Overcomers," or "Bereans"? Would they know the difference between "pneumatology" and "eschatology" or between an "invocation" and a "benediction"? If the pastor mentions the "Pauline epistles," would they wonder who "Pauline" was? The fact of the matter is that the larger culture is more "pagan" than "Christian." This means that the cultural distance between the average church and the folks next door is huge. They are "not like us" and we are "not like them." They enter our world as "outsiders"—the same status we enjoy in theirs.

This leads to the second lesson for insiders: We must confess our reluctance to welcome outsiders, especially those with problematic pasts or presents. Normally, we Christians settle into comfortably snug small groups of friends who are like us. Even if we avoid forming actual cliques, we tend to associate with people with whom we have a lot in common. This is "normal" behavior for most human beings.

Few of us have faced prostitutes or enemy military leaders on the church doorstep, but we usually can spot people with other kinds of baggage who show up. They may be people who live on the economic margins, often in low-paying jobs or bouncing around from job to job. They may be mentally ill or emotionally damaged—people very different from us (or so we think). They may be recovering alcoholics whose faces still bear the scars of their past defeats and current struggles. Their clothes, speech, personal habits, or story may give them away. Such people may be as foreign to most of us as Rahab was to the Israelites. Their differences unsettle us because our normal ways of relating to people do not quite work with them.

Another difficulty is that relationship with them requires more time than we are used to giving to relationships. Quite simply, such people are demanding of time and energy, and they rarely get better. Americans are "fix-it" kind of people—the world's best problem solvers—and that is one reason that we avoid these kinds of outsiders. Fix-it people find it difficult to hang in with less-than-fixable people.

But Joshua let Rahab live in Israel, and our Lord Jesus models a lifestyle of hanging in with people in trouble, people in need, people on the margins, people others avoid. We, his followers, can do no less. How can we do this? We need to overcome our natural skittishness about such people. As Rahab welcomed the Israelite spies, outsiders in her world, so we are to welcome outsiders into ours. Initially, Israel may not have been overjoyed to have Rahab and her family among them, and our challenge is a similar one. Prayerfully, we need to swallow our pride, set aside our preferences, and set out to cross the boundaries. We need to prepare ourselves to get our holy hands dirty to do the work of the kingdom. We need to remake our church life to make anyone who walks in off the street feel welcome.

We must remember as well that Jesus hung out with "tax collectors and sinners"—a motley crew if there ever was one. The crowd that surrounded Jesus included a Zealot (Simon, a man whose party espoused violence against Rome) and a tax collector (Matthew). Remember, further, that without embarrassment the Bible includes Rahab in the ancestry of Jesus himself. Kingdom work may require us to hang out with people whom fellow believers might deem "the wrong crowd." It may require us to include people usually unwelcome in our hallowed halls.

The third lesson for insiders is that God not only welcomes outsiders but also uses them to encourage his people. That is how powerful and caring God is! Through Rahab, Yahweh confirmed that victory at Jericho was certain because he had already sent panic among the Canaanites. Through her, he boosted the morale of his people in anticipation of the long conquest ahead, displaying that, prior to their arrival in Canaan, God had already paved the way for them. God's providential introduction of faithful Ruth into Judah from Moab reminded Israel of God's faithfulness to them. Her winsome life signaled that God was still at work in their midst, regardless of what chaos or change might swirl surround them.

Naaman's newfound faith likewise verified that Yahweh was, indeed, the only true God—the only one able to heal incurable diseases. Naaman's healing showed Israel just how much more powerful Yahweh is than other gods like Baal and, thus, how right it is to worship Yahweh alone. Similarly, Nebuchadnezzar's testimony of God's sovereign power would have encouraged God's people, at the time enduring a long, dispiriting exile.

In short, one lesson for insiders is that God is at work abroad in his world, not just within the Christian community, and that some of his activities benefit his people. This truth is both humbling and inspiring—humbling in reminding the church that it is not the only arena of God's dealings, and inspiring in reminding us just how very much God cares for his world. Further, this truth encourages us that whatever we may be doing to serve him, God may already be paving the way ahead of us to enhance the effectiveness of our efforts.

How do we respond to these lessons concerning outsiders? (1) We need to embrace and celebrate the idea that God is at work in all kinds of ways and with all kinds of people. To do so is simply to expand our mental horizons and to open our eyes to things he is doing that we might otherwise miss. God may, in fact, be preparing us to involve ourselves in one of those "missed" things. At least, seeing them confirms that God is in the neighborhood, so to speak—an important message for times when he seems very absent.

(2) We need to work hard at getting past first impressions. As with any human beings, behind the outward appearance—unkempt, smelly, offensive, demanding—is a person for whom Jesus died. Here are a few suggestions. Pray that God will help you get past the unpleasant sights, smells, and habits. Get to know the people on their terms, not yours. Find out what they like or dislike. Ask them to tell you their story, and listen to it without reacting. Ask them to share their dreams, if they have any. Above all, take them seriously. Treat them as a genuine human being, not as some category or type or project.

(3) See them as people whom God has on the way somewhere, not people who have reached their final destination in life. Pray for them as people in whom God's Spirit can miraculously cultivate more Christlikeness. Pursue the relationship expectantly. Expect to see signs in their attitudes and behavior that reveal Christ's love at work in them. Tell them how you see God at work in them. This is important because they may be too down on themselves to recognize the signs.

(4) Work with them to meet their practical needs. Rahab provided the spies protection, hospitality, and guidance. According to Hebrews 11:31, that was the way she showed her faith and confirmed her righteousness (cf. James 2:24—26). Similar practical deeds act out our own trust in God. They show tangibly that he truly has transformed us and confirm that our faith is the real deal. At the same time, do not hesitate to say "no" or to set boundaries whenever requests for help exceed your means or violate your sense of what is appropriate. The needs are always greater than the means available, so focus your attention on what you deem to be doable.

(5) The final lesson that Rahab teaches is that God continues to work to woo outsiders inside. In retrospect, a sense of hidden providence is subtly evident in the Rahab narrative. Looking back, the sparing of her life and her settlement in Israel seem to enjoy God's approval—in my view, a harbinger of all the Gentiles who would later join God's people.[100] They include us! Given the gentle wooing of the Holy Spirit and the persuasive power of the gospel, no one is doomed to be an outsider forever. Anyone willing to surrender to the wooing can become an insider free of charge.

In summary, an open door to the usually unwelcomed demonstrates that God cares for outsiders—that he is truly an inclusive God. This is the God visible in the book of Joshua—a God who uses a Canaanite prostitute and opens the door for her to become part of Israel. This God is also visible in the book of Jonah—a God who goes to great lengths to dispense

---

100. As we will see, the sparing of the Gibeonites marks a second such harbinger in the book of the Joshua (ch. 9).

mercy even to people like the hated Assyrians. Our open door to outsiders is nothing less than God's always-open door to them. Remember that the church is not an exclusive club of elites who preserve their own special status by keeping the Rahabs of this world out. Rather, over its doors hangs the welcoming words of Jesus, "Come to me, all you who are weary and burdened, and I will give you rest" (Matt. 11:28). Its doors are open to prostitutes, warmongers, egotists, broken hearts, failures, and the successful.

Rahab's reminder. Surprisingly, to look at Rahab is to look in a mirror at ourselves. In Paul's words, " ... that is what some of you were" (1 Cor. 6:11). Rahab the outsider reminds us of what we were all like once — "outsiders," pure and simple. To look at her is to glimpse ourselves as God saw us before we came to Christian faith. In fact, that glimpse confronts us with an uncomfortable truth: Our natural bent toward rebellion still occasionally drives us back across the line into our old outsiders' ways. It shreds all our claims to righteousness and purity; it shatters all our pretensions. Granted, most of us were not prostitutes before Christ, but in God's eyes we were just as awful in our own way.

This glance in the mirror called Rahab is important for two reasons. (1) The fresh confrontation with the ugliness of our sin (both then and now) leads us to appreciate all the more the work of God's grace in us. It gives us a fresh glimpse of how far we have come since we first believed the gospel. The then-and-now contrast highlights how profound and life-changing have been its effects. We were all once prisoners pardoned from death sentences. We owe our very lives to God, the pardon-giver (see John 3:18). As a result, we will sing "Amazing Grace" with deeper feelings of gratitude than ever before. In turn, those grateful feelings will find arms and legs to live out thankfulness in practical service for Christ.

(2) Some years ago, I read a humorous story that took place aboard an aircraft carrier at sea. The flight deck was a hubbub of activity, with pilots trying to qualify for carrier duty. Back aft, plane after plane landed fast, their tail hooks catching the cable across the runway to slow down to taxi speed. At the bow, the steam-driven catapult hurled plane after plane off the end of the ship fast enough so each could fly. Radio communications between pilots and the ship blared over speakers on deck. But unexpectedly, one launch did not go smoothly. In silent horror, the crew watched as the just-launched aircraft like a wounded bird valiantly struggled to stay in the air. Precious seconds passed as the plane's fate hung in the balance. The pilot radioed nothing during the battle to stay aloft. Finally, the plane leveled off and began to fly normally, much to the relief of everyone. (Occasionally, aircraft are lost on take-off). Finally, the pilot broke his silence: "OK, God, I'll take over from here."

This story illustrates the second reason for glancing in the mirror that is Rahab: She steers us clear of our bent toward self-righteousness. The pilot credits God's flying skills with sparing him a possibly fatal plunge into the sea. But, once rescued, he takes over from God, as if God were no longer needed. In my view, long-time Christians often experience a similar change in attitude. At first, they feel greatly thrilled and relieved to be "saved by grace"—like the pilot snatched from death at a critical moment. As time passes, however, an attitude of spiritual self-confidence creeps in, as if to say, "OK, God, I'll take over from here."

Worse, a subtle self-satisfaction also may come into play. I would put the unspoken assumption this way: "We were saved by grace, but in retrospect, God really did a smart thing to do so." From there a subtle, small step may follow from thinking our salvation was deserved to looking down self-righteous noses at others as if we were spiritually superior. The prophet Ezekiel faced a similar problem among the exiles to whom he ministered in Babylon. He addressed it in an allegorical story about the history of Jerusalem, the city whose imperiled fate so concerned his audience (Ezek. 16).

Jerusalem, he reminds them, was born a baby girl whose gender and mixed racial ancestry led her to be despised and abandoned rather than cleaned and cuddled (Ezek. 16:2–5). But Yahweh passed by and commanded the girl, "Live!" then raised her to become a strikingly beautiful young woman (vv. 6–7). When he passed by again, Ezekiel continues, Yahweh saw that she was old enough to marry, so he himself married her. A generous, loving husband, he showered her with all kinds of wonderful gifts and tasty delicacies (vv. 8–13). Under his tender care, she became a queen renowned worldwide for her stunning beauty (v. 14).

Alas, however, the queen trusted, not in her loving husband, but in his gifts—her beauty and her fame. She thought they were hers by right, so she abandoned her husband and became a prostitute (Ezek. 16:15). Here Ezekiel joins Hosea in portraying idolatry—the worship of gods other than Yahweh—as an unfaithful wife turned prostitute (vv. 16–34).[101] Twice Ezekiel voices Jerusalem's big mistake: "You did not remember the days of your youth" (vv. 22, 43). She had forgotten her own story, a story of rescue from certain death by the grace of a generous, loving, committed God. Similarly, Rahab reminds us of our story—that God saves by grace—to underscore that we still live by that same grace regardless of how long we

---

101. Ezekiel's allegory goes beyond Hosea, however, in also describing as prostitution Jerusalem's trust in international diplomacy for survival rather than in dependence on God (vv. 26–30).

have been Christians. As people ever sustained by grace, we have no reason whatsoever to don robes of self-righteousness. On the contrary, we were born sinners and we will die sinners—but sinners "being saved" by God's wonderful grace (cf. Eph. 2:8).

The fateful choice. Finally, Rahab marks an early example of a larger biblical theme, an individual who faces a radical choice for or against submission to God. As Stek notes, the agents of two conflicting kingdoms knocked on her door that fateful night—that of Yahweh (the Israelite spies), and that of Canaan's religio-political system (Jericho's king and his men). He writes: "This same radical choice faces everyone wherever, whenever, and however the kingdom of God comes knocking on the door."[102] Only those willing to risk their lives—to throw away their past lives, their selfish dreams, their previous identity—receive inclusion in God's people and enjoy the "rest" that comes with belonging to that kingdom.

I hasten to add that that is a choice Christians must make every day. Granted, at a certain moment we may have "decided to follow Jesus," as the song says. But in another sense, we face the same choice in small ways—every time we face a choice between doing what would please Jesus or what would please someone or something else. Outsiders came abruptly into Rahab's life and she chose to give them hospitality—protection, shelter, information, and good advice. We face a similar choice when outsiders intrude into our lives. Jesus clearly models the welcoming of outsiders, so the choice confronts us as to whether or not to follow his example or that of someone else.

Canadian singer Shania Twain captures the choice in her hit song, "Dance with the One That Brought You." The song tells the reflections of a young woman whose date has taken her to a dance but left her to watch while he dances with other women. Her natural instinct is to abandon him and find someone else. But, in the song's thematic refrain, the girl quotes the sage advice her mother gave her about loyalty and commitment: "Dance with the one that brought you, and you can't go wrong." That is good advice for Christians: Remember the gracious God who got us to where we are. He is, indeed, the one who "wants you" and "loves you" and "brought you." He is the one with whom "you can't go wrong." His is the grace that draws every Rahab from outside to inside; his is the grace that sustains us every step of the way. He is truly someone with whom to stick forever.

---

102. J. H. Stek, "Rahab of Canaan and Israel: The Meaning of Joshua 2," *CTJ* 37 (2002): 48.

Joshua 3:1–5:1

EARLY IN THE morning Joshua and all the Israelites set out from Shittim and went to the Jordan, where they camped before crossing over. ²After three days the officers went throughout the camp, ³giving orders to the people: "When you see the ark of the covenant of the LORD your God, and the priests, who are Levites, carrying it, you are to move out from your positions and follow it. ⁴Then you will know which way to go, since you have never been this way before. But keep a distance of about a thousand yards between you and the ark; do not go near it."

⁵Joshua told the people, "Consecrate yourselves, for tomorrow the LORD will do amazing things among you."

⁶Joshua said to the priests, "Take up the ark of the covenant and pass on ahead of the people." So they took it up and went ahead of them.

⁷And the LORD said to Joshua, "Today I will begin to exalt you in the eyes of all Israel, so they may know that I am with you as I was with Moses. ⁸Tell the priests who carry the ark of the covenant: 'When you reach the edge of the Jordan's waters, go and stand in the river.'"

⁹Joshua said to the Israelites, "Come here and listen to the words of the LORD your God. ¹⁰This is how you will know that the living God is among you and that he will certainly drive out before you the Canaanites, Hittites, Hivites, Perizzites, Girgashites, Amorites and Jebusites. ¹¹See, the ark of the covenant of the Lord of all the earth will go into the Jordan ahead of you. ¹²Now then, choose twelve men from the tribes of Israel, one from each tribe. ¹³And as soon as the priests who carry the ark of the LORD—the Lord of all the earth—set foot in the Jordan, its waters flowing downstream will be cut off and stand up in a heap."

¹⁴So when the people broke camp to cross the Jordan, the priests carrying the ark of the covenant went ahead of them. ¹⁵Now the Jordan is at flood stage all during harvest. Yet as soon as the priests who carried the ark reached the Jordan and their feet touched the water's edge, ¹⁶the water from upstream stopped flowing. It piled up in a heap a

great distance away, at a town called Adam in the vicinity of Zarethan, while the water flowing down to the Sea of the Arabah (the Salt Sea) was completely cut off. So the people crossed over opposite Jericho. [17]The priests who carried the ark of the covenant of the LORD stood firm on dry ground in the middle of the Jordan, while all Israel passed by until the whole nation had completed the crossing on dry ground.

[4:1]When the whole nation had finished crossing the Jordan, the LORD said to Joshua, [2]"Choose twelve men from among the people, one from each tribe, [3]and tell them to take up twelve stones from the middle of the Jordan from right where the priests stood and to carry them over with you and put them down at the place where you stay tonight."

[4]So Joshua called together the twelve men he had appointed from the Israelites, one from each tribe, [5]and said to them, "Go over before the ark of the LORD your God into the middle of the Jordan. Each of you is to take up a stone on his shoulder, according to the number of the tribes of the Israelites, [6]to serve as a sign among you. In the future, when your children ask you, 'What do these stones mean?' [7]tell them that the flow of the Jordan was cut off before the ark of the covenant of the LORD. When it crossed the Jordan, the waters of the Jordan were cut off. These stones are to be a memorial to the people of Israel forever."

[8]So the Israelites did as Joshua commanded them. They took twelve stones from the middle of the Jordan, according to the number of the tribes of the Israelites, as the LORD had told Joshua; and they carried them over with them to their camp, where they put them down. [9]Joshua set up the twelve stones that had been in the middle of the Jordan at the spot where the priests who carried the ark of the covenant had stood. And they are there to this day.

[10]Now the priests who carried the ark remained standing in the middle of the Jordan until everything the LORD had commanded Joshua was done by the people, just as Moses had directed Joshua. The people hurried over, [11]and as soon as all of them had crossed, the ark of the LORD and the priests came to the other side while the people watched. [12]The men of Reuben, Gad and the half-tribe of Manasseh crossed over, armed, in front of the Israelites, as Moses had

directed them. ¹³About forty thousand armed for battle crossed over before the LORD to the plains of Jericho for war.

¹⁴That day the LORD exalted Joshua in the sight of all Israel; and they revered him all the days of his life, just as they had revered Moses.

¹⁵Then the LORD said to Joshua, ¹⁶"Command the priests carrying the ark of the Testimony to come up out of the Jordan."

¹⁷So Joshua commanded the priests, "Come up out of the Jordan."

¹⁸And the priests came up out of the river carrying the ark of the covenant of the LORD. No sooner had they set their feet on the dry ground than the waters of the Jordan returned to their place and ran at flood stage as before.

¹⁹On the tenth day of the first month the people went up from the Jordan and camped at Gilgal on the eastern border of Jericho. ²⁰And Joshua set up at Gilgal the twelve stones they had taken out of the Jordan. ²¹He said to the Israelites, "In the future when your descendants ask their fathers, 'What do these stones mean?' ²²tell them, 'Israel crossed the Jordan on dry ground.' ²³For the LORD your God dried up the Jordan before you until you had crossed over. The LORD your God did to the Jordan just what he had done to the Red Sea when he dried it up before us until we had crossed over. ²⁴He did this so that all the peoples of the earth might know that the hand of the LORD is powerful and so that you might always fear the LORD your God."

⁵:¹Now when all the Amorite kings west of the Jordan and all the Canaanite kings along the coast heard how the LORD had dried up the Jordan before the Israelites until we had crossed over, their hearts melted and they no longer had the courage to face the Israelites.

Original Meaning

AS CHAPTER 3 OPENS, dawn is breaking over the Israelite camp six miles east of the Jordan at Shittim. By now the details of the spies' report have probably spread through every tent. Joshua's public standing probably remains mixed, mainly because of divided opinions on the value of his spy mission. Indecision also probably divides popular opinion about the spies' conduct during the adventure. Meanwhile, the sunrise gives early risers a broad, distant glimpse of the landscape of Canaan rising up west of the Jordan. All this soon changes, however, in one of the Bible's most dramatic episodes. The spectacular display of divine power removes a water barrier to God's plan, an echo of the crossing of the Red Sea (Ex. 13–15; see 4:23).[1] This episode marks Israel's long-awaited, historic transition from the wilderness to the Promised Land, a transition begun at the Exodus from Egypt.[2] Indeed, the Red Sea and Jordan crossings form bookends around the long story of how Israel finally arrives in Canaan.

A steady drumbeat of repeated language drives home the narrative's key motifs: that the priests stood (*ʿamad*) holding the ark in the Jordan (3:3, 6, 8, 13, 14, 15, 17; 4:9, 10, 16, 18); that the Jordan's waters "stood (still)" (*ʿamad*; 3:13, 16) and were "cut off" (*karat* ni.; 3:13, 16; 4:7); that Israel crossed on dry land (3:17; 4:18; cf. v. 23); and that twelve men carried twelve stones from the riverbed (4:3, 5, 6, 7, 8, 20, 21; cf. 3:12; 4:9). Two other important motifs include the beginning of Joshua's rise in stature as the sequel to his possible false start in chapter 2 (3:7; 4:14), and Israel's future remembrance of the crossing event.

Literarily, a schema of instruction-obedience drives the action throughout.[3] Joshua (3:5, 6, 9; 4:5–7) and Yahweh (3:7–8; 4:2, 15) issue instructions that Joshua, the Israelite priests, or the people carry out (3:14–15; 4:8–13). Indirect instructions concerning future remembrance of this episode also stand out, although expressed as explanations in support of other statements (3:6–7; 4:21–24). More important, the narrative presents the episode, not primarily as a gigantic military invasion or a large-scale migration, but as a religious procession. The people must ritually prepare themselves (3:5) because the "amazing things" about to appear imply the holy presence of Yahweh himself. The ark's dominant role symbolizes that same presence and also dictates that the people keep a respectful distance from it (v. 4).

But this narrative also represents a complex literary piece. Nelson complains that the narrative crams too many topics together, leaving "the thematic threads ... tangled and knotted."[4] Two particular curiosities are

---

1. A similar miracle opens up the Jordan for Elijah and Elisha to cross, albeit in the opposite direction (2 Kings 2:8), but the narrative merely reports it and moves on.

2. J. Wagenaar, "Crossing the Sea of Reeds (Exod 13–14) and the Jordan (Josh 3–4)," in *Studies in the Book of Exodus*, ed. M. Vervenne (Leuven: Leuven Univ. Press, 1996), 470 ("the transition from the desert to the inhabitable land").

3. Nelson (*Joshua*, 57) favors a pattern of "narrative action (obedience and miracle) interwoven with associated speech (command, prediction, and explanation)." Howard, *Joshua*, 133, suggests a pattern of "anticipation/confirmation or command fulfillment."

4. Nelson, *Joshua*, 55; cf. J. F. D. Creach, *Joshua* (Louisville: John Knox, 2003), 44. Nevertheless, Nelson adds that "by using moderate effort the reader actually has no trouble making sense out of the story line."

---

striking: an appearance of disorder as various characters issue commands, and several actions that seem to not quite fit the context.[5] For example, it is curious that the officers rather than Joshua initiate Israel's preparations for entering Canaan (3:2–4). Equally curious, Joshua commands Israel to select a man from each tribe without specifying their mission (3:12), while Yahweh issues virtually the same command to Joshua and specifies the mission (4:1b–3). Further, the report that Joshua himself erected twelve stones in the Jordan riverbed (4:9) seems to appear out of the blue and without explanation or motivation.

Literary critics theorize that the present text either combines two originally separate texts or comprises a simple original text plus various additions.[6] The lack of a consensus, however, suggests that "further attempts to reconstruct the literary history of chapters 3–4 are probably doomed to failure."[7] An earlier consensus that rooted parts of the narrative in cultic ceremonies at Gilgal has likewise recently fallen into disfavor as too speculative.[8] Occasional literary roughness notwithstanding, the narrative for the most part makes clear narrative sense. Some phrases might subtly reflect the incorporation of an original cultic ceremony, but we cannot be certain.[9]

Structurally, the text consists of two main sections — the report of the Jordan crossing (3:1–17) and Yahweh's two commissions of Joshua (4:1–24) — followed by a one-verse epilogue (5:1). The focus of the first section falls on the crossing events, the second on the means to remember

---

5. For full discussion of the literary roughness, see L. D. Hawk, *Joshua* (Berit Olam; Collegeville, Minn.: Liturgical, 2000), 54–55.

6. For the former, cf. Butler, *Joshua*, 41–42; E. Vogt, "Die Erzählung vom Jordanübergang, Josue 3–4," *Bib* 46 (1965): 125–48; for the latter, cf. Fritz, *Josua*, 43–56; J. Dus, "Die Analyse zweier Ladeerzählungen des Josuabuches (Jos 3–4 und 6)," *ZAW* 72 (1960): 107–34. Cf. Wagenaar ("Crossing the Sea of Reeds," 466–68) and Nelson (*Joshua*, 55, n.2) for further discussion and additional bibliography.

7. Nelson, *Joshua*, 57; followed by Howard, *Joshua*, 118, n.173, who regards chapter 3 as a "fairly straightforward" narrative but concedes that authorial concern with theological reflection leaves it repetitive and chronologically difficult (118). Alternatively, according to P. Saydon, "The Crossing of the Jordan, Jos. Chaps. 3 and 4," *CBQ* 12 (1950): 194–207, the text has no notable incongruities, while for Polzin (*Moses and the Deuteronomist*, 94–99) the alleged discrepancies merely reflect shifting time perspectives and viewpoints. Cf. also B. Peckham, "The Composition of Joshua 3–4," *CBQ* 46 (1984): 413–31 (the story's elaborate thematic structure simply overpowers its plot).

8. Fritz, *Josua*, 43–46; against e.g., H.-J. Kraus, "Gilgal: Ein Beitrag zur Kultgeschichte Israels," *VT* 1 (1951): 181–99; J. R. Porter, "The Background of Joshua 3–5," *SEÅ* 36 (1971): 5–23.

9. E.g., (lit.) "from this (place), from the middle of the Jordan" (Josh. 4:3), "this Jordan" (4:22), "these stones" (4:6, 7, 20, 21).

it in the future. The epilogue reports the paralyzing panic that news of the crossing spreads among kings in Canaan. The twice-repeated child's question (4:6, 21) shows that the narrative's purpose is to teach Israel the meaning of this dramatic episode.[10]

The Report of the Jordan Crossing (3:1 – 17)

PREPARATIONS FOR CROSSING (3:1 – 8). To open, the narrative reports Israel's preparations for the upcoming exciting events (vv. 1 – 8). The morning after the spies' return, Joshua and Israel shift their camp from Shittim, about six miles west, to the Jordan itself (v. 1). The early morning start may imply corporate eagerness energized by the spies' debriefing finally to "get moving." Three days later, the officers pass through the camp a second time to instruct Israel about the crossing (vv. 2 – 3; cf. 1:10 – 11). As noted above, the narrator specifically quotes their words without explaining how they came by them (vv. 3 – 4). They order the people to watch for the ark with its priestly bearers and follow it (v. 3b). This comment marks the book's first mention of the ark of the covenant, the well-known golden box that will also figure prominently in the ritual conquest of Jericho (6:6, 12 – 13; cf. 7:6) and the covenant renewal ceremony at Shechem (8:33). Israel understood the space between the winged cherubim to be the royal throne over which Yahweh invisibly reigns (1 Sam. 4:4; 2 Sam. 6:2; Ps. 99:1).[11]

Here it symbolizes Yahweh's royal presence with Israel and his sovereign leadership of the coming invasion.[12] The ark (i.e., Yahweh) led Israel out of Egypt and through the wilderness (Num. 10:35), and now it will lead them across into Canaan.[13] But, surprisingly, Israel is to follow the ark at a distance of about two thousand cubits (over half a mile).[14] Keeping this

---

10. Creach, *Joshua*, 44. A similar child's question forms part of the Passover remembrance (see Ex. 12:26), so the question-answer exchange here further links the Exodus and crossing stories. For additional question-answer examples, see below.

11. For additional background on the ark, see the Bridging Contexts section below.

12. The phrase "ark of the covenant of the LORD" is a common one (Num. 10:33; Deut. 10:8; 31:9, 25, 26; Josh. 3:3, 11, 17; 4:7, 18; 6:6; 8:33; 1 Sam. 4:4; 1 Kings 16:19; 1 Chron. 15:25; 16:37; 17:1; 22:19; 28:2, 18; Jer. 3:16).

13. For an overview of the ark's history, parallels, and theology, see C. Seow, "Ark of the Covenant," *ABD*, 1:386–93; for its role, see G. Coats, "The Ark of the Covenant in Joshua: A Probe into the History of a Tradition," *HAR* 9 (1985): 137–57.

14. Syntactically, the restrictive adverb *ʾak* ("only") introduces what follows as further clarification of the instruction that precedes; cf. WO§39.3.5d. According to Nelson (*Joshua*, 60), this stipulation renders the crossing impossible, but the stated rationale ("so you will know which way to go") suggests that the stipulation probably only applies until the ark stops in the middle of the Jordan, not while the people cross. Certainly, to my knowledge, the Pentateuch requires no such distance when Israel followed the ark in the wilderness.

distance serves a practical purpose: It enables Israel to know the proper entry route since this event will mark their first time in Canaan (v. 4). Theologically, the stipulation presupposes divine familiarity with Canaan, as if, unlike Israel, Yahweh *has* been on this road before. But it is one thing for Yahweh to lead, quite another for Israel to follow. Thus, the command sets a pattern for subsequent events—that Israel, indeed, must always follow Yahweh and fully depend on his presence. Such consistent obedience will set this generation apart from the prior one now buried in the desert sands along the road behind them.

Specific instructions follow in three brief narrative snapshots (vv. 5–8). Literarily, their brevity creates a sense of forward motion and momentum. Their quick succession and the lack of reported execution may also portray how helter-skelter were the camp's preparations for departure. (1) Joshua commands the people (v. 5) to prepare themselves personally—to "consecrate yourselves" (Heb. *qadaš*, hithp., lit. "make yourselves holy"). This self-consecration is necessary because "tomorrow the LORD will do amazing things among you." "Amazing things" (*nipla'ot*) are stunning feats that only God can do, deeds so incredible as to leave their witnesses gasping, "How'd you do that, LORD?"[15] Biblical writers know Yahweh as the Wonder Worker par excellence (Judg. 13:19; 1 Chron. 16:9; Ps. 86:10). As examples, they often cite the Exodus from Egypt (Ex. 3:20; Judg. 6:13; Ps. 78:11; 106:7, 22; Mic. 7:15) and his mysterious work in creation and history (Job 5:9; 9:10; 37:5, 14; Isa. 28:29). But that Yahweh will soon do marvels "among you" promises the close proximity of his holy presence, and that puts sinful Israel at great risk. The threat is that "the LORD will break out against them" (Ex. 19:22)—that his holiness will ravage them.[16]

To avoid that catastrophe, Israel must become ritually clean ("consecrate yourselves!"), a ritual washing that commonly precedes biblical theophanies (Num. 11:18; Josh. 7:13; 1 Sam. 16:5; 1 Chron. 15:12; 2 Chron. 29:5; 35:6). Presumably, Israel will also abstain from sexual relations and don clean clothes the next day (Ex. 19:10). The requirement for ritual purity signals that this river crossing is a solemn religious ritual, not an ordinary military invasion.

(2) Joshua's next command, this one to the priests (v. 6), confirms this—and invokes a thematic wordplay. They are to pick up the ark and "cross" (Heb. *'abar*) to the head of the line with the people behind them. This "crossing" positions them to lead the river "crossing" (or, better, to act out *Yahweh's* leadership).

---

15. Cf. Ex. 34:10; Ps. 40:5; 72:18; 78:4; 98:1; 111:4; Jer. 21:2; Joel 2:26. For more on "amazing things," see the Contemporary Significance section on ch. 23.
16. Cf. H.-P. Müller, "קדשׁ," *THAT*, 2:605–6; J. Nanne, "קדשׁ," *NIDOTTE*, 3:885.

(3) In the final snapshot, Yahweh addresses Joshua with a personal promise (v. 7). "Today" will mark a momentous new beginning for Joshua, too.
By doing "amazing things," Yahweh will "exalt you in the eyes of all Israel."
The Lord will enhance Joshua's stature in Israel to confirm that he enjoys
the same close relationship with Yahweh as Moses did.[17] With their own
eyes Israel will recognize Joshua as their new Moses, the divinely appointed
leader to trust and to obey. Shortly — and in dramatic fashion — they will
demonstrate their willingness to follow him.

Yahweh concludes the final snapshot with a terse instruction through
Joshua for the priests carrying the ark. At first glance, it makes little sense
(v. 8). Rather than stop at the water's edge, the priests are to stand (Heb. ʿamad)
in the middle of the Jordan. But how can they possibly do that, given the
river's current flow at flood stage (v. 15)? Will they have to lift the ark above
their heads to keep it dry? Will they have the strength to prevent the water
from sweeping it from their hands downstream? The vague, curious instruction anticipates what follows, especially the stunning event soon to ensue.

The crossing (vv. 9–17). The crossing event forms the heart of chapter 3. Joshua assembles the Israelites ("come here") to hear "the words of
the LORD your God" (v. 9). Apparently, we are not to understand his short
speech (vv. 10–13) as a prophetic oracle since it lacks the messenger formula ("Thus says the LORD"; cf. 24:2). He also refers to Yahweh in the third
(rather than first) person. But Joshua still claims that his words are Yahweh's
words. For the first time Joshua speaks as the mouthpiece of Yahweh just
as Moses did (Ex. 4:28; 24:3, 4; Num. 11:24).[18] If Israel believes him, this
speech significantly elevates him as leader in their eyes. It confirms that
Yahweh is indeed "with [Joshua] as [he] was with Moses" (v. 7).

After Israel has assembled, Joshua addresses them (vv. 9–13), immediately driving home the key point: "The living God . . . among you" is, indeed,
about to drive out the seven peoples inhabiting Canaan (v. 10).[19] As evidence
Joshua simply points (Heb. *hinneh*, lit., "Look!") to the ark of the covenant,

---

17. For the use of *gadal* pi. "to exalt, promote, enhance the stature of," see also Est. 5:11;
10:2; cf. Gen. 12:2; 1 Kings 1:47; 1 Chron. 29:12.

18. In conveying Yahweh's words, Joshua also anticipates Samuel (1 Sam. 8:19; 15:1) and
the prophets Semaiah (2 Chron. 11:4), Jeremiah (Jer. 36:4, 6, 8, 11; 37:2; 43:1; cf. 23:36),
and Ezekiel (Ezek. 11:25); cf. Amos 8:11.

19. In my view, the initial "Joshua said" (v. 10) implies a separate (but closely related)
occasion for what follows, although LXX lacks it. For "living God," see only Ps. 42:2; Hos.
1:10. Several texts list the same seven inhabitant peoples in different orders (Deut. 7:1; Josh.
12:8; 24:11), while others vary in the total number and the names of peoples listed (Gen.
15:19–20; Ex. 3:8; 13:5). Interestingly, the Jebusites always appear last in the above lists,
perhaps a reflection of their late conquest by David (2 Sam. 5:6–10). For a glimpse of the
inhabitants' geographical distribution, see Num. 13:29.

at that moment standing before them borne by priests.[20] Earlier references introduced the ark's prominence in the crossing (vv. 3, 6, 8), but here Joshua underscores its singular role as symbol of God's presence (v. 11; cf. v. 12).

The unusual, relatively rare title "the Lord of all the earth" (cf. also v. 13) highlights Yahweh's sovereign lordship over a geographic sphere—the whole earth.[21] Contextually, this is not an unimportant theological qualifier. It affirms that Israel's covenant God—the one whose portable throne "will go into the Jordan ahead of you" (v. 11b)—is no local divine despot but the world's only sovereign. Implicitly, it offers theological justification for his expulsion of the seven peoples and his gift of their land to Israel. His dominion over the whole earth means that he owns everything in it and, hence, has the authority to distribute any particular piece—Canaan, in this case—as he wishes. The title also creates the expectation that whatever happens when the ark enters the Jordan derives from that dominion. Next, Joshua commands Israel to select one man from each tribe for a purpose unstated here (v. 12) but probably clarified by 4:1–9.[22] He ends his speech climactically with an astounding announcement: The Jordan is to stop flowing past the waiting Israelites (v. 13)!

Three wordplays in v. 13 underscore the significance of the amazing event. (1) According to Joshua, the event's trigger is the entry of the (lit.) "soles of the feet" of the priests into the river, a key phrase in both vv. 8 and 13. The Old Testament often associates that term (NIV "set foot") with the conquest of enemies (Deut. 2:5; 11:24; 1 Kings 5:3; Mal 4:3). The motif here may stamp the present story with a similar sense of conquest (cf. Josh. 1:3; 4:18): Yahweh asserts his authority over the Jordan River and all land westward.

(2) A second wordplay connects the "standing" (*ʿamad* [v. 8b]) of the priests with the ark mid-river as the actual cause of the "standing (still)" (*ʿamad*) of the Jordan's flow (v. 13; cf. vv. 15–16).[23]

---

20. In Joshua's statement ("This is how ..."), "this" (*zoʾt*) probably refers to the ark; cf. *DCH*, 372. Here *hinneh* expresses a presentative exclamation, whose vividness and immediacy directs the reader to its object; cf. WO §40.2.1.

21. For the title elsewhere, cf. only Ps. 97:5; Mic. 4:13; Zech. 4:14; 6:5; O. Eissfeldt, "אָדוֹן," *TDOT*, 1:61–62; G. Johnston, "אָדוֹן," *NIDOTTE*, 1:257–58. Semantically, the title foregrounds the idea of lordship (with ownership in the background) while with its synonym *baʿal* ("husband, owner, master"), the idea of ownership predominates.

22. "Now then" (*weʿattah*) syntactically signals the transition from instruction to the call for action. As noted above, the omitted purpose suggests the likelihood that a complex literary history stands behind the present text.

23. "Come to rest" (*nuaḥ*, v. 13; NIV "set foot in") and "stand [still]" (*ʿamad*, v. 8b) are synonyms since the former basically means "to cease activity, come to rest"; cf. G. Robinson, "The Idea of Rest in the OT and the Search for the Basic Character of the Sabbath," *ZAW* 92 (1980): 32–42; H. Preuss, "נוּחַ," *TDOT*, 9:279; cf. Num. 10:36.

(3) A third wordplay makes an even wider, more important connection. The waters are to stand in a "heap (of water)" (*ned*), a term that elsewhere only describes what Yahweh did at the Red Sea (Ex. 15:8; Ps. 78:13). The pun hints that Yahweh is about to perform at the Jordan as stunning a miracle as he did at the Exodus. It also implies that the Jordan and Red Sea crossings are somehow connected, a point made explicit later (see 4:23). In short, the river's waters are to be "cut off" and "stand up in a heap" upstream—an incredibly stunning way for the sovereign "Lord of all the earth" to open the gates of Canaan for Israel to enter!

Suddenly, the speech ends and the narrator steps forward to report that the crossing proper takes place exactly as expected (vv. 14–17). His literary style gives the report of the "amazing things" (cf. v. 5)—the stoppage of the Jordan's flow—a slow, majestic, dramatic feel.[24] A single, complex sentence rich with thematically important, repeated words opens the scene (vv. 14–16).[25] The priests and ark lead the procession to the Jordan once Israel breaks camp (v. 14). At the river, a dramatic confrontation of the priests and ark (and Yahweh) versus the mighty river occurs (v. 15). The Jordan is at its mightiest—at flood stage (cf. 1 Chron. 12:15), angrily swollen by melting snow and spring rains. That makes a transit via known fords (2:7, 23) out of the question. It is almost as if the river defiantly dares Israel to attempt a crossing! But the trigger that ignites the miracle is the moment that the priests' "soles" wade into (lit., "are dipped in") the water's edge.[26] That instant marks the clash for sovereignty between ark and river, a conflict that the ark easily wins ("the water from upstream stopped flowing" [lit., "stood still"]; v. 16).

Up river "a great distance," the water "piled up in a heap" (or dam) at the city of Adam near Zarethan (see 1 Kings 4:12; 7:46). Adam is probably Tell ed-Damiyeh (modern Damiya, Jordan), in antiquity a strategic

---

24. A directional motif also seems evident. Initially, the action moves westward from the Jordan's east bank as the people break camp and the ark-bearers reach the Jordan (v. 14; cf. v. 6). In v. 16 the details of the stoppage introduce a north-south orientation.

25. E.g., "the Jordan" (vv. 14a, 15a, 15b) and variations of "the priests who carried the ark" (vv. 14b, 15a; cf. v. 17). Grammatically, the sentence begins with two long temporal clauses (vv. 14–15) both subordinate to v. 16a ("the water ... stopped flowing"). V. 16b (a disjunctive sentence) reintroduces the people from v. 14, forming a nice thematic inclusio. Sadly, NIV's translation obscures this structure, apparently to produce a smooth translation. For further discussion, cf. Howard, *Joshua*, 129–30; Nelson, *Joshua*, 62.

26. The change of preposition from *be* "with" (v. 14) to *ke* "about" (v. 15) may intend to sharpen the sense of temporal coincidence (and implied causality) within vv. 15–16. In temporal clauses *be* indicates general temporal proximity, *ke* events immediately preceding those of the main clause; cf. WO §36.2.2b. A good paraphrase of vv. 15–16 might be, "No sooner had the priests' feet waded in than the water stopped."

city forty-five miles north of Jericho and just south of the Jabbok River. Important trade routes intersected there, and landslides there were known to dam the Jordan.[27] Its association here with Zarethan, another important ancient city about thirty miles farther north, is curious. First Kings 4:12 invokes a similar phrase to locate Beth Shean, so perhaps—and for reasons unknown to us—Zarethan served as a common ancient reference point (cf. 1 Kings 7:46).

Whatever the case, the geographical comment assumes authorial knowledge gained after the fact, probably from local tradition around that area. The water upstream "stood (still)" (*amad*), causing the Jordan's flow downstream toward "the Sea of the Arabah (the Salt Sea)"—today, the Dead Sea—(lit.) to "cease" and "be cut off."[28] The gigantic disruption enables "the people [to cross] over opposite Jericho." As the decamping of the people opens this stunning scene (v. 14), so their crossing here concludes it. After all, the people are the ultimate beneficiaries of the entire episode.

Finally, the narrator repeats a word to underscore the single astounding result of the stoppage (v. 17). The priests holding the ark "stood" mid-river and all Israel crossed "on dry ground" (*beḥorabah*; cf. 4:18). Elsewhere, "dry ground" (*ḥorabah*) designates nonwatery terrain—the opposite of "flood" or "sea" (Gen. 7:22; Hag. 2:6). Thus, for the writer, the "amazing thing" here is that the events transform naturally watery (and normally impassible) terrain into its dry opposite. The simple physical fact of dry soil underfoot confirms the reality of the miracle and symbolizes the victory of the ark (and its resident king, Yahweh) over the waters.

The "dry ground" motif also echoes another mighty, salvific act of Yahweh, his stunning parting of the Rea Sea at the Exodus (Ex. 14:21).[29] Further, the crossing apparently transforms "the whole nation" of Israel itself. Verse 17 marks the first time that the book calls Israel a "nation" (*goy*) rather than "people" (*am*), perhaps a signal that "crossing the Jordan to become a landed people has meant a change in national status."[30]

Strikingly, however, the author omits direct mention of Yahweh's role. The priests' feet and the ark are the stars—as it were, his stand-ins. Literarily, the omission casts the spotlight on the spectacular event itself—the breathtaking, dramatic scene Israel witnesses—rather than its divine

27. Boling, *Joshua*, 112 (map), 169; M. Fretz, "Adam," *ABD*, 1:64.

28. NIV ("completely cut off") captures the emphatic pairing of the verbs *tamam* ("cease") and *karat* ni. ("be cut off").

29. Fritz, *Josua*, 52. For "the whole nation," cf. 4:1; 5:6, 8. The "dry ground" motif also anticipates the later parting of Jordan's water when Elijah and Elijah crossed (2 Kings 2:8).

30. Nelson, *Joshua*, 62; cf. Ex. 19:6; Deut. 26:5; Josh. 5:6, 8; 10:13.

source. But that, too, redounds to the glory of Yahweh: He need not be visible to wield overwhelming power. The reality of his powerful, invisible presence with Israel will prove to be a prominent theme in Joshua.

Yahweh's Two Commissions of Joshua (4:1–24)

YAHWEH'S FIRST COMMISSION (VV. 1–14). As soon as the last Israelite emerges from the Jordan's dry bed, Yahweh again speaks to Joshua (v. 1).[31] Yahweh's first commission breaks a long divine silence and follows up his last statement (3:7–8). It also introduces a new subplot into the story, the origin of the twelve memorial stones (vv. 2–14). The literary effect of the addition is to freeze the main action (the crossing) until verse 10.[32] Also, Yahweh's direct speech enhances the narrative in two ways: it gives the commission solemn importance, and it invests the memorial to be erected with Yahweh's own authority.

Specifically, Yahweh commissions Joshua to select twelve men, one from each tribe (v. 2), and commands them to undertake a special mission (v. 3).[33] The men are to carry twelve stones (presumably one per man [cf. v. 5b]) from the spot where the priests' feet rested in the dry Jordan and deliver them to Israel's next campsite (as yet, unnamed). Clearly, the importance of the stones is their connection with that historic spot. Contextually, the specific instructions seem to follow up and supplement 3:12 (see 4:4).[34] But it seems odd that Joshua's command (3:12) would chronologically precede Yahweh's (4:1–3).[35] The present order almost pictures Yahweh as picking up Joshua's idea rather than vice versa. Howard suggests that "in real time" (i.e., the actual chronology of events) Yahweh's words did precede Joshua's but that the present order conforms to a pattern of "antici-

---

31. The repetition of language from the end of 3:17 implies that the completion of the crossing spurs Yahweh to speak. Initial *wayehi ka'ašer* + perfect signals the contemporaneity of the completed crossing (temporal clause) and Yahweh's new statement (main clause); cf. WO §38.7a; Judg. 3:18. Structurally, Boling (*Joshua*, 170) regards 3:17–4:8 as a literary unit "separate from the main story."

32. So Nelson, *Joshua*, 65, who rightly observes how 4:10–11a "unfreezes" the central plot by resumptive repetition of language from 3:16b–17.

33. The phrase (lit.) "take for yourselves" + a number occurs in another cultic context, Yahweh's command that Job's friends make sacrifices (Job 42:8).

34. The wording of v. 2 closely resembles that of 3:12, including a plural imperative (so, too, v. 3) even though it apparently addresses only Joshua. LXX and Vulgate show singular imperatives in vv. 2 and 3 (Syriac concurs in v. 3 but not in v. 2), while LXX omits the number "12" (v. 2) and "priests" (v. 3).

35. The plural imperatives in vv. 2–3 pose an additional problem. The simplest (but not fully satisfactory) explanation is to assume that 4:2 simply borrows language from 3:12 (plural imperative included) and 4:3 invokes a plural imperative for consistency.

pation/confirmation or command/fulfillment" evident in Joshua 3 – 4.[36] In my view, this merely sidesteps the issue. The reader still finds it curious, if not theologically problematic, that Yahweh "confirms" or "fulfills" the command of Joshua.

Nevertheless, one must recall that the narrator introduces Joshua's command (3:12) as the "words of Yahweh" (see 3:9). Thus, the text apparently assumes that Yahweh "speaks" both through Joshua and on his own. Further, the present picture (Yahweh's confirmation/fulfillment of Joshua's command) may in fact also serve a thematic purpose — to enhance the portrait of Joshua as leader and close divine confidant (see 3:7; 4:14). What would "exalt" Joshua more in Israel's eyes than to hear Yahweh repeat something Joshua had said to them?

In addition, the text clearly assumes that, ultimately, Joshua is subordinate to Yahweh. Joshua orders the selection of the twelve (3:12), but it is Yahweh who specifically details what they are to do (4:3). Even more important, it is Joshua who in 4:4 – 5 executes all of 4:2 – 3. He summons the twelve men chosen earlier (v. 4; cf. 3:12) and reissues Yahweh's command with added details (v. 5). The men are to cross (back!) to the middle of the Jordan where the priests stand holding the ark. Each is to pick up one stone on his shoulder, the total number of stones (12) equaling the number of Israelite tribes. The numerical comment signals that the stones symbolize Israel as a whole nation and associate that unity with the miracle of the dry ground. After all, it was the latter that made the stones available.

Joshua hastens to explain the purpose (initial *lemaʿan*, "so that") of this unusual mission "as a sign among you" (v. 6). In the Old Testament, a "sign" (*ʾot*) is a visible object, action, or event that conveys information to authenticate something else.[37] For example, the rainbow after a rainstorm recalls God's covenant with earth's living creatures (Gen. 9:11 – 12), while the weekly Sabbath reminds Israel of its covenant obligations to Yahweh (Ex. 31:13, 17; Ezek. 20:12, 20). The plagues in Egypt serve to inform Pharaoh that "I the LORD am in this land" (Ex. 8:22; cf. vv. 19, 23; 7:3, 5; 10:2), and Isaiah offers King Ahaz a sign to authenticate Yahweh's announced destruction of the king's enemies in order to buck up the king's wavering faith (Isa. 7:11).

Here the stones serve as both "sign" and "memorial" (*zikkaron*, v. 7; cf. Ex. 13:9). They authenticate that the past event actually happened and remind

---

36. Howard, *Joshua*, 133, who sees Joshua's command as fitting best between 4:2 and 4:4 – 7 (133, n.220).

37. F. Helfmeyer, "אוֹת," *TDOT*, 1:168 – 70, and his discussion of the various functions of signs (170 – 86); P. Kruger, "אוֹת," *NIDOTTE*, 1:331 – 33.

Israel of its continuing significance for later generations.[38] But the stones bear no self-explanatory inscription (cf. 8:32). Instead, their mute testimony will cause curious Israelite children to ask in the future, "What do these stones mean?" This is significant: The text assumes visits to the site by future generations, probably for some ritual remembrance if not reenactment, of the river crossing. Such visits served to keep alive its meaning over the centuries. Probably the rituals took place at Gilgal, the site where Israel first camped in the land, but the text prevents our saying anything more.[39]

The adults' lengthy reply, however, supplies the missing meaning (v. 7).[40] These stones recall that, when the ark crossed the Jordan, its waters were cut off. Once again, nothing is said of Yahweh's involvement in the miracle, and presumably the child is to make that connection here. Probably, the author saves explicit theologizing to give the story a dramatic, final flourish (see v. 23).

The twelve men carry out Joshua's orders (v. 8). Each carries a stone from the middle of the Jordan and (per Yahweh's orders, vv. 2–3) deposits it at Israel's campsite (again, unnamed). Parenthetically (and probably at the same time), twelve other stones unexpectedly merit mention (cf. the emphatic Hebrew word order). These are ones that Joshua himself unilaterally erects in the middle of the Jordan, right where the priests' feet stood (v. 9).[41] As with the other dozen, nothing is said about the shape or size of Joshua's creation, but the author observes that these stones "are there to this day." The comment almost tempts later readers to find the site and see for themselves. Thus, two groups of twelve stones remember the ark's crossing (and drying) of the Jordan, one amid its bed, the other nearby.

With those symbolic memorials in place, the narrative resumes the main plot, the dramatic crossing. It does so by repeating language from 3:17 and 4:1 (lit., "until all ... ceased") and by returning to the priests holding

---

38. As C. A. Keller says, the purpose of a *zikkaron* is "to prevent something from being forgotten which deserves to be handed down, and to make it real over and over again"; quoted in Helfmeyer, "אות," 1:168.

39. For an overview of the alternatives, see Helfmeyer, "אות," 1:180–81. Fritz (*Josua,* 43–46), however, breaks with the earlier consensus, denying that Joshua 3–4 either founds a later cultic celebration or legitimates a specific cultic site.

40. The format "when your child/ren ask ... you shall say ..." seems at home in several formal settings, such as the Passover (Ex. 12:26), the redemption of the firstborn (Ex. 13:14), and instruction on obeying the law (Deut. 6:20). In each case, the adult's answer is either to report some events connected with the Exodus (the death of the firstborn [Ex. 13:14–15], the deliverance from slavery and gift of the land [Deut. 6:21–24]) or to make a simple declaration (Ex. 12:26–27).

41. In my view, the object-initial sentence structure (*waw* + a non-verb) sets v. 9 off as parenthetical (so NRSV) and suggests its contemporaneity, although other views are also possible (see NIV).

the ark in the Jordan's dry bed (v. 10). Here the point is that they stood there until everything commanded by Yahweh through Joshua was finished. Indeed, the author underscores that, by obeying Yahweh, Joshua also obeyed Moses (cf. Num. 27:22 – 23; Josh. 1:7).

Finally, the comment that the people crossed in a hurry (v. 10b) leads to verses 11 – 14, which hurries to lower the curtain on the crossing scene. The ark itself and the priests cross over as the people watch from the west bank (v. 11). The narrative even singles out the crossing of Israel's vanguard, the fully-armed Transjordanian tribes (Reuben, Gad, and half-Manasseh). Their crossing confirms that they kept their earlier promise to Moses (1:12 – 18; Num. 32:25 – 32) and signals that a united, obedient Israel has, indeed, entered Canaan. About forty thousand fully-equipped Israelite soldiers also cross into the plains of Jericho, the large level area between that city and the river (v. 13).

In the Old Testament, "forty thousand" is a round number meaning "huge army" (Judg. 5:8; 2 Sam. 10:18//1 Chron. 19:18; 1 Kings 4:26; 1 Chron. 12:36). This throng passes in review "before Yahweh," their commander, armed and ready for war.[42] The pass portrays the force as a holy army ready to do battle behind Yahweh, the holy warrior himself.[43] These comments cast Israel's crossing not as a migration but as an invasion by a numerically formidable force. The reader now better understands Jericho's terror and the reaction of Canaan's kings to these stunning events (see 5:1). The plains of Jericho also offer Israel's army a clear, level path westward toward Jericho, their first target.

Most importantly, that day Yahweh keeps his promise to exalt Joshua before Israel (v. 14a echoes 3:7). Indeed, henceforth, Israel accords Joshua the same consummate respect given Moses during his lifetime (cf. Ex. 14:31; 34:30). Granted, like Moses, Joshua benefits from the "halo effect," his mediation of Yahweh's miraculous deeds heightening his personal reputation in Israel. But that simply serves to confirm his divine appointment as Moses' successor. This new, high stature makes it easier for Israel to follow him. Of course, theologically Joshua merely represents in human form the loving sovereignty of Israel's covenant lord, Yahweh.

Yahweh's second commission (vv. 15 – 24). According to v. 11, the ark and the priests crossed after the people, but now a flashback details how

---

42. The phrase "armed for war" always designates fully armed soldiers (Num. 31:5, 27; 1 Chron. 12:24 [cf. v. 23]; 2 Chron. 17:18). For "plains of Jericho," see Josh. 5:10; 2 Kings 25:5; Jer. 39:5; 52:8; cf. "plains of Moab opposite Jericho" (Num. 22:1; 26:3, 63; 31:12; et al.).

43. NIV breaks up the Hebrew phrase "before Yahweh for the war" by inserting "to the plains of Jericho" between "Yahweh" and "for." This obscures the fact that MT here applies to all Israel language that Moses had earlier used for the Transjordanian groups alone (Num. 32:20, 27, 29).

the ark came to cross. Yahweh commissions Joshua to command the priests with the ark to "come up out of the Jordan" (vv. 15 – 16), a commission that Joshua immediately executes in a terse, almost verbatim command (v. 17). Strikingly, "come up" (*ʿalah*) replaces "cross over" (*ʿabar*) as the key verb, both for the priests (vv. 16, 17, 18) and for the people (v. 19).[44] It makes perfect sense to order the priests to ascend the west bank from the middle of the river, but "came up" would not describe their crossing from the east to the west bank. Thus, *ʿalah* probably intends to evoke memories of the Exodus (Ex. 12:38; 13:18; Judg. 11:13, 16; Isa. 11:16; Hos. 2:17). It says, "Israel came up out of the Jordan, just as they came up out Egypt."[45]

As soon as the priests set foot on dry land (v. 18a), the Jordan's waters return to their former place, again swelling its banks (cf. 3:15). "Waters returned" probably marks another allusion to the Exodus, the return of waters over the dry path through the Red Sea (see the same phrase in Ex. 14:26, 28; 15:19; cf. Gen. 8:3). If so, linguistically the author twice signals his view that the entrance into Canaan is on par with, if not the climax of, the exodus from Egypt.

The timing of the momentous event—the tenth day of the first month (v. 19a)—also makes this connection. "First month" confirms a spring time frame for the episode (March-April) with spring runoff the reason for the Jordan's swollen current. The date also recalls dates associated with Passover, thus forging a further link between the Red Sea and Jordan crossings. The crossing date also anticipates and explains the Passover celebration four days later (5:10 – 12).

Meanwhile, the narrator finally names the site where Israel camped—Gilgal, on the eastern edge of the territory (not the city) of Jericho.[46] This marks the debut of the town that in Joshua 5 – 10 will provide

---

44. After 4:15, only in vv. 22 and 23; but cf. 3:1, 2, 4, 6, 11, 14, 16, 17; 4:1, 3, 5, 7, 8, 10, 11, 12, 13. This is also the only occurrence of *ʾaron ʿedut* (lit., "ark of the testimony"; elsewhere only Ex. 25:22; 26:33, 34; 30:6, 26; 40:3, 5, 21; Num. 4:5; 7:89; et al.); cf. forms of *ʾaron berit* "ark of the covenant" (3:3, 6, 8, 11, 14, 17; 4:7, 9, 18; 6:6, 8; 8:33).

45. Cf. also Num. 32:11; 33:38; Judg. 19:30; 1 Sam. 15:2, 6. For the use of *ʿalah* for Israel's entrance into Canaan, see Ex. 33:3; Num. 13:20; Deut. 1:21; for Israel's return from exile, see 2 Chron. 36:23; Ezra 1:3, 5; 2:1, 59; 7:7; Neh. 7:5, 6, 61; 12:1; cf. Isa. 11:16; Ezra 7:6, 28; 8:1.

46. Cf. R. L. Hubbard, Jr., "Gilgal," *DOTHB*, 334 – 36. The name derives from *galal*, "to roll" (*DCH*, 348, 355), which accounts for the suggested meanings "The Circle" (Boling, *Joshua*, 185) or "circle (of stones)" (KB, 183; cf. "wheel," Isa. 28:28). Y. Yadin suggests that the name was a generic term for a mobile campsite fortified by a circle of stones; cited by A. Malamat, "Israelite Conduct of War in the Conquest of Canaan according to the Biblical Tradition," in F. M. Cross, ed., *Symposia Celebrating the 75th Anniversary of the American Schools of Oriental Research (1900 – 1975)* (Cambridge, Mass.: ASOR, 1979), 44. But 5:9 relates it to *galal* pi. ("to remove [Israel's shame]").

Israel "both a bridgehead in Canaan and a springboard to the mountainous interior."[47] Finally, the writer returns to the chapter's symbolic center, the twelve stones, reiterating their origin in the Jordan and their erection by Joshua, but now locating them specifically at Gilgal (v. 20; cf. v. 9).

Joshua's statement to the people (vv. 20–21) reprises the question-and-answer ritual from verses 6–7. The child's question ("What do these stones mean?") repeats its counterpart almost verbatim (v. 21b; cf. v. 6), but the language and length of the adult's answer here differs significantly (vv. 22–24; cf. v. 7). The answerer is to "inform" (*yada*ᶜ causative)—to improve their knowledge (v. 22a)—not just "say" something (*ʾamar* qal). The answerer is also to reply with a specific formula ("Israel crossed the Jordan on dry ground" [v. 22b]). The final, emphatic word spotlights the dry land Israel traversed, not the stopped waters.

Further, unlike verse 7, in verse 23 Joshua explicitly credits Yahweh with drying up the Jordan's waters and compares the act to his drying up of the Red Sea at the Exodus. The words "Yahweh dried up [the Red Sea]" echo those of Rahab (2:10) and anticipate the report circulating among Canaanite kings (5:1). Strikingly, Joshua compares the experience of his audience (e.g. "the LORD *your* God," "until *you* [pl.] had crossed") with his own at the Red Sea ("before *us*," "until *we* had crossed"). In my view, such language may echo the cultic ceremony on which parts of chapters 3–4 draw. The author of Joshua understands the connection between Exodus, Jordan crossing, and Yahweh just as the psalmist did in Psalm 114:

> When Israel came out of Egypt,
>> the house of Jacob from a people of foreign tongue . . .
> The sea looked and fled,
>> the Jordan turned back. . . .
> Why was it, O sea, that you fled,
>> O Jordan, that you turned back. . . .
> Tremble, O earth, at the presence of the Lord,
>> at the presence of the God of Jacob. . . . (Ps. 114:1, 3, 5, 7)

At least, Joshua's rhetoric aims a passionate, highly personal appeal at the listeners (and readers) to engage, if not reexperience, both events.[48]

---

47. M. Rooker, "Gilgal," *NIDOTTE*, 4:684; cf. Malamat, "Israelite Conduct of War," 43–44. Its exact location is still unknown, but it plays a prominent role in the book (5:10; 9:6; 10:6, 7, 9, 15, 43). For possible sites, see Boling, *Joshua*, 112, 147, 185; W. Kotter, "Gilgal," *ABD*, 2:1023, who conveniently reviews the city's history (1022–23) and concludes that "its exact location remains enigmatic."

48. Cf. Helfmeyer, "אות," 1:180–81, for whom the question-answer format confirms the text's "parenetic intention."

More important, it links them as two turning points of the same history, making the experience of his audience as crucial as that of their ancestors. Climactically, Joshua states the episode's twofold informational purpose (v. 24): Both dryings dramatically display Yahweh's dreadful, breathtaking supremacy (cf. Ex. 13:9; Deut. 5:15; 7:8; cf. Deut. 4:10; Jer. 31:11). Thus, it seeks to inform "all the peoples of the earth" that "the hand of the LORD is powerful"—that Yahweh is a mighty, awesome God with whom they must reckon. Since "you (Israelites)" already know Yahweh's power, however, the episode seeks to elicit the proper response of such knowledge, the very response of Israel's ancestors at the Exodus (Ex. 14:31; cf. 15:11)—to fear Yahweh always. To "fear" Yahweh is to hold him in the highest respect—yes, with a realistic touch of terror—and to act accordingly. In sum, whenever Israel sees the stones—whenever the child asks and the adult answers—Israel remembers the might of Yahweh and rekindles their awe of that great God.

Epilogue: International Reaction (5:1)

THE DRIED-UP JORDAN AND Israelite crossing do not escape the notice of the kings on the west bank (the Amorites) and along the Mediterranean (the Canaanites). On the contrary, the report sparks the very reaction described by Rahab (5:1b virtually repeats 2:11a)—paralyzing terror and physical despair. The present comment both confirms Rahab's earlier diagnosis and anticipates a chain reaction of defensive moves by Canaanite kings to which Israel will respond and from which they will benefit (9:1; 10:1; 11:1).

Here the comment stresses that Israel's presence in Canaan—and especially the miracle that opened the entry gates—is no secret to their prospective adversaries. With the crossing, the die is cast: Conflict with the land's inhabitants is inevitable. The swollen Jordan also bars any chance of an Israelite retreat. Israel's only choice is to "do-or-die" on the west bank. Of course, memory of the miracle at the Jordan—a spectacular "amazing thing" done by Yahweh—buoys Israel's confidence of victory in whatever battles that lie ahead.

THE ARK OF THE covenant. The ark of the covenant stands at the center of this dramatic story and is clearly the key to everything happening around it. The ark serves as a kind of "divine crossing guard," stopping the Jordan's flow until all Israel, including the priests, have safely crossed into Canaan. Basically a gilded wooden box, the ark represents the footstool to God's throne and symbolizes the presence of Yahweh, otherwise invisible to human sight, amid Israel. The Old Testament narrates the ark's long, storied history: its construction at Mount Sinai by the artisan Bezalel (Ex. 25:10; 37:1); its placement within the tabernacle's Most Holy Place (26:33); its role as the place where God spoke to Israel through Moses (25:22; Num. 7:89) and repository of the law tablets (Deut. 10:2, 5; 1 Kings 8:9; cf. Heb. 9:4); its guidance of Israel through the wilderness (Num. 10:33–36; 14:44); its long residence in Solomon's temple (1 Kings 8:6); and its apparent role in cultic rituals (Ps. 132:8).

The ark is often called "the most sacred object in ancient Israel," a statement that several later episodes confirm.[49] The first is 1 Samuel 5–6, the somewhat humorous account of how, while in Philistine hands, the ark so disrupted Philistine life that they gladly returned it to Israel (see below). Three minor incidents illustrate the overwhelming power associated with the ark. For failing to pay it due respect, Yahweh killed seventy members of one family (1 Sam. 6:19), as he did a man named Uzzah, who touched it without authorization (2 Sam. 6:6–7). Small wonder that the dangers of possessing such a holy object terrified Israel, David included (1 Sam. 6:20; 2 Sam. 6:9).

By contrast, when treated properly, the Lord's blessing comes to those who treat it properly, as did Obed-Edom (2 Sam. 6:11). David retrieved the ark from its twenty-year exile at Kiriath Jearim and brought it to Jerusalem with great ceremony, installing it in a tent until its move into the temple (2 Sam. 6:16–19; 1 Kings 8:4). Interestingly, once there it apparently vanishes from history except for its mention by King Josiah three centuries later (2 Chron. 35:3). Jeremiah's prophecy that after Israel returns from exile the ark will not be remembered, missed, or remade (3:16) seems to have come true.[50] But Hebrews 9:4 remembers it, and John sees it in the heavenly temple (Rev. 11:19). Of course, it becomes the prized object in the motion picture *Raiders of the Lost Ark*, and some Ethiopian Christians claim that during Solomon's reign an Israelite priest secretly brought it to Ethiopia where it still resides today.[51]

---

49. These texts originally comprised a prebiblical source called "The Ark Narrative," a series of episodes that 1–2 Samuel incorporate (1 Sam. 4–6 + 2 Sam. 6). For contrasting views of its purpose, see A. Campbell, *The Ark Narrative* (Missoula, Mont.: Scholars Press, 1975); P. Miller, *The Hand of the Lord* (Baltimore: Johns Hopkins Univ. Press, 1977); cf. R. P. Gordon, *1 & 2 Samuel* (OT Guides; Sheffield: JSOT Press, 1984), 30–34; C. Seow, *Myth, Drama, and David's Dance* (Atlanta: Scholars Press, 1989), 55–76, who argues that 1 Samuel 4–6 intend to legitimate an early Israelite shrine at Kiriath Jearim.

50. Cf. R. Friedman, *Who Wrote the Bible?* (New York: Summit, 1987), 156: "There is no report that the Ark was carried away or destroyed or hidden.... The most important object in the world, in the biblical view, simply ceases to be in the story."

51. For one journalist's fascinating search for the ark in Ethiopia, see G. Hancock, *The Sign and the Seal* (New York: Simon and Schuster, 1992).

As fascinating as the ark is, modern Bible readers find the idea strange that a gilded wooden box would command such wonder and exude such power. Intrepid searches for the ark or the holy grail may make great movies but have little to do with daily life today. Since the Protestant Reformation (sixteenth cent. A.D.), many Christians (especially evangelical ones) no longer hold religious objects in special awe. Granted, they may wear lapel pins or necklaces with a cross, fish, or dove; or they may treat the church's altar or communion table with more respect than, say, a folding table for church suppers. But they are not afraid to approach, touch, or handle the altar or communion table lest they die on the spot. And at the end of the day they probably store the pin or necklace with their other jewelry. Though symbolic of sacred themes, these objects enjoy no direct touch of God's holiness or endowment of his frightening power. They are mere symbols — physical objects whose shape or associations point to events or meanings elsewhere.

Israel associated the ark with both the presence and the "hand (i.e., the power) of Yahweh" (e.g. Josh. 4:24).[52] Because of this, some readers may wonder how the ark differs from an idol. The key issue with idols is that ancient rituals made them into a repository for the divine essence. A deity's image was thought to actualize the deity himself or herself — to make it real or actual in a physical object. That is why ancient peoples treated them with such careful respect, for they thought that the image before them was a god. That is why idols formed the center of ancient worship. Through various cultic means, non-Israelites sought the intervention of treasured idols in their troubled lives. At the same time, they also felt free to carry the images around and to have them in their homes.

On one occasion Israel came close to treating the ark as if it were at least a magical good-luck charm, if not an actual idol. The Philistines had just inflicted a shattering defeat and great loss of life on Israel (1 Sam. 4). After the debacle, the response of Israel's leaders was to ask why Yahweh had done this to them and to order that the ark be sent to the next battle. That way, "it [the ark] will save us ... from ... our enemies" (4:3). The implication of their words is telling: Their reliance was not on the presence of Yahweh with the ark but on "it" (the ark itself). Like their idolatrous neighbors, they felt free to move it around as they wished — in this case, to a battlefield. They seemed close to believing that the ark somehow actualized Yahweh and his mysterious powers — surely, perceptions akin to idolatry.

---

52. This is particularly true of the ark narratives; cf. 1 Sam. 5:7, 11; 6:3; 2 Sam. 6:6; Seow, 73–74. For similar phrases in the Ancient Near East, see J. J. M. Roberts, "The Hand of Yahweh," *VT* 21 (1971): 244–51.

But the example from 1 Samuel 4 represents Israel's distorted view of the ark, not the biblical view of it. Their error was to equate the invisible Yahweh with the physical ark and to presume upon his powerful presence with it. It was their sincere perception of things, but a perception woefully out of touch with reality nonetheless. Subsequent events plainly show it as illusory. In the next battle, with the ark on scene, the Philistines again routed Israel and—worse—actually captured the ark and took it home (vv. 10–11). Its capture gave the lie to Israel's distorted perception. Apparently, the ark possessed no (or, at least, not enough) inherent power to defend itself against humans.

The biblical truth, by contrast, is that its powerful influence so evident on other occasions always derives from Yahweh's presence with it. Thus, the first key way in which the ark differs from idols is this: The ark may be *in* God's presence but it does not directly *mediate* God's presence as idols were thought to do. The ark also differs from idols in a second key way: As a physical object, the ark does not offer a physical representation of Yahweh—that is, what Yahweh actually looks like. In the ancient world, bulls might visually present other gods (Baal, for example), but a gilded box in no way presents a visible image of who Yahweh is. On the contrary, the Bible stresses that Yahweh is completely *invisible*, unavailable to human sight, and hence impossible to represent.

Indeed, behind the prohibition against idols (Ex. 20:4; Deut. 5:8) stands an assumption: Yahweh's majesty so defies physical representation by humans as to make all such attempts both futile and blasphemous. That was the error of the golden calves promoted by Aaron and King Jeroboam as representations of Yahweh (Ex. 32; 1 Kings 12:28; 2 Kings 10:29). They horribly *mis*represented him! They were nothing but ugly, grotesque, silly forgeries—insults to God himself—and earned both promoters just punishment.

One should also remember another related, important biblical idea. People who attempt to "look at God" himself run the risk of instant death simply for doing so (Judg. 13:22; cf. John 1:18). Two thoughts may underlie this. (1) To look on God means for sinful eyes to look starkly at divine holiness, and that clash accounts for the death feared. (2) To look on God may imply human control, however limited, over him. In the ancient world, to "look on" something was, in a sense, to exercise some control over it. Our expression to "keep (something) in our sights" offers a helpful analogy. To keep a danger or a foe in our sights is to deprive it of the element of surprise, to subject it to our intimidating counterlook, and to give us time to sort out our options. In other words, it gives us more control over the situation than we would have otherwise.

By the same token, our human experience may mislead us into thinking that to look on God somehow shifts some sovereignty into our hands. That, of course, is a blasphemous thought, one also worthy of sudden death. Humans exercise not even one scanty scintilla of sovereignty over God. To even entertain such a thought offends God's majesty and rightly earns his wrath. The whole idea of eyes connecting physically with God is out of the question. Thus, to look on the physical ark is not to look on God himself.

In other words, the ark is not an idol from the Bible's viewpoint. It is a symbol of Yahweh's invisible presence, not an actual physical representation of him. Neither individually nor as a whole do its physical properties (i.e., wood, gilding, adhesives, nails, cherubim, etc.) have any inherent powers. They are just inert physical objects. In short, as a symbol, the ark is like an arrow pointing away from itself to the invisible God hovering unseen above it. Despite the suggested similarities, it is not in fact an idol.

Remembrance of historic past events. Joshua 3 – 4 also stresses the remembrance of historic past events by God's people. Indeed, though dimly glimpsed, the text seems to reflect some ancient Israelite practice, perhaps at Gilgal, as the occasion for the question-and-answer dialogue (4:6 – 7, 21 – 22). Deuteronomy 16:16 requires that all Israelite men meet at the temple in Jerusalem three times each year — at the annual Feasts of Unleavened Bread (i.e., Passover), Weeks (or Pentecost), and Booths (cf. Ex. 34:23; 2 Chron. 8:13). Each festival remembers some important event in Israel's past, an event foundational to their national identity. In my view, such annual celebrations serve three purposes: (1) They ensure that Israel remembers the basic history; (2) they remind Israel of the unique identity and sovereignty of their God; and (3) they reaffirm the kind of conduct that pleases Yahweh and through which they are to live out their unique covenant identity.

For example, Moses commands Israel to "commemorate this day [the Exodus], the day you came out of Egypt, out of the land of slavery" (Ex. 13:3). The Passover reviews what happened at the Red Sea, reminds Israel of the overwhelming might of her covenant God, and reaffirms the availability of that power on any day. It also recalls Israel's hardship as oppressed slaves and, thus, cultivates an attitude of Yahweh-like compassion toward fellow Israelites suffering hardship (see, e.g., Lev. 25:25 – 28, 35 – 38, 39 – 43).

Consider also the brief liturgy that Israelites recite in bringing their offering of firstfruits during the Festival of Weeks (Deut. 26:3 – 11). Each sets his basket of grain before the altar at the temple and goes through a liturgical summary of Israel's early history. The summary runs from the patriarchs ("my father was a wandering Aramean . . ."), through the Egyptian oppression, the miraculous Exodus, and the settlement in Canaan (vv. 5 – 9). The offerer affirms that his grain gift acknowledges that the whole harvest is Yahweh's gift to Israel (v. 10).

Once again the ritual recalls the long historical scenario that led to this moment. It reaffirms Yahweh's identity and sovereignty — specifically, his "mighty hand and . . . outstretched arm" (Deut. 27:8) and generosity — and reasserts Israel's unique identity in practical terms. By confessing his slave background and his presence in Canaan, the Israelite confesses his dependence on Yahweh's goodness and, through his gift, acknowledges Yahweh's sovereign sway over his own life. In sum, this liturgy links the individual's personal story and faith with Israel's national story and identity.

The fear of God. Finally, Joshua stresses the purpose of the twelve stones for Israel — to cultivate the fear of God in Israel (4:24b). At first glance, modern readers squirm uncomfortably at the idea of having to "fear" God. Such a thought seems to set up a theological clash between the angry God of the Old Testament and the loving God of the New. It seems to clash with our image of Jesus as loving and compassionate. To speak of fearing God also conflicts with the values of our contemporary "feel-good" culture.

I offer three comments to help us engage this concept realistically. (1) The cold, hard reality is that the "fear of God" is a central biblical teaching. God deems it so fundamental that he even put Abraham through a severe test — the sacrifice of his only son, Isaac — to find out whether Abraham truly feared God (Gen. 22:12). To fear God is one of God's basic expectations of Israel (Deut. 10:12, 20; 1 Sam. 12:24; Prov. 24:21), and Peter also commands Christians to "fear God" (1 Peter 2:17). Thus, like it or not, Christians must "fear God" — whatever that means.

(2) That leads to my second comment — to define what "fear" means. In the Old Testament, the word "fear" means to treat with the highest respect or to hold in awe. In "fear" one responds to the greatness, majesty, and mystery of God. One squarely faces the gaping gap that divides Almighty God from puny humans. Biblical "fear" includes an element of "dread" or "alarm" at the thought of God. One senses a slight quickening of the pulse, a little sweating, a minor tensing of muscles, a feeling of being ill-at-ease. But such feelings derive from the awe that God's wondrous nature inspires in us, not from a dread of divine irritability. They reflect visceral recognition that God truly is awesome! In sum, to fear God is simply to take him very, very seriously — and to live accordingly.

(3) My final comment concerns how we do that. According to the Bible, the fear of God is more than just an abstract idea. On the contrary, believers

demonstrate that they fear God in specific actions. Consider a few selected biblical examples of such practical actions. Like Pharaoh's officials, to fear God is to take his word seriously (Ex. 9:20); like Israel's ancestors, it means to believe in him personally (Ex. 14:31; Ps. 40:3). To fear him compels one neither to insult the deaf verbally nor to trip up the blind (Lev. 19:14); it drives one to pay respect to old people (19:32) and to refrain from cheating others (25:17). It requires one to serve only him (1 Sam. 12:24) and to back up oaths by his name alone (Deut. 6:13), even when to do so hurts (Ps. 15:4). It is to affirm that

> the LORD your God is God of gods and Lord of lords, the great God, mighty and awesome, who shows no partiality and accepts no bribe. He defends the cause of the fatherless and the widow, and loves the alien, giving him food and clothing. (Deut. 10:17–18)

It means to put away other gods, to devote oneself exclusively to Yahweh (Josh. 24:14; Judg. 6:10), and to affirm, despite life's ups and downs, that Yahweh's "love endures forever" (Ps. 118:4). In short, we demonstrate that we fear God by doing specific things because we know that they please him.

MEMORY. "THERE ARE THREE things I can't remember," the old professor said. "I can't remember names, I can't remember faces, and ... hmm, let's see ..., well, I guess I can't remember the other thing I can't remember!" The human mind is a truly remarkable organ. The longer I live, the more amazed I am at the surprising things that my brain recalls. Even more amazing, scientists say that we only use a small percentage of our brain's total capacity.

We all face the problem of remembering—or, put differently, our tendency to forget. Part of the problem is that we have so much to remember these days. Modern media bombard our brains with all kinds of facts and claims, some of which ideally one ought to store away in memory. We must recall our social security number for official forms, our PIN number to retrieve cash from the ATM, and both our regular and cell phone numbers to tell others. Important dates also beckon for recall. The larger our family, the more birthdates and anniversaries require remembering, and the larger our circle of friends and coworkers, the more data about them we store away for recollection at the right moment. Many a spouse has paid a heavy price for forgetting an anniversary! Many an employee has suffered embarrassment for failing to match the right information with the right client!

Worse yet, we all live enslaved under a modern pharaoh known as "the tyranny of the urgent." Besides the media bombardment, "urgent" matters constantly crowd our consciousness jockeying for attention. We spend our days like a firefighter answering one alarm bell after another, leaving some of life's really important matters undone. The constant data bombardment and tyranny of the urgent leaves us with an uneasy feeling that our minds are hopelessly cluttered. Sadly, we recognize ourselves in Hazel, a character novelist John Steinbeck describes:

> ... casting about in Hazel's mind was like wandering alone in a deserted museum. Hazel's mind was choked with uncatalogued exhibits. He never forgot anything but he never bothered to arrange his memories. Everything was thrown together like fishing tackle in the bottom of a rowboat, hooks and sinkers and line and lures and gaffs all snarled up.[53]

The cluttered mind poses a unique danger to our lives. It makes us forget things which matter most, including our walk with Christ.

Joshua erected twelve stones at Gilgal so that future Israelite generations would remember what had happened there. He wanted Israel not to forget an astounding miracle (i.e., an "amazing thing")—that Israel had entered Canaan on dry ground because the ark stopped the Jordan's flow. Remembering that miracle would remind Israel of the unstoppable might of their warrior God and challenge them to reaffirm his sovereignty over their lives. It would drive them back to a firm, steady, convinced, life-altering fear of him. But we might ask, what miracles should we remember? And how should we remember them so that our fear of God remains high?

Of prime importance for Christians is the atoning death of Jesus Christ. The cross marks the crucial event, the historical watershed, that brought humanity salvation. It comprises the Christian counterpart of the Red Sea-Jordan crossing sequence for the Israelites. Further, like Joshua, Jesus took pains to ensure that his followers remember his death. At the Last Supper, he declared, "This is my body given for you" (Luke 22:19), in retrospect an allusion to his willing submission to crucifixion. But he adds, "Do this in remembrance of me," thereby instituting what we now practice as communion or the Eucharist.

Early Christians took his command literally, including the "breaking of bread" (i.e., communion) among their several acts of devotion (Acts 2:42). The apostle Paul quotes the above words of Jesus in his instructions concerning the Lord's Supper (1 Cor. 11:24). He even extends them to apply

---

53. J. Steinbeck, *Cannery Row* (New York: Bantam, 1945), 20.

to the cup of wine; we are to drink it in remembrance of him, too (v. 25). In short, the observance of the Lord's Supper is the prime way in which we remember "amazing things" God has done. They include the fact that Jesus voluntarily died so that, in the mysterious workings of God's plan, his followers might enjoy release from their slavery to sin. They include the close relationship with their Creator and loving Heavenly Father that faith in Christ restores. More important, Paul adds, our times of remembrance in reality constitute times of proclamation: ". . . whenever you eat this bread and drink this cup, you proclaim the Lord's death until he comes" (v. 26).

How can we make our communion observances both remembrance and proclamation? Joshua 3–4 and the Old Testament's practice of remembering suggest several things. (1) They remind us to include a review of the historical event(s) behind communion as part of our observance of it. Without the events of Passion Week, there is no crucifixion, and without the crucifixion there is no point to the Lord's Supper. In planning communion occasions, church leaders would do well to include Scriptures that narrate the events. I suggest that each occasion focus on one or two scenes from the gospel accounts of Jesus' final two days, thus reviewing the entire story over several months. In part, observances should feature the reading of those scriptural accounts.

But Scripture can be read in some creative ways. For example, Scripture may be read by groups on the model of a Greek chorus, by using a narrator and readers, by a minidrama acted out, by a leader and congregational response, and the like. Such creative, carefully thought-through readings can enhance communion times significantly. The participation each time of a few audience members or the whole congregation can deepen the experience for everyone.

The point is that the repetition of Scripture over time—and by "time," I mean years—will go a long way toward firmly fixing the events of Jesus' death in the minds of the congregation. Indeed, this practice may be more crucial than we might think in light of the pervasive influence of postmodern thought in the larger culture. In a world that has little interest in "the past," especially the distant past, churches would do well to keep the past alive among its members. It is essential that believers remember how Jesus went to the cross—and that his passion is actual history, not to be equated with *Star Wars* or *Beauty and the Beast*.

(2) Communion observances could be more family-centered. In Joshua 4, the remembrance of the Jordan crossing centers around a child's question and an adult's answer. Practical necessity probably led to it. Unlike today, each Israelite family did not have their own copy of the narrative about the Jordan crossing. Understanding of it had to pass from one generation to the

next through liturgies performed on site annually such as that (or those?) that I speculate underlie Joshua 3–4. Families had to pass it on by telling the story again and again over the years. Such family observances offer an obvious educational advantage: *Everyone* learns what happened and what it means, not just adults.

But an underlying theological assumption merits mention as well. To include children as participants in remembrance says that that remembrance has meaning for children as well as adults. Now, this suggestion to make communion occasions more family-centered may raise an unsettling ecclesiastical issue for some churches. Many bodies discourage, if not prohibit, children from taking communion before they complete confirmation or make their own personal profession of faith. But my point is not necessarily that children *take* communion but that they somehow *participate* in its observance. With proper instruction, they can fully enjoy their role in the church's remembrance while fully understanding the reason why they cannot take communion.

Further, I suggest the question-and-answer pattern of Joshua 4 as a pattern for a family communion reading. As an example, I offer the following:

Leader: We meet at this table because Jesus passed on this practice to his disciples who passed it on to us. We meet to remember what happened on the night that he was betrayed.

Child: (*holding up the bread*) This bread—what does it mean to you? Why do you eat it?

Parents: (*taking the bread*) We eat it because Jesus said, "This is my body given for you." We eat it to obey Jesus' command, "Do this in remembrance of me."

Child: (*holding up the cup*) This cup—what does it mean to you? Why do you drink it?

Parents: (*taking the cup*) We drink it because Jesus said, "This cup is the new covenant in my blood." We drink it to obey Jesus' command, "Do this, as often as you drink it, in remembrance of me."

Everyone: And so let us remember the death of Jesus. Let us eat and drink in his memory and, in so doing, "proclaim his death until he comes."

If done well and wisely, such simple ceremonies celebrate that Jesus died for everyone, young and old, even though only confirmed members or those of personal faith may actually take the elements. In addition, there are other ways to make the Lord's Supper more family-centered. Traditionally, church elders and/or clergy serve communion, but churches whose ecclesiology so allows might enlist families to serve communion and create appropriate ways for them to do so. I suggest also the inclusion of single-parent families, single adults, and senior citizens in these creative observances, for example, by forming them into symbolic families. The point is that, as everyone participates, everyone comes to learn and relearn the fundamental fact that Jesus died so that everyone, whatever their age or status, might have the forgiveness of sins.

Author William Barton illustrates why we observe communion in a parable by his fictional teacher, Safed the Sage, entitled "Things Not to Be Forgotten." One day Safed was traveling by train through Kansas when the train stopped for lunch. Disembarking, the wise man noticed a little park by the station in which stood a white post three feet high. Affixed on top Safed recognized an old-time draw-bar, coupling pin, and link used to couple train cars together. The post bore the inscription, "Lest We Forget." The Sage surmised that this was a memorial to the man who had invented the safety coupler, but the station clerk said he could not confirm that—he had never seen the post. The station manager said that he had forgotten whom it honored. Later, aboard the departing train, Safed mused on his experience:

> And I considered the days of my boyhood, when I played about the Cars, and I knew Railway men; and many of them lost fingers that were crushed in coupling cars; and many lost their hands, and others lost their lives.
>
> And I said, Behold, there was a man who considered all these things, and sat up nights, and peradventure pawned his Shirt that he might invent a method of avoiding all this. And here is his memorial, marked, Lest We Forget, and some men pass it every day and never see it; and others once knew its meaning but they have forgotten.
>
> And I looked out of the car window, and I beheld a Church, and upon the Church was a Spire, and upon the Spire was a Cross.
>
> And I thought of the multitudes who continually pass it by, and I was grieved in mine heart; for I said, Among them are those who say, I have never seen it; and others say, I have seen it, but what it meaneth, behold I know not. And others say, Behold I once knew, but I have forgotten.[54]

But I aver that, besides the cross of Christ, we remember our own personal "historic events." By this I mean the stories of events that mark crucial turning points in our spiritual pilgrimage. Perhaps it is the story of how we came to personal faith in Christ, how God healed us of some grave disease,

---

54. W. Barton, *Safed and Keturah* (Atlanta: John Knox, 1978), 52–53. The parables of Safed and his wife, Keturah, originally appeared as Barton's column in early issues of the *Christian Century*.

how God guided us to important decisions, how he shielded us from physical or spiritual dangers, or how he shepherded us through some deep, dark valley of despair. Granted, our stories do not have the saving significance of biblical events. They may also lack the miraculous element of biblical ones. But they have two important elements: They mark *memorable* life-changing events, and they are *ours*. They lead us to say, with young Pip in Charles Dickens' *Great Expectations*:

> That was a memorable day for me, for it made great changes in me. But it is the same with any life. Imagine one selected day struck out of it, and think how different its course would have been. Pause you who read this, and think for a moment of the long chain of iron or gold, of thorns or flowers, that would never have bound you, but for the formation of the first link on one memorable day.[55]

These memorable events confirm that the mighty God who parted the Red Sea and stopped the Jordan still does "amazing things" today. Furthermore, I advise us to find our own twelve stones — some tangible, symbolic object — to memorialize that event. Like Joshua's twelve stones, such symbols should obviously reflect some design and intention and be publically displayed in our homes, workplaces, or churches. But they should be subtle, usually without any inscription (unless it be a vague one). They are not a billboard or bumper sticker that puts out a relatively clear message in words. No, their critical function is to cause those who see them, who do not know their meaning, to ask questions. The questions then give us the opportunity to tell the personal story to which the symbol points.

I am aware of two examples in which believers follow the example of Joshua 3 – 4. My wife's mother has a friend who in his living room displays, in plain sight, a simple pile of stones. Their configuration reflects design and presupposes careful arrangement, which means that they are not there by accident. There is nothing written around them to explain their meaning. Nor does the man direct attention to them or prod his guests to pay the piled stones special notice. The stones sit silently, emitting a mute message that soon pricks the visitor's curiosity. When the latter finally asks, "What do these stones mean?" the host picks them up, sets them down on the coffee table, and replies, "Please sit down. Whew, have I got a story to tell you!" He then tells his curious guest his personal testimony of how Christ rescued his life from self-destruction.

Also, a simple, pleasantly configured arrangement of large stones stands in front of Community Bible Church in Central Point, Oregon. It bears

---

55. C. Dickens, *Great Expectations* (London: Oxford Univ. Press, 1978 [1861]), 67.

a bronze plaque that quotes the question-and-answer verses from Joshua 4, but it does not detail the "amazing thing" in the life of the church that occasioned it. At the time, significant numerical growth was straining the church's facilities, so the congregation launched a building program that required the raising of a quarter-million dollars to meet a series of large, monthly financial obligations. The dollar amount needed stretched the church's resources, but God faithfully provided it and the building program reached its goals. The simple stone monument remembers God's faithful provision during those critical months and, according to Pastor Pete Slusher, reminds the congregation that "the God who could supply a quarter-million dollars can take care of us."[56]

Both these examples model ways for us to bear witness to our experiences of God's "amazing things." By following their example, we ensure that our family and friends learn of God's work in our lives, and we testify that God still opens up our impassable Red Seas and puts a stop to our Jordans so that we can move ahead for God. These symbols demonstrate in tangible form that we do, indeed, fear God. Just as Joshua wanted.

God's presence among his people. Finally, the ark of the covenant plays such a prominent role in Joshua 3–4 that we might ask whether it might have a modern equivalent. In more liturgical churches, burning altar candles and incense symbolize God's presence among his people, while Roman Catholics affirm the "real presence" of Christ—his actual body and blood—in the elements of the Eucharist. More informal churches associate the presence of God with the presence in one place of his gathered people.

Two theological truths undergird this assumption: (1) Jesus' teaching that he is present whenever two or three believers meet together (Matt. 18:20); and (2) Paul's idea that both the corporate church (1 Cor. 3:16–17; 2 Cor. 6:16; Eph. 2:21) and the individual Christian (1 Cor. 6:19) constitute the temple in which God lives. Thus, according to this view, the presence of God becomes evident when the church gathers for worship. Jesus joins the assembled group in a special way, and the gathering, as it were, forms a mystical temple in which God dwells and in whom his Spirit works.

More commonly, Christians associate God's power with the Scripture and with the Holy Spirit. Both the Old and New Testaments acknowledge the power of God's Word to cause its announced events to happen (Num. 11:23; Isa. 24:3; 55:11; Heb. 4:12). That assumed power undergirds the preaching of the prophets and the proclamation of the gospel, especially when empowered by the Holy Spirit (1 Cor. 2:4–5; 1 Thess. 1:5; cf. Zech.

---

56. I am grateful to Pastor Slusher for sharing this story with me.

4:6). It also gives force to the gospel witnessing and Christian service that we do today. But one might argue that some Christian behaviors seem to treat the printed Bible itself as a sacred icon endowed with mysterious power. That assumption helps explain why some believers prominently enshrine it in their homes—and why they would not dare throw one away. They are too afraid that something akin to poor Uzzah's fate might befall them if they do!

Despite such questionable conduct, the point to remember is that, even without ark-like holy objects in our possession, God remains a powerful presence in our lives. He channels that power through Scripture and empowers both the Word and God's people through the Holy Spirit. It might be nice to have a spiritual magic wand that would, on command, release wonderful blessings or unleash terrible destruction. But Christians are not powerless. In Scripture they have the mighty Word of God, and in their midst moves the Spirit of God, both of which have power to work "amazing things" even today.

Joshua 5:2–6:27

§

At that time the LORD said to Joshua, "Make flint knives and circumcise the Israelites again." ³So Joshua made flint knives and circumcised the Israelites at Gibeath Haaraloth.

⁴Now this is why he did so: All those who came out of Egypt—all the men of military age—died in the desert on the way after leaving Egypt. ⁵All the people that came out had been circumcised, but all the people born in the desert during the journey from Egypt had not. ⁶The Israelites had moved about in the desert forty years until all the men who were of military age when they left Egypt had died, since they had not obeyed the LORD. For the LORD had sworn to them that they would not see the land that he had solemnly promised their fathers to give us, a land flowing with milk and honey. ⁷So he raised up their sons in their place, and these were the ones Joshua circumcised. They were still uncircumcised because they had not been circumcised on the way. ⁸And after the whole nation had been circumcised, they remained where they were in camp until they were healed.

⁹Then the LORD said to Joshua, "Today I have rolled away the reproach of Egypt from you." So the place has been called Gilgal to this day.

¹⁰On the evening of the fourteenth day of the month, while camped at Gilgal on the plains of Jericho, the Israelites celebrated the Passover. ¹¹The day after the Passover, that very day, they ate some of the produce of the land: unleavened bread and roasted grain. ¹²The manna stopped the day after they ate this food from the land; there was no longer any manna for the Israelites, but that year they ate of the produce of Canaan.

¹³Now when Joshua was near Jericho, he looked up and saw a man standing in front of him with a drawn sword in his hand. Joshua went up to him and asked, "Are you for us or for our enemies?"

¹⁴"Neither," he replied, "but as commander of the army of the LORD I have now come." Then Joshua fell facedown to

the ground in reverence, and asked him, "What message does my Lord have for his servant?"

¹⁵The commander of the LORD's army replied, "Take off your sandals, for the place where you are standing is holy." And Joshua did so.

⁶:¹Now Jericho was tightly shut up because of the Israelites. No one went out and no one came in.

²Then the LORD said to Joshua, "See, I have delivered Jericho into your hands, along with its king and its fighting men. ³March around the city once with all the armed men. Do this for six days. ⁴Have seven priests carry trumpets of rams' horns in front of the ark. On the seventh day, march around the city seven times, with the priests blowing the trumpets. ⁵When you hear them sound a long blast on the trumpets, have all the people give a loud shout; then the wall of the city will collapse and the people will go up, every man straight in."

⁶So Joshua son of Nun called the priests and said to them, "Take up the ark of the covenant of the LORD and have seven priests carry trumpets in front of it." ⁷And he ordered the people, "Advance! March around the city, with the armed guard going ahead of the ark of the LORD."

⁸When Joshua had spoken to the people, the seven priests carrying the seven trumpets before the LORD went forward, blowing their trumpets, and the ark of the LORD's covenant followed them. ⁹The armed guard marched ahead of the priests who blew the trumpets, and the rear guard followed the ark. All this time the trumpets were sounding. ¹⁰But Joshua had commanded the people, "Do not give a war cry, do not raise your voices, do not say a word until the day I tell you to shout. Then shout!" ¹¹So he had the ark of the LORD carried around the city, circling it once. Then the people returned to camp and spent the night there.

¹²Joshua got up early the next morning and the priests took up the ark of the LORD. ¹³The seven priests carrying the seven trumpets went forward, marching before the ark of the LORD and blowing the trumpets. The armed men went ahead of them and the rear guard followed the ark of the LORD, while the trumpets kept sounding. ¹⁴So on the second day they marched around the city once and returned to the camp. They did this for six days.

¹⁵On the seventh day, they got up at daybreak and marched around the city seven times in the same manner, except that on that day they circled the city seven times. ¹⁶The seventh time around, when the priests sounded the trumpet blast, Joshua commanded the people, "Shout! For the LORD has given you the city! ¹⁷The city and all that is in it are to be devoted to the LORD. Only Rahab the prostitute and all who are with her in her house shall be spared, because she hid the spies we sent. ¹⁸But keep away from the devoted things, so that you will not bring about your own destruction by taking any of them. Otherwise you will make the camp of Israel liable to destruction and bring trouble on it. ¹⁹All the silver and gold and the articles of bronze and iron are sacred to the LORD and must go into his treasury."

²⁰When the trumpets sounded, the people shouted, and at the sound of the trumpet, when the people gave a loud shout, the wall collapsed; so every man charged straight in, and they took the city. ²¹They devoted the city to the LORD and destroyed with the sword every living thing in it—men and women, young and old, cattle, sheep and donkeys.

²²Joshua said to the two men who had spied out the land, "Go into the prostitute's house and bring her out and all who belong to her, in accordance with your oath to her." ²³So the young men who had done the spying went in and brought out Rahab, her father and mother and brothers and all who belonged to her. They brought out her entire family and put them in a place outside the camp of Israel.

²⁴Then they burned the whole city and everything in it, but they put the silver and gold and the articles of bronze and iron into the treasury of the LORD's house. ²⁵But Joshua spared Rahab the prostitute, with her family and all who belonged to her, because she hid the men Joshua had sent as spies to Jericho—and she lives among the Israelites to this day.

²⁶At that time Joshua pronounced this solemn oath: "Cursed before the LORD is the man who undertakes to rebuild this city, Jericho:

"At the cost of his firstborn son
will he lay its foundations;

at the cost of his youngest
will he set up its gates."

²⁷So the LORD was with Joshua, and his fame spread
throughout the land.

WITH ISRAEL NOW CAMPED at Gilgal and Israel's
first target reconnoitered, readers expect an
attack on the small town of Jericho only a few
miles away. They are not disappointed, but two
militarily strange but crucial preparations apparently must precede the
assault. Rather than a single, continuous narrative, the text comprises two
brief reports of preparations at Gilgal (5:2–12) and the report of the ritual
siege of Jericho (6:2–27). The preparations include circumcision (5:2–8)
and the celebration of Passover (5:9–12), while the main report of Jericho's
fall has its own preface—Joshua's curious encounter with a mysterious
stranger (5:13–6:1).

Exodus 12:48–50 clearly provides the background for the circumcision
scene, Leviticus 23:5–6 for the Passover observance. The writer's transparent but unstated concern is that the arriving Israelites line up properly
with the Instruction of Moses. Like chapters 3–4, the present narratives
follow a pattern of divine command and human obedience (see 5:2, 3; 6:2,
6) and clearly intend to portray what follows, not as a military venture, but
as a religious one. Given their concern with cultic matters, some scholars
believe that they reflect the contributions of Israelite priests to the book
of Joshua.

Chapter 6 requires special introductory comment.[1] As with the Jordan
crossing (Josh. 3–4), a command-execution schema structures the passage literarily.[2] Orders flow down the chain of command from Yahweh
to Joshua (6:2–5) and from him to the priests (v. 6) and the people (vv. 7,
16–19), who execute them (vv. 8–15, 20–21).[3] Thematically, the schema

---

1. The Greek and Hebrew texts of Joshua 6:1–15 differ in some details but tell the same
basic story. LXX is much shorter than MT, but MT also clarifies some important points. For
further discussion, see E. Noort, "The Disgrace of Egypt: Joshua 5:9a and Its Context," in *The
Wisdom of Egypt*, ed. A. Hilhorst and G. H. van Kooten (Leiden: Brill, 2005), 12–13; Nelson,
Joshua, 83–85 (with parallel English translations of LXX). In Nelson's view (87), LXX offers
"the earliest recoverable text" of the story, MT an "expanded version."

2. Nelson, *Joshua*, 91–92; Hawk, *Joshua*, 88, who provides a convenient chart of the
schema (88–89).

3. The narrator also reports two of Joshua's commands in retrospect (vv. 10, 22), followed by reports of compliance (vv. 20, 23, 25).

underscores the intimate connection between divine directives and promises, human obedience, and successful outcomes.[4]

Further, like the crossing, the conquest procedure bears all the earmarks of a ritual procession rather than a typical military assault (cf. 8:2).[5] Yahweh prescribes a solemn seven-day ceremony featuring priests bearing the ark and blowing trumpets (6:4–5). The statistical prominence of the number "seven"/"seventh" (vv. 4, 6, 8, 13, 15, 16) is striking, and the number's association with religious rituals gives Joshua 6 a distinctly cultic feel.[6] But ancient parallels, especially the Keret text from Ugarit, suggest that this seven-day format comprises a common literary convention for war under divine guidance—not a battle report but a narrative of Yahweh's war.[7] Its intention is not to report a siege but to celebrate Yahweh.[8] The sacred number also may signal the totality, completeness, and perfection of Yahweh's victory over Jericho.[9] However, notwithstanding the many literary connections with the Jordan crossing narrative, the ark's role here is clearly less prominent than in chapters 3–4. In fact, it completely disappears after v. 13 and plays no role in the collapse of the city wall. Instead, the spotlight falls on the symbolic processional, the trumpet blasts, and the people's shout.

The striking use of trumpets and shouts reflects the combined military and ritual background of Yahweh's war. Elsewhere, the two noisemakers prominently figure in both martial and cultic contexts and, hence, give the present report military and religious connotations. Joshua 6, therefore, marks the literary culmination of the rituals in chapter 5 by which Israel sanctifies themselves for Yahweh's war and Yahweh sets aside Jericho as "holy" (dedicated to him through destruction).[10] Thematically, Joshua 5–6

---

4. Hawk, *Joshua*, 92.

5. For an insightful exploration of the tension between the text's cultic and military aspects, see R. B. Robinson, "The Coherence of the Jericho Narrative: A Literary Reading of Joshua 6," in *Konsequente Traditionsgeschichte*, ed. R. Bartelmus et al. (Göttingen: Vandenhoeck & Ruprecht, 1993), 322–30.

6. *Seven* priests are to carry *seven* trumpets on each of *seven* days and then on *seven* circuits of Jericho on the *seventh* day (v. 4 [4x]; vv. 6, 8, 13 [2x]; v. 15 [3x]; v. 16 [1x]); cf. P. P. Jenson, "שֶׁבַע," *NIDOTTE*, 4:34–37.

7. D. E. Fleming, "The Seven-Day Siege of Jericho in Holy War," in *Ki Baruch Hu*, ed. R. Chazan, W. W. Hallo, and L. H. Schiffman (B. A. Levine Festschrift; Winona Lake, Ind.: Eisenbrauns, 1999), 211–28. Fleming stresses that such narratives have no specific cultic setting, including Gilgal (the oft-proposed candidate).

8. Ibid., 214.

9. Howard, *Joshua*, 169. For additional background on seven/seventh and on trumpets and shouts, see Bridging Contexts below.

10. For the suggestion that the present text combines three original versions of a ritual, cf. J. Wilcoxsen, "Narrative Structure and Cult Legend: A Study of Joshua 1–6," in *Transitions in Biblical Scholarship*, ed. J.Rylaarsdam (Chicago: Univ. of Chicago Press, 1968), 52–53. For other critical views, see Fritz, *Josua*, 68; Nelson, *Joshua*, 88.

emphasizes that Israel must ritually prepare for Yahweh's war and for what proves to be a unique theophany. Joshua also further establishes himself as Israel's respected leader.

Preparations at Gilgal (5:2 – 12)

THE CIRCUMCISION CEREMONY (VV. 2 – 9). How does Israel prepare for the coming attack on Jericho? In his first speech since 4:15 – 16, Yahweh decrees that Joshua must lead Israel in a circumcision ceremony using flint knives (vv. 2 – 9).[11] As is well known, Yahweh instituted this rite — the ritual removal of the foreskin of the penis — as the sign of his covenant with Abraham's descendants and the symbol of Israel's unique identity (Gen. 17:10 – 14; Lev. 12:3).[12] "At that time" apparently places the present ceremony during the four days between Israel's arrival at Gilgal and the Passover observance (Josh. 5:10 – 12). But the comment (v. 2b) that this marks a *second* occasion of circumcision ("again," is *šenit* [lit., "a second time"]) is puzzling since the Bible records no *first* circumcision of Israel by Joshua. Probably the text speaks broadly, counting preexodus circumcision in Egypt as the "first" time and Joshua's circumcision here as the "second" (cf. 4 – 5).[13]

But the real question is why Yahweh commands that circumcision be done *now*. Amid Israel's risky intrusion into Canaan, why perform a religious rite that would sideline Israel's soldiers for days of painful recovery? (1) The risk may in fact not be all that great. Recall that news of the miraculous crossing had immobilized the Canaanite monarchs with fear (5:1), so they apparently pose no real threat to the Israelite camp.

(2) Joshua 4:19 dates the crossing to the tenth day of the first month, creating the expectation of a Passover observance four days later (Lev. 23:5). That only the circumcised could participate (Ex. 12:44, 48) explains the

---

11. For background on flint knives, see Howard, *Joshua*, 148, n.257. The LXX of Josh. 24:31 says that these knives were buried with Joshua in his tomb. For an in-depth summary of the scholarly discussion concerning this passage, see M. N. van der Meer, *Formation and Reformulation: The Redaction of the Book of Joshua in the Light of the Oldest Textual Witnesses* (VTSup 102; Leiden: Brill, 2001), 249 – 327.

12. Egyptians and West Semites commonly practiced it, but the Philistines did not (Judg. 14:3; 1 Sam. 14:6). For discussion of its possible background as a marriage or fertility rite (cf. Gen. 34; Ex. 4:24 – 26), see R. Hall, "Circumcision," *ABD*, 1:1025 – 27; Boling, *Joshua*, 188, 189, 193 – 94.

13. So Howard, *Joshua*, 148; but cf. J. Sasson, "Circumcision in the Ancient Near East," *JBL* 85 (1966): 473 – 76, who suggests an actual second circumcision of Israelites who had been circumcised the Egyptian way. Alternatively, the LXX omits "second time" and explains that some Israelites of the Exodus generation had not been circumcised at all.

attention that the author devotes to the procedure here.[14] Unlike their ancestors who died in the wilderness, the generation born in the wilderness had not been circumcised (vv. 4–7).[15]

(3) Circumcision ensures the ritual fitness of Israel's soldiers (lit., "men of war," vv. 4, 6), a requirement for the upcoming war of Yahweh. The evocative phrase "a land flowing with milk and honey" (v. 6b), a tasty echo of Israel's ancient hopes, reminds the reader that ultimately possession of the land is at stake here.[16] In short, at issue is a question that echoes throughout the book: Will *this* generation — the one Yahweh graciously preserved in the wilderness (v. 7) — obey him and keep (not lose) the land? Joshua himself obeys by circumcising the "nation," ensuring that the earlier sad history not repeat itself (v. 8), at least not for now. The ritual marks this younger Israel as Yahweh's covenant people and ritually fit to occupy the land.

A solemn pronouncement by Yahweh ("Today I have rolled away ...") gives it even greater meaning for all Israel ("you" is plural) and ties it to the place name "Gilgal" (v. 9). What is this "reproach of Egypt" that Yahweh declares as rolled away? Two similar phrases suggest that the reproach here is the scorn that Egypt has heaped on Israel (Ezek. 16:57; Zeph.2:8; Ps. 89:50), but the reason for it is unclear. One possible reason is Israel's slavery in Egypt, but that seems unlikely, since the present wilderness generation would not have personally suffered Egyptian scorn for slavery.[17] Verses 4–6 suggest another possible reason for the humiliation — the terrible judgment that befell the Exodus generation for disobedience. Certainly, the text seems to imply that the present circumcision ends that sad era.[18]

But, in my view, the best explanation factors in all the motifs of vv. 4–7: the dead generation's failure and judgment, Yahweh's gift of land, and the younger generation's uncircumcised status. The uncircumcision symbolizes the whole sorry period of landless wandering and the cynical interpretive spin that Egypt gave it. The "reproach of Egypt" would be Egypt's biting ridicule that Yahweh had royally snookered poor Israel, promising the

---

14. The formal opening formula "Now this is why ..." introduces explanations (Ex. 29:1; Judg. 21:11; 1 Kings 11:27; Isa. 38:7).

15. Since Num. 14:29 condemns only men twenty-one and older to die in the wilderness, there is a possibility that some men of the Exodus generation twenty or younger might also have survived; cf. Noort, "The Disgrace of Egypt," 12–13.

16. For the phrase, see Ex. 3:8, 17; 13:5; 33:3; Lev. 20:24; Num. 13:27; 14:8; 16:13, 14; Deut. 6:3; 11:9; 26:9, 15; 27:3; 31:20.

17. Against Hertzberg, *Josua*, 33; Boling, *Joshua*, 190; *Butler*, Joshua, 59. Vv. 4–7 mention the exodus from Egypt but not the oppression in Egypt. For a list of alternative interpretive options and discussion, see Noort, "The Disgrace of Egypt," 14–18.

18. So Hess, *Joshua*, 122.

moon but leaving their high hopes bogged down in the desert sands (see Ex. 32:12; Num. 14:13 – 16; Deut. 9:28).[19] Through circumcision (and in Canaan, too!), this generation confirms its obedient spirit and gives Yahweh warrant to declare the past humiliation dead and buried, never to be thrown accusingly at Israel again. In essence, Yahweh welcomes this generation to his covenant and grants it a fresh start in his land. Henceforth, Israel will call the site where Yahweh "rolled (it) away" Gilgal, the name evoking memories of Yahweh's historic declaration.[20]

The Passover observance (vv. 10 – 12). The observance of Passover marks the second important prebattle activity (vv. 10 – 12). This takes place four days after Israel's arrival, with the people encamped at Gilgal in the plains of Jericho. They celebrate it "on the evening" of the fourteenth day, testimony to their careful conformity to divine instructions (Ex. 12:6; Deut. 16:4, 6).[21] This is further evidence that an obedient spirit guides the younger generation, at least thus far.

Indeed, Israel as a people temporarily replaces Joshua at center stage in the scene. Their prominence leaves the impression that Israel initiates Passover on their own, without prompting from either Yahweh or Joshua. The symbolic importance of this event for the new arrivals merits mention. Passover remembers the night when the tenth plague — the death of the firstborn — struck Egypt but spared Israel (Ex. 12). On that night Israel actually left slavery behind and entered a new era, life as a free people. The last recorded observance of Passover took place at the beginning of Israel's second year out of Egypt (Num. 9).[22] Thus, as Israel's first Passover in the new land, this celebration signals a new beginning for their national life.[23]

---

19. Cf. Howard, *Joshua*, 151 – 52; Noort, 18 – 19.

20. "Roll away" and "Gilgal" both derive from the root *galal*; cf. *DCH*, 348, 355.

21. Scholars who attribute this text to Israelite priests appeal to this and other ties between 5:2 – 12 and Mosaic instructions as evidence; cf. J. A. Wagenaar, "The Cessation of Manna: Editorial Frames for the Wilderness Wandering in Exodus 16,35 and Joshua 5,10 – 12," *ZAW* 112 (2000): 200 – 201.

22. Hess (*Joshua*, 123) and Howard (*Joshua*, 153) rightly argue that the present observance recalls the first Passover in Egypt rather than any later celebrations in the wilderness. For recent literary-critical discussion of vv. 10 – 12, see van der Meer, *Formation and Reformulation*, 315 – 29, 393 – 408; Wagenaar, "Cessation of Manna," 198 – 209; and C. Brekelmans, "Joshua v 10 – 12: Another Approach," *OTS* 25 (1989): 89 – 95.

23. Within the larger DH, it also anticipates the next reported observance six centuries later under King Josiah (2 Kings 23:21 – 23). The Chronicler reports that King Hezekiah also led an observance in the previous century, especially inviting northern tribes to join (2 Chron. 30). A comment in v. 5 ("it had not been celebrated in large numbers") suggests either that Israel had observed it infrequently or that the turnout of worshipers was often poor.

Indeed, the narrator highlights two notable events in successive days to confirm the dawning of a new day for Israel.

The day after Passover the people feed themselves for the first time with food grown in their new land (Josh. 5:11).[24] They eat two Middle Eastern staples, "unleavened bread [cakes]" and "roasted [i.e., cooked] grain."[25] How Israel comes by this food is not stated, although we know that they arrive at harvest time (3:15). The mention of unleavened bread presupposes both access to and use of grain milled into flour. The point is that the food is "homegrown" in Canaan, not provisions brought with them (cf. 1:11). At the same time, the two specific items constitute a kind of ancient "fast food"—simple, easy-to-fix fare ideal for people in a hurry.[26] Once settled, Israel will have time enough fully to savor Canaan's diverse, rich bounty.

The second notable event occurs the next day. Since Israel now eats off the land, their daily supply of manna, that mysterious food that fed them through the wilderness, stops (v. 12; cf. Ex. 16:31–33; Deut. 8:3).[27] The note that "there was no longer any manna for the Israelites" interprets this event as the end of an era—the Exodus-wilderness period. Indeed, literarily the events that end the wilderness wandering—crossing, circumcision, Passover (Josh. 3–5; see comment on ʿabar on 6:7)—actually mirror those that precede it (i.e., the Exodus), albeit in reverse order (Ex. 12–14).[28]

Ahead lies the new era ("that year") of living off the land of Canaan (see Ex. 16:35). "Harvest" and "produce" here are not yet "milk and honey," but for these veteran desert nomads every fresh, tasty bite confirms that they are home. Yahweh has kept his promise to get them there, and full enjoyment of the land lies near at hand (cf. Deut. 6:11). "Produce of Canaan" may also have a military connotation here. The food supply of ancient armies besieging a city came from local fields, orchards, and vineyards (Deut. 20:19–20). Thus, the term may specifically relate to the land conquest motif of Joshua—Israel's army feeding itself from local food stocks.[29]

---

24. The Hebrew of v. 11 is emphatic ("the next day ... on that very same day").

25. "Unleavened bread" (*maṣṣot*) is a common food item (Judg. 6:19; 1 Sam. 28:24) and also given as an offering (Lev. 2:4; Num. 6:15). It comprises part of the required diet during Passover (Ex. 12:15; Deut. 16:8; Ezek. 45:21), although eaten along with bitter herbs (Ex. 12:8; Num. 9:11). For "roasted grain," see Lev. 2:14 and a related word in Ruth 2:14; 1 Sam. 25:18.

26. Nelson, *Joshua*, 79; Howard, *Joshua*, 154; cf. Gen. 19:3; Ex. 12:34; 1 Sam. 17:17; 25:18. According to Wagenaar ("The Cessation of Manna," 204), this two-part list may derive from a similar list of food in Lev. 23:14.

27. NRSV dates the events of vv. 11 and 12 to the same day, but MT and LXX seem to support NIV's rendering "the day after the Passover ... they ate...."

28. See Wagenaar, "The Cessation of Manna," 208, who credits the so-called priestly writer with this self-conscious patterning; cf. Brekelmans, "Joshua v 10–12," 91–92.

29. Cf. Wagenaar, "The Cessation of Manna," 204–5.

In other words, in these brief events, sunset falls across Israel's sorry past forty years while a joyous new day dawns on the Israelite camp. Yes, battles lie ahead, but for the moment Israel pauses to reflect on Passover, celebration of salvation in the past, and to relish the present goodness of their new land and of the God who had brought them there.

The Ritual Siege of Jericho (5:13 – 6:27)

THE MYSTERIOUS STRANGER (5:13 – 6:1). A brief scene involving a mysterious stranger shifts attention from preparation to conquest.[30] As preface to the conquest of Jericho, the scene signals the transition from Israel's arrival in Canaan to its movement inland. But from the outset, the scene has an eerie, otherworldly feel to it. We are told neither what Joshua is doing there, nor how this episode relates chronologically to its context. We do not even know whether it is day or night.[31] Somewhere "near Jericho," Joshua spots a man standing across from him holding his sword unsheathed (v. 13).[32] The sword tells Joshua that the man is a soldier ready for combat, but the reader wonders how he can take a savvy Joshua by surprise. Has he suddenly appeared "out of thin air"?

Interestingly, the phrase "drawn sword" elsewhere occurs only with "the angel of the LORD" (Num. 22:23; 1 Chron. 21:16) and, thus, creates the expectation in readers (but in not Joshua) that the "man" is in fact a divine messenger in human form. It is almost comic to watch Joshua, oblivious to the other party's true identity, commandingly confront and interrogate him. Two other surprises await Joshua later, the first no laughing matter (7:1–6), the second yielding unexpectedly good results for Israel (chs. 9–10).

Joshua's question ("Are you for us or for our enemies?") seeks the man's military affiliation. He answers "Neither" (v. 14), then identifies himself as the "captain of the army of the LORD," a title that occurs only here and in v. 15.[33] The title "army commander" usually designates a man who

---

30. Wagenaar (ibid., 205) and others compare it to the vision report in which the goddess Ishtar appears to the Assyrian king, Ashurbanipal, before a military campaign. She also bears a drawn sword as does the figure in Josh. 5:13. For a critical assessment of past scholarly approaches to Joshua 6, see Robinson, "The Coherence of the Joshua Narrative," 312–20.

31. Perhaps, like any good commander, Joshua is there to gather intelligence concerning the city's size, layout, and defenses. He is, after all, the one who sent the spies (Josh. 2).

32. Lit., "he [Joshua] raised his eyes and looked, and—look!—a man...." The "look!" voices Joshua's perspective, especially his astonishment (so Howard, *Joshua*, 156). For the use of *hinneh* to indicate surprise, see WO §40.2.1.

33. We need not emend MT *lo'* ("no, not") to *lo* ("to him") after LXX and Syriac. NIV and NRSV ("Neither") are misleading since they wrongly imply that the messenger does not support Israel's cause (so Howard, *Joshua*, 156, n.285).

leads the army of a king, someone famous enough to be remembered by name.[34] But the Old Testament also understands that Yahweh has a heavenly army (his "hosts," hence his title "LORD of hosts," NRSV; 1 Kings 22:19; Ps. 103:19−21), that Israel, too, is his "army" (Ex. 7:4; 12:41; 1 Sam. 17:45), and that Yahweh leads both as king.[35]

The visitor's answer underscores what is important, his identity as God's on-site commander, not his loyalties to either Israel or Canaan. Once the stranger's words hit home, Joshua falls face down on the ground and worships him (v. 14b; see below), a gesture of high respect that an inferior pays a superior (i.e., Ruth 2:10; 2 Sam. 9:6; 14:22; 2 Chron. 20:18). Joshua acts out his recognition that the "army" is God's almighty, invisible host and the stranger is an angelic figure in human form (see also Gen. 18; Judg. 13). Joshua no longer needs to ascertain the man's loyalty—the man is clearly a "friend" come to support Israel.

But Joshua knows that Yahweh only dispatches such a commander for a high purpose, so he asks (lit.), "What is my Lord commanding his servant to do?" (v. 14c). "My Lord" and "his "servant" show Joshua's submission to the stranger's authority; Joshua requests marching orders for battle. Yahweh has already commissioned Joshua to lead Israel into the land (Josh. 1), so the present question seeks specific direction from his superior for the immediate moment.

Surprisingly, the commander orders, "Take off your sandals, for the place where you are standing is holy" (v. 15a). The command virtually quotes Yahweh's familiar orders to Moses at the burning bush (Ex. 3:5). Literarily, the echoed wording links the two scenes, reconfirming Joshua as Moses' successor and—more important—forever marking this episode as Joshua's "burning bush experience."[36] Moreover, it creates the huge expectation of an imminent theophany, perhaps one comparable to Yahweh's descent on Mount Sinai (Ex. 19).[37]

"Holy [ground]" is a sure sign that Yahweh is present and about to speak (cf. Ex. 3:2−4:17; 6:2−5), since his holy presence is the only thing able to sanctify space. It remains to be seen whether this place as "holy" also defines the status of Jericho in God's eyes. Surrounded by holiness, Joshua

---

34. Gen. 21:22 (Phicol); Judg. 4:2 (Sisera); 1 Sam. 14:50 (Abner); 2 Sam. 10:16 (Shobach); 1 Kings 1:19 (Joab); 16:16 (Omri); 2 Kings 5:1 (Naaman); but cf. 2 Kings 4:3; 25:19; 2 Chron. 33:11; cf. Robinson, "The Coherence of the Joshua Narrative," 321.

35. For discussion of "army" (Heb. *ṣabaʾ*), see conveniently Howard, *Joshua*, 157−58; T. Longman III, "צָבָא," *NIDOTTE*, 3:734−35.

36. Contrast Butler, *Joshua*, 62, who stresses Joshua's dependence on Moses ("Wherever he turns, Joshua cannot escape the Mosaic shadow").

37. Robinson, "The Coherence of the Joshua Narrative," 321.

wisely removes his sandals in adoration and awaits the divine voice (v. 15b). Instead, the writer interposes a short parenthesis to inform us that Israel's threatening presence has caused the city to shut its gates tight, barring both entry and exit (6:1).[38]

This is no throw-away line. Chapter 5 lays out Israel's transition to the land and preparations for doing Yahweh's war. It ends with the surprising, climactic arrival on scene of Yahweh and his invisible army. Jericho senses the severe threat, seals itself off, and trusts its fate to its walled defenses. So, an ancient combat scene once again repeats itself—an invading army poised at the gates and a city sealed for a siege. In Boling's words, "All is at last in readiness for the warfare."[39]

The ritual siege of Jericho (6:2–25). The central scene, the ritual siege of Jericho proper (6:2–25), now follows, and, as expected, the supreme commander speaks (vv. 2–5). He reassures Joshua with the assurance-of-victory formula ("I have delivered Jericho into your hands," v. 2).[40] Grammatically, the formula paints Jericho's "fall" as an already "done deal," and it echoes Yahweh's earlier promise to Joshua to be with him and never leave him (1:2–5).[41] Jericho's demise is Yahweh's gift to them, not Israel's own military achievement. Fittingly, those destined for Israel's hands include both Jericho's king and soldiers, both of whom earlier sought to capture the two spies (Josh. 2:2, 3, 7, 22).[42] This time the tables are turned: Those who attempted that capture will soon suffer capture themselves.

God's instructions (vv. 3–5) sketch a general overview with few details. Israelite soldiers are specifically to "encircle" (not merely "march around") the city once each day for six days (v. 3)—a six-day, symbolic siege of Jericho.[43] For six days seven priests are each to carry a ram's horn trumpet

---

38. This reading presumes that Exodus 3 and Joshua 5:13–15 closely parallel each other. Alternatively, the subject-initial syntax of 6:1 might signal the opening of a new episode rather than a parenthesis.

39. Boling, *Joshua,* 194.

40. For the formula, see Fritz, *Josua,* 69. Similar formulae occur in Assyrian and Babylonian texts. Later, Yahweh will voice the same reassurance in sending Israel against Ai (8:1); cf. Deut. 2:24 (concerning the Amorite King Sihon); Josh. 2:24.

41. Cf. Hawk, *Joshua,* 91–92.

42. Joshua 2 calls the soldiers simply "men" or "pursuers," not the more specific military phrase "fighting men" (Heb. *gibbor ḥayil*), as here. For the latter, see also Josh. 1:14; 8:3; 10:7; 2 Kings 24:14; but cf. 2 Kings 15:20 (NRSV "the wealthy"); Ruth 2:1; 1 Kings 11:28. For other uses, see H. Kosmala, "גָּבַר," *TDOT,* 2:374; R. Wakely, "גָּבַר," *NIDOTTE,* 1:810–11.

43. By itself, *sabab ʾet haʿir* could mean either "to march around the city" (cf. Ps. 48:13) or "to surround" it (Gen. 37:7; Job 40:22; Ps. 22:12). But the parallel, causative verb *naqap* hi. ("to encircle, surround"; Job 19:6; 2 Kings 6:14; 11:8 // 2 Chron. 23:7; Ps. 17:9; 88:18; Lam. 3:5) favors the second sense (cf. LXX *peristeson* ["stand around in a circle"]).

---

ahead of the ark of the covenant (v. 4a). Their small numbers cannot "encircle" the city, so presumably their task each day is to march around the city already "besieged" by the prepositioned soldiers. In effect, the circuits of the ark enclose Jericho in a deadly ring of Yahweh's power and doom it to fall before that power.[44] The seventh day marks the ceremony's climax. On that day, with the troops in place, the trumpet-bearing priests are to march around the city seven times, blowing steadily on their instruments (v. 4b–5). After the last circuit, they are to sound a long blast, the signal for the people to raise a mighty shout (v. 5a).

Interestingly, the instruction details the movements of the soldiers and priests but not of the people. But since they are each to attack the city straight ahead, they presumably either trail the ark on its daily circuits or (more likely, in my view) participate with the soldiers in the symbolic siege. Elsewhere similar shouts issue a war cry that signals the beginning of battle (1 Sam. 4:5). That sense fits here, too: Their shout announces the attack—the tumbling of the massive wall of Jericho and the Israelite onslaught inside the city (v. 5b). The wall is literally to "fall under itself"—to collapse right where it stands—opening easy access inside Jericho. The connection between the people's cry and the fall of Jericho seems fitting in two respects. It represents the people's participation, however limited, in Yahweh's war; the victory is *their* victory, too. It also symbolizes that the land—here personified by the city of Jericho—will, indeed, become theirs.

Immediately, Joshua issues an order to execute Yahweh's battle plan (vv. 6–7). Seven priests, each with a ram's horn, are to lead the priests carrying the ark of the covenant (v. 6; cf. v. 4). Joshua also commands the people, "Move out! Surround the city" (v. 7, my translation).[45] Strikingly, the first command invokes ʿabar ("to cross over"), the dominant verb in the Jordan crossing narrative, with the relatively rare sense "to proceed" (see Gen. 18:5; Num. 22:26; Judg. 12:1). Its repetition here marks the advance on Jericho as a continuation of the inexorable forward momentum unleashed at the riverside.[46] "Surround the city" repeats the instruction given the soldiers (v. 3); the people, too, are symbolically to besiege the city. Later, a retrospective comment will note that Joshua also orders them to remain totally silent until told to shout (v. 10).

---

44. Fleming, "The Seven-Day Siege," 218.

45. Reading the Qere *wayyomer* ("he said") rather than the Ketib plural ("they said"). By contrast, LXX has Joshua ordering the priests to tell the people to advance.

46. Howard, *Joshua*, 170. The verb occurs 19 times in the crossing narrative (e.g., 3:1, 2, 6, 14, 16, 17; 4:1, 3, 5, 7; et al.; cf. 1:2, 11, 14, 15; 5:1; 24:11).

For now, Joshua adds a further detail: an armed vanguard and "rear guard" are, respectively, to precede and follow the ark in its daily circuits of the city (vv. 7b, 9b). Again, ʿabar ("move out") links the vanguard's action to the narrative forward momentum begun at the Jordan. But here the Jericho narrative departs slightly from the earlier narrative. In the latter, the ark preceded the people into the Jordan without human protection (3:14–17), but here human soldiers precede the ark around Jericho. Since the ark needs no human defense, this gesture must be symbolic. In my view, the vanguard, rear guard, and ark together personify that Israel as a whole is engaging in Yahweh's war.

Jericho: Day One (vv. 8–11). Now the action starts, with Israel dramatically obeying the commands of Yahweh and Joshua.[47] Participles portray the movement of the ark, its priests and armed escorts as ongoing (vv.8–9), as if the reader were actually watching the scene. Word repetition keeps the priestly trumpets blaring raucously, a perpetual reminder of Yahweh's presence and readiness for battle.[48] But, on Joshua's orders, the people keep silent as stones; no traditional war whoops for them today (v. 10).[49] Why the silence? Probably, Joshua wants to preserve the sober, sacred solemnity of the ceremony. This is no festive family outing, no leisurely outdoor stroll, no boastful taunting of Jericho's barricaded residents. It is solemn Yahweh war—a ceremonial siege soon to yield his enemy's defeat. Eventually, Israel will enjoy their joyous victory shout, but only on the day Joshua orders it (v. 10b).

The combination of blowing ram's horns and dead silence may also aim to strike terror in the hearts of the Canaanites watching the scene (cf. 1 Sam. 4:8–10). And so, Jericho Conquest–Day One ends. Strikingly, the closing summary (v. 11) features the star of the drama, the ark—specifically, that Joshua has it circle the city once that day. It then reports that all other participants return to camp for the night.[50] The ark's symbolic circuit of Jericho may anticipate its later, final victory lap. Granted, the human

---

47. Though grammatically ambiguous, the opening phrase (vv. 8–9) clearly reports actions against Jericho on the first day, actions that v. 11 summarizes in conclusion.

48. Fleming, "The Seven-Day Siege," 218. Both NIV and NRSV obscure MT's double reference to the priests blowing the trumpets. Given the context, the subject of the concluding pair of infinitive absolutes (lit., "going and blowing") certainly is the priests, not the rear guard; so Howard, *Joshua,* 171; against Nelson, *Joshua,* 88, who wrongly alleges a narrative discrepancy by claiming that the rear guard also blew trumpets.

49. The threefold prohibition could not be any stronger: (lit.) "Don't shout, don't make a peep, don't utter a word"—in other words, observe dead silence.

50. NRSV ("the ark of the LORD went around the city") apparently follows LXX in reading *wayyasseb* as a qal rather a causative hiphil (so MT; NIV). NIV reads the MT as a hiphil ("he [Joshua] had the ark of the LORD carried around"), a rendering that slightly enhances the role of Joshua in the story; cf. Nelson, *Joshua,* 84.

actors—soldiers, priestly trumpeters and ark-bearers, vanguard and rear guard, ordinary people—play important roles. But ultimately, that wooden box, symbol of Yahweh's powerful presence, commands center stage and identifies him as Jericho's true attacker.

Jericho: Days Two to Seven (vv. 12–25). Day Two sees Joshua up early, no doubt to guarantee an early resumption of the ritual, and the priests again carry the ark (v. 12). Virtually repeating vv. 8–9, v. 13 again parades the seven priests blowing the seven trumpets ahead of the ark. The word repetition confirms that Day Two conforms to procedures standardized for Day One—that Israel continues to obey Yahweh and Joshua. Interestingly, here the focus falls on the seven priestly trumpeters, their ongoing sounds, and the ark's front and rear guard details (v. 14a). All other participants—the soldiers (v. 2), the people (vv. 7a, 10), even Joshua himself—remain off stage.

Granted, the context certainly presumes their participation. But, as on Day One, it is the ark's trumpeting priestly heralds and armed guards that interest the narrator on Day Two. It is as if only the ark and its entourage march around Jericho that day—or, at least, the writer deems only them worthy of mention. As with Day One, however, "they" (all the participants) return to camp. Rather than report the remaining days' rituals, the narrator simply reports that Israel repeated the exact same procedure on Days Three through Six (v. 14b). The prominence accorded the priests fits the chapter's pattern and sounds an important theme: Israel participates ceremonially in this episode of Yahweh's war, but it is Yahweh's presence that is decisive in toppling Jericho.

Day Seven, indeed, marks the ceremonial climax of the entire week. The formal, formulaic opening of v. 15 (lit., "It happened on the seventh day …") fixes the chronology and hints at the decisive moment to follow. Two new narrative tidbits imply camp-wide, eager excitement. The day begins not just "early" but at "daybreak," and today the whole camp ("they"), not just Joshua, rises to greet it (cf. v. 12). Today, however, all Israel ("they") takes center stage rather than the ark. The procedure is the same as Days One to Six, but today—and only today—they circle Jericho a climactic seven times as Yahweh has commanded (v. 15b; cf. v. 4).[51]

More important, a second formal formula ("[it happened] the seventh time around") dramatically sets off the decisive, electric, long-awaited moment—the seventh and final walk round the city (v. 16). Per Yahweh's

---

51. Heb. *raq* applies its restrictive sense ("only") to the temporal phrase "on that day"; cf. Williams, §390; vv. 17, 18, 24. Oddly, NIV renders v. 15b as an exception clause, which makes little sense (i.e., they "marched around the city seven times … *except that* [italics, mine] on that day they circled the city seven times"). LXX lacks this comment altogether.

instructions (v. 4), the priests sound the long-expected trumpet signal, but—against expectations (cf. v. 5)—the next voice is Joshua's, not the people's. He commands them, "Shout!"—but then issues his final instructions concerning the city's fall (vv. 16–19). The surprising digression abruptly postpones the climactic war cry and the falling of the wall (v. 20). The literary effect is to heighten the scene's suspense and to underscore the importance of his instructions.

In fact, this marks the first instruction in the book concerning the treatment of conquered Canaanites and the debut of the important concept of *ḥerem* (NIV "devoted things").[52] Essentially, Joshua reiterates the edict of Moses issued long ago concerning it (Deut. 7:1–7; 20:16–18). But, though narratively awkward, it is narratively necessary that the people clearly understand what Yahweh expects of them. The next chapter will show what happens when Israel disregards those expectations. According to Joshua, Jericho falls in a special category, "devoted to the LORD" (*ḥerem*), meaning that "it and everything in it belongs to Yahweh" (v. 17).[53] *Ḥerem* is an intangible quality or state that attaches to a person or an object like the paired opposites holy/profane and clean/unclean (Lev. 27:21; Deut. 7:26; Josh. 7:12; 1 Sam. 15:21). The heart of *ḥerem* is Yahweh's exclusive ownership, an ownership not subject to redemption. To violate that ownership—to keep, rather than devote, *ḥerem*—is tantamount to robbing Yahweh and seriously imperils the violator (Josh. 7:15; cf. Lev. 27:28–29; 1 Sam. 15:23, 26).

In a context of Yahweh's war, *ḥerem* takes on a specific religious meaning. It requires the devotion to Yahweh of anything classed as *ḥerem* either through special custody provisions (e.g., Josh. 6:19) or through its total destruction.[54] Destruction denies the distribution of conquered people and goods classed as *ḥerem* as plunder among the conquerors. Such destruction does not

---

52. The root first debuts in Rahab's reference to Israel's utter destruction (*ḥaram* hi.) of the two Amorite kings, Sihon and Og (Josh. 2:10), but is absent from the narrative detailing those events (Num. 21:21–35). Thus, in Rahab's comment it probably means "to utterly destroy" without the special religious connotations it has in Josh. 6:17. Of course, fear of ritual destruction may still underlie the panic of Rahab and the Canaanites (2:10–11; 5:1). Joshua makes a veiled reference to *ḥerem* at the Jordan (3:10).

53. This reads the Hebrew of v. 17a as two parallel statements ("the city is *ḥerem*"//"it and everything in it belongs to Yahweh"), which NIV and NRSV combine. I am indebted for some of what follows to the insightful essay by R. D. Nelson, "*Ḥerem* and the Deuteronomic Social Conscience," in *Deuteronomy and Deuteronomic Literature*, ed. M. Vervenne and J. Lust (Leuven: Leuven Univ. Press, 1997), 39–54. Cf. also N. Lohfink, "חָרַם," *TDOT*, 2:180–99; C. Brekelmans, "חָרַם," *THAT*, 1:635–39; J. A. Naudé, "חָרַם," *NIDOTTE*, 2:276–77.

54. One special custody provision permits a priest to own *ḥerem*—for example, a field that became Yahweh's at the Year of Jubilee (Lev. 27:21). For more on *ḥerem*, see Bridging Contexts below.

constitute a religious sacrifice to atone for some past offense or rebellion. Rather, it simply constitutes the way Yahweh requires Israel to implement his exclusive ownership. Thus, Joshua's declaration of Jericho as *ḥerem* affirms that Yahweh owns it exclusively and seals the fate of everything in it.

Everyone, of course, except "Rahab the prostitute," as Joshua quickly clarifies (v. 17b). She and her family receive a special exception because Rahab hid (*ḥaba'*) the young Israelite "messengers" (not "spies") when they reconnoitered Jericho (see ch. 2).[55] Unlike the rest of Jericho, "all who are with her in her house shall be spared"—the key stipulation of the spies' oath (2:18−20). The exception contains two striking elements. (1) The verb "hide" (*ḥaba'*) echoes Rahab's advice that the spies "hide themselves" (*ḥaba'* reflexive [ni.]) in the hills to elude their pursuers (2:16). The word choice might suggest that Joshua views her advice as a more noteworthy act than her hiding of them (*ṭaman*) on the roof (2:6; cf. 7:21). (2) Compared to the familial terms of 2:18, the more general phrase "all who are with her" may hold open the door of escape to people beyond Rahab's family (cf. v. 25).

In any case, in Joshua's view, the hiding justifies the sparing (lit., "shall live") of Rahab and anyone found in her house. A kind of poetic justice is at work: As Rahab spared the lives of the spies, so Israel will spare those found with her. Otherwise, Joshua emphatically orders Israel to "keep away from" all material goods (*ḥerem*) in Jericho (v. 18, my rendering). To *take ḥerem* will *make* Israel itself *ḥerem* and "bring trouble" on the whole camp (v. 18b).[56] Literarily, *'akar* ("to bring trouble") thematically foreshadows the terrible trouble (also *'akar*) that the following chapter narrates (7:25).

In sum, Rahab's family marks the lone human exception to *ḥerem* destruction, and precious metals constitute the lone material one (v. 19). Joshua declares the latter to be "sacred [*qodeš*] to the LORD"—set apart from all profane use for sacred use alone.[57] This statement contains a surprise on at least two accounts. (1) It marks the first and only biblical reference to the

---

55. The spies were "messengers" in that they brought back a report of their experience at Jericho to Joshua (2:23−24; cf. 2 Kings 7:15); cf. R. Ficker, "מַלְאָךְ," *THAT*, 1:902−3; D. N. Freedman and B. E. Willoughby, "מַלְאָךְ," *TDOT*, 8:313.

56. NRSV reads *taḥmedu* ("you covet") instead of MT *taḥarimu* (*ḥaram* hi. "to cause *ḥerem*"; NIV "bring about your own destruction"). This reading apparently follows LXX ("to ponder deeply") and implies that MT reads an original *d* as *r* and juxtaposed the last two letters (i.e., LXX *ḥadam* > MT *ḥaram*). If correct, 6:18a would nicely anticipate the repetition of the same verb sequence *ḥadam* + *laqaḥ* in Achan's confession (7:21), implying that he succumbed to the very temptation against which Joshua had warned.

57. This is the same sacral category as other items elsewhere declared "set apart" for specific people by the formula "it is holy to ..." (Heb. *qodeš hu' le*). Examples include: the Sabbath for Israel (Ex. 31:14; cf. Gen. 2:1−3), ordination food, anointing oil, and a portion of the

existence of such a "treasury" in connection with the tabernacle. (2) The phrase "house of the LORD" (v. 24) most often refers to the temple in Jerusalem, whether the one built by Solomon (1 Kings 7:12, 48) or rebuilt by the returned exiles (Ezra 3:11; 8:29; Zech. 8:9).[58] David includes treasuries in his plans for the temple (1 Chron. 26:20; 28:11–12), and over time they become the repository of gold and silver objects (29:8) and money paid at the temple (2 Kings 12:4).[59]

Thus, Joshua 6:19 and 24 may comprise an anachronism, a reference to the later temple treasury as the ultimate destination of all metallic plunder from Jericho. Nevertheless, it may be significant that most later references to the temple treasury are plurals (lit., "treasuries"; 1 Kings 7:51; 14:26; 2 Kings 12:18; 1 Chron. 26:22; 28:12), not singular as here (cf. also only 1 Chron. 29:8; Zech. 11:13). If so, Joshua 6:19 and 24 may concern a tabernacle treasury seeded by goods from Jericho, an event about which the Bible is elsewhere silent.[60] Its purpose and long-term destiny remain a mystery, as does the wisdom of encumbering Israel, a mobile infantry just beginning a long campaign, with Yahweh's treasures. But the point here is clear: Joshua classes metallic objects from Jericho as *ḥerem* (i.e., "devoted to Yahweh") but destined for his treasury, not for destruction.

At last, the people answer the trumpet's call with their long-awaited victory shout (v. 20).[61] And, as v. 5 promised, the wall collapses where it stands, each Israelite marches straight into Jericho, and Israel captures the city.[62] The mound of Jericho measures about ten acres—in reality, a "town"

Nazirite's offerings for the priests (Ex. 29:34; 30:32; Num. 6:20). Things set aside for Yahweh include the priests, Nazirites, and a day to read the Torah (Lev. 21:7; Num. 6:8; Neh. 8:9) and the holy district in eschatologically restored Israel (Ezek. 45:1); cf. Ex. 3:5; Josh. 5:15.

58. Cf. "treasury of the LORD's house" (Josh. 6:24). It is difficult to determine whether other pretemple references to the "house of the LORD" refer to the tabernacle or to a temporary temple about which the Bible is silent (Ex. 23:19; 34:26; 1 Sam. 1:24; 3:15; 2 Sam. 12:20). References in the law probably anticipate the later temple or reflect later updating of terminology (Ex. 23:19; 34:26; Deut. 23:19). One should probably read Judg. 19:18 after the LXX (so NRSV "to my own house"; cf. NIV "the house of the LORD").

59. Later, conquering kings plunder its treasures (and those of its royal counterpart) to enrich their own royal treasuries (1 Kings 14:26; 2 Kings 14:14; 24:13; cf. Dan. 1:2; Hos. 13:15); cf. V. P. Hamilton, "אצר," *NIDOTTE*, 1:488.

60. Howard, *Joshua*, 173–74, capably argues against an anachronistic reference here, but in my view his evidence does not convince.

61. As observed earlier, MT v. 20 seems disordered (cf. its reordering by NIV). LXX suggests one possible solution, the omission of the initial terse "and the people shouted." Alternatively, one may read the latter as the people's expected response to the trumpet blast of v. 16a and v. 20b as a brief recapitulation of the entire blast-shout sequence.

62. Heb. *ʿalab* "to go up" (NIV "charged") may imply awareness that to attack Jericho required ascent up the mound on which it sat.

rather than a "city."[63] Since Rahab's house survives intact, the "fall" probably was either a breach in the wall or a kind of chain reaction of collapsing along it.[64] Inside, Israel obeys Joshua's instructions, and the slaughter is total: everything living in the city — both humans and animals — are devoted to Yahweh (v. 21).[65] Indirect-object-first syntax singles out the lone exception (v. 22), Rahab and (lit.) "her entire family," whom the spies lead safely from Jericho (v. 23). They locate them somewhere "outside the camp of Israel" (v. 23b), presumably to maintain its ritual cleanness.

Two further disjunctive sentences dramatically lower the curtain on Jericho. The first contrasts the fates of the city (a terrible conflagration) and the metal items (safely in the sanctuary treasury; v. 24; cf. v. 19). The second highlights the ultimate fate of "Rahab the prostitute" and company (v. 25): Joshua "spares" them, and Rahab still lives in Israel ("to this [the writer's] day"). "Spared" echoes Rahab's condition for protecting the spies (cf. 2:13) and confirms that Joshua fulfills it.[66] The remark quietly portrays Joshua as a man of integrity (he keeps oaths) and free of any consequences for waiving the ḥerem mandate. It also confirms his full authority as Moses' successor to do so.

What justifies Rahab's survival? The narrator reiterates: She hid the spies (cf. v. 16; 2:16). That action apparently has obligated Israel to reciprocate in kind ("Our lives for your lives!" [2:14]), and Israel did so. More subtly, Rahab embodies the opportunity that larger Jericho squandered: Had the city welcomed rather than pursued Joshua's "messengers," it might have survived, too (cf. Deut. 20:10–15). Literarily, her fate foreshadows Israel's next close encounter with Canaanites (Josh. 9) and holds out hope for their survival. Meanwhile, the spared treasury items anticipate the role other items from Jericho will play in Joshua's next military venture (Josh. 7–8).

---

63. Among archaeologists, the rule of thumb for population estimates is two hundred persons per acre, so Jericho probably had about two thousand residents at the time. Additional Canaanites from the city's environs who probably sought refuge from Israel there might increase its population by five-hundred or so.

64. For further details on the settlement's structure, see K. A. Kitchen, *On the Reliability of the Old Testament* (Grand Rapids: Eerdmans, 2003), 187–88.

65. The list of victims compares to the divine mandate given Saul against Amalek (1 Sam. 15:3) and Saul's killing of the priests of Nob (1 Sam. 22:19). In my view, the ḥerem policy of Joshua 6:21 (and Deut. 7 and 20) seems harsher than that articulated elsewhere (cf. Ex. 23:23–33; 34:11–16; Num. 33:50–55).

66. Lit., "caused them to live" [ḥayah hi.]). In fact, henceforth Rahab enters a narrative eclipse, reappearing only in Jesus' genealogy (Matt. 1:5), in the so-called "Hall of Faith" (Heb. 11:31), and as an example of someone justified by works (James 2:25). For further discussion, see ch. 2 (Bridging Contexts).

Postscript: Joshua's curse and reputation (vv. 26–27). To conclude, the narrator returns Joshua to center stage to pronounce a curse on Jericho (v. 26). The vague reference "at that time" loosely connects the event with the city's fall (cf. 5:2; 11:10, 21), and Joshua's reference to "this city" possibly assumes a public occasion there. The pronouncement of curses was common in the ancient biblical world. Officials in ancient Israel would invoke the curse formula ("cursed is the one who does X") to outlaw certain behaviors. Their pronouncement would also detail the dire consequences to befall violators (Deut. 27:15; 1 Sam. 14:24, 28; cf. Jer. 11:3; 20:15).[67] The phrase "before the LORD" here (also 1 Sam. 26:19) makes explicit what all Israelite curses assume—that Yahweh himself enforces them. His backing is what gives the oath and its stipulations popular credibility.[68]

Joshua's curse may follow a specific ancient custom attested in two Hittite texts—the cursing of a city just destroyed.[69] It condemns anyone who rebuilds Jericho by again laying its foundations and erecting it gates. It exacts a heavy price from the violator—the loss of his "firstborn" and "youngest" sons—but the exact means of payment remain obscure. The curse may allude to a pagan ceremony involving child sacrifice at the founding of a city or to a high rate of infant mortality caused by the water from Jericho's spring.[70]

Interestingly, later Israelites continued to inhabit Jericho despite the curse (see 18:21; Judg. 3:13; 2 Sam. 10:5). Evidently, the curse only condemned any attempt to rebuild the city as a fortified city, not just to live there.[71] That would explain why the curse later exacted its terrible toll on Hiel from Bethel (1 Kings 16:34), a fulfillment that Joshua 6:26 literarily anticipates.[72]

But why single out Jericho for cursing? Certainly, the city has great symbolic value. Near a natural ford of the Jordan, the city marks one of the primary gateways into Canaan (cf. 4:19; 2 Sam. 10:5), a role it played for

---

67. Cf. J. Scharbert, "אָרַר," *TDOT*, 1:405–18; F. R. Magdalene, "Curse," *EDB*, 301–2.

68. Human curses, however, did not work automatically but might be overturned (see Deut. 23:5; Judg. 17:2), and stiff legal penalties follow the misuse of curses (Ex. 22:28[27]; Lev. 19:14; 20:9; 24:10–23). For the liturgical use of curses, see Ps. 37:22 and 109:6–15.

69. Fritz, *Josua*, 74. He also cites examples of ancient curses that trace the destruction of cities to the curses of the gods.

70. Cf. Boling, *Joshua*, 210, 214–15, who cites approvingly the proposal that the spring may have been contaminated by a parasite carried by snails attested in excavations at Jericho; cf. E. V. Hulse, "Joshua's Curse and the Abandonment of Ancient Jericho: Schistosomiasis as a Possible Medical Explanation," *Medical History* 15 (1971): 376–86. Concerning later problems with water at Jericho, see 2 Kings 2:19.

71. Similarly, Howard, *Joshua*, 176.

72. For scholarly discussion of the redactional history behind both references, cf. A. F. Campbell and M. A. O'Brien, *Unfolding the Deuteronomistic History* (Minneapolis: Fortress, 2000), 123 n.38 and 391 n.109.

nearly eight thousand years.[73] To foreign passersby, the charred ruins were evidence of judgment by some deity, to passing Israelites mute testimony to Yahweh's first great victory in Canaan.[74] The ruins would also remind them of the city's status as *ḥerem*; to rebuild it would rob Yahweh of a sizeable war prize and risk his retaliation.[75] Finally, Deuteronomy 13:17[16] might lead some Israelites to read Jericho as a city destroyed and abandoned for heresy. From this angle, ruined Jericho would silently warn Israel of the terrible fate awaiting those who abandon Yahweh for other gods.

Finally, Yahweh's stunning victory further enhances Joshua's public stature. It confirms convincingly that "the LORD was with Joshua" just as he promised (v. 27a; cf. 1:5). An Israelite leader can have no better reputation. It also secures Joshua's stature among the land's inhabitants (v. 27b; cf. 4:14). All in all, Joshua is "on a roll" — apparently, a leader so blessed and brilliant as to be unstoppable. Under Joshua, the reader expects a relentless juggernaut soon to sweep all of Canaan clean of resistance. Sadly, chapter 7 will soon show that leaders who presume upon the divine presence do so to their shame. Joshua's triumphal moment as king of the world will soon prove to be surprisingly short-lived.

THE BRIDGE FROM JOSHUA 5–6 to Contemporary Significance traverses some difficult terrain. First, it returns us briefly to the use of the number seven and noises in Joshua 6. Second, it discusses two controversial subjects, the archaeology of Jericho and the troubling issue of violence in Joshua.

Of sevens and noises. The prominence of "seven"/"seventh" is not surprising. Several Israelite cultic festivals last seven days,[76] as did the celebration that dedicated Solomon's temple (1 Kings 8:62–66). Mesopotamian literature prominently features seven in lists associated with gods and in reports of seven-day festivals or sevenfold ritual actions.[77] More important, both Akkadian and Ugaritic literatures attest the pattern of an action

---

73. The city's earliest archaeological remains go back to the Neolithic era (ca. 9000 B.C.); cf. P. F. Jacobs, "Jericho," *EDB*, 689–90.

74. Cf. Nelson, *Joshua*, 91, who thinks of the treatment of Jericho "as a paradigm for the entire conquest."

75. Cf. Nelson, *Joshua*, 95. Alternatively, cf. Hess, *Joshua*, 135, for whom the curse symbolizes "the totality of divine judgment against Jericho" for refusing to worship Yahweh (cf. Deut. 13:17[16]).

76. E.g., the Feasts of Unleavened Bread (Ex. 23:15; 34:18; Deut. 16:1–8) and Booths (Lev. 23:34–43; Deut. 16:13–15).

77. P. P. Jenson, "שֶׁבַע," *NIDOTTE*, 4:34.

repeated for six days followed by a decisive event on the seventh. In the Gilgamesh Epic, the seventh day marks the moment the storm subsides, and Gilgamesh offers the gods seven bowls of offerings and forfeits immortality for sleeping for seven days.[78] The six-day ritual with seventh-day climax, therefore, follows this ancient Near Eastern pattern.

As for the noise makers, the term *teru‘ah* (Josh. 6:5, 20) apparently means "sharp, loud sound," whether a trumpet blast, clashing cymbal (Ps. 150:5), or human shout.[79] In military contexts, trumpet blasts sound simple signals for troops (Num. 10:5–6; Judg. 3:27; 6:34; 7:18) or alarms in cities under attack (Ezek. 33:4, 5; Neh. 4:20). Israel also uses battle cries to terrify their enemies (Judg. 7:20–22; 1 Sam. 4:5–6; 17:20), especially as a battle begins (17:52), and also hears their attacking enemies' shouts (Zeph. 1:16; cf. Amos 1:14; 2:2). In cultic contexts, blowing trumpets accompany Yahweh's dramatic descent on Mount Sinai (Ex. 19:13, 16), the entrance of the ark into Jerusalem with David (2 Sam. 6:15), and Israel's songs of praise (Ps. 47:5–6[6–7]; 98:5–6). Trumpet blasts across Israel also announce the opening of the important Year of Jubilee (Lev. 25:9).[80] Shouts of praise accompany sacrifices and ceremonies in the temple (Ps. 27:6; 89:15[16]; cf. Num. 29:1; Job 8:21) and celebrate the laying of the temple's foundation (Ezra 3:11). It is no surprise, then, that the present act of Yahweh's war, the ritual conquest of Jericho, combines these military and cultic customs. The dramatic climax of the seven-day ceremony is surely something worth making noise about!

The problem of ḥerem.[81] Many Bible readers find the wholesale killing of Canaanites in Joshua 6 repulsive and disturbing. They find it hard to accept that their loving God sanctioned the brutal annihilation of an entire city. Hard, disquieting questions arise concerning the morality of their God. If given the chance, some might even vote Joshua completely

---

78. W. W. Hallo and K. L. Younger, eds., *The Context of Scripture* (Leiden: Brill, 1997), 1:458–60; *ANET*, 95–96; cf. S. E. Lowenstamm, "The Seven-Day Unit in Ugaritic Epic Literature," *IEJ* 13 (1963): 121–33.

79. The root *rw‘* ("to raise a war cry") occurs in vv. 5, 10, 16, 20.

80. According to Hawk, *Joshua*, 94–95, the term *yobel* ("ram's horn") and the repeated "sevens" here allude to the Jubilee Year with its concern for preserving family land ownership ("Jubilee" is a transliteration of that Hebrew word; cf. Lev. 25:8–55; Josh. 6:5, 6, 8, 13). In his view, the allusions both "confirm Israel's rightful possession of the land" and rebut the mistaken notion that Israel, not Yahweh, owns it.

81. Some of what follows originated in a lecture given on February 5, 2000, at the "Conference on the Contextualization of Scripture" hosted by Denver Seminary. I gratefully acknowledge the seminary's kind invitation to address these matters and the invaluable assistance of my teaching assistant, Dr. Liang-her Wu, in its preparation. A briefer discussion of the issue is available in the Introduction ("Now, About All That Killing . . .").

out of the canon. A review of three biblical ideas—Yahweh's war, the concept of *ḥerem* (or "the ban"), and God's mandate—launch us on the road to reckoning with the violence in Joshua.

The term "Yahweh's war" describes the biblical theme that God has enemies whom he defeats militarily, usually with Israel's participation and for their benefit.[82] In Joshua, the concept shapes its narration of the defeats of Jericho (ch. 6), Ai (ch. 8), Gibeon (10:1–15), and southern and northern Canaan (10:16–11:23). It assumes that such war is a sacred act and, hence, requires ritual purity in Israel's war camp (Deut. 23:9–14; cf. Josh. 3:5; 1 Sam. 7:9–10; 13:8–14; 2 Sam. 11:11).[83] Yahweh himself issues the command for Israel to attack (e.g., Num. 14:39–45; Josh. 6:1–5; 8:8; 10:40; 11:12, 15, 20, 23), but he alone (not Israel) actually fights and wins the victory.[84] Israel is simply to trust Yahweh for victory, not depend on their own devices.

Basically, the word *ḥerem* means "utter destruction" (Isa. 43:28; Zech. 14:11; Mal. 4:6 [3:24]) or "plunder" (Ezek. 26:5) and derives from the root *ḥaram* hi. ("to utterly destroy annihilate" [cities, nations, people, livestock]").[85] In Leviticus and Joshua, however, the root has a specifically religious sense. The verb connotes "to devote to destruction" (e.g., Lev. 27:21; Josh. 6:21), the noun an "object devoted to destruction" or "banned object" (e.g., Lev. 27:28, 29; Num. 18:14; Josh. 6:17). Whatever is "devoted to destruction" or "banned" is assumed to be consecrated to Yahweh for his exclusive ownership and use. In essence, it has been transferred from the profane realm of humans to the holy realm of Yahweh (Josh. 8:26, 28; cf. Mic. 4:13).

As God's exclusive property, *ḥerem* enjoys the highest degree of holiness ("most holy to the LORD" [Lev. 27:28]) and cannot be redeemed for return to the profane sphere. Thus, the only humans who may possess it are Israel's priests, who had custody of land consecrated to Yahweh (Lev. 27:21; cf. v. 28; Num. 18:14; Ezek. 44:29). However strange it sounds, this religious practice was not unique to Israel. In the Mesha Inscription (ninth cent. B.C.), King Mesha of Moab also invokes the cognate verb: He "devoted to destruction"

---

82. Cf. the valuable overview by G. H. Jones, "The Concept of Holy War," in *The World of Ancient Israel: Sociological, Anthropological, and Political Perspectives*, ed. R. E. Clements (Cambridge: Cambridge Univ. Press, 1989), 299–321.

83. This assumption also explains why Israel's crossing of the Jordan River (chs. 3–4) and conquest of Jericho (ch. 6) both involve ritual processions. For other features, see J. Holloway, "The Ethical Dilemma of Holy War," *Southwestern Journal of Theology* 41 (1998): 49–50.

84. The book of Joshua highlights how Yahweh hands/handed over his enemies to Israel (8:7, 18; 10:19, 30, 32; 11:6, 8) and how "Yahweh fought for Israel" (10:14, 42; 23:2).

85. For details, see S. Niditch, *War in the Hebrew Bible: A Study in the Ethics of Violence* (New York: Oxford Univ. Press, 1993), 28–77; P. D. Stern, *The Biblical Ḥerem: A Window on Israel's Religious Experience* (BJS 211; Atlanta: Scholars Press, 1991).

(*ḥerem*) an Israelite city to his god, Ashtar Chemosh.[86] But one crucial qualification concerning the practice in Israel bears mentioning: The Old Testament does not understand every Israelite destruction of a city or people as an act of religious *ḥerem*. No Israelite leader can on his own decide to impose *ḥerem* on an enemy—only Yahweh himself can designate what is *ḥerem*.

The divine mandate (Deut. 20:16–18) probably raises the reader's theological queasiness the most. Yahweh allows offers of peace to foreign cities under Israelite siege (vv. 19–20) but mandates that Israel "not leave alive anything that breathes" among Canaan's six peoples (vv. 16–18). There is no getting around that cold hard fact. No humane provisions exempt women, children, the disabled, or the elderly. The reason is that they will lead Israel into apostasy (cf. Deut. 7:2; 13:16, 18; Josh. 6:17, 18, 21). In other words, *ḥerem* in this case concerns not judgment on Canaanites for abhorrent practices but protection of Israelites from their persuasive instruction.

This sweeping mandate sparks many questions. Was this slaughter really necessary? Was Canaanite religion so attractive—and Israel's faith so fragile—as to make Israelite apostasy inevitable? And, most important, what does this policy imply about the moral character of Yahweh? Does it suggest that God considers other—if not all—human life as of similar low value? Does it expose God as a cold, forbidding, irascible deity—a kind of cosmic Darth Vader eerily possessed of an erratic "dark side"?

Three recent scholars have proposed ways to understand Joshua's violent ethnic cleansing. Rowlett suggests that we read Joshua as a special kind of rhetoric, the rhetoric of violence, not necessarily the report of actual events. In her view, its military language borrows the rhetoric of violence from Assyria to help Judah rebuild its identity under Josiah (seventh cent. B.C.) after centuries of foreign domination.[87] The rhetoric warns Josiah's subjects that his government would suppress anyone in the kingdom that resisted his control.

---

86. Cf. the translation by K. P. Jackson, "The Language of the Mesha Inscription," in *Studies in the Mesha Inscription and Moab*, ed. J. A. Dearman (Archaeology and Biblical Studies 2; Atlanta: Scholars Press, 1989), 97–98; *ANET*, 320–21. For an evaluation of other parallels, see J. S. Kaminsky, "Joshua 7: A Reassessment of Israelite Conceptions of Corporate Punishment," in *The Pitcher Is Broken: Memorial Essays for Gösta Ahlström*, ed. S. W. Holloway and L. K. Handy (JSOTSup 190; Sheffield: Sheffield Academic Press, 1995), 332–36. Cf. also G. F. Del Monte, "The Hittite Herem," in *Memoriae Igor M. Diakonoff*, ed. L. Kogan et al. (Winona Lake, Ind.: Eisenbrauns, 2005), 21–45.

87. L. Rowlett, *Joshua and the Rhetoric of Violence* (JSOTSup 226; Sheffield: Sheffield Academic Press, 1996), especially 181–83. Her work follows up the suggestion of other scholars that Joshua in the book is a "thinly disguised King Josiah" (13); cf. R. D. Nelson, "Josiah in the Book of Joshua," *JBL* 100 (1981): 531–40; R. Sutherland, "Israelite Political Theory in Joshua 9," *JSOT* 53 (1992): 67.

At first glance, Rowlett's thesis takes some of the sting out of Joshua's violence by reducing it to mere rhetoric. But, ultimately, her proposal offers no satisfactory relief. If her thesis holds, the book still threatens real violence, albeit against opponents rather than Canaanites. Further, the alleged ties between Joshua and Josiah are by no means certain. Were royal ideology driving the book, one would expect many more connections with later kings than it has.[88] In short, while suggestive, Rowlett's view does not fully satisfy.

The quite different approach of Knierim starts by comparing the treatment of other nations in Joshua with their treatment elsewhere in the Old Testament.[89] He notes how other texts speak of Yahweh as righteous, the merciful ruler of all peoples (Ps. 96; Jonah), a defender of the weak of all nations (Ps. 82), a God whom the nations seek and, thereby, abandon war (Isa. 2:1–4). That view of God, Knierim claims, would drive those biblical voices to grant the Canaanites continued life and dignity. The war and land policy of Joshua are, thus, theologically out of step with the God of the wider Old Testament.[90] Knierim asks readers to set them aside in favor of the Old Testament's majority view.

In a sense, this intriguing, bold proposal compares to what many readers do anyway—ignore the book of Joshua as irrelevant. Knierim's advocacy of Canaanite dignity also appeals to a modern sense of human rights, and one cannot fault his reading of Joshua within its larger Old Testament context. But why give the other texts greater weight on the issue of violence than Joshua? Is there no way to retain all Old Testament voices in the discussion?[91]

In my view, Knierim's hermeneutical approach is correct, but I would nuance his conclusion slightly. Knierim rules Joshua out of bounds theolog-

88. Cf. N. Habel, *The Land Is Mine: Six Biblical Land Ideologies* (Minneapolis: Fortress, 1995), 67: "By the end of the book, Joshua has established no centralized court, temple, militia, or administration. Rather he encourages each ancestral house, family, and tribe to claim and conquer its own lands."

89. Knierim, "Israel and the Nations," 309–21.

90. In his view, they represent an Israelite faction—the "holy war and get tough with people of the land" party; cf. Knierim, ibid., 320.

91. For example, Brueggemann's interpretation is the exact opposite of Knierim's. In his view, Joshua offers a critique of the terrible socioeconomic oppression of Israel by corrupt Canaanite city-states. If so, the conquest of Canaan represents a victory for oppressed people, Israel among them. Joshua's view of God, then, would seem compatible with that of the texts Knierim cites and actually commend its acceptance by the reader; cf. W. Brueggemann, "Revelation and Violence: A Study in Contextualization," in *A Social Reading of the Old Testament: Prophetic Approaches to Israel's Communal Life*, ed. P. D. Miller (Minneapolis: Fortress, 1994), 285–318. Brueggemann builds on the sociological analysis of N. Gottwald, *The Tribes of Yahweh* (Maryknoll, N.Y.: Orbis, 1979), 389–419.

ically because it departs from the consensus of the larger Old Testament. But I would argue from that consensus that Joshua's war and land policy be understood as time-specific and limited. It applies only to the conquest and settlement periods and, hence, cannot be used as a precedent elsewhere. This does not settle the theological question of God's morality, but it does explain Joshua's policy as rooted in a specific context and serving a narrow intention.

Stone offers a completely different approach from those of Rowlett and Knierim.[92] He argues that texts within Joshua itself reflect discomfort with the idea of holy war and the annihilation of the Canaanites among those who edited the book. They amount to a subtle downplaying of the martial and territorial motifs of Yahweh war. For example, the book starkly contrasts the acceptance of Yahweh's plan for Canaan by Rahab and the Gibeonites (2:9–11; 9–10) with resistance to it by Canaanite kings (5:1; 9:1–2; 10:1–5; 11:1–5). The contrast, Stone says, intends to make the case that the Canaanites perished for resisting Yahweh, not for religious decadence or economic oppression of peasants. Thus, the book's message promotes responsiveness to Yahweh's actions and warns against resistance to them.[93]

Indeed, Stone argues, the book's reshaping within the DH introduces the law as the object of Israel's acceptance or resistance.[94] Thus, in its present form Joshua's main message is that holy war (Stone's term) is ultimately more about "uncompromising obedience to Yahweh's law" than about "territory or warfare."[95] In sum, Stone's view offers not only a way around our horror of the conquest but a persuasive articulation of the original meaning of Joshua.

I find myself in agreement with Stone's observations concerning Rahab and the Gibeonites. His thesis that the book links the Canaanites' fate to their rejection of Yahweh's actions is certainly correct. Elsewhere, I have argued from a reading of Joshua 7–10 that the book actually affirms divine acceptance of foreigners like Rahab and the Gibeonites within Israel.[96] Amid

---

92. L. G. Stone, "Ethical and Apologetic Tendencies in the Redaction of the Book of Joshua," *CBQ* 53 (1991): 25–35.

93. Ibid., 34, 35.

94. Ibid., 34–36. In his view, additions to the text concerning the law (Josh. 1:1–9; 8:30–35; ch. 23) by Deuteronomic editors achieved this reshaping. If so, the book reached its present form in three stages: to the original holy war narratives (Josh. 2–11) later editors added six passages about foreigners; the Deuteronomic editors then finished the book.

95. Ibid., 36.

96. R. L. Hubbard Jr., "'What Do These Stones Mean?': Biblical Theology and a Motif in Joshua," *BBR* 11 (2001): 25–49.

the catastrophe around them, they alone receive compassion—indeed, *salvation*. Their very survival strongly implies that Yahweh permits exceptions to the mandate of Deuteronomy 20 to those who acknowledge Yahweh's greatness.

Thus, rather than promote violence as the standard Israelite treatment of foreigners who reside within Israel, Joshua teaches two things: (1) Those who honor Yahweh's greatness and do not teach Israel idolatry may remain in the land, and (2) rigorous obedience to the law is Yahweh's supreme expectation for all peoples in the land. The cases of Rahab and the Gibeonites exemplify the first teaching, the book's repeated references to the law and to Moses spotlight the second.[97] Thus, Joshua's openness to non-Israelites parallels the inclusive themes of Knierim's texts and anticipates the New Testament's emphasis on the international ethnic inclusivity of the gospel (e.g., Acts 1:8; Rev. 5:9; 14:6).[98] More important, I would argue that the book of Joshua reflects two aspects of God's nature, his righteous anger against opponents and his mercy and compassion toward those who turn to him. In my view, Christians come to experience both aspects of God's character through their relationship with Jesus Christ.

Jericho and archaeology. A second troubling matter besides the practice of *ḥerem* concerns the archaeology of Jericho (or Tell es-Sultan). A century of excavations has unveiled the history of Jericho's occupations in great detail.[99] Though small in area (about ten acres), the town is among the world's oldest (founded ca. 8000 B.C.), a fact easily explained by its location near an important Jordan crossing, its warm climate, and the spring that supplies its water. In the mid-1930s, J. Garstang excavated Jericho, dating the ruins of both a double city wall atop the mound and a residential area on its southeast slope ("City IV") to 1400 B.C.[100] He credited their destruction to the Israelites under Joshua.

But excavations two decades later led Kathleen Kenyon to revise the date of Garstang's double wall upward to ca. 2400 B.C. and City IV's

---

97. See Josh. 1:7, 8, 17; 4:10, 12; 8:30–35; 9:24; 11:12, 15; 20:2; 21:2, 8; 22:2, 5; 23:6; 24:6, 26. The call to obedience to the law fits well with the larger biblical stress on the duty of believers to obey Scripture as God's Word (e.g., Deut. 8:3; Ps. 1:2; Prov. 30:5; Matt. 4:4; John 2:22; 1 Tim. 4:13; 2 Tim. 3:15–16; James 2:8).

98. For the Bible's treatment of Ruth the Moabite as an example, see Hubbard, *Ruth*, 64–65, 116–21.

99. See conveniently, Kitchen, *The Reliability of the Old Testament*, 187–88; T. A. Holland and E. Netzer, "Jericho," *ABD*, 3:723–40; Jacobs, "Jericho," *EBD*, 690–91.

100. Garstang did not publish a formal excavation report, but he and his son published a popular account of his excavations in J. Garstang and J. B. E. Garstang, *The Story of Jericho* (2nd ed.; London: Marshall, Morgan, & Scott, 1948).

destruction to ca. 1550 B.C.[101] Spectacular evidence from its nearby tombs attests the town's great prosperity during the early Middle Bronze Age (ca. 2000 B.C.), but the mound itself shows only a few traces of that heyday. A violent conflagration (ca. 1550 B.C.) left the town a barren, uninhabited ruins for two centuries, and erosion washed away all but a few traces of the Late Bronze occupation (fourteenth-thirteenth cent. B.C.).[102]

The question is, Was Jericho inhabited during the next four centuries (thirteenth to ninth cent. B.C.) until its rebuilding during Ahab's reign by Hiel (1 Kings 16:34)? The current scholarly consensus follows the conclusion of Kenyon: Except for a small, short-lived settlement (ca. 1400 B.C.), Jericho was completely uninhabited ca. 1550−1100 B.C. In other words, notwithstanding Joshua 6, there was no fortified city of Jericho for Joshua and Israel to conquer.[103] This is true whether one opts for an "early" (fifteenth cent.) or "late" (thirteenth cent.) date for Israel's arrival in Canaan.

The absence of a "fortified city," however, may not necessarily mean that Jericho was completely uninhabited in the Late Bronze Age. As noted above, most Late Bronze Age towns were small and unwalled, and there is in fact evidence of such a settlement at Jericho (fourteenth cent. B.C.).[104] The "wall" of Joshua 2 and 6 might be (or, at least, somehow relate to) the contiguous outer walls of houses that together formed a protective circle around the city. If so, this evidence would tend to favor a "late" date for Jericho's fall.

Along a different line, however, B. G. Wood has recently argued that the archaeological reports of both Garstang and Kenyon reflect evidence for a Joshua-era Jericho.[105] On that basis, he reaffirms Garstang's original dating of City IV and its walls to ca. 1400 B.C., thus lending support to an "early date" for Jericho's destruction. Further, he finds evidence in the reports that remarkably parallels the biblical account. For example, Kenyon

---

101. B. G. Wood, "Did the Israelites Conquer Jericho? A New Look at the Archaeological Evidence," *BAR* 16/2 (March−April 1990): 49. For a convenient summary of the evidence, see Hess, *Joshua*, 137−38; K. M. Kenyon, "Jericho," *NEAEHL*, 2:674−81.

102. Cf. the careful assessment of P. Bienkowski, *Jericho in the Middle Bronze Age* (Warminster: Aris & Phillips, 1986), 120−25.

103. E.g., Jacobs, "Jericho," 691: "Attempts to identify archaeological remains at Tell es-Sultan with Jericho depicted in Joshua 6 flounder on the absence of archaeological data."

104. Herzog ("Cities in the Levant," 1:1037) lists Jericho among the five LBA cities "protected by a belt of houses instead of a city wall." Gonen, "Urban Canaan," 65 (Table 1) lists Jericho's size as "tiny" (ca. 1−3 acres). For further discussion, see the Original Meaning section of Josh. 2.

105. Wood, "Israelites Conquer Jericho?" 50−53. These walls are not the same ones that Kenyon dated to ca. 2400 B.C. (see above).

suggested that a heap of red mudbricks found at the base of the revetment wall below City IV originally came from the city's collapsed parapet wall. (They had tumbled down the slopes.) The combination of fallen bricks and timbers and evidence of a violent conflagration also suggested to Kenyon that the eastern walls collapsed before the fire scorched them. That scenario certainly compares to the biblical report that the walls fell before Israel burned the city (Josh. 6:20, 24).[106]

Wood's reading of the archaeological evidence is still subject to dispute.[107] His dating of Jericho's destruction to the Late Bronze Age depends heavily on carbon – 14 dating of remains from Jericho's burn layer. But a subsequent study applied high-precision radiocarbon dating to eighteen samples of carbon and six charred cereal grains from that same source and twelve other carbon samples. The results confirmed Kenyon's original dating (ca. 1550 B.C.) rather than that of Wood (ca. 1400 B.C.).[108] By implication, they also undermine the force of Wood's observation that the city's archaeological data favorably compares to the biblical data.

But even if Wood's thesis survives this finding, it would not *prove* the claims of Joshua 6. To show that City IV suffered terrible destruction does not verify that Israel was responsible for it, but it does leave the possibility open. In short, though often cited with appreciation, Wood's thesis that Jericho was inhabited ca. 1400 B.C. is in doubt. But suppose one prefers (as do many scholars) a "late date" for the conquest? Kitchen is among them and offers an alternate theory. He deems it highly likely that erosion has washed away the remains of Late Bronze Age Jericho — the Jericho usually linked with Joshua. In his view, those ruins now lie under the modern road and farmland along the site's eastern side.[109] Kitchen concludes:

---

106. Wood (ibid., 56) speculates that an earthquake toppled the walls, and he provides evidence that seismic disturbances were typical in the region. He also draws some intriguing inferences (56–57) from the unexpectedly large quantities of grain that Garstang and Kenyon found.

107. See the spirited rebuttal of P. Bienkowski, "Jericho Was Destroyed in the Middle Bronze Age, Not the Late Bronze Age," *BAR* 16/5 (September–October 1990): 45–46, and Wood's equally spirited response, "Dating Jericho's Destruction: Bienkowski is Wrong on All Counts," *BAR* 16/5 (September–October 1990): 45, 47–49, 68–69.

108. H. J. Bruins and J. van der Plicht, "Tell Es-Sultan (Jericho): Radiocarbon Results of Short-Lived Cereal and Multiyear Charcoal Samples from the End of the Middle Bronze Age," *Radiocarbon* 37/2 (1995): 213–20.

109. Kitchen, *Reliability of the Old Testament*, 187. Kenyon herself also notes the heavy erosion at Jericho; cf. K. M. Kenyon, *Archaeology in the Holy Land*, 5th ed. (Nashville: Nelson, 1985), 181–82. The only Middle Bronze age buildings still on the mound are the "palace" (Garstang's term), the so-called Middle Building, and the ruins of a house floor in Square Hill (Kenyon's term); for structures cf. Holland and Netzer, "Jericho," 3:736.

There may well have been a Jericho during 1275–1220, but above the tiny remains of that of 1400–1275, so to speak, and *all* of this has long, long since gone. We will never find "Joshua's Jericho" for that very simple reason.[110]

In short, the archaeological evidence bears four interpretations, depending on one's view of Jericho's layout at the time as well as whether one prefers an "early" or "late" date for the Joshua era. The lack of evidence for the former means either that Jericho was uninhabited at the time (Kenyon) or that erosion has removed it (Kitchen). But if the evidence Wood offers holds, the early date would remain a possibility. Finally, if one assumes that LBA Jericho (fourteenth cent. B.C.) was a small, unwalled city, a destruction date in the 1300s B.C.—a "later," if not a "late," date—becomes a possibility. A decision between the options will depend on the persuasion of evidence and arguments beyond the scope of this commentary.[111]

THE CONTEMPORARY MEANING OF Joshua 5–6 centers on four important themes: the wilderness experience, the problem of fitness before God, the end of Israel's shame, and the reality of the Jesus war that engages us (on Jesus war, see below).

The past: the wilderness backdrop. Above, I indicated that the two scenes at Gilgal (circumcision and Passover) symbolize Israel's historic transition from the wilderness to the Promised Land. The participants are all people who, having endured and survived desert life, now prepare to move forward. Joshua 5 reports the end of the wilderness period, but what had the Israelites now camped near the Jordan learned during that time? How were they different from their rebellious ancestors, and what can their experience teach us today? Deuteronomy 8:2–3 summarizes God's perspective on the purposes of their wilderness experiences:

> Remember how the LORD your God led you all the way in the desert these forty years, to humble you and to test you in order to know what was in your heart, whether or not you would keep his commands. He humbled you, causing you to hunger and then feeding you with manna, which neither you nor your fathers had known, to

---

110. Kitchen, *Reliability of the Old Testament*, 187.

111. Chavalas and Adamthwaite ("Archaeological Light on the Old Testament," 78–90) argue for the superiority of a fourteenth-century date for the Exodus-Conquest events. Whether their view will gather a consensus remains to be seen.

teach you that man does not live on bread alone but on every word that comes from the mouth of the LORD. (Deut. 8:2 – 3)

What God wanted—and what the wilderness was to produce—was a spiritually healthy, fit Israel. The first thing they had learned in the desert was humility (to "humble you"). They had learned to depend totally on God rather than on themselves. Indeed, the only reason they are now safely in Canaan at all is because they have depended completely on God.

The wilderness of Sinai is a barren, hostile desert without the requisite rainfall to cause crops to grow. No human effort can transform it into a lush garden spot. Underground water from wells at oases is available in sufficient quantity to keep humans and animals from dying of thirst. They must, of course, reach an oasis to access it. But those life-giving wells cannot support agriculture able to feed large groups like Israel. People starve to death in the wilderness unless they bring food with them or obtain it from passersby. In that hostile environment, Israel came to trust God to provide them with food and water to sustain them. God gave them water from rocks and manna from the sky. It is that trust that got them to the west bank of the Jordan. Thus, the group that drank from the Jordan rather than desert springs and ate food from Canaan rather than manna are more spiritually fit than they were before.

A brief glance back across the Jordan also gives us some good news from Israel's experience. It teaches us that as we move forward, what we really need is more than just better technology or more creative ideas, as useful and necessary as they may be in their own way. What we really need is spiritual fitness—a firm trust in God himself to sustain us through what lies ahead just as he did Israel in the wilderness. Our God is one whose quiet, loving presence supports us through all the experiences through which he leads us, even wilderness ones. As he supplied wandering Israel with manna, so he provides for our basic needs, too. However difficult the days, he gently keeps us alive. Indeed, the entire experience aims to create in us a hunger for God himself—to learn to depend on him and to trust that in a pinch he will come through for us. God's purpose is to cultivate in us the same spiritual health he did in Israel—a fitness for what comes next.

Second, God used the desert days to "test" Israel—to see what is "in [their] heart." Here Moses has in mind the heart as the center of their will—the place where Israel makes choices. Time and again, the Israelites faced the choice of whether or not to obey God's Instruction. The long journey to Canaan taught Israel much about how double-minded their hearts were—devoted to Yahweh one day, in rebellion the next. The group camped along the Jordan had not fully purged themselves of sin, and they needed circumcision and the Passover observance to further round out their fitness for Canaan and its battles. But enroute to those moments they had learned how fickle and easily-swayed their heart was. They had learned how central (or peripheral) God's will was to their life-choices.

A brief look back across the Jordan from Gilgal will teach us similarly to take stock of what really is in our own heart. The fact is that, like Israel, we are often prone to fickleness and subject to bad influences, especially when things are going well for us. Sometimes, like Israel, we may rebel outright against God's wishes, at other times the list of "what's important" in our hearts may differ radically from God's. Too often we are like kids who, if left on their own, easily do what they want rather than what their parents do. We easily give in to our own hungers for status, wealth, approval, freedom, or fulfillment. Those are the things that grip our heart. But Israel learned in the wilderness—and teaches us today—what is truly of value and what our heart really wants. The Israelites soon bound for Jericho knew the difference between their own hungers ("bread alone") and a focused hunger on what God wanted ("every word that comes from the mouth of the LORD"). Their experience points us in the right direction—to make obedience to God's Word our number one priority.

In short, God used the wilderness period to sift and sort Israel, and the band that survived it learned much. Like them, our task is also to respond willingly to the experiences through which God leads us—to enhance and maintain our spiritual fitness. We must persereve, tightly clutching his guiding hand as we navigate our way enroute to the battles ahead. In Joshua 5, Israel tooks steps to get spiritually fit for those battles, and so should we.

The problem of fitness. What is spiritual fitness, and how can we can improve ours? Many readers may associate the idea of "fitness" with the grueling physical training in the military that readies troops for the rigors of combat. Since the late twentieth century, however, physical fitness has become a cultural priority in the general population. Today a growing industry of fitness centers offers ordinary people places to strengthen their cardiovascular system, lose weight, and improve their self-esteem. There is a large, heavily utilized fitness center connected with the hospital near my home, and I have seen such centers in shopping malls and in downtown buildings. Corporations and businesses also provide access to fitness facilities for their employees since good physical conditioning improves their attitude and productivity. For some people their neighborhood is their gym. They exercise by walking several miles from their home and back, often with like-minded friends.

As we saw above, Israel had to acquire a different kind of fitness — ritual fitness — to live in Canaan. That is why at their camp at Gilgal they circumcised all Israelite males and celebrated the Passover (5:2 – 12). It judged them fit on Yahweh's scale of holiness to participate in Yahweh's war and to reside there as his people after the Conquest. Israel's example challenges Christians today to pursue a similar self-assessment and self-improvement — their *spiritual* fitness for Jesus' war and kingdom life.

What is Christian spiritual fitness? A comparison of the latter with physical fitness helps illumine the idea. A program of regular exercise seeks to improve an individual's physical and emotional health. Weight loss is a key contributor to both, since shedding extra flab decreases the strain on the heart and reduces cholesterol. Those who lose weight also feel good about themselves, especially when other people notice the change. Further, regular exercise also significantly reduces stress, a silent, sinister strain on the body that may cause headaches and even heart attacks. Stress reduction noticeably brightens the exercisers' outlook on life and increases their energy level. The ultimate goal of physical activity, however, is to strengthen the heart muscle and stave off serious diseases.

Similarly, spiritual fitness aims to strengthen the hearts of believers — their heart for God and for doing his will. It also seeks to rid them of spiritual flab that they sometimes drag around as part of their identity. By this I mean the bad habits, little slaveries, gloomy outlooks, divided loyalties, and cynicism that sap our energy. Left unattended, they engender doubts, feed our fears, and rob us of focus. To shed them, however, frees that sapped energy to energize our lives with Christ. Spiritual fitness substitutes energy (or "passion") for lethargic spiritual laziness. Above all, it strengthens our heart — our resolve to live for Jesus as faithfully as we can. It replaces the Bread Alone Diet with the more nourishing Word Alone Diet.

What exercises maintain one's spiritual fitness? In my view, a regular regime of five basic activities promotes good spiritual health. The first two items offer healthy spiritual nutrition. (1) Of first importance is weekly worship with a local Christian congregation. Hebrews 10:25 urges us not to neglect meeting together as believers to encourage each other in our growth in fitness. Amazingly, Jesus promises to join us whenever we do so (Matt. 18:20)! More important, as our Creator, Savior, and heavenly Father, God simply deserves our honor and praise, and public worship is an important way to do that. Corporate worship benefits us in two specific ways: It gives us a break from everything else so we can focus on God, and it gives us extended contact with his very presence.

(2) A second basic nutritional exercise is to practice a love for the Bible as God's Word. Regular Bible reading hits the pause button on our often

frenetic preoccupation with "bread alone" so we can nurture our souls with God's words. Typically, we get to know people through conversation over time, and those conversations also teach us things about ourselves. A pattern of Scripture reading opens an ongoing conversation with God. It allows him to speak to us personally so we get to know him better—and to know ourselves better, too. Some believers set aside devotional times to read the Word, while others prefer listening to Bible readings from CDs en route somewhere. Whatever one's method, consider it a supplement to our daily diet of news; the latter keeps us abreast of what is going on, God's Word tells us what he thinks about it all. Time with Scripture also reminds us that he is right in the thick of all those other things.

I also recommend three strengthening exercises to supplement the nutritional ones. (3) Some form of ongoing service for Christ, preferably outside the church, is a necessary practice. We may start by praying for God to guide us to find an activity in which we may put our faith in action and visibly live out the love of Christ. In my view, priority should go to service done for people outside the church, particularly those who do not yet confess Christ as savior. For example, consider some way to bring justice to people whom your city or town tends to ignore if not disadvantage. In any case, the point is to do something that we enjoy or that stretches us. "Stretching" is always a good spiritual practice!

(4) Participation in a small accountability group is good for our spiritual health. The Christian life is, after all, a team sport, and small groups are essential to any spiritual fitness program. Such groups pick us up when we fall, applaud us when we succeed, and challenge us when we need a swift kick. Consider it like going to the gym, spiritually speaking.

(5) Regular offerings to support God's work financially are also an important spiritual exercise. The outside world may rag on Christian organizations for being "all in it for the money," but we know better. We know that God expects us to invest a portion of the resources that he gives us in his ongoing work.[112] Jesus teaches us to put our money in a safe, secure place—where rust cannot corrode it or thieves steal it (Matt. 6:19–20). It is in good hands with God for God will make it "grow" hugely through what he is doing in the world.

(6) Finally, an occasional Spiritual Fitness Test, an honest look in the mirror at how we are doing (perhaps in a group), is always a good idea.

The end of shame. One special highpoint, God's removal of Israel's shame (5:9), also has something to say to us. In Israel's case, the shame

---

112. For a convenient survey of biblical teaching on giving, see my 'The Art of Giving Well: How Can We Give When the Culture Says 'Get'?," *Moody Magazine* 101/4 (March/April 2001): 18–21.

in view is Egypt's ridicule of them for (in Egypt's view) stupidly following Yahweh, given his burial of a whole generation in the desert. What a relief to have Yahweh remove the humiliation wrongly heaped on them and to receive divine vindication for their faithfulness.

That humiliation by others is not unlike what Christians sometimes experience today. As I read the popular press, I pick up vibes that reflect a mood critical of Christians. Two recently dominant values probably drive this spirit: an increasingly secular worldview and religious pluralism as the cultural norm. Secularism excludes God from having a voice in anything and, by implication, looks down on anyone who claims that God already runs everything. The humiliating message its devotees send Christians is, "Oh, don't tell me you still believe in *that* old stuff?" Pluralism embraces all religions as good and ridicules anyone who asserts Christianity's unique claims about Jesus. Pluralism's followers tell Christians, "Shame on you! What arrogance to think that your religion is better than any other!" Indeed, my "gut feel" is that they perceive such claims to be insulting and a threat to the culture.

Some readers may have personally experienced touches of disdain from coworkers, neighbors, friends, and family. To my knowledge, no North American has gone to jail for holding on to faith in Jesus, but people do occasionally look down on us for our beliefs. Recent political activism by some highly visible evangelicals has probably made things worse for us.[113] Suddenly, evangelicals are on everyone's radar screen plugging their favorite hot-button issues in the political arena. Alas, the high profile creates the impression that we are out to force our beliefs on everyone else by political means.

Of course, popular hostility to followers of Jesus is nothing new. Jesus himself warned us to expect it: "Everyone will hate you because of me, but those who stand firm to the end will be saved" (Matt. 10:22 TNIV; cf. vv. 16−25). Emotionally, the rejection by the culture, and particularly people we know personally, is difficult to take. A section in Malcolm Gladwell's recent bestseller, *Blink: The Power of Thinking without Thinking*, captures the pain well. Gladwell briefly reports one fascinating result of research on marriage by Professor John Gottman of the University of Washington.[114]

Over many years, Gottman has analyzed videotaped conversations between marriage partners about some ordinary topic. From his studies,

---

113. For further, brief comment on this phenomenon, see the Contemporary Significance section of 24:1−28.

114. M. Gladwell, *Blink: The Power of Thinking without Thinking* (New York: Back Bay, 2005), 20−34, esp. 30−34.

Gottman claims that he can predict whether a marriage is in trouble merely by hearing a brief snippet of a couple's conversation (what Gladwell calls a "thin-slice"). For Gottman, the key signs of serious marital trouble are four negative emotions—defensiveness, stonewalling, criticism, and contempt—and of these Gottman believes contempt to be the most important indicator. (By "contempt," he means insulting comments in which one partner from a stance of superiority puts down the other). Gottman has found that if contempt infects a marriage, he can actually predict how many colds the husband and wife may suffer. In other words, the stress of receiving contempt from someone one loves is so great that it even takes its toll on the recipient's immune system. Says Gottman, "Contempt is closely related to disgust, and what disgust and contempt are about is completely rejecting and excluding someone from the community."[115] All this is to say that the experience of contempt and its impact on one's emotional side are things to be taken seriously.

Here again the gospel gives us good news that God also removes our moments of humiliation. Jesus reminds us that he himself calls us not "servants" but "friends" (John 15:15). Knowing that I am one of Jesus' friends eases the traces of shame left by our culture's rejection. So does remembering God's declaration concerning me: "Therefore, there is now no condemnation for those who are in Christ Jesus" (Rom. 8:1). In Christ, I have nothing to be ashamed of for following Jesus. On the contrary, I look forward to the vindication of my faith that Paul anticipates when he writes about every knee bowing and every tongue confessing that Jesus is Lord (Phil. 2:10–11; cf. Rom. 14:11). As a forgiven sinner, of course, I have no reason to gloat, but every reason to feel satisfaction. The satisfaction derives not from the fact that those who rejected Jesus "finally get theirs," but from the smiling approval of my Lord Jesus, for the fact that I hung in there with him.

A dose of reality: the Jesus War. The final theme about which Joshua 5–6 speaks to us concerns the unpleasant fact that we are not at peace but at war, the Jesus War. The contempt discussed above marks the iceberg tip of a harsh reality: The enemies of the gospel comprise a vast, truly cruel and truly tyrannical foe with vast strength (see Eph. 6:12). They are spiritual powers that cruelly enslave human beings and which, if unconquered, doom their captives to terrible eternal punishment.

These powers underlie every international war, rotting jail, violent crime, terrible torture, smutty movie, drug addiction, broken marriage, tragic suicide, and arrogant bureaucrat. They thwart our attempts to share

115. See ibid., 33.

the gospel, to reconcile fractured families, to better our neighborhoods, to serve the poor, and to win justice for the oppressed. Internationally, they imprison and oppress our sisters and brothers in contexts where real, live war rages. In short, with Joshua, we share the theological assumption that there is a war on and that God fights for his people.[116] The Jesus War actually continues the Yahweh war of the Old Testament.[117] Warrior Jesus exercises the same power on our behalf today as Warrior Yahweh did for Israel at Jericho. It is both a spiritual and political one, demanding that its troops engage God's enemies in both arenas.[118]

Now, a "decisive battle" is the central turning point in any war, the single event that turns the tide of victory in favor of one side, however many battles still remain to be fought. In early June, 1942, the U.S. won such a decisive battle against Japan at the Battle of Midway.[119] Having crippled the U.S. Pacific Fleet at Pearl Harbor, the Japanese navy hoped to lure American carriers to defeat by attacking U.S. forces on Midway Island. Instead, decoded secret messages and a little good luck enabled U.S. planes to surprise and sink four Japanese carriers, a defeat that crippled the Japanese navy for the rest of the war.

This history illustrates one important thing about the Jesus War: Jesus Christ has already won its decisive battles. To us, the tide of war often seems turned against us, but his victories have in reality decisively turned it in our favor.[120] To paraphrase Joshua, Jesus has already "given the enemy into our hands" (cf. 6:2; 8:1; 10:8). The healing of the Gerasene demoniac marks one such victory (Luke 8:27–36). This man's tormenters were so despotic that he lived pathetically alone among ritually unclean tombs. They

---

116. Witness the retrospective claims that "the LORD was fighting for Israel" (Josh. 10:14, 42) and "the LORD your God ... fought for you" (Josh. 23:3; cf. v. 10; Deut. 3:22; Zech. 14:3).

117. Cf. V. Eller, *King Jesus' Manual of Arms for the Armless* (Nashville: Abingdon, 1973) 116, who argues that the Old Testament tradition of Yahweh war gave early Christians "the framework within which they found their understanding of what God did do, is doing, and will do through Christ and for the world."

118. For a brief critique of the relationship of Christians to the modern secular state, especially its "neat division between sacred and secular spheres in life," see Holloway, "The Ethical Dimension of Holy War," 64–65. He rightly observes (64), "While the western world sees holy war as a primitive and threatening religious concept, others see the secular state — void of transcendent purpose and divine guidance — as inherently more dangerous."

119. For personal accounts by battle survivors from both navys, see "Ghosts and Survivors Return to the Battle of Midway," *National Geographic* (April 1999), 80–103.

120. For further details, especially concerning exorcisms by Jesus as victories, see Longman and Reid, *God Is a Warrior*, 97–103.

---

were, in fact, a demon horde by the name of "Legion," the Roman term for a fearful military unit.[121] Jesus banished the spiritual legion to nearby pigs, a conquest akin to those of Yahweh's war against Israel's human enemies. He proved them to be powerless before his wondrous power.

The cross and the resurrection mark Jesus' most decisive victory—in Eller's words, "The Victory of Skull Hill."[122] At Calvary and the empty tomb God through Christ decisively defeated humanity's bitterest enemies, sin and death. In Colossians 2:15, Paul imagines three invisible events happening on Skull Hill when Jesus died.[123] God, first, disarms the "powers and authorities," stripping off their might like an old, frayed, useless garment.[124] Then he "made [them] a public spectacle" (*deigmatizo*, "to expose to public shame, disgrace"). He imagines the once-powerful authorities slowly trudging, naked and downcast, past the crowds in disgrace (cf. Matt. 1:19).[125] What irony! At the time, Jesus' disciples mourned a terrible loss, but in retrospect it marked the stunning, humiliating defeat of all evil powers. Finally, Paul imagines God "triumphing over them" (*thriambeuo*, "to celebrate a triumph" or "to lead in triumph"). This phrase pictures a general leading his victorious army and its vanquished foes in public celebration after a battle (cf. 2 Cor. 2:14; Eph. 4:8). It recalls the happy, relieved celebrations after the conclusion of World War II or the more recent Gulf War of the early 1990s.

The point of Paul's imaginary scenario is this: At the time, Jesus' death and resurrection seemed a colossal setback for God's salvific plan, but in retrospect it emerges as the decisive defeat of his enemies. It defeated, dethroned, and disarmed the Prince of Darkness, a great victory that has paved the way for humans to receive salvation.

---

121. Cf. H. Priesker, "λεγιών," *TDNT*, 4:68−69. Elsewhere the term describes angels (Matt. 26:53).

122. Eller, *King Jesus' Manual of Arms*, 115−45; cf. Longman and Reid, *God Is a Warrior*, 119−35. In my view, the New Testament treats them as two phases of a single event, so what follows treats them likewise.

123. For detailed discussion of interpretive nuances, see J. D. G. Dunn, *The Epistles to the Colossians and to Philemon* (NIGTC; Grand Rapids: Eerdmans, 1996), 166−70; D. Garland, *Colossians and Philemon* (NIVAC; Grand Rapids: Zondervan, 1998), 152−54. For Jesus' own statements concerning the disarming of Satan, see Luke 10:18; 11:21−22.

124. Cf. Dunn, *Colossians and Philemon*, 168: "For the Colossians ... the point would be clear: the spiritual powers, including the elemental forces (2:8), should be counted as of no greater value and significance than a bunch of old rags."

125. Dunn (ibid., 168) compares the picture to the requirement of Cyprian law that the hair of an adulteress be cut off publicly and that the community henceforth treat her as a prostitute. Israel also practiced similar public punishment (e.g., Ezek. 16:38−40; Hos. 2:2−3).

What are the implications of Paul's images for us? (1) It means that we are not responsible for winning the final victory for God—Christ has already won that. Our responsibility is simply to carry out our duties as faithful soldiers of the cross.

(2) It means that our spiritual enemies—Satan and all his hosts—need no longer paralyze us with fear. Though to be taken seriously, Satan today is an enemy already defeated and disarmed by the Warrior Jesus. We need not cower in fear before him. We dishonor Christ—and deny the reality of his great victory at Skull Hill and the Empty Tomb—when we treat the devil as a spiritual boogeyman who haunts our every step. In trying not to underestimate the threat that he and his army pose, we sometimes overestimate their power. We need to remember just how defeated and powerless they are. Imagine them as dazed, humiliated soldiers firmly under the authority of Jesus and sing with Martin Luther in his "A Mighty Fortress":

> The Prince of Darkness grim? We tremble not for him!
> His rage we can endure, for lo, his doom is sure.
> One little word shall fell him!

(3) Finally, Christ's victory reminds us of just how great is the power working in us. At Skull Hill and the Empty Tomb, God displayed firepower so overwhelming that it released all creation from the grip of sin and death. And that same power undergirds our faithful service as spiritual soldiers. Thus, we should fight our battles with the same confidence that Israel had in marching around Jericho. Our enemy is already on the run, so our task is, like Israel at Jericho, to enter enemy territory, follow up, and consolidate Jesus' victory there. I once met a man who used to greet people by saying "Praise God, the devil's on the run!" The greeting often took its recipients by surprise, but it also aimed to encourage them. Christians may take Satan's power seriously but need not live in terror of him. He is "on the run," fleeing in retreat, still reeling from his thrashing at Skull Hill and the Empty Tomb.

The year 1971 found me far from home in the hot, humid Mekong Delta of Vietnam. I was a "circuit-riding preacher," a Navy chaplain assigned to pastor personnel on small bases and repair ships along the delta's rivers and criss-crossing canals. My travels took me one day to visit a new base at Cho Moi. Militarily, the area was fairly safe, so a group of us took an afternoon stroll from the base to the village nearby. After passing various shops, we entered the local Catholic church where mass was being said in Vietnamese. The language barrier led me to quietly worship on my own. Frankly, a few months in country had left me discouraged. The ministry seemed to be difficult, and my efforts seemed to yield few results. A few times no one showed up for church! I had begun to wonder why God had sent me there—and why instead I could not be home with my lovely young wife of one year.

As I prayed, suddenly the Lord brought Jesus' reassuring words to mind: "On this rock I will build my church, and the gates of Hades will not overcome it" (Matt. 16:18). A small dawn of hope opened in my weary soul. It reminded me of Christ's commitment to "build my church," a church that hell itself could not defeat. I went on with my duties encouraged that God was building it through me, however imperceptible the signs of progress. I soldiered on, confident that God's efforts through me were unstoppable.

And so should we. Indeed, remembrance of Jesus' wonderful victories reassures us that we are on the winning side, however difficult the Jerichos we face may seem. Our confidence and persistence derive from the fundamental biblical fact that Jesus has won the decisive battle. Jesus has triumphed; our enemy has been stripped of his weapons and publicly humiliated. People may erect walls to keep Jesus out, but no walls can withstand his overwhelming power. So, daily we enter the field of battle, wherever God sends us, knowing that his powerful presence surrounds our every step. We plod on humbly and patiently, knowing that God already has the enemy on the run. He is, in fact, quietly and gently wooing many of them to surrender willingly to his loving lordship.

Joshua 7:1 – 8:29

B UT THE ISRAELITES acted unfaithfully in regard to the devoted things; Achan son of Carmi, the son of Zimri, the son of Zerah, of the tribe of Judah, took some of them. So the LORD's anger burned against Israel.

²Now Joshua sent men from Jericho to Ai, which is near Beth Aven to the east of Bethel, and told them, "Go up and spy out the region." So the men went up and spied out Ai.

³When they returned to Joshua, they said, "Not all the people will have to go up against Ai. Send two or three thousand men to take it and do not weary all the people, for only a few men are there." ⁴So about three thousand men went up; but they were routed by the men of Ai, ⁵who killed about thirty-six of them. They chased the Israelites from the city gate as far as the stone quarries and struck them down on the slopes. At this the hearts of the people melted and became like water.

⁶Then Joshua tore his clothes and fell facedown to the ground before the ark of the LORD, remaining there till evening. The elders of Israel did the same, and sprinkled dust on their heads. ⁷And Joshua said, "Ah, Sovereign LORD, why did you ever bring this people across the Jordan to deliver us into the hands of the Amorites to destroy us? If only we had been content to stay on the other side of the Jordan! ⁸O Lord, what can I say, now that Israel has been routed by its enemies? ⁹The Canaanites and the other people of the country will hear about this and they will surround us and wipe out our name from the earth. What then will you do for your own great name?"

¹⁰The LORD said to Joshua, "Stand up! What are you doing down on your face? ¹¹Israel has sinned; they have violated my covenant, which I commanded them to keep. They have taken some of the devoted things; they have stolen, they have lied, they have put them with their own possessions. ¹²That is why the Israelites cannot stand against their enemies; they turn their backs and run because they have been made liable to destruction. I will not be with you anymore unless you destroy whatever among you is devoted to destruction.

¹³"Go, consecrate the people. Tell them, 'Consecrate yourselves in preparation for tomorrow; for this is what the LORD, the God of Israel, says: That which is devoted is among you, O Israel. You cannot stand against your enemies until you remove it.

¹⁴"'In the morning, present yourselves tribe by tribe. The tribe that the LORD takes shall come forward clan by clan; the clan that the LORD takes shall come forward family by family; and the family that the LORD takes shall come forward man by man. ¹⁵He who is caught with the devoted things shall be destroyed by fire, along with all that belongs to him. He has violated the covenant of the LORD and has done a disgraceful thing in Israel!'"

¹⁶Early the next morning Joshua had Israel come forward by tribes, and Judah was taken. ¹⁷The clans of Judah came forward, and he took the Zerahites. He had the clan of the Zerahites come forward by families, and Zimri was taken. ¹⁸Joshua had his family come forward man by man, and Achan son of Carmi, the son of Zimri, the son of Zerah, of the tribe of Judah, was taken.

¹⁹Then Joshua said to Achan, "My son, give glory to the LORD, the God of Israel, and give him the praise. Tell me what you have done; do not hide it from me."

²⁰Achan replied, "It is true! I have sinned against the LORD, the God of Israel. This is what I have done: ²¹When I saw in the plunder a beautiful robe from Babylonia, two hundred shekels of silver and a wedge of gold weighing fifty shekels, I coveted them and took them. They are hidden in the ground inside my tent, with the silver underneath."

²²So Joshua sent messengers, and they ran to the tent, and there it was, hidden in his tent, with the silver underneath. ²³They took the things from the tent, brought them to Joshua and all the Israelites and spread them out before the LORD.

²⁴Then Joshua, together with all Israel, took Achan son of Zerah, the silver, the robe, the gold wedge, his sons and daughters, his cattle, donkeys and sheep, his tent and all that he had, to the Valley of Achor. ²⁵Joshua said, "Why have you brought this trouble on us? The LORD will bring trouble on you today."

Then all Israel stoned him, and after they had stoned the rest, they burned them. ²⁶Over Achan they heaped up a large pile of rocks, which remains to this day. Then the LORD turned from his fierce anger. Therefore that place has been called the Valley of Achor ever since.

⁸:¹Then the LORD said to Joshua, "Do not be afraid; do not be discouraged. Take the whole army with you, and go up and attack Ai. For I have delivered into your hands the king of Ai, his people, his city and his land. ²You shall do to Ai and its king as you did to Jericho and its king, except that you may carry off their plunder and livestock for yourselves. Set an ambush behind the city."

³So Joshua and the whole army moved out to attack Ai. He chose thirty thousand of his best fighting men and sent them out at night ⁴with these orders: "Listen carefully. You are to set an ambush behind the city. Don't go very far from it. All of you be on the alert. ⁵I and all those with me will advance on the city, and when the men come out against us, as they did before, we will flee from them. ⁶They will pursue us until we have lured them away from the city, for they will say, 'They are running away from us as they did before.' So when we flee from them, ⁷you are to rise up from ambush and take the city. The LORD your God will give it into your hand. ⁸When you have taken the city, set it on fire. Do what the LORD has commanded. See to it; you have my orders."

⁹Then Joshua sent them off, and they went to the place of ambush and lay in wait between Bethel and Ai, to the west of Ai—but Joshua spent that night with the people.

¹⁰Early the next morning Joshua mustered his men, and he and the leaders of Israel marched before them to Ai. ¹¹The entire force that was with him marched up and approached the city and arrived in front of it. They set up camp north of Ai, with the valley between them and the city. ¹²Joshua had taken about five thousand men and set them in ambush between Bethel and Ai, to the west of the city. ¹³They had the soldiers take up their positions—all those in the camp to the north of the city and the ambush to the west of it. That night Joshua went into the valley.

¹⁴When the king of Ai saw this, he and all the men of the city hurried out early in the morning to meet Israel in battle at a certain place overlooking the Arabah. But he did not

know that an ambush had been set against him behind the city. ¹⁵Joshua and all Israel let themselves be driven back before them, and they fled toward the desert. ¹⁶All the men of Ai were called to pursue them, and they pursued Joshua and were lured away from the city. ¹⁷Not a man remained in Ai or Bethel who did not go after Israel. They left the city open and went in pursuit of Israel.

¹⁸Then the LORD said to Joshua, "Hold out toward Ai the javelin that is in your hand, for into your hand I will deliver the city." So Joshua held out his javelin toward Ai. ¹⁹As soon as he did this, the men in the ambush rose quickly from their position and rushed forward. They entered the city and captured it and quickly set it on fire.

²⁰The men of Ai looked back and saw the smoke of the city rising against the sky, but they had no chance to escape in any direction, for the Israelites who had been fleeing toward the desert had turned back against their pursuers. ²¹For when Joshua and all Israel saw that the ambush had taken the city and that smoke was going up from the city, they turned around and attacked the men of Ai. ²²The men of the ambush also came out of the city against them, so that they were caught in the middle, with Israelites on both sides. Israel cut them down, leaving them neither survivors nor fugitives. ²³But they took the king of Ai alive and brought him to Joshua.

²⁴When Israel had finished killing all the men of Ai in the fields and in the desert where they had chased them, and when every one of them had been put to the sword, all the Israelites returned to Ai and killed those who were in it. ²⁵Twelve thousand men and women fell that day—all the people of Ai. ²⁶For Joshua did not draw back the hand that held out his javelin until he had destroyed all who lived in Ai. ²⁷But Israel did carry off for themselves the livestock and plunder of this city, as the LORD had instructed Joshua.

²⁸So Joshua burned Ai and made it a permanent heap of ruins, a desolate place to this day. ²⁹He hung the king of Ai on a tree and left him there until evening. At sunset, Joshua ordered them to take his body from the tree and throw it down at the entrance of the city gate. And they raised a large pile of rocks over it, which remains to this day.

ONE MAY IMAGINE THAT Jericho gave Israel a "high" and boosted their confidence. Another resounding victory seems in the offing, turning the invasion into something of a juggernaut. Joshua selects Ai as Israel's next target, but its conquest hits a serious snag because of something secretly done at Jericho but as yet unreported.[1] Once the snag is removed, however, Yahweh gives Israel a second chance at Ai, and a positive outcome results.

Structurally, the text comprises reports concerning the first (7:1–26) and second attacks on Ai (8:1–29). In the former, the short battle report (Ai I) merely sets the scene for the well-known story of Achan, while the latter recounts the actual fall of Ai to Israel (Ai II). As with the first spy story (ch. 2), here again Joshua acts on his own, dispatching spies and launching Ai I (ch. 7). But it is Yahweh who orders the second, and he also dictates the military tactic to use (8:1–2). In fact, the command-obedience pattern dominant in Joshua 3–7 recurs in chapter 8. The plot of Joshua 7–8, in which a faked retreat and ambush reverse an earlier military defeat, is a traditional one both in Israel and in classical sources.[2] But the chronology of Joshua 8 merits brief comment because of possible confusion.[3]

The action of Ai II begins at night. Joshua issues instructions, sends the ambush team off to Ai, and spends the night with the rest of the army (8:3–9). The group presumably secretly reaches the ambush site in the middle of the night (Night 1).[4] The next morning (Day 1), Joshua and the elders lead the remaining troops to Ai, where they encamp (vv. 10–13).

---

1. Concerning the literary history and archaeological background of chs. 7–8, see Z. Zevit, "Archaeological and Literary Stratigraphy in Joshua 7–8," *BASOR* 251 (1983): 23–35. For the literary interplay of Outsider and Insider between Rahab (Josh. 2, 6) and Achan, cf. Spina, *The Faith of the Outsider*, 52–71; L. Rowlett, "Inclusion Exclusion and Marginality in the Book of Joshua," *JSOT* 55 (1992): 19–23.

2. Cf. Judg. 20:15–48; Nelson, *Joshua*, 111–12; Hess, *Joshua*, 160–61, who cites several ancient Near Eastern examples. For Greco-Roman examples and in-depth treatment of military tactics in Joshua, see A. Malamat, *A History of Biblical Israel* (CHANE 7; Leiden: Brill, 2001), 80–96.

3. This is not to say, as Nelson does (*Joshua*, 110), that "this narrative is rough and confused."

4. The conflicting sizes given for the ambush group — 30,000 (vv. 1, 3) versus 5,000 (v. 12) — pose a problem that defies solution. Woudstra (*Joshua*, 137) and Howard (*Joshua*, 203) attribute it to a scribal error and accept the smaller figure as correct. That is possible, but no manuscript evidence supports it (as Howard concedes). Butler (*Joshua*, 84), however, traces the difference to the text's prehistory, each figure marking a thematic symbol. The latter figure would underscore Israel's faith in relying on only 5,000 to defeat a city of 12,000, the former ten times the number sent for Ai I (7:4).

They make their presence obvious in front of the city to draw its attention to them and away from their comrades hidden behind it (v. 11). That night Joshua descends into the valley for some unstated purpose (Night 2).[5]

The next morning (Day 2), the king of Ai sees something threatening, probably Joshua's presence in the valley, and the battle is on (8:14 – 29). Repetitions of the positions of the ambushers (vv. 9, 12, 13) and main force (vv. 11, 13) seem superfluous but probably serve to raise reader anticipation of the coming drama. Since verses 4 – 8 detail the course of events in verses 9 – 19 but not verses 20 – 29, the latter literarily take the reader by (pleasant) surprise. Literarily, 8:1 – 2 and 8:27 – 29 bracket the chapter with a satisfying thematic inclusio, and its many geographical details enrich the narrative and confirm the location of Ai (see Bridging Contexts). The clever use of alternating viewpoints (Ai versus Israel) creates "the disorienting impression of a confusing melee."[6] Finally, Joshua 7 – 8 voices the theological paradigm that undergirds the entire book: Disobedience stirs Yahweh's anger and incurs his judgment (Achan), but obedience guarantees national success.

Ai Attack I (Joshua 7:1 – 26)

A DEADLY SECRET (7:1 – 15). Without preface or fanfare, the narrator reveals a shocking, deadly secret (v. 1): "Israel acted unfaithfully in regard to the devoted things [*ḥerem*]" (v. 1). At Jericho, someone apparently kept them as spoils of war rather than hand them over to Yahweh as he commanded.[7] The language is blunt, emphatic, and fraught with terrible consequences; it casts an "atmosphere of foreboding" over the chapter.[8] The priestly theological term *maʿal* ("to act faithlessly") describes a highly serious, treacherous breach of trust between Yahweh and Israel (cf. 22:16, 22).[9] In this case,

---

5. The ancient versions apparently found the end of v. 13 ("That night Joshua went into the valley") problematic. For full discussion, cf. Nelson, *Joshua*, 112, who omits the sentence and times Israel's arrival (v. 11) and their discovery by the king of Ai to the same day, rather than the next morning (so MT; NIV; NRSV; NLT). For alternative chronological readings, see Woudstra, *Joshua*, 136 – 40; Howard, *Joshua*, 200 – 201.

6. Nelson, *Joshua*, 112 – 13 (quote 113); Hawk, *Joshua*, 127 – 28. Nelson also sees an inclusio frame around Joshua's speech (vv. 3 – 10).

7. For more details on the practice of *ḥerem*, see Bridging Contexts in chs. 5 – 6. For in-depth discussion of Josh. 7 – 8, see Hubbard, "What Do These Stones Mean?" 25 – 49.

8. The phrase comes from G. Mitchell, *Together in the Land* (JSOTSup 134; Sheffield: Sheffield Academic Press, 1993), 67.

9. The root describes unfaithfulness both toward other humans—e.g., the sexual infidelity of a spouse (Num. 5:11 – 31), the deceptive withholding of a deposit (Lev. 5:21 [6:2]; cf. also Job 21:34; Prov. 16:10)—or toward God (1 Chron. 5:25; 2 Chron. 26:16; Ezek. 14:13 – 20; 18:24; 20:27; et al.); cf. R. Knierim, "מָעַל," THAT, 1:920 – 22; H. Ringgren, "מָעַל," TDOT, 8:460 – 63.

ma°al ("disloyalty, infidelity") amounts to stealing Yahweh's money right out of the offering plate.[10]

The culprit, the one who took items from Jericho, is a man named Achan with an impressive, prestigious pedigree ("son of Carmi, the son of Zimri, the son of Zerah, of the tribe of Judah"; cf. v. 18). His tribe will soon produce Israel's royal dynasty, so he is "as Israelite as Rahab is Canaanite, which makes his violation ... even more egregious."[11] For the first time in the book, God is furious with the Israelites. In Butler's words, "Israel has become the enemy rather than the people of God."[12] Readers know about the crime, the criminal, and God's fury (v. 1), but Joshua and Israel remain in the dark, oblivious to the readers' sense of foreboding.[13] They only learn about them when — to their great surprise! — the foreboding becomes an unhappy reality in unexpected events at Ai.

As with Jericho, Joshua acts on his own, dispatching another reconnaissance team to spy out the region around Ai (Heb. *ha°ay*, lit., "the ruin"; v. 2). Thus far such initiative has been rare in Joshua: Yahweh has orchestrated virtually all the events of chapters 1–6.[14] The reader wonders how the outcome of this spy mission will compare to that of the last one (Josh. 2). The selection of Ai, a town in the central mountains just east of better-known Bethel, makes good military sense.[15] A victory there will drive an Israelite wedge into the very heart of the land and give Israel access to the main roads in all directions.

Again, as at Jericho (2:24), the spies' report on Ai is positive (7:3): no need to march the whole army up there; a force of two or three thousand will easily overwhelm Ai's small garrison ("only a few men"). Of course, physically this attack is far more demanding than that against Jericho. A few miles across flat terrain hardly compares to an uphill trek thirteen miles inland to three thousand feet elevation. On the spies' advice, Joshua

---

10. Cf. Yahweh's characterization of the act in v. 11 as "to sin" (*hata°*), "to steal" (*ganab*), and "to act deceitfully" (*kahaš*, pi.); and Milgrom's definition of *ma°al* as "trespassing upon the divine realm, either by poaching on his sancta [holy things] or breaking his covenant oath; it is a lethal sin which can destroy both the offender and the community"; cf. J. Milgrom, *Cult and Conscience: The Asham and the Priestly Doctrine of Repentance* (Leiden: Brill, 1976), 16–21 (quote 21).

11. Spina, *The Faith of the Outsider*, 65.

12. Butler, *Joshua*, 84.

13. This literary device of informing readers while characters remain oblivious occurs elsewhere in Hebrew narrative; cf. Gen. 3:1; 22:1; Ruth 2:1.

14. For Yahweh's initiative, cf. 1:1; 3:7; 4:1, 15; 5:2, 9; 6:2. Joshua apparently acts on his own in 2:1; 5:13; 6:26.

15. The location of the other reference point, Beth Aven (lit., "house of iniquity [or wealth?]"), is uncertain; cf. P. M. Arnold, "Beth-Aven," *ABD*, 1:682.

---

sends "about three thousand" soldiers (actually about five hundred) to Ai but with shocking results: Ai's "few" defenders send the group of soldiers packing (v. 4).[16]

The author drops a few details to highlight the irony. The greatly out-numbered "few" kill about thirty-six Israelites, then go on the offensive, chasing the invaders from their front gate. They overtake the Israelites at the nearby town quarries and clobber them as they retreat downhill (v. 5a).[17] Worse, enemy hearts had melted in fear of Israel (2:11; 5:1), but now wishy-washy courage haunts Israel ("hearts . . . melted and became like water"; v. 5b). So much for the Israelite invasion juggernaut! Grave doubts suddenly plague Israel: Will God enable them to take even one more city, much less the whole land? Right before the reader's eyes, frightened Israel is looking more and more like the Canaanites.[18]

Joshua himself acts out his own bitter grief over the crisis (and perhaps over his personal responsibility for it). He tears his clothes and joins the tribal leadership ("the elders") in tossing dust on their heads and in laying face down before the ark until the evening (v. 6). (Presumably, they also wail loudly or keep deathly quiet the whole time.) These gestures typically express great sorrow over a death or a grievous setback (Gen. 37:34; 44:13; Lam. 2:14; Ezek. 27:30). The dramatic prostration of Israel's leadership before the ark probably aims to enlist God's attention to the tragedy — the mourners (unlike the reader) oblivious to its root cause. Defeat in only the second battle of the campaign bodes ill for Israel and certainly marks the scene as the saddest thus far in the book.

About nightfall, Joshua finally speaks (v. 7), addressing God with a typi-cal formula of deference, "Ah, Sovereign LORD" (cf. Judg. 6:22; Jer. 1:6; 4:10; Ezek. 4:14; 9:8). He then asks an accusatory question: Why did Yahweh bring "this people" across the Jordan only to hand "us" over to the Amorites for destruction? The question echoes questions Moses also raised when his obedience resulted in a crisis rather than success (i.e., Ex. 5:22; 32:11; cf. Num. 11:11).[19] In wishing ("If only . . .") "we" had "been content" to stay on the Jordan's other side (v. 7b), Joshua also sounds like Israel's grumbling

---

16. The shock of this defeat is not lessened if one assumes (with many scholars) that Heb. *'elep* "thousand" actually means more vaguely "sizeable group" or "company" (ca. 200–250 soldiers). See further comments below.

17. It is uncertain whether Heb. *haššebarim* is a plural noun of place (NIV "quarries") or a proper noun (NRSV "Shebarim"). It occurs nowhere else, but the root *šabar* ("to smash, shat-ter") favors a place of "shatterings" or "quarries" (so NIV, NLT).

18. Cf. Spina, *The Faith of the Outsider*, 65–66.

19. The people several times ask Moses why he brought them out of Egypt into the barren desert; cf. Ex. 17:3; Num. 20:4–5.

against God and Moses in the wilderness (Num. 14:2; 20:3; cf. Job 6:2).[20] His preference for Transjordan over Canaan equates to the earlier generation's hankering for Egypt over the desert (Num. 14:2; cf. 20:3).

Given Joshua's ignorance of Achan's perfidy, one may forgive him the frustration and indignation with which his words ring. Indeed, unlike his ancestors whose grumbling voiced rebellion, Joshua here simply invokes the hyperbole of lament and regret. Besides, he still addresses Yahweh with a formula of respect ("O Lord" [Heb. *bi ʾadonay*, "by your leave"]), bowing to Yahweh's authority as a preface to his next cry of frustration (v. 8).[21] He does not know what to say after Israel has turned tail (Heb. *ʿorep*, "back of the neck") and fled from their enemies. What command or pep talk can he possibly give to drive the invasion forward?

Worse, the retreat has damaged Israel's psychological advantage over the peoples of Canaan (v. 9). Israel's self-confidence and popular perception of invincibility are gone. One imagines them fearfully huddled in their tent camp at Gilgal with no fortified cities to run to. Joshua himself fears the camp's vulnerability to easy encirclement and annihilation by the enemy ("wipe out [lit., cut] our name"). Rhetorically, the subtext of Joshua's lament argues that Yahweh has a huge stake in Israel's survival and, hence, that God should consider — perhaps even feel obliged to — intervene. Here Joshua sounds like Moses, who twice interceded to win Yahweh's forgiveness and end his threatened judgment — once at Sinai after the golden calf episode (Ex. 32:11 – 14), and once at Kadesh Barnea after the spies' report (Num. 14:13 – 19). The irony is that, unlike Moses, Joshua argues for Israel's survival without knowing the real threat to Israel — Yahweh's anger over Achan's sin.

Finally, Joshua ends his soliloquy the way he began it — with a question (but a more personal and pointed one than before) to drive home what he sees as ultimately at stake here for Yahweh. He plays on the word "name" (*šem*): If "*our name*" is gone, he asks, "what then will you [Yahweh] do for *your* own great name?" (italics mine) A "great name" is what people today call a "good reputation." It connotes the positive standing or reputation that friends, coworkers, and even total strangers who have "heard something" accord someone they respect (e.g., Gen. 12:2; Deut. 26:19; 2 Sam. 7:9; 8:13).

Obviously, Yahweh's reputation in Israel (Ps. 76:1; cf. 1 Sam. 12:22) and among the nations is solid (1 Kings 8:42; 2 Chron. 6:42; Mal. 1:11, 14). The Gibeonites will shortly cite that fame as their reason for proposing a

---

20. Grammatically, Heb. *lu* + verb means "Oh, I wish that …"; cf. WO §38.2e.
21. Cf. Ex. 4:10, 13; Judg. 6:15; 13:8.

peace treaty with Israel (Josh. 9:9–10). It is the respect (lit., "name") that Yahweh won in Egypt and east of the Jordan. But, as Moses once argued, that reputation may suffer if the nations (esp. Egyptians and Canaanites) hear about Israel's misfortunes and interpret them as signs of Yahweh's weakness or even malevolence (Ex. 32:12; Num. 14:13–16).

So Joshua makes the same pitch. If we grant Yahweh's absolute sovereignty, Joshua's subtext implies that the loss of Israel will tarnish the greatness of Yahweh in the nations' eyes. Unflattering, cynical rumors of his catastrophic failures will spread. He will become the laughingstock of his enemies. Like it or not, his reputation hangs on Israel's quality of character and historical success, so with Israel gone, Joshua asks, "What then will you do for your own great name?" For a human addressing God, the argument is amazingly bold and personal—very much like those of Moses. As Boling puts it, "Here at the climax of his complaint Joshua means to hit where it will hurt the most. And it brings a response."[22]

Response, indeed! "Stand up! What are you doing down on your face?" Yahweh barks with obvious irritation (v. 10). In God's eyes, Joshua's posture and procedure are totally out of line—in modern terms, he "just doesn't get it." This is not about divine inattention but about Israel's sin ("Israel has sinned"; v. 11). In highly provocative words, Yahweh rapidly ticks off what has him so ticked off:[23] Israel's "sin" involves covenant breach (i.e., the keeping of "devoted things")—in other words, theft, trickery, and presumed ownership of things that belong to him.[24] To put "holy" things (i.e., items set aside for God's use alone) to "profane" use particularly offends God's holiness.

This outrage explains the disaster at Ai (v. 12)—why Israel lacks the courage to take on their enemies, turning tail and running instead (cf. v. 8). In short, Israel itself has now become what it stole—*ḥerem* ("destined for destruction")—and unless they do what they should have in the first place (i.e., destroy the hidden *ḥerem*) Yahweh refuses to be with them. They can go wherever they like, but they do so without his powerful, protective presence ("I will not be with you anymore")—the ultimate vulnerability! They

---

22. Boling, *Joshua*, 224. In my view, this is the opposite of Butler's claim (*Joshua*, 85): "Israel depends for its name on Yahweh. Yahweh does not depend for his name upon Israel."

23. Strikingly, five short sentences strung together by the emphatic particle *gam* ("also, indeed") fire a rapid rhetorical barrage (i.e., "They did this, *and* they did this, *and* they did this …"). The verbal volley explains how "Israel has sinned."

24. "To steal" (*ganab*) plainly violates the well-known prohibition from the Decalogue (Ex. 20:15; Deut. 5:19) and "to act deceitfully" (*kaḥaš*, pi.) is "an infringement of sacral law" and, by implication, "a transgression of Yahweh's covenant"; cf. K.-D. Schunck, "כָּחַשׁ," *TDOT*, 7:134; V. Hamp, "גָּנַב," *TDOT*, 3:42–45.

have "a serious and malignant presence"—a virtual Canaanite—within their ranks (i.e., Achan). Their annihilation as a people hangs in the balance![25]

But Yahweh spells out the conditions to be met to satisfy the divine "unless" (vv. 13–15). Joshua must "consecrate (*qadaš* pi.) the people," ordering them to "consecrate yourselves" (*qadaš* hith.) for a ceremony the next day (v. 13a). To underscore its absolute importance, its rationale comes in a prophetic-like oracle ("this is what the LORD ... says"). Yahweh addresses the people directly, as if throwing his full weight behind it. He bluntly confronts Israel with two painful facts of life: There is *ḥerem* somewhere in the camp right now, and they will not win another victory until they completely "remove" it (v. 13b). As Hess writes, "Either Israel must destroy the devoted things ... or it will be destroyed as devoted things."[26]

The oracle also details the removal procedure (vv. 14–15). Tomorrow morning, Israel is to present themselves before God by tribes so that Yahweh may sift out (lit. "take" [*lakad*, "capture, trap"]) the mystery man's tribe, clan, and family step by step. Then, each man in the family is to pass until the lot "takes" the one hiding *ḥerem*. Probably, Yahweh "takes" through the casting of lots, although the text does not so specify.[27]

An interesting ancient Near Eastern parallel suggests what the process may have been like.[28] The lots would have been two stones, one white and one black, respectively signifying a "yes" or "no" answer to the question, "Is this tribe/clan/family/individual the one?" As Joshua presided, someone (perhaps a priest) would draw out one stone hidden in his clothing to evaluate each candidate. A "no" would exclude the party from further consideration, while a "yes" would lead to further winnowing until the individual was "taken." Theologically, the procedure assumes that Yahweh's hand invisibly guides the lot drawing to flush out the secret crook. The officiant might even repeat the process three times with each candidate to verify that divine guidance rather than mere chance lay behind the result.[29] Elsewhere *lakad* describes the capture of cities, so the text

---

25. Spina, *The Faith of the Outsider*, 67–68.

26. Hess, *Joshua*, 150.

27. Cf. 1 Sam. 10:20–21; 14:14–15, 41–42. Later, Joshua will cast lots to distribute the land (14:2; 15:1; chs.18, 19, and 21).

28. Cf. W. Horowitz and V. Hurowitz, "Urim and Thummim in Light of a Psephomancy Ritual from Assur (LKA 137)," *JANES* 21 (1992): 95–115; cf. also V. Hurowitz, "True Light on the Urim and Thummim," *JQR* 88/3–4 (1998): 263–74. Admittedly, Joshua 7 does not specify the use of Urim and Thummim.

29. Horowitz and Hurowitz, "Urim and Thummim," 108. For discussion of the process of casting lots in the division of land, see the Original Meaning section concerning 18:11–19:48.

may also portray this "capture" as a unique act of Yahweh's war against an internal enemy.[30]

The penalty is severe: the individual and everything he has will be burned — and for two reasons: He has violated the covenant (cf. v. 11) and "did a disgraceful thing [*nebalah*] in Israel" (v. 15b).[31] Elsewhere, *nebalah* ("folly, outrage") describes sexual immorality (e.g., Deut. 22:21) and more general foolish acts that violate accepted norms of fairness. Phrases like "such a thing is not done (in Israel)" often further explain the word, showing that *nebalah*-action transgresses a commonly accepted standard of conduct. The act here amounts to an egregious intrusion into Yahweh's sacral sphere, one worthy of execution by fire.

In short, this is not a petty crime but deadly serious business, and the direst of consequences follow. Singlehandedly, the man has returned Israel to their precrossing state of uncleanness (see 3:5) and driven Yahweh from their midst.[32] They are no longer "holy" enough to wage Yahweh's war. Worse, without Yahweh fighting for them, they are doomed to disastrous defeat (cf. vv. 7–9). The only antidote is to unmask the mystery man whose disgraceful, secret theft of Yahweh's *ḥerem* now imperils Israel's very survival.

Joshua's discovery (7:16 – 26). Early the next morning, Joshua executes the plan. Strikingly, impersonal, passive verbs ("was taken") replace the active verbs ("Yahweh takes") of the instruction. The scene is high drama, the atmosphere tense. Huge numbers of nonwar veterans — women, children, and nonmilitary males — probably turn out to witness it. One can imagine nervous glances of suspicion among the groups "taken" and sighs of relief by those not.

Quickly, the process identifies the tribe (Judah; v. 16), the clan (the Zerahites), and the family (Zabdi; v. 17). Finally, the lot nabs the traitor from among Zabdi's males, Achan, and the narrator ticks off his illustrious lineage (v. 18). Subdued comments probably ripple through the crowd at the shocking revelation, and a mini-trial ensues. Joshua addresses Achan as "my son" (v. 19), the way superiors speak to subordinates (1 Sam. 3:16; 4:16; 2 Sam. 18:22). He commands him to "give glory to the LORD ... and ... praise" (cf. 1 Sam. 6:5). The command assumes that Achan's crime

---

30. Cf. H. Gross, "לָכַד," *TDOT*, 8:2–3. The verb plays a prominent role in Yahweh's war in Joshua (6:20; 8:19, 21; 10:1, 28, 32, 35, 37, 39, 42; 11:10, 12, 17; 15:16, 17; 19:47).

31. For the phrase *ʿaśah nebalah beyiśrael* ("to do folly in Israel"), see Gen. 34:7; Deut. 22:21; Judg. 20:6, 10; 2 Sam. 13:12; Jer. 29:23.

32. The virtual identity of the commands in 3:5 and 7:13 suggest this. Elsewhere, the purification procedure prepares Israel for a theophany (cf. Ex. 19:10, 14), but here it anticipates a cult-legal procedure, including the removal of the contaminating *ḥerem* (Josh. 7:13–14); cf. Mitchell, *Together in the Land*, 71; H.-P. Müller, "קָדֵשׁ," *THAT*, 2:605.

somehow violates Yahweh's honor and praiseworthiness, so now Achan must offset that offense by repaying Yahweh the proper respect. In short, Achan must make a full confession ("Tell me what you have done . . .").[33]

Achan does so (v. 20), invoking a typical confession declaration formula ("I sinned against Yahweh"; cf. Ex. 10:16; 2 Sam. 12:13) and then fully confessing his crime (v. 21). For the first time, and from the now-unmasked traitor's own lips, all Israel and Bible readers hear a full accounting of his secret crime (cf. v. 1). Roaming Jericho's ruins, he spotted three things: "a beautiful robe from Babylonia, two hundred shekels of silver and a wedge of gold weighing fifty shekels."[34] He "coveted them"—clearly, a violation of the Decalogue (Ex. 20:17; Deut. 5:21)—and took them to his tent and hid them underground (notice the details concerning quantities and storage). Achan's greed simply got the better of him.

Joshua dispatches messengers, who "run" to Achan's tent and—yes, indeed!—they find the stuff hidden there just as he had said (v. 22).[35] They bring them to Joshua and all the Israelites and "spread [lit., poured] them out before the LORD" (v. 23). "Before the LORD" is appropriate in two respects. First, the goods really belong to him, so in essence the action returns them to their rightful owner. Second, Yahweh is the judicial authority sponsoring the trial, so the gesture also presents him with the incriminating evidence that confirms Achan's admission of guilt.

Quickly, the legal conversation ends and the scene changes. All Israel joins Joshua as he leads Achan, the stolen goods, his children, animals, tent, and everything he owns from Jericho to the Valley of Achor (v. 24), a short walk away.[36] The full list of people and items creates an impression of totality (i.e., everything associated with Achan) and pictures a lengthy procession strung along the road. At Achor, Joshua pronounces the death sentence, rhetorically punning on the root behind the place name (ʿakar "to bring trouble," v. 25a). He declares: "Why have you brought this trouble on us? The LORD will bring trouble on you today." The wordplay affirms

---

33. C. Westermann, "כָּבַד," *THAT*, 1:803. The giving of "glory" and "praise" to Yahweh after a crime makes this expression "tantamount to a confession"; cf. M. Weinfeld, "כָּבֵד," *TDOT*, 7:26. For "son" see H. Haag, "בֵּן," *TDOT*, 2:152; J. Kühlwein, "בֵּן," *THAT*, 1:319.

34. To list the "beautiful robe" (ʾadderet šinʿar "a cloak of Shinar" [cf. NRSV; TNK]) with the silver and gold implies that it was an especially valuable article of clothing; cf. D. M. Stec, "The Mantle Hidden by Achan," *VT* 41 (1991): 359. For the link between Shinar and Babylon, see Gen. 10:10; 11:2.

35. NIV's "and there it was" captures the force of the Heb. particle *hinneh* ("Look there!" or "Yes, indeed!").

36. The Valley of Achor is one of the wadis that empty into the Arabah north of (but reasonably close to) Jericho, most probably modern El Buqeʿah (Josh. 15:7); cf. C. J. Pressler, "Achor," *ABD*, 1:56; Kallai, *Historical Geography of the Bible*, 118–21.

the justice of the sentence. "Trouble" (the crime) is repaid by "trouble" (the punishment), with the offended party (Yahweh) the executioner. Appropriately, Achan's innocent victim, the entire community, stones him to death, burns him with fire, and then stones everything else (25b).[37] Thus, Israel meets Yahweh's demands (cf. v. 13): They remove the *ḥerem*, source of their current troubles, and in so doing, restore the community to its pre-Achan ritual cleanness.

Finally, they "heap up" over Achan's charred remains a great pile of stones, "which remains to this day" (v. 26a). Stones still visible "to this day" mark the locales of several key events in the larger narrative of Joshua (cf. 4:7 – 8; 10:27).[38] In this case, they mark the gravesite of Achan, by ancient standards a humiliating form of burial. Apparently, Israel reserved such burials for prominent rebels (2 Sam. 18:17 [Absalom]) and enemies (Josh. 8:29 [the king of Ai]; cf. Job 8:17).[39] Such burial mounds were common in ancient times and alerted passersby to the proximity of death and defilement.

Fittingly, Yahweh turns "from his fierce anger," the driving force behind the catastrophe (cf. v. 1b), a divine signal of Israel's safe return to his good graces. To draw down the curtain, the narrator notes that the name "trouble" (*ꜥakor*) stuck, presumably because popular memory associated the site with the infamous Achan episode (v. 26b). Even at the time the author wrote ("to this day"), people still called the spot "Trouble Valley." But Joshua's wordplay (v. 25) makes this particular heap a monument to "double trouble" — the trouble that Achan caused Israel (i.e., defeat at Ai), and the trouble that Yahweh caused him (i.e., his execution).

Achan's simple greed has pushed Israel to the brink of disaster, sullying their holiness and souring their relationship with Yahweh. Its secrecy makes it particularly fiendish: There is no protection against a secret crime whose existence only comes to light through unexpected disaster. Thus, the stones also remind Israel that they are by nature not a collection of individuals but a community — a fragile, carefully woven fabric in which disobedience by one thread strains or tears at the integrity of the whole.

Literarily, the Achan episode anticipates the later altar episode (ch. 22), where *maꜥal* ("to break faith") and Achan reappear (cf. comments on ch. 22).

---

37. Unless v. 25 is somehow corrupt, MT seems to assume that the instructions to burn the guilty party with fire entail stoning as well, though v. 15 leaves the latter unstated.

38. For a theological study of this motif, see Hubbard, "What Do These Stones Mean?" 25–49.

39. E. Bloch-Smith, "Burials: Israelite," *ABD*, 1:787, who assumes the stones to be in a circle rather than a heap. The Assyrians accorded their defeated foes similar treatment; cf. Younger, *Ancient Conquest Accounts*, 224; Hess, *Joshua*, 155–56. Cf. Gen. 31:46.

By then the Achan affair has become a cautionary tale about the deadly seriousness of apostasy, holiness, and corporate culpability.[40] In sum, the stone heap at Trouble Valley forewarns "potential Achans"[41] within Israel's ranks to practice the fear of God by doing what he commands. The theme echoes in the pleas of obedience in Joshua's farewell speech (ch. 23) and his speech at the covenant ceremony (ch. 24).

Finally, unlike Joshua 3 – 4, chapter 7 establishes no institution or formal process to interpret these stones to future generations. They may or may not recognize them as a burial mound of someone notorious. Only the narrative links the grave to the evocative name ("Trouble Valley"), Joshua's explanatory wordplay on *ʿakar* ("to bring trouble"), and possibly the name Achan.[42] The still-visible stones confirm the authenticity of the old story, but only the story itself interprets their meaning.

Ai Attack II (Joshua 8:1 – 29)

YAHWEH'S COMMANDS (8:1 – 2). With Achan's crime a thing of the past, the question arises as to what Yahweh now expects of Israel. Does the execution wipe the slate clean, or must Israel do something else? Joshua launched the first attack, but who will initiate things this time? Joshua chose Ai as the target, but might Yahweh have other plans?

Yahweh immediately takes charge, addressing Joshua with language typical of Yahweh war. To encourage him, he invokes the twofold formula of reassurance ("Do not be afraid/discouraged"). Leaders commonly invoke it to encourage those under them, often before going into battle, especially in Yahweh's war (Josh. 8:1; cf. Deut. 1:21; 2 Chron. 20:15, 17; 32:7).[43] Later, Joshua himself will do so to reassure his military leaders at Makkedah prior to the southern campaign (Josh. 10:25).

---

40. "It is a paradigmatic illustration of the priestly admonition: 'Be sure your sins will find you out' (Num. 32:23)"; cf. R. E. Clements, "Achan's Sin: Warfare and Holiness," in *Shall Not the Judge of All the Earth Do What Is Right?* ed. D. Penchansky and P. L. Redditt (Winona Lake, Ind.: Eisenbrauns, 2000), 117.

41. The phrase is that of Rowlett, "Inclusion, Exclusion, and Marginality," 23.

42. LXX and Syriac consistently read *Achar* instead of *Achan* (7:1, 18 – 20, 24; 22:20; 1 Chron. 2:7) while MT reads *Achar* only in 1 Chron. 2:7. Hess suggests that "Achan" was the story's original name, "Achar" a nickname for Achan derived from the "trouble" he caused Israel in the Valley of Achor; cf. R. S. Hess, "Achan and Achor: Names and Wordplay in Joshua 7," *HAR* 14 (1994): 89 – 98. The explanation seems likely for 1 Chron. 2:7, but MT's persistent reading of *Achan* and its resistance to emendation that would enhance the wordplay on *ʿakar* commend its originality in Josh. 7.

43. H. F. Fuhs, "יָרֵא," *TDOT*, 6:304 – 5; F. Maass, "חתת," *TDOT*, 5:280 – 81. Cf. 1 Chron. 22:13; 28:20; Isa. 51:7; Jer. 30:10; 46:27; Ezek. 2:6.

Yahweh also orders Joshua to lead "the whole army" up to attack Ai—ironically, the exact opposite advice given Joshua the last time by the returning spies (7:3). Perhaps, Yahweh sends the entire army to share in the victory and, thus, to restore their confidence as preparation for the battles yet to come. He decrees that the king of Ai, his city, and his land are already in Joshua's hands. The idiom "See, I have handed over to you ..." (NRSV) exactly echoes Yahweh's prebattle decrees concerning the defeats of the Amorite king, Sihon (Deut. 2:24; cf. Num. 21), and Jericho (Josh. 6:2). Indeed, Yahweh mandates that Ai, both king and city, receive "the Jericho royal treatment" but with one exception: This time, Israelites may help themselves to plunder and livestock (Josh. 8:2). If only Achan had been patient and not given in to greed!

Finally, Yahweh dictates a specific tactic, an ambush from behind the city (Heb. *ʾoreb*, "a lying in wait"; cf. Judg. 20:33; Jer. 51:12). The "element of surprise" makes ambushes standard operating procedure in ancient and modern warfare (Judg. 9:25, 43; 20:29; 1 Sam 15:5).[44] "Behind the city" probably assumes that Ai has one (or, at least, one main) gate—the city's "front." Militarily, it marks its most vulnerable (and, hence, most heavily defended) point. With the city's defenses focused on the front gate, the ambush team hidden behind it has a good chance of escaping detection.

Joshua's compliance (8:3 – 9). Joshua promptly prepares the whole army for Ai II (v. 3). He selects thirty elite units—militarily, "the best and the brightest"—as an ambush team and sends them to Ai at night.[45] The nighttime march probably aims to guard against detection en route and, hence, to retain the element of surprise. Later, a similar move will spring an effective surprise attack on unsuspecting armies besieging Gibeon (10:9).

Before the elite force embarks, Joshua issues crucial orders ("Listen carefully") that flesh out Yahweh's general concept ("an ambush") into a detailed, coordinated battle plan (8:4 – 9). The ambushers are to hide behind the city but within easy striking distance (v. 4). They are to remain alert, presumably to prevent discovery. The deep ravines that line several sides of Ai enable the troops to keep out of sight. While they wait, Joshua is

---

44. Assassins and marauders also avail themselves of it (Judg. 9:25; Ps. 10:8; Hos. 6:9). Later, Israel's King Jeroboam I (tenth cent. B.C.) uses the same rear ambush stratagem against Judah, although in open country (2 Chron. 13:13).

45. The size of Hebrew numbers continues to pose interpretive problems. Since "thirty thousand" (so NIV) seems too large and unwieldy for an ambush team, Heb. *ʾelep* here probably designates an elite military "unit," perhaps roughly the size of an extended family (perhaps 150–200), not the statistical number "thousand." By contrast, "about five thousand men" (8:12) probably furnishes the numerical strength of the "thirty units." P. P. Jenson, "אֶלֶף," *NIDOTTE*, 1:416–18, conveniently summarizes the various scholarly solutions.

to lead the remaining force in what is to look like a replay of the first attack (cf. 7:4–5). But this time, their luring of Ai's defenders from the city and feigned retreat baits a trap (8:5).[46] Psychologically, Joshua's plan uses the confidence buoyed by Ai's earlier victory to Israel's advantage. Seeing only the attacking force, the defenders are to think that the second battle will turn out like the first (v. 6).[47] They have no inkling of the ambush group hiding out of sight behind them.

But once the feigned retreat lures them out, the hidden force is to "rise up from ambush" and take (lit., "possess") the city. Indeed, Yahweh will hand it over to them (v. 7). With the people of Ai distracted by events out "front," the ambushers can easily slip unseen from "behind" and enter the now-unprotected city. Once they fully control it, they are to set it on fire — the full "Jericho treatment" that Yahweh commands (v. 8; cf. v. 2; 6:24).[48] As if worried about a second Achan, Joshua barks a closing charge: "See to it; you have my orders" (my paraphrase). Verse 9 restates Joshua's dispatch of the ambushers to their hidden spot west of Ai toward Bethel, while he himself spends that night (Night 1) with his other troops (v. 9). The stage is set for Israel's second attack on Ai.

The trap: set and sprung (8:10–23). Early the next morning (Day 1), carefully crafted narration unfolds the dramatic scene. An opening wide shot shows Joshua mustering the army, then a close-up follows him and Israel's elders leading the troops uphill toward Ai (v. 10). The view then quickly widens to show the ascent and dramatic arrival of the entire force with Joshua at the very front of the city (v. 11).[49] Undoubtedly, Israel's arrival leads Ai to shut its gates in siege mode, as had Jericho (6:1). Tactically, the open show of force probably serves to draw the city's defensive focus toward Joshua's group in front and away from the group hidden behind.

Israel then camps across a ravine on Ai's northern side, the ravine probably providing security against a preemptive surprise attack. Joshua then proceeds to position his forces per the battle plan. The narrative now builds tension in anticipation of the coming battle. It briefly backtracks, review-

---

46. Pronouns used emphatically—"I and the whole army" versus "you" (pl.)—distinguish the tactical roles of the Israelite "attackers" and ambushers (vv. 5 and 7, respectively).

47. The threefold repetition of the root *nus* ("to flee") and the twofold repetition of *yaṣaʾ* ("to exit") underscore the crucial importance of the "retreat" in luring the army of Ai away from the city (vv. 5–6).

48. Alternatively, the "command" may refer to Yahweh's command to conquer Ai (v. 1; so Howard, *Joshua*, 204) or to commands given by Joshua on Yahweh's behalf (so Butler, *Joshua*, 87).

49. The subject-first sentence structure opening 8:11 suggests contemporaneous action.

ing the prior, secret placement of the ambush team of "about five thousand men" (v. 12; cf. v. 9). It then reports the final double checks by Joshua's officers (NIV "they"), ensuring that everyone is ready and in position. That night (Night 2) Joshua himself spends the night in the valley, perhaps positioning himself to lead his troops into battle (v. 13). Everyone quietly awaits the dawn.

The next morning (Day 2), the king of Ai sees something threatening ("this"), probably Joshua's presence in the valley. Why this might pose a threat is unclear, but the king and his army immediately "hurry" out to battle Israel somewhere east of the city (v. 14).[50] Parenthetically, the author comments that the king knows nothing of the ambush awaiting him behind the city. The brief remark implies, "So far, so good." Joshua and all Israel feign being routed (the matter-of-fact verb [lit., "were being beaten"] is tongue-in-cheek) and flee eastward down the wilderness road.

Meanwhile, "lured away" from Ai (cf. v. 6) just as Joshua planned, Ai's entire military force hotly pursues him (v. 16). The fact that every male from Ai and nearby Bethel have abandoned the city to pursue Israel leaves its gates open and its inhabitants defenseless (v. 17). Unexpectedly, Yahweh himself speaks, ordering Joshua to stretch out the "javelin" (Heb. *kidon*, "scimitar") in his hand toward Ai because "I will give it into your hand" (v. 18 NRSV). His order marks this as the decisive turning point in the raging battle. *Kidon* is not the usual word for "sword" (*ḥereb*) or "spear" (*ḥanit*) and, hence, probably designates a distinctive weapon.[51] Mesopotamian and Egyptian art frequently display a crescent-shaped sword, an obsolete, ancient weapon symbolic of divine or human sovereignty.[52]

The sovereignty-symbol idea fits Yahweh's declaration, itself a reiteration of his earlier promise of victory (cf. v. 1). If so, Joshua's scimitar uplifted toward Ai symbolically targets the city for Yahweh's war, with Yahweh himself providing Israel the decisive margin of victory. As if on cue (i.e., just as Joshua's arm extends), the hidden ambush team suddenly appears, runs into the city, captures it, and sets it on fire (v. 19).[53] The forms of *mahar* ("to hurry")—"rose quickly," "quickly set it on fire"—convey how fast they

---

50. The Arabah (cf. "overlooking the Arabah") is the wide Jordan River Valley.

51. In the Old Testament, *kidon* seems to be the weapon of non-Israelites, e.g., Goliath (1 Sam. 17:6, 45), Jeremiah's "enemy from the north" (Jer. 6:23; 50:42); cf. Job 39:23; 41:21. Sir. 46:2 remembers this dramatic moment.

52. For full discussion, see Boling, *Joshua*, 240–241 and Plate III.

53. The subject-first sentence structure portrays the symbolic sword gesture and the appearance of the ambush group as contemporaneous events. The LXX reads Joshua's dramatic gesture as a signal to launch the ambush, but that seems unlikely since the city (to say nothing of the swarming crowd of soldiers downhill) would surely block the ambushers' view.

set it ablaze. The sounds and sights of the inferno apparently cause the Ai forces to look back, and—look at that!—they see smoke ascending skyward from the city.

The visible conflagration confirms the successful ambush, so the fleeing Israelites turn around. They deny Ai's stunned forces any hope of escape and spring the fatal trap (vv. 20–21). The arrival of the ambush team from the city swamps Ai's helpless troops in a sea of Israelites (v. 22). The resulting slaughter, the narrator stresses, is total—no survivors or escapees—with one exception. The Israelites single out the king of Ai and bring him alive to Joshua, an action that signals absolute victory (v. 23; cf. 10:26–27; 1 Sam. 15:8).

The king's fate (8:24–29). A retrospective summary of the day's events draws the account to a close. Israel has killed all Ai's inhabitants, some in the open country ("the fields") and some in the wilderness, ironically the very places in which Ai had originally chased Israel. Israel does a thorough job, putting everyone—the army on the battlefield and the people in the city—to the sword (v. 24). The day's casualty count of "the fallen"—Ai's total population of men and women—totals twelve thousand (v. 25). By ancient standards, that figure makes Ai a large city, unlike the rather small outpost of Bethel the book of Joshua portrays. But, as with the earlier thirty thousand figure (v. 3), twelve thousand probably means "twelve (undefined) units"—a considerably smaller population.

As for Joshua, the narrator adds, he does not lower the symbolic scimitar until "he" has "utterly destroyed" (*ḥaram* hi.) all Ai's inhabitants (v. 26). The comment implies that, as Israel's leader, ultimate responsibility for the execution of *ḥerem* falls on his shoulders. The crescent-shaped sword represents "both human signal and medium of divinely assisted victory."[54] It symbolizes a key theological theme in Joshua: divine promise and empowerment working in concert with human planning and execution.

Unlike Jericho, however, Yahweh permits Israel to keep plunder and livestock from Ai, a policy Israel gladly carries out (v. 27; cf. v. 2). Certainly, Israel can keep any luxury items found, but the policy's purpose aims to increase Israel's supply of food, clothes, pottery, utensils, and so on. The seeming preoccupation with slaughter and plunder may disturb some readers. But the accounting probably contrasts Israel's conduct at Ai with that at Jericho. At Ai Israel obeys Yahweh, meticulously carrying out *ḥerem*. They have truly learned the lesson of Achan.

---

54. Nelson, *Joshua*, 113–14, who compares it to the upraised arms of Moses in Israel's victory over the Amalekites (Ex. 17:8–15) and the arrows given King Jehoash by Elisha as promissory symbol of Yahweh's defeat of the Arameans.

In short, Joshua accomplishes two key things. (1) He reduces Ai to a permanent pile of burnt rubble—a state still evident in the writer's day (v. 28). He pronounces no curse over it as he had at Jericho, but perhaps because the site's utter devastation precludes any thought of rebuilding. Strategically, the removal of Ai as an outpost guarding the road to cities farther inland increases the latter's vulnerability to Israel's advance. The political shock waves emanating from Ai's fall will shortly become evident (9:1–2).

(2) Joshua executes the king of Ai, impaling him on a post until evening (v. 29). At sunset, Joshua has his corpse taken down and thrown down at the entrance of Ai's city gate, exactly obeying Moses (Deut. 21:22–23). As the day's final act, the Israelites raise a "large pile of rocks" over it, just as they had over the corpse of Achan (the wording matches Josh. 7:26; cf. 1 Sam. 18:17). Both rock piles were still there in the biblical writer's day.[55] But, unlike the Achan episode, which ended in defeat, this episode need not report the end of Yahweh's anger from Israel (cf. Josh. 7:26). Instead, the royal rock-pile tomb at Ai testifies to a great victory by Yahweh the warrior. Barring the perfidy of another Achan, more victories—some perhaps even more astounding—may soon follow.

TWO ASPECTS OF THIS passage merit further comment here—the archaeology of the city of Ai, and the question of justice that arises when apparently innocent or uninvolved people suffer for Achan's crime. Two further comments concerning *ḥerem* will also be helpful.

The archaeology of Ai. As noted above, Ai means "the Ruin," probably a nickname given the site later in retrospect rather than what its occupants would have called it. The huge site at et-Tell (27.5 acres) is commonly identified as biblical Ai. But the fact that extensive excavations there have found no evidence of its occupation at the time of this episode creates a historical problem.[56] For that reason, some scholars regard the biblical narrative as either fictional—a legend told to explain the enormous ruins

55. Joshua will shortly follow a similar procedure of punishment and rock-pile memorial when punishing the five kings of other captured, rebellious cities (10:26–27).

56. For alternative sites and discussion, see R. L. Hubbard Jr., "Ai," *DOTHB*, 21–22; Kitchen, *Reliability of the Old Testament*, 188–89. Three decades of vigorous defense of alternative locations for Ai (e.g., Khirbet Nisya or Khirbet el-Maqatir) and Bethel (e.g., el-Bireh) have apparently not weakened the consensus accepting the traditional identifications of both cities.

familiar to the audience — or a simple error (i.e., the author confuses the destruction of nearby Bethel with that of Ai). The topographical details of Joshua 7 – 8, however seem to fit the terrain of et-Tell better than that of Bethel, a blow to the simple-error proposal. Further, the Bible commonly pairs Ai with Bethel, so the latter's mention (7:2) may in fact imply the conquest of both cities.[57]

Finally, some details in Joshua 7 – 8 suggest that the then-extant ruins of Ai may actually have served as a temporary defensive outpost for Bethel. Joshua 8:17, for example, implies that defenders from Bethel joined Ai's forces against Israel. That might explain why the spies initially found "so few" at Ai (7:3) and that only twelve "units" (not "thousands") of Ai perished (8:25). Further, if "his land" (8:1) alludes to royal farmland around Ai, the town may also have been the base for summer workers tending the fields. Such seasonal work would require only temporary shelters rather than permanent stone homes.[58] If so, the lack of evidence of occupation makes sense, in that such a small, ad-hoc defensive detail or seasonal work force would require few permanent structures and, thus, probably leave few, if any, archaeological traces. Over two millennia of erosion may also have simply washed away some evidence of occupations at Ai. Thus, as elsewhere, so with Ai: The absence of evidence is not necessarily the evidence of absence.

To die with Achan. So what about the justice of apparently innocent people suffering Achan's punishment? This question arises right in the first verse. Joshua 7:1 first blames the Israelites for the crime, but then identifies Achan as the culprit. Worse, the context makes clear that Joshua and Israel know nothing about it, yet all Israel suffers the defeat and loss of life of Ai I while Achan escapes unscathed. Further, in his confession Achan names no accomplices or co-conspirators, yet his children, livestock, and personal property share his punishment.

Some readers may view this as unfair (the punishment does not fit the crime) and mystifying. The problem is that in Joshua 7 our modern, individualistic worldview bumps into the more corporate worldview of the Bible. The former says that individuals benefit from or suffer for what they themselves do (or do not do). Usually, they are exempt from the benefits or deficits of what others do (or do not do). For it to be otherwise, individualism says, would be unjust. (American culture particularly prizes a strong

---

57. In fact, Joshua 12:16 celebrates the conquest of Bethel, but the book of Joshua nowhere reports how it happened.

58. Kitchen, *Reliability of the Old Testament*, 189, who also notes that Ai may have provided "a strong point for those whose lands adjoined it."

variety of this worldview called "rugged individualism.") In the Bible's world, however, whole groups benefit or suffer because of the actions of an individual, and no one reckons this unjust.

It is crucial that we understand the contrast between these two perspectives; otherwise we will not understand Joshua 7 – 8 and much of the Bible.[59] More important, we moderns finally need to catch up with the Bible and see things as God sees them. Only then will his transformation of us approach his vision for us as Christian people. As a first step, we need to retool our perspective by reviewing other indicators of God's corporate perspective at work.

To begin, recall that in the beginning God created not individuals but collective humanity personified by an individual (Heb. *haʾadam*, "the Human"; Gen. 2:7, 15). Even when God introduced the gender distinction "man" and "woman" (*ʾiš* and *ʾiššah*; Gen. 2:21 – 23), "the Human" still comprises "male" and "female" (*zakar* and *neqebah*; Gen. 1:27). We rightly recognize ethnic diversity today, but theologically God still regards humanity as a single group. Yes, the Bible reports — and we experience — his relationship with individuals. But those experiences do not deny the prior fact of God's corporate viewpoint. Several well-known Scriptures illustrate the persistence of this thought.

For example, Paul urges Christian husbands to love their wives "just as Christ loved the church [not individuals] and gave himself up for her [as a whole]" (Eph. 5:26). Similarly, John 3:16 affirms God's love for "the world" (corporate perspective) but also envisions that everlasting life may be claimed by "whoever believes in him [the Son]" (individualistic perspective). Consider, further, Paul's explanation of humanity's sin problem and its solution in Christ:

> For if, by the trespass of *the one man*, death reigned through that one man, how much more will those who receive God's abundant provision of grace and of the gift of righteousness reign in life through the *one man*, Jesus Christ.... For just as through the disobedience of *the one man the many* were made sinners, so also through the obedience of *the one man the many* will be made righteous. (Rom. 5:17, 19 TNIV, my italics)

Paul contrasts the acts and outcomes of two men, each "(the) one man." The sinful act of the first (Adam) introduced sin, death, and condemnation to "many" (all humanity). But the righteous act of "one man" (Jesus Christ) brings abundant grace, justification, and righteousness to "many"

---

59. For further discussion on this topic, see Bridging Contexts section of ch. 22.

(all believers in him). In both cases, the action of "the one" produces results for the "many."

A key assumption underlies these claims: Each "man" acts as a representative of the whole group. All humanity sinned when Adam (or "the Human") did, and all humanity benefits when Christ ("the last Adam," 1 Cor. 15:45) died and rose again. The act of each determines the destiny of their kind: God imputes Adam's sin to every human and Jesus' righteousness to everyone who confesses Jesus as Lord. The collective worldview clearly undergirds Paul's theology, and that perspective also explains the troubling elements in Joshua 7–8.

Ḥerem: two further thoughts. The concept of *ḥerem* in Joshua 7–8 leads me to add two further comments. (1) An important theological assumption behind the concept challenges contemporary readers to catch up with the Bible in one respect. Recall that Yahweh applied *ḥerem* to Jericho and Ai differently. He decreed all of Jericho to be *ḥerem* ("devoted to destruction") and off-limits to Israel as plunder. He also exempted silver and gold and objects of bronze and iron from destruction (they went into Yahweh's treasury; 6:19, 26). Recall, further, that at Ai Yahweh also exempted from destruction any objects or animals the Israelites desired to keep for themselves. The latter surely marks an act of God's grace intended to benefit his people.

But behind his varied applications of *ḥerem* stands the important theological truth that God owns everything. That presumed ownership gives him the authority to decide whether and to what extent humans may enjoy the use of his property. Psalm 24:1–2 almost sounds like a deed of ownership when it acclaims:

> The earth is the LORD's, and everything in it,
>   the world, and all who live in it;
> for he founded it upon the seas
>   and established it upon the waters.

The "earth" refers to all its oceans and dry lands—what we call "property" today—and "everything in it" designates ... well, everything. This includes everything that humans have created using the raw materials of creation since the latter all belong to God. "All who live in it" refers to all earth's inhabitants, including humans and animals.[60] In short, there are no areas marked "Property of X" or "Belonging to Y"; everything is marked "Property of God," and no footnotes or exception clauses complicate that simple fact. He owns everything, and we humans own nothing.

---

60. Cf. Yahweh's claim that "every living soul belongs to me" (Ezek. 18:4).

The reason is that God created everything. At the same time, however, God has entrusted the care of the earth and its inhabitants to the descendants of *ha'adam*. The Old Testament calls that care "rule" or "dominion" (Gen. 1:26, 28; Ps. 8:6–8). Ultimately, humans are not owners but stewards of God's property, including birds, animals, and fish. As stewards, our responsibility is to manage divine property wisely and, above all, in line with their owner's wishes. Given our culture's promotion of ownership, the Bible here challenges us to view what we call "our property" from a different perspective — God's. We will return to this theme below in discussing the Contemporary Significance.

(2) Let us reflect briefly on the attitude toward property implicit in Achan's explanation of his actions. In his confession, he weaves together three verbs to summarize the process that led to them: "I saw ... I coveted ... and [I] took ..." (cf. Gen. 3:6). This captures biblical coveteousness in a nutshell. It begins with human eyes seeing something the viewer would really like to have, either for its appearance or value (cf. Gen. 3:6; Matt. 5:28). What caught Achan's eye at Jericho were the special beauty of an imported robe and the high value that silver and gold carry. As the sun outshines all lesser lights, their beauty and value blinded him to lesser things (cf. 2 Chron. 21:20). As Wallis notes, the verb *ḥamad* ("to covet") "reflects the suggestive power of observation, which takes possession of someone and incorporates the deed within itself, despite the best will and intentions."[61] The seeing quickly stirs up the covetous desire to possess the object and thus to perpetuate the pleasure, to impress friends by its display, and to enjoy the enhanced security of wealth (cf. Mic. 2:2). The inflamed desire causes temporary memory loss, blocking recollection of the divine prohibition against possession (cf. Gen. 3:2). The fateful step soon follows — the "taking" and hiding of the goods.

But besides the psycho-spiritual process just described, there is something more profound theologically going on. First, Achan's desire seduces him into a subtle arrogance of which he is probably consciously unaware. He thinks that he is smarter than God! He thinks that he can possess things and resist the danger of them possessing him. Second, he assumes himself justified in taking possession, as if he were a peer of "god" in authority, if only for the moment. As with Adam and Eve, ultimately his covetous act reveals that he simply does not trust God's goodness. He suspects that by denying him something obviously good (in his eyes), God is self-centered and petty, not generous and beneficent. He thinks that God is untrustworthy because he refuses to share and because he never explains himself.

---

61. Cf. G. Wallis, "חָמַד," *TDOT*, 4:452–61 (quote 457).

In the end, Achan's conduct protests that God should be accountable to him in the present matter—the truth is perfectly obvious to Achan!—and, in essence, elevates himself above God. Such is the theology that underlies human covetousness. It introduces us to a theme that we will pursue below, the dark side of human nature, a side even Christians experience. Achan's tragic fate attests that this is no unimportant matter.

The stunning reversal of the fates of the Israelite Achan and the Canaanite Rahab brings into sharp focus exactly what is at stake in Achan's actions. Achan—heir to a renowned Israelite family line—suffers the fate of Canaanite Jericho, while Rahab—as Canaanite as they come—escapes it. Rahab, the ultimate "outsider," becomes an "insider" in Israel by submitting to Yahweh's authority, while Achan, "the exemplary insider," makes himself an "outsider" by rejecting it.[62] In effect, Achan's rebellion trumps his ethnic membership in Israel. His fate implies that Yahweh prizes obedience far more than ethnicity.[63] Put differently, in Yahweh's eyes to be "true Israel" is to fear God; to not fear God is, in effect, to renounce membership in true Israel. The identity of a true Israelite derives from a serious, ongoing commitment to divine lordship, not simply from birth into an Israelite family.

IT IS TIME FOR Christians today to catch up with the Bible. That is the challenge for today that emerges from Joshua 7–8, and the important themes in the Achan and Ai episodes point the way.

The dark side: human sin. Achan confronts us with the dark side of human nature—sin. People today avoid talking about sin, perhaps because to do so seems harsh and judgmental. Since "guilt" goes along with "sin," and guilt is thought to reflect psychological immaturity, the word "sin" seems irrelevant. When street preachers passionately invoke it, passersby usually respond with silence or (occasionally) amusement. In my view, contemporary culture seems highly aware of the reality of evil but in deep denial about the reality of personal and corporate sin.

But God calls Achan's actions "sin" (7:11), and so does Achan himself in his confession (7:20). Sin is a central biblical theme, and the Achan-Ai episode confronts us with it eyeball to eyeball. To catch up with the Bible is to face our sin squarely, for only then can we truly appreciate the marvelous grace that God has given through his Son, Jesus. To minimize the wretch-

62. Rowlett, "Inclusion, Exclusion, and Marginality," 20, 22; cf. Howard, *Joshua*, 211: "Achan was expelled from Israel and treated as a Canaanite."
63. Similarly, Stone, "Ethical and Apologetic Tendencies," 34–36.

edness of our sin is to devalue the huge sacrifices that God the Father and Jesus made to deal with it.

A full reckoning with sin rightly begins with hearing some sobering biblical voices that illumine this ugly side of our humanity. The Bible diagnoses the problem as, at root, a deadly heart ailment. Jeremiah says, "The heart is deceitful above all things and beyond cure. Who can understand it?" (Jer. 17:9). In his view, nothing exceeds the human heart in capacity for deception (or, conversely, its incapacity for truth and justice). He regards the heart's disease as both incurable and even beyond understanding.

Elsewhere, Jeremiah asks, "Can the Ethiopian change his skin or the leopard its spots?" The answer, of course, is obviously "No." Neither vigorous washing nor the strongest soap can in any way change the Ethiopian's skin color or make the leopard spotless. By the same token, Jeremiah concludes, "Neither can you (pl.) do good who are accustomed to doing evil" (Jer. 13:23). Ethiopians and leopards have a better chance of changing their looks than people and societies do of loosening the vise grip of the sin habit. No chance at all! Jesus also traces all human sinful acts—"evil thoughts, murder, adultery, sexual immorality, theft, false testimony, slander"—to that same heart malady (Matt. 15:19–20). In short, what makes sin so deadly is that it is hidden and secretive, as Achan's was.

An important question to ask at this point is this: What sins today might compare to Achan's? As we saw, Achan sinned by keeping to himself things that Yahweh had declared to be his own exclusive property (*ḥerem*). The answer to our question, thus, lies in identifying things that God today claims to be his own. Certainly, God's claim that the taking of revenge against enemies belongs exclusively to him (Rom. 12:19) comes to mind. For us to do so, thus, is tantamount to taking something that belongs to God—to make the mistake that Achan made—rather than trusting God to take care of us. For us to transgress this truth is seriously to breach our relationship with God.

Also, the church and other Christians ultimately belong to only God and not to us. The church is the bride of Christ himself (Rev. 19:7), a spiritual union based on Jesus' loving sacrificial death on the cross on behalf of the church (Eph. 5:25, 29). Jesus deeply cares for his bride, so it would be Achanesque to do anything to harm the church, as Achan's sin did grave harm to Israel. Therefore, the example of Achan warns against doing anything that sullies the public reputation of the church, puts a strain on its relationship with God himself, or brings disunity to the body. What applies to the church as a whole likewise applies to our treatment of fellow believers. Woe to us if we lead them astray, confuse their minds, harm their walk with Christ, or disillusion them about the gospel.

Finally, I suggest that poor stewardship—the selfish hoarding of our time, abilities, resources, and the like—similarly robs God of things that belong to him. Poor stewardship diverts to our own selfish ends things that belong to God, things that he has entrusted to us to use for the sake of the kingdom, not just for ourselves. To squander what God has given us is to commit a sin comparable to Achan's.

The poet Henry David Thoreau wrote, "Like cuttlefish we conceal ourselves, we darken the atmosphere in which we move; we are not transparent."[64] Thoreau compares humans to a common marine animal, the cuttlefish. The cuttlefish lacks the defenses of other fish—speed, size, shells, or poisonous spines—so as it moves, it pours out a dark, inky liquid to protect itself. The murky camouflage hides the cuttlefish from the view of dangerous predators. Thoreau puts his finger on our human avoidance of transparency, and that is especially true of sin. Rarely does someone stand up in church and say publicly, "I confess that I sinned this week. I did such-and-such, and I need forgiveness." Some sins carry less of a stigma and are easier to confess (e.g., "I lost my temper at work," "I broke a promise to my spouse," "I took the Lord's name in vain," etc.). But the more shameful sins remain—as in Achan's case—hidden, unconfessed, and perhaps even unacknowledged.

Who openly says, for example, "I cheated my employer," "I'm addicted to ...," "I committed adultery"? In ancient Israel, pilgrim groups recited an entrance liturgy before entering the temple to affirm their worthiness to approach God.[65] Were the technology available, one wonders what hidden sins a spiritual X-ray machine might detect among entering worshipers. Church attendance would probably go down!

Some years ago, I knew a dynamic pastor of a growing church in a major American city. The larger Christian community greatly admired his passion for the lost, inspiring vision for the church, and the deep impact of his ministry. The pastor was in great demand as a speaker nationwide and had published a highly popular and widely read book on church growth. But one day a sad, secret truth came to light: That enormously effective pastor had carried on, undetected, a ten-year affair with a church member. The revelation of the secret shocked the community, and the pastor is no longer in ministry today. Sins can be kept secret, but instead of a spiritual X-ray machine, Scripture outlines the detection process that God prefers.

---

64. B. Terry, ed., *The Writings of Henry David Thoreau: Journal Vol. 4* (Boston/New York: Houghton Mifflin, 1906), 315 (August 24, 1852).

65. The two extant biblical examples feature a question-and-answer liturgical format (Ps. 15; 24:3–6; cf. Mic. 6:6–8).

(1) *Trust enough to confess to each other.* The apostle James commands us to "confess your sins to each other and pray for each other so that you may be healed. The prayer of a righteous person is powerful and effective" (James 5:16). This is easier said than done, of course. Pride prevents us from readily risking our reputations by confessing our faults, especially really bad ones. But participation in a caring, trustworthy small group often frees people to stop being cuttlefish and to start showing what is really going on inside. (A candid confession need not be made before the whole church unless, as with Achan, the sin affects the entire body.) The telling of one's struggles brings a huge sense of relief, and it also empowers other believers to unburden themselves. More important, James stresses, confession allows others to unleash the powerful medium of prayer for us that God will "heal" us—that is, permanently rid us of the sin and its effects.

(2) *Tell each other the truth.* Beside the need for confession, another biblical antidote to sin is for Christians to "[speak] the truth in love" (Eph. 4:15). Unfortunately, weasel words and pleasant diplomacy govern many of our serious conversations with each other. Afraid of rejection, we pull our punches or hem and haw rather than call something what it is. Paul calls for conversation in which fellow Christians tell each other the truth—that they truly engage in honest conversation about things that really matter. He urges that the truth-telling be done "in love" (i.e., gently and with the other person's best interests at heart). Again, this straight talk about our lives is probably best experienced in a small group of trusted friends. The important thing is that it should happen—and happen as often as needed.

(3) *Hold each other accountable.* One particular highlight of the Achan incident concerns the dramatic process of lot-casting. Imagine again the huge gathering before Joshua, with all Israel probably silent and sober in tribal groups because of the grave matter at hand. Feel the mixture of tension and relief that sweeps the crowd with each lot drawn. Those eliminated from consideration instantly relax, as those still on the hook tense ever more nervously.

For us, several observations are pertinent. (a) Recall that Israel as a whole suffered because of the sin of one Israelite, Achan. God held the entire nation accountable for Achan's sin; according to Yahweh, "the Israelites acted unfaithfully" (Josh. 7:1). This implies that what Achan did was a corporate concern, not an individual one.

(b) That assumption explains the second observation: This is an all-Israelite occasion. Israel as a whole people meets to do serious business—to remove the *ḥerem* secretly hidden somewhere in the camp—in order to restore their collective relationship with Yahweh. That restoration is the key to the future success Israel hopes to achieve in its attempt to conquer

Canaan. In short, the people of Israel meet to hold someone — Achan, it turns out — accountable for his actions. In so doing, Joshua 7 – 8 commends to Christian communities the importance of similar mutual accountability.

(c) The process for doing that need not, however, involve lot drawing, execution, and burning as with Achan. Each community should prayerfully consider what process best fits its situation. Israel had its unique way of handling this particular matter, and many churches have written procedures for handling sins in the congregation.[66] Joshua 7 suggests that such procedures focus on sins that greatly affect the entire church body — sins that justifiably offend mature people or disturb congregational unity. Sins that damage the public reputation of the church in the larger community also merit corporate attention. I hasten to add that they need not concern only sexual immorality; other issues with roots in sin also call for community accountability (e.g., ethical lapses, severe family problems, financial malfeasance, abuses of power, etc.).

(d) Each community also will need to decide how corporate the process is to be. The example of Joshua 7 need not require a public airing of every such sin before the whole church. The incremental process outlined by Jesus for handling a sin against a fellow believer (Matt. 18:15 – 17) offers a wise, helpful model for problems touching the larger body. Issues of confidentiality may deem some situations too sensitive for open discussion. In such cases, the matter may be assigned to a small group of individuals in whose wisdom, integrity, and compassion the congregation has great trust. The point that Joshua 7 forces on us is that our communities practice some carefully thought-out mutual accountability when sin harms (or threatens to harm) the body of Christ.

The big picture: the mystical unity. The earlier discussions have brought to the surface the corporate understanding of the people of God that undergirds aspects of the Achan narrative. That understanding explains why Yahweh charged Israel with treachery because of Achan and why the entire nation participated in the legal process of discovery and execution. It also explains why Achan had to be executed and burned: The community needed to rid itself of his sinful contamination. The narrative assumes that

---

66. For possible models of church discipline, see A. Poirier, *The Peacemaking Pastor: A Biblical Guide to Resolving Church Conflicts* (Grand Rapids: Baker, 2006); E. and S. Wilson, et al., *Restoring the Fallen: A Team Approach to Confronting and Reconciling* (Downers Grove, Ill.: Inter-Varsity Press, 1997); T. C. Oden, *Corrective Love: The Power of Communion Discipline* (St. Louis, Mo.: Concordia, 1995).

a mystical unity binds individuals like Achan within the larger community of Israel.

According to the New Testament, a similar mystical bonding binds members of the body of Christ today. Alas, treacherous Achans also populate Christian communities and openly or secretly disturb their unity and impede their forward momentum. The Achan episode, thus, marks a good moment briefly to review the features of that mystical unity and to reaffirm our commitment to the corporate ideal of God's people. In Joshua 8 the Israelite community—no longer dragging Achan's secret, sinful baggage—successfully conquered Ai, a testimony to its full restoration by Yahweh (see below). A review of our unity in Christ will also remind us of what our communities are to look like when free of Achanesque baggage.

This review will yield two important benefits. (1) It will encourage us to work hard at maintaining that unity and corporate identity. After all, according to Jesus, what will catch the world's eye—the unique identification mark that sets off Jesus' followers from nonfollowers—is our love for each other (John 13:34–35). The present brief review will make us watchful for signs of an Achan among us whose public or private actions are harming the body's wholeness. It will keep us alert to ways in which to strengthen our unity in Christ.

(2) As a second benefit, to understand our mystical unity will help to build a bridge to the upcoming generation. One of the characteristics of the so-called Generation X is the high premium it places on community, so a church whose common life centers around community will catch their attention.

The terms for Israel in Joshua 7 are (lit.) "the children of Israel" (vv. 1, 12, 23) and "the people" (vv. 5, 7, 13). In this context, the latter describes either the "people" of Israel as a whole (v. 5, 7) or "people" as opposed to Joshua as leader (v. 13). The former describes the people genealogically as the descendants of "Israel" (i.e., Jacob)—in other words, as members of his extended family household.

Paul also invokes the ancient metaphor of the household for the church (Eph. 2:19), but perhaps his best-known metaphor for the nature of the church is as a "body" (1 Cor. 12:12–27). Several of his general points flesh out a Christian understanding of the mystical union of believers in the people of God and add further illumination to the comments on Joshua 7 above. (1) He stresses that, like any body, the church combines unity and diversity. A human body has many parts (e.g., eyes, ears, hands, feet, etc.), each with its unique function, yet remains a single, unified whole. In the book of Joshua, Israel as a body included descendants of Jacob as well as several other groups that had joined them along the way. Among them were resident aliens from other countries (Josh. 8:33, 35), Rahab and her family, and the Gibeonites from Canaan (for the latter, see ch. 9). Descendants of the so-called "mixed multitude" (Ex. 12:38 KJV) that had escaped Egypt with the Israelites may also have been among them. As we will soon learn, the Gibeonites worked at the sanctuary of Yahweh, and the other non-Israelites presumably had their places in Israel, although we know no details. Together they comprised "all Israel."

By the same token, the church has many members, each with his or her own history prior to salvation. Each plays at least one role essential to the corporate life of the church, yet the church retains its unity (1 Cor. 12:12, 14, 20). God has simply planned it to be that way (v. 18), and it marks one of the strengths of the church of Christ. If a body had only eyes, Paul writes, it would be unable to hear sounds or smell smells (v. 17). What a sadly impoverished sensory experience! Similarly, the diverse membership of the church enhances its effectiveness as God's vehicle for showing his love to the world. If everyone were a pastor, who would teach children, counsel hurt people, pray for the sick, bring the gospel to neighbors, stand up for justice, or manage the money? (And imagine the intense competition for time in the pulpit!)

(2) Paul affirms that, regardless of its function, every part of the body of Christ enjoys the same full membership as the others. In this regard, the church differs from the Israel in the book of Joshua, for Rahab, the resident aliens, and the Gibeonites probably did not enjoy "full membership" in it. At least, the Old Testament provides no information from which one might infer that they ever became "Israelites" in an ethnic sense.[67] In the church, the reality of full membership for everyone means that no one can say, "Because my role's not important, I'm not really an integral part of the church" (cf. 1 Cor. 12:16). There are no longer any Rahabs, resident aliens, Gibeonites, or "mixed multitudes" (cf. Gal. 3:28). Nor can any member tell another member, "I don't need you" (1 Cor. 12:21). On the contrary, Paul says, all parts are indispensable since God himself has joined them together. Rather than have a "division" disrupt the body's unity, God intends that "its parts should have equal concern for each other" (vv. 22–25). Indeed, the body's parts are so integral to the whole that Paul can write, "If one part suffers, every part suffers with it; if one part is honored, every part rejoices with it" (v. 26).

---

67. Rahab's place in Jesus' genealogy (Matt. 1:5), however, seems to imply full membership, but 2 Sam. 21:2 expressly states that the Gibeonites "were not a part of Israel." Israelite laws and narratives suggest that resident aliens participated fully in Israel's social and cultic life but for the most part remained non-Israelites ethnically; cf. C. van Houten, *The Alien in Israelite Law* (JSOTSup 107; Sheffield: JSOT Press, 1991), 160–62.

(3) Now, Paul's body metaphor is so well known that one may easily miss some of its important implications for modern church life. Paul understands the church's unity to be something organic, not merely associational. An "association" comprises a group of individuals who voluntarily join it — for example, a club or society. Such groups are bound by a common interest (e.g., music or the arts, hobbies, civic concerns, etc.) and the continuing commitment of its individual members. When changes occur — such as when a member no longer has time, moves away, or loses interest — his or her "unity" with that entity ends. That is why such associations are not organic; rather, they are based on shared interest and voluntarism.

By contrast, birth, blood, or adoption bind an organic unity — for example, family kinship. The organic connection is what guarantees admission to family events and activities. A connection with that "body" persists whether one attends them, feels estrangement, or moves away. Similarly, the church comprises an organic unity because one gains membership in the body of Christ by new birth and baptism into God's family. Membership in the universal church is a key prerequisite for membership in a local church body. The choice not to attend or to join a local church in no way alters one's membership in the church of Jesus Christ.

(4) Further, Paul's body metaphor means that Christians have to make the church work, otherwise, God is dishonored. We must deal seriously and wisely with the Achans among us, although, of course, not in the way that Israel did with the son of Carmi. One may "take or leave" a choral society or bird watchers' club, but a Christian is stuck with the church of Jesus, like it or not. "Now you are the body of Christ," writes Paul, "and each one of you is a part of it" (v. 27). End of discussion!

In addition, fierce competition may drive contemporary culture, but one-upmanship has no place in the church of Jesus Christ, the one who gave himself for others. Our challenge is to avoid being an Achan — a greedy, self-centered "troubler" of the church whose thoughtless actions or negative attitudes may injure the health of the body's corporate life. On the contrary, our task is to work hard at maintaining unity in God's people. After all, as Jesus taught us, our love for each other is what displays that we are truly his followers for all to see.

The bright side: God holds no grudges. Joshua 7 – 8 speaks not only about sin but about God's magnificent grace. Once the stone pile over the late Achan ben Carmi is complete, the narrator remarks that Yahweh's anger, initially stirred by the crime, also ends (7:26; cf. v. 1). God immediately reassures Joshua: "Do not be afraid; do not be discouraged. . . . For I have delivered into your hands the king of Ai, his people, his city and his land" (8:1). What a relief to Israel and Joshua! The legal process of ch. 7 has satisfied Yahweh, and Israel is no longer *ḥerem* ("devoted to destruction"). There are no grudges to overcome, no probationary period to serve. Israel again enjoys full standing with Yahweh, and his commitment to give them the land still stands, too. In short, God had again extended his gracious mercy to Israel.

The victory of Ai II confirms that Yahweh means what he says. Biblically, this is no surprise. The popular impression is that the Old Testament's God is a God of wrath. But here is a glimpse of that God, post-Achan, showing wonderful mercy and forgiveness. Similarly, after condemning Israel's unfaithfulness at length, the book of Micah closes with beautiful reassurance:

> Who is a God like you,
>> who pardons sin and forgives the transgression
>> of the remnant of his inheritance?
> You do not stay angry forever
>> but delight to show mercy.
> You will again have compassion on us;
>> you will tread our sins underfoot
>> and hurl all our iniquities into the depths of the sea.
> You will be true to Jacob,
>> and show mercy to Abraham,
> as you pledged on oath to our fathers
>> in days long ago. (Mic. 7:18–20)

"Who is a God like you?" Micah asks. "No one"! is the answer. Yahweh has no peer, human or divine, when it comes to pardon and forgiveness. Other gods typically vent anger and nurse grudges, but Yahweh prefers to show mercy rather than anger. Micah promises his readers, no doubt in despair over their sin, that God will extend mercy to them as he did long ago to Abraham and Jacob. Most striking, however, is the metaphor Micah invokes to picture what God does with forgiven sin: He treads them into the ground (they cannot be recognized) and throws them to the bottom of the sea (they cannot return).

This image recalls a brief experience I had during my preteen years. My family was attending a summer family reunion in the Sierras of central California. One day several of us rented a rowboat to enjoy the beauty of the nearby lake. The boat came equipped with a crude anchor—a six-inch piece of railroad track attached to a thick rope with a loop tied at the other end. After rowing us out a ways, my dad told me to cast off the anchor, which I did. Oops! I forgot to attach the end-loop to the bow of the boat. To this day, I can still picture the anchor towing the waving, vertical rope to the bottom of the lake out of sight. I felt pretty stupid. The anchor was gone, lost in the depths of the lake with no way to recover it. I imagine it today—a rusting iron chunk still tethered to its fraying rope, both overgrown with algae, out of sight, lying on the lake bottom.

Imagine God throwing our sins into the far deeper depths of the sea. Imagine the fresh start that results for Israel post-Achan—and for us, too, after our sins. God's forgiveness dumps them overboard; they are gone, buried, forgotten, unrecoverable. They cannot be thrown accusingly in our faces again. Good-bye, sins! Hello, forgiveness! Of course, it is one thing to *know* we are forgiven, and quite another to actually *embrace* that forgiveness. The challenge is to let God's truth erase our memories of failure and silence our self-criticism. Great relief follows when we do so, the elated feeling of a newly freed prisoner throwing off tight handcuffs and heavy leg irons.

But perhaps the greatest challenge is to give our forgiveness to someone who has wronged us. We enjoy nursing our grievances, using them to our advantage, or plotting our revenge. That makes it imperative for us to remember Jesus' teaching on forgiveness. (1) He directly links the forgiveness we receive from God with the forgiveness that we dispense to each other: "For if you forgive others when they sin against you, your heavenly Father will also forgive you. But if you do not forgive others their sins, your Father will not forgive your sins" (Matt. 6:14 – 15 TNIV). Clearly, our failure to forgive sin against us denies us God's forgiveness of our sins against him. His teaching is: "Forgive, and you will be forgiven" (Luke 6:37).

(2) God's willingness to forgive us never stops, and neither should ours (Matt. 18:21 – 22). That is the point of the parable of the unforgiving servant (18:23 – 35). The master had forgiven the huge debt of his servant, graciously absorbing the financial loss himself. But the very next moment he finds the just-forgiven man angrily demanding the immediate repayment of a trivial sum owed him by another man. When the poor man refuses, the servant has him thrown in jail until he pays back every cent. No wonder that, learning of this, the master throws the servant in jail until he, too, pays everything owed—an impossible task.

Jesus goes on to say that that is exactly the way our heavenly Father will treat us "unless you forgive your brother or sister from your heart" (Matt. 18:35 TNIV). To not forgive a fellow believer means that we really do not "get it." We show ourselves clueless to the huge, impossible debt that God's forgiveness has wiped out for us. Only the painful, humiliating defeat at Ai persuaded Israel that something was dreadfully wrong in the camp. And when we "get" how dreadfully wrong we have been—how much like Achan we really are!—the enormity of God's forgiveness will grab us as never before. Our gratitude for that unbelievable grace will drive us to forgive each other of offenses that, beside our Achanesque treacheries against God, seem pitifully trivial.

In one of his novels about amateur detective Easy Rawlins, Walter Mosley recounts the funeral for Reese Corn, a murder victim in the small town of Pariah, Texas. Rev. Nathaniel Peters is the officiating pastor:

> "Reese Corn was a solitary man in his last years. He didn't come much to Ethiopia Baptist Church. And those of you who don't have faith," and Rev. Peters looked out over the congregation, "might say that he had lost the way of the Lord. But brother Reese didn't lose his way. He knew death was comin' an' on his last Sunday in the world Reese came back to the Lord." ...
>
> The minister looked up at the ceiling and shook his head as if he were arguing with the next words the Lord was putting in his mouth. Finally he returned his gaze to earth. "What is our lesson? That's what you wanna know. What is God trying to say to me here today? Well ... no one can truly understand the mind of God because the mind of God is what we call infinite. That means he's everywhere. As far as you can go—God is there. He's at the bottom of the ocean and he's way out past the moon and stars. He's in the room right now, sittin' next to ya. Reese is with him now, and if Reese could pierce the veil I think he'd say the lesson is the infinite forgiveness of the Lord."[68]

The "infinite forgiveness of the Lord" is one of the truths from ancient Ai that still speaks to us today. In receiving and dispensing it, we experience the thought of hymn writer Horatio Spafford:

My sin, oh, the bliss of this glorious thought!
My sin, not in part but the whole,
Is nailed to the cross, and I bear it no more.
Praise the Lord, praise the Lord, O my soul!

---

68. Walter Mosley, *Gone Fishin'* (Baltimore: Black Classic, 1997), 202, 206.

Joshua 8:30–35

‮❦‬

THEN JOSHUA BUILT on Mount Ebal an altar to the
LORD, the God of Israel, [31]as Moses the servant of
the LORD had commanded the Israelites. He built
it according to what is written in the Book of the Law of
Moses—an altar of uncut stones, on which no iron tool had
been used. On it they offered to the LORD burnt offerings
and sacrificed fellowship offerings. [32]There, in the presence
of the Israelites, Joshua copied on stones the law of Moses,
which he had written. [33]All Israel, aliens and citizens alike,
with their elders, officials and judges, were standing on both
sides of the ark of the covenant of the LORD, facing those
who carried it—the priests, who were Levites. Half of the
people stood in front of Mount Gerizim and half of them in
front of Mount Ebal, as Moses the servant of the LORD had
formerly commanded when he gave instructions to bless the
people of Israel.

[34]Afterward, Joshua read all the words of the law—the
blessings and the curses—just as it is written in the Book of
the Law. [35]There was not a word of all that Moses had commanded that Joshua did not read to the whole assembly of
Israel, including the women and children, and the aliens who
lived among them.

Original Meaning

THIS BRIEF TEXT REPORTS a covenant renewal ceremony led by Joshua on Mount Ebal above
Shechem.[1] The ceremony comprises three parts:
Joshua builds an altar of uncut stones and Israel
sacrifices on it (vv. 30–31); Joshua writes a copy of Moses' Instruction on
the altar's stones (vv. 32–33); and Joshua reads the entire Instruction to

---

1. Judg. 9:7 connects Mount Gerizim with Shechem, whereas Deut. 11:30 seems to
locate it and Mount Ebal in the mountains immediately west of Gilgal. The present exposition assumes the former location. For full discussion on the geographical issue, see E. Noort,
"The Traditions of Ebal and Mount Gerizim: Theological Positions in the Book of Joshua,"
in *Deuteronomy and the Deuteronomic Literature,* ed. M. Vervenne and J. Lust (Leuven: Uitgeveru
Peeters, 1997), 161–80.

Israel listening in the valley below (vv. 34—35).[2] Though short, the text certainly ranks as one of the more important in the book. Its contents and theological perspective compare to texts thought to be shaped by the DH editors (cf. Josh. 1; 24:1—28). Their editorial work probably underlies its present placement between Ai II (8:1—29) and war planning by the Canaanite kings (9:1—2).[3]

Three striking literary features stamp the episode with special significance. (1) Two long notices underscore that all Israel fully participates: priests, national leaders (v. 33), women, children, and even resident aliens (vv. 33, 35).[4] The lists picture the episode as a momentous, national event for all Israel.

(2) Three prominent "footnotes" stress that Joshua's actions fulfill specific commands of Moses (vv. 31, 33, 35; cf. v. 32).[5] Joshua himself models the absolute priority of obedience to Moses' Instruction. Together, the footnotes, the dramatic writing and reading of Moses' Instruction, and the central geographical location of Mount Ebal all say, "Sinai is coming home."[6] They signal the formal recognition of the Instruction as the "law of the land" in geographical Israel.

(3) Though 8:30—35 closely follows Deuteronomy, it also surprisingly departs from it in important details.[7] For example, Joshua (not the people of Israel) builds the altar, writes the law, and reads it aloud. Further, the ceremonial locations of the two groups of Israelite participants differ. In Deuteronomy 27:12—13, the groups are pictured atop Mounts Gerizim and Ebal with Moses, while in my view Joshua 8 positions Joshua alone on Mount Ebal and the Israelite groups in the valley below the two moun-

---

2. I prefer to render Heb. *torah* as "the Instruction" because it conveys the content ("teaching") and social standing (i.e., an accepted, familiar literary work) of Moses' written legacy better than the ambiguous term "the law."

3. Scholarly discussion questions whether the text best "fits" here. In the Vulgate, it comes after 9:1—2, while the longer text at Qumran (4QJosh[a]) has it before 5:2 (i.e., between the Jordan crossing and the circumcision at Gilgal); cf. Nelson, *Joshua*, 116—17, who prefers the MT and Vulgate locations.

4. The two lists echo language from Deut. 29:10—11[9—10].

5. They primarily cross-reference Deut. 11:29 and 27:2—13 (but cf. 31:11—12), an indication that Deuteronomy comprises the "Book of the [Instruction] of Moses" (Josh. 8:31). I owe the footnote metaphor to Nelson, *Joshua*, 118.

6. See Noort, "The Traditions of Ebal and Mount Gerizim," 178—79 (quotes 179, 178), who views the scene as the formal transfer of the Instruction and its message from outside the land (Mount Sinai, the Plains of Moab) to the Promised Land proper.

7. Cf. the divergences noted by Hawk, *Joshua*, 133—34; and the comment of Nelson (*Joshua*, 118) that the text is "the product of creative writing based on a string of revered texts."

tains. Also, Deuteronomy 27 makes no provision at all for the reading of the law, but in Joshua 8 Joshua reads it as the people listen below.[8] These surprising departures create a striking scene: Joshua atop the mountain reading the law, the people below receiving its words. In short, Moses' commands dictate most of the ceremonial steps, but the narrative spotlight falls brightly on Joshua. In my view, the image of Joshua on the mountain reading the Instruction plays on an idealized memory of Moses on Mount Sinai (e.g., Ex. 19:20–25; 24:1–8, 13–18). As Moses mediated Yahweh's Instruction on Mount Sinai with Israel encamped below, so does Joshua on Mount Ebal.[9]

The scene elevates Joshua (literally!) to a stature and authority approaching that of Moses. That Joshua rather than the priests reads the Instruction strikingly portrays him as Moses' ideal successor (cf. Deut. 31:9–13). He is the one who "wrote down the whole torah, the one who recited the torah, and made it present in Israel."[10] This motif is important; it prepares the reader to accept Joshua's innovative application of Moses' instructions in the next chapter.[11] Reader acceptance of that ruling hinges on the level of authority that Joshua 8:30–35 accords Joshua. Finally, through the ceremony Israel receives the Instruction anew, thereby renewing its covenant with Yahweh.

Joshua 8:30–35, in other words, constitutes the second of three covenant anchor points in the book (cf. 5:2–9, 10–12 and 24:1–28). Spiritually, it ensures that Israel has shaken off the ill effects of Achan in preparation for the battles and temptations that loom ahead.[12]

---

8. Deut. 31:11 commands that the priests publicly read the law to Israel every seven years, and the report of Joshua's doing so (Josh. 8:34) might draw on that command. The stark (and I believe symbolic) simplicity of having Joshua the sole reader is all the more striking when compared to the long, complex process that Deut. 27 teaches.

9. If so, the picture compares to the narration of Elisha's succession of Elijah as a replay of the transition between Moses and Joshua (1 Kings 2); cf. R. L. Hubbard Jr., *First and Second Kings* (Chicago: Moody, 1991), 139–41; T. R. Hobbs, *2 Kings* (Waco, Tex.: Word, 1985), 19, 27. Alternatively, Nelson ("Josiah in the Book of Joshua," 531–40) argues that the narrative portrays Joshua as a royal figure in anticipation of King Josiah (2 Kings 22–23).

10. Noort, "The Traditions of Ebal and Mount Gerizim," 175.

11. This important theme first sounded in 3:7 and 4:14 awaits two even louder echoes in 10:14 and 24:29 (on which see the commentary).

12. Many scholars concur with Butler (*Joshua*, 91, 94–95) that the present ceremony enables Israel to repair its covenant relationship after Achan's serious breach (Josh. 7). But, in my view, God's reassurance and instructions (8:1–2) imply that Israel already enjoys full divine favor and needs no "repair."

The Altar-building and Sacrifices (8:30–31)

THE OPENING REPORT IS straightforward: About the time that Ai fell, "Joshua built on Mount Ebal an altar to the LORD, the God of Israel" (v. 30).[13] At first glance, however, the remark seems abrupt and out-of-the-blue. Instantly and without explanation, it transports readers to Mount Ebal, the large mountain just north of Shechem in the central hill country.[14] Many scholars assume that Israel returned to their base camp at Gilgal after the victory at Ai (cf. Josh. 9:6). If so, the present text assumes that Israel made a possibly risky thirty-mile trek northwest from the Jordan Valley to reach Mount Ebal. But the context more likely assumes that Israel has proceeded there directly from Ai (ca. 23 mi.) along the main north-south highway nearby.[15]

The defeat of Ai (and possibly Bethel) would have made the road safer, especially if royal resistance to Israel (9:1–2) had not yet jelled. The central hill country was sparsely inhabited at the time, so the only military risk would at best be limited to the area around Shechem, an ancient regional power.[16] But Joshua 8 may assume that through circumstances unknown to us, Shechem was already safely in Israelite hands (cf. Josh. 17:2, 7; Judg. 9). Later, Shechem will host the book's final covenant renewal ceremony (Josh. 24:1, 25).

The altar building carries out Moses' commands, especially the stipulation that only large, uncut fieldstones be used (Josh. 8:30–31; cf. Deut. 11:26–32; 27:1–26).[17] The people immediately offer on it the "burnt offerings" and "fellowship offerings" that Moses commanded (Deut. 27:6, 7; cf. Ex. 24:5). The purpose for the prohibition of reworked stones is uncertain. In my view, if the physical alteration of the stones transmits defilement (likely), the preference for unaltered ones serves to preserve the holiness of space set aside for God.[18]

---

13. The opening syntax approximates the date of the event ("about that time ..."; NIV "then"), leaving a loose connection with the context. For the syntax, cf. WO §31.6.3; JM §113i; 1 Kings 11:7; 2 Kings 12:18; 16:5. The use of *'az* and a finite verb introduces an episode or pause over a remark elsewhere in Joshua (Josh. 10:12, 33; 22:1).

14. Shechem is the mountain's traditional location, but some dispute that assumption. See note 1 above.

15. This assumes, of course, that Israelites who remained at Gilgal during the attack on Ai somehow rendezvoused with the army for the ceremony at Mount Ebal.

16. Cf. Howard, *Joshua*, 212, who sees a greater risk in the trip from Ai to Shechem. It bears mentioning, however, that the author focuses on the mountain but ignores the city (but see Josh. 24:1, 25, 32). The Amarna letters (fourteenth cent. B.C.) reflect Shechem's regional hegemony; cf. Kuhrt, *The Ancient Near East*, 1:319, 324–28.

17. The altar law (Ex. 20:24–26) similarly prohibits cut-stone altars in favor of earthen ones. It also forbids the use of steps to ascend them.

18. So S. Olyan, "Why an Altar of Unfinished Stones? Some Thoughts on Ex 20:25 and Dtn 27:5–6," *ZAW* 108/2 (1996): 161–71. Other scholarly suggestions include: to keep

A wordplay in 8:31 seems to underscore the point: Only "uncut [*šelemot*] stones" make an altar suitable for "fellowship offerings" (*šelamim*). The "fellowship offering" burns only parts of the animal, leaving the rest to be eaten by worshipers in a communal meal (Lev. 3:1–17; 7:11–12).[19] It is an occasion to "rejoice in the presence of the LORD your God" (Deut. 27:7)—a simple, happy scene, with God and his people sharing a joyful, friendly fellowship meal.

In a "burnt offering," a wood fire on the altar completely consumes the animal, sending "a pleasing aroma" skyward to Yahweh (Ex. 29:18; Lev. 1:9, 13, 17). It usually functions as a prelude either to other offerings or (more commonly) to the presentation of petitions. But what purpose does the pair of offerings serve here? Elsewhere, they describe an act of worship in Yahweh's honor (see Num. 10:10; chs. 28–29; Judg. 20:26; 21:4; 1 Sam. 10:8). So, "burnt offerings and . . . fellowship offerings" may simply state generally that Israel worships Yahweh through appropriate rituals.[20]

It is striking, however, that the wording in Joshua 8:31 echoes language in the covenant-making ceremony at Mount Sinai (Ex. 24:5). Since the offerings mark the people's only direct action here, their actions probably signal their recommitment to the covenant. But consider also the great symbolic significance of building an altar on Mount Ebal in the very heart of Canaan. The elevation of Mount Ebal (2,867 feet) offers a commanding view of virtually all of Canaan except the Negev.[21] Mounts Ebal and Gerizim flank the strategic east-west pass that connects Shechem in both directions. Whoever controls the pass at Mount Ebal controls the north-central hill country from just north of Jerusalem to just south of the Valley of Jezreel.[22]

More important, Shechem also has ties to Israel's patriarchs. Both Abraham and Jacob built altars there when they, too, entered Canaan (Gen. 12:7; 33:20). Patriarchal altar-building underscores the connection between

---

out Canaanite influences from Israelite worship; to avoid luxury; and to maintain a semi-nomadic lifestyle.

19. This explains why it is called the "fellowship offering." But some translations (e.g., KJV, NLT) render the term as "peace offerings" since Heb. *šelamim* derives from the same root as *šalom* ("peace").

20. The meaning of the burnt offering and its relationship to the fellowship offering is the subject of much discussion. For a recent summary and critique, see J. W. Watts, "ʿolah: The Rhetoric of Burnt Offerings," *VT* 56/1 (2006): 126–32. Cf. Howard (*Joshua*, 215), who avers that here the burnt offering atones for Israel's sins while the fellowship offering reestablishes a positive relationship with Yahweh.

21. For an entrancing first-person account of the view, see G. A. Smith, *The Historical Geography of the Holy Land* (New York: Armstrong & Son, 1901), 94–95.

22. Boling, *Joshua*, 247.

entering the land, the promise of land, and the true worship of Yahweh. As Noort observes, "The altars are fixed points in the theological geography of the land. They claim the land for YHWH, his chosen one and his descendants."[23]

The altar raised by Joshua on Mount Ebal probably stakes a similar claim for the present generation. This may explain why Joshua 8 gives primacy to the altar construction (Josh. 8:30 vs. Deut. 27:5–6) rather than to the writing of the law on plastered stones (Josh. 8:32 vs. Deut. 27:1–4). The reordering makes the altar a powerful symbol of Israel's land claim on Canaan, signals the end of Israel's old nomadic society, and inaugurates a new one in Israel's new land.[24]

Archaeology attests the presence atop Mount Ebal of a massive rectangular structure reached by a ramp, but whether it relates to Joshua's altar (or is even an altar at all) remains a matter of dispute.[25] But archaeological evidence does suggest that, whatever its precise nature, the site was probably a major cultic one.[26] For example, the four corners of the main structure there point precisely to the four points of the compass. Further, the amount of burned animal bones found exceeds what one would expect at an ordinary small settlement. Some of the ceramic ware also compares to vessels known elsewhere to serve cultic functions.

The Writing of the Law (8:32–33)

ONCE THE SACRIFICES CONCLUDE, the people apparently descend the mountain since they next appear in the valley below (v. 33). Joshua then writes on the stones a copy of the "Instruction of Moses" (my translation) that the latter had himself written "in the presence of the Israelites" (v. 32).[27] The

23. Noort, "The Traditions of Ebal and Mount Gerizim," 171; cf. his full discussion (170–72); Gen. 13:4; 26:25; 35:1–7.

24. Cf. Hawk, *Joshua*, 133.

25. The claim by Zertal in the mid-1980s to have found Joshua's altar on Mount Ebal has not won scholarly acceptance; cf. A. Zertal, "Has Joshua's Altar Been Found on Mt Ebal?" *BAR* 11/1 (January–February 1985): 26–43. For example, what Zertal interpreted to be an altar Kempinski argues was instead a watchtower; cf. A. Kempinski, "Joshua's Altar: An Iron Age I Watchtower," *BAR* 12/1 (January–February 1986): 42, 44–49; response by A. Zertal, "How Can Kempinski Be So Wrong," *BAR* 12/1 (January–February 1986): 43, 49–53. For further discussion and bibliography, see Noort, "The Traditions of Ebal and Mount Gerizim," 168–69.

26. Noort, "The Traditions of Ebal and Mount Gerizim," 169–70; cf. A. Mazar, *Archaeology of the Land of the Bible 10,000–586 B.C.E.* (New York: Doubleday, 1992), 348–50.

27. Howard (*Joshua*, 215) believes that Joshua had written the copy, but grammatically Moses is the closest antecedent of the relative pronoun "which" (ʾašer) and the most likely subject of "wrote."

reference may be to Moses' writing of "the Book of the Covenant" (Ex. 24:4, 7), apparently at the Israelite camp though not specifically "in the presence of the Israelites," as Joshua 8:32 says. The term "Instruction of Moses" more likely recalls his writing of "this law" at the plains of Moab since the context has the Israelites present (Deut. 31:7, 9).

The "stones" probably refer to the altar's stone components, although Deuteronomy 27:2–4 may suggest a separate set of plastered stones.[28] The ancient Near East certainly attests the practice of writing on plastered surfaces (e.g., walls, stone slabs, etc.), especially legal texts.[29] But any writing posted outdoors, even on a plastered surface, would require occasional retouching because of the elements. In any case, Joshua writes this copy of the law with Israel present, just as Moses did. The double repetition of the verb "to write" (*katab*) — the third occurrence thus far (vv. 31, 32 [2x], 34; cf. "written" [vv. 31, 34]) — sounds a key theme, the primacy of Moses' written teaching in Israel's national life.[30] To use a modern analogy, it provides Israel's constitution, the written document that defines their identity and destiny. Their future hangs on obedience to it.

Subject-first syntax quickly leads the reader from Mount Ebal to "all Israel" standing in the valley below (v. 33).[31] Deuteronomy 27:12–13 describes the people by tribal names (e.g., Dan, Judah, etc.), but the present report (Josh. 8:33–35) invokes common social terms. Literarily, the latter terms make the description more personal and appealing and imply that the Instruction cuts across all tribal lines. The participants include everybody: leaders ("elders, officials and judges"), priests, Israelite citizens, resident aliens (vv. 33, 35), as well as "women and children" (v. 35). Everyone is present for this public, corporate event.

The inclusion of "aliens" twice underscores the inclusiveness of membership within the religious "assembly [*qahal*] of Israel" (v. 35). "Foreigners"

---

28. Howard (*Joshua*, 215–16) favors the latter because of Deut. 27, as does Nelson (*Joshua*, 119), who believes the author presumes that audience familiarity with Deut. 27 will guide it to distinguish the stones in v. 32 from those in v. 31. The grammar favors the former option, but the latter is also grammatically possible (but, in my view, less likely). The question is whether the author is closely following Deut. 27 and assumes knowledge of its contents, or whether his silence signals his intentional omission of the provision for plastered stones.

29. One example is the writings about Balaam that once covered plastered walls at Tell Deir ʿAlla in the central Jordan Valley; cf. Hess, *Joshua*, 173; Nelson, *Joshua*, 120.

30. Cf. Noort, "The Traditions of Ebal and Mount Gerizim," 179.

31. This assumes that Heb. *ʾel-mul* means "in front of" (so Ex. 34:3; 1 Sam. 17:30; LXX *plesion* ["near, nearby"]) rather than simply "opposite." In my view, it makes more linguistic and contextual sense to visualize each half-group of Israelites as positioned directly "in front of" one of the mountains. That would imply locations in the valley, not together on Mount Ebal.

(*nokrim*) merely pass through Israel, but resident aliens (*gerim*) live there permanently. The Instruction guarantees them access to fields for gleaning (Lev. 19:10; 23:22) and protects them from oppression (Ex. 21:22; Deut. 10:17−22). It supports its protections by invoking the memory of Israel's own terrible experience as "aliens" in Egypt (Ex. 23:9; Lev. 19:34; Deut. 10:10).

More surprising, Moses' teaching authorizes the participation of aliens in Israel's worship life—Sabbaths (Ex. 20:10), Passover (Ex. 12:19, 48, 49), and other major festivals (Deut. 16:10−14; 26:10−11). As Howard notes, "This shows—as does the story of Rahab—that Israel's faith was not a closed system; it was open to outsiders."[32] (For Joshua's possible extension of resident alien status to an unexpected group, see Josh. 9.) Later, aliens also will receive protection under the system of cities of refuge (20:9). Meanwhile, whether native-born citizen or immigrant, all stand side by side in two large groups, half at the foot of Mount Gerizim and half at the foot of Mount Ebal. They wait patiently below as Joshua writes.

Note, however, the purpose that the author assigns to this assembly: Per Moses' instructions, it convenes "to bless the people of Israel." Here the author slightly (and significantly) departs from Deuteronomy 27. The latter orders six tribes to pronounce blessings and six tribes the curses (vv. 12−13), but here Joshua himself will soon read both (8:34). Further, Deuteronomy 27 ends with the Levites reading the long list of painful curses (vv. 16−26), but in Joshua 8 the spotlight falls exclusively on blessing for the present assembly of people.[33] In short, this ceremony serves a single purpose, to bestow on the people Yahweh's blessings. As the words of Joshua's reading cascade like a waterfall on the people below, they drench them in the power of God to bless. (For more on blessing, see Bridging Contexts).

The Reading of the Law (8:34−35)

LATER ("AFTERWARD") JOSHUA TURNS from writing to reading.[34] He reads aloud (lit., "called out") "all the words of the [written] Instruction" (my translation; cf. NLT), specifically the blessings and curses (v. 34; cf. Deut. 28). The act is momentous—the first recorded public reading of the Instruction since the death of Moses. In spirit, it implements Moses' mandate that the priests publicly read the Instruction every seven years (Deut. 31:11).[35] Implicitly,

---

32. Howard, *Joshua*, 217.

33. Nelson, *Joshua*, 118.

34. The time marker "afterward" (*ʾaḥare-ken*) highlights the chronological distinction between the writing and reading phases; cf. Gen. 23:19; 25:26; Ex. 34:32; 2 Chron. 33:14; Jer. 49:6.

35. Cf. Nelson, *Joshua*, 120.

the phrase "the blessings and the curses" confronts Israel with the life-and-death choice to be for or against Yahweh that Moses gave them:

> This day ... I have set before you life and death, blessings and curses. Now choose life, so that you and your children may live and that you may love the LORD your God, listen to his voice, and hold fast to him. (Deut. 30:19–20a)

Again, the emphasis falls on the Instruction written in a book. The authoritative teaching of Moses is permanently available for instruction and consultation—if Israel chooses.

Finally, the author underscores that Joshua reads the entire Instruction—every single word (v. 35). The comment both enhances the portrait of Joshua as a worthy successor to Moses and pictures the Instruction of Moses as consummately authoritative. A "Moses for Dummies" will not do; Israel needs to hear every word. To conclude, the author again returns briefly to describe the audience before whom Joshua reads. It is the "assembly [*qahal*]"—the religious congregation of Israel gathered for an important religious ceremony.[36] To the earlier list of participants (v. 33) the narrator adds "women and children" and reiterates the presence of "the aliens who lived [lit., 'walked'] among them." "Among" may, in fact, allude to Rahab since 6:25 has a similar phrase ("among Israel"). The Instruction applies to *everyone*, regardless of gender, age, or social standing.

In short, the ending reasserts the religious importance and inclusive participation of the ceremony. It leaves out neither a single word from Moses nor a single member of "all Israel"—in Hawk's words, "men, women, children, and even Canaanites, indeed all who express obedient devotion to YHWH."[37] Generations of future readers will "see themselves in their ancestors' situation at Ebal and Gerizim." The glance back at ancestral infidelity and renewal will challenge them to "renewed allegiance to the land and rejuvenated hope in the power of Yahweh's blessing."[38]

 **Bridging Contexts**

COVENANT AND COVENANT RENEWAL. The idea of covenant renewal may strike some readers as strange. In modern thinking, a commitment is a commitment; one either does or does not keep it. Some may even recoil at the term "renewal," since the word most

36. F.-L. Hossfeld and E.-M. Kindl, "קָהַל," *TDOT*, 12:553–54.
37. Hawk, *Joshua*, 134.
38. Nelson, *Joshua*, 120.

commonly applies to newspaper and magazine subscriptions or club memberships. They reject the implication that Christian commitment compares to a subscription. To them it sounds ridiculous (if not impossible) that someone might actually decide some December 31 *not* to be a Christian in the new year. In short, the Christian experience of many readers may create a disconnect between themselves and Joshua 8 concerning the concept of covenant renewal. It is striking, however, that moments of renewal are typical of Israel's religious life. One theme of contemporary meaning, therefore, concerns the blessings that flow from the practice of periodic renewal.

We should recall that two other moments of covenant renewal occur in the book of Joshua. The first is the circumcision ceremony at Gilgal in which Joshua circumcised all Israelite males of military age (5:2–9). Militarily, the move makes little sense since it disables the soldiers. But along with physical fitness, they needed ritual fitness both for the holy war ahead and for later settlement in Yahweh's holy land. Submission to the painful ceremony signals the younger generation's commitment to the covenant, and Yahweh confirms their full membership in it by declaring their "shame" gone (see comments on ch. 5).

The second renewal moment in the book (24:1–28) more closely echoes Joshua 8.[39] Joshua convenes an all-Israelite ceremony at Shechem (see comments on ch. 24). The generation circumcised at Gilgal will soon confront a major change, life without Joshua. As his death approaches, he will urge them to renew their commitment to Yahweh and the covenant in the post-Joshua period. He demands that they choose which God they will serve in the future (Josh. 24:14–15). In short, the dawn of a new day confronts Israel with a fork in the road and a choice for or against Yahweh.

What makes such renewals advisable? The reason is that life is full of changes, and those changes alter the context of one's commitment. One may come to faith as a child, but childhood soon yields to the independence and challenges of adulthood. Education, job, family, and longer life experience all require new choices. Each stage tests the adequacy and relevance of that childhood faith, and each such test in essence demands a new choice.

Life also has its own natural rhythms or phases. Chronological rhythms—the day, week, month, and year—are easily measured by cal-

---

39. The similarities suggest to some scholars that Joshua 8:30–35 and 24:1–28 (5:2–9, too) derive from the same editorial activity; cf. Campbell and O'Brien, *Unfolding the Deuteronomistic History,* 117–18, 127, 160–63. Fritz (*Josua,* 57–59, 95–99, 239–49) basically concurs but advances a more complex history, especially with ch. 24.

endars and universally shared by the culture. At age eighteen one achieves legal emancipation—the legal landmark of adulthood. But life also has unmarked "stages"—phases experienced in the moment as common among humans. Not everyone experiences every stage, and stages differ in the length and sequence experienced. The perspective of young adulthood certainly differs from those of middle and old age. The eyes of youth focus forward on the future, the eyes of middle age both forward for planning and backward for perspective, and those of old age primarily backward.

In each stage, the influences on our decision making also change. The Joshuas of early life (family, Sunday school teachers, youth pastors, etc.) soon give way to the opinions of peers. Adult independence allows us to choose which authorities to believe and which leaders to follow. Each stage challenges one's faith in unique ways and, as noted above, forces the question, "Is Jesus still Lord here and now?"

Now, I hasten to add that the above discussion presumes a modern view of individualism—a worldview that shapes and guides the way most of us think. That perspective, however, differs radically from the corporate worldview of both the covenant and the gospel. Thus, understanding the covenant will further aid our understanding of the benefits of practices of renewal.

The term "covenant" (Heb. *berit*) designates the kind of relationship that binds Yahweh and Israel. This Hebrew word basically means "imposition, liability, obligation."[40] In biblical usage, it appears synonymously with words like "law" and "commandment" (e.g., Deut. 4:13; Isa. 24:5; Ps. 50:16; 103:18). Its usage excludes any idea that the relationship between Yahweh and Israel is in any way a mutual one. The covenant does not presuppose that Yahweh and Israel are peers who have entered their relationship on equal footing. Rather, Yahweh's role is that of the master or suzerain, who rightfully imposes the terms of the agreement on his subordinate or vassal (cf. Josh. 9:26; 1 Sam. 11:1–2).[41]

The so-called "covenant formulary" and its variations summarize their relationship: "I will be your God, and you shall be my people" (Ex. 6:7; Deut. 29:13; Jer. 7:23; Ezek. 36:28). The terms "God" and "people" reflect the roles, respectively, of sovereignty and subordination inherent in their relationship. Typically, to confirm a covenant requires that the latter take

---

40. M. Weinfeld, "בְּרִית," *TDOT*, 2:255–56.

41. This is true even if human mediators sponsor the covenant, as do Moses (Ex. 24) and Joshua (Josh. 24). The Old Testament also attests covenants between individuals (Gen. 21:22–23; 1 Sam 18:3; 23:18), nation-states (1 Kings 5:12[26]; 15:19), kings and subjects (2 Sam. 5:3; 2 Kings 11:17), and husbands and wives (Ezek. 16:8; Mal. 2:14); cf. Weinfeld, ibid., 264.

an oath that imposes terrible consequences for any violations (Deut. 29:10–13[9–12]; Josh. 9:15–20; 2 Kings 11:4). The oath comprises a conditional curse—for example, "May such-and-such happen to me if I break this obligation." It confirms that the subordinate will truly comply with the terms of the agreement. The underlying theory is that only someone willing to abide by them would voluntarily take a curse upon himself. In the covenant between Yahweh and Israel, the Instruction of Moses constitutes the terms of the agreement.

Important illumination on the form and content of the covenant comes from ancient Near Eastern treaties, especially those of the Hittites in Anatolia (fourteenth and thirteenth cent. B.C.).[42] The structural elements of Hittite treaties have striking analogies in biblical texts about the covenant (e.g., Ex. 19–24 and Deuteronomy).[43] Hittite treaties open with a historical introduction in which the suzerain reviews the history of his relationship with the vassal. He surveys promises made by his royal predecessors, gifts of land in the past, and their present borders. Treaties also list the stipulations—the suzerain's promises and the "do's and don'ts" expected of the vassal—and call on gods to witness the transaction. Blessings and curses for keeping or breaching the treaty follow. Finally, the treaty provides for its contents to be read periodically to the public and for its documents to be stored.

As for content, the vocabulary of treaties also has biblical analogies. Treaties invoke "love" as a metaphor for the loyalty of vassals to the suzerain. Phrases like "hearken to the voice of," "go after," "serve," "fear," and "not turn to the right hand or the left" figure prominently.[44] This vocabulary has obvious echoes in Deuteronomy, including the repeated appeals to "love the LORD" (Deut. 11:1; 19:9; cf. Josh. 22:5; 23:11) and to "serve" and "fear" him (Deut. 6:13; 10:20; cf. Josh. 24:14).

As for structure, no single Old Testament covenant text completely matches the format of ancient treaties, but they do share several important elements. Exodus 19 and Deuteronomy 1–11 function as historical prologues to the stipulations (i.e., the laws) that follow (Ex. 20:1–23:19; Deut. 12–26). Deuteronomy also summons "heaven and earth" as witnesses to the covenant (Deut. 4:26; 30:19; 31:25–26) and mandates the deposit

---

42. Ibid., 265–70. According to Weinfeld (267–68), the Neo-Assyrian treaties (first millennium B.C.) seem particularly analogous to Deuteronomy. In particular, the content and order of the curses in Deut. 28 compare closely to the curses in a treaty of the Assyrian king Esarhaddon with his eastern vassals (627 B.C.). For a translation of the latter, cf. *ANET*, 534–41.

43. For translations of examples, cf. *COS*, 2:93–106.

44. Weinfeld, "בְּרִית," 268–69.

of the Book of the Law in the ark of the covenant (10:1–5; 31:25–26). As in Hittite treaties, Deuteronomy commands that the law be read publicly (31:9–13) and orders the king to read it (17:18–19). Similarly, Deuteronomy includes a long section of blessings and curses (27:15–26; ch. 28), a section that Joshua 8:34 apparently mentions.

One final point needs making about the covenant. The covenant formulary defines the agreement as between God and "his people." Since "people" is a single collective noun (Heb. *ʿam*), the entity it describes is the corporate body of Israel. That is, it presents Israel as a single whole, not a collection of individuals. Granted, individuals participate in the covenant and are responsible individually to obey its demands, but the Bible understands Israel to be a single, corporate entity. Further, it understands that corporateness to extend across generations. Notice something Moses says: "I am making this covenant, with its oath, not only with you who are standing here with us today in the presence of the LORD our God but also *with those who are not here today*" (Deut. 29:14–15, my italics).

"Those not here today" refers to future generations of Israelites. Though not present the day Moses made the covenant in the plains of Moab, they are parties to it, too. A similar corporate understanding underlies Paul's statement that "Christ loved the church and gave himself up for her" (Eph. 5:25). Though individuals can receive salvation, Jesus did not die for individual "Christians" but for "the church" as a corporate body. Jesus presupposes this, too, in his prayer for the disciples: "My prayer is not for them alone. I pray also for those who will believe in me through their message, that all of them may be one" (John 17:20–21). In the future, people will become believers in Jesus. By faith they will join "the church" and become part of the new covenant. So Jesus prays that they may all be "one"—that they will function as the collective "people" they are.

This corporate understanding of the people of God helps explain the importance of covenant renewal. Once inaugurated, both the old and new covenants remain in force across the centuries. Through circumcision, newborn Israelites become members of the old covenant, and through baptism newly born-again Christians become members of the new covenant. But for the covenants to work, each new generation of the collective Israel or the church must truly understand its terms for their day. They must also, so to speak, agree to keep its terms in their own lives just as past generations did.

Further, in so doing, they affirm the transgenerational nature of the body of which they are a part. They celebrate their membership in a larger corporate body—that they received the faith from spiritual ancestors and pass it on to descendants. Those past and future connections motivate each generation to renew its commitment to the faith. They embrace their responsibility to ensure its safe passage into the future.

Blessings (and curses). Finally, earlier I indicated that the focus of the ceremony at the end of Joshua 8 falls on blessing. Theologically, the narrative portrays the power of God's blessing flowing from the words of the Instruction over the people hearing them. The idea of blessings and curses, thus, merit brief additional clarification.[45]

In the ancient world, one typically uttered a curse in response to gross violations of the basic ethical norms of one's clan, religious community, or people. The curse aimed to destroy the solidarity previously enjoyed with them by the violator or to undermine his or her ability to resist powerful enemies. The blessing intended the opposite—to strengthen an individual's solidarity with individuals or groups in two directions. The solidarity might concern persons with whom close social, ethnic, and religious relationships existed or were sought. Or, it could concern persons to whom the individual wished to express special thanks or appreciation.

Now, the ancient world highly regarded magic—the belief that to utter solemn words released the power to make the utterance a reality almost automatically. By contrast, in the Old Testament spoken words (curses and blessings) possess no such inherent power. They are subordinate to the sovereignty of God and take effect only because he empowers the words. So, Israelites utter only blessings that Yahweh alone can bring to reality, and the speaker must be in personal fellowship with God. Otherwise, the blessing will not achieve the strengthening of solidarity sought.

The subordination of spoken words to God's authority and power also means that blessings and curses are revocable—that blessings may become curses and vice versa. The case of the seer Balaam is a case in point (Num. 22–24). His sponsor, King Balak of Moab, hired him to curse Israel, at the time camped within his territory and (in his view) posing a threat. Several times and in several places Balak pressed Balaam to curse Israel, but each request required Yahweh's approval. Each time Yahweh replied that Balaam could say only what Yahweh wanted—to bless Israel. Toward the end of the narrative, Balaam explained to Balak, "I have received a command to bless; he [Yahweh] has blessed, and I cannot change it" (Num. 23:20). In all, Balaam pronounced four oracles of blessing on Israel just as Yahweh commanded, much to Balak's unhappiness!

Suppose a speaker utters a blessing in appropriate words and with an aim that pleases God. In that case, the spoken words release a power—Yahweh's power—to bring "happiness, prosperity, respect, fertility, etc., to

---

45. Cf. the discussion in J. Scharbert, "בָּרַךְ," *TDOT*, 2:303–4.

the person being blessed."[46] In short, Israel regarded words and power as inseparably related—the vehicle of Yahweh's beneficent powers. This understanding also undergirds the Old Testament view of the power of the word of God. Recall the well-known claim from the book of Isaiah:

As the rain and the snow
   come down from heaven,
and do not return to it
   without watering the earth
and making it bud and flourish,
   so that it yields seed for the sower and bread for the eater,
so is my word that goes out from my mouth:
   It will not return to me empty,
but will accomplish what I desire
   and achieve the purpose for which I sent it. (Isa. 55:10–11)

The prophet compares the power of the word of God to the effects of rain and snow. Rather than simply evaporate immediately heavenward, rain and melted snow always water the earth first. The moisture empowers the earth to produce seeds for sowing future crops and grains to be eaten as bread. When spoken, God's word also always achieves God's purposes; it never returns to him without doing so ("empty"). This background suggests that the very reading of the Instruction by Joshua actually does something to the Israelites below. It sows among them seeds of divine blessing destined to flourish, unless, of course, their disobedience causes Yahweh to substitute curses for blessing.

In conclusion, it is worth noting how tangible and practical are the blessings of Deuteronomy 28. They apply to all kinds of places—the city and the country and everything in between (v. 3)—and life's routine entrances and exits (v. 6). They concern the gamut of human concerns for fertility: new children, crops, and livestock (v. 4). In the ancient world, crops and livestock marked a family's basic livelihood, and besides simple joy children also augmented the labor force needed to sustain it. The blessings concern a family's having daily fruit and bread (v. 5) and its success in the many tasks required by agricultural life (v. 8). They thwart the disasters with which enemy invasions threaten families (v. 7).

Two major campaigns await Israel (Josh. 10–11), so the blessing of enemies being defeated would certainly ease the fears of soldiers in Joshua's audience. For the most part, however, the blessings look beyond the battles to the coming "abundant prosperity ... in the fruit of your womb, the young

---

46. Ibid., 304.

of your livestock and the crops of your ground" (v. 11). That prosperity depends on the generosity of the rain showers God sends (v. 12). Through blessings, Yahweh makes Israel "the head, not the tail"—that is, he keeps Israel "always ... at the top, never at the bottom" (v. 13).

As Israel listens in the valley below Mount Ebal, the practical benefits of God's powerful blessings resonate deeply throughout the audience. Rather than sending magical powers, the reading of God's words releases his power to empower Israel for the future—for the imminent battles and the later settlement ahead.

THE BLESSING OF RENEWAL. Joshua 8:30–35 features a dramatic moment of covenant renewal in which Israel receives Yahweh's blessing afresh. The ceremony welcomes the Instruction to the Promised Land and empowers Israel for the days ahead. This ceremony suggests that similar moments of renewal might likewise benefit Christians today.

To a certain extent, congregations that follow the liturgical church year already incorporate renewal in their worship life. But the practice has happily also found a home in more low-church congregations like mine. During Advent, the advent wreath symbolizes the weeks of anticipation before Christmas Day. Each Sunday, members or families read Scriptures and light a new candle. During the week, some families also read Scripture and light candles on wreaths at home (we did when our sons were young). The tradition prepares the congregation to welcome the Christ child anew into their lives and homes. It extends the reach of Christmas from an "eve" and a single "day" to a four-week "season" of Sundays. It keeps at bay the pressing commercial preoccupation of the larger culture and keeps our observance of Christmas genuinely Christian. It fosters an attitude of expectant waiting and excited anticipation. It marks one good way that churches annually renew their commitment to Jesus as the Christ.

This starkly contrasts with my experience of Easter growing up in a low-church congregation. Easter celebrates the final, climatic week of Jesus' redemptive ministry on earth. Theologically, it marks the central turning point of human history, the opening of unimaginable, radically new possibilities for humanity. Victory over sin, and victory over death—what could be more important? But my memories are that Easter always seemed to arrive out of the blue. All of a sudden it was Palm Sunday, and then Holy Week began in earnest without much anticipation.

Granted, as kids my sisters and I often got new clothes, which we proudly wore Easter Sunday. And we always had a big meal that day. But, unlike Christmas, no long "season" preceded it. I only knew Easter was coming when the choir started rehearsing for the annual cantata. (And I only knew that because my mother was the organist!) Of course, with liturgical traditions the forty-day season of Lent offers a season of preparation and anticipation. And, for a time, some low-church congregations adopted a kind of "evangelical Lent"—special programs such as the "Fifty-Day Spiritual Adventure" that led up to Easter. But, recently such programs seem less tied thematically to Easter and may be scheduled at other times.[47]

My point is not to criticize such programs—they offer churches useful resources that do much good. My concern is twofold. (1) I rue the absence in many congregations of a moment set aside periodically for corporate renewal of their commitment to Christ. Many married couples today renew their covenant with each other by repeating wedding vows at milestone anniversaries. But when do church bodies as a whole renew their commitment to the new covenant as Israel did to the old?

(2) I rue the lack of a meaningful action to symbolize that renewal, one that Christians of different faith traditions share in common. Communion services certainly mark times for sober reflection and the renewal of our commitment to the new covenant that Jesus initiated on the cross. They also invoke the emotionally powerful symbols of broken bread and poured-out wine. But I have in mind something done annually rather than weekly or monthly—more like an anniversary or commemorative holiday.

Along that line, the Advent season offers a likely moment, but I myself prefer to leave the themes of wonder, expectancy, and welcome as is. Easter offers another candidate, but I myself prefer to leave it as the joyous victory celebration it traditionally is. I picture covenant renewal as a sober, solemn moment with a feeling—positive and hopeful, to be sure—of "signing one's life away." The traditional Watch Night Service held on New Year's Eve probably offers the best occasion. The timing and setting are appropriate. Our culture promotes the making of New Year's resolutions as the old year runs out. They also occur at night, and the darkness outside sets a tone for serious reflection and resolve. The trick is how to Christianize the celebration.

A short scene in *Mrs. Miniver* by novelist Jan Struther contributes an important insight here. The Minivers are a middle-class British family

---

47. As I write, the "50-Day Spiritual Adventure" website (http://www.sundaysolutions.com/index.html) offers "Sermon Series on Christmas and Advent," but none of its "50-Day Spiritual Adventure Campaigns" is specifically designed for Easter.

struggling to survive the darks days of World War II. One episode finds Mrs. Miniver and her husband, Clem, on a car trip to Scotland, a drive they had made every year for fifteen years. The passing of familiar places triggers "little memory-flags with which, on their minds' map, the road was studded." Some spots are places where earlier cars had unhelpfully broken down and stranded them temporarily. Other locales recall pleasant picnics in past years, and one in particular calls up memories of the beautiful double rainbow they had seen. Their present journey brings them to a summit where, as is their custom, they stop to stretch and enjoy the wide expanse of majestic countryside below. Refreshed, she and Clem resume their journey northward down the long descent from the summit. As she drives, Mrs. Miniver muses about the importance of memories:

> In the convex driving mirror she could see, dwindling rapidly, the patch of road where they had stood; and she wondered why it had never occurred to her before that you cannot successfully navigate the future unless you keep always framed beside it a small clear image of the past.[48]

Israel would agree with Mrs. Miniver. Israel's renewal celebration always begins with *a look backward at the past*. They review the great things God has done for them during their history—the call of Abraham, the Exodus, and the gift of Canaan (cf. Josh. 24:2–13). Implicitly, this review celebrates the goodness of God and gives grateful thanks for it. It explains from where and how far has been the journey to the present. The review also leads to *a call to renewal in the present* (24:14–15). The call compels Israel to take stock of the lessons of its history. Were they good days or bad days? Did Yahweh in any way fail, or did our ancestors fail him? And where does the present generation stand with him? Has it perpetuated the past failures or broken with them? *And what about the future?* Is today's generation ready to reembrace Yahweh and recommit to their covenant with him? Is that recommitment rooted only in self-interest—not to lose Yahweh's generosity—or genuine love for him? No movement into the future can succeed without shame-faced *confession of past sins and rebellions*.

Further, Israel answers the call with *a solemn reaffirmation* to abide by the covenant's terms. In Joshua 24, the reaffirmation takes the form of a long liturgy in which Israel renounces all connections with other gods (vv. 16–24). The back-and-forth dialogue between Joshua and the people ritually acts out Israel's firm resolve. Finally, the ceremony ends with Joshua writing down some rules, making a record of the transaction, and erecting a stone

---

48. Jan Struther, *Mrs. Miniver* (New York: Harcourt, Brace & World, 1942), 120.

witness to it (vv. 25−27). This stage formally makes the covenant official and records it for posterity. The records may become the subject of public readings during future renewal ceremonies. It also involves a symbolic representation of the event, the stone witness. In short, the pattern of Israel suggests the following phases to any covenant renewal ceremony: a review of the past, a call to renewal, confession of sin, a solemn reaffirmation for the future, and a record of the event, and a symbol that it occurred.

I propose, however, that congregations consider an alternate form of contemporary covenant renewal, a *baptism renewal ceremony*. By this I mean a special ceremony that enables previously baptized Christians symbolically to reaffirm their earlier baptismal commitment. This makes good theological sense since baptism marks the symbolic event through which people today commonly enter the Christian faith. In the practice of infant baptism, committed Christian parents present their child for inclusion in the community of faith. A decade or so later, the baptized child completes confirmation, a special process of education that culminates in the child's personal affirmation of her or his own faith in Jesus Christ.

Now, I am aware that some denominations celebrate a form of baptismal renewal. In some churches such celebrations occur annually on the Sunday in January that remembers the baptism of Jesus. But I believe the practice worthy of wider observance, since otherwise the only reminder of one's baptism is the witness of new ones.[49]

By contrast, my impression is that churches practicing believer's baptism—the Christian "tribe" in which I grew up—rarely if ever offer such occasions. Their worship life includes no symbolic way for already baptized members to connect with their own baptism in the past. But my proposal is that whatever a church's form of baptism, it include some occasion for renewal of baptismal commitment.

For example, my home church recently celebrated several baptisms. When the baptismal service ended, the pastor invited worshipers to come forward to the portable baptismal pool. The invitation was to pause there a moment to remember their own baptism. People were encouraged even to dip their hands in the water as a tangible connection with that past experience. It was a meaningful, moving moment of worship and renewal. With infant baptisms, the font can serve as the site for baptismal remembrance and renewal. Churches can decide how and when to offer such ceremonies.

---

49. A. D. Duba, "Take Me to the Water: Ideas for Keeping Baptism Front and Center," *Reformed Worship* 62 (Dec. 2001): 22−52, reviews the meanings associated with baptism and suggests ways to practice baptismal renewal. Implicitly, his article confirms that such celebrations either are uncommon or need increased emphasis.

Churches that have several baptisms each month may prefer a monthly or yearly observance. The incorporation of baptisms and baptism reconnection in an annual Watch Night Service is another possibility. Churches that practice immersion baptisms in pools recessed behind the choir loft may need to provide a small, symbolic pool accessible to worshipers. Whatever the case, I suggest a baptism renewal or remembrance as one way to renew our commitment to Christ today. It offers another way to apply the themes of Joshua 8 to Christian life now.

Word incarnate: God with us. A moment of special drama in Joshua 8 is the reading of the Instruction. The words of God echo down from Mount Ebal and imbue the people below with divine blessing. That scene reminds readers that God's word is powerful, a theme as relevant today as it was then.

A mountaintop scene much later in Israel's history offers a good vantage point from which to view this theme. There a later Joshua named Jesus stands with his three key disciples, Peter, James, and John.[50] Suddenly, something strange happens before their eyes: Jesus is "transfigured" (Gk. *metamorphoomai*, "to be changed in appearance"). His face "shone like the sun" (Matt. 17:2) and his clothes became "dazzling white, whiter than anyone ... could bleach them" (Mark 9:3). The imagery recalls the radiant appearance of Moses when he descended from Mount Sinai after forty days and nights of talking with Yahweh (Ex. 34:29–30).[51] Immediately, Moses and Elijah—representatives, respectively, of the Old Testament law and prophets—join the scene. The three discuss Jesus' imminent "departure" (Gk. *exodos*) to fulfill his mission in Jerusalem (Luke 9:31), a reference to his coming death, resurrection, and ascension.[52] An excited Peter proposes the erection of three temporary shelters, one each for Jesus, Moses, and Elijah (Matt. 17:4; Mark 9:5). But a bright cloud suddenly envelops them and God speaks from it: "This is my Son, whom I love. Listen to him!" (Mark 9:7). The next instant, the disciples look, and the only person present is Jesus (Matt. 17:8; Mark 9:8).

In short, God has sent a new Moses for us to listen to and demands that we do so. What the Instruction of Moses was to Israel, the Instruction of Jesus, the new Moses, is to us. He is the mediator par excellence of God's Word—the one to listen to now as someone to whom Moses, Elijah, and

---

50. Recall that "Jesus" (*Iesous*) is the Greek form of the Hebrew name "Joshua" (*yehošuaᶜ*).

51. Cf. Ex. 19:9, 16; 24:15–18; 34:5, 29–30. They may indirectly also allude to Elijah's experience of a theophany there (1 Kings 19:8–21).

52. C. A. Evans, *Luke* (NIBCNT; Peabody, Mass.: Hendrickson, 1990), 153.

Joshua are subordinate. As the writer of Hebrews says, "In the past God spoke ... through the prophets ... but in these last days he has spoken to us by his Son" (Heb. 1:1–2). "These last days" identifies him as the latest of God's spokespersons, and "last days" may also locate him in history's closing eschatological age.

More important, unlike the prophets, who were human, this is God's "Son." He wears human flesh as they did, but only he is God living right here among humans (see John 1:14; 1 John 1:1). He is "the Word" incarnate. Consider what an improved means of divine revelation the term "Son" implies. Moses, Elijah, and Joshua were certainly God's servants. When Joshua read the Instruction from Mount Ebal, Israel listened seriously to it as God's word because of Joshua's status. But the access a "son" has to a "father" far surpasses that of any servant. On Mount Sinai Moses spent more time talking directly with God than any human in history. But God's own Son—he knows the Father like no one else!

A popular story reports the bedtime scene in a child's bedroom. Susie has prayed her usual prayer ("Now I lay me down to sleep ..."), and her mother is tucking her in for the night. Though solemn and sincere, the prayer has not allayed Susie's deathly fear of the dark. She pleads with her mother to stay with her until she falls asleep. But her mother kisses Susie goodnight, turns off the light, and pauses at the door for a final word.

"There's no reason to be afraid, Susie," she says. "Remember: God is right here with you."

Susie ponders that thought a moment, then from the dark says, "But I want somebody with skin."

Jesus is God "with skin" speaking to us. It is an obvious point, but one worth making: "This is my Son, whom I love. Listen to him!" Many voices beckon for our ear every day. People on the street ask to explain their legislative petitions and get our signature. Clever, carefully crafted media commercials entice us to buy Brand X. Media entertainers seek to hold our attention to expose us to all those commercials! Meetings at work discuss all manner of important matters, as do the many phone calls one makes and receives daily. The world, it seems, everywhere echoes an incessant "Blah, blah, blah, blah...." But we must not let the surrounding din drown out Jesus' voice in our ears. We must hear him! So, let us meditate carefully on Scripture to hear the quiet sounds of his voice. Let us spend time in quiet prayer listening for the gentle whisper of his voice. Let us keep ever before us the question: What is Jesus saying to me? Above all, hear him!

Written Word and Spirit: blessing with us. Jesus has left his Instruction in written form just as Joshua 8 reports that Moses did. Its reading by Joshua released God's power of blessing on his Israelite audience. The New

Testament also understands the Word of God to be powerful, and it captures that power in a single metaphor—the sword. Thus, Joshua 8 points us
forward through that canonical stopping point en route to today. Consider
these two familiar texts:

> Take the helmet of salvation and the *sword* of the Spirit, which is the
> word of God. (Eph. 6:17, my italics)

> For the word of God is living and active. Sharper than any *double-
> edged sword*, it penetrates even to dividing soul and spirit, joints and
> marrow; it judges the thoughts and attitudes of the heart. (Heb. 4:12,
> my italics)

These two texts prompt several observations. (1) The "word of God"
as "the sword of the Spirit" occurs in Paul's portrait of the ideal Christian
soldier fully outfitted for combat (Eph. 6:10–20). That person obeys Paul's
exhortation to "be strong in the Lord and in his mighty power" (v. 10). The
command compares to the exhortations given Joshua by Moses, Yahweh,
and the Transjordanian tribes (Deut. 31:7, 23; Josh. 1:6, 7, 9, 18). The prospect of imminent and protracted warfare stands behind all these exhortations. Joshua faced actual physical combat, but Paul's exhortations assume
ongoing spiritual combat between God and his opponents (e.g., "the devil's
schemes" [Eph. 6:11–12]). The implication is that without God's power,
Christians risk being overpowered and defeated. They engage in a life-and-
death struggle of eternal consequences for people. Tapping God's might,
however, makes survival, if not victory, certain.

(2) This soldier belongs to the infantry, not the artillery (ancient armies
had both). The latter fire objects from a safe distance, but the former always
face close, hand-to-hand, deathly sword play. The metaphor reminds Christians that most spiritual battles involve personal, face-to-face encounters
with people battling to keep God away. In hand the Christian wields the
"word of God" visualized by Paul as "the sword of the Spirit." The metaphor
compares God's word to a sword wielded by no less than the Holy Spirit
himself. Notice that this marks the only *offensive weapon* in the Christian's
armor—everything else is *defensive*, designed to protect the soldier.

A video clip of spiritual warfare might show a human quoting or reading
words of Scripture aloud, but unseen are the Spirit's expert hands pressing
those words home like a sword. The spoken words of God, so to speak,
"take on" the enemies and engage them. Notice also that the sword brings
impressive firepower. It is "living and active" and incredibly sharp ("sharper
than a two-edged sword"). It passes right through defenses—shields, armor,
and skin and bones—as if they were paper. Nothing can stop it from get-

ting inside someone and sticking. Like a modern surgical scalpel, it opens up even the most hidden, secret places—one's whole inner self ("soul and spirit," "joints and marrow"). It can even render judgment on one's inner thoughts and intentions. In the Spirit's hands, it forms an incredible weapon for getting to people!

Several implications for today flow from this truth. (1) It reminds us that all Christians are soldiers in a grand cosmic struggle between God and the forces of evil.[53] None of us is, in military terms, "in the rear" (and safe)—we are all on the front lines. Now, frontal attacks may be infrequent, but the struggle goes on behind the scenes and beneath the surface. This truth about cosmic struggle should dispel any illusions that "all is [spiritually] right with the world." On the contrary, it compels us to be on our spiritual guard and rely daily on God's power, lest God's enemies overpower us.

(2) The sword metaphor reminds us of the incredible power in our hands. In the Bible, we have the Word of God with its inherent divine power, and we have the Spirit whose mighty hand drives its words home. My exhortation is that we maintain (if not redouble) our efforts to store God's words in our memory for future use. The psalmist said, "I have hidden your word in my heart that I might not sin against you" (Ps. 119:11). The secret hiding place for the word that the psalmist selected was his heart, in biblical anthropology, the seat of human thought and will. There its words could whisper divine promptings to his mind and tug on the levers of his will. To store God's words there kept him from sinning by easing him away from his own (sinful) inclinations.

(3) But I also suggest that we draw on our memory bank of God's Word as the subtle, powerful offensive weapon that Paul imagines. I propose we find ways to quote it in everyday conversations—to unleash its Spirit-driven power to penetrate the hearts and lives of people who need to hear it. Now, let me be clear on one thing. I am not calling for a new wave of Bible-bashing or a kind of "Bible-ese" in which we speak mostly in Bible verses. The verbal violence of the first approach dishonors Jesus, and the second would make us sound like freaky aliens.

I also do not assume that the Bible's words have mystical powers that magically create effects simply by saying the words aloud. I eschew the magical mentality that undergirds the amusing story told by John Steinbeck in his delightful cross-country travel memoir, *Travels with Charlie*. One dark, rainy night he and Charlie, his faithful dog, camp in an eerie forest

---

53. For more on being a Christian soldier, see the Contemporary Significance section of chs. 9–10. The Contemporary Significance section of ch. 11 also discusses the larger spiritual struggle behind human history.

in Maine. The conjunction of darkness and loneliness stir memories of the forest of giant madrona trees on his ranch in the coastal mountains of California. He remembers how the dense forest and dim light conjure up the spooky feelings of a haunted place. He recalls asking the Filipino man who worked for him whether the spot terrified him. The man claimed that a charm given him by a witch doctor made him unafraid of evil spirits. Steinback replays the conversation:

> "Let me see that charm," I asked.
>
> "It's words," he said. "It's a word charm."
>
> "Can you say them to me?"
>
> "Sure," he said and he droned, *"In nomine Patris et Fillii [sic] et Spiritus Sancti."*
>
> "What does it mean?" I asked.
>
> He raised his shoulders. "I don't know," he said. "It's a charm against evil spirits so I am not afraid of them."[54]

Unlike Steinbeck's story, I do not regard God's words as a kind of magical charm. So, my call is to quote God's words so the Holy Spirit can do its gentle surgery in human hearts. I suggest two practical ways to pursue this lifestyle of conversation. (a) One might display a Scripture quotation or two in one's home, car, and workplace. I would advise the posting of some less familiar but thought-provoking ones. It would be wise to select Scriptures that have personal meaning or that somehow tie directly into one's own life story. Once they are up, pray that God will use them, perhaps even as discussion starters. Indeed, those public words of God might well deserve a brief daily prayer. It would also be a good idea to change them every so often to sow more biblical seed and to foster more conversation. Finally, be prepared for those expected follow-up conversations. Get ready to explain why you selected that text and what it means to you or how it intersects with your life story.

(b) One might weave Scripture quotations into ordinary conversations at appropriate moments—but not so often as to be obvious. But do this only if it feels genuine rather than forced or uncomfortable. Whatever the method, the point is to avail ourselves of the power of God's words to work inside people.

To conclude, it is customary in some churches for a reader who finishes reading a Scripture passage during worship to say, "This is the word of the

---

54. John Steinbeck, *Travels with Charlie in Search of America* (New York: Penguin, 1962), 48–49. This Latin phrase means "In the name of the Father, and the Son, and the Holy Spirit."

Lord." The congregation responds, "Thanks be to God!" Joshua 8 and the sword of the Spirit are "the word of the Lord." They give us powerful words with which to unleash the quiet, gentle, healing, surgical work of the Spirit. God's command on the Mount of Transfiguration was: "Listen to him!" I propose a lifestyle in which we appropriately and genuinely expose friends, family, and coworkers to some of God's very words. My advice is: "Speak them!" Thanks be to God, indeed!

Blessings for today. Whatever their liturgical style, most Christian church services conclude with a blessing of the people. This continues the Old Testament tradition evident in Joshua 8:33 and typified by the priestly blessing of Numbers 6:24–27. In fact, that Aaronic blessing finds frequent use in contemporary benedictions (another word for "blessing"), along with New Testament ones (e.g., 2 Cor. 13:14; Eph. 3:20–21; Heb. 13:20–21; Jude 1:24–25). Those blessings are somewhat general, but the blessings in Deuteronomy 28:3–13 flesh out the kinds of things that comprise God's blessings. Inspired by Moses' words, I offer the following blessings for your life today:

> May God's blessings shadow you in the city and in the coun-
> try—indeed, wherever you go.
> May God bless you when you leave for work and when you get back
> home.
> May God bless you with children—and bless them, too.
> May God shepherd them safely through childhood and protect them
> from the dangers of youth.
> May God bless you at work or at school to get everything done—and
> on time.
> May your boss reward your efforts generously.
> May your teacher give you good grades for good work.
> May God bless you with abundant rain for your fields, gardens, and
> lawns.
> May you never go hungry but have plenty of fruit and bread.
> May you always be grateful.
> May God always keep your enemies at bay.
> May God even give you genuine love for them.
> May God walk close beside you through grief and great loss.
> May God make your savings and investments grow.
> May God keep you dependent on him and not on them.
> May God guide your children to make wise choices.
> May God grant your children mature, happy marriages.
> May God also grant you many doting grandchildren.

May God grant you success in everything, even projects at home.

May God so bless you that neighbors will notice, their respect for you
rise, and their hunger for God increase.

May God walk with you gently through your later years.

May God's loving blessings shadow whatever you do and wherever
you go.

Amen.

Joshua 9:1 – 10:43

‹‹

NOW WHEN ALL the kings west of the Jordan heard about these things—those in the hill country, in the western foothills, and along the entire coast of the Great Sea as far as Lebanon (the kings of the Hittites, Amorites, Canaanites, Perizzites, Hivites and Jebusites)—²they came together to make war against Joshua and Israel.

³However, when the people of Gibeon heard what Joshua had done to Jericho and Ai, ⁴they resorted to a ruse: They went as a delegation whose donkeys were loaded with worn-out sacks and old wineskins, cracked and mended. ⁵The men put worn and patched sandals on their feet and wore old clothes. All the bread of their food supply was dry and moldy. ⁶Then they went to Joshua in the camp at Gilgal and said to him and the men of Israel, "We have come from a distant country; make a treaty with us."

⁷The men of Israel said to the Hivites, "But perhaps you live near us. How then can we make a treaty with you?"

⁸"We are your servants," they said to Joshua.

But Joshua asked, "Who are you and where do you come from?"

⁹They answered: "Your servants have come from a very distant country because of the fame of the LORD your God. For we have heard reports of him: all that he did in Egypt, ¹⁰and all that he did to the two kings of the Amorites east of the Jordan—Sihon king of Heshbon, and Og king of Bashan, who reigned in Ashtaroth. ¹¹And our elders and all those living in our country said to us, 'Take provisions for your journey; go and meet them and say to them, "We are your servants; make a treaty with us." ' ¹²This bread of ours was warm when we packed it at home on the day we left to come to you. But now see how dry and moldy it is. ¹³And these wineskins that we filled were new, but see how cracked they are. And our clothes and sandals are worn out by the very long journey."

¹⁴The men of Israel sampled their provisions but did not inquire of the LORD. ¹⁵Then Joshua made a treaty of peace

with them to let them live, and the leaders of the assembly ratified it by oath.

[16]Three days after they made the treaty with the Gibeonites, the Israelites heard that they were neighbors, living near them. [17]So the Israelites set out and on the third day came to their cities: Gibeon, Kephirah, Beeroth and Kiriath Jearim. [18]But the Israelites did not attack them, because the leaders of the assembly had sworn an oath to them by the LORD, the God of Israel.

The whole assembly grumbled against the leaders, [19]but all the leaders answered, "We have given them our oath by the LORD, the God of Israel, and we cannot touch them now. [20]This is what we will do to them: We will let them live, so that wrath will not fall on us for breaking the oath we swore to them." [21]They continued, "Let them live, but let them be woodcutters and water carriers for the entire community." So the leaders' promise to them was kept.

[22]Then Joshua summoned the Gibeonites and said, "Why did you deceive us by saying, 'We live a long way from you,' while actually you live near us? [23]You are now under a curse: You will never cease to serve as woodcutters and water carriers for the house of my God."

[24]They answered Joshua, "Your servants were clearly told how the LORD your God had commanded his servant Moses to give you the whole land and to wipe out all its inhabitants from before you. So we feared for our lives because of you, and that is why we did this. [25]We are now in your hands. Do to us whatever seems good and right to you."

[26]So Joshua saved them from the Israelites, and they did not kill them. [27]That day he made the Gibeonites woodcutters and water carriers for the community and for the altar of the LORD at the place the LORD would choose. And that is what they are to this day.

[10:1]Now Adoni-Zedek king of Jerusalem heard that Joshua had taken Ai and totally destroyed it, doing to Ai and its king as he had done to Jericho and its king, and that the people of Gibeon had made a treaty of peace with Israel and were living near them. [2]He and his people were very much alarmed at this, because Gibeon was an important city, like one of the royal cities; it was larger than Ai, and all its men were good fighters. [3]So Adoni-Zedek king of Jerusalem appealed to

Hoham king of Hebron, Piram king of Jarmuth, Japhia king of Lachish and Debir king of Eglon. ⁴"Come up and help me attack Gibeon," he said, "because it has made peace with Joshua and the Israelites."

⁵Then the five kings of the Amorites—the kings of Jerusalem, Hebron, Jarmuth, Lachish and Eglon—joined forces. They moved up with all their troops and took up positions against Gibeon and attacked it.

⁶The Gibeonites then sent word to Joshua in the camp at Gilgal: "Do not abandon your servants. Come up to us quickly and save us! Help us, because all the Amorite kings from the hill country have joined forces against us."

⁷So Joshua marched up from Gilgal with his entire army, including all the best fighting men. ⁸The LORD said to Joshua, "Do not be afraid of them; I have given them into your hand. Not one of them will be able to withstand you."

⁹After an all-night march from Gilgal, Joshua took them by surprise. ¹⁰The LORD threw them into confusion before Israel, who defeated them in a great victory at Gibeon. Israel pursued them along the road going up to Beth Horon and cut them down all the way to Azekah and Makkedah. ¹¹As they fled before Israel on the road down from Beth Horon to Azekah, the LORD hurled large hailstones down on them from the sky, and more of them died from the hailstones than were killed by the swords of the Israelites.

¹²On the day the LORD gave the Amorites over to Israel, Joshua said to the LORD in the presence of Israel:

"O sun, stand still over Gibeon,
    O moon, over the Valley of Aijalon."
¹³So the sun stood still,
    and the moon stopped,
    till the nation avenged itself on its enemies,

as it is written in the Book of Jashar.

The sun stopped in the middle of the sky and delayed going down about a full day. ¹⁴There has never been a day like it before or since, a day when the LORD listened to a man. Surely the LORD was fighting for Israel!

¹⁵Then Joshua returned with all Israel to the camp at Gilgal.

¹⁶Now the five kings had fled and hidden in the cave at Makkedah. ¹⁷When Joshua was told that the five kings had been found hiding in the cave at Makkedah, ¹⁸he said, "Roll large rocks up to the mouth of the cave, and post some men there to guard it. ¹⁹But don't stop! Pursue your enemies, attack them from the rear and don't let them reach their cities, for the LORD your God has given them into your hand."

²⁰So Joshua and the Israelites destroyed them completely—almost to a man—but the few who were left reached their fortified cities. ²¹The whole army then returned safely to Joshua in the camp at Makkedah, and no one uttered a word against the Israelites.

²²Joshua said, "Open the mouth of the cave and bring those five kings out to me." ²³So they brought the five kings out of the cave—the kings of Jerusalem, Hebron, Jarmuth, Lachish and Eglon. ²⁴When they had brought these kings to Joshua, he summoned all the men of Israel and said to the army commanders who had come with him, "Come here and put your feet on the necks of these kings." So they came forward and placed their feet on their necks.

²⁵Joshua said to them, "Do not be afraid; do not be discouraged. Be strong and courageous. This is what the LORD will do to all the enemies you are going to fight." ²⁶Then Joshua struck and killed the kings and hung them on five trees, and they were left hanging on the trees until evening.

²⁷At sunset Joshua gave the order and they took them down from the trees and threw them into the cave where they had been hiding. At the mouth of the cave they placed large rocks, which are there to this day.

²⁸That day Joshua took Makkedah. He put the city and its king to the sword and totally destroyed everyone in it. He left no survivors. And he did to the king of Makkedah as he had done to the king of Jericho.

²⁹Then Joshua and all Israel with him moved on from Makkedah to Libnah and attacked it. ³⁰The LORD also gave that city and its king into Israel's hand. The city and everyone in it Joshua put to the sword. He left no survivors there. And he did to its king as he had done to the king of Jericho.

³¹Then Joshua and all Israel with him moved on from Libnah to Lachish; he took up positions against it and attacked it. ³²The LORD handed Lachish over to Israel, and Joshua took it

on the second day. The city and everyone in it he put to the sword, just as he had done to Libnah. ³³Meanwhile, Horam king of Gezer had come up to help Lachish, but Joshua defeated him and his army—until no survivors were left.

³⁴Then Joshua and all Israel with him moved on from Lachish to Eglon; they took up positions against it and attacked it. ³⁵They captured it that same day and put it to the sword and totally destroyed everyone in it, just as they had done to Lachish.

³⁶Then Joshua and all Israel with him went up from Eglon to Hebron and attacked it. ³⁷They took the city and put it to the sword, together with its king, its villages and everyone in it. They left no survivors. Just as at Eglon, they totally destroyed it and everyone in it.

³⁸Then Joshua and all Israel with him turned around and attacked Debir. ³⁹They took the city, its king and its villages, and put them to the sword. Everyone in it they totally destroyed. They left no survivors. They did to Debir and its king as they had done to Libnah and its king and to Hebron.

⁴⁰So Joshua subdued the whole region, including the hill country, the Negev, the western foothills and the mountain slopes, together with all their kings. He left no survivors. He totally destroyed all who breathed, just as the LORD, the God of Israel, had commanded. ⁴¹Joshua subdued them from Kadesh Barnea to Gaza and from the whole region of Goshen to Gibeon. ⁴²All these kings and their lands Joshua conquered in one campaign, because the LORD, the God of Israel, fought for Israel.

⁴³Then Joshua returned with all Israel to the camp at Gilgal.

Original Meaning

AFTER THE DRAMA OF covenant renewal, Joshua 9–10 takes Israel on another adventure of faith with a curious twist at the outset and an astounding result at the end. Topically, the text is a sequel to the story of Rahab because it features the Gibeonites, a local people on the ḥerem hit-list. Their starring role again raises the thorny question of how Israel is to relate to non-Israelites and yet not surrender their own unique religious identity, a question that still confronts Christian believers everywhere. With Rahab, the required application of ḥerem lurked in the background, but here it surfaces even more pointedly.

Joshua 9–10 also echoes a telling pattern from the Achan-Ai narrative (Josh. 7–8), an echo that creates tension here. In both cases, initiatives taken by Joshua and Israel produce problematic results—an unexpected rout at Ai (Josh. 7) and a potentially compromising treaty with Gibeon (Josh. 9). As the reader follows Israel's rush to rescue Gibeon (ch. 10), the nagging question is: Will events there replay Ai I (divine anger) or Ai II (divine pleasure)?[1] Achan imperiled Israel by secretly bringing *ḥerem* "among" (*beqereb*) Israel (7:12–13), and the peace treaty with Gibeon possibly keeps *ḥerem* "among" (*beqereb*) Israel (9:7, 16, 22). The comparison raises the haunting specter of possible disobedience and eventual divine wrath.[2] As it turns out, the problems of ch. 9 set the scene for the huge victory sequence of ch. 10, just as those of ch. 7 (Achan) did for Ai II (ch. 8). When ch. 10 ends, Israel has snatched victory from the jaws of defeat; they now control virtually the southern half of Canaan.

Structurally, Joshua 9–10 has two main parts: the report of the Israelite treaty with Gibeon (9:1–27) and the report of Israel's rescue of Gibeon and the resulting southern campaign (10:1–43). The first part features the story of how the Gibeonites, one of the peoples slated for annihilation under *ḥerem*, tricks Israel into making a peace treaty. It comprises two subsections, the Gibeonite trick (9:1–15) and the Gibeonites' indenture (9:16–27). It raises a troubling question: Did the treaty violate the *ḥerem* policy and displease Yahweh?

The second reports the rescue of Gibeon and the scattering of its attackers (10:1–14), the capture and execution of the five royal ringleaders (vv. 15–27), and the capture of six southern cities (vv. 28–39). It concludes with a summary of the conquest (vv. 40–43), confirmation that Yahweh did indeed fight for Israel. The famous episode of the sun standing still (10:8–15) reports a phenomenal event that astounds even the narrator (10:12–14).[3]

---

1. Nelson (*Joshua*, 128–31) proposes a helpful reading of Josh. 9 as two movements, each of which passes from initial action (9:1–5, 16–17) through dialogue (vv. 6–13, 22–25) to decision (vv. 14–15, 26–27). In his view, vv. 18–21 offer an ancillary movement.

2. Cf. Nelson, *Joshua*, 131–32. The book later echoes the theme of the continuing presence of unconquered peoples (15:63; 16:10; 17:12–13; 23:4, 7, 12–13).

3. Joshua 10:15 creates a major chronological problem that requires a brief comment. The LXX lacks it completely (also in v. 43), and if vv. 16–27 report the rest of the day's events (likely), the narrative takes a strange turn if Joshua now descends to Gilgal as the battle rages only to reappear out of the blue leading the Israelite blitzkrieg through the lowlands (vv. 20–27). In my view, the narrative makes far better sense when read without it, so I reckon v. 15 as a later addition (e.g., a copyist's error) and omit it from discussion below. Cf. Howard, *Joshua*, 251, who accepts this solution as among two good possibilities.

The Gibeonites: Trick and Treaty (9:1–27)

THE GIBEONITE TRICK (9:1–15). News of Israel's capture and destruction (*ḥaram* hi.) of Ai (and perhaps Jericho) galvanizes Canaan's kings into action (v. 1). Lists of the land's main regions and its six main peoples create a double image: They underscore how widespread is the awareness of Israel's presence and how formidable is the foe gathering to oppose them (v. 1; cf. 12:8).[4] The threat Israel poses is a real one: Further victories in the Canaanite heartland could swing the strategic balance against its inhabitants. At stake is the Canaanites' ancient way of life, precisely what Yahweh intends to replace with a whole new society.

In self-defense, the kings join forces to battle Joshua, their leadership counterpart, and Israel (v. 2). Theologically, their war plans reveal a fateful decision — the rejection of Yahweh — and sharply contrast the alternative, conciliatory approach soon to appear. In 5:1 the kings are terrified of Israel, but 9:1–2 mentions no fear factor, as if these monarchs are no longer cowed by them. Perhaps, as Hess suggests, Israel's defeat at Ai I has encouraged the Canaanite kings that Israel can be beat in battle.[5]

But a subject-first sentence in verse 3 quickly shifts from the massing armies to report the reaction of a single group, "the people of Gibeon," who have also heard the same news. The narrative move contrasts the "kings" of the cities (9:1–2; 10:1–5) with the people (lit., "inhabitants") of Gibeon, a city that apparently has no king (vv. 3–4).[6] Politically, Gibeon breaks from the pattern of domineering city-states with kings (see below and v. 17).[7]

---

4. Concerning the geography, see Howard, *Joshua*, 220–21. The geography here anticipates the conquest summary to follow in 10:40. Unlike 5:1, however, of nineteen biblical lists of nations, the present one corresponds only to that of Deut. 20:17 (Butler, *Joshua*, 101). This is significant in that it represents one of several key links between Deut. 20 and Josh. 9.

5. Hess, *Joshua*, 175–76; cf. Howard, *Joshua*, 218. If so, another casualty of Ai I, besides Achan, was the popular perception of Israelite invincibility. But, against Hess (176) and Howard (218), it seems to me unlikely that a victory at Ai I would have led other Canaanite nations to respond as Rahab and the Gibeonites did.

6. In v. 4, Heb. *gam hemmah* (lit., "they, too"; NRSV "for their part") also underscores this contrast, as if to say, "The Gibeonites responded, but along different lines." Their account describes their leaders as "our elders and all those living in our country" (v. 11). According to Hess (*Joshua*, 179–80), the rule by elders may point to the group's origin in Anatolia where, unlike among Canaanites, nonroyal government was typical of the Hittites. The Philistines, who probably came to Canaan from Mycenean Greece, had a five-city federation ruled by "lords" (*seranim* [a non-Hebrew word]); cf. Josh. 13:3; Judg. 3:3; 1 Sam. 6:16–18.

7. Gibeon is not among the cities in Canaan that the Amarna tablets (fourteenth cent. B.C.) mention. It first appears on the lists of Egyptian conquests in Canaan under Sheshonq I (tenth cent. B.C.); cf. *ANET*, 242–43. In Josh. 12:8 the writer rhetorically invokes the traditional hit-list of Canaan's nations, including the Hivites.

The latter, several of whom are named here, are the villains of Joshua 2 – 11 because they plan war to resist Israel (e.g., 2:3; 5:1; 8:14; 11:1).

Like Rahab, the Gibeonites thrust the reader eyeball-to-eyeball with real live Canaanites and their real live fears (cf. v. 24). Indeed, the narrator's preferred term for them is "Gibeonites" (vv. 3, 16, 22, 27)—that is, with the people themselves, not the city or its leaders—and the narrative speaks from the Gibeonite (not Israelite) point of view.[8] Gibeon is, in fact, home to a specific subgroup of Canaan, the Hivites (v. 7; cf. v. 1), and a kind of capital city to a confederation of four small towns (cf. the list in v. 17).[9]

The city of Gibeon (modern el-Jib) sits in the central mountains about seven miles southwest of Ai (also nine miles northwest of Jerusalem). That explains why the word about Ai so easily reaches them. An important east-west road passes Gibeon, ascending from Jericho and descending through the Valley of Aijalon along the Beth Horon ridge to the coastal plain. The news of Joshua's threat also galvanizes the Gibeonites into action, but with a difference. They eschew the violence of the warrior kings in favor of a simple "ruse" (*beᶜaremah*, "with cunning"), an ambiguous term whose morality depends on how the parties involved see the matter (v. 4a).[10] What the Gibeonites considered "cleverness" Israel will call "treachery" here. The clever trick aims to win them better treatment from Israel than they can expect as Canaanites. Notice the amusing irony: Israel, whose trick victimizes unsuspecting Ai (ch. 8), themselves soon fall victim to one.

The Gibeonites present quite a bedraggled, woeful picture as they enter the Israelite camp at Gilgal to meet Joshua and Israel (v. 6a).[11] Their donkeys bear worn-out sacks and wineskins, the latter even showing stitches that mend tears (v. 4). The "travelers" themselves wear worn-out, patched sandals and tattered clothes, and their food is dry and crumbly (v. 5).[12] They apparently expect their looks to do the talking, for they open with

---

8. Butler, *Joshua*, 99. For the archaeology of Gibeon, see Hess, *Joshua*, 177.

9. Hivites apparently also lived around Shechem (Gen. 34:2) and in the land of Mizpah at the foot of Mount Hermon (Josh. 11:3). For details on these cities, see Boling, *Joshua*, 266–67; Butler, *Joshua*, 103.

10. Butler, *Joshua*, 101. In 1 Sam. 23:22 Saul applies it to David in a negative light, while the narrator admires it; cf. (positive regard) Prov. 15:5; 19:25; (negative regard) Job 5:13; Ps. 83:4.

11. According to Hess (*Joshua*, 178), the Gilgal here must be a different location from the one in Josh. 4–5, otherwise the story is out of sequence. He deems it unlikely that, after gaining a strategic foothold in central Canaan at Ai II, Israel would go back down to the Jordan valley. Howard (*Joshua*, 224) concurs and surveys all the Gilgals in the Old Testament. While possible, the book seems everywhere to presuppose the same well-known Gilgal.

12. Younger, *Ancient Conquest Accounts*, 200–204, defends the historicity of the ruse motif here, appealing to Ancient Near Eastern parallels.

an abrupt, vague introduction: "We have come from a distant country," they lie. Then they boldly ask that Israel make a treaty with them (v. 6b).[13]

Interestingly, their approach sounds much like Moses' permission for Israel to make peace with foreign cities who seek it (Deut. 20:10 – 15).[14] The whole tattered display aims to convince Israel that the visitors "are not from around here" and, hence, pose no threat to Israel. The subsequent conversation pits wary Israelites against cagey Gibeonites. "Perhaps you live near us" puts the Israelites' wariness into words and explains their reluctance to enter a treaty (v. 7). They apparently have in mind texts that prohibit the making of treaties with the indigenous peoples of Canaan (Ex. 34:11 – 12; Deut. 20:15 – 18). They also may have learned something from the Achan incident after all! To dispel Israelite misgivings, the Hivites reply by, in essence, surrendering themselves fully into Israel's hands ("We are your servants"; v. 8a; cf. vv. 11, 24).[15] But Joshua still presses them for details about their identity ("who are you") and homeland ("where do you come from"; v. 8b).

Their answer is at the same time expansive and evasive. They completely breeze past the request for an ethnic name, and "very distant country" names no specific homeland. They emphasize the reason for their trip: The magnet of Yahweh's "fame" has drawn them to visit the Israelites (v. 9a; cf. 7:9). They cite reports of his victories over Egypt (v. 9b) and Sihon and Og east of the Jordan (v. 10; cf. Num. 21:21 – 35). Their words echo Rahab's similar affirmation during her own negotiations for her life (2:10). Their historical review of Yahweh's great deeds cleverly masks a diversion meant to distract Israel from finding their true status. News of Ai and Jericho gave birth to their plan (9:2 – 3), but here they mention only events from outside Canaan. Subtly, they feign ignorance of the latest local news, thus reinforcing their claim of being foreigners.[16]

Still, they claim, what they heard drove the elders and people back home to authorize the long trip and to supply them with provisions. They are empowered to surrender their people into Israel's hands ("We are your servants") and make a treaty (v. 11). Curiously, from prior knowledge or (more likely) dumb luck, the Gibeonite appeal may have slim support in Moses' instructions concerning Israelite sieges of foreign cities

---

13. Their claim may mark a half-truth, since the Hivites may in fact have arrived from the north (perhaps Armenia in Asia Minor) shortly before Joshua and Israel entered Canaan from the east (Boling, *Joshua*, 264 – 65).

14. Cf. Howard (*Joshua*, 223), who thinks the Gibeonites' actions show that they "knew something about Israelite law."

15. In 9:8, 11, 24, "servant" reflects ancient, polite deference, unlike the servitude the term carries in v. 23; cf. 2 Kings 10:5; 16:7.

16. Howard, *Joshua*, 226; Nelson, *Joshua*, 133.

(Deut. 20:10–15).[17] Implicitly, their pitch seeks to score points with the Israelites: While the local kings mass for war, the Gibeonites "acted on the basis of what Yahweh had done."[18] How could Israel ever deny a treaty to a people who honor Yahweh and want peace?

But Israelite suspicions remain: Why is this bedraggled group so evasive? Why the unexpected revelation about Yahweh's fame? Why did that not come out when they first arrived? Why should Israel deal with a delegation (not actual authorities) whose only accreditation is their spoken word and shabby condition?[19]

To allay such suspicions once and for all, the visitors point out hard evidence that verifies their "very long journey": dry, moldy (not warm) bread, patched (not new) wineskins, and tattered clothes and worn shoes (vv. 12–13). Some Israelite men (but not Joshua) take the bait. They sample the alleged provisions but (alas) do not seek Yahweh's advice (lit., "mouth") on the matter (v. 14; cf. Isa. 30:2).[20] Their actions naively trust the matter to their human senses rather than to divine guidance.

For his part, Joshua fails to avail himself of Yahweh's earlier provision for seeking advice through Eleazar the priest (Num. 27:21). Suddenly, a sense of foreboding overshadows the story, for the last time Israel followed human sense the disastrous defeat at Ai resulted (7:1–5). Is history repeating itself here? Will the treachery of Gibeon put Israel at risk as did the treachery of Achan? Or might Yahweh's providence actually be behind the conversation?

Whatever his misgivings, Joshua makes a treaty to spare the lives of these pathetic strangers, and Israel's leaders ratify it with an oath (v. 15; cf. v. 18; 2 Sam. 21:1–14).[21] Presumably, the oath invokes the name of Yah-

---

17. The instructions authorize Israel, when besieging a city, first to offer the city peace and, if it surrenders, to compel its inhabitants to work for the Israelites (vv. 10–11). But the present case only seeks to head off a future siege, not to resolve a present one. Also, unlike Deut. 20, here the "besieged" party (the Gibeonites) requests peace from Israel rather than receiving an offer of peace from them.

18. Boling, *Joshua*, 263.

19. Butler, *Joshua*, 103.

20. According to Nelson (*Joshua*, 133), the object-first order of v. 14b ("but did not inquire") highlights "Israel's rash carelessness." Since Joshua participates in the interrogation, he is probably still present and, hence, tacitly concurs with the nonconsultation.

21. These "leaders of the assembly" comprise a leadership group usually associated with Moses and priests who participate in decisions of national importance (Josh. 22:30; cf. Ex. 16:22; Num. 31:13; 32:2). The "assembly" (ʿedah) comprises all free Israelite males eligible for military service (Num. 1:2–3), an assembly that is consulted on important community matters (Ex. 12:3; 35:1–4; Num. 10:1–7) and legally adjudicates murder cases (Num. 15:32–36; Josh. 20:6–9); cf. Boling, *Joshua*, 268.

weh to enforce it—the same Yahweh whom Israel has failed to consult.[22] The treaty's provisions are unstated here but evident from the larger biblical context: an agreed-upon peace, mutual self-defense (cf. 10:6–7), and punishment for violations (2 Sam. 21:18).[23] Oblivious to the Gibeonite ruse, Israel understands the agreement to guarantee the visitors safe passage through Canaan en route home. Little do they know that they have just been "had."

The Gibeonites' indenture (9:16–27). The Gibeonite point of view of 9:3–15 now gives way to an Israelite one in this section. The text quotes the Gibeonites, but they make no actual appearance in what follows.[24] Clearly, the "hearing" of news about Israel by Canaanites drives the plot in Joshua (2:10–11; 5:1; 9:1, 3, 9), but this time, ironically, it is Israel who hears something about Canaanites. The treaty is only three days old, and Israel learns that their new "foreign" partners are in fact Gibeonites, a people on the *ḥerem* hit-list (v. 16). Exactly how Israel learns this is unstated, but a sticky dilemma now confronts them. The *ḥerem* mandate requires the extermination of the Gibeonites, but to do so would violate the oath sworn in Yahweh's name and risk his wrath.

Nevertheless, Israel sets off from Gilgal, reaching the Hivites' four cities three days later (v. 17).[25] The oath prohibits Israel from attacking their treaty partner but does not prevent the Israelite community at large from grumbling against the leaders who took it (v. 18). The verb "grumble" (*lwn* ni.) links this grumpy group with Israel's famous ancestral grumbling against Yahweh, Moses, and Aaron in the wilderness.[26] But as Butler observes, "Here the wilderness motif has been turned upside down, for in the wilderness the leaders were justified, while the congregation was guilty. Here the congregation is justified, while the leaders are at fault."[27]

A crisis of confidence in Israel's leadership (but not in Joshua) now looms large: How can leaders so easily duped into disobedience still lead? In reply, the leaders reiterate that the oath prohibits Israel from laying so much as

---

22. Butler, *Joshua*, 99.

23. Probably, the treaty compares to the suzerain-vassal type well known in the ancient Near East (see Bridging Contexts section of 8:30–35; cf. Howard, *Joshua*, 219). Alternatively, it may constitute a "pact with a protegé" by which peoples end a potentially disastrous siege by agreeing to military service with the attacking army; cf. J. M. Grintz, "The Treaty of Joshua with the Gibeonites," *JAOS* 86 (1966): 113–26 (quote 122).

24. Butler, *Joshua*, 100.

25. For the locations of the towns (all within the later territory of Benjamin), cf. Hess, *Joshua*, 182.

26. Cf. Ex. 15:24; 16:2, 7, 8; 17:3; Num. 14:2, 27; 16:11, 41 [17:6]; 17:5[20]).

27. Butler, *Joshua*, 104.

a finger on the Gibeonites (v. 19). Israel's only alternative is to let them live (the oath's main provision [v. 15]) lest they incur "wrath" (presumably Yahweh's judgment) for breaking an oath (v. 20). The leaders apparently assume that Israel may not simply declare the treaty "null and void" because it was concluded under false pretenses.[28]

Again, no one consults with Yahweh, who could have either voided the treaty or voiced approval of it. Instead, leaders publically pronounce their formal decision ("Let them live"), but they also limit the Gibeonites to a specific social role—to serve the community as "woodcutters and water carriers" (vv. 21, 27). Typically, those menial tasks are the province of resident aliens (*gerim*) who are members of the covenant with Yahweh (Deut. 29:11[10]; cf. 19:5; Josh. 8:33, 35; 20:9). So, Joshua 9:20 may actually extend the legal principle of alien inclusion to the Hivites as an exception to the *ḥerem* mandate.[29] If so, it establishes the precedent that peoples in Canaan on the hit-list may be treated the same as resident aliens from outside it.

With Israel present in force in the Hivite heartland, Joshua summons the Hivite leaders and addresses them (v. 22). His question amounts to an accusation, as if they are on trial: Why have they deceived Israel? It invokes the typical formula by which victims of deceit confront their deceivers.[30] Implicitly, Joshua indicts the Gibeonites for cunningly covering up crucial facts to gain personal advantage. He may even imply that the betrayal has brought serious injury to Israel—for example, compromised its relationship with Yahweh. Not surprisingly, Joshua next does what victims of deceit typically do: He curses the whole Hivite people ("You [pl.] are now under a curse"). The curse distances victims from the deceivers, their deceptions, and the divine judgment due them (v. 23a; cf. 6:26).[31]

---

28. Howard (*Joshua*, 229) sees a parallel to the oath's inviolability in the irrevocability of the blessing that Jacob won from Isaac via trickery (Gen. 27).

29. Similarly, Butler, *Joshua*, 104. Alternatively, it may simply implement the servitude mandated for foreign cities under Israelite siege who surrender (Deut. 20:10–11). But cf. Nelson, *Joshua*, 132 ("a sort of toleration, albeit one that sounds suspiciously colonialist and oppressive to modern ears"); Boling, *Joshua*, 269 ("precisely what the covenant liturgy [Deut. 29:11(10)] was originally designed to counteract").

30. The formula is *lamah* ("why?") + *ramah* pi. ("to deceive"); cf. Gen. 29:25 (Jacob to Laban); 1 Sam. 19:17 (Saul to Michal); 1 Sam. 28:12 (the Endorite witch to Saul); 2 Sam. 19:26–27 (Mephibosheth to David).

31. The combination of accusatory question and oath may borrow a legal pattern whereby an aggrieved party gains revenge for a crime through a curse; cf. Butler, *Joshua*, 100; Gen. 4:9–16. For other ethnic curses, see Gen. 4:11–12 (Kenites) and Canaanites (9:25). Howard (*Joshua*, 230) compares this curse to those supporting the Mosaic covenant (Deut. 27–28).

But Joshua's curse adds an important detail to the leader's earlier community-service theme (cf. v. 21). He decrees that the Gibeonites' wood-cutting and water-carrying will always serve "the house of my God" (v. 23). Now, in effect, the curse demotes the Gibeonites from treaty partners to menial slaves (Heb. *ᶜebed*) serving the whole congregation. They will do the dirty work in support of the sanctuary on behalf of the congregation. In a sense, poetic justice prevails: A ruse wins the Gibeonites continued life but at a price—reduction to permanent slavery at menial tasks (but see below). Finally, Joshua's handling of the matter—his response to their complaints with open dialogue—regains the community's confidence in his leadership.[32]

The ambiguous phrase "the house of my God" (v. 23; cf. "house of the LORD" [6:24]) may comprise an anachronism, a reflection of the author's knowledge of the Gibeonites' eventual destination (Jerusalem; cf. 1 Kings 6:5; Isa. 2:2). Usually, "house" (*bayit*) designates a permanent structure (Judg. 18:31), and the psalmist invokes "tabernacle" as a metaphor for "the house of the LORD" (the temple) where one finds refuge (Ps. 27:4, 6). Alternatively, here "house" may simply mean "sanctuary"—a reference to the tabernacle—although the Old Testament nowhere else equates "house of my God" with "the tabernacle." Other possibilities include Shiloh, later Israel's central meeting place (Josh. 18:1; 21:2; 22:9, 12) and a sanctuary under Eli (1 Sam. 1:7), or the important mountain-top sanctuary at Gibeon, where Solomon will later offer sacrifices (1 Kings 3:4; cf. 2 Sam. 21:6).[33]

Whatever the case, the curse destines the Hivites to support the worship of Yahweh with a steady supply of wood for sacrificial fires and water for ritual washing. That is the penalty they bear for their perfidy, but again it beats the alternative! From another angle, to work at the sanctuary represents something of a promotion—from great distance from Yahweh to close proximity to his presence. Surely, there are blessings to be had from working up close and personal with him (cf. the case of Obed-Edom [2 Sam. 6:11]).

Finally, in assigning the Gibeonites to the sanctuary, the sacred realm over which only priests preside, Joshua exercises an authority akin to that of Moses.

The Hivites, however, defend their actions before Joshua (v. 24): They have simply responded to what someone had told them. The comment

---

32. Butler, *Joshua*, 104.

33. Howard (*Joshua*, 230) prefers the tabernacle or Shiloh, while Boling (*Joshua*, 269) accepts Gibeon as a possibility. Butler (*Joshua*, 104) reckons the reference as an anachronism but concedes (*Joshua*, 105), "At least one stage of the tradition probably referred this to Gibeon."

supplements their earlier remarks (v. 9), although neither specifies the source of their information. Their knowledge proves somewhat accurate — and also differs from what Rahab knew (2:10). They knew that Yahweh had ordered Moses both to give Israel "the whole land" and to "wipe out" (*šamad* hi.) its inhabitants (cf. Deut. 7:23–24; 33:27). They confess that the news terrified them ("we feared for our lives") and drove them to treachery.

However, their explanation falls considerably short of Rahab's ringing affirmation of Yahweh's supreme sovereignty (see 2:11). In fact, their word choice seems subtly to distance them from Yahweh. Yahweh is usually the subject of *šamad* hi., but their statement puts Moses between them and Yahweh, naming him as the one giving land and doing annihilation. It is almost as if they preferred to deal with a human rather than a divine opponent.[34] They concede that Joshua's "hands" hold their fate and submit to "whatever seems good and right" for him to do (v. 25).[35] Joshua (lit.) "did for them accordingly" (v. 26) — in other words, what he deemed "good and right" under the circumstances. Specifically (if not surprisingly) he (lit.) "saved them from the hands of the Israelites" in whose grip revenge, if not death, might be likely. ("Israelites" here refers to the people in general, not the leaders). Implicitly, this comment further justifies the Gibeonites' decision to pursue their duplicitous ploy.

A change to more formal literary style ("That day he made ...") brings the scene to a close (v. 27). From distant hindsight ("to this day"), the narrator reiterates Joshua's twofold assignment of the Gibeonites: to provide wood and water "for the community" (i.e., for daily life) at large and "for the altar of the LORD" (i.e., for sacrifices). In a sense, this honors them: Their tasks may be lowly, but their workplace enjoys the highest rank and serves Yahweh Most High himself (Ps. 47:2[3]). The phrase "the place the LORD would choose" echoes a key formula from Deuteronomy — a reference to Jerusalem, in the view of many scholars. On its own, however, the phrase may designate any locale where Yahweh authorizes worship, including the apparently orthodox high place at Gibeon mentioned above.[36]

The point is that Joshua, not the leaders or people, decides the Gibeonites' fate. As Moses' successor, he enjoys Mosaic authority (cf. his cursing of

---

34. Butler (*Joshua*, 104) offers a different view: "The Gibeonite defense shows their Yahwistic piety, as they paraphrase the Deuteronomic credo."

35. For other occurrences of the phrase "whatever seems good and right," see Gen. 16:6; Jer. 26:14; 1 Sam. 24:4; Job 1:12; 2:6.

36. That is, "only at sanctioned Israelite cultic centers ... and not Canaanite ones" (Howard, *Joshua*, 231). Certainly, Shiloh had a "temple" (1 Sam. 1:3, 9), and Boling (*Joshua*, 269) claims that Gilgal did, too.

Jericho [6:26]). In my view, he also exercises that highest level of authority when he exempts the Gibeonites from *ḥerem*. Given his dilemma—to break an oath sworn in Yahweh's name or to disobey the *ḥerem* mandate—Joshua apparently believes it "good and right" to spare the Hivites and incorporate them as "aliens" within Israel.

The theology of the Gibeonites may fall short of Rahab's, but their explanation and acceptance of Joshua's decision (cf. vv. 24–25) remain important. It compels readers to wrestle with a key theme, Israel's relationship with foreigners. The Gibeonites put a human face on the annihilation policy, just as the conversation with Rahab did. Seen up close, at least some Canaanites are not the whoring, incorrigible idolaters of popular impression. Rather, they are ordinary people who know a little about Yahweh, find that knowledge terrifying, and wish only to live at peace with Israel in the land. As with Rahab, the Gibeonite episode suggests that the *ḥerem* principle is not absolute—that exceptions may be made where elementary knowledge of Yahweh could mature into something larger.

In my view, the Deuteronomist (the book's editor) has apparently included this episode both to explain a historical reality (i.e., why the Gibeonites still survive in Israel) and to argue that the decision by Joshua to permit it is "good and right."[37] More important, the story anticipates Yahweh's response to the whole treaty episode in chapter 10.

Duped but Not Defeated (10:1–39)

AS YET, NOTHING IS known of Yahweh's attitude toward the pact with Gibeon. He has not spoken since 8:18, and Israel did not seek a word from him prior to making the treaty (cf. 9:14). The silence leaves one to wonder whether a Jericho-like victory or an Ai-like defeat now awaits Israel. Israel soon learns into what trouble their treaty with Gibeon has gotten them.

Israel to the rescue (vv. 1–14). The scene opens in Jerusalem, nine miles south of Gibeon, where news of the treaty and of Ai's capture and destruction (*ḥaram* hi.) has reached King Adoni-Zedek (v. 1). The fall of Ai signals that Israel is bent on conquest, and the treaty means that Gibeon has "fallen" peacefully to them. Two things terrify the king. (1) He knows that the Gibeonites "were living near" (lit., "among") the Israelites—that is, the two are now allies.[38] (2) Gibeon is a hugely important city (v. 2).

---

37. Cf. Butler, *Joshua*, 99 ("a position of treaty partner protected by the might of Israel's army").

38. The spread of news among Canaan's inhabitants about Israel's advances marks a common theme in Joshua and drives the plot of chapters 2–11 (cf. 2:10–11; 5:1; 9:1–2; 11:1).

Larger than Ai, it compares to "one of the royal cities"—that is, the heavily fortified capitals of kings who ruled city-states (cf. 1 Sam. 27:5)—and all its male residents are "good fighters" (*gibborim,* "mighty ones").[39]

All this is terrifyingly bad news to Adoni-Zedek, who fears a domino effect of falling cities—a seismic shift in the balance of power—that threatens his own kingdom. The king's fears have roots in reality: Control of Ai-Bethel and Gibeon has given Israel strategic control of central Canaan and its major highways. Israel can now easily maneuver by road throughout the land. So Adoni-Zedek rallies the kings of four other powerful city-states—Hebron, Jarmuth, Lachish, and Eglon (all south and southwest of Jerusalem)—to rendezvous at Jerusalem and join him in attacking Gibeon (vv. 3–4). His message that Gibeon has "made peace with Joshua and the Israelites" (v. 4b) captures the sizeable threat that an Israelite-Gibeonite force poses.[40] As in 9:1–2, these royal war plans also make a fateful decision—the rejection of Yahweh—and sharply contrast the Gibeonite approach.

The five Amorite kings do, indeed, muster their armies at Jerusalem, proceed to Gibeon, set up camp, and lay siege to it (v. 5).[41] The author's formal, city-by-city listing of the pentapolis highlights the five-against-one odds in their favor against Gibeon. In response, Gibeon's leaders (lit., "men," not "king") send word to Joshua camped at Gilgal, pleading for him to rush to their rescue (v. 6). The wording echoes the plea of Adoni-Zedek (v. 4), but the addition of "quickly," "save," and "do not abandon us" stamps the message as "Urgent!"[42] Presumably, the plea invokes a treaty provision for protection against enemies ("servants" recalls their earlier self-references [9:8, 9, 11, 23, 24]).

The citation of "all the Amorite kings from the hill country" seems exaggerated (Lachish, Jarmuth, and Eglon are in the lowlands, not the

---

39. That Pharaoh Sheshonk I (late tenth cent. B.C.) lists Gibeon among the cities in Canaan that he either conquered or dominated further attests the city's importance; cf. *ANET,* 242; 1 Kings 14:25; 2 Chron. 12:2–4.

40. Hess further discusses the rulers' names (*Joshua,* 29–30) and the geography (*Joshua,* 188–90). Compared to the Amarna letters from Egypt between Pharaoh and local rulers (fourteenth cent. B.C.), the letters dispatched here (v. 4) are brief; cf. Hess, *Joshua,* 190–91.

41. "Amorite" here probably refers to Canaan's inhabitants in general since, of the five cities, two cities lie in the central mountains (Jerusalem, Hebron), the others in the western lowlands (Jarmuth, Lachish, Eglon); contrast Howard, *Joshua,* 235 (only peoples in the central mountains). Literarily, "kings of the Amorites" may link them with Sihon and Og (Josh. 9:10) and imply that the same fate awaits them (so Hess, *Joshua,* 191).

42. "Do not abandon" (lit., "do not relax your hands from [us]") suggests that the failure to act will deprive the Gibeonites of Israel's steadying, protective military power and leave them to stand or fall on their own.

hill country) but rhetorically conveys the sender's panic and urgency. In response, Joshua leads the entire army, including all its "best fighters" (*gibborey beḥayil*), on an all-night march to defend Israel's beleaguered ally, Gibeon. The reader wonders, however, whether—as at Ai, when Joshua proceeds without consulting Yahweh—defeat may again shadow Israel in the present ambiguous circumstances (cf. 9:14).

The fear of a replay of Ai I vanishes when, at last, Yahweh breaks his silence since Joshua 8:18 sometime during the force's long, arduous ascent. God invokes the common biblical formula of reassurance ("Do not be afraid of them"; v. 8a; cf. v. 25; 8:1; 11:6), the soothing words directly addressing Joshua's anxiety about the battle ahead. The kings need not terrify Joshua because their defeat is a done deal (v. 8b): Yahweh has already doomed them to disaster ("given them into your hand"), making Joshua unstoppable just as he promised him in the beginning (cf. 1:5). One can hardly imagine a more encouraging word for a general and his troops to hear en route to the battlefield.

Joshua's unexpected, early-morning arrival takes the encamped besiegers by complete surprise. Given the treaty, they probably expect Israel to show up but not to make an all-night march to do so (v. 9).[43] No sooner has Israel arrived than Yahweh unleashes a terrifying vanguard to lead Israel's advance (v. 10). The report draws vocabulary from the Old Testament tradition of Yahweh's war and follows its typical two-stage assault.[44] Yahweh first hurls "holy terror" (*hamam*, "to vex, confuse, panic") at the enemy, scattering them in panicked retreat (cf. Deut. 7:23).[45] Then Israel slaughters those still at Gibeon and pursues troops fleeing down the Beth Horon ridge road to Azekah and Makkedah in the lowlands twenty miles away (v. 10).[46]

The narrator enriches the account with two details about the battle scene. (1) He reports that as the enemy flees from Israel, Yahweh showers them with huge hailstones (v. 11; cf. Isa. 30:30). The comment that the latter killed more enemy than did Israelite swords (v. 11b) sounds the theme

---

43. At least, that seems to be the assumed connection between the all-night march and the enemies' reported surprise.

44. For more on Yahweh war, see Longman and Reid, *God Is a Warrior*; T. B. Dozeman, *God at War: Power in the Exodus Tradition* (New York: Oxford Univ. Press, 1996).

45. Cf. H.-P. Müller, "הָמַם," *TDOT*, 3:419–21. The means used to panic the enemies is not clear here, but elsewhere it includes the frightening presence of the pillar of fire and cloud (Ex. 14:24), a deathly dread (Ex. 15:16; 23:27; cf. Josh. 2:9), loud thunder (1 Sam. 7:10), or fierce lightning (2 Sam. 22:15 = Ps. 18:14[15]; 144:6); cf. Sir. 48:21.

46. Hess (*Joshua*, 194–95) details the geography. For the phrase "inflict a great slaughter" (NIV "defeated them in a great victory") see v. 20; Judg. 15:8; 1 Sam. 6:19; 2 Chron. 28:5.

that Yahweh is fighting on Israel's behalf. Since Israel could not have won it on their own, the victory is ultimately Yahweh's.[47]

(2) He highlights something memorable that Joshua said as Israel witnessed the momentous day when Yahweh handed the Amorites over to them. Certainly, the phenomenon marks one of the book's best-known and most-discussed parts (vv. 12–13). Chronologically, it is probably contemporaneous to the hailstorm, although the two may be one and the same.[48] As one might expect, this intriguing and important text has stirred much discussion.[49] The literary challenge is to determine which lines comprise poetry or prose, as well as to define where Joshua or the narrator speaks. My comments below assume the following structure of vv. 12–14 (and my own translation):

I. The Poem (vv. 12–13a)
A. Extended report formula (v. 12a)
B. The poem proper (vv. 12b–13a)
1. Twofold plea (v. 12b):

"'O, Sun, at Gibeon stand still,
O, Moon, at the Valley of Aijalon.'"[50]

2. Compliance report (v. 13a):

"So the sun stood still,
and the moon stopped,
until a nation avenged itself on its enemies."

II. Authorial Comments (vv. 13b–14)
A. Citation formula (v. 13b): "Isn't it written in the Book of Jashar?"
B. Summary-Report (v. 13c):

"The sun stood still in mid-heavens;
it didn't rush to set for about a full day."

C. Implication (v. 14): "There's never been such a day before or since when the LORD heeded a human voice. Indeed, the LORD fought for Israel!"

---

47. The Hittite and Assyrian examples in Younger (*Ancient Conquest Accounts*, 207–11) confirm how ancient battle reports commonly include the motif of divine intervention, with one account (210) actually mentioning divinely sent hailstones.

48. According to WO §33.3.3b, Heb. ʾ*az* ("at that time") plus an imperfect refers to "a (con)sequent or explanatory situation in the past time ..."; cf. v. 33; 8:30; 22:1. For the view that Yahweh (not Joshua), is the speaker, see Howard, *Joshua*, 240–41.

49. See the summaries and bibliography in M. K. Hom, "A Day Like No Other: A Discussion of Joshua 10:12–14," *ExTim* 115/7 (2004): 217–23; H. Kruger, "Sun and Moon Marking Time: A Cursory Survey of Exegetical Possibilities in Joshua 10:9–14," *JNSL* 26/1 (2000): 137–52.

50. Alternatively, according to Hom ("A Day Like No Other," 223), v. 12b reports Yahweh's response to Joshua's prayer, reading "Yahweh" as the subject of "and he said."

In my reading, five lines of a poem that Joshua quotes (vv. 12b+13a) comprise the centerpiece of vv. 12 – 14. The author reminds the reader (v. 13b) that the lines are preserved in the Book of Jashar, apparently a collection of early Israelite epic or lyric poetry. Given its usage elsewhere, the formula (v. 13b) probably means that Jashar is not quoted but "appealed to" for legitimation either of the poetic lines or the entire chapter.[51]

In essence, the poem voices his plea ("Sun, Moon, stand still!") and reports the luminaries' compliance ("So the sun stood still ..."). The parallel lines in vv. 13b+c—ʿamad ("stand, come to a standstill") and "didn't rush to set"—clarify that the key verb in Joshua's plea to the sun and moon (damam, v. 12b) means simply to "stand still."[52] It calls for a cessation (or, at least, a significant slowing) of their motion—that the two great lights halt in mid-course, respectively, over Gibeon (sun) and the Aijalon Valley (moon)—and they obediently do so.[53] The final line of the compliance report features a temporal clause ("until a nation avenged itself ...") that states the duration and implied purpose of their pause mid-sky.[54] They are given "about a full day" to take revenge on their enemies, a phrase that might draw on an ancient, hyperbolic literary convention to underscore magnitude of the military victory.[55] The lights in the sky stand still so that Israel may keep moving.

Strikingly, while the cosmic scale of the text's claims are what amaze modern readers, what stuns the narrator is the terrestrial scene—that Joshua prays and (unbelievable!) Yahweh obeys (šamaʿ beqol, "to hearken to, obey") by fighting for Israel (v. 14).[56] He views it as an event without past precedent or likelihood of future recurrence, a comment that needs further clarification since, for example, Yahweh also "heeded" Rachel's voice (the same Heb. phrase) by ending her barrenness (Gen. 30:6). As I see it, what astonishes the author is not simply that God answers a plea—the OT attests that he often answers human prayers—but that he heeds a request

---

51. Hom, ibid., 221, 223, who favors the latter. Cf. D. L. Christensen, "Jashar, Book of," *ABD*, 3:646–47. Elsewhere it appears only once (2 Sam. 1:18), although a couplet in Solomon's prayer dedicating the temple may be a third excerpt (1 Kings 8:12–13 LXX). But cf. Howard (*Joshua*, 239–40), who questions the consensus view that the lines are poetry.

52. The verb has two main senses, "to be quiet" or "to be still" (i.e., motionless), or "to cease"; cf. *DCH*, 450–51. The LXX reflects the same understanding.

53. The book of Joshua often associates ʿamad ("to stand") with obedience to Yahweh; cf. Hom, "A Day Like No Other," 221, esp. n.41.

54. The original poem says "a nation," but the reference is clearly to Israel ("the nation" [NIV, NRSV]; "the nation of Israel" [NLT]; "the people" [KJV]).

55. For examples, see Younger, *Ancient Conquest Accounts*, 215–16; cf. Hom, "A Day Like No Other," 221, who also discusses alternative understandings of the phrase.

56. The idiom can connote either "a willing and attentive listening that manifests itself in obedience or ... actual obedience"; cf. K. T. Aitken, "שָׁמַע," *NIDOTTE*, 4:178.

---

of such cosmic magnitude.[57] He readily deploys cosmic forces, his two primary celestial lights, to help fight his great battle on Israel's behalf. In effect, he fully honors Israel's covenant renewal at Mount Ebal (8:30–35) and leaves the treaty with Gibeon out of consideration.

Finally, the "neither-before-nor-since" motif of Joshua 10:14 may echo the praise of Moses' unique relationship with God that concludes Deuteronomy (Deut. 34:10–12). If so, it hints that Joshua enjoys a similar closeness, further enhancing his Moses-like stature, a prominent theme in the book (cf. 3:7, 14; 11:15, 23; 24:31; Judg. 2:7).[58] As Moses' protégé, Joshua here comes off as being in the same league as his mentor—that the two occupy a league of their own.

Scholars, however, have interpreted verses 12–13 variously. The traditional view, one still held by many today, assumes that the earth literally stops rotating, thereby lengthening the day to give time to attain victory.[59] Others find that view implausible because the universe apparently shows no traces of such a cosmic event and, besides, such a cosmic stoppage of nature seems out of keeping with God's character.[60] Instead, they propose solutions involving natural phenomena: (1) that the text reports a refraction of light that prolongs the daylight hours for Israel to be victorious; (2) that the sun "ceases shining" (not "ceases moving"), either from a solar eclipse or cloud cover (cf. the hailstorm, v. 11), thereby giving Israel (and, of course, their enemies!) relief from the sun's heat; (3) that, consistent with ancient Near Eastern beliefs, Joshua seeks an omen—an extraordinary alignment of sun and moon in the same sky that Israel reads as favorable and/or the Amorites as unfavorable.[61] In response, nothing in the text points to light refraction, protective cloud cover, or a solar eclipse.[62] An Israelite (but not

---

57. Alternatively, the astonishment might derive from the fact that Joshua took initiative in the strategy of Yahweh war. The author might have regarded that as an audacious move for a human.

58. Cf. Hom, "A Day Like No Other," 222.

59. For bibliography, cf. Howard, *Joshua*, 241–42, who narrates some of the urban legends that this view has spawned, including the oft-told (but untrue) claim that NASA has discovered a missing "day" in some of its space-flight calculations. What follows draws on his fine discussion (242–48 with bibliography).

60. Howard also notes (*Joshua*, 246) that the sun and moon share the sky in the early morning, an odd time for Joshua to request a long day. For full discussion of the numerous interpretive options, see Hom, "A Day Like No Other," 217–20.

61. On this latter view, see J. H. Walton, "Joshua 10:12–15 and Mesopotamian Celestial Omen Texts," in *Faith, Tradition, and History*, ed. A. R. Millard, J. K. Hoffmeier, and D. W. Baker (Winona Lake, Ind.: Eisenbrauns, 1994), 181–90.

62. In addition, the solar eclipse and cloud cover views assume that *damam* means "to cease shining" or "to darken," senses unattested elsewhere. They also fit poorly with the

an Amorite) perception of the phenomenon as an omen may offer the best possibility, but even that view is not problem-free.[63]

The interpretation of verses 12–14 is difficult, but an important starting point is to take seriously its poetic nature—that its thought world is phenomenological and metaphorical rather than historical or scientific. The best option is to read verses 12–13 figuratively as a poetic depiction of the military conflict on a cosmic scale.[64] It compares to the claim of another poem, the Song of Deborah, that "from the heavens the stars fought, from their courses they fought against Sisera" (Judg. 5:20).[65] The poetic excerpt invokes cosmic terms rhetorically to magnify the majestic power of God that won this great victory.[66] Specifically, they symbolize the boundaries of the "battle theater" (Nelson's term) from which the enemy cannot escape and the cosmic divine power flooding it on Israel's behalf.[67]

The text assumes the common human observation that the sun and moon seem to traverse the sky themselves (see Job 31:26; Ps. 19:4–5[5–6]). Its poetic nature also helps explain why Joshua surprisingly addresses the sun and the moon rather than Yahweh, as "said to the LORD" implies. Literarily, they function as personifications, a role the Old Testament also accords them elsewhere: They personify harmful threats from which Israel needs divine protection (Ps. 121:6) and prominent witnesses to Yahweh at war (Hab. 3:11). Like Joshua, the psalmist actually addresses them, commanding them to join the rest of creation in praising Yahweh (148:3). Habakkuk 3:11 probably offers the closest literary parallel, reporting that "sun and moon stood still in the heavens," as if they were "people" awestruck at the

---

parallel verb *ᶜamad*, "to stand still" (v. 13). Further, none of the known eclipses correspond chronologically to the date of this incident; cf. Howard, *Joshua*, 247.

63. The fact that the language of 10:12b–13 differs significantly from the phraseology of the suggested ancient Near Eastern parallels undermines this view (cf. Hom, "A Day Like No Other," 219). An additional problem concerns its assumption that the same phenomenon would have been interpreted as favorable by Israel and as unfavorable by the Amorites. While possible, this seems unlikely. At least the text clearly states the positive Israelite perception of it.

64. After an in-depth discussion of options, Howard reaches the same conclusion (*Joshua*, 247–48).

65. Sisera was the Canaanite general defeated by Barak and Deborah (Judg. 4–5). Strikingly, Josh. 10 combines prose and poetic descriptions as does Judg. 4 (prose) and 5 (poetry); cf. also Ex. 14 (prose) and Ex. 15 (poetry).

66. For an alternative figurative view, cf. Nelson, *Joshua*, 144–45.

67. Cf. Hom, "A Day Like No Other," 222–23; Nelson, *Joshua*, 144, who compares the luminaries to the symbolic or victory-inducing actions of Moses' upheld arms (Ex. 17:11–12) or Joshua's upraised sword (Josh. 8:18). The boundary motif derives from the posting of the sun over Gibeon (east) and the moon over the Aijalon Valley (west).

power of Yahweh the warrior.[68] In sum, as two of creation's prominent features, in Joshua 10 the sun and moon personify the cosmic sovereignty of Yahweh for whose intervention Joshua appeals.[69]

The fate of the royal ringleaders (vv. 15–27). Amid the furious general retreat, the narrator focuses on the five kings who have attacked Gibeon. They flee for their lives and hide in the cave at Makkedah (v. 16), the town along with nearby Azekah where the fleeing troops sought refuge from their Israelite pursuers (cf. 10). In reporting royal flight and hiding, the narrative includes motifs typical of ancient Near Eastern conquest accounts.[70]

The Old Testament mentions Makkedah only here and in the list of towns belonging to Judah (15:41). Of course, Israel does not know the area, having just arrived in country and perhaps never having scouted out the western lowlands. The kings' desperate ploy presumably takes advantage of Israel's geographical unfamiliarity. They hope to hide themselves out of sight until the crisis passes and Israel leaves the area. Alas, information as to their whereabouts reaches Joshua at the Israelite camp ("Joshua was told"; v. 17a; cf. v. 21). The NIV and TNK (but not NRSV) obscure the fact that MT quotes the actual report (v. 17b): "The five kings have been found hiding in the cave at Makkedah." How this crucial piece of intelligence falls into Israel's hands is not said (Israelite scouts or the interrogation of local residents?), but to protect this unexpected windfall Joshua issues orders to his troops on the scene.

The author quotes them at length (vv. 18–19): They are to roll large stones over the cave opening—an instant prisoner-of-war cell!—and to post men to guard the captured kings. This will prevent any rescue by loyal troops or an escape by the monarchs themselves (v. 18). Urgently, Joshua also addresses "the rest of you" (TNK; lit., "you" plural, i.e., those not needed as guards) not to stop (lit., "stand still"; v. 19). They are to chase after "your enemies," attack them from the rear, and cut off their escape to safety in fortified cities. The reason is that "the LORD your God" has handed them over to "you" (pl.) Israelites, the very word of assurance Joshua gave before Israel's successful victory at Ai (8:7). It aims to ease their fears and to spur a vigorous, strategic pursuit. Rather than describe the ensuing battle,

---

68. Cf. Kruger, "Sun and Moon Marking Time," 148–49, who suggests that the concept of a solar chariot underlies Joshua's address of the sun and moon. If so, "the passage ... could represent a prayer by Joshua asking Yahweh ... traveling on his sun-chariot through the skies, to pause for some time until his enemies are defeated." He concedes, however, that this view fails to include the moon in it.

69. The phrase "Valley of Gibeon" in Isa. 28:21 may allude to this remarkable event (or to David's rout of the Philistines [2 Sam. 5:20=1 Chron. 14:11]).

70. For examples, see Younger, *Ancient Conquest Accounts*, 220–22.

however, the narrator skips ahead to underscore its results (v. 20) — (lit.) a "very great slaughter," a term reprised from v. 10.

But two additional touches here — the emphatic ("very") and the phrase "almost to the last man" (lit., "until they had completely perished"; cf. 5:6; 8:24) — makes this victory sound even more significant than the earlier rout at Gibeon. "Almost" recognizes, however, that some fleeing survivors elude Israel's grasp — at least, for the moment (cf. vv. 28 – 39). The whole victorious Israelite army returns safely to the camp at Makkedah where Joshua is, and no one utters a word of criticism against the Israelites (v. 21). The sense of the latter comment is uncertain but probably amplifies the previous comment about a safe return. Exodus 11:7 has the only other use of (lit.) "to move [?] a tongue against" (i.e., "not a dog will bark" [NIV] or "snarl" [TNK]). The metaphor contrasts the peace and quiet among the Israelites against the loud cries among the Egyptians grieving their lost firstborn. Here "no one moved (?) a tongue against the Israelites" probably contrasts the fates of the Israelites and their enemies — something like "no (Israelite) suffered so much as a scratch" in the fighting.[71]

That is what happens when God fights for Israel (vv. 14b and 42b). Israel can now peacefully camp in the Amorite heartland, surely a harbinger of their later, larger settlement there. But the five kings must be dealt with, so Joshua orders the caves opened and kings brought outside to him (v. 22). As if to heighten the drama and highlight how momentous the moment, the narrator slows down the narrative pace in verses 22 – 24a. He follows up Joshua's commands by spelling out his troops' compliance (vv. 22 – 23, 24b). He includes a short but dramatic statement by Joshua — surely, the scene's dramatic climax (v. 25). Each verse features *yaṣaʾ* hi. ("to bring out"): "bring … out" (v. 22); "they brought … out" (v. 23); "when they brought … out" (v. 24). He takes time to list "these five," but this time by title ("king of city-X") rather than by name (v. 23; cf. v. 3; 12:7 – 24). The impersonal treatment may signal that, for all their prior prominence, (lit.) "these five kings" (vv. 16, 22, 23, 24) — from Jerusalem, Hebron, Jarmuth, Lachish, and Eglon — are about to become history.[72] The word repetition, list, and formal style seem to present the scene in slow motion.

Joshua, however, seizes the moment for a symbolic action to benefit his troops. Surrounded by the entire force, he commands the troop commanders to step forward and place their feet on the necks of the

---

71. So REB. NIV ("no one uttered a word against the Israelites") seems improbable given the huge slaughter and huddling of survivors in their towns.

72. For a study of namelessness as a literary device, see R. L. Hubbard, Jr., "'Old What's His Name': Why the King in 1 Kings 22 Has No Name," in *God's Word for Our World*, ed. J. H. Ellens et al. (JSOTSup 388; London/New York: Continuum, 2004), 1:294 – 314.

presumably prostrate kings (v. 24). In the Old Testament, the foot symbolizes the sovereignty of the imposer and the subjection of the one under it (1 Kings 5:3[17]; Ps. 8:6[7]; 47:4[3]).[73] In connection with battles, it marks a key metaphor for resounding victory (foot imposed) or crushing defeat (underfoot; 2 Sam. 22:39 = Ps. 18:38[39]), and that is the symbolism here.[74]

Joshua then addresses his men, urging them to be neither "afraid" nor "discouraged" (v. 25), the very two-word assurance Yahweh gave Joshua before Ai II (Josh. 8:1; cf. Deut. 1:21) and that the Levite Jahaziel will later give Jehoshaphat before a big battle (2 Chron. 20:10; cf. Jer. 30:10=46:27). Rather, they are to be "strong and courageous," a two-word charge that echoes Joshua's own commissioning by Yahweh and Moses (Deut. 31:7, 23; cf. 3:28; Josh. 1:6, 7, 9; cf. 1:18).[75] It is not going too far to call "be strong and courageous" the main theme of Joshua's life under God.

Finally, with a simple, emphatic "this" (*kakab*, "like thus") — as if verbally pointing down to their feet poised on enemy necks — Joshua brings home its significance. They can be strong and courageous because Yahweh will similarly defeat all the enemies they are now battling (the participle stresses current, ongoing activity; v. 25b). Joshua again sounds the key theme of Yahweh's fighting Israel's enemies, the key factor that assures victory and inspires Israel to show strength and courage (vv. 14, 42; cf. Ex. 14:25).

Joshua next strikes and kills the five kings, then hangs (probably impales) their corpses on wooden stakes until evening (v. 26). At sunset, he has the corpses taken down per the Instruction (Deut. 21:22 – 23) and thrown back into the cave (v. 27; cf. 16). The Israelites again reseal it with a pile of large stones over the mouth. Ironically, the "mouth" in which they sought to escape death has now swallowed them forever. This time the place forms a grave, not a jail cell (cf. v. 18), so no guards need be posted. In closing, the author observes that at the very time he wrote, they are still there.[76] Yahweh has, indeed, fulfilled his promise to give Canaan's kings into Israel's hands (Deut. 7:24).

---

73. F. J. Stendebach, "גָּלַל," *TDOT*, 13:319–20.

74. The same gesture appears in the annals of an Assyrian king (thirteenth cent. B.C.): "I captured Kaštiliaš, king of the Kassites (alive). I trod with my feet upon his lordly neck as though it were a footstool" (quoted from Younger, *Ancient Conquest Accounts*, 317, n.86).

75. David invokes both word pairs ("don't fear" + "don't be discouraged"; "be strong and courageous") in handing over royal leadership to Solomon (1 Chron. 22:13; 28:20; cf. 2 Chron. 32:7).

76. For a comparable extrabiblical example, see Younger, *Ancient Conquest Accounts*, 224–25.

Though inhumane to modern readers, the gesture was typical of ancient warfare.[77] The public humiliation of defeated enemies probably served the victors' propaganda purposes—to discourage the attacks of other enemies and to inspire courage in their own troops.[78] Theologically (and perhaps also offensive to some readers), it attests the victory of Yahweh the warrior over his present and future enemies—exactly the point Joshua's symbolic action makes.

The southern blitzkrieg (vv. 28 – 39). Despite an astounding day of victory, other battles remain for Joshua and Israel. But to treat them the narrator adopts a style with repeated formulae (but not slavishly or in lock-step order) and occasional hyperbole (e.g., "everyone in it").[79] The following comprise its core items (in general order of occurrence):

1. The city's capture (vv. 28, 32, 35, 37, 39)
2. The siege and attack (vv. 29, 31, 34, 36, 38)
3. The city, everyone put to the sword (vv. 28, 30, 32, 35, 37, 39)
4. No survivors remain (vv. 28, 30, 33, 35, 37, 39)
5. Israel implements the "ban" (vv. 28, 35, 37, 39)[80]
6. The king suffers the same fate as the king of city-X (vv. 28, 30, 32, 35, 37, 39)

Obviously, the stress falls on the capture of each of the six cities and the annihilation of its inhabitants, but several literary features are striking. In statement 6 the author compares the treatment of both Makkedah and Libnah to that of Jericho, whereas each of the next three are compared only to the one destroyed just before it. The literary effect of this motif is to portray Israel's campaign procedure as consistently effective and the victims as sharing the same terrible fate.[81] With the final city, however (Debir [vv. 38 – 39]), the comparison is to both Libnah (city 2) and Hebron (city 5). That wrinkle plus the report's wordy repetition gives it a fitting rhetorical flourish for the last conquest report. That Lachish took two days to subdue (v. 32) makes sense and redounds especially to Israel's credit since

---

77. Cf. ibid., 222 – 23, who quotes Sennacherib's report of his treatment of Ekron's leaders: "the governors (and) nobles who had sinned I put to death; and I hung their corpses on poles around the city."

78. Cf. R. S. Hess, "תָּלָה," *NIDOTTE*, 4:295.

79. The use of stereotyped, hyperbolic phrases like these is typical of ancient Near Eastern victory reports; cf. Younger, *Ancient Conquest Accounts*, 227 – 28. They overstate in order to persuade or to be emphatic and so are to be understood figuratively, not literally.

80. The "ban" (Heb. ḥerem "utter destruction") is God's mandate to annihilate the inhabitants of Canaan (Deut. 7:2; 20:17).

81. Cf. Hess, *Joshua*, 204.

it is the largest, most prominent, and perhaps most heavily fortified, of the conquests.[82]

Younger has shown that verses 28–39 form the following structural chiasm:[83]

A Makkedah (v. 28)
  B Libnah (vv. 29–30)
    C Lachish (vv. 31–32)
    X Gezer (v. 33)
    C' Eglon (vv. 34–35)
  B' Hebron (vv. 36–37)
A' Debir (vv. 38–39)

The center of a chiasm (the member with no parallel) marks its emphasis, in this case the report of Israel's rout of King Horam of Gezer who had marched his army in defense of Lachish (v. 33).[84] Israel never conquered Gezer (16:10), so the chiasm singles out the event as a major and especially memorable one, given the city's ancient importance.[85]

Geographically, Israel hits Makkedah first since it lies near the cave, then picks off Libnah, Lachish, and Eglon—each only six to seven miles apart—in a sweeping arc basically southwest to southeast. The longest march is to Hebron (thirty-two miles east), followed by a short one (ca. five miles southwest) to Debir.[86] Given the logistics involved, the conquests probably take several weeks (or even months) to complete.

The hit-list shows some striking omissions and inclusions. All five original royal conspirators die at Makkedah, but for some reason neither Jerusalem (home of the ringleader) nor Jarmuth are attacked.[87] Three uninvolved

---

82. When Sennacherib (late eighth century B.C.) wanted to besiege Jerusalem, he first had to destroy both Lachish and Libnah; cf. Boling, *Joshua*, 294. Apparently, he especially relished his conquest of Lachish since he had a wall relief celebrating it made for his palace at Nineveh.

83. K. L. Younger Jr., "The 'Conquest' of the South (Jos. 10:28–39)," *BZ* 39 (1995): 255–64 (esp. 259–64). Howard (*Joshua*, 256–57) proposes a six-member chiastic structure also centered around Gezer; cf. Boling, *Joshua*, 294.

84. Horam is probably a West Semitic name; cf. R. S. Hess, "Non-Israelite Personal Names in the Book of Joshua," *CBQ* 58 (1996): 207.

85. For example, the Amarna Letters (fourteenth cent. B.C.) mention Gezer, and Pharaoh Merneptah apparently considered it a strategic site, listing it among his campaign's conquests on his victory stele (ca. 1207 B.C.); cf. Hess, *Joshua*, 204.

86. These directions and estimated distances are based on Y. Aharoni and M. Avi-Yonah, *The Macmillan Bible Atlas*, rev. ed. (New York: Macmillan, 1977), map #58.

87. The book of Joshua is well aware of Jerusalem as an island within Israel, terming it "the Jebusite city" (Josh. 15:8; 18:16, 28; cf. Judg. 19:11) and acknowledging that the Jebusites still held it (Josh. 15:63; cf. Judg. 1:21).

kings/cities (Makkedah, Libnah, Debir) suffer destruction but nothing is said as to why they have made the list. Presumably strategic considerations (i.e., size, location, prominence, etc.) came into play.

Summary of the Conquest (Joshua 10:40–43)

THE STORYTELLER'S RETROSPECTIVE COMMENT now rings down the curtain on an amazing series of events. Since victories at Jericho and Ai, Israel has rung up a stunning string of additional victories, effectively destroying many of southern Canaan's leading cites and decimating its population.[88] Up front, he credits Joshua with the achievement ("Joshua subdued the whole region"), sounding again the theme of Joshua's rise to Moses-like stature (see above). He lists what "the whole region" comprises (v. 40): "the hill country" (i.e., the central mountain backbone), "the Negev" (the southern desert), "the western foothills" inland from the coastal plain, and "the mountain slopes" (the ridges that connect the foothills with the central backbone), and all their kings.

Borrowing terms from verses 28–39, the author credits Joshua with leaving "no survivors" (10:40) — that is, with annihilating "all who breathed" — in obedience to Yahweh's command. The author stakes out the boundaries of Joshua's swath of victory with the typical Old Testament way of describing large territory ("from ... to ..."; e.g., 11:17; 13:26; et al.). Kadesh Barnea was an oasis in the southern Negev — Israel's home base during the wilderness wanderings (cf. Num. 32:8; 34:4); Gaza was a large state in the coastal plain northwest of Kadesh. Though as yet unidentified, the "region of Goshen" probably lay somewhere in the central Negev (see 11:16; 15:51), while Gibeon was the city in the strategic Central Benjamin Plateau (CBP), the city whose ruse lit the firestorm of vv. 28–39.

Verses 41–42 celebrate Israel's conquest (but not necessarily control) of the land. Their conquest includes the mountainous spinal cord (south to north) from the lower Negev to the CBP (less Jerusalem, among others, of course) and (east to west) from the backbone to the coastal plain. The reason "one campaign" (lit., "one time") suffices to achieve it is "because the LORD, the God of Israel, fought for Israel" — a verbal echo of verse 14b and, hence, a major theme in the chapter. The narrator awards the heroic victor's crown to Joshua, but ultimately it is Yahweh who has given the decisive margin of victory.

---

88. Ancient Near Eastern conquest accounts typically conclude with summary statements, often exaggerated, akin to this one; cf. Younger, "'Conquest' of the South," 264; idem, *Ancient Conquest Accounts*, 230–32.

Finally, after a remarkable blitzkrieg that, in essence, won them the southern half of Canaan, Joshua and Israel return to base camp at Gilgal (v. 43). Certainly, their families welcome their return for a period of rest, but further momentous events soon follow (ch. 11).

THREE IMPORTANT MATTERS SURFACE in the fascinating events of chapters 9 – 10 that merit follow up. Does the biblical writer view the ruse by which the Gibeonites win their treaty with Israel in a positive, neutral, or negative light? Why does Israel regard their oath as still valid given Gibeon's obvious deception? And what about all the violence that chapter 10 seems to celebrate?

Unforgivable trick or providential wisdom? Elsewhere, the key term (Heb. ʿormah "ruse") occurs only five times, with a positive sense in Proverbs (i.e., "prudence, shrewdness"; Prov. 1:4; 8:5, 12) and a negative one in Exodus 21:14 ("treachery" [i.e., a murder scheme]). Which sense best fits the present context? On the one hand, a contextual case can certainly be made for a negative connotation here. On the heels of Jericho and Ai, the divine mandate of annihilation clearly hangs like a sword of Damocles over the scene, casting any deviation from that mandate, whether by its victors or potential victims, in a negative light. Further, there is no escaping the fact that the Gibeonites plainly lie about being from a "distant country" (vv. 6, 9) and only fully disclose their identity after being discovered.[89]

On the other hand, to call their approach "treacherous" does not sound quite right. Though self-serving, it masks no malice or malevolence toward Israel—unlike the military machinations of the kings. The negotiations are no stalling tactic to enable a hidden Gibeonite army to overwhelm unsuspecting Israel as the latter did to Ai.

Some indicators suggest that the narrative may even aim to portray the Gibeonites and their ruse in a somewhat sympathetic light. The scene featuring their fake old clothes and phony moldy bread strikes me as comical. Indeed, once Israel learns of the trick, the public recriminations (9:18 – 20) pale in comparison with the bitter grumbling that bedeviled Moses. Surely, there is nothing here of the magnitude of the humiliated prostration and mourning Joshua and the leadership did after the rout at Ai.

Ultimately, however, the question of authorial sympathy depends on how one answers a larger question: How does the author interpret the

---

89. Such thinking probably underlies the view of H. Niehr, "עָרַם," *TDOT*, 11:361 – 66 (esp. 362 – 64). Inexplicably, A. Luc, "עָרַם," *NIDOTTE*, 3:539 – 41, omits mention of Joshua 9:4.

events theologically? Does the author present them with approval or disapproval? Several indicators may imply the latter. (1) The treatment of the Gibeonites runs afoul of two Mosaic instructions — the prohibition against making treaties with the nations in Canaan and the command to annihilate them without exception (Deut. 7:2; 20:16–17). The Hivites clearly make the ḥerem hit-list to which both provisions apply (7:1; 20:17), so Israel's actions toward them (Josh. 9) clearly violate those instructions.

(2) The narrator's remark that Israel's leaders "did not inquire of the LORD" (9:14) might characterize their inaction as unwise, if not reprehensible, especially if read in light of the Achan episode (ch. 7). The stakes for Israel are high — the potential loss both of Yahweh's favor and of the land itself. Thus, the failure to consult might be read as reckless and imply Israelite overconfidence. Why roll the dice on Israel's future when a simple ritual would allow Yahweh to reveal the true identity of the Gibeonites and head off Israelite disobedience?

But other indicators suggest that the situation is not so cut-and-dried. The authorial remark about Israel's failure to consult Yahweh is in fact ambiguous. The reading cited above assumes that, if consulted, Yahweh would unmask the Gibeonites and command Israel to kill them. It is also possible, however, that consultation with Yahweh would yield a surprising exception to the ḥerem demand and articulate divine rationale for it. Remember that, notwithstanding popular impression, the Instruction of Moses is, in fact, more a statement of policy (i.e., the basic, overarching values Yahweh wishes to cultivate in Israel) than a full-blown legal code.[90] Yahweh could permit an exception to the policy, especially taking into account the Hivites' knowledge, without annulling its applicability to other situations.

In fact, do Yahweh's subsequent words and/or actions say anything about his approval or disapproval of the treaty with the Gibeonites? In reply, his very first words since 8:18 — his reassurance of Joshua and promise of victory at Gibeon (10:8) — are telling. He says nothing directly about the treaty, but his word choice clearly echoes 8:1 and, therefore, implies that Israel enjoys the same good standing (i.e., restored status) it did after Achan's removal.

Yahweh's actions confirm this implication. On Israel's behalf, he unleashes his arsenal of cosmic weapons (10:10–11) and empowers Israel's capture of the Amorite kings (vv. 15–27) and the surprising conquest of all of southern Canaan (vv. 28–39). His relationship with Joshua, if anything, actually seems to have become stronger — witness the astounding fact that

---

90. I owe this concept to E. F. Campbell Jr., *Ruth* (AB 7; Garden City, N.Y.: Doubleday, 1975), 132–35 (citing George Mendenhall); cf. Hubbard, *Ruth*, 50–51.

Yahweh maneuvers the sun and moon in response to Joshua's poetic petition (vv. 12 – 14). Further, the Joshua who orchestrates the symbolic action with the captured kings acts as a commander who feels the full confidence of his Commander-in-Chief, Yahweh (v. 25). In short, the surprising success that follows the treaty suggests at least divine acquiescence to the reality, if not actual approval of it.

Moreover, Joshua 11 clearly tips the evidentiary scales toward the "approval" side. In that chapter, the author remarks that throughout the conquest Joshua "left nothing undone of all that the LORD commanded Moses" (11:15). Since the context mentions the Hivites in Gibeon (v. 19), verse 15 seems to imply that the treaty with Gibeon actually *did* something that Moses commanded—or, at least, did not violate the Mosaic Instruction. More telling is the author's explanation for why the Gibeonites escaped destruction: They were the only city in Canaan to make a peace treaty with Israel (v. 19). Further, the reason for the fallen cities' resistance was that Yahweh had "hardened their hearts to wage war" so he might destroy them (v. 20).[91]

These remarks have startling implications for understanding chapters 9 – 10. Joshua 11:15 and 19 clearly voice approval of the Gibeonite treaty and seem to apply to Hivite Gibeon Moses' instruction concerning how Israel is to conquer foreign cities (Deut. 20:10 – 15).[92] The rationale for *not* applying that policy to cities within Canaan—that the cities might lead Israel into idolatry (Deut. 20:18)—may also supply the underlying rationale for the acceptance of the treaty. Gibeon shows a rudimentary understanding of Yahweh. Further, instead of luring Israel into idolatry, Gibeon historically served as a major center of the worship of Yahweh before the temple was built (1 Kings 3:4 – 5). (Presumably, the Gibeonites provided water and wood for worship there [Josh. 9:26 – 27]).

Also, Joshua 11:20 implies that since Gibeon survived destruction, Yahweh chose *not* to harden the hearts of the Gibeonites—surely, a mysterious act of sovereign divine grace—and may provide a missing piece to the puzzle of chapters 9 – 10. Yahweh's sovereign guidance accounts both for the Gibeonites' request for peace and Israel's agreement to a treaty.[93]

---

91. Obviously, the phrase "to harden [their] hearts" alludes to Yahweh's sovereign intervention in Egypt (cf. Ex. 4:21; 9:12; 10:20, 27; 11:10; 14:8, 17). See comments on ch. 11.

92. For scholars who see Deut. 20 as the key background to this episode, see Nelson, *Joshua*, 124 (with bibliography). Nelson himself (124, n.2), however, argues that the story still makes good sense even without that assumption.

93. Subsequently, the Gibeonites make a cameo appearance in an episode that further verifies the above interpretation (2 Sam. 21). In trying to annihilate them, Saul had incurred bloodguilt that led Yahweh to punish the land with a three-year drought. Clearly, Yahweh's

In conclusion, I hold that the biblical writer regards the Gibeonite "ruse" as "clever" or "prudent" rather than "treacherous." Over against the "kings" and their "cities," what distinguishes the Gibeonites is their serious respect of Yahweh, their lack of offensive idolatry, their desire for peace rather than war, and their appeal for "good and right" treatment from Joshua (9:25). In essence, their appeal marks a call for mercy, consciously or unconsciously an appeal to the character of Yahweh as "good and right" (i.e., merciful). The entire episode provides an opportunity for Yahweh to demonstrate whether or not his *ḥesed* ("mercy, loyalty, [covenant] commitment") might somehow extend to non-Israelites.

Why honor the oath? The second matter is to sort out why, when Israel discovers the Gibeonite deception, they still regard the oath they have sworn as valid. Modern readers probably presume that anything done under false pretenses is invalid, but that seems not to be the case here. By definition, an oath is a self-imprecation sworn to authenticate the seriousness with which one party (or several) enter an agreement with another (or others).[94] By an oath one voluntarily accepts that dire consequences will rightly follow any violations of it. Oaths are sworn in the name of a deity (e.g., 9:15, 19), who serves as its guarantor (i.e., the enforcer of its consequences, when necessary).

Now, as strange as it may seem today, the text plainly accepts that the Gibeonite deception does not annul the oath, despite Israel's acceptance of it under false pretenses (9:18–21). That is Israel's explanation for why they cannot attack and kill the Gibeonites, despite grumbling in the Israelite camp (vv. 18–19). Such actions, the leaders argue, would violate the treaty and incur the punitive "wrath" of Yahweh (v. 19). The phrase "by the LORD, the God of Israel" may offer the only clue to the underlying rationale of their hesitation. To their credit, they clearly take Yahweh (and their own actions) seriously.

Genesis 27, however, does provide an illuminating parallel. Pretending to be Esau, Jacob deceived Isaac and received from his father the blessing of the firstborn that rightfully belonged to Esau. Like the oath in Joshua 9, the blessing involved a spoken word that formally effected a transaction—the patriarchal blessing (i.e., positive rather than negative consequences). Despite the false pretenses under which Jacob obtained it, Isaac was apparently only able to give Esau a different blessing, not annul and

---

enforcement of Israel's oath regarding Gibeon confirms his acceptance of their special status within Israel, as does David's dealings with them to resolve the guilt and remove the famine. Unselfconsciously, the text identifies them as leftover Amorites and accepts them as a "given" in Israel.

94. I. Kottsieper, "שָׁבַע," *TDOT*, 14:314–16.

reissue the first (and official) one. For whatever reason, once spoken, the blessing could not be voided; trembling, the frail Isaac cried, "I blessed him—and indeed he will be blessed!" (27:33). This example suggests that the ancient idea that spoken words cause effects that cannot be changed may underlie what happens in Joshua 9.

A related subject concerns the phenomenon parallel to the oath, the curse that Joshua pronounces on the Gibeonites (9:23). The provision may strike some readers as harsh and vindictive, but the present writer proposes that ancient legal logic may underlie it. As Scharbert notes, the curse formula constitutes a powerful "decree" whereby an authority may impose misfortune on an individual or group guilty of a serious offense.[95] Literarily, the present example follows a formal sequence of accusatory-question (v. 22), transition ("Now therefore" [NRSV]), and curse-formula in the indicative mood ("You are under a curse …"; v. 23).[96] The accusatory-question ("Why did you deceive us…?") states the reason for which the curse is pronounced. In this case, Joshua refers to the Gibeonites' false claim of being foreigners, a serious offense that misled Israel into a treaty they may not have otherwise made.

Typically, the principle of proper proportion guides ancient (and modern) legal penalties (i.e., "the punishment fits the crime"). So, one expects the curse to impose a consequence commensurate with the nature and seriousness of the offense. To mandate, say, the complete annihilation of the offenders (i.e., *ḥerem*) would constitute disproportionate punishment—like executing someone today for fraud. By contrast, the treaty is to govern Israelite-Gibeonite relations in perpetuity, so one expects the penalty likewise to apply permanently. Further, since the fraudulently executed treaty subordinates the Gibeonites to Israel, it would make sense for the penalty to perpetuate that subjection in a punitive way.

In this view, the curse conforms to the above principles. The penalty specifically repays the deception that produced the treaty not to Israel's liking. What would be an appropriate penalty for such an offense? The curse condemns the Gibeonites to a permanent, servile social role—as "slaves" manually providing wood and water for Yahweh's sanctuary. It corresponds to the permanent subordination of the original treaty.

At the same time, Joshua introduces a striking alteration to the servitude Israel's leaders impose on the Hivites (9:21). He stipulates that their

---

95. J. Scharbert, "אָרַר," *TDOT*, 1:411–12. People probably assumed that the curse became effective in the very act of pronouncing it, implemented through Yahweh's intervention.

96. For other examples of the pattern, see Gen. 3:13–14; 4:10–11; cf. 3:17.

service as woodcutters and water-carriers take place at "the altar of the LORD" (v. 27). The implications of this provision are uncertain. It might imply that, ultimately, their offense was thought to be against Yahweh, not Israel, so they appropriately serve him as their penalty. According to verse 26, Joshua's assignment of them to Yahweh's altar "saved" the Gibeonites from being killed by Israelites. Perhaps their sacred location also gave them sanctuary under Yahweh's protection from moves by future generations to exact revenge (cf. 2 Sam. 21). Another possibility is that the assignment of the Gibeonites to work at the altar put them under priestly oversight, thus limiting the possibility of their promoting idolatry in Israel.[97]

But what are the implications of positioning a non-Israelite people in this proximity? What level of holiness does it assume for or require of the Gibeonites? What might it suggest about their status in Israel? Does it, in fact, constitute a kind of "promotion" above the resident aliens who normally provided Israel with wood and water, although not at the holy place? Perhaps the best one can say is that the Gibeonites performed menial tasks at a prestigious site, certainly a vocation both they and Israel would regard as an honor.

Yikes! More slaughter! Finally, the slaughter and humiliation of the seven kings (10:22 – 27) may leave some Christian readers uncomfortable. In reply, it bears repeating that however offensive to Christian sensibilities, the scene is typical of the conquest accounts of the literature of its day.[98] Joshua 10 merely reflects the warfare practices common in the ancient world, the cultural milieu that shaped the book of Joshua. The practice of violence in antiquity differs greatly from that of today. It is, thus, frankly unfair to judge practices commonly accepted three thousand years ago (or at any time in past history) by modern standards.

Moreover, it is important to remember exactly who these kings are. Joshua portrays them clearly as steadfast opponents of God's plan for his people, rulers willing to make alliances and muster armies to annihilate Israel. In essence, they seek to do to Israel what Israel intends to do to them (a military form of *ḥerem*). Jews today might compare them to the Russian czars and Adolph Hitler, while Christians might compare them to Nero in the first century and to recent religious extremists in India and Kenya. In my view, the religious freedom that Western Christians enjoy sometimes blinds us to the fact that truly evil people still exist—and that their not-so-subtle goal is to stop the spread of Christianity. As a result, there are in fact many Christians who suffer under the cruel hegemony of their own "Amorite kings."

---

97. I am grateful to Professor John H. Walton for this suggestion.
98. For examples, see Younger, *Ancient Conquest Accounts*, 220 – 25.

Finally, recall that the final consummation of history involves the destruction of God's enemies, scenes in John's Revelation even more horrible than those in Joshua 10.

In short, while no Christian should ever be comfortable with violence, it is helpful to remember that the present chapter reflects its own ancient culture, that it should be accepted on its own ancient terms, and that God's warfare against evil still has one final, climatic chapter planned for the future. At the same time, the merciful welcome accorded the Gibeonites anticipates the inclusive welcome that the gospel offers all nations. Thankfully, the Gibeonites already have many spiritual descendants, including the present writer, and by God's grace more are accepting God's offer of mercy every day.

 JOSHUA 9–10 HELPFULLY sounds three important themes crucial for contemporary Christians to hear. All three center around the topic of identity. To begin, however, one implication that does *not* flow from the passage merits comment.

Don't do this! Joshua 9–10 in no way justifies the use of violence to achieve Christian goals. This seems obvious, of course, given the nonviolent ethic of Jesus, until one remembers that not too long ago the cross and the sword sought in tandem to conquer lands in the so-called "New World," Asia, and Africa in the name of Christ. One historical lesson of that sorry colonial period of Christian history is that the gospel does not advance by military coercion.

Nevertheless, in recent memory a few Christians (among them, a former student of mine) took it upon themselves to bomb abortion clinics and kill several physicians. The bombings might have even continued had the Christian community not realized that such violence is ill-advised (and illegal). What sense does it make to take human life in order (allegedly) to save it?

Recall, further, the Old Testament understanding of Yahweh's war. It consists of warfare that God himself wages against his enemies on behalf of his people (and with their participation). But it is not an ongoing Israelite institution. That is, it is not warfare that Israel initiates and executes on its own under the banner of Yahweh's war. The authority to pursue it remains the exclusive province of Yahweh, so that to pursue it today would require nothing less than a direct divine revelation, not just biblical teaching.

Also, the Bible regards the conquest of Canaan as a one-time-only event to achieve a specific purpose — to provide Israel a homeland and God a geographical base from which eventually to bless the world. There is no justification for adopting the Conquest as a paradigm for the use of violence as part of spiritual warfare today. Instead, Paul points in the right direction when he commends the gospel as "the power of God for ... salvation" (Rom. 1:16). It is more powerful than anything humans can do and, hence, needs neither sword nor political system to achieve its conquests.

Similarly, Isaiah got it right when he warned late eighth-century Judah against dependence on Egyptian military aid rather than on Yahweh for survival. He said, "The Egyptians are mortals and not God; their horses are flesh and not spirit" (Isa. 31:3a TNIV). According to Isaiah, the real power lies not in "flesh" (i.e., "mortals"//"horses") but in "spirit" (i.e., in God's mighty power). In sum, Joshua offers no justification for the use of violence to achieve Christian ends. It might be tempting for a local congregation to bomb city hall when city planners deny its petition for some variance or rezoning, but Joshua in no way justifies the acting out of "righteous indignation" in violence. The nonviolent plan may frustrate us, but it is Jesus' way of doing things.

The big picture: there's a war out there! To eschew violence is not to deny that there is a spiritual war going on as I write this. *Au contraire!* There is, in fact, a war out there (and "in here," too). Indeed, the first aspect of contemporary meaning is to recognize how Joshua 9 – 10 offers a microcosm of the "big picture," the gospel enterprise in history. Whatever one's moral compunctions about the Conquest, theologically it marks a step forward in God's plan to establish his kingdom on earth. It confronts the ruling powers of the day (the "Amorite kings") with the demand that they submit to Yahweh's sovereign rule. It puts his representatives — his chosen people, warts and all — smack dab in the middle of the nations of the world.

Two major international highways, the Coastal Highway (along the Mediterranean) and the King's Highway (along the Jordan's east bank), border it and offer access in all directions. That brings many nations to Israel's doorstep, sometimes for peace, other times for war. Israel's presence confronts one of the local nations, the Hivites of Gibeon, with a choice: To avoid annihilation, they can either join the forming military alliances or somehow sue the invaders for peace. The request for a treaty marks the only time since the Exodus that another nation has greeted Israel peacefully. In Joshua 9 – 10 the battle between Yahweh and his enemies is both historical and cosmic. It pits earthly kings against Yahweh's cosmic powers (i.e., the sun and moon). The conquest and settlement of the Promised Land anticipate God's sending of Jesus to teach, live, die, and rise again. It also prepares a place for the giving of the Great Commission, the day of Pentecost, and the carrying of the gospel in all directions.

For Christians the war is a spiritual one. Rather than confront enemies of "flesh and blood," they face "the rulers ... the authorities ... the powers of this dark world and ... the spiritual forces of evil in the heavenly realms" (Eph. 6:12). Their enemies are both political leaders and cosmic evil forces whose opposition to the gospel is as fierce as—if not greater than—that of the Amorite kings. Like Israel, God has also dispersed his representatives—his own redeemed people—right in the middle of the world's many nations. The arrival of gospel messengers anywhere provokes modern Amorites to hostile opposition and people like the Gibeonites to peaceful inquiry.

In one sense, all Christians (except for Jewish ones) are the spiritual descendants of the Gibeonites—"Gentiles," or people who once "were separate from Christ, excluded from citizenship in Israel and foreigners to the covenants of the promise" (Eph. 2:12). But then they met Jesus Christ, and that changed everything. With the Gibeonites in mind, savor Paul's poignant description of the transformation of Gentiles from their pre- to post-Christian status:

> But now in Christ Jesus you who once were far away have been brought near by the blood of Christ.... For through him we both have access to the Father by one Spirit. Consequently, you are no longer foreigners and aliens, but fellow citizens with God's people and also members of his household, built on the foundation of the apostles and prophets, with Christ Jesus himself as the chief cornerstone. (Eph. 2:13, 18–20 TNIV)

People both "far away" (Gibeonites/Gentiles) and "near" (Jews) have been "brought near [to God] by the blood of Christ" (vv. 13, 17). Christ has come and "preached peace" to them, so "peace" (the ultimate treaty!) has replaced "the dividing wall of hostility" (e.g., the fearful threat of *ḥerem*) that once had Gibeonites and Israelites at loggerheads. Indeed, Christ has united Gibeonites and Israelites into "one new humanity" in fellowship with God through Christ's salvific work (vv. 14, 17). As a result, Gibeonites are no longer "foreigners and aliens"—people on God's hit-list—but "fellow citizens with God's people" and even "members of his [personal] household" (v. 19). No more lowly "woodcutters and water carriers" laboring on the periphery of the sanctuary! Now they have full "access to the Father" (v. 18), relating to him not as "people" to "God" but as "child" to "Father"! Indeed, gone is the circumspect, low-profile life on the margins; now Gibeonites comprise part of the temple itself, the very place "in which God lives by his Spirit" (vv. 21–22).

What a stunning portrait of the marvelous change in status given by God to all believers as a free gift of his grace through their faith in Christ.

They enjoy the full standing before God of which the Gibeonites may only have dreamed. Nevertheless, as in Joshua 9–10, God is engaged in spiritual warfare today, seeking Gibeonites to believe in him while battling the vicious Amorite kings. The sweeping triumph of Joshua 9–10 reminds believers that since God the Warrior leads the way, final victory is certain.

To cite Paul again, the Christian hope of final triumph derives from God's "incomparably great power for us who believe," "the working of his mighty strength" that raised Christ from the dead and seated him at God's right hand" (Eph. 1:19–20). Christ (our Joshua as we fight for the kingdom's advance) enjoys that exalted seat of cosmic authority. It includes God's placement of "all things under his feet" (remember the fate of the five kings!) and his appointment as head of the church (1:22). It means that Christ decisively outranks "all rule and authority, power and dominion, and every title that can be given, not only in the present age but also in the one to come" (1:21). As Yahweh's power and authority empowered Israel to execute his plan, so for Christians the power and authority of Christ emboldens us with confidence and hope whatever the circumstances. Thanks be to God!

The ideal troops: the kind soldier. The kind of spiritual warfare engaging Christians today calls for a soldier with certain character traits. In Joshua 9–10, the conduct of the leaders, both Joshua and the others, illustrates several of them. (1) The ideal troops are *people of their word.* Though deceit had led Israel into the treaty, they refused to invoke it as an excuse for bailing out of it later. Whatever their motive—not to risk Yahweh's wrath or not to dishonor his name—they stuck with their agreement, even when it drew them into war against half of Canaan.

Jesus taught something similar when he said, "Simply let your 'Yes' be 'Yes,' and your 'No,' 'No'; anything beyond this comes from the evil one" (Matt. 5:37). The apostle James put it a little more strongly: "Above all ... do not swear—not by heaven or by earth or by anything else. Let your 'Yes' be yes, and your 'No,' no, or you will be condemned" (James 5:12). Both Jesus and James underscore that Christians are to be people of their word. They are people who follow through on their commitments made by saying "Yes" and do not second-guess themselves on commitments declined with a "No." The world is filled with phony Yes-People—people who accept a commitment but cannot be counted on to carry it out—and Maybe-people—people who are afraid to say "No" so they say "Maybe" (a polite "No").

This trait is more than just human decisiveness. It is, in fact, a spiritual one because it mirrors the nature of God as trustworthy. As Balaam put it,

"God is not a human, that he should lie, not a human being, that he should change his mind. Does he speak and then not act? Does he promise and not fulfill?" (Num. 23:19 TNIV; cf. 1 Sam. 15:29). The seer gives two key insights. (a) He affirms that what God "promises" he "fulfills." Put in modern terms, "he says what he means and he means what he says." (b) Balaam states that lying is typical of human beings. His assumption is either that their evil side asserts itself in lies or that they are too weak to speak with consistency (or both). That is why we humans need the alternative model of constancy in truth-telling that God himself provides. That is why we need the power of the Holy Spirit to overcome our evil bent and weakness.

The trait of straight speaking is also spiritual in another sense. It reflects our trust in the guidance of God through the Holy Spirit to discern whether "Yes" or "No" is the best answer at the time. The life of faith draws on the Spirit's help to know when each response is appropriate — even times when "Maybe" might genuinely allow time for a prayerful quest for God's guidance. The latter would be appropriate when facing a life-altering decision — a move, marriage, job change, financial venture, and so on.

(2) The second trait for today's soldiers is to be *people of mercy*. Joshua exemplifies this trait when the Gibeonites, owning their duplicity, gently cast their fate in his hands ("We are now in your hands"; 9:24–25). They accept that Joshua holds all the cards — that they are completely at his mercy (cf. Jer. 26:14a). Subtly, they appeal to the great leader's compassionate side. Further, accepting their powerlessness, they willingly submit to his decision ("Do to us whatever seems good and right to you"). Both "good" and "right" entail an ethical appeal; the former implies "do what you think best," whereas "right" assumes action according to a standard ("do the right thing").[99]

This word pair asks Joshua for an outcome that benefits him and Israel and that also treats the Gibeonites fairly. At first glance, "fairly" might bring up the prospect of the dreaded *ḥerem*, but the question for Joshua is: "How should I treat people who chose peace over war and who accept some basic truths about our God?" Or, "Given that, might Yahweh make an exception as he did with Rahab?" In the end, Joshua shows mercy: He "saves" the Gibeonites from Israelite revenge and accords them a unique social role in Israel's worship. Israel knows Yahweh as a God of mercy, and in my view Joshua 9–10 display that mercy, too. On Mount Sinai Yahweh proclaimed himself as "the compassionate and gracious God, slow to anger, abounding in love and faithfulness" (Ex. 34:6), words that Psalm 103:8–10 echoes:

---

99. Cf. L. Alonso-Schökel, "יָשָׁר," *TDOT*, 6:464–71; for "good," cf. K.-D. Schunck, "טוֹב," *TDOT*, 5:308–9.

> The LORD is compassionate and gracious,
>   slow to anger, abounding in love.
> He will not always accuse,
>   nor will he harbor his anger forever;
> he does not treat us as our sins deserve
>   or repay us according to our iniquities.[100]

David, in fact, gambled on that very mercy when Yahweh permitted him to choose his punishment for taking a census (2 Sam. 24). He opted for three days of plague rather than three years of famine or three months of pursuit by enemies. His rationale was clear: "Let us fall into the hands of the LORD, for his mercy is great; but do not let me fall into the hands of men" (2 Sam. 24:14). He knew the character of his God, and his gamble paid off. Though seventy thousand Israelites died, it so grieved Yahweh to destroy Jerusalem that he ended the plague (24:16).

Joshua knew that side of Yahweh, too. He (and Israel) had experienced it after the Achan episode (Josh. 7–8). Also, as noted above, Joshua 9–10 seem to put on display the mercy of God also toward the Gibeonites doomed to die under ḥerem, the same mercy he also showed Rahab, because they submitted to his will. The episodes involving David, Rahab, and the Gibeonites remind us that God himself is the example par excellence of mercy and the standard against which to measure ours.

Although ḥerem was not involved, Jesus' himself once confronted a non-Israelite outsider, a Canaanite woman, who sought his mercy (Matt. 15:22–28). She cried out desperately on behalf of her demon-possessed daughter, but Jesus ignored her, claiming that his mission was only for "the lost sheep of Israel" (v. 24). Though she persisted, he resisted, even appearing to insult the woman: "It is not right to take the children's bread and toss it to their dogs" (v. 26). But she replied cleverly, "Yes, Lord, but even the dogs eat the crumbs that fall from their master's table" (v. 27). The rejoinder amazed Jesus, and he immediately praised her faith. He readily granted her request, and her daughter recovered (v. 28). As Joshua extended mercy to the Gibeonites, so Jesus did to the Canaanite woman, and good soldiers of the cross always strive to put Jesus' beatitude into practice: "Blessed are the merciful, for they will be shown mercy" (Matt. 5:7).

(3) Good soldiers are also *people of prayer*. Someone recently dialed a phone number and received this message: "I am not available right now, but thank you for caring enough to call. I am making some changes in my life. Please leave a message after the beep. If I do not return your call, you

---

100. See also Num. 14:18; Ps. 86:15; Jonah 4:2; James 5:11.

are one of the changes." Well, God never answers people that way. Again, Joshua's poetic prayer—his petition concerning the sun and moon amid the chaos of battle (10:12b)—exemplifies this truth. As the biblical writer stresses, the astonishing thing is that God "obeyed" a human voice.[101] Truly astonishing, indeed! Autobiographically, the psalmist frames the question that fuels the astonishment:

> When I consider your heavens,
>> the work of your fingers,
> the moon and the stars,
>> which you have set in place,
> what are mere mortals that you are mindful of them,
>> human beings that you care for them? (Ps. 8:3–4 TNIV)

Given the vast nightly, celestial display, the psalmist finds it unbelievable that God, the Creator of the cosmos, even notices humans at all.[102] How can God not only notice them but also actually *hear* their words and—most astounding—even *act* in response? But the simple biblical fact is that he does, as this refrain from a song by Johnny Cash affirms:

> I talk to Jesus everyday,
> And he's interested in everything I say;
> No secretary ever tells me,
> 'He's been called away.'
> I talk to Jesus every day.

That is why the apostle James exhorts Christians to pray about practical needs:

> Is anyone among you in trouble? Let them pray.... Is anyone among you sick? Let them call the elders of the church to pray over them and anoint them with oil in the name of the Lord. And the prayer offered in faith will make them well; the Lord will raise them up.... The prayer of a righteous person is powerful and effective. (James 5:13–15a, 16b TNIV)

---

101. In the Original Meaning section, I interpreted the author's "never-before, never-since" comment (10:14) either as simple rhetorical hyperbole or as a reference to the cosmic content of the prayer. It does not mean that God had never nor would never again listen to a human prayer.

102. The equally astonishing observation, he adds, is that God even puts humans in charge of the earth (Ps. 8:5–8). Citing ordinary birds and lilies of the field as evidence, Jesus adds that God even knows our human needs for food, drink, and clothing before we ask him (Matt. 6:25–32).

James calls believers to pray in trouble and in sickness caused by sin. He says that the prayer of someone in right standing before God is "powerful and effective" (James 5:16). As proof he cites the case of Elijah, whose earnest prayers — first for drought, then for rain — each proved effective because God answered them (5:17 – 18; cf. 1 Kings 17:1; 18:36 – 37).

Such prayers and answers are not merely nice things God does. They are also weapons in the cosmic battle in which we Christians are now engaged. Answers to prayer testify not only that God exists but that we are in personal contact with him. That sends the message that God somehow cares about humans. They confirm that "God [indeed] so loved the world ..." (John 3:16). In short, an ongoing life of prayer marks a believer as a soldier of the cross, someone ready to offer services to people outside the faith.

Today's Gibeonites. In another way, the situation of Israel and the Gibeonites compares to our contemporary situation as Christians. There are Gibeonites near us — people outside the kingdom who, according to Jesus, at this present moment stand condemned to eternal death because of their unbelief (John 3:18). Like the Gibeonites, they may have some knowledge of the Bible's God but, unlike them, have not yet exchanged their rebellion against him for a relationship with him.

Of course, this analogy has several important limitations. Israel was to impose *ḥerem* on the Gibeonites, while Christians have no authorization to impose judgment on anyone. Indeed, our instructions are to leave judgment to God (Deut. 32:35; Rom. 12:19), who has a final judgment day already planned (Rev. 20:11 – 15). Further, the Gibeonites approached Israel, not the other way around, whereas Jesus' mandate to us is to "go and make disciples of all nations" (Matt. 28:19). Nevertheless, Joshua 9 – 10 show the contrasting fates of those who surrender to God and those who rebel — the Gibeonites versus the kings of Canaan — and God's use of Israel (a reluctant Israel, to be sure) to initiate a relationship with himself. For us the question is: With regard to the Gibeonites of today, what do we do?

In a recent book, George Hunter aptly described the contemporary culture in which Christians live and minister:

> The Church, in the Western world, faces populations who are increasingly "secular" — people with no Christian memory, who don't know what we Christians are talking about. These populations are increasingly "urban" — and out of touch with God's "natural revelation." These populations are increasingly "postmodern"; they have graduated from Enlightenment ideology and are more peer driven, feeling driven, and "right-brained" than their

forebears. These populations are increasingly "neo-barbarian"; they lack "refinement" or "class," and their lives are often out of control. These populations are increasingly receptive — exploring world-view options from Astrology to Zen — and are often looking "in all the wrong places" to make sense of their lives and find their soul's true home.[103]

Hunter's description implies that to reach such populations — our Gibeonites — will require a new approach. In my view, reflection on Joshua's relationship with the Gibeonites and the Celtic model of Hunter may point the way. Recall that the Gibeonites knew only a few basic things about Israel and about God. They also preferred peace to war and tricked Israel into a treaty. Israel let them live, and Joshua's curse assigned them permanently to humble service at Yahweh's sanctuary. Whether intended or not, that assignment gave the Gibeonites a glimpse of Yahweh's work in human lives at street level. They could closely observe daily worship, annual festivals, sacrifices, readings of the Instruction, legal processes, and so on. In short, Israel incorporated them into its community, albeit in a restricted sense.[104]

Hunter studied how St. Patrick won the barbarian Celts in Ireland to Christianity and also, through missionaries sent from his community, he reestablished it in Europe (fourth to fifth cent. A.D.). Rather than build a church or a monastery, St. Patrick set up "monastic communities" in locales accessible to traffic (e.g., near main roads, villages, etc.). The community was remarkably diverse: It had monastic priests and nuns, but also nonascetic priests and a variety of laypeople (e.g., "scholars, teachers, craftsmen, artists, farmers, families, and children").[105] Worship, study, and work comprised the average day, making the communities beehives of all sorts of activities — unlike the typical cloistered monasteries.

These communities intentionally cultivated ongoing contacts with outsiders and welcomed visitors. Hospitality to guests of all kinds (e.g.,

---

103. G. G. Hunter III, *The Celtic Way of Evangelism: How Christianity Can Win the West — Again* (Nashville: Abingdon, 2000), 9.

104. Unfortunately, the lack of biblical data denies us knowledge of the Gibeonites after their cameo appearance in 2 Samuel 21. For example, we do not know whether they were at Gibeon when David visited there (1 Chron. 16:39; 21:29) — during the tabernacle's time there — or when Yahweh appeared there to Solomon in a dream (1 Kings 3). First Chronicles 12:4 lists "Ishmaiah the Gibeonite" among the "Thirty" warriors who joined David's guerrilla band at Ziklag. His name ends in "-yah," the sign of a Yahwistic name, but "Gibeonite" refers to the town, not the ethnic group. The Judean prophet Hananiah also hailed from Gibeon (Jer. 28:1).

105. Hunter, *The Celtic Way of Evangelism*, 28.

pilgrims, refugees, seekers, etc.) was a priority.[106] They evangelized as a team, who supported each other and pursued good relationships with the nearby settlement. Community activities (e.g., solitary spiritual exercises, peer accountability, small groups, work and worship, etc.) prepared members for sharing the gospel. Community prayer life prominently featured imaginative prayer—prayer that touched emotions and engaged the imagination, including poetry with vivid visual images (in modern terms, "right-brained"). Through contact with the community, outsiders learned some Scripture, came to understand Christian beliefs, were prayed for regularly, and eventually asked about making a commitment to Christ. In short, what Robin Gill observes about most new Christians today was true of monastic communities: "Belonging comes before believing."[107]

Hunter's study suggests that the way local churches relate to outsiders may need revision. The "revivalist" model that seeks to draw a crowd to hear a message must give way to a more relational model. The focus should be less on attracting people to hear preaching and more on drawing them relationally into ongoing contact with some form of Christian community. For some, the "community" may be weekly worship or a creative, city-wide outreach activity. For others it may be an Alpha Course, a small discussion group or Bible study, a special lecture series, a community-oriented social activity, a church-sponsored community project, a divorce recovery group, and the like. Church members "out there" in the neighborhood constitute the key bridge linking these Christian communities to people outside the church.

Many churches use creative means to encourage and counsel Christians on how to make friends, pursue relationships, answer serious questions, meet practical needs, and offer prayer for needs. The point is that local churches may need to think of themselves differently. Rather than places for mainly Christians, they should see themselves as worshiping communities that intentionally seek, welcome, and incorporate Gibeonites. Through community participation, they will observe the Christian life in action and engage Christian beliefs without pressure. Their priority should be to make seekers feel welcome and cared for—to cultivate "belonging" before "believing." The words of an ancient Chinese poem summarize the Gibeonite/Celtic model:

Go to the people.
Live among them.

---

106. They followed the Benedictine Rule #53: "All guests who present themselves are to be welcomed as Christ, for he himself will say: 'I was a stranger and you welcomed me'"; quoted from ibid., 52.

107. Quoted from Hunter, ibid., 55.

Learn from them.
Love them.
Start with what they know.
Build on what they have.[108]

Some years ago, Ed Dobson—a traditional, older pastor of a traditional church in Grand Rapids, Michigan—led his church to try a four-month experiment called "Saturday Night Live." It was a Saturday night worship service geared for the street people, prostitutes, and the homeless near the church. Before beginning, Ed warned the Sunday morning congregation not to attend Saturday evening. He said that the music would offend and that he would talk fifteen minutes about God, not give a sermon. He would also pass out 3 x 5 cards for people to submit their questions about God. They would put their name on the card, and Ed would answer them that night. Ed asked the Sunday morning folks to pray for the experiment, and the experiment began.

The street-people audience, over-the-top music, short talk about God, and question-and-answer time was just as Ed had said. But during the first two months, Ed was dumbfounded to see three ladies from the Sunday morning congregation up in the balcony every Saturday night. Finally, he went up there one night to find out why.

"Oh, Pastor, it's about the questions," one said.

"About the questions?" he asked. "You all know the answers to these questions. You've been Christians for years—longer than I have, in fact."

"No, Pastor," they said, "it's the names. We write down the names you read from the cards. And every Tuesday morning in our prayer group, we pray for each name. We pray for their salvation."

After four months, twenty people had received eternal life through Saturday Night Live and the prayers of those three ladies. The church voted to continue the experiment, and it eventually became a church plant on its own, a church that continues to thrive today.[109] Surrounded by a growing sea of contemporary Gibeonites, Joshua would call churches today to engage them through their own creative outreach strategies.

---

108. Quoted from Hunter, ibid., 120.

109. I am grateful to my friend and former pastor, the Rev. Debra Gustafson, for sharing this story.

Joshua 11:1–23

W HEN JABIN KING of Hazor heard of this, he sent word to Jobab king of Madon, to the kings of Shimron and Acshaph, ²and to the northern kings who were in the mountains, in the Arabah south of Kinnereth, in the western foothills and in Naphoth Dor on the west; ³to the Canaanites in the east and west; to the Amorites, Hittites, Perizzites and Jebusites in the hill country; and to the Hivites below Hermon in the region of Mizpah. ⁴They came out with all their troops and a large number of horses and chariots—a huge army, as numerous as the sand on the seashore. ⁵All these kings joined forces and made camp together at the Waters of Merom, to fight against Israel.

⁶The LORD said to Joshua, "Do not be afraid of them, because by this time tomorrow I will hand all of them over to Israel, slain. You are to hamstring their horses and burn their chariots."

⁷So Joshua and his whole army came against them suddenly at the Waters of Merom and attacked them, ⁸and the LORD gave them into the hand of Israel. They defeated them and pursued them all the way to Greater Sidon, to Misrephoth Maim, and to the Valley of Mizpah on the east, until no survivors were left. ⁹Joshua did to them as the LORD had directed: He hamstrung their horses and burned their chariots.

¹⁰At that time Joshua turned back and captured Hazor and put its king to the sword. (Hazor had been the head of all these kingdoms.) ¹¹Everyone in it they put to the sword. They totally destroyed them, not sparing anything that breathed, and he burned up Hazor itself.

¹²Joshua took all these royal cities and their kings and put them to the sword. He totally destroyed them, as Moses the servant of the LORD had commanded. ¹³Yet Israel did not burn any of the cities built on their mounds—except Hazor, which Joshua burned. ¹⁴The Israelites carried off for themselves all the plunder and livestock of these cities, but all the people they put to the sword until they completely destroyed them, not sparing anyone that breathed. ¹⁵As the LORD commanded his servant Moses, so Moses commanded Joshua,

and Joshua did it; he left nothing undone of all that the LORD commanded Moses.

¹⁶So Joshua took this entire land: the hill country, all the Negev, the whole region of Goshen, the western foothills, the Arabah and the mountains of Israel with their foothills, ¹⁷from Mount Halak, which rises toward Seir, to Baal Gad in the Valley of Lebanon below Mount Hermon. He captured all their kings and struck them down, putting them to death. ¹⁸Joshua waged war against all these kings for a long time. ¹⁹Except for the Hivites living in Gibeon, not one city made a treaty of peace with the Israelites, who took them all in battle. ²⁰For it was the LORD himself who hardened their hearts to wage war against Israel, so that he might destroy them totally, exterminating them without mercy, as the LORD had commanded Moses.

²¹At that time Joshua went and destroyed the Anakites from the hill country: from Hebron, Debir and Anab, from all the hill country of Judah, and from all the hill country of Israel. Joshua totally destroyed them and their towns. ²²No Anakites were left in Israelite territory; only in Gaza, Gath and Ashdod did any survive. ²³So Joshua took the entire land, just as the LORD had directed Moses, and he gave it as an inheritance to Israel according to their tribal divisions.

Then the land had rest from war.

THIS CHAPTER DRAWS THE long saga of Israel's conquest of Canaan to a close. It opens with the last Canaanite coalition massing for war (vv. 1–5) and ends on the peaceful note that war no longer ravages the land (v. 23b). Structurally, it comprises a report of the northern campaign (vv. 1–15) and a summary of the geographical sweep of the conquest that began at 5:1 and culminates here (11:16–23).

The chapter includes two special notices, the conquest of Hazor (vv. 10–11) and the destruction of the people known as the Anakites (vv. 21–22), each loosely linked to the surrounding narrative by the phrase "at that time" (cf. 5:2; 6:26). The latter phrase presents the two events as contemporary to the main event (the battle at Merom) but without chronological precision.[1] The chapter's literary structure and content mirror that

---

1. Cf. Younger, *Ancient Conquest Accounts*, 229 ("a type of flashback so that the materials ... can be linked together").

of chapter 10. News of Israelite advances spurs the king of a leading city (Hazor) to rally allies (11:1–5 // 10:1–3); Yahweh gives Joshua an oracle of assurance (11:6 // 10:8); Israel attacks the bivouacked enemy by surprise (11:7 // 10:9); Yahweh gives Israel the victory (11:8 // 10:10–14); Israel captures the enemy's cities and destroys its inhabitants (11:10–15 // 10:28–39); a concluding summary ends the narrative (11:16–20, 23 // 10:40–42).[2]

At the same time, chapter 11 strikes readers as sketchy compared to chapter 10.[3] It supplies neither an explanation for Jabin's attack (Heb. lacks the "this" of NIV in 11:1) nor a location for the place where God addresses Joshua (v. 6). Its information about the enemy is similarly vague, naming only two kings (Jabin of Hazor and Jobab of Madon) and lumping others together as "the northern kings" (v. 2). This sketchiness may reflect either the limited source materials available to the writer or simply his intention to focus the account on God's involvement and strategy for victory. Whatever the reason, his report successfully rounds out the book's conquest account.[4] One notable exception to the spare details is the geographical terms that identify places to which the defeated enemies flee (see below). Certainly, the political prominence of Hazor at the time marks its fall to Israel as a memorable moment.

With considerable skill, the writer pictures the battle as the decisive, stunning climax of the entire conquest. His particular concern is to bring a literary crescendo to one of the book's main themes — Joshua's attainment of Mosaic-like stature through exemplary, faithful leadership. Finally, the writer also provides something new, the book's lone theological explanation for the universal opposition to Israel among Canaan's monarchs (v. 20; cf. 2:3; 9:1–2; 10:1–5; cf. 5:1). In short, much remains to be done, but the author seizes the victory at Merom and its aftermath as the fitting moment to pause, albeit briefly, to voice satisfaction in God's blessings throughout the battles.

The Northern Campaign (11:1–15)

THE BATTLE OF MEROM (vv. 1–9). Like earlier narratives, this one opens with a report of the enemy's mustering for battle based on what they have "heard" of Israel's advances (vv. 1–5; cf. 5:1; 9:1; 10:1). Here the "hearer"

---

2. Nelson, *Joshua*, 151. The burning and plundering of Hazor (11:14), however, more closely compares to the treatment given Ai (8:27–28).

3. Cf. Campbell and O'Brien, *Unfolding the Deuteronomistic History*, 134, 136.

4. References to the "hill country of *Judah*" and the "hill country of *Israel*" (11:21) also imply a date of composition no earlier than the divided kingdom, since elsewhere the term is "hill country of *Ephraim*" (i.e., a tribal [not political] term); cf. 17:15; 19:50; 20:7; 21:21; 24:30, 33; et al.

is King Jabin of Hazor (cf. Judg. 4; Ps. 83:9[10]), a city-state ca. ten miles north of the Sea of Galilee in the southwest corner of the Huleh Valley.[5] In the late Bronze Age, Hazor undoubtedly was the largest, most influential city in all of Canaan. Its size was huge—200 acres, an estimated population of 30,000—and ideally situated for economic and political dominance:

> The north eastern [sic] branch of the via maris, which comes from Megiddo, leads via Hazor and forks here. The western connection leads north to Lebo Hamath and Kadesch [sic]. The eastern junction leads via the Jordan to Damascus, then … via Tadmor and Mari to Babylon. From Hazor roads lead to the Phoenician coast towards the north (Tyre and Sidon). There is an ancient connection to the south via Kinneret to Beth Shean. Hazor is like a fat spider in a wide-strung web. The strategic importance of this geographic position can hardly be overestimated.[6]

At the time Hazor controlled the entire northern Jordan Valley as far southeast as the Yarmuk River.[7] Its strategic location and hegemony over a wide swath of northern Canaan made Hazor an unavoidable Israelite target.[8] Precisely what Jabin has heard is unstated, but coming on the heels of chapter 10, the news probably concerns Israel's sweeping victories over the Amorites in the south. Like Adoni-Zedek (10:3), Jabin rallies other kings who presumably owe him fealty, dispatching messengers to King Jobab of Madon (cf. 12:19), the (unnamed) kings of Shimrom and Acshaph, and other (also unnamed) northern kings (11:1–2).

Where are these cities? Though disputes remain, Madon probably is Tel Qarnei Hittin, a site on the northern flank of the Horns of Hattin about

---

5. Jabin is the Hebrew form of Ibni, a known West Semitic name, and the Mari archives attest the name Jabin (or Jabni). Since Jabin was Hazor's king during Deborah's lifetime (Judg. 4; cf. Ps. 83:9[10]), "Jabin" may have been the dynastic name of Hazor's kings; cf. P. Benjamin, "Jabin," *ABD*, 3:595–96; Hess, "Non-Israelite Names," 206–7.

6. C. Schäfer-Lichtenberger, "Hazor—A City State Between the Major Powers," *SJOT* 15 (2001): 111; cf. A. Ben-Tor and T. Rubiato, "Excavating Hazor II: Did the Israelites Destroy the Canaanite City?" *BAR* 25 (May–June 1999): 24–25. Given the significant decline of the number and size of urban centers in the Late Bronze Age, Hazor's large size and population seems enigmatic. It represents "an abnormally large settlement," four times as large as Lachish, the land's second largest city; cf. Gonen, "Urban Canaan," 68.

7. Na'aman, *Borders and Districts*, 124; Amarna Letter (EA 364). Hazor lies seventeen miles south of Dan, the city that later marked Israel's northern border (Judg. 20:1; 2 Sam. 3:10). Both the Mari texts (eighteenth cent. B.C.) and the Amarna Letters (fourteenth cent. B.C.) picture Hazor as a prominent city-state.

8. The city was destroyed in the thirteenth cent. B.C., perhaps by the Israelites (Y. Yadin), the Sea Peoples (V. Fritz), Pharaoh Rameses II (C. Schäfer-Lichtenberger), or Deborah and Barak (Y. Aharoni); cf. J. M. Hamilton, "Hazor," *ABD*, 3:87.

five miles west of the Sea of Galilee.[9] By listing Madon first and by naming its king, the author presents Jobab as Hazor's most important vassal.[10] If Merom and Madon mark the same place, this city-state was prominent enough to make the list of kingdoms subject to Thutmose III (fifteenth cent. B.C.) and destroyed by Rameses II (thirteenth cent. B.C.).[11]

Acshaph probably lies in the plain of Acco at modern Tell Kisan, territory later allotted to the tribe of Asher (12:20; 19:25).[12] Though biblically unimportant outside of Joshua, its mention in various Egyptian texts confirms its political importance in ancient Canaan.[13] The prominent city-state of Shimron (sometimes Shimʿon; modern Khirbet Sammuniyeh) is located in the Jezreel Valley about seven miles northeast of Jokneam (five mi. west of Nazareth), the southeast corner of land later assigned to Zebulun (12:20; 19:15).[14] Like its allies, it also receives mention in Egyptian sources, an indication of its importance as a Canaanite kingdom at the time.[15]

More important, the locations of Acshaph and Shimron — both twenty-five to thirty miles southwest of Hazor across the rugged mountains of Galilee — attest the wide region that the kingdom of Hazor dominated. The powerful alliance of Hazor, Madon, Acshaph, and Shimron easily enlisted the region's lesser rulers ("the northern kings") to join their endeavor (v. 2). These lesser rulers hail from "the mountains" (probably areas surrounding the Jezreel Valley), from the Jordan Rift Valley south of the Sea of Galilee, the western foothills, and the far west (Naphoth Dor; v. 2).[16] An important Canaanite seaport, Naphoth Dor lies in the Sharon Plain twelve

---

9. Naʾaman, *Borders and Districts*, 119, 120 (cf. his full discussion [119–43]); Boling, *Joshua*, 305; Hess, *Joshua*, 209. For "Madon" LXX and Syriac have *marron*, which compares to "Meron" (vv. 5, 7).

10. Hess, *Joshua*, 208.

11. *ANET*, 243, 256.

12. Naʾaman, *Borders and Districts*, 123, 141.

13. At Karnak Thutmose III (fifteenth cent. B.C.) lists Acshaph among the kingdoms under his domain (*ANET*, 242), and the city also receives mention in the Execration Texts (*ANET*, 329, n.8, along with Hazor) and in two Amarna letters (*ANET*, 484, 487).

14. Naʾaman, *Borders and Districts*, 141; cf. P. Benjamin, "Shimron (Place)," *ABD*, 5:1218.

15. Cf. Amarna Letters EA 225 and 367 (Hess, *Joshua*, 209, n.3). Another letter relates that the prince of Shimron conspired with the king of Acco to attack and plunder a Babylonian caravan at Hannathon in Galilee; cf. Benjamin, "Shimron (Place)," 5:1218.

16. Usually, "western foothills" (Heb. *šepelah*) designates a specific region of Judah, the transitional slopes and intersecting valleys between the central mountains and the coastal plain. Here, however, the reference is probably either to the low hills between the hill country of Samaria and the Carmel Range (today, Ramot Manasseh) or (more likely) the north-south foothills between the mountains of western Galilee and the coastal plain of Tyre in southern Lebanon; cf. D. Brodsky, "Shephelah (Place)," *ABD*, 5:1204.

miles south of Carmel.[17] Roughly, the total territory of the northern kings extends north from the mountains between Dor and the Jordan Valley and north to Upper Galilee above Hazor.

Ethnically, the entire army features Canaanites from the west coast and Jordan Valley (lit., "from east and from west"), four peoples from the central mountains (Amorites, Hittites, Perizzites, and Jebusites), and Hivites from somewhere south of Mount Hermon (i.e., northeast of Hazor; v. 3).[18] Notwithstanding the lack of details (cf. ch. 10), the text clearly locates the episode geographically as northern. Technically, two peoples listed are usually reckoned as southern (Hittites, Jebusites), but here the author probably draws on a typical list of Canaan's peoples to underscore the large size of the force being mustered.[19]

Skillfully, the writer traces developments leading up to the impending battle. All the above kings answer the summons of Jabin; each leaves his home base with his entire army (v. 4). Briefly, the author emphasizes the vast size and frightening technology of the gathering force. The threefold repetition of the Hebrew word *rab* ("much, many, great"), the last climactically emphatic (*rab-me'od*, "a *very* great [number]"), presents it as "a huge [*rab*] army." It numbers as many (*rab*) soldiers as there are sand grains on the seashore, along with "a large number" of horses and chariots.[20]

This marks the debut of horses and chariots in Joshua — an ominous note for poor Israel, who faces the enemy on foot. Of course, horses and chariots are precisely the technological superiority enjoyed by Pharaoh at the Red Sea, and look what happened to him! The kings and their forces rendezvous ("joined forces") and bivouac together at the Waters of Merom (v. 5), the staging area from which they will launch an attack on Israel somewhere farther south. The location of the Waters of Merom remains uncer-

---

17. P. Benjamin, "Naphoth-Dor (Place)," *ABD*, 4:1020. Napthoth-Dor means either "dune/district of Dor" or (if in the language of the Sea Peoples) "wooded country of Dor"—the equivalent of Hebrew "Dor of Sharon."

18. Other texts also locate the Canaanites in the west, including the coast, and in the Jordan Valley (Num. 13:29; Deut. 11:30; Josh. 5:1), the Amorites and Perizzites in the central mountains (Deut. 1:7; Josh. 10:5; 13:2–4; 16:10; 17:15), and the Hivites in the Lebanon mountains (Judg. 3:3). The Hittites appear in narratives at Hebron (Gen. 23) and Beersheba (Gen. 26:34; 27:46), both in the central mountains (Beersheba at their southern edge). The Jebusites reside in their fortress-city of Jebus (i.e., Jerusalem), also part of the central mountains (Num. 13:29; Josh. 15:8, 63; Judg. 1:21).

19. Of course, it is also possible that, for reasons unknown to us, clans of the Hittites and Jebusites resided in the north, thus explaining their inclusion by the writer.

20. For other references to Canaanites and chariots, see Josh. 17:16, 18; Judg. 4:3. Amarna Letter RA 19 mentions the prince of Acshaph as one of two leaders who provided fifty chariots for a rebellion against the local Egyptian ruler (*ANET*, 487).

tain, but the evidence slightly favors a spring near modern Tell el-Khirbeh, the suggested site for Merom ca. fourteen miles northwest of Hazor in the highlands of Upper Galilee.[21]

The reader rightly imagines a dramatic scene around the Merom spring: a huge military force determined to stop Israel's advance into Galilee. Verses 1–5 create the impression that everyone has come from everywhere—and with frightening firepower. The reader knows that this scene is no mere "show-of-force" to intimidate Israel. The biggest battle—the dramatic denouement of the entire conquest—is about to begin. The result could be Canaan's last stand or Israel's final triumph.

Suddenly, the text ushers the reader to the Israelite side at an unknown location. The unexpected change signals that the anticipated battle is about to begin at last (vv. 6–15). The narrative assumes that Joshua knows the enemy's moves, because Yahweh opens the battle report with a word of assurance, a promise, and an instruction for Joshua (v. 6). The assurance and promise echo similar reassuring statements given before the battles of Ai and Gibeon (8:1; 10:8): "Do not be afraid of them because by this time tomorrow I will hand all of them over to Israel, slain" (11:6; cf. 6:1).[22]

But the wording ("by this time tomorrow," "all," and "slain") gives the present promise immediacy and certainty. Unlike Yahweh's instructions before battles at Jericho (6:2–5) and Ai (8:1–2, 18), here they concern not the battle proper (the victory is his to achieve) but the mop-up afterward.[23] Once Israel finds the enemy "slain" (lit., "pierced") right before their eyes, they are to put the previously ominous horses and chariots permanently out of commission. The horses are to be hamstrung and the chariots burned, the typical way in warfare both ancient and modern to disable both. Since these actions follow the enemy's retreat, they symbolize the overwhelming

---

21. *CBA*, 54–55. The campaign reports of Thutmose III (*ANET*, 243), Rameses II (*ANET*, 256), and Tiglath-Pileser (*ANET*, 283) mention Merom, and Rameses' report suggests this vicinity. If so, as Liid notes, "Merom held a strategic place in the control of Canaanite upper Galilee"; cf. D. C. Liid, "Merom, Waters of (Place)," *ABD*, 4:705. Other scholars favor the spring just north of Tel Qarnei Hittin in Wadi el-Hamam; cf. Naʾaman, *Borders and Districts*, 126; Hess, *Joshua*, 211.

22. They also echo Moses' words to all Israel (Deut. 20:1). Younger (*Ancient Conquest Accounts*, 229) compares 11:6 to the Zakkur text with its oracle of Baʿalshamayn to the king: "Do not be afraid because I have made you king, and I will stand with you, and I will deliver you from all these kings who have raised a siege against you." Unlike the latter, however, in Joshua 11:6 Yahweh promises to "deliver the enemy into Israel's hands."

23. Yahweh also had instructed Joshua concerning the crossing of the Jordan (3:7–8; 4:2–3, 17), on that occasion more directly than in the later battles.

victory won.[24] So, Joshua and the whole Israelite army take the offensive (v. 7), launching a surprise attack as they did at Gibeon (cf. 10:9). It catches the enemy camp off-duty, unprepared for battle. If the location of Merom proposed above is correct, the Israelites may have suddenly fallen upon the unsuspecting soldiers from the highland forests near their campsite.[25]

True to his word, Yahweh gives the coalition troops into Israel's hands (v. 8). Israelite soldiers rout them and chase the retreating enemy in two directions. Some Israelites pursue them northwest ca. twenty miles, later branching into two subgroups. One subgroup goes as far as "Greater Sidon," the coastal region above the Litani River dominated by the powerful city-state of Sidon (cf. 19:28). The other subgroup chases the enemy to a coastal town on Greater Sidon's southern border, Misrephoth Maim (lit., "lime kilns by the water"), probably modern Khirbet Musheirefeh at the northern end of the Plain of Acco.[26]

A second Israelite band heads northeast from Merom into the Valley of Mizpeh, probably a valley ca. twenty miles away in the Lebanon Mountains east of the Litani.[27] (Apparently, Israel has blocked all escape routes to the south.) Relentlessly, Israel strikes the fleeing enemy "until no survivors were left," the latter phrase a formulaic echo of chapter 10 and typically deuteronomic (10:28, 30, 33, 37, 39, 40; cf. 8:22; Num. 21:35; Deut. 2:34; 3:3; 2 Kings 10:11). The northern coalition has suffered the same disastrous fate as its southern counterpart.

To close the scene, the author stresses that Joshua does to them precisely what Yahweh commanded (v. 9), thereby sounding a theme heard earlier—Joshua's unwavering obedience to Yahweh.[28] The object-first word order makes the point emphatically: "Their *horses* he hamstrung and their *chariots* he burned with fire" (my translation). The reader imagines a scene of fire, rising smoke, hobbled warhorses, and no enemy in sight. Israel owns the battlefield—a great victory, indeed!

---

24. To "hamstring" is piel of Heb. ʿaqar ("to tear out by the roots"); cf. Gen. 49:6; 2 Sam. 8:4=1 Chron. 18:4. Today one hamstrings horses by severing the large tendon above the hoof at the back of the lower leg; a similar practice is in mind here.

25. D. C. Liid, "Merom," *ABD*, 4:705. This forest may be the "forest of the Gentiles" (cf. Judg. 4:16) in upper Galilee's southern highlands.

26. P. Benjamin, "Misrepoth-Maim," *ABD*, 4:873. Alternatively, Misrephoth Maim may designate the Litani River itself; cf. *CBA*, 54. Benjamin also acknowledges the latter possibility.

27. *CBA*, 54. This location is uncertain, however. "Mizpah" ("watchtower"?) could also designate a city either east or way north of Merom; cf. P. M. Arnold, "Mizpah (Place)," *ABD*, 4:881.

28. The same formula reports Joshua's obedience of Moses (Ex. 17:10) and Balak's of Balaam (Num. 23:30). The command-and-obedience pattern—God commanding and Joshua executing—is typical of chapters 1, 3–4, 6, and 8.

Special notice: Hazor (vv. 10–11). Sometime later,[29] Joshua "turns back" from wherever he is (e.g., chasing enemy troops, disabling their horses and chariots, etc.) and captures the city of Hazor (v. 10). The combination of "turn" (*šub*) and "capture" (*lakad*) echoes the language of 10:38–39, the report of the last southern city to fall (Debir). The shared terminology links the two-city conquest scenes literarily (i.e., Conquest Phases I and II) and also marks the fall of Hazor as the battle's climatic event.[30] Given the gigantic importance of Hazor in antiquity, the short chiastic headline—(lit.) "[he] captured Hazor" // its king [he] killed"—smacks of stunning understatement!

The writer quickly explains that Hazor fell not because of an Israelite preemptive strike but because of its long-standing, regional dominance ("head of all these kingdoms").[31] The remark implies that Hazor sustained its lengthy, regional hegemony (see vv. 1–3) by violent oppression of its underlings—and that here Hazor finally receives its just desserts for the bloodshed. Its demise ends the last bastion of Canaanite rule—a very, very big deal for Israel—and inaugurates the Israelite period.

The narrator tells the story behind the headline in a slow-paced, solemn statement and restatement that weave in key wording from chapter 10 (11:11). Together they picture the treatments of north and south as identical. With swords Israel (lit.) "struck down" everyone in Hazor as *herem* (*haram* hi.), leaving no survivors (cf. 10:28, 30, 32, 35, 37).[32] Also, Hazor shares a dubious distinction with Jericho and Ai: It is only the third city in Canaan that Joshua sets ablaze (cf. 6:24; 8:28).

Conclusion (vv. 12–15). The other cities and kings suffered the same fate as Hazor (v. 12).[33] This is what Moses commanded, the writer adds (cf. Deut. 20:16–18), and he alone (so far) bears this unique title of the highest authority ("the servant of the LORD").[34] Again, the narrator sounds

---

29. Heb. *ba'et hahi'* ("at that time") approximates the chronology ("about that time") between the battle proper, the mop-up scene, and the event to follow; cf. 5:2; 6:26; 11:21.

30. Other linguistic echoes of ch. 10: "its [X-city's] king" (10:28, 30, 37, 39) and "put to the sword" (10:28, 30, 32, 35, 37, 39)

31. Heb. *lepanim* ("before, time past"). Unfortunately, the NIV is vague ("Hazor had been the head ...") and fails to convey this nuance. The defeat of Hazor's army undoubtedly would have left the city defenseless and vulnerable to attack. Interestingly, EA 228 uses the phrase "Hazor together with its other cities," presuming it to be a kind of capital over a region of cities.

32. The vocabulary of annihilation here clearly concerns the *herem* tradition (Deut. 7:2; 20:16–17).

33. Literarily, the object-first syntax in v. 12 (cf. vv. 10–11) reintroduces the other defeated powers after the focus on Hazor, links their fate to its fate, and signals that they fell about the same time as their "head."

34. In fact, Moses, Joshua, and David are the only Old Testament characters to bear it. For more on the title, see comments at 24:29–32.

one of the book's main themes, Joshua (and Israel's) completion of Moses' mandates (cf. v. 15; 1:7, 13; 4:10, 12; 8:30–33; 20:2; 21:2, 8; 22:2).

But two exceptions limit the destruction carried out here (v. 13).[35] (1) Israel does not burn any northern cities built atop mounds except for Hazor, with whose destruction the writer credits Joshua. Presumably, this proviso leaves the Israelites ready-made cities in Galilee in which to settle after the land distribution. (2) Language echoing the same provision at Ai (8:2, 27) permits Israel to keep for their own personal use plunder (i.e., food, clothes, pottery, valuables, etc.) and livestock from the cities (v. 14).[36]

But, again, object-first word order underscores an exception even to this provision: Israel cannot keep any humans. Instead, "all the people" suffer the same fate as their armies (v. 8) exactly as their counterparts in the south (10:28, 30, 33, 37, 39, 40). Israel strikes them down with the sword until they are wiped out—precisely what the Gibeonites had feared (9:24)—not sparing "anyone that breathed" (lit., "all breath"). The reader imagines cities everywhere "breathless"—empty, silent, void of the rhythmic respiration-pulse of human activity.

A concluding comment retraces the historical chain of command that authorized the above scene (v. 15). Yahweh commanded Moses, Moses commanded Joshua, and Joshua did it. Indeed, the writer stresses, he did it perfectly: "He left nothing undone" of what Yahweh had commanded Moses. With unswerving devotion, he fully executed his divine commission (1:7), anticipating David's similar obedience (1 Kings 15:15; cf. Deut. 28:14). Fittingly, the conquest enterprise that began with Joshua now ends with a brief word of commendation for his faithful service to Yahweh (cf. v. 23). He achieves the stature in Israel that Yahweh promised him (3:7).

In Praise of Joshua: Conquest Summary (11:16–23)

TO CELEBRATE THE STATURE of Joshua, the narrator now summarizes his impressive accomplishments (vv. 16–23; cf. 10:40–42). "Joshua took this entire land," a claim that verse 23 repeats almost verbatim, thus bracketing vv. 21–23 with an inclusio. What the young spies excitedly told Joshua before Jericho had come true (2:24).[37]

Geographical summary (vv. 16–17a). A survey of Canaan's major geographical regions asserts the extent of Joshua's conquests. It seems to reflect

---

35. For the restrictive use of *raq* ("except") in Joshua, see vv. 14, 22; 6:17, 24; 8:2, 27; WO §39.3.5c. For wider usage, cf. Gen. 47:42; Ex. 8:7; 9:26; Deut. 2:35, 37.

36. The language also echoes a similar provision in Deut. 20:14 concerning the treatment of cities outside Canaan proper that refuse Israel's offer of peace. The lone difference is that the latter permits the keeping of women and children.

37. "Took (*laqaḥ*) the land" contrasts with "struck (*nakah* NIV "subdued") the land" in 10:40.

a Judahite perspective, beginning with a traditional southern survey that echoes verse 2 (e.g., Deut. 1:7; cf. 10:40): the central mountains (*hahar* "the hill country"), the whole Negev (the southern desert), all the land of Goshen (see comments on 10:41; cf. 15:51), the western foothills (*šepelah*), and the Arabah (the Jordan Rift Valley).

The author then tacks on two general northern references, "the mountains (*hahar*) of Israel" (a term used only here and in v. 21) and their foothills (*šepelah*). He invokes a typical "from X to Y" schema to trace the sweep of the land from border to border (v. 17a). It begins way south at Mount Halak (ca. thirty miles southeast of Beersheba; cf. 12:7) that ascends eastward to Seir (i.e., Edom) and reaches way north to "Baal Gad in the Valley of Lebanon" (the modern Beqaꞌ Valley), a town apparently north of Israelite Dan and "below" (i.e., northwest of) Mount Hermon.[38]

Noticeable by their absence are the coastal plain and details about Galilee, the latter all the more unusual since the battle report above takes place there. The latter two regions will dominate the list of Canaan's unconquered areas (Josh. 13:1 – 7), and the silence here may reflect similar awareness that they have eluded conquest. This chapter's closing summary anticipates the even more comprehensive conclusion in 21:43 – 45.

An interpretive surprise (vv. 17b – 20). Clearly, Joshua is the author's main interest, but he also has an interpretive surprise up his sleeve. In the narrative, it is Israel who does everything,[39] but as Joshua's unique, memorable act the author singles out his capture and execution of enemy kings (v. 17b).[40] Those moments befit his role as commander-in-chief, but they also serve further to enhance his stature in Israel's eyes (cf. 3:7; 6:27) and to encourage the people that Yahweh truly is on their side (cf. 10:25). That Joshua battled all these kings "for a long time" attests his persistence and perseverance in pursuit of Yahweh's plan (v. 18).

But, the writer adds, the ultimate reason for the long conquest is the Canaanite kings' refusal to seek peace[41] with the Israelites: Not one city (except

---

38. *CBA*, 69; R. H. Smith, "Lebanon," *ABD*, 4:269.

39. They fall on the enemy (v. 7b), receive the victory from Yahweh (v. 8a; cf. v. 6), strike blows and chase the retreating enemy (v. 8), kill Hazor's inhabitants (v. 11), burn no other cities (v. 13a), seize plunder and livestock (v. 14a), and annihilate everyone that breathes (v. 14b).

40. Cf. vv. 10, 12; 8:29 (Ai); 10:26 (5 kings), 28 (Makkedah), 30 (Libnah), 32 (Lachish). According to ch. 11, he also led Israel to Merom (v. 7), did the chariot-burning and hamstringing that Yahweh ordered (vv. 6b, 9), and captured and burned Hazor (vv. 10, 13b). Interestingly, ch. 10 credits the Israelites with the royal executions at Eglon (10:35), Hebron (10:37), and Debir (10:39).

41. Heb. *šalem* hi., lit., "to make complete"; cf. G. Gerleman, "שָׁלֵם," *THAT*, 2:925 – 26; P. J. Nel, "שָׁלֵם," *NIDOTTE*, 4:131; Deut. 20:12; Josh. 10:1, 4; 2 Sam. 10:19; 1 Kings 22:45[44].

for the Hivites of Gibeon) did so. That explains why the Israelites have to take all of them militarily (v. 19). This is a startling statement, for it applies Moses' instruction on making peace with cities outside Canaan (Deut. 20:10–15) to peoples inside it, something Moses expressly forbad (vv. 16–17).[42] Further, the reports of conquest in Joshua 11 echo its language, implying that Israel's actions obey it. Even more important, the author now springs the chapter's real surprise (v. 20)—something truly new—the book's only theological explanation for why Canaan's kings universally opposed Israel.

In short, God did it (lit., "from the LORD it was" [emphatic word order]).[43] He himself stiffened their resolve (lit., "hardened their hearts") to meet Israel in battle. The same phrase describes how Yahweh hardened Pharaoh's heart to not release the Israelites (Ex. 4:21; 10:20, 27; 9:12; 11:10; 14:4, 8, 17). A person with a "hard heart" is intractable, obdurate, stubbornly resistant to outside influences.[44] The intended result of this Canaanite obduracy was to "destroy them totally" (Heb. *ḥaram* hi.)—to carry out the religious slaughter of "the ban." The cries of the Canaanites to God for mercy fell on deaf divine ears because he intended their annihilation, just what Yahweh had commanded Moses (Deut. 7:2; 20:16–17).[45]

Now, the claim about heart-hardening by God raises some important questions, questions to be dealt with in the Bridging Contexts section. For now, the point of the text must be grasped: The Canaanites could have escaped disaster by making peace with Israel, but they refused because Yahweh steeled their resolve to attack instead. By the same token, the comment also implies that God did *not* harden the heart of the Hivites of Gibeon, leaving them free to seek peace rather than rally for war. Theologically, the comment suggests divine awareness of the Hivites' inclination in that direction, an inclination that God permits to run its course. Indeed, it seems tantamount to an act of divine grace toward an otherwise condemned people. In short, amid the dark horrors of war and *ḥerem* a small candle of mercy shines on a group of humans whose attitude pleases God.

Special notice: the Anakites (vv. 21–22). Finally, the chapter concludes with a special notice concerning the Anakites (vv. 21–23). About the same time as the above events ("at that time"; cf. 5:2; 6:26), Joshua also destroys (lit., "cuts off") the Anakites from the southern central mountains (v. 21; see comment at v. 2). They apparently did not attack Israel or

---

42. Deut. 20:15 stipulates: "This is how you are to treat all the cities that are at a distance from you and do not belong to the nations nearby."

43. For similar statements, see Judg. 14:4; 2 Kings 6:33; Ps. 118:23; Mic. 1:12; Hab. 2:13.

44. F. Hesse, "חָזַק," *TDOT*, 4:308; R. Wakely, "חָזַק," *NIDOTTE*, 2:70.

45. T. E. Fretheim, "חָנַן,"*NIDOTTE*, 2:204: "The nom. *teḥinnah* and *taḥanun* almost always refer to supplications for favor made to God (usually) and human beings."

conspire with others to do so, so their fame and iconic status in Israelite memory probably motivate Joshua's action.

The Anakites were descendants of Anak son of Arba (Josh. 15:13) and, ultimately, of the fabled Nephilim (Num. 13:33; cf. Gen. 6:4).[46] Their stunning height and gigantic size had especially terrified the Israelite spies (Num. 13:28; Deut. 1:28; 2:10, 21; 9:2, 3).[47] The author underscores the completeness of the destruction, listing the areas from which Joshua cut off these long-dreaded enemies. The Bible locates the main concentration of Anakites in and around their capital at Hebron in southern Canaan (Gen. 23:2; 35:27), and the list of three cities (Hebron, Debir, Anab) and the "hill country of Judah" fit that picture.[48] But the Bible nowhere else locates Anakites in the "hill country of Israel" (see v. 16), so the writer may be invoking the word pair "hill country of Judah and ... Israel" as hyperbole to underscore the comprehensiveness of the destruction.[49]

Joshua "totally destroyed" them and their cities under the "ban" (*ḥaram* hi.), just as he had the northern coalition (cf. v. 20). Whether he burned the Anakite towns as he did Jericho, Ai, and Hazor (6:24; 8:28; 11:11) is not stated, but the results are devastating (v. 22): No Anakites survive except in Gaza, Gath, and Ashdod, three Philistine cities along the Mediterranean where they either lived or fled for refuge.[50] The mention of Gath is significant: It anticipates the later debut of Goliath, who (along with other giants) presumably descended from the Anakite remnant in Philistia (1 Sam. 17:4, 8, 23; 2 Sam. 21:16–22; cf. 1 Chron. 20:4–8).[51]

---

46. Cf. E. C. B. MacLaurin, "Anak/Anaks," *VT* 15 (1965): 468–74, who suggests that Heb. *ʿanaq* is not a proper name but a Philistine word designating an official position (cf. Gk. *anax*).

47. The Egyptian Execration Texts (*ANET*, 328–29) identify several princes with Semitic names as rulers of *Iy-ʿanaq*. The latter might be a tribal name somehow related to the Anakites, or (more likely) the name of a town or settlement of clans; so E. Lipiński, "ʿAnaq-Kiryat ʾArbaʿ-Hébron et ses sanctuaires tribaux," *VT* 24 (1974): 47; cf. also G. L. Mattingly, "Anak (Person)," *ABD*, 1:222. For Caleb's later expulsion of them from their capital city of Hebron, see 14:12–15; 15:13–14; Judg. 1:10.

48. Hebron and Debir are also among the Anakite cities taken later by Caleb (Josh. 15:14–15). Hebron's ancient name, Kiriath Arba (lit., "city of Arba"), implies that Arba founded it; cf. Josh. 14:15; 15:13.

49. The term "hill country of Israel" (*har yiśraʾel*) is itself unusual, occurring only here and in v. 16. It implies that the author writes sometime after the onset of the divided kingdom (late tenth cent. B.C.).

50. Joshua apparently did not attack them there, but the cities do play a minor role in the book. In 10:41, Gaza marked the western boundary of Joshua's conquest (cf. 15:47), and 11:22 marks the biblical debut of Gath (cf. Judg. 6:11; 1 Sam 5:8; et al.) and Ashdod (cf. Josh. 15:46, 47; 1 Sam. 5:1, 5).

51. Mattingly, "Anak (Person)," 1:222.

"**The end**" (v. 23). With this long-dreaded enemy gone, Joshua's triumph is now complete. Again, the author reaffirms that "Joshua took the entire land" just as Yahweh commanded Moses (cf. vv. 15, 21). By this, the author means that he has faithfully executed the *ḥerem* or ritual destruction of the land's inhabitants (v. 23; cf. Deut. 7; 20).[52] Further, to round out his encomium to Joshua, the writer adds that Joshua gives the land as an inheritance to Israel "according to their tribal divisions" (cf. Josh. 12:7). This comment seems slightly out of place since the land distribution report comes later (chs. 13–19). Perhaps it formed part of the author's original source and could not be excluded. Thematically, it does anticipate the book's second half, the settlement narrative and its inheritance theme, and thus helps unify the book's two halves.

A closing rings down the curtain on the conquest narrative (chs. 1–11): "Then the land had rest [*šaqaṭ* "be quiet"] from war," which introduces the quiet that will allow the settlement (chs. 13–24) to proceed peacefully. Later, the DH will again invoke the phrase to end the report of Caleb's defeat of the Anakites (15:14) and to set off phases of the era of the judges (Judg. 3:11, 30; 5:31; 8:28; 18:7). Israel will not enjoy its final, complete "rest" (a different word) until each tribe has received its inheritance land (see Josh. 21:43–45).[53]

The present campaign had been long and grueling, but in Yahweh's mighty power Joshua has won the victory at last. The "quiet" gives Israel a chance to rest, replenish supplies, reconnoiter the land, and think about the future. They can now "beat their swords into plowshares and their spears into pruning hooks." They can stop being soldiers and start being farmers, vineyard owners, and cultivators of fruit trees.

 FOUR IMPORTANT MATTERS MERIT follow up in transition to the Contemporary Significance section: a summary of the archaeology of Hazor, further discussion concerning the Canaanite kings, comments about the portrayal of Joshua, and a closing glimpse on the "rest from war."

The archaeology of Hazor. It is clear that after a long, prestigious history, Canaanite Hazor suffered a violent, fiery destruction sometime in the thirteenth century B.C. But the identity of its destroyers, including the rele-

---

52. Repetition of *ḥaram* hi. ("to destroy totally") weaves a thematic thread through the chapter (vv. 11, 12, 20, 21).

53. For more on this phrase, see Bridging Contexts below.

vance of Joshua 11 to the question, remains a matter of scholarly dispute.[54] Two centuries later (eleventh cent. B.C.), a new population of unknown size settled on the vacant site, but it occupied only ten acres of Hazor's western hill. Its evidently short stay left behind comparatively meager architectural remains, most prominently many round pits three by five feet in diameter and depth that probably served for disposal of refuse.[55] The pottery styles from this period differ significantly from the Canaanite tradition of the previous occupiers and suggest inhabitants of a different ethnic group. Further, the new arrivals apparently lived in tents and temporary structures — an encampment of transients rather than long-term residents. Later, they vacated the site voluntarily, since it shows no evidence of destruction.

Ben-Ami tentatively interprets this settlement as one of the temporary Israelite camps evident in Joshua and Judges (e.g., Gilgal [Josh. 2−10], Shiloh [Josh. 18:1−10; Judg. 21:12], and Dan's two camps [Judg. 13:25; 18:12]). From biblical evidence he speculates that the site may represent an early settlement of the tribe of Naphtali or a group of tribes. If so, the term "camp of Israel" (e.g., Josh. 6:18, 23; 18:9) may reflect part of the historical reality of how the Israelites settled: encampments as preparation for and transition to permanent settlement.[56]

But Ben-Ami also observes an especially striking phenomenon. Typically, subsequent settlements raise their buildings on earlier foundations and reutilize building materials and walls left by former residents. At Hazor, however, both the Israelite encampment and the later Israelite city (ca. 950 B.C.) do nothing with the ruined Canaanite palace in their midst. He suggests that both may have believed it to be under a curse or ban, a belief that persisted over several centuries.[57] In short, the archaeological picture of Hazor comprises three phases: the Canaanite city that ended violently (thirteenth cent. B.C.), two centuries without occupation, a short-term

---

54. D. Ben-Ami, a colleague of the present excavator (A. Ben-Tor), argued from recent archaeological evidence that Hazor had already been destroyed when Israel arrived; cf. D. Ben-Ami, "The Iron Age I at Hazor in Light of the Renewed Excavations," *IEJ* 51/2 (2001): 168−69. In two earlier articles, Ben-Tor affirmed the Israelites (or perhaps proto-Israelites) as the most likely destroyers of Hazor as Joshua 11 claims, a view also held by his predecessor, Yigael Yadin; cf. A. Ben-Tor and T. Rubiato, "Excavating Hazor II: Did the Israelites Destroy the Canaanite City?" *BAR* 25 (May−June 1999): 36; idem, "Excavating Hazor I: Solomon's City Rises from the Ashes," *BAR* 25 (March−April 1999): 26−37, 60; and Y. Yadin, *Hazor* (London: Oxford Univ. Press, 1972), 108. For other views, see Schäfer-Lichtenberger, "Hazor," 116.

55. Ben-Ami, "The Iron Age I at Hazor," 165−66. Cf. also D. Ben-Ami, "Early Iron Cult Places — New Evidences from Tel Hazor," *Tel Aviv* 33/2 (2006): 121−33.

56. Ben-Ami, "The Iron Age I at Hazor," 169−70.

57. Ibid., 167−68.

Israelite encampment (eleventh cent. B.C.), and a permanent Israelite city (tenth to eighth cent. B.C.).

Now, the question is: Did the Israelites destroy Canaanite Hazor? Ben-Ami denies any cause-and-effect relationship between that destruction and the later Israelite encampment. He assumes (without apparent rationale, in my view) no connection between the two parties and, in effect, denies that the destroyers were Israelites. His view is that the biblical author wrote Joshua 11 as an etiology—simply to explain how the once-great city of Hazor became well-known, impressive ruins.[58] However, Ben-Ami rightly allows another possible scenario—that the city's destroyers and later encampment occupants were both Israelite groups, albeit centuries apart.

In my view, Ben-Ami's suggestion concerning the curse or *ḥerem* ban might provide the link between them. If, as he suggests, the populace maintained such a belief, later Israelite settlers would likely have known it, too. One could imagine, for example, the possibility that an oral tradition about the destruction passed down from earlier Israelites, perhaps even from the destroyers themselves. At present, certainty eludes us in the matter, and the continuing excavation may require revisions, but my inclination is toward the second of Ben-Ami's two proposed scenarios.[59]

Hard-hearted Canaanite kings. Once again the reader confronts a scene of widespread death and destruction done in God's name. Joshua 11, however, lays the blame at the feet of Canaan's kings. In Gamaliel's words, they were "fighting God" (Acts 5:39). They all represented the old order of Canaan: city-states, each ruled by a prince or king but still subject to the Egyptian pharaoh until the mid-twelfth cent. B.C. Each city-state held sway over territory and small villages in the surrounding countryside. Occasionally, they squabbled with the others for their own benefit (and perhaps to curry Egypt's favor).[60]

Each dynasty required taxation of the populace to support it, usually in the form of grain, wine, oils, and other goods, but occasionally slaves were also drafted for royal service. As part of the Egyptian empire, local rulers had to pay the required periodic tribute to staff Egyptian farms and vineyards within Canaan, and on demand to supply the Egyptian home-

---

58. Ibid., 168, 169.

59. For more on the archaeology of Hazor, see the Bridging Contexts section of ch. 12. The archaeological picture presented above seems to leave no obvious historical period for the other, presumably later, battle involving Hazor (Judg. 4). Since excavations continue there, however, it seems wise, first, to face that a problem exists and, second, to withhold judgment on the apparent conflict between Josh. 11 and Judg. 4 until the digging ends and a scholarly consensus emerges concerning the history of Hazor.

60. Kuhrt, *The Ancient Near East*, 1:318, 326; cf. EA 354.

land with highly valued goods.[61] The local leaders felt strong pressure to meet royal demands, whether local or Egyptian, and so did the populace. Our knowledge of pre-Israelite Canaan is limited, but the general situation seems a good seedbed for abusive oppression of ordinary people. Even without such injustices, however, the fact is that God had decreed the death of the old order and the birth of a new one (Josh. 2−11). Canaan's rulers opposed that new order and so set themselves to "fighting God." The issue was whether or not they would submit to God's authority.

As noted above, the narrator explains why the kings of Canaan went down to defeat (v. 20): Yahweh "hardened their hearts" to attack Israel and suffer certain doom. Literarily, this motif echoes the same divine scheme against Pharaoh and links the Exodus and Conquest as two triumphs of Yahweh within a single larger plan (cf. Josh. 4:23−24; Ps. 114:3−6). But this explanation may trouble modern readers, as John Goldingay says:

> Making the king resistant ... could suggest that the king is Yhwh's toy, to be manipulated in such a way as to serve Yhwh's purpose, without regard for his personal desires. Is Yhwh playing mind games, or working like a hypnotist who gets people to do something they would not otherwise do by planting ideas in their subconscious minds that they would not otherwise generate, or treating the king like a computer to be programmed at will?[62]

Did the kings have no choice in the matter? Did God manipulate them into doing something against their wishes? If so, is that not unfair to the kings? Given God's character, how could he simply railroad them to disobey his will? Indeed, at first glance, the kings seem faced with a no-win situation: If they do nothing, Israel will annihilate them anyway, but if they attack they face certain defeat by Yahweh.

In response, Goldingay carefully reviews the scenario in Exodus. The underlying issue, he argues, is the authority of Yahweh: "Is the king of Egypt the great sovereign, or is the God of Israel?"[63] From the outset God knows that he will inevitably have to compel Pharaoh to let Israel go (Ex. 3:19), so he declares upfront his intention to strengthen Pharaoh's resolve to not release Israel. He does this so that, in the end, he may kill Pharaoh's firstborn son for his refusal to free Yahweh's firstborn son, Israel (Ex. 4:21−23). To demonstrate his superiority—that is, to get Pharaoh to

---

61. Kuhrt, *The Ancient Near East*, 1:328.

62. J. Goldingay, *Israel's Gospel* (Old Testament Theology 1; Downers Grove, Ill.: Inter-Varsity Press, 2006), 353.

63. Ibid., 350.

acknowledge "that there is no one like me in all the earth" (Ex. 9:14) — Yahweh chooses through the plagues "to maneuver the king [Pharaoh] into acting stupidly."[64]

One might add that their stupidity betrays a blind self-confidence born of a deadly delusion — the conviction that they can beat Yahweh at any game. In the case of Joshua 1 – 11, Yahweh also launches Israel's invasion to demonstrate his superiority ("so that all the peoples of the earth might know that the hand of the LORD is powerful" [Josh. 4:24]) and to force the kings of Canaan similarly to "act stupidly."

Further, Goldingay observes an interesting pattern in the plague narrative. Twice Yahweh declares his intention to stiffen Pharaoh's resolve (Ex. 4:21; 7:3), but a series of subsequent statements report that "Pharaoh hardened his heart" or "his heart was tough" (e.g., Ex. 7:13, 14, 22; 8:15[11], 19[15], 32[28]; 9:7, 34, 35). These statements reveal strong symptoms of stupid, royal resistance and willfulness, after which later comments add that "Yahweh stiffened [Pharaoh's] resolve" (10:1, 20, 27; 11:10; cf. also 9:12). In short, the latter acts serve to firm up the stupidity toward which Pharaoh was inclined on his own and also to punish him. This is the key point: The juxtaposition of Yahweh-hardened and Pharaoh-hardened reports implies that things are turning out just as Yahweh anticipated, not that Yahweh caused them. The very juxtaposition cleverly "draws attention to the mystery about human stupidity."[65] Goldingay concludes:

> [Yhwh's] decision stands as the background to what happens, yet it does not force people to take a path they would not otherwise have taken. Even if Yhwh had done nothing, the opening of Exodus suggests that the king likely had quite enough stupidity to resist a change of policy. So Pharaoh is responsible for his acts, yet they take place within Yhwh's purpose.[66]

Now, the book of Joshua has nothing like the rich, detailed narrative tracing the face-off between Yahweh and Pharaoh. But Goldingay's discussion nevertheless illumines the claim of divine hardening in Joshua 11:20. Yahweh's decision to have Israel invade Canaan forces the kings of the land to respond according to their natural inclination — either to acknowledge Yahweh's authority or to fight back. A pattern soon emerges in the book: Each Israelite victorious forward step provokes responses from the land's leadership — in every case, a military move to stop Israel (except

---

64. Ibid., 351.
65. Ibid., 355.
66. Ibid., 357.

for the Gibeonites).[67] Canaan's kings show the same stupidity as Egypt's Pharaoh—despite the obvious knowledge of Yahweh, his evident power, and his will for Canaan that Rahab and the Gibeonites voice (see 2:10−11; 9:24). Rather than manipulate or override each leader's will, God simply gives them good reasons to follow their own inclinations, however foolish they may prove to be. As with Pharaoh, the disastrous defeats that the Canaanite leadership suffers signal God's displeasure with their resistance and result in divine punishment.[68]

The portrait of Joshua. A brief review of the theme of Joshua's rise in stature will lay the groundwork for the Contemporary Significance section. Yahweh himself introduces it, informing Joshua that the Jordan crossing will elevate him in Israel's eyes (3:7−8). He marks the event as the decisive demonstration that God is with Joshua just as he was with Moses. Perhaps doubts about Joshua haunted some Israelite minds; the transition from Moses to Joshua, they reasoned, was no guarantee of Yahweh's blessing, especially if Joshua messed up badly. The entry into Canaan showed that Yahweh truly backs Joshua and accords him maximum credibility with the Israelites. Indeed, Israel "revered him all the days of his life, just as they had revered Moses" (4:14).

The loss of Moses meant no loss of quality leadership. Israel's first victory at Jericho further confirmed that "the LORD was with Joshua" and also spread "his fame ... throughout the land" (6:27). Even in the dark shadow of Israel's defeat at Ai, Joshua unhesitatingly picked up the Mosaic mantle to represent Israel's interests before God (7:6−9). Finally, the rout at Gibeon in answer to Joshua's bold prayer dispelled all doubt that Yahweh listened to him (10:12−14). Later, the book will close with a concluding eulogy at his death (see comments on 24:29−31).

What made Joshua so great? To the narrator, Joshua is first and foremost an obedient servant of Yahweh. The repeated literary schema, Yahweh's instructions followed by Joshua's execution of them, portrays this trait.[69]

---

67. If Rahab is any indicator, the Exodus and Israel's defeat of Sihon and Og sparked Jericho's terrified resistance (2:9−11). The miraculous crossing of the Jordan struck fear in the hearts of other kings (5:1), as did the fall of Ai (9:1−2). The Gibeonites cite the falls of Jericho and Ai (9:3−4), the Exodus, and the defeats of Sihon and Og (vv. 10−11), as well as Yahweh's gift of the land and *ḥerem* mandate (v. 24) as their motives for seeking peace. The southern kings respond to the destruction of Jericho and Ai and (more importantly) the treaty between Gibeon and Israel (10:1, 4), and the defeat of the southern kings stirs the northern kings to resist.

68. Hess, *Joshua,* 214.

69. See the commentary at ch. 3; cf. other patterns suggested by Nelson (*Joshua,* 57) and Howard (*Joshua,* 133).

So, Joshua carries out divine orders concerning the Jordan crossing (ch. 3), the memorial of twelve stones (4:1–8), the ark's exit from the Jordan (4:15, 17), the circumcision at Gilgal (5:2–3), the method of taking Jericho (ch. 6), the way to expose Achan's secret sin (ch. 7), the tactics and plunder policy at Ai (ch. 8, esp. v. 27), and the treatment of chariots and horses left by the northern coalition (11:6, 9). Joshua accepts his place in the chain of command below Moses and Yahweh, respectively (11:15; cf. 4:10; 11:23).

The same three-level command structure undergirds two later special appeals for Joshua to allocate inheritance land (14:2–6, 12; 17:4) and probably one to allocate cities to the Levites (21:1–3, 8). The Yahweh-Moses-Joshua chain probably goes all the way back to Joshua's emergence as Moses' aide (Ex. 17:14; 27:18, 22; Deut. 31:14; cf. 33:11).[70] It seems to govern larger policy matters (i.e., the Instruction; see 1:7; 23:6), but concerning immediate tactical matters Yahweh addresses Joshua directly as he did Moses. Later, Joshua will carry out Yahweh's direct orders to distribute the land among the tribes (13:6–7; chs. 14–19) and to designate cities of refuge (ch. 20).

Joshua is also an obedient servant of Moses. One prominent motif in Joshua traces how Joshua obediently carried out specific Mosaic instructions. That obedience underlies Joshua's dealings with the Transjordanian tribes (1:12–18; 22:1–4, 9; cf. 12:6), his initiation of the covenant ceremony on Mount Ebal (8:30–25; cf. Deut. 11:29; 27:4, 13), the destruction of the northern kingdoms (11:12), and the distribution of land (14:2, 5), including special allocations for West Manasseh (17:4).[71]

But one striking feature of Joshua's portrait is that he occasionally accommodated Moses to Israel's current reality in Canaan. For example, in the case of the Gibeonites, Joshua made a decision that, on the face of it, seems not quite in keeping with Moses' instructions. Rather than subjecting the Gibeonites to *ḥerem*, he let them live and work as suppliers of wood and water for Yahweh's altar. In my view, Joshua 9 portrays him as creatively applying two Mosaic provisions to them, the role assigned resident-aliens (*gerim*) and the making of treaties with foreign peoples. Ultimately, the theme of Yahweh's elevation of Joshua may aim to give him the Moses-like authority to make such judgments. In other words, he is free to act in the "spirit" (though not the "letter") of Moses (see comments on ch. 9).

---

70. Even Yahweh's formal appointment of Joshua (Josh. 1:2–9) echoes Moses' own charge to his aide-designate (Deut. 31:7).

71. By contrast, Moses was merely the mediator of Yahweh's commands to establish cities of refuge (20:2) and to allocate cities to the landless Levites (21:2, 8). Joshua's circumcision of Israelites born in the desert after the Exodus (5:1–9) meets the law's requirement (Lev. 12:2–3), but the writer makes no explicit connection of that action with Moses.

At the same time, in making such exceptions, Joshua still operates within the Instruction of Moses rather than freelance. Such episodes serve only to enhance the picture of Joshua as the paradigmatic obedient servant of Moses. Thus, he has much to teach leaders of future generations.

Rest from war. Both occurrences of "the land had rest from war" (11:23; 14:15) invoke the verb *šaqaṭ*, "to be quiet, undisturbed" (cf. 2 Chron. 14:5; Isa. 14:7; Zech. 1:11).[72] A variation of the phrase, primarily in Judges, substitutes lengths of time (usually, forty years) for "from war" (Judg. 3:11, 30 [eighty years]; 5:31; 8:28; 2 Chron. 13:23 [ten years]). All the above occurrences describe the state of peace, quiet, and calm that follows the end of military threats or oppression. Notice one striking aspect about the biblical phrase: Its subject is not the people but "the land"—a collective reference to a whole, wide geographical area, the physical region that people populate. The phrase's true sense becomes a little clearer if one ponders the picture conveyed by its opposite—for example, "the land was greatly disturbed by war."

War "disturbs" or "disquiets" not just people but the entire environment—the people, the animals, the birds, the plants, the trees, the grass, the air, and the soil itself. It completely disrupts the world's natural state. The cheerful songs of songbirds and children at play fall eerily silent. Across the usually quiet landscape erupts a horrible cacophony of angry shouting, the clangs of clashing weapons, the grunts and groans of soldiers' grappling, and the cries and moans of the maimed and dying. The smoky smell of burning homes, the crackle of harvest fields ablaze, and the stench of dead flesh shove aside the sweet smells of new-mown grass, freshly cut stalks, spring flowers, and the pleasant breeze. For a few hours (or days) the land becomes ugly—a living hell: "The land is greatly disturbed."

Against this background, the reader more fully appreciates how good it was that "the land had rest from war." The horrible cacophony falls silent, the gut-grabbing dread and wrenching grief are gone, and nature's sweet smells return. The giddy sense of relief—the heady rush of having survived death—is one of life's most powerful experiences. It is a kind of victory appreciated most fully against the dark, harsh reality that preceded it. And it points toward an even greater victory and an even more wonderful peace to be discussed below.

---

72. E. Bons, "שָׁקַט," *TDOT*, 15:453–54; P. J. Nel, "שָׁקַט," *NIDOTTE*, 4:234–35. Though their meanings overlap (see 1 Chron. 22:9; 2 Chron. 14:6[5]; 20:30), *šaqaṭ* ("to be quiet") is not the root behind the larger idea of "rest" from enemies that God promised Israel in the land (*nuaḥ*; Deut. 3:20; 12:10; 25:19; cf. Ps. 95:11). For the latter, see comments on 1:15; 21:43–45.

WHENEVER I TELL MY students that "God is a warrior," a spirited discussion always breaks out. They reckon texts like Exodus 15:2 ("The LORD is a warrior") as an oxymoron. The "God of love" they know and the term "warrior" simply do not go together. The statement strikes them as nonsense — like saying, "Elephants fly," "men birth babies," or "white is dark."

Their reaction is, however, a typical one for Christians, followers of Jesus Christ, a man who refused to fight his enemies though it cost him his life. He was also a man who taught his followers to endure abuse rather than retaliate — in his words, to "turn the other cheek" (Matt. 5:39; Luke 6:29). They buy his ethic of quiet nonviolence and nonretaliation, and talk of Christians engaged in war understandably makes them uneasy. Further, consistent with that view, the words they (and readers) associate with Jesus include "loving," "gentle," "kind," "compassionate," "caring," and "truthful." Those words capture a pattern of conduct they themselves pursue as disciples of Jesus. But the contemporary relevance of Joshua 11 begins with recognition that behind the confrontation between Canaan's rulers and Joshua and the Israelites stands the same cosmic struggle of God against willful human rebellion that goes on today. The same eternal question still confronts people: Will you surrender to Jesus' authority?

The battle still rages. Joshua and the Canaanites may be long gone, but Jesus himself threw down the gauntlet, signaling that the battle over his authority — the same issue that divided Joshua and his enemies — had begun with his coming:

> Do not suppose that I have come to bring peace to the earth. I did not come to bring peace, but a sword. For I have come to turn
>
> "a man against his father,
>   a daughter against her mother,
> a daughter-in-law against her mother-in-law —
>   a man's enemies will be the members of his own household."
>   (Matt. 10:34 – 36, quoting Mic. 7:6)

Granted, Jesus was addressing everyone rather than just rulers, and in this case the "battle" is a spiritual rather than a military one. But Jesus' point is that he came swinging a sword for war, not peace. The war is about his lordship — whether people will surrender to it or fight against it. The battle, he says, will split families; some members will surrender and serve him, others will not. The Gospels report the unfolding of that split. Over time, confrontations with Jesus unleashed a momentum among the "will-nots" that eventuated in his trial and execution. More than a millennium after Joshua 2–11, people still found themselves "fighting God," a battle still raging today every time someone hears the gospel and Jesus' demand that a person make him their Lord.

Joshua faced the kings of Canaan's city-states, but who are the enemies we face today? Enemy Number One is the "power of Satan" (Acts. 26:18) still at work around us. He is the one who fires the fiery darts against which the "shield of faith" protects us (Eph. 6:16), and his schemes lie behind failure by Christians to forgive each other and be reconciled (2 Cor. 2:10–11). He is also an expert at disinformation, blinding the minds of unbelievers so they cannot see the gospel's light (2 Cor. 4:4) and cleverly masquerading as an "angel of light" to lead believers away from the truth (2 Cor. 11:14). Cunningly, he sets traps to capture and keep unrepentant believers unrepentant (2 Tim. 2:26); roaring loudly, he roams about like a lion eager to pounce on unsuspecting spiritual prey (1 Peter 5:8). Through unstated means, he stopped Paul and Silas from revisiting Thessalonica, a place they had fled from earlier because of an uproar (Acts 17:1–9; 1 Th. 2:18). Two millennia may have passed since the New Testament era, but Satan—the master spiritual terrorist—still stealthily stalks believers behind the scenes. His aim remains the disruption of God's salvation plan for the world.[73]

Some governments, political systems, and businesses also today oppose the gospel and the new world order it represents. Recall the concept of hell that C. S. Lewis describes in the introduction to the *Screwtape Letters*:

> The greatest evil is not now done in those sordid "dens of crime" that Dickens loved to paint. It is not done even in concentration camps and labour camps.... But it is conceived and ordered (moved, seconded, carried, and minuted) in clean, carpeted, warmed, and well-lighted offices, by quiet men with white collars and cut fingernails and smooth-shaven cheeks who do not need to raise their voice. Hence, naturally enough, my symbol for Hell is something like the bureaucracy of a police state or the offices of a thoroughly nasty business concern.[74]

Lewis goes on to describe how this Hell operates:

> "Dog eat dog" is the principle of the whole organization. Everyone wishes everyone else's discrediting, demotion, and ruin; everyone is an expert in the confidential report, the pretended alliance, the

---

73. For discussion of Satan as an already disarmed enemy with limited power since Christ's decisive victories against him, see the Contemporary Significance section of Josh. 5–6.
74. C. S. Lewis, *The Screwtape Letters* (New York: Macmillan, 1959), x.

stab in the back. Over all this their good manners, their expressions of grave respect, their "tributes" to one another's invaluable services form a thin crust. Every now and then it gets punctured, and the scalding lava of their hatred spurts out.[75]

Lewis paints the picture in the extreme, but people who have lived under recent communist or totalitarian regimes will immediately identify with it. The sad fact is that there are still regimes that forbid, or at least heavily regulate, the access to Bibles of their populace. There are still places in which Christians must keep a low profile for fear of imprisonment or death. There are also regimes that promote other religions as superior to and to be preferred to Christianity. Other governments sponsor a secular religion, one that worships human reason and creativity as supreme and excludes the God of the Bible from their realms.

As for businesses, some readers may recognize something of their own hellish workplace in it. The dog-eat-dog competition pits them against coworkers whom they would otherwise like to befriend in the name of Christ. They live daily with pressures to produce that all too often collide with their ethics as Christians. They may face the awkward choice between company loyalty and loyalty to Christ. The choice is not exactly outright persecution, but the "wrong" choice might cost them their precious livelihood.

Some enemies are more intellectual. One of the themes of the science fiction novel *Contact*, by the late, popular astronomer Carl Sagan, is scientific skepticism about God's existence and about Christian claims about God. One well-known scene features a conversation between two Christian ministers, the Reverend Billy Jo Rankin and the Reverend Palmer Joss, and Dr. Eleanor ("Ellie") Arroway, director of Project Argus. That project had set up radio telescopes in New Mexico to search for evidence of extraterrestrial intelligence in the universe and had received one such communication. In the discussion, Dr. Arroway says:

> When I say I'm an agnostic, I only mean that the evidence isn't in. There isn't compelling evidence that God exists—at least your kind of god—and there isn't compelling evidence that he doesn't. Since more than half the people on the Earth aren't Jews or Christians or Muslims, I'd say that there aren't any compelling arguments for your kind of god. Otherwise, everybody on Earth would have been converted. I say again, if your God wanted to convince us, he could have done a much better job.[76]

75. Ibid., x–xi.
76. C. Sagan, *Contact: A Novel* (New York: Simon and Schuster, 1985), 175.

It is fitting to respect and honor Sagan's brilliant scientific career and widespread popularity, but fitting also to beware of views antithetical to faith. On the more popular level, the early twenty-first century has also seen Jesus in the headlines, albeit by popular media promoting unorthodox views. Dan Brown's novel *The Da Vinci Code* builds on the assumption that Jesus married Mary Magdelene and fathered a child. This claim has been around for centuries, but Brown's novel has repackaged it for a new generation to consider.

Similarly, in 2007 the Discovery Channel aired a documentary, "The Lost Tomb of Jesus," which claimed that the bones of Jesus and Mary Magdalene had been found in a family tomb near Jerusalem. The lively debate that ensued, including a critical assessment by Ted Koppel, seemed to undermine the thesis and subject the show's producers to much criticism. Whatever the motives behind such phenomena, both clearly contradict traditional Christian beliefs. They are "enemy" in that they feed skeptics fresh ammunition and spread confusion about the gospel's real claims. Most of us, however, experience an "enemy" more personally: a neighbor who keeps aloof because we are Christians, a friend who rejects our attempts to talk about Jesus, or a coworker who ridicules our faith because of bad experiences with a church.

These cases lead me to voice two words of caution. (1) The purpose for pursing this theme is to remind us of an oft-forgotten aspect of reality, the larger spiritual struggle over Jesus' lordship. Through Joshua, God demanded that Canaan's kings bow to his authority, and through the gospel Jesus likewise demands surrender today. Opposition is really about him, not about us.

(2) While honestly reckoning with this reality, no paranoia or panic need result. No one needs to scrutinize relatives, neighbors, coworkers, or friends to root out possible enemies. The thoughtless labeling of anyone as an "enemy" demeans a person whom Jesus loves and for whom he died. It may also wrongly skew our perception of him or her and needlessly lead us warily to keep our distance. Clearly, that amounts to a retreat of the gospel rather than its advance. Instead, we should simply understand that we may occasionally experience conflict over our commitment to Jesus Christ. We should also draw confidence from God's powerful presence with us through his Holy Spirit. As God was with Moses and Joshua, so he is with us. Though vigilant, we need fear no ambush or rout because the Spirit who lives in us is greater than the warring spirits in the world (1 John 4:4; cf. 2 Kings 6:16).

This second word of caution is actually a strong warning. Christian readers should never demonize anyone with whom conflict arises.

Labeling someone in unflattering terms harms rather than advances the gospel's interests. It is needlessly offensive, if not insulting, and cuts off the possibility of further conversations of any sort, much less about our faith. Jesus told it straight: "Love your enemies, do good to those who hate you, bless those who curse you, pray for those who mistreat you" (Luke 6:27; cf. Matt. 5:44).

In other words, surprise the heck out of such people! Give them the one response they do not expect—kindness for unkindness, warmth for coldness, love for hate. That unexpected response demonstrates how different—indeed, how startlingly transformed—Christians are compared to other people. It will spark their curiosity and open them up a little to consider the gospel. In military terms, Jesus orders us to use a surprise attack—to react in an unexpected way that knocks them a little off balance. Surprise worked militarily at Ai and Gibeon, and it can work nonmilitarily for us, too.

Some Christian refugees from Sudan in a town near Chicago illustrate the spirit of Jesus at work.[77] Before emigrating, they suffered greatly at the hands of the pro-Islamic government of Sudan that violently sought to force southern Sudan to become Muslim and culturally Arab. Many Sudanese refugees watched in horror as strafing aircraft, bombardments, and infantry assaults claimed the lives of loved ones. Between 1983 and 2005, merciless attacks on defenseless southern villages killed two million people and forced four million into exile, some in America. That horrible history notwithstanding, every Christmas and Easter the Sudanese Community Church of Wheaton invites Muslim Sudanese for a lamb dinner (the Muslims reciprocate after Ramadan). Since participants speak various tribal languages, the event is conducted in a mixture of Arabic (many speak it) and other languages (for non-Arabic speakers). According to one Christian from the Dinka tribe, the tribe of the well-known "Lost Boys," a spiritual imperative led the Christians to initiate the semiannual celebration: "Even though they are Muslim," said Wilson Lual, "Jesus says, 'Love your enemies.'"[78] And Jesus still says that.

The promise still applies. Joshua 11 traces Joshua's military success to a simple promise (my paraphrase): "Don't be afraid of them because I'm handing all of them over to you dead" (Josh. 11:6). "Don't be afraid" (*'al-tira'*) is a typical formula of warfare, the reassurance of victory that Yahweh gives his on-site commander shortly before the battle begins (Num. 21:34; Josh.

77. R. Working, "Bridging Sudanese Divide—in Wheaton," *Chicago Tribune* (Sunday April 8, 2007), 1, 20.
78. Ibid., 20.

10:8; 11:6). A promise ("because [*ki*] I'm handing them over to you") typically supports the reassurance.[79]

The encouraging words "Don't be afraid" also echo elsewhere across the biblical landscape. Angels reassured Mary and Joseph not to worry about the ramifications of her mysterious pregnancy (Matt. 1:20; Luke 1:30). They encouraged Zechariah that God had answered his prayer—that barren Elizabeth would bear a son (Luke 1:13). "Don't be afraid" calmed the fears of the shepherds frightened by the angelic singing in the sky above (Luke 2:10), and bucked up the disciples before they dispersed on their mission (Matt. 10:26, 28, 31). The words gently dispelled whatever doubts Jesus' "little flock" (i.e., the disciples) might have about actually seeing God's kingdom come (Luke 12:32). "Don't be afraid" eased John's terror at seeing God's awesome majesty in a vision (Rev. 1:17), and through John's vision eased the fears of Christians at Smyrna about to suffer severe persecution (Rev. 2:10).

One night at Corinth God spoke those soothing words to Paul in a vision: "Do not be afraid; keep on speaking, do not be silent. For I am with you" (Acts 18:9−10). Reassured, Paul taught God's word there for a year and a half (v. 11). "Don't be afraid" permits us, as we face our own battles, to respond with confidence, "The Lord is my helper; I will not be afraid. What can human beings do to me?" (Heb. 13:6 TNIV; cf. Ps. 27:1; 118:6).

Fears plague us all, especially when we are keenly aware that a spiritual battle swirls around us. Some Christians may fear actual physical harm for their faith in Christ. Certainly, believers who suffer under oppressive regimes know that fear intimately. The dark, ugly specter of brutal beatings, long imprisonment, and even death still haunt them. I have a friend whose wife became a Christian as a teenager in a central Asian country, and her family immediately threw her out in the street, never to return. Three decades later, they still refuse contact with her, a terrible grief for her to bear. Many from nonreligious or antireligious homes in the West face a similar fear. Those who toy with accepting the gospel often must fearfully weigh their family's reaction before deciding.

Still yet another fear of Christians is the fear of failing and disappointing God. Behind this lies a deep sense of inadequacy in light of the imagined enormity of what God expects. It is true that the Christian life is no lazy stroll through the park. Sexuality and materialism preoccupy the surrounding culture, not an easy arena in which to remain pure before God and to avoid the lure of excessive material goods. Small wonder that some

---

79. H. F. Fuhs, "ירא," *TDOT*, 6:304−5; cf. also assurances by human leaders to their commanders (Josh. 10:25; 2 Chr. 32:7).

believers live with worry over not being good enough in God's eyes. But the reassuring "Don't be afraid" spoken by Jesus applies to fears of persecution, ostracism, and personal inadequacy. It offers us a powerful antidote to the stresses they inflict on us, his daily presence with us.

Those who occasionally give a gospel witness fear the negative reactions of their hearers. The possibility of rejection—not only of the gospel but of us personally—is ever-present and anxiety-producing, especially if our witness puts an important personal relationship at risk. The popular press tends to tar evangelicals with the brush of intolerance, a craving for power, and hypocrisy. To humiliate women thought guilty of adultery, the New England Puritans used to put them in stocks in the public square wearing an "A" (for adultery).[80] In today's popular media, the terms "evangelical" or "fundamentalist" often carry their own set of negative connotations. Some might even regard such people as a "threat to the Republic."

All this means that it is politically incorrect to say that someone "needs Christ." Behind the popular mood lurks a fear among nonevangelicals that evangelical critic Robert Lanham recently called "evangophobia." This is the fear that the evangelical right is not a new counter-culture but the new cultural mainstream.[81] What particularly troubles Lanham are beliefs that that culture cherishes what he deems destructive (e.g., opposition to gay rights). He believes such teachings create divisions between people rather than bring them together. Given such fears and fully aware of the Christian task, one is tempted in despair to invoke that line from Paul, "And who is equal to such a task?" (2 Cor. 2:16).

One night during my tour in Vietnam as a circuit-riding Navy chaplain, I witnessed an awesome display of military might. Thankfully, the show aimed to impress dignitaries visiting the small riverboat base in the Mekong Delta rather than to repel attackers in an actual firefight. Hovering over the base, a single Huey helicopter fired its Gatling-style minigun into the empty forest behind it at a rate of four thousand rounds per minute. The whole area echoed with a frightening racket, and tracer rounds cast a laser-like light beam from the chopper to its pretended target. Between minigun bursts, the helo's rocket pods fired their small, destructive missiles into the dark treeline. A loud "whoosh!" and short vapor trail quickly produced a sudden flash in the trees, each explosion further lighting up the night sky.

---

80. This practice underlies the nineteenth-century romance, N. Hawthorne, *The Scarlet Letter* (New York: Bantam, 1981).

81. R. Lanham, *The Sinner's Guide to the Evangelical Right* (New York: Penguin, 2006), xix, 205, 220. The book is a satirical look at such highly visible evangelicals as James Dobson and Pat Robertson.

As I watched, I quivered inside at the overwhelming firepower on display. I imagined myself as the enemy recipient of the fiery fury raining down from the sky. I imagined the frozen grip of deathly terror and the frightened urge to seek shelter or escape. To this day I can still hear the ear-splitting racket, smell the gunpowdery smoke, and see the fireworks display. It was a dazzling/tantalizing demonstration of human wizardry.

But that display pales into harmless puffs of smoke and kids' sparklers alongside the awesome, unstoppable power of God. It is that power that backs up God's "Don't be afraid" to us and eases our fears. It is that power that, in the face of our daily struggles, bucks up our confidence, relaxes our tense muscles, relieves our troubled minds, and lifts our sagging spirits. Remember that this is the true evidence that the gospel has transformative power; to outsiders it seems at first glance as foolish (How can someone who dies on a cross save people? [1 Cor. 1:18–24]), weak (i.e., its messengers are frail humans [2 Cor. 4:7]), and unimpressive (i.e., its proclaimers lack eloquence and impressive learning [1 Cor. 2:1–8]). The only plausible explanation for the credibility and effects of the gospel message is not its intellectual persuasiveness, its stunning spokespersons, its dazzling display of miracles, its dramatic religious rituals, its impressive list of well-known believers, or its down-to-earth practical advice. The gospel's credibility derives from its amazing power—the "amazing grace that saved a wretch like me"—to transform human lives. It heals the hurting, repairs the broken-hearted, makes the ugly beautiful, and softens the hard-hearted into tenderness.

The story told by friends of mine who live in a Muslim country illustrates this point well. My friends had just attended the funeral of a Christian woman from their church, the only believer in her entire family. Though her family was Muslim and animist, they decided to honor the woman's choice of religion by having a Christian funeral rather a Muslim one. Muslims have a saying that if someone becomes a Christian, they will have a bad funeral (no one will come). This claim discourages many Muslims from following Christ because to do so would risk great humiliation at death. That explains why the family was shocked at how many people turned out for the celebration—almost the entire church. By my friends' account, the service was wonderful, the good news of Jesus Christ infusing each of aspect of the event. During a Muslim funeral, people come to the house of the deceased and pray all night that Allah will mercifully allow the person into heaven. The deceased's family were therefore surprised that all the church people came to celebrate all night that the woman was *already* in heaven with her Savior.

The turnout for this old woman's memorial services showed the family that a Christian does have a good, honorable funeral. As a result, her Muslim family came to church the following Sunday. That day, her son announced to the church that he wanted to follow Christ. Through the powerful Christian testimony of his mother's funeral God had transformed his heart. The power lay in the simple truths of the gospel message — as Paul put it, "the power of God for the salvation of everyone who believes" (Rom. 1:16). That transformative power enables us to do whatever God sets in front of us to do. With such power available, we respond to it by affirming with renewed confidence, "If God is for us, who can be against us?" (Rom. 8:31). According to popular speaker Michael Pritchard, "Fear is that little darkroom where negatives are developed."[82] But God's "Don't be afraid" brightens our lives, leaving no room for "negatives."

The best soldiers: humble, obedient servants. Joshua 11 highlights how Joshua faithfully carried out God's instructions, whether given directly by Yahweh or through Moses. Literarily, he stands in stark contrast to all the kings whose attempts to stamp out Israel Joshua soundly defeated. Two aspects of his obedience make him an especially good example of good soldiering in God's service today.

(1) Joshua *humbly subordinated himself* to the leadership of Moses. In his biblical debut, Joshua had won Israel's first military victory, the defeat of the Amalekites at Rephidim (Ex. 17:8 – 13). Thereafter the Bible remembers him as Moses' "aide" (Heb. *mešaret* "servant"; Ex. 24:13; Num. 11:28), a position he filled from his youth until Moses died (Josh. 1:1). Biblical chronology for the Mosaic era is uncertain, but Joshua probably served at Moses' side — and in his shadow, too — about forty-five to fifty years. That's a long time for Joshua to await his turn to lead Israel. A more ambitious man might have cleverly played the "Bye, Moses! Back to Egypt!" rebellion against Moses (Num. 14) to his advantage and replaced him as leader. Instead, he (and Caleb) defended Moses against the mob and became the only two of their generation actually to enter the land. Joshua 11 praises Joshua for doing "just as the LORD commanded Moses" (vv. 15, 23). Even when he finally got to "sit in Moses' seat" (Matt. 23:2), he still carried out the agenda of Moses rather than his own. He models a unique humility for a leader, the humility to support someone else as a subordinate.

Jesus taught his disciples (and us) something similar in two well-known episodes. In the first, his disciples ask him to settle a disagreement among them as to who of them is the greatest in the kingdom of God (Matt. 18:1 – 6; Mark 9:33 – 37; Luke 9:46 – 48). In retrospect, it is almost laughable

---

82. Cited from www.quotationspage.com/quote/1920.html.

to imagine them even asking such an arrogant question. In reply, Jesus surprises them by bringing a little child into their midst and saying, "Whoever humbles himself like this child is the greatest in the kingdom of heaven. And whoever welcomes a little child like this in my name welcomes me" (Matt. 18:4−5). Jesus contrasts the sweet simplicity of a child's devoted love for Jesus with the adult power games of his adult disciples.

Granted, the disciples later would constitute the apostolic pillars of the infant community of Jesus. But notwithstanding their exalted position in the church, they were never to lose their basic stance toward Jesus—the simple, trusting, loving devotion of a little child. Karl Barth, a theological giant of the twentieth century, never lost that simplicity. During a visit to America, someone once asked the brilliant Swiss theologian what was the most profound theological idea he had ever encountered. Without missing a beat, Barth replied, "Jesus loves me, this I know, for the Bible tells me so." He was a theological genius—but still a "child" in what he deemed the essential Christian truth.

In a second episode, Jesus contrasts the leadership model of the scribes and Pharisees with the model his followers were to pursue (Matt. 23:1−12). The religious leaders of his day, Jesus says, command obedience as Moses' successors, but they are corrupt. They do not "practice what they preach"; they saddle humans with "heavy loads" (i.e., their strict interpretation of the Torah) but do not "lift a finger" to help humans manage them. In other words, they are great experts at making demands but rank amateurs at compassion. Also, what drives them is not service of God's people but adoration by them. They wear exaggerated religious clothes simply to get noticed. They gush inside when people pay them special attention—upfront seats at banquets, the solemn address as "Rabbi."

Not so among you (and us), Jesus counters, because you are to understand yourselves differently. We serve one Master, Jesus, below whom we share the same rank—peers within a family. We have one "father," our heavenly Father, and one "teacher" (Jesus, the Messiah), and neither shares his title with anyone. Our world is an upside-down one: The "greatest" is the servant of the others, and ladder climbers end up at the bottom. The winners in this competition are those who go lower than anyone else, not those who reach the top!

This teaching cuts across the common tendency of human organizations to create "pecking orders" and status symbols. In business, the ultimate prize is the proverbial key to the executive washroom and the title "CEO," but the size and location of one's office and parking space scores big status points, too. In academia, the rank of "professor" marks the professional pinnacle, a delicacy garnished with lots of invitations to write important books and to give lectures before adoring crowds. In churches, "senior pastor" or "chairman of the board" top the pecking order, with all the respect (if not adoration) of "associate pastors" and laity alike. All such pecking orders subtly cause ego-inflation, the confident feeling — never voiced publicly, of course — that "I'm good at what I do, so I'm entitled to all this."

Against this, Jesus challenges both leaders and followers to be servants who regard others as more important than themselves. In his kingdom, there is no ladder to be scaled or mountain to be climbed, only the simple drudgery of ensuring that the needs of everyone else are met first. Such submission cuts across the grain of the self-centered, entrepreneurial, competitive spirit of contemporary Western culture. Jesus bypasses that spirit and leads his people in the opposite direction. It is terribly counter-cultural, but there is no getting around it: That is precisely the way Jesus wants it.

(2) The second aspect of Joshua's obedience is his *consistent surrender* to God's will. The simple reports about Joshua in Joshua 11 in effect toss accolades his way on this topic. He is thorough: He "left nothing undone" (v. 15) and even dealt with the Anakites (vv. 21−22). He shows remarkable endurance: "Joshua waged war against all these kings for a long time" (v. 18). God honors his thoroughness and endurance by giving him success: "Joshua took the whole land" (vv. 16, 23).

It is striking that Joshua 11 credits Joshua so highly. Earlier chapters have Yahweh in the forefront, at key points issuing reassurances as well as tactical orders (chs. 3−4; 6; 8; 9−10). But unlike 10:42, here Yahweh steps into the background to spotlight Joshua's faithfulness. As a whole, the book of Joshua portrays a Joshua who consistently does God's will once he succeeds Moses as leader. In that context, the land descriptions that follow (chs. 13−19) read like long lists of his sparkling achievements — an impressive resumé of leadership, indeed. Certainly, his life pursued what Eugene Peterson calls "a long obedience in the same direction."[83]

Joshua offers a good model of obedience, but all too often our lives more resemble Achan than Joshua. The contrast between the two men confronts us with a basic but important biblical reality: Obedience does not come naturally to us humans. Achan knew the rules concerning *ḥerem*, but he still secretly kept some booty from Jericho for himself. Adam and Eve knew that God had set that special tree off-limits, but the prohibition apparently rankled them. In my view, that is why they fell for the serpent's clever pitch: They already suspected that God was keeping something

---

83. Cf. E. H. Peterson, *A Long Obedience in the Same Direction*, 2nd ed. (Downers Grove, Ill.: InterVarsity Press, 2000).

good from them—that he was neither "good" nor "generous." And, alas, I find myself siding with them.

Candidly, some early disillusionment with Christian leaders whose guidance and example I had trusted has scarred my soul. Painfully, I learned that not all of what my guides taught me was true, so I still suffer occasional suspicions about God's good intentions. But a recent book by David Benner has helped me understand obedience in a new way. My soul nods "yes" when Benner writes that "most of us harbor a deep-seated suspicion that God's desires for us and ours for ourselves share no common ground."[84] So willfulness, with its motto of "my way or no way," rules our lives: "Living life 'our way' appears to be the hard-wired default option for all of us.... And often—at least in the short term—it seems to work reasonably well."[85] We simply kick our steely self-discipline into gear, following the spiritual disciplines we deem necessary to a healthy spiritual life. But, Benner notes, that approach treats those routines as ends in themselves, not as means to the true, God-honoring end—our inner transformation.[86] They simply live out the "kingdom of self" rather than the kingdom of God.

In the kingdom of God, however, self-discipline must give way to total surrender to God. It requires us to pray with Jesus, "Not as I will, but as you will" (Matt. 26:39). But how does such a submission of our will happen? According to Benner, God wants us to love him, not out of obligation, but out of an inner willingness born of deep desire for God. Benner describes this as a "love-shaped willing"—deep, "inner longings for relationship and intimacy" with God that our external spiritual practices live out.[87] The reason is, quite simply, that God first and foremost wants our heart—our surrender to him out of our love for him—not just our determination to obey him.

As humans, we devote ourselves totally and most passionately to the things we desire deep down inside—the things for which we long, the things whose absence leaves a gaping hole, the things that propel us to action. As Thomas Merton wrote, "Life is shaped by the end you live for. You are made in the image of what you desire."[88] The book of Joshua exposes none of Joshua's inner thoughts or struggles of the heart. But it does demonstrate that his full surrender to the important task God had given him shaped the great leader that he became. His devotion to God spurred his growth into a stature on par with Moses.

---

84. David G. Benner, *Desiring God's Will* (Downers Grove, Ill.: InterVarsity Press, 2005),
83. I am grateful to my wife, Pam, for introducing me to this helpful book.
85. Ibid., 24, 32.
86. Ibid., 30–31.
87. Ibid., 50–51.
88. T. Merton, *Thoughts in Solitude* (Boston: Shambhala, 1993), 55.

Now, some approaches to the Christian life require the crucifixion of our desires, but Benner avers that actually God seeks their "distillation" and purification. When we surrender our will to God's will, his love shapes, as it were, a "love-shaped place deep within us. Our fundamental longing will be a thirst for Living Water."[89] Facing myself squarely in the mirror, I feel embarrassed by some of my desires — for example, to be liked or to please, to experience adventure, to command respect, to have status, to enjoy good health in old age. They seem self-centered and less than godly, if not just plain evil. But Benner reads them as "disordered," surface desires that actually derive from the core spiritual needs I received from God because he created me that way. In other words, my surface desires are simply distorted, "residual traces of God's desires for us and always therefore point toward God."[90]

But how do we purify or distill from our "disordered" desires the "ordered" or purified desires at their roots? To launch a spiritual self-improvement plan will not do. We have all tried those before, and our sinful, human weakness always dooms them inevitably to failure. No, instead of self-reformation we need the transformation of our disordered and confused state. We need to hand ourselves over to God in sincere prayer. By this I do not mean a simple "OK, God, please take over. Amen." With Benner, I suggest prayers over time that ask God to sort out our desires and that also leave times of silence to listen for God's voice speaking to us.[91] The transformation from willful rebel to willing soldier of God's love begins with such a prayer season.

Recent radio commercials in my city promote a special cardiological evaluation called "Heart Check." Through a thorough series of tests, their doctors are said to diagnose reliably the most life-threatening heart problems, even those other doctors might miss. Now, I have no expertise to assess the program, but I wholeheartedly commend a regular spiritual "heart check" for myself and my Christian readers. This spiritual self-examination aims to diagnose how close our heart is to God's heart. Test #1 asks: What are my desires — to feel safe and secure, to know who I really am (i.e., my identity), to feel significant, to find ways of self-expression, or to attain a feeling of fulfillment? Test #2 asks: Do I really love God, or am I just serving him out of obligation or duty? Test #3 asks: Do my suspicions or hurts keep God at arms' length? If so, will I pray to move closer to him? If the diagnosis shows an openness to loving God more deeply, I would tell God that in prayer. Your transformation is already underway. You are becom-

---

89. Benner, *Desiring God's Will*, 79–81, quote 81.
90. Ibid., 84–85.
91. Ibid., 85–88.

ing the same kind of willing soldier as Joshua. For those who feel a little tongue-tied talking to God, perhaps this prayer of Thomas Merton might suggest some words to use:

> My Lord God, I have no idea where I am going. I cannot see the road ahead of me. I cannot know for certain where it will end. Nor do I really know myself, and the fact that I think I am following your will does not mean that I am actually doing so. But, I believe that the desire to please you does in fact please you. And I hope I have that desire in all that I am doing. I hope that I will never do anything apart from that desire. And I know that if I do this you will lead me by the right road, though I may know nothing about it. Therefore I will trust you always though I may seem to be lost and in the shadow of death. I will not fear, for you are ever with me and you will never leave me to face my perils alone.[92]

The result: peace. Joshua 11 ends with the comment that "the land had rest from war" (v. 23), a comment that also closes the report of Caleb's capture of his inheritance (14:15). In both cases, God's victories brought peace, albeit temporarily. It compares to the brief respite that the early church in Judea, Galilee, and Samaria enjoyed after its archenemy, Saul of Tarsus, became a Christian. Spirit-filled vitality, buoyed confidence, and numerical growth resulted (Acts 9:28−31).

In God's plan, however, Christians enjoy a more profound, unshakeable inner peace that the temporary quiet in Joshua's day only anticipates. Jesus' reassuring words to his disciples speak of it: "Peace I leave with you; my peace I give you. I do not give to you as the world gives. Do not let your hearts be troubled and do not be afraid" (John 14:27). Even when trouble strikes, as it inevitably will, his followers have peace "in me" (John 16:33). At the heart of this peace is the peace that we have with God through faith in Christ's redemptive work, a peace that inspires hope even amid sufferings (Rom. 5:1−4).[93] What great confidence Paul shows—almost an echo of Joshua 10:24−25—when he promises the believers in Rome that "the God of peace will soon crush Satan under your feet" (Rom. 16:20). Wow! A powerful pep talk to people facing strong spiritual opposition!

The challenge, however, is to keep that marvelous inner peace vital while at war. By nature, war of any kind unnerves, dispirits, and terrorizes us. How, then, can soldiers of Christ maintain it while still battling? Paul's

---

92. Merton, *Thoughts in Solitude*, 89.
93. For Paul insights on how Jesus' crucifixion brought peace to the age-long conflicts between Jews and Gentiles and created a single, new humanity, see Ephesians 2:14−17.

sage advice to the Philippians is helpful. Instead of sinking helplessly into the grip of anxiety, he counsels, constantly "present your requests to God," giving God proper thanks in the process (Phil. 4:6). By so doing, we will experience "the peace of God, which transcends all understanding" (v. 7). A breathtaking experience that dispels all anxiety! And, like a soldier who bars admission to an inner sanctum, that astounding calm will "guard [our] hearts and minds," denying fear access inside. The key lesson is this: an ongoing prayer life is our peacekeeper. A consistent habit of petition and thanksgiving keeps the guard on duty. It makes space for "the peace of Christ [to] rule in [our] hearts," thereby leaving no room for fear (Col. 3:15).

Conclusion. So, the spiritual war continues. God's powerful presence keeps our courage up, and the experience of his love enlivens us to faithful obedience. Keeping in touch with God through prayer keeps our inner peace alive, despite the struggles. Remember that the triumph of Jesus Christ is certain, a point that buoyed Paul's spirits at a particular low point in his ministry:

> But thanks be to God, who always leads us in triumphal procession in Christ and through us spreads everywhere the fragrance of the knowledge of him. For we are to God the aroma of Christ among those who are being saved and those who are perishing. (2 Cor. 2:14–15)

Joshua 12:1–24

T here are the kings of the land whom the Israelites had
defeated and whose territory they took over east of
the Jordan, from the Arnon Gorge to Mount Hermon, including all the eastern side of the Arabah:

²Sihon king of the Amorites,
who reigned in Heshbon. He ruled from Aroer on
the rim of the Arnon Gorge—from the middle of the
gorge—to the Jabbok River, which is the border of
the Ammonites. This included half of Gilead. ³He also
ruled over the eastern Arabah from the Sea of Kinnereth to the Sea of the Arabah (the Salt Sea), to Beth
Jeshimoth, and then southward below the slopes of
Pisgah.

⁴And the territory of Og king of Bashan,
one of the last of the Rephaites, who reigned in
Ashtaroth and Edrei. ⁵He ruled over Mount Hermon,
Salecah, all of Bashan to the border of the people of
Geshur and Maacah, and half of Gilead to the border
of Sihon king of Heshbon.

⁶Moses, the servant of the LORD, and the Israelites conquered them. And Moses the servant of the LORD gave their
land to the Reubenites, the Gadites and the half-tribe of
Manasseh to be their possession.
⁷These are the kings of the land that Joshua and the Israelites conquered on the west side of the Jordan, from Baal Gad
in the Valley of Lebanon to Mount Halak, which rises toward
Seir (their lands Joshua gave as an inheritance to the tribes of
Israel according to their tribal divisions—⁸the hill country,
the western foothills, the Arabah, the mountain slopes, the
desert and the Negev—the lands of the Hittites, Amorites,
Canaanites, Perizzites, Hivites and Jebusites):

⁹the king of Jericho	one
the king of Ai (near Bethel)	one
¹⁰the king of Jerusalem	one
the king of Hebron	one

¹¹the king of Jarmuth	one
the king of Lachish	one
¹²the king of Eglon	one
the king of Gezer	one
¹³the king of Debir	one
the king of Geder	one
¹⁴the king of Hormah	one
the king of Arad	one
¹⁵the king of Libnah	one
the king of Adullam	one
¹⁶the king of Makkedah	one
the king of Bethel	one
¹⁷the king of Tappuah	one
the king of Hepher	one
¹⁸the king of Aphek	one
the king of Lasharon	one
¹⁹the king of Madon	one
the king of Hazor	one
²⁰the king of Shimron Meron	one
the king of Acshaph	one
²¹the king of Taanach	one
the king of Megiddo	one
²²the king of Kedesh	one
the king of Jokneam in Carmel	one
²³the king of Dor (in Naphoth Dor)	one
the king of Goyim in Gilgal	one
²⁴the king of Tirzah	one
thirty-one kings in all.	

THE OPENING SUBJECT-FIRST SYNTAX sets this chapter off as a retrospective review of the past, not a report of the next events. Structurally, it comprises two sections, each introduced by the same formula ("These are the kings of the land whom the Israelites/Joshua and the Israelites had defeated/conquered . . ."; vv. 1, 7). The first section reviews the kings defeated east of the Jordan and describes the lands Moses distributed (vv. 1–6; a brief retelling of Deut. 2:26–3:8). The second reviews those defeated west of the Jordan whose lands Joshua allotted (vv. 7–24; a retelling of Josh. 6–11). In general, both lists correspond to the order of biblical reports (Num. 21; Deut. 1–3; Josh. 6–11), but the second includes twelve cities that lack conquest reports.[1] Both sections share parallel language (e.g., *nakah* hi. ["defeat," vv. 1, 6–7], *natan* ["give," vv. 6, 7]), and the literary effect of the whole is to link the work of Moses and Joshua.[2]

Kings in the ancient Near East commonly celebrated their conquests by listing the cities they captured, destroyed, and burned. In Egypt, for example, Thutmose III initiated the practice of listing conquered cities and countries at the Temple of Amon at Karnak, a practice his successors continued there and elsewhere.[3] While similar, Joshua 12 rhetorically differs from such listings in two respects. (1) In the royal lists, the king speaks in the first person (e.g., "I captured, destroyed, etc...."), using the lists as a vehicle to extol royal greatness. By contrast, Joshua 12 speaks in the third person, crediting the victories to corporate action ("the Israelites" [v. 1], "Joshua and the Israelites" [v. 7])—in other words, more matter-of-fact and less bombastic.

(2) Joshua 12 spotlights kings of capital cities rather than the cities by themselves. Theologically, the list of kings seems to see behind Joshua 1–11 a larger contest between King Yahweh and the human kings listed, a motif also true of the plague narratives (see Ex. 6:1; 9:16; 10:3), from which Yahweh also emerges victorious. If Joshua 11 (vv. 16–20, 23) wraps up the conquest in geographical and theological terms, Joshua 12 highlights the royal leadership and capital cities that fell to Israel in chapters 1–11. For good reason the book portrays Israel's victories as responses to regional royal military alliances (see 5:1–2; 9:1–2; 10:1–5; 11:1–5).

The chapter draws together the book's central thematic threads and motifs: the unity of Moses and Joshua (1:1–2, 5, 17; 3:7; 4:10, 14; 8:32, 35; 11:12, 15, 23; 22:7), resistance by Canaan's kings (2:10; 5:1, 9:1–2; 10:1–5, 42; 11:1–2, 17–18), lists of enemy peoples (3:10; 9:1; 11:3; 24:11), echoes of Yahweh war, special provisions for the eastern tribes (1:12–17; 4:12; 22:1–34), and land distribution (1:6; 11:23; chs. 13–19). It underscores the astounding result of their faithful leadership—in essence, a kind of "golden age" for Israel spanning Moses' triumphant last years and Joshua's heyday.[4]

1. For details of the lists, locations, and background, see Tables 2–4 in Hess, *Joshua*, 222–28. The conquest of Arad is especially interesting. It apparently resulted from a pre-conquest-era Israelite incursion into the Negev, the only city in Cisjordan so conquered (Num. 21:1–3).

2. Nelson, *Joshua*, 159. For Howard (*Joshua*, 277), chapter 12 presents the "raw data"—the "supporting evidence"—that backs up the author's claims in the conquest narrative.

3. Cf. the translation of the preface by Thutmose III and the table of conquests claimed by him and his successors in *ANET*, 242–43. For other examples, see Younger, *Ancient Conquest Accounts*, 230–32.

4. Nelson, *Joshua*, 159.

Clearly, the prior political order of petty kingships ruling city-states is gone, replaced by a united Israel in full possession of all the land on both sides of the Jordan. Within the book, chapter 12 marks a decisive literary turning point. Battle reports give way to tedious (at least, to moderns!) lists of tribal boundaries and towns (chs. 14 – 19). The literary change signals the dawn of a new day for Israel; the days of war (i.e., the Conquest) give way to the days of land distribution (i.e., the settlement). Chapter 22 may imply the dominance of Cisjordan as true Israel, but here one celebrates greater Israel proudly settled astride both Jordan banks.[5]

Two Fallen Eastern Kings (12:1 – 6)

THE RECAPITULATION OF ISRAELITE royal conquests begins at the beginning, with their victories over two kings and land acquisitions "east of the Jordan" (v. 1).[6] Literarily, geographical descriptions ("from X to Y") echo language from Deuteronomy 1 – 4; the author apparently relishes the citation of well-known landmarks to map out the vast territories. The spectacular Arnon Gorge through which the Arnon River empties into the Dead Sea marks the southern border, with Mount Hermon, Syro-Palestine's highest point (9232 feet) about 130 miles away, its northern one (v. 1). The territory includes "all the eastern side of the Arabah" (cf. 11:16), the land east of the Jordan between those boundaries (i.e., northern Jordan and southern Syria).

Ruling this territory was the first king, the Amorite Sihon, from his capital city of Heshbon on the wide plateau parallel to the Jordan.[7] His domain on the plateau above the Jordan is described from north to south (except for the "eastern Arabah" below). It ran from Aroer (v. 2), an ancient fortress on the northern rim of the gorge (Deut. 2:36; 4:48; Josh. 13:16), north about fifty miles to the Jabbok River, a feeder of the Jordan River midway between the Dead Sea and the Sea of Galilee and southern border of Ammonite territory.[8] Sihon also held sway over "the eastern Arabah," land between the east side of the Sea of Kinnereth (i.e., Galilee) and the "Sea of the Arabah (Salt Sea)" (or Dead Sea), including the east-west road to Beth Jeshimoth and land south as far as the slopes of Mount Pisgah (v. 3).

The second Amorite king is "Og king of Bashan" with two royal cities, Ashtaroth and Edrei. The latter locate his domain east and southeast of

5. Cf. Howard, *Joshua*, 277: the chapter "reviews all [Israel's] gains ..., whether east or west of the Jordan" and thereby "reinforces the theme of national unity mentioned in chap. 1."

6. Heb. *mizreḥah haššameš*, lit., "toward the sun" (cf. 21:19).

7. For details on the identification of this site, cf. Hess, *Joshua*, 225 – 26.

8. G. I. Mattingly, "Aroer (Place)," *ABD*, 1:399. The biblical author identifies the "middle of the gorge" as the specific boundary and remarks that the land includes "half of Gilead."

the Sea of Kinnereth and east of and parallel to that of Sihon. The author identifies him among "the last of the Rephaites," a storied ancient race of giants or warrior kings like the Anakim (see 11:21–22).[9] Deuteronomy 3:11 remembers Og's gigantic bed—thirteen feet long by six feet wide and (at the time) still to be seen in Rabbah of the Ammonites! The description of his domain runs from north to south (the opposite of Sihon's) and encompasses eastern Mount Hermon (presumably the eastern side), the town of Salecah (its southeast border point [Deut. 3:10; Josh. 13:11; 1 Chron. 5:11])—i.e., "all of Bashan" that abutted the border of the Geshurites to his immediate west and northwest, as well as the half of Gilead that bordered Sihon's half to the south (v. 2).[10]

Finally, the writer recalls the important past history of Sihon, Og, and Israel. Moses and the Israelites struck down both kings, and Moses gave their lands as the inheritance of the tribes of Reuben, Gad, and East Manasseh (v. 6; Num. 21; 32:33; Deut. 1:4; 3:1–17). Recall that word of the fates of Sihon and Og inspired earlier conciliatory actions toward Israel by Rahab (Josh. 2:10) and the Gibeonites (9:10). Besides the Exodus, biblical tradition also remembers Sihon and Og as a paradigmatic victory of Yahweh on behalf of Israel.[11] Literarily, they comprise a "down payment" on the eventual realization of Israel's full inheritance, assert the tribes' claim to their land, and confirm God's promise of land.[12]

The Fallen Western Kings (12:7–24)

NARRATIVE PREFACE (VV. 7–8). Now comes the list of the thirty-one kings whom Joshua and the Israelites struck down west of the Jordan (lit., "seaward")—a recapitulation of Joshua 6–11. The narrative preface by the Deuteronomistic Historian (vv. 7–8) begins by invoking the "from X to Y" formula to map out the territory won by the defeat of Canaan's kings (vv. 7–8). The description echoes 11:17 and 23 and runs from way north to way south—from Baal Gad in the Valley of Lebanon to Mount Halak (see comments at 11:17). The report is anachronistic, affirming in advance what is to come later (see also 11:23), namely, that Joshua did in Cisjordan

---

9. Gen. 14:5; Deut. 2:10–11 (cf. Num. 13:33); 3:11, 13; Josh. 13:12; cf. M. S. Smith, "Rephaim," *ABD*, 5:675; R. F. Youngblood, "Giants, Heroes, Mighty Men," *NIDOTTE*, 4:677, who cites an illuminating background text from Ugarit. Goliath may have been a Rephaim (2 Sam. 21:19; 1 Chron. 20:5).

10. *CBA*, 34, 53, 68.

11. For later memories of Sihon and Og, see Judg. 11:19–21 (Sihon only); 1 Kings 4:19; Neh. 9:22; Ps. 135:11; 136:19–20; Jer. 48:45 (Sihon only).

12. Howard, *Joshua*, 278.

what Moses did in Transjordan (v. 6b). Joshua gave it to Israel tribe-by-tribe as their "(family) inheritance" (Heb. *yerussah;* NIV "possession"; cf. v. 6).[13]

In addition, the Deuteronomistic Historian invokes a traditional list of Canaan's main geographical regions (see 10:40; 11:16) to picture all the places where their new inheritance lands lie: the hill country, the western lowlands, the Great Rift Valley, the mountain slopes, the desert, and the Negev (v. 8a). The literary effect is to reaffirm the earlier claim that "Joshua took the whole land" (Josh. 11:16, 23) and to foreshadow its upcoming distribution.[14]

Finally, the text offers a traditional list of the six peoples over whom the kings presided and who went down to defeat with them — the Hittites, Amorites, Canaanites, Perizzites, Hivites, and Jebusites (v. 8b).[15] Literarily, the wedding of geography and people groups underscores how impressive and complete the Conquest is.[16]

The list proper (vv. 9 – 24). To reinforce this point, a stylized list of kings now follows (vv. 9 – 24), and its formal layout in MT is particularly striking (see NIV).[17] Except for v. 24 (one king plus the total), each line lists two kings in stereotyped form — "The king of City-X ... one ... the king of City-Y ... one" — as if the reader/audience were counting them.[18] The conquest narrative (Josh. 6 – 11) occasionally names the kings (see 10:3, 33; 11:1), but the list here only identifies each king by his city (or, in one case, by region). The literary effect is to highlight their social position and the fact they are all gone. In Nelson's words, "The incessant repetition 'king of' nails down the total defeat of the system of Canaanite city-states."[19]

---

13. The Hebrew term refers not to the land of Canaan as a whole but specifically to the "territory possessed by subgroups in Israel" (e.g., a family's inheritance land); cf. N. Lohfink, "יָרַשׁ," *TDOT,* 6:376, 384.

14. The inclusion of "mountain slopes" (*'asedot*) is an unusual term, since elsewhere it describes mountains in western Transjordan (Num. 21:15; Deut. 3:17; 4:49; Josh. 12:3; 13:20). It does occur, however, in the list of Cisjordanian regions in Joshua 10:40.

15. Cf. the same list of six in Deut. 20:17 and Josh. 9:1; cf. 3:10.

16. Howard, *Joshua,* 280 – 81.

17. Cf. also a similar layout of the list of Haman's ten sons (Esth. 9:7 – 10) and number in each tribe within the 144,000 (Rev. 7:4 – 8).

18. In classroom instruction, I have students read it as a liturgy, individual students reading each king's name and the entire class responding "one." Interestingly, the LXX lacks "one" in verses 9 – 24a, lists thirty kings (omitting the kings of Bethel and Madon [vv. 16, 19] and adding a king of Marron [v. 20]), but gives a total of only twenty-nine. No biblical manuscripts of Joshua 12 exist among the Dead Sea Scrolls, so one cannot know whether or not the layout noted above precedes MT; cf. F. García Martínez, *The Dead Sea Scrolls Translated,* trans. W. G. E. Watson, 2nd ed. (Leiden: Brill, 1996), 476 – 77.

19. Nelson, *Joshua,* 161.

As for genre, the list compares to two ancient types of lists, the royal list of conquests (see above) and the lists of names or items followed by numbers or tally marks.[20] As noted above, however, the list specifically concerns the kings (not the cities) conquered. In fact, the king of Gezer met defeat at Lachish, not at his capital (10:33; cf. 12:12), while the king of Jerusalem died with his four royal allies outside the cave of Makkedah (10:23, 26).[21] Also, the list includes nine cities not mentioned in the conquest narrative and presents four in an order different from that in the narrative.[22] As Nelson notes, the inclusion of previously unmentioned cities suggests that "the stories told represent only an illustrative sample of a larger struggle."[23]

This also suggests that the list may derive from an ancient source from which the conquest narrative drew its basic outline.[24] The existence of a prior list might explain why 12:19−20 lists Hazor second among the four-king northern coalition whereas 11:1 has Hazor as its head. Further, readers familiar with Joshua 6−11 readily recognize four sections within the list: (1) Jericho and Ai mark a kind of basic pattern for what follows (12:9);[25] (2) verses 10−12a list the five-city, Jerusalem-led coalition executed at Makkedah (and in the same order as 10:3); (3) verses 12b−16a incorporate four cities (Makkedah, Libnah, Gezer, Debir) conquered in the southern campaign (albeit in different order from 10:28−33) but whose kings escaped execution at Makkedah; (4) verses 19−20 list the four-party northern coalition from Josh. 11 (but with Hazor second, as noted above). The inclusion of five cities from the land's center unmentioned in Joshua 6−11

---

20. The ostraca from Arad exemplify this; cf. Y. Aharoni, *Arad Inscriptions* (Jerusalem: Israel Exploration Society, 1981), nos. 38, 49, 72.

21. Biblical tradition credits David with the conquest of Jerusalem (2 Sam. 5:6−7), and Gezer first debuts as an Israelite city during Solomon's reign (1 Kings 9:15−17). How Gezer fell to Israel after dogged resistance by its Canaanite inhabitants (Josh. 16:10; Judg. 1:29; cf. 2 Sam. 5:25) is unknown.

22. The unmentioned cities include four southern cities (Geder, Hormah, Arad, and Adullam) and five northern ones (Bethel, Tappuah, Hepher, Aphek, and Lasharon); cf. the discussion in Howard, *Joshua*, 281. The four cities whose order varies are Gezer (v. 12; cf. 10:33), Debir (v. 13; cf. 10:38), Libnah (v. 15; cf. 10:29), and Makkedah (v. 16; cf. 10:28).

23. Nelson, *Joshua*, 161−62 (quote, 162).

24. Nelson (ibid., 162) thinks that the list may have supplied the names of the coalitions led by Jerusalem (10:3, 5; 12:10−12a) and Hazor (11:1; 12:19b−20), but that the author added Jericho and Ai; cf. Fritz (*Josua*, 137), who concurs on the addition but also avers that the author compiled the present list from lists available but unrelated to the conquest tradition.

25. Cf. Nelson, *Joshua*, 161 ("paradigmatic conquests"). The addition "near Bethel" with Ai continues the book's consistent association of Ai and Bethel (7:2; 8:9, 12; cf. Gen. 13:3). For later reports that refer back to both foundational episodes, see 8:2; 9:3; 10:1, 28, 30.

(vv. 16b–18) gives the list a smooth geographic flow through Canaan's southern, central, and northern parts.[26]

Finally, brief clarification concerning the cities omitted from the conquest begins with the four Judean ones. That the Hebrew root *gadar* underlies several city names (e.g., Beth-gader, Gederah, etc.) makes identification of Geder (v. 13b; lit., "wall") difficult. If Geder equals Gedor (15:58), it would lie about six miles north of Hebron,[27] but its context within the list also suggests possible locations in the southern Judean foothills (i.e., near Debir [12:13]) or in the northern Negev (near Arad and Hormah [v. 14]).[28] Hormah (v. 14a; cf. Num. 14:45) also defies precise identification but may be Tel Masos, a site a few miles east of Beersheba,[29] while archaeological evidence firmly establishes Arad (v. 14b) at Tel-Arad, northeast of Tel Masos.[30] Adullam (v. 15b) lies in Judah's western lowlands about twelve miles northwest of Hebron. The locations of two cities in the central hill country are well established: Bethel (v. 16b) is tel-Beitin ten miles north of Jerusalem, and Tappuah (v. 17a) stands twelve miles north of Bethel. Less certain but probable are the locations of Hepher (v. 17b) at Tel-Muhafar, a few miles south of Megiddo,[31] and Aphek (v. 18a) in the Sharon Plain about eighteen miles west of Tappuah, with Lasharon (v. 18b) probably somewhere nearby.[32]

Of the six northern cities, the identification of four are fairly certain. Taanach (v. 21a; Tel-Ti'innik), Megiddo (v. 21b), and Jokneam (v. 22b) all sit a few miles apart along the ridge overlooking the Jezreel Valley. Taanach and Megiddo guard a heavily-traveled mountain pass that connects the valley with the Sharon Plain.[33] Tirzah (v. 24a), the first capital of the later northern kingdom (1 Kings 14:17; 15:21, 33; 16:8, 15, 23), is probably Tel el-Far'ah North, about seven miles northeast of Shechem. It occupies a hilltop between two springs at the head of the Wadi Far'ah, a small, fertile valley whose river flows down to the Jordan.[34]

---

26. Nelson, *Joshua*, 161; Howard, *Joshua*, 281–82.

27. So, Fritz, *Josua*, 133; Hess, *Joshua*, 227. This identification presumes that the site's modern Arabic site name preserves the Hebrew original.

28. C. H. Ehrlich, "Geder (Place)," *ABD*, 2:924, surveys possible locations.

29. Hess, *Joshua*, 227; Boling, *Joshua*, 327; cf. J. M. Hamilton, "Hormah (Place)," *ABD*, 3:289.

30. Fritz, *Josua*, 133; Hess, *Joshua*, 227.

31. A. Zertal, "Hepher (Place)," *ABD*, 3:139.

32. Alternatively, Fritz (*Josua*, 135) and Nelson (*Joshua*, 158) follow LXX, reading Heb. *lašaron* as clarifying which among several ancient Apheks is meant (i.e., "Aphek of the Sharon Plain") rather than a separate place. But, as Howard notes (*Joshua*, 282), MT identifies each with it own king.

33. Boling, *Joshua*, 328–29.

34. D. W. Manor, "Tirzah (Place)," *ABD*, 6:574; Hess, *Joshua*, 227.

Kedesh (v. 22a) is probably Tel Abu Qudeis, a small mound in the Jezreel Valley between Taanach and Megiddo.[35] Finally, Goyim in Gilgal (v. 23b) strikes some readers as a strange name since Goyim in Hebrew means "non-Israelite peoples," and the Bible attests no northern city of Gilgal. "Goim of Galilee" in LXX compares stylistically to the two places it follows in the list and makes a little more sense. It could designate a city (cf. Harosheth Haggoyim, the hometown of Sisera [Judg. 4:2]), or a region (cf. "Galilee of the Goyim" [Isa. 9:1(8:23)]) somewhere in the north.[36]

With "the king of Tirzah ... one ... thirty-one kings in all" the curtain falls on the long conquest narrative, leaving a moment of silence on stage. In that moment, the reader senses how vast was the sweep of Joshua's victories. As Hawk writes, "the repetitive listing of defeated kings creates a cumulative effect much greater than the sum of its parts."[37] Further, the juxtaposition of thirty-one kings and the repeated word "one" serves to contrast Canaan's royal plurality with Israel's oneness. Again, Hawk captures the point: "The list thus sets the multiplicity of Canaan against the constancy of oneness."[38]

The total triumph comes from one God, Yahweh, and one united people, Israel. Besides drawing the conquest to a close, the list also literarily anticipates what follows. With Tirzah, the list returns the reader to the Israelite heartland, the place where the long process of allocation will soon begin. Further, the roster omits significant ancient cities — notably, Shechem — thus foreshadowing the theme of *un*conquered land with which the following chapter opens.[39]

Bridging Contexts

JOSHUA 12 IS ABOUT kings whom Israel defeated, events whose importance earned them mention in Psalms 135 and 136. Those passages single out the east-bank Amorite kings, Sihon and Og, as representative of the larger group of fallen monarchs, and both credit the victories to Yahweh alone rather than to human heroes.[40] In Psalm 135, an

---

35. R. Arav, "Kedesh (Place)," *ABD*, 4:11; Boling, *Joshua*, 329. Alternatively, Howard (*Joshua*, 282–83) identifies it with the later city of refuge and Levitical city northwest of Lake Huleh in northern Naphtali (19:37; 20:7; 21:32).

36. Hess (*Joshua*, 228, n.1) says that Gilgal and Galilee may be variations of the same name, specifically a region, whose ruler would have reigned from a capital city. He suggests that the name Jiljuliyey, a site three miles north of Aphek, might preserve the ancient city's name.

37. Hawk, *Joshua*, 176.

38. Ibid., 176, n.24.

39. Hess, *Joshua*, 229.

40. This contrasts the litany of fallen monarchs in Joshua 12, which credits them to Moses, Joshua, and the Israelites (vv. 1, 6, 7). For other memories, see Ps. 68:12[13]; 105:43–44;

individual affirms Yahweh's greatness and authority over both creation and history: "He struck down many nations and killed mighty kings ... and ... gave their land as an inheritance ... to his people Israel" (135:10, 12). In Psalm 136, a group thanksgiving liturgy, the parallel claims "[he] struck down great kings" // "and killed mighty kings" evoke the audience reply, "His love [*ḥesed*] endures forever" (136:17).

Interestingly, similar phrases about the same events evince associations with at least two different truths about Yahweh's character—his sovereign greatness and his covenant love (*ḥesed*). To prepare for the next section, however, we explore two themes: Yahweh's unquestioned authority, and the realities of human kingship.

Yahweh's unquestioned authority. Nebuchadnezzar learned the hard way that Yahweh does not share his sovereignty with anyone—period! Recall the scene in which Daniel both "tells" and "interprets" the king's dream (in contrast to only "interpreting"). The prophet affirms before the king that besides controlling times and seasons and dispensing wisdom and knowledge, Yahweh also "sets up kings and deposes them" (Dan. 2:21; cf. Ps. 47:9[10]).

Two chapters later, surveying greater Babylon from his palace roof, Nebuchadnezzar forgets that truth and sadly runs afoul of Yahweh. Enchanted by the sparkling scene below, he blurts out his true feelings: "Is not this the great Babylon I have built ... by my mighty power and for the glory of my majesty?" (Dan. 4:30). In essence, the king sings a praise chorus in his own honor—"How Great I Art!" (4:30). That very bad insult of Yahweh reveals how out of touch with reality the unfortunate king is and makes his punishment—temporary insanity as a grazing wild animal—fitting poetic justice. He remains so until he regains his senses—until he acknowledges that "the Most High is sovereign over the kingdoms of earth and gives them to anyone he wishes" (Dan. 4:32 TNIV).

This is no isolated incident. Two centuries earlier, the arrogant message that King Sennacherib of Assyria sent to intimidate Jerusalem into surrender similarly demeans Yahweh, an insult for which the king later paid with his life (2 Kings 18:29–35; 19:32–37). Other texts warn kings not to overstep their boundaries as subordinate to Yahweh. The Song of Deborah (Judg. 5) directly addresses kings ("Hear this, you kings!" [v. 3]), then sings a victory song about Yahweh's defeat of "the kings of Canaan" under Sisera's

---

Amos 2:10. For a larger study of later biblical memories of events in Joshua, see Hubbard, "Only a Distant Memory," 131–48. Biblical tradition often remembers the defeats of Sihon and Og as paradigms of Yahweh's victories and/or gift of land (Deut. 1:4; 29:7; 31:4; Josh. 2:10; 9:10; Neh. 9:22; cf. 1 Kings 4:19).

command at Taanach (v. 19; cf. Judg. 4). Yahweh's cosmic forces engage them ("from the heavens the stars fought ... against Sisera" [v. 20]) and his natural forces—in this case, the river Kishon—"swept them away" (vv. 20, 21). To conclude, the poet addresses Yahweh ("So may all your enemies perish, O LORD!" [v. 31]). By singing of Yahweh's past victory the writer forewarns other kings of the dire consequences of crossing the line from subordinate to "enemy."[41]

Psalm 2 issues a similar warning. At the outset, the writer finds the royal foolishness incredible ("Why do the nations conspire ... in vain?" [v. 1]); to rebel against the Davidic king ("the LORD's anointed") is to attack Yahweh himself! (vv. 2 – 3).[42] The sight of this foolhardiness causes God, enthroned in heaven, to burst out laughing (v. 4). Laughter gives way to rebuke—and to Yahweh's reassertion of his prior decree that designated the Israelite king as his on-site ruler for earth (vv. 5 – 9; cf. 2 Sam. 7).[43] The psalmist concludes the poem with a warning for earth's kings. If they are wise and wish to escape destruction, they will "serve the LORD with fear" and "kiss the Son"—i.e., acknowledge the king's supreme authority—and enjoy the blessing of his protection (vv. 11 – 12).

Behind this psalm stands the important theme of Yahweh's kingship over all creation and all creatures. "The LORD reigns" ensures the continuation of a stable universe (Ps. 93:1; 96:10). It also provides them a cosmic Supreme Court from which to receive justice for their complaints and vengeance on their oppressors (Ps. 94:2, 23; 99:4).

The experience of abuse and oppression underscores an additional aspect of God's reign, his role as rescuer. "The LORD reigns" gives the oppressed a refuge to which to flee for protection, an ear alert to hear anguished cries, and a mighty deliverer from deathly dangers (Ps. 9:9, 12, 13 [10, 13, 14]; cf. 97:10; 99:6, 7). Several times the psalmists address Yahweh with a special title, "God our Savior," in appeals for deliverance from trouble (Ps. 65:5[6]; 68:19[20]; 79:9; 85:5; cf. 1 Chron. 16:34 – 36). Other psalmists cry, "Help me [*hošiʿah*], O king!" invoking the traditional Israelite appeal for help (lit., "Save!") from Yahweh and his human, royal representative (2 Sam. 14:4; 2 Kings 6:26).[44]

---

41. As with 11:23, this victory also yields peace throughout the land, in this case, for forty years (Judg. 5:31).

42. The term "Messiah" transliterates Heb. *mašiaḥ* ("anointed one"), a key word to which we will return in the Contemporary Significance section.

43. The decree also affirms the special father-son relationship Yahweh shares with the Davidic kings.

44. J. F. Sawyer, "יָשַׁע," *TDOT*, 6:445; R. L. Hubbard Jr., "יָשַׁע," *NIDOTTE*, 2:556 – 57, 559 – 61.

Similarly, the psalmists invoke the word in anguished cries ("Help!") to King Yahweh (Ps. 12:1[2]; 20:9[10]; 28:9; 60:5[7]; 108:6[7]). The situations from which such cries for divine intervention arise are practical and down-to-earth: ongoing enemy attacks, recent military defeats, and malicious talk within Israel; the defense of good people against bad people; and the restoration of Israel to divine favor. But one important clarification merits mention: Sometimes God's salvation involves rescue (i.e., removal) from the danger, but in most cases it brings divine help "into a situation of distress or danger, to people where they are and where they need it."[45] This distinction will illumine our discussion in the next section.

Finally, Psalm 146:6 singles out two qualities of Yahweh that anchor his role as Savior and lead those who seek him to praise him. (1) Only he is the Creator, "the Maker of heaven and earth, the sea, and everything in them." In other words, he has the means sufficient to save. If he acts, he can get the rescue job done without question. But how does one know that he *will* respond if called upon? (2) His second quality, his faithfulness (he "remains faithful forever") affirms his unwavering commitment to the well-being of his people. He simply keeps his promises.

In other words, as awesome Creator, God has the means to help, and as faithful covenant-partner he has the will to help. That is why the psalmist exhorts fellow Israelites, "Do not put your trust in princes, in mortal men, who cannot save" (Ps. 146:3). The mortality of human rulers, says the biblical poet, makes them an unreliable source for salvation ("who cannot save"). They may die suddenly before executing their rescue plan (v. 4)—unlike the eternal reliability of Yahweh, who "reigns forever" (v. 10). Small wonder the psalmist brackets Psalm 146 with appropriate calls to "Praise the LORD!" (vv. 1, 10b). He is, indeed, the only reliable Savior!

The truth that "the LORD reigns" and does what good kings do (i.e., rescues from danger, protects the weak from abuse, provides for the poor, etc.) gives earth's people a prime reason to rejoice (Ps. 97:1). What a good, kind king he is:

> He upholds the cause of the oppressed
> > and gives food to the hungry.
> The LORD sets prisoners free,
> > the LORD gives sight to the blind,
> the LORD lifts up those who are bowed down,
> > the LORD loves the righteous.

---

45. Sawyer, "יָשַׁע," 6:462; cf. 445, 463; Hubbard, "יָשַׁע," 2:556.

The LORD watches over the alien
  and sustains the fatherless and the widow,
  but he frustrates the ways of the wicked. (Ps. 146:7–9)

Yahweh feeds the hungry, frees prisoners held against their will (as was Israel in Egypt), gives the blind their sight, and steadies those bearing heavy loads. He protects the especially vulnerable—the resident alien, the orphan, the widow—by stymieing cruel attempts to take unfair advantage of weakness. And he expects his earthly royal representatives—that is, any king, Israelite or otherwise, whom he appoints—to exercise a similar benevolent rule. Indeed—and this is an important point to which we will return below—there are two quick ways for a king to lose his throne: by denying Yahweh's supremacy (Dan. 4:31) and by abusing his power (i.e., by favoring elites over the lowly; see Dan. 4:27).

The realities of human kingship. The human need for Yahweh's salvation derives from this second theme. Above I briefly mentioned what kind of kings those listed in Joshua 12 were, and here I amplify this further. Susan Zuckerman aptly describes the larger historical scene at the time:

Syria and Canaan in the second millennium B.C.E. were divided into local kingdoms, ruled by local kings and managed by ruling elites. This situation is vividly reflected in the Amarna archive. The lavish lifestyles of these kings and their sometimes-extravagant palaces are often mentioned. The King of Hazor held a special position among his Canaanite peers. Abdi-Tirshi of Hazor is the only Canaanite vassal to be called "king" by other rulers and by himself. He aspired to acquire additional territories from his neighbors, the rulers of Tyre and Ashtaroth.[46]

Clearly, a social hierarchy headed by kings and a powerful bureaucracy dominated the daily lives of people in Syria and Canaan.[47] One can imagine the kinds of demands placed on ordinary people to support such lavish royal lifestyles. Certainly, one demand was taxes on levied goods produced, and a levy of labor for royal building projects was another. A military draft of young men also probably preceded the king's attempts to extend his

---

46. S. Zuckerman, "Where Is the Hazor Archive Buried?" *BAR* 32/2 (March–April 2006): 34. For discussion and interpretation of the palace precinct at Hazor, see pp. 34–37. Ben-Ami proposes that the standing stones at Hazor may "commemorate some high-ranking individuals who were part of the government bureaucracy" (i.e., among Zuckerman's "ruling elites"); cf. D. Ben-Ami, "Mysterious Standing Stones: What Do These Ubiquitous Things Mean?" *BAR* 33/2 (March–April 2006): 45 (entire article: 38–45).

47. Cf. the discussion of this in the Introduction.

realm into territory ruled by his competitor-kings. (Or the king may have had a standing army supported by taxes). Undoubtedly, many young troops paid the ultimate price in such royal ventures. One glimpses something of the cruelty that competing kings inflicted on each other in the comment of Adoni-Bezek, a king captured by Judah: "Seventy kings with their thumbs and big toes cut off have picked up scraps under my table. Now God has paid me back for what I did to them" (Jdg. 1:7).[48]

The acropolis at Hazor shows three temples — the "Southern" and "Long" temples, and the "Royal Sanctuary" — that together comprise "a ceremonial religious precinct."[49] Although distance separated the palace from the temple precinct at Hazor, ancient kings typically sponsored the local cultic site and received religious legitimation from it for their rule. Socially, the gap between the rich (the king, the elites) and the poor was no doubt wide, with the latter vulnerable to the whim of the powerful — and powerless to defend themselves.

Palaces like those at Ugarit, Megiddo, and Hazor feature "royal portals" where special visitors performed religious rituals. They are entrances reserved exclusively for international VIPs: royal ambassadors from other leading cities, international businessmen, and other distinguished guests of the king. Of course, these entrances were off-limits to ordinary residents.[50] Implicit in this description is an indictment of oppressive royal hegemony and also of the alliance between the kings and their gods. These mark the underbelly of the realities of ancient royal leadership. They offer justification for the dismantling of this system in Joshua 2 – 11 and perhaps imply that dismantling as divine judgment.

Two primary biblical voices, each in a farewell speech, warn Israel of the risky dangers in having a king. Moses instructs Israel *not* to have a king like those of other nations, while Samuel surveys the downside of monarchical leadership. But the following chart of their main points further fleshes out what the Canaanite kings of Joshua 12 were like.

According to Moses, the typical trappings of ancient monarchy include: intimidating military might (many horses), enviable prestige embodied in a large harem (many wives, including marriages to seal international alli-

---

48. The prospect of attack by well-known military powers also terrified cities (2 Kings 7:6; 10:4), and enemy propaganda played on such fears to win their surrender (2 Kings 19:11). For further discussion of the social situation in Canaan, see the Introduction (the Historical Setting of Joshua).

49. Zuckerman, "Where Is the Hazor Archive Buried?" 32 – 34. Zuckerman believes (pp. 35 – 37) that an area previously identified as the city's gate area actually marks the entry to a large royal palace.

50. Ibid., 37.

Moses	Samuel
Things Forbidden (Deut. 17:14–20)	Things To Expect (1 Sam. 8:11–18)
Chosen by people, not God (v. 15a)	Draft of sons as enlisted military (v. 11)
Possible non-Israelite king (v. 15b)	Commission of sons as military officers (v. 12a)
A large stable of horses (v. 16a)	Draft of sons to tend and harvest royal lands (v. 12b)
Return trips to Egypt to buy them (v. 16b)	Draft of sons into war industries (v. 12c)
Multiple, foreign-born, royal wives (v. 17a)	Draft of daughters to serve the royal palace (v. 13)
Large silver and gold holdings (v. 17b)	Demand for the best agricultural products to supply his personal staff (v. 14)
Lack of reverence for God (vv. 18–19a)	Ten-percent tax to pay other royal officials (v. 15)
Disobedience of God's law (v. 19b)	Demand for laborers and "best" cattle/donkeys for himself (v. 16)
Social superiority over fellow Israelites (v. 20)	Ten-percent tax of flocks (v. 17a)
	Enslavement of the populace (v. 17b)
	A deaf-ear from God to their cries (v. 18)

ances), and very great wealth (silver and gold). In Wright's words, "Weapons, women, and wealth. Why else be a king?"[51] Samuel's description underscores the perks that kings pursue and their price tag for the populace. It repeats the key phrase "he (the king) will take …," implying the victims of his "taking" have no say in the matter. It is the people whose sons man his military and tend his lands, whose daughters serve in his palace, whose fields and flocks supply his royal table and fund his lavish lifestyle. In essence, they are slaves to his demands. Thus, the list of defeated kings in Joshua 12 memorializes the end of Canaan's corrupt, oppressive social system—in itself, a kind of "salvation." Their fall should not surprise us, for as Elihu told Job:

51. C. J. H. Wright, *Deuteronomy* (Peabody, MA: Hendrickson, 1996), 209.

> Can he who hates justice govern?
>> Will you condemn the just and mighty One?
> Is he not the One who says to kings, 'You are worthless,'
>> and to nobles, 'You are wicked,'
> who shows no partiality to princes
>> and does not favor the rich over the poor...?
> Without inquiry he shatters the mighty
>> and sets up others in their place....
> He punishes them for their wickedness
>> where everyone can see them....
> They caused the cry of the poor to come before him,
>> so that he heard the cry of the needy. (Job 34:17 – 19, 24, 26, 28)

The implication is that when God deposes kings, it is because they ignored the cries of people in need and favored the rich over the poor. They were partial. "He who hates justice" cannot govern at all.

And so Joshua 12 remembers their just demise. It recalls the end of their royal pretensions much as Shelley's poem "Ozymandias" does:

> I met a traveller from an antique land
> Who said: — Two vast and trunkless legs of stone
> Stand in the desert. Near them on the sand,
> Half sunk, a shatter'd visage lies, whose frown
> And wrinkled lip and sneer of cold command
> Tell that its sculptor well those passions read
> Which yet survive, stamp'd on these lifeless things,
> The hand that mock'd them and the heart that fed.
> And on the pedestal these words appear:
> "My name is Ozymandias, king of kings:
> Look on my works, ye mighty, and despair!"
> Nothing beside remains: round the decay
> Of that colossal wreck, boundless and bare,
> The lone and level sands stretch far away.[52]

Now, at the end of the day, when the reader finishes reading "thirty-one kings in all" (v. 24), is there really *no* king left? No, there is one still standing—Almighty King Yahweh, Israel's God. In fact, he is the only real "King of all the earth," who "reigns over the nations"—the Greatly Exalted One to whom earth's kings belong (Ps. 47:7 – 9). All others are mere pretenders. And, as we will now see, his royal sovereignty still continues.

---

52. Quoted from en.wikipedia.org/wiki/Ozymandias.

IN MY VIEW, YAHWEH still reigns today through another king, Jesus Christ, the Son of God. The New Testament portrays Jesus' entry into the city of Jerusalem — the event we celebrate each year on Palm Sunday — as the arrival of Israel's long-awaited messianic king (Matt. 21:1 – 11; cf. Isa. 11:1 – 5; Zech. 9:9). But John's Revelation also recognizes in the Lamb (i.e., Jesus) someone who is more than just a Jewish king. He is the supreme king — "King of kings and Lord of lords" (Rev. 19:16; cf. 17:14). Thus, the affirmation "there is no king but Jesus" (see below) forms the basis for the contemporary significance of Joshua 12.

The New Testament reports that Jesus came announcing that the long-awaited kingdom of God had finally arrived (Mark 1:14 – 15; Luke 4:18 – 21). More important, it accords him a level of honor that smacks of kingship — for example, Paul's comment that one day every knee will bow before the name of Jesus (Phil. 2:10). Four questions will guide the discussion that follows: Do we need a king? Why call Jesus "king"? What kind of king is King Jesus? If Jesus is king, so what?

Do we need a king? Some time ago, a senior enlisted person retired from the Navy after nearly three decades of service. She permanently entered the day-to-day civilian world for the first time in a long time. After few weeks, she returned to the base to visit the office from which she had retired.

"How's it going out there in the civilian life, Chief?" someone asked.

"Oh, it's just terrible," she said straightforwardly.

"'Terrible'? What's wrong?"

"Well," the chief said, "just think about it a moment: all those people running around and nobody in charge!"

Every society navigates between the magnetic poles of order on the one hand, and chaos on the other. In my view, behind this stands something inherent in the cosmos since creation. In fact, the concept of chaotic forces formed part of the worldview of ancient peoples. Biblically, one glimpses this in two well-known passages, the first creation account (Gen. 1) and the flood story (Gen. 6 – 9). The former has watery chaos in mind when it describes the earth as "formless and empty," covered with deep waters, and shrouded in darkness (Gen. 1:2). Through creation, God bends the forces of chaos to his will and permanently establishes an orderly, stable (i.e., nonchaotic) universe.

In the flood story, however, in judgment God releases the "springs of the great deep" and throws open the "floodgates of the heavens" (Gen. 7:11). He temporarily returns the earth to its former, watery, chaotic state. Much ancient Near Eastern religion aimed at keeping the frightening forces of chaos at bay, and in my opinion, similar, primal fears of disorder still lurk in the human psyche. Nothing more unsettles people than the frightening feeling that things are somehow "out of control" with no one in charge.

Recent events in North America probably have stirred the same feelings. Since the events of September 11, 2001, a series of terrorist attacks in various countries have kept Western democracies on high alert to thwart new threats. Some politicians continue to warn that "we're at war"—the war on terror—and counsel a high level of vigilance. Passage through airport security checkpoints reminds ordinary people that they are less secure than they once were. At the same time, some worry about the possible erosion of historic civil liberties as governments pursue potential terrorists through exceptional means.

Meanwhile, unexpected violent events at schools and businesses, in some cases with multiple fatalities, certainly raise popular anxiety about the threat that emotionally troubled people might suddenly pose to the safety of one's family. Economic globalization, including the shift of many jobs to places outside North America, signals that the world is changing—and beyond one's control. Many North Americans experience this personally (as I did recently) when consulting a telephone help desk with the speaker in India. The influx of immigrants and their increasing visibility even in small towns creates situations where cultural misunderstandings, and perhaps even suspicions, unsettle people with limited prior cross-cultural experience.

Finally, a concern is growing that global warming may, in fact, be a threatening reality caused by human lifestyles and that we may be approaching (or have already passed) the point of no return in reversing it.

In short, rapid modern communications means that the world is very much with us—and not happily so. An uneasiness, if not outright fear, simmers beneath the surface of many hearts. The need for "kings"—for able prime ministers, presidents, governors, business leaders, pastors, school teachers, parents, and so on—is enormous. People are eager for them to take charge, to solve problems, and to reduce popular anxiety. But a nagging feeling persists that the size of some problems may ultimately be beyond human resolution.

What particularly moves me, however, are the ongoing pressures I sense people face today. The schedules young families keep, especially when both parents work or when one parent home-schools several children, are daunting. The demands of school (or home-school) are big enough, but the addition of healthy after-school activities significantly increases the strain. At an intersection near my home, I occasionally see their vans dutifully shuttling kids to ballet or music lessons, soccer or swimming practice, church activities or shopping trips to the mall. To say they live "busy lives" is an understatement. The organizational skills and sheer physical stamina required can prove challenging.

What about the financial pressures to fund the feeding, clothing, educating, entertaining, and multiactivity expected of them? Then come the standardized tests that, at least in my state, determine whether their eighth-graders can enter the best public high school. Parents often have to help kids deal with disappointment over the results, but then the crusade to gain admission to a good college or university begins. It requires its own relentless pursuit of academics and activities, all while the teens traverse the emotional highs and lows of high school relationships. Both parents and kids truly need a strong and wise king to help them navigate the fleeting years and all that life and society throw at them. Thankfully, instead of the self-centered kings of ancient Canaan, they have Jesus Christ as their potential friend and guide.

Why call Jesus "king"? In the popular movie *The Lion King*, King Mufasa proudly rules the Pride Lands as king of the jungle from his home at Pride Rock. His son is Simba, a fun-loving, rambunctious lion cub whose childhood adventures and maturing process mark a central theme of the film. In one delightful scene, Simba and the hornbill Zazu discuss the fact that the cub will one day succeed his father as king. Much to Zazu's dismay, Simba revels in the happy prospect of becoming king in the song, "I Just Can't Wait to be King." Proudly, he looks forward to being the one in charge rather than having to obey the orders of others. To that end, he is practicing looking down on people and sharpening the terror of his roar. His special joy will be the freedom to do whatever he wants and to hold the spotlight of everyone's attention. He can hardly wait to have all eyes riveted on him as he publicly struts his royal stuff. In the song, thoughts of his wonderful royal future erupt in his repeated, enthusiastic cry, "Oh, I just can't wait to be king!"

Simba's understanding of kingship approaches that of the Canaanite kings. His goal is to terrify enemies and to boss people around with his "roar." It brings a freedom to do whatever one pleases rather than to obey the orders of others. It guarantees him the starring role in the spotlight at center stage, all eyes on him alone. Alas, Simba and the Canaanite kings have many descendants today, each thinking, "Oh, I just can't wait to be king!" Politicians, religious leaders, famous athletes, film idols, rock stars, and founders of movements all proclaim, "Follow me!" They eagerly beckon for enthronement as king—or, at least, as "kingpins." Given the felt-need for either, many garner sizeable followings.

What rightful claim does Jesus have to being king? Why choose him over modern Canaanite ones? The simple answer is that the God whom

the Old Testament celebrates as king appointed him as David's successor. Recall that, for all practical purposes, the four-century-long run of the
Davidic monarchy ended with the death of King Jehoiachin in Babylon
(mid-sixth cent. B.C.). When Judah returned from exile in 538 B.C., it did
not reestablish the monarchy, but the prophetic hope of a future new David
remained strong (see Isa. 11:1; Am. 9:11; Mic. 5:2). Recall, further, that the
Old Testament refers to each ruling Davidic descendant as the "anointed of
the LORD" or "his/your/my anointed one" (*mašiaḥ*). The LXX translates *mašiaḥ*
literally as *christos* ("anointed one"), which becomes "Christ" or "the Christ"
in English (e.g., Matt. 2:4; 16:16; Luke 23:35; Acts 2:36).[53] In short, when
his contemporaries quizzed Jesus about being "the Christ," they wanted to
know if he was the long-awaited new David or (in our terms) "the Messiah"
(Mark 14:61; Luke 22:67).[54]

By tracing Jesus' genealogy to David ("son of David," Matt. 1:1), Matthew connects Jesus with the prophecies and undergirds his identification
of Jesus as "Christ" and "the Christ" (Matt. 1:16–17). Those seemingly
simple words stamp Jesus as the long-expected king sent by God himself
to transform history. They form the context in which to hear two early
confessions of Jesus—in reality, two surrenders to his kingship. The first
is by Peter ("You are the Christ, the Son of the living God" [Matt. 16:16]),
the second by Nathaniel ("Rabbi, you are the Son of God; you are the King
of Israel" [John 1:49]). They still supply the words by which people of all
times and places may voice their own submission to this king.

Jesus—what kind of king? Joshua 5–11 pictures the kings of Canaan
as monarchs willing to go to war against Israel and Yahweh in order to preserve their political power (cf. Josh. 2:2–3). As noted above, the Amarna
Letters from Egypt (fourteenth cent. B.C.) portray them as conspiratorial
royal rivals of each other and somewhat abusive of their subjects. The really
important question for us, however, concerns how Jesus compares to other
kings familiar to us, including modern Canaanite ones. One thing, first of
all, sets the reign of Jesus apart: He is a *good king*. Ponder a statement from
Peter's talk before the household of the Gentile, Cornelius:

> You know what has happened throughout Judea, beginning in Gali-
> lee after the baptism that John preached—how God anointed Jesus
> of Nazareth with the Holy Spirit and power, and *how he went around*

---

53. Cf. "anointed of the LORD" (1 Sam. 24:7, 11; 2 Sam. 19:22; Lam. 4:22), "his/your/
my anointed one" (1 Sam. 2:10, 35; 2 Sam. 22:51; Ps. 2:2; 18:50 [51]; 132:10, 17), and "an
anointed one" (Dan. 9:25–26).

54. The word "Messiah" transliterates into English the Gk. word *messias*, a term that
occurs only twice (John 1:41; 4:25) and is itself a transliteration of Heb. *mašiaḥ*.

doing good and healing all who were under the power of the devil, because God was with him. (Acts 10:37 − 38, my italics)

Empowered by the Holy Spirit and God's presence, Peter says simply, Jesus "went around doing good...." Several things strike me about this simple testimony. (1) "Went around" (Gk. *dierxomai*, lit., "went *through*") seems to picture Jesus as passing through the midst of the places he visited. My mind, thus, imagines him mobbed by crowds as he enters and makes his way through each town or village. The people are thinking, "Wow, the famous Rabbi has come to *our* backwater!" It is a Jesus who mills among the locals shaking hands, giving occasional hugs, joking with the crowd, and asking about what has been going on. It is a Jesus who loves ordinary people and loves to be with them.

That picture could not more starkly contrast what I witness when today's kingpins venture out in public: a helicopter gently lands them behind an impenetrable wall of security personnel; or a phalanx of siren-squealing, lights-flashing motorcycle police leads a caravan of black limousines with darkly-tinted, bullet-proof windows to the protective wall waiting a short drive away. Most of the eager crowd will barely catch a quick glimpse of the famous passenger. A walk to shake hands, much less josh, with onlookers is still done occasionally but thought awfully risky. The only "handlers" are aides and security agents who crowd around their celebrity through his or her every move.

(2) As he passed through the crowd, Jesus was "doing good." Peter omits details, but, again, my imagination pictures something other than an aloof, security-conscious Jesus. I see him pausing along the way to teach the crowds, to pray for individuals in particular need, to encourage the elderly with a smile or kind word, and to listen to what is on everyone's mind. I imagine him stopping to play with children, to kid the street merchants about giving him a good bargain, to discuss local problems with the village elders, and to wave smilingly at people on the rooftops. I picture him organizing the disciples into impromptu work groups to help repair a home, pave a street, fetch needed water, or do some heavy lifting. Definitely not the smiling, waving, aloof modern kingpin who in reality seems to be fleeing for his or her life! Instead, he models for us a down-and-dirty, feet-on-the-ground, up-close-and-personal engagement in the lives and struggles of the people around us today.

Peter singles out one "good" activity, his "healing [of] all who were under the power of the devil, because God was with him." Rare is the kingpin today who bothers with the mentally ill, the unclean, the unkempt, the depressed, the lonely, and the grieving. But not so with Jesus. He not only bothered, but he brought God's powerful presence wherever he went. A kingpin's fear or loathing might avert his eyes from looking and quicken his steps to escape the danger, but not Jesus. He went right up to the demon-possessed, the deranged, and the dirty. He even—are you ready for this?—touched them! To him the demons, dirt, and derangement smacked of a cruel servitude reminiscent of Canaan's ancient kings. His power healed them, freeing them from racking torments and restoring them to joyous health and sound minds. And Jesus is still the great healer. He can still put shattered lives back together, repair brokenness, restore lost hope, sweeten bitter grief, and cast out all our inner demons. Listen to this, one of his royal decrees:

> Come to me, all you who are weary and burdened, and I will give you rest. Take my yoke upon you and learn from me, for I am gentle and humble in heart, and you will find rest for your souls. For my yoke is easy and my burden is light. (Matt. 11:28–30)

What a different king is this Jesus! Canaanite-type kings ride in luxury on the bent backs of weary workers, but Jesus promises refreshing "rest"—a break from back-breaking labor—and only "light" and "easy" burdens. That is the kind of king that pressured people today want—a "good king" unlike any other.

Jesus is also a *king who saves.* This dimension of Jesus' kingship first appears among the Bible's most familiar texts, the birth narratives. For example, as Joseph ponders a quiet divorce from his pregnant fiancé, Mary, in a dream an angel advises him instead to marry her. The angel also commands him to give her son the name Jesus, "because he will save his people from their sin," and he did so (Matt. 1:21, 25). The angel puns on the name, Jesus (Gk. *Iesous*), the LXX word for "Joshua" (Heb. *yešuʿa*, probably "Yahweh is help").[55] The wordplay connects him with the promised "help" (i.e., salvation) from sin. Similarly, the angel announces to the shepherds the birth in Bethlehem of "a Savior"—"Christ the Lord" (Luke 2:11). These texts echo the Old Testament idea of salvation as rescue out of danger.

Later, in his home at Jericho, the once-corrupt tax collector Zacchaeus responds to Jesus' surprising visit by repenting of his shady past. He promises to contribute half his net worth to the poor and to repay his victims four times the amount he cheated them—apparently, obeying the law of theft (Ex. 22:1). Jesus then announces, "Today salvation has come to this house"—"salvation" in the sense of divine help that transforms one's way of life so that he escapes punishment. It all results, Jesus adds, from the fact that Jesus' mission is to "seek and to save what was lost" (Luke 19:8–10). As

---

55. KB, 379–80.

Evans says, "Jesus calls all to repentance, religious and irreligious, healthy and sick, rich and poor."[56]

Our Palm Sunday celebrations also remember that Jesus is a king who saves. As is well known, in Matthew's view Jesus' entry into Jerusalem amid the approving, palm-waving throng fulfills Zechariah 9:9. The latter foretells the coming of a future, gentle king (the Messiah) who enters the city on a donkey as had Solomon at his accession (1 Kings 1:38, 44). The donkey is not a war horse and, hence, signals that the king is on a goodwill mission.[57] The people's spreading of cloaks and branches on the roadway probably also marks the moment as a festive one like the Feast of Tabernacles (cf. 2 Kings 9:13).

For our purposes, however, the item to highlight is the series of cries that sweep the crowd as the royal procession escorting Jesus inside proceeds. They shout: "Hosanna!" "Blessed is he who comes in the name of the Lord!" "Blessed is the King of Israel!" (John 12:13). "Hosanna" is the Greek transliteration of the Aramaic form of *hoši‘a na'* from Psalm 118:25, the traditional cry to Yahweh for help discussed in the previous section. By invoking that formula, the throng unwittingly welcomes the long-awaited new David with the shout that once greeted the old Davidic kings.[58] They also unknowingly recognize him as Savior, the one whose royal procession will end with him hanging on a cross bearing the ironic sign, "King of the Jews." He is, indeed, a king—but one who saves by giving his own life. And he still saves people today.

Above I pointed out that "to save" in the Old Testament has two senses, "to rescue" out of trouble and "to help" in the midst of it.[59] As Savior, Jesus rescues us from all kinds of things. I know this from long years of personal experience, as do (I presume) many readers. His forgiveness unshackles the chains of sin that bind me, freeing me from my slavery to it. His power bails me out of the messes which I sometimes create for myself. His grace gently lifts me up when I fall so he and I can go on together. His patience also warmly embraces me when I fail him, and his smile dispels the dark clouds of discouragement and shame that often envelop me. His soothing presence shepherds me through the dark valleys of despair through which I sometimes must pass.

As Savior, Jesus also helps all of us persevere and survive amidst the troubles so common in daily life. He wisely helps us endure difficult job

56. Evans, *Luke*, 281. In his view, Luke 19:10 recapitulates the central themes of Luke 15.
57. R. H. Mounce, *Matthew* (Peabody, Mass.: Hendrickson, 1991), 194–95.
58. J. A. Motyer, "ὡσαννά," *NIDNTT*, 1:100; cf. Matt. 21:9; Mark 11:9.
59. Sawyer, "יָשַׁע," 6:462; cf. 445, 463; Hubbard, "יָשַׁע," 2:556.

situations from which we find escape impossible. He firmly sustains us through trying circumstances that might otherwise overwhelm us. He lovingly lifts our spirits through moments when we get down on ourselves. He patiently reminds us that we belong to him when doubts or uncertainties weaken our faith. In short, Jesus is a Savior sufficient for our needs.

The highly-regarded movie *Amazing Grace* portrays the life of William Wilberforce, a member of the British Parliament whose dogged, determined efforts in the early nineteenth century ended slavery in the British empire. John Newton, the spiritual mentor from whom Wilberforce often sought guidance, also figures prominently in the film. (Its title derives from the title of the still popular hymn written by Newton). Newton was the leading evangelical Anglican clergyman at the time, a man who had himself once commanded British slave ships.

In his biography of Newton, John Pollock recounts the events surrounding Newton's last days. Long known as a powerful preacher, at age eighty-two Newton insisted on trying to deliver one more sermon. But his feeble mind failed him, he lost his train of thought, and had to be led bewildered and confused down from the pulpit. Eventually, as he lay dying a few days before Christmas in 1807, he joked that he was all packed and waiting for the stagecoach to arrive. Then, his life ebbing away and heaven beckoning, he tried to say something. His friend William Jay leaned across the bed to catch Newton's last words. Almost inaudibly he whispered, "My memory is nearly gone, but I remember two things: that I am a great sinner," and, pausing to catch his breath, he managed to gasp: "and that Christ is *a great Savior!*"[60]

The quality of King Jesus leads me to respond in grateful surrender to that "great Savior." The joy is so great, the wonder so vast, that the words fail fully to voice my experience of that king. But the theme of the song "Lord Reign in Me" by Brenton Brown does express my longing for his lordship — that he both rein me in and reign in me.

Finally, the final destiny of King Jesus is as *victor over all other kings*. The angry mob that dragged Jason and several other early Christians before the city officials in Thessalonica were right: Besides (indeed, in defiance of) Caesar, "there is another king, one called Jesus" (Acts 17:7). The cross and empty tomb signal his reality-transforming power that triumphs over sin, death, and the invisible powers currently at war with God (see Col. 2:15). Those triumphs pave the way for the spread of the gospel, the extension of his loving rule to people worldwide who accept his salvation and commit to his lordship.

---

60. J. Pollock, *Amazing Grace: John Newton's Story* (San Francisco: Harper & Row, 1981), 182.

Every day, my newspaper chronicles the chaos of today's world: political uncertainty, the breakneck speed of change, wars between nations, economic competition between established and emerging nations, tyranny and oppression over the poor. As Joshua 12 remembers the final victory of Joshua and Israel over Canaan's kings, so John's vision of the end anticipates Jesus' final victory over earth's anti-God nations and economic interests at the second coming. Their demise brings long-waited relief to oppressed believers (Rev. 17–19).

In the vision, John sees "the [coming] punishment of the great prostitute" or Babylon. She is a stunning woman robed in the rich colors and glittering jewels of royalty—but also grotesquely drunk on the blood of Christian martyrs (Rev. 17:1, 4, 5). The "kings of the earth" have been her steady customers, the heady wine that her adulteries provide intoxicates the whole earth (v. 2), and its merchants became filthy rich by supplying her extravagant luxuries (18:3; cf. vv. 11–13). The woman's title is Babylon, "the great city that rules over the kings of the earth" (vv. 5, 18), ruled by "the beast." John's audience would read the prostitute as Rome and its global empire, but she also symbolizes "the 'global village' of godless power, which determines daily life for every person at any time in human history."[61] In order that the new Jerusalem may replace Babylon (21:2), "the Lamb" and his followers will decisively defeat Babylon, the beast, and their royal allies. The defeat is certain precisely because the Lamb is "the Lord of lords and King of kings" (17:14).

Suddenly, an angel announces Babylon's coming fate: "Fallen! Fallen is Babylon the Great" (18:2; cf. 14:8; Am. 5:2). She is justly going to receive back what she cruelly dished out to the world—a fiery end from God's hand for all her killing (18:6, 8). The angel warns Christians to leave the city immediately, lest her sins stain them and they share her doom (Rev. 18:4; cf. Gen. 18–19). The warning follows up one of the book's central themes, the call for Christians to resist strong social pressures bent on the corruption of their faith (Rev. 2:10, 13; 3:21; 14:12). The announcement of Babylon's fate plunges into mourning her royal allies, her suppliers of luxury, and the merchant fleet that delivered the goods (18:9–19).

But the angel calls for "saints and apostles and prophets" to rejoice because "God has judged her for the way she treated you" (Rev. 18:20). Suddenly, John hears the reaction in heaven to Babylon's fall, a huge throng shouting, "Hallelujah! Salvation and glory and power belong to our God" (19:1). From the heavenly throne a voice calls, "Praise our God, all you his servants, you who fear him, both small and great!" (19:5). The heavenly

61. R. W. Wall, *Revelation* (Peabody, Mass.: Hendrickson, 1991), 202.

381

multitude obeys with a thunderous shout: "For the wedding of the Lamb has come, and his bride has made herself ready" (19:6−7).

But another event intervenes before the wedding supper, the second coming of Christ, which John displays in three short visions (19:11−16, 17−18, 19−21).[62] Only the first one will concern us here. In it John sees a white horse in heaven, a symbol of victory, with a rider called Faithful and True (19:11a). He leads heaven's armies, also arrayed in white and riding white horses (v. 14). In pursuing justice and war, his fiery, blazing eyes can penetrate human pretensions and facades truly to discern guilt from innocence (vv. 11b−12). His name is "the Word of God," a reference to his incarnation as Messiah (v. 13; cf. John 1), and he defeats the nations with an unconventional sword. It comes out of his mouth, probably a reference to the proclamation of the gospel message about Christ's faithfulness to God. That proclamation exposes the contrary claims of the anti-Christian kingdom and its rulers for what they are—lies and deceptions. It also confirms that God's condemnation of nations that operate similarly is just (cf. Heb. 4:11−12).

Strikingly, unlike Joshua 2−11, no battles and bloodshed take place (but see Rev. 19:21). Instead, the focus falls on God's judgment of evil and the display of the rider's royal rule as "King of kings and Lord of lords" (vv. 15−16). The overthrow of royal Canaanite hegemony introduced a completely new order in Canaan (Josh. 1−11). What Wall calls "the future apocalyptic eruption of God's salvation within human history" through the return of Jesus will likewise shove phony kings and their elites aside, end their cruelty toward common people, establish God's kingdom on earth, and vindicate the messianic work of Jesus Christ.[63] God's final triumph radically alters human existence, both its social and spiritual dimensions, and brings it into alignment with the good wishes that the creator intends for it.[64]

These events are the source of hope for all who struggle to remain faithful to Jesus and of personal vindication for all who have suffered injustice. It resoundingly answers the anguished prayers of Christians who have rotted in stinking prisons for their faith in Jesus. It satisfies the longing of anyone socially slighted or subtly demeaned for their ethnicity, gender, physical limitations, or religious faith. It holds out pleasant reward for the faithful, patient endurance of anyone whose commitment to Jesus has been ridi-

---

62. Four other visions follow these three (20:1−3, 4−10, 11−15; 21:1−22:6a), a total of seven visions, all on a single topic, the second coming of Christ; cf. Wall, *Revelation*, 227.

63. Ibid., 226.

64. Ibid., 227−28.

culed. It finally brings justice to every innocent slave secretly hung beside some lonely American road. It firmly avenges the deaths of helpless would-be immigrants who died at the hands of unscrupulous smugglers. It holds out hope to those engaged in the cause of social justice of a future final justice to rid the world of its evils. Indeed, it lifts the spirits of all who worship and serve Jesus as King of kings and Lord of lords.

From all corners of the globe, all who anxiously await this grand day of final salvation joyously add their voice to that of the heavenly chorus: "Hallelujah! For our Lord God Almighty reigns. Let us rejoice and be glad and give him glory!" (Rev. 19:6-7). With Tertullian, their spirits soar on the wings of the conviction that "Christ's name is extending everywhere, believed everywhere, worshiped by all the ... nations, reigning everywhere, adored everywhere, conferred equally everywhere upon all."[65]

In the spirit and form of Joshua 12, the reading below puts the hope of King Jesus' final triumph into words for today. The format makes it suitable as a reading for public worship.

In Celebration of the King of Kings: A Reading

Leader: The final conquest of evil human rulers awaits the return of our Lord Jesus. Today we celebrate that coming great day of victory by our Savior in a way that Joshua 12 celebrated that of an earlier "savior." We do so to embrace Jesus as our triumphant King of kings and Lord of lords. Let me inquire ...
How many pharaohs remain who cruelly enslave God's people?

Women: None.

Leader: How many Caesars who martyr the Christian faithful?

Men: None.

Leader: How many tyrants who beat, maim, and imprison believers?

All: None.

Leader: How many mayors who cater to the rich and ignore the poor?

Men: None.

Leader: How many scoundrels who defraud the weak, vulnerable, and elderly?

Women: None.

Leader: How many kings, presidents, tsars, and premiers remain besides Jesus?

---

65. Tertullian, *Adv. Jud.* 7 (*Ante-Nicene Fathers*); quoted from G. Gilbert, "The List of Nations in Acts 2: Roman Propaganda and the Lukan Response," *JBL* 121/3 (2002): 509.

All: None.

Leader: How many kings other than Jesus rule in our hearts and lives?

All: None.

Leader: John wrote in his vision, "Then I heard what sounded like a great multitude, like the roar of rushing waters and like loud peals of thunder, shouting: 'Hallelujah! For our Lord God Almighty reigns." [PAUSE]

How many kings will we serve?

All: One! [PAUSE]

Now to the King eternal, immortal, invisible, the only God, be honor and glory for ever and ever. Amen. (1 Tim. 1:17)

Joshua 13:1–19:51

WHEN JOSHUA WAS old and well advanced in years, the LORD said to him, "You are very old, and there are still very large areas of land to be taken over.

²"This is the land that remains: all the regions of the Philistines and Geshurites: ³from the Shihor River on the east of Egypt to the territory of Ekron on the north, all of it counted as Canaanite (the territory of the five Philistine rulers in Gaza, Ashdod, Ashkelon, Gath and Ekron—that of the Avvites); ⁴from the south, all the land of the Canaanites, from Arah of the Sidonians as far as Aphek, the region of the Amorites, ⁵the area of the Gebalites; and all Lebanon to the east, from Baal Gad below Mount Hermon to Lebo Hamath.

⁶"As for all the inhabitants of the mountain regions from Lebanon to Misrephoth Maim, that is, all the Sidonians, I myself will drive them out before the Israelites. Be sure to allocate this land to Israel for an inheritance, as I have instructed you, ⁷and divide it as an inheritance among the nine tribes and half of the tribe of Manasseh."

⁸The other half of Manasseh, the Reubenites and the Gadites had received the inheritance that Moses had given them east of the Jordan, as he, the servant of the LORD, had assigned it to them.

⁹It extended from Aroer on the rim of the Arnon Gorge, and from the town in the middle of the gorge, and included the whole plateau of Medeba as far as Dibon, ¹⁰and all the towns of Sihon king of the Amorites, who ruled in Heshbon, out to the border of the Ammonites. ¹¹It also included Gilead, the territory of the people of Geshur and Maacah, all of Mount Hermon and all Bashan as far as Salecah—¹²that is, the whole kingdom of Og in Bashan, who had reigned in Ashtaroth and Edrei and had survived as one of the last of the Rephaites. Moses had defeated them and taken over their land. ¹³But the Israelites did not drive out the people of Geshur and Maacah, so they continue to live among the Israelites to this day.

¹⁴But to the tribe of Levi he gave no inheritance, since the offerings made by fire to the LORD, the God of Israel, are their inheritance, as he promised them.

¹⁵This is what Moses had given to the tribe of Reuben, clan by clan:

¹⁶The territory from Aroer on the rim of the Arnon Gorge, and from the town in the middle of the gorge, and the whole plateau past Medeba ¹⁷to Heshbon and all its towns on the plateau, including Dibon, Bamoth Baal, Beth Baal Meon, ¹⁸Jahaz, Kedemoth, Mephaath, ¹⁹Kiriathaim, Sibmah, Zereth Shahar on the hill in the valley, ²⁰Beth Peor, the slopes of Pisgah, and Beth Jeshimoth ²¹—all the towns on the plateau and the entire realm of Sihon king of the Amorites, who ruled at Heshbon. Moses had defeated him and the Midianite chiefs, Evi, Rekem, Zur, Hur and Reba—princes allied with Sihon—who lived in that country. ²²In addition to those slain in battle, the Israelites had put to the sword Balaam son of Beor, who practiced divination. ²³The boundary of the Reubenites was the bank of the Jordan. These towns and their villages were the inheritance of the Reubenites, clan by clan.

²⁴This is what Moses had given to the tribe of Gad, clan by clan:

²⁵The territory of Jazer, all the towns of Gilead and half the Ammonite country as far as Aroer, near Rabbah; ²⁶and from Heshbon to Ramath Mizpah and Betonim, and from Mahanaim to the territory of Debir; ²⁷and in the valley, Beth Haram, Beth Nimrah, Succoth and Zaphon with the rest of the realm of Sihon king of Heshbon (the east side of the Jordan, the territory up to the end of the Sea of Kinnereth). ²⁸These towns and their villages were the inheritance of the Gadites, clan by clan.

²⁹This is what Moses had given to the half-tribe of Manasseh, that is, to half the family of the descendants of Manasseh, clan by clan:

³⁰The territory extending from Mahanaim and including all of Bashan, the entire realm of Og king of Bashan—all the settlements of Jair in Bashan, sixty towns, ³¹half of Gilead, and Ashtaroth and Edrei (the royal cities of Og

in Bashan). This was for the descendants of Makir son of Manasseh—for half of the sons of Makir, clan by clan.

³²This is the inheritance Moses had given when he was in the plains of Moab across the Jordan east of Jericho. ³³But to the tribe of Levi, Moses had given no inheritance; the LORD, the God of Israel, is their inheritance, as he promised them.

¹⁴:¹Now these are the areas the Israelites received as an inheritance in the land of Canaan, which Eleazar the priest, Joshua son of Nun and the heads of the tribal clans of Israel allotted to them. ²Their inheritances were assigned by lot to the nine-and-a-half tribes, as the LORD had commanded through Moses. ³Moses had granted the two-and-a-half tribes their inheritance east of the Jordan but had not granted the Levites an inheritance among the rest, ⁴for the sons of Joseph had become two tribes—Manasseh and Ephraim. The Levites received no share of the land but only towns to live in, with pasturelands for their flocks and herds. ⁵So the Israelites divided the land, just as the LORD had commanded Moses.

⁶Now the men of Judah approached Joshua at Gilgal, and Caleb son of Jephunneh the Kenizzite said to him, "You know what the LORD said to Moses the man of God at Kadesh Barnea about you and me. ⁷I was forty years old when Moses the servant of the LORD sent me from Kadesh Barnea to explore the land. And I brought him back a report according to my convictions, ⁸but my brothers who went up with me made the hearts of the people melt with fear. I, however, followed the LORD my God wholeheartedly. ⁹So on that day Moses swore to me, 'The land on which your feet have walked will be your inheritance and that of your children forever, because you have followed the LORD my God wholeheartedly.'

¹⁰"Now then, just as the LORD promised, he has kept me alive for forty-five years since the time he said this to Moses, while Israel moved about in the desert. So here I am today, eighty-five years old! ¹¹I am still as strong today as the day Moses sent me out; I'm just as vigorous to go out to battle now as I was then. ¹²Now give me this hill country that the LORD promised me that day. You yourself heard then that the Anakites were there and their cities were large and fortified, but, the LORD helping me, I will drive them out just as he said."

¹³Then Joshua blessed Caleb son of Jephunneh and gave him Hebron as his inheritance. ¹⁴So Hebron has belonged

to Caleb son of Jephunneh the Kenizzite ever since, because he followed the LORD, the God of Israel, wholeheartedly. [15](Hebron used to be called Kiriath Arba after Arba, who was the greatest man among the Anakites.)

Then the land had rest from war.

[15:1]The allotment for the tribe of Judah, clan by clan, extended down to the territory of Edom, to the Desert of Zin in the extreme south.

[2]Their southern boundary started from the bay at the southern end of the Salt Sea, [3]crossed south of Scorpion Pass, continued on to Zin and went over to the south of Kadesh Barnea. Then it ran past Hezron up to Addar and curved around to Karka. [4]It then passed along to Azmon and joined the Wadi of Egypt, ending at the sea. This is their southern boundary.

[5]The eastern boundary is the Salt Sea as far as the mouth of the Jordan.

The northern boundary started from the bay of the sea at the mouth of the Jordan, [6]went up to Beth Hoglah and continued north of Beth Arabah to the Stone of Bohan son of Reuben. [7]The boundary then went up to Debir from the Valley of Achor and turned north to Gilgal, which faces the Pass of Adummim south of the gorge. It continued along to the waters of En Shemesh and came out at En Rogel. [8]Then it ran up the Valley of Ben Hinnom along the southern slope of the Jebusite city (that is, Jerusalem). From there it climbed to the top of the hill west of the Hinnom Valley at the northern end of the Valley of Rephaim. [9]From the hilltop the boundary headed toward the spring of the waters of Nephtoah, came out at the towns of Mount Ephron and went down toward Baalah (that is, Kiriath Jearim). [10]Then it curved westward from Baalah to Mount Seir, ran along the northern slope of Mount Jearim (that is, Kesalon), continued down to Beth Shemesh and crossed to Timnah. [11]It went to the northern slope of Ekron, turned toward Shikkeron, passed along to Mount Baalah and reached Jabneel. The boundary ended at the sea.

[12]The western boundary is the coastline of the Great Sea.

These are the boundaries around the people of Judah by their clans.

¹³In accordance with the LORD's command to him, Joshua gave to Caleb son of Jephunneh a portion in Judah—Kiriath Arba, that is, Hebron. (Arba was the forefather of Anak.) ¹⁴From Hebron Caleb drove out the three Anakites—Sheshai, Ahiman and Talmai—descendants of Anak. ¹⁵From there he marched against the people living in Debir (formerly called Kiriath Sepher). ¹⁶And Caleb said, "I will give my daughter Acsah in marriage to the man who attacks and captures Kiriath Sepher." ¹⁷Othniel son of Kenaz, Caleb's brother, took it; so Caleb gave his daughter Acsah to him in marriage.

¹⁸One day when she came to Othniel, she urged him to ask her father for a field. When she got off her donkey, Caleb asked her, "What can I do for you?"

¹⁹She replied, "Do me a special favor. Since you have given me land in the Negev, give me also springs of water." So Caleb gave her the upper and lower springs.

²⁰This is the inheritance of the tribe of Judah, clan by clan:

²¹The southernmost towns of the tribe of Judah in the Negev toward the boundary of Edom were:

Kabzeel, Eder, Jagur, ²²Kinah, Dimonah, Adadah, ²³Kedesh, Hazor, Ithnan, ²⁴Ziph, Telem, Bealoth, ²⁵Hazor Hadattah, Kerioth Hezron (that is, Hazor), ²⁶Amam, Shema, Moladah, ²⁷Hazar Gaddah, Heshmon, Beth Pelet, ²⁸Hazar Shual, Beersheba, Biziothiah, ²⁹Baalah, Iim, Ezem, ³⁰Eltolad, Kesil, Hormah, ³¹Ziklag, Madmannah, Sansannah, ³²Lebaoth, Shilhim, Ain and Rimmon—a total of twenty-nine towns and their villages.

³³In the western foothills:

Eshtaol, Zorah, Ashnah, ³⁴Zanoah, En Gannim, Tappuah, Enam, ³⁵Jarmuth, Adullam, Socoh, Azekah, ³⁶Shaaraim, Adithaim and Gederah (or Gederothaim)—fourteen towns and their villages.

³⁷Zenan, Hadashah, Migdal Gad, ³⁸Dilean, Mizpah, Joktheel, ³⁹Lachish, Bozkath, Eglon, ⁴⁰Cabbon, Lahmas, Kitlish, ⁴¹Gederoth, Beth Dagon, Naamah and Makkedah—sixteen towns and their villages.

⁴²Libnah, Ether, Ashan, ⁴³Iphtah, Ashnah, Nezib, ⁴⁴Keilah, Aczib and Mareshah—nine towns and their villages.

⁴⁵Ekron, with its surrounding settlements and villages; ⁴⁶west of Ekron, all that were in the vicinity of Ashdod,

together with their villages; ⁴⁷Ashdod, its surrounding settlements and villages; and Gaza, its settlements and villages, as far as the Wadi of Egypt and the coastline of the Great Sea.

⁴⁸In the hill country:

Shamir, Jattir, Socoh, ⁴⁹Dannah, Kiriath Sannah (that is, Debir), ⁵⁰Anab, Eshtemoh, Anim, ⁵¹Goshen, Holon and Giloh—eleven towns and their villages.

⁵²Arab, Dumah, Eshan, ⁵³Janim, Beth Tappuah, Aphekah, ⁵⁴Humtah, Kiriath Arba (that is, Hebron) and Zior—nine towns and their villages.

⁵⁵Maon, Carmel, Ziph, Juttah, ⁵⁶Jezreel, Jokdeam, Zanoah, ⁵⁷Kain, Gibeah and Timnah—ten towns and their villages.

⁵⁸Halhul, Beth Zur, Gedor, ⁵⁹Maarath, Beth Anoth and Eltekon—six towns and their villages.

⁶⁰Kiriath Baal (that is, Kiriath Jearim) and Rabbah—two towns and their villages.

⁶¹In the desert:

Beth Arabah, Middin, Secacah, ⁶²Nibshan, the City of Salt and En Gedi—six towns and their villages.

⁶³Judah could not dislodge the Jebusites, who were living in Jerusalem; to this day the Jebusites live there with the people of Judah.

^{16:1}The allotment for Joseph began at the Jordan of Jericho, east of the waters of Jericho, and went up from there through the desert into the hill country of Bethel. ²It went on from Bethel (that is, Luz), crossed over to the territory of the Arkites in Ataroth, ³descended westward to the territory of the Japhletites as far as the region of Lower Beth Horon and on to Gezer, ending at the sea. ⁴So Manasseh and Ephraim, the descendants of Joseph, received their inheritance.

⁵This was the territory of Ephraim, clan by clan:

The boundary of their inheritance went from Ataroth Addar in the east to Upper Beth Horon ⁶and continued to the sea. From Micmethath on the north it curved eastward to Taanath Shiloh, passing by it to Janoah on the east. ⁷Then it went down from Janoah to Ataroth and Naarah, touched Jericho and came out at the Jordan. ⁸From Tappuah the border went west to the Kanah Ravine and ended at the sea. This was the inheritance of the tribe of the Ephraimites, clan by clan. ⁹It also included all the towns and their villages that were set aside for the Ephraimites within the inheritance of the Manassites.

¹⁰They did not dislodge the Canaanites living in Gezer; to this day the Canaanites live among the people of Ephraim but are required to do forced labor.

¹⁷:¹This was the allotment for the tribe of Manasseh as Joseph's firstborn, that is, for Makir, Manasseh's firstborn. Makir was the ancestor of the Gileadites, who had received Gilead and Bashan because the Makirites were great soldiers. ²So this allotment was for the rest of the people of Manasseh—the clans of Abiezer, Helek, Asriel, Shechem, Hepher and Shemida. These are the other male descendants of Manasseh son of Joseph by their clans.

³Now Zelophehad son of Hepher, the son of Gilead, the son of Makir, the son of Manasseh, had no sons but only daughters, whose names were Mahlah, Noah, Hoglah, Milcah and Tirzah. ⁴They went to Eleazar the priest, Joshua son of Nun, and the leaders and said, "The LORD commanded Moses to give us an inheritance among our brothers." So Joshua gave them an inheritance along with the brothers of their father, according to the LORD's command. ⁵Manasseh's share consisted of ten tracts of land besides Gilead and Bashan east of the Jordan, ⁶because the daughters of the tribe of Manasseh received an inheritance among the sons. The land of Gilead belonged to the rest of the descendants of Manasseh.

⁷The territory of Manasseh extended from Asher to Micmethath east of Shechem. The boundary ran southward from there to include the people living at En Tappuah. ⁸(Manasseh had the land of Tappuah, but Tappuah itself, on the boundary of Manasseh, belonged to the Ephraimites.) ⁹Then the boundary continued south to the Kanah Ravine. There were towns belonging to Ephraim lying among the towns of Manasseh, but the boundary of Manasseh was the northern side of the ravine and ended at the sea. ¹⁰On the south the land belonged to Ephraim, on the north to Manasseh. The territory of Manasseh reached the sea and bordered Asher on the north and Issachar on the east.

[11]Within Issachar and Asher, Manasseh also had Beth Shan, Ibleam and the people of Dor, Endor, Taanach and Megiddo, together with their surrounding settlements (the third in the list is Naphoth).

[12]Yet the Manassites were not able to occupy these towns, for the Canaanites were determined to live in that region. [13]However, when the Israelites grew stronger, they subjected the Canaanites to forced labor but did not drive them out completely.

[14]The people of Joseph said to Joshua, "Why have you given us only one allotment and one portion for an inheritance? We are a numerous people and the LORD has blessed us abundantly."

[15]"If you are so numerous," Joshua answered, "and if the hill country of Ephraim is too small for you, go up into the forest and clear land for yourselves there in the land of the Perizzites and Rephaites."

[16]The people of Joseph replied, "The hill country is not enough for us, and all the Canaanites who live in the plain have iron chariots, both those in Beth Shan and its settlements and those in the Valley of Jezreel."

[17]But Joshua said to the house of Joseph — to Ephraim and Manasseh — "You are numerous and very powerful. You will have not only one allotment [18]but the forested hill country as well. Clear it, and its farthest limits will be yours; though the Canaanites have iron chariots and though they are strong, you can drive them out."

[18:1]The whole assembly of the Israelites gathered at Shiloh and set up the Tent of Meeting there. The country was brought under their control, [2]but there were still seven Israelite tribes who had not yet received their inheritance.

[3]So Joshua said to the Israelites: "How long will you wait before you begin to take possession of the land that the LORD, the God of your fathers, has given you? [4]Appoint three men from each tribe. I will send them out to make a survey of the land and to write a description of it, according to the inheritance of each. Then they will return to me. [5]You are to divide the land into seven parts. Judah is to remain in its territory on the south and the house of Joseph in its territory on the north. [6]After you have written descriptions of the seven parts of the land, bring them here to me and I will cast lots for you in the presence of the LORD our God. [7]The Levites, however, do not get a portion

among you, because the priestly service of the LORD is their inheritance. And Gad, Reuben and the half-tribe of Manasseh have already received their inheritance on the east side of the Jordan. Moses the servant of the LORD gave it to them."

⁸As the men started on their way to map out the land, Joshua instructed them, "Go and make a survey of the land and write a description of it. Then return to me, and I will cast lots for you here at Shiloh in the presence of the LORD." ⁹So the men left and went through the land. They wrote its description on a scroll, town by town, in seven parts, and returned to Joshua in the camp at Shiloh. ¹⁰Joshua then cast lots for them in Shiloh in the presence of the LORD, and there he distributed the land to the Israelites according to their tribal divisions.

¹¹The lot came up for the tribe of Benjamin, clan by clan. Their allotted territory lay between the tribes of Judah and Joseph:

¹²On the north side their boundary began at the Jordan, passed the northern slope of Jericho and headed west into the hill country, coming out at the desert of Beth Aven. ¹³From there it crossed to the south slope of Luz (that is, Bethel) and went down to Ataroth Addar on the hill south of Lower Beth Horon.

¹⁴From the hill facing Beth Horon on the south the boundary turned south along the western side and came out at Kiriath Baal (that is, Kiriath Jearim), a town of the people of Judah. This was the western side.

¹⁵The southern side began at the outskirts of Kiriath Jearim on the west, and the boundary came out at the spring of the waters of Nephtoah. ¹⁶The boundary went down to the foot of the hill facing the Valley of Ben Hinnom, north of the Valley of Rephaim. It continued down the Hinnom Valley along the southern slope of the Jebusite city and so to En Rogel. ¹⁷It then curved north, went to En Shemesh, continued to Geliloth, which faces the Pass of Adummim, and ran down to the Stone of Bohan son of Reuben. ¹⁸It continued to the northern slope of Beth Arabah and on down into the Arabah. ¹⁹It then went to the northern slope of Beth Hoglah and came out at the northern bay of the Salt Sea, at the mouth of the Jordan in the south. This was the southern boundary.

²⁰The Jordan formed the boundary on the eastern side.

These were the boundaries that marked out the inheritance of the clans of Benjamin on all sides.

²¹The tribe of Benjamin, clan by clan, had the following cities:

Jericho, Beth Hoglah, Emek Keziz, ²²Beth Arabah, Zemaraim, Bethel, ²³Avvim, Parah, Ophrah, ²⁴Kephar Ammoni, Ophni and Geba—twelve towns and their villages.

²⁵Gibeon, Ramah, Beeroth, ²⁶Mizpah, Kephirah, Mozah, ²⁷Rekem, Irpeel, Taralah, ²⁸Zelah, Haeleph, the Jebusite city (that is, Jerusalem), Gibeah and Kiriath—fourteen towns and their villages.

This was the inheritance of Benjamin for its clans.

¹⁹:¹The second lot came out for the tribe of Simeon, clan by clan. Their inheritance lay within the territory of Judah. ²It included:

Beersheba (or Sheba), Moladah, ³Hazar Shual, Balah, Ezem, ⁴Eltolad, Bethul, Hormah, ⁵Ziklag, Beth Marcaboth, Hazar Susah, ⁶Beth Lebaoth and Shar-uhen—thirteen towns and their villages;

⁷Ain, Rimmon, Ether and Ashan—four towns and their villages—⁸and all the villages around these towns as far as Baalath Beer (Ramah in the Negev).

This was the inheritance of the tribe of the Simeonites, clan by clan. ⁹The inheritance of the Simeonites was taken from the share of Judah, because Judah's portion was more than they needed. So the Simeonites received their inheritance within the territory of Judah.

¹⁰The third lot came up for Zebulun, clan by clan:

The boundary of their inheritance went as far as Sarid. ¹¹Going west it ran to Maralah, touched Dabbesheth, and extended to the ravine near Jokneam. ¹²It turned east from Sarid toward the sunrise to the territory of Kisloth Tabor and went on to Daberath and up to Japhia. ¹³Then it continued eastward to Gath Hepher and Eth Kazin; it came out at Rimmon and turned toward Neah. ¹⁴There the boundary went around on the north to Hannathon and ended at the Valley of Iphtah El. ¹⁵Included were Kattath, Nahalal, Shimron, Idalah and Bethlehem. There were twelve towns and their villages.

¹⁶These towns and their villages were the inheritance of Zebulun, clan by clan.

¹⁷The fourth lot came out for Issachar, clan by clan. ¹⁸Their territory included:

Jezreel, Kesulloth, Shunem, ¹⁹Hapharaim, Shion, Anaharath, ²⁰Rabbith, Kishion, Ebez, ²¹Remeth, En Gannim, En Haddah and Beth Pazzez. ²²The boundary touched Tabor, Shahazumah and Beth Shemesh, and ended at the Jordan. There were sixteen towns and their villages.

²³These towns and their villages were the inheritance of the tribe of Issachar, clan by clan.

²⁴The fifth lot came out for the tribe of Asher, clan by clan. ²⁵Their territory included:

Helkath, Hali, Beten, Acshaph, ²⁶Allammelech, Amad and Mishal. On the west the boundary touched Carmel and Shihor Libnath. ²⁷It then turned east toward Beth Dagon, touched Zebulun and the Valley of Iphtah El, and went north to Beth Emek and Neiel, passing Cabul on the left. ²⁸It went to Abdon, Rehob, Hammon and Kanah, as far as Greater Sidon. ²⁹The boundary then turned back toward Ramah and went to the fortified city of Tyre, turned toward Hosah and came out at the sea in the region of Aczib, ³⁰Ummah, Aphek and Rehob. There were twenty-two towns and their villages.

³¹These towns and their villages were the inheritance of the tribe of Asher, clan by clan.

³²The sixth lot came out for Naphtali, clan by clan:

³³Their boundary went from Heleph and the large tree in Zaanannim, passing Adami Nekeb and Jabneel to Lakkum and ending at the Jordan. ³⁴The boundary ran west through Aznoth Tabor and came out at Hukkok. It touched Zebulun on the south, Asher on the west and the Jordan on the east. ³⁵The fortified cities were Ziddim, Zer, Hammath, Rakkath, Kinnereth, ³⁶Adamah, Ramah, Hazor, ³⁷Kedesh, Edrei, En Hazor, ³⁸Iron, Migdal El, Horem, Beth Anath and Beth Shemesh. There were nineteen towns and their villages.

³⁹These towns and their villages were the inheritance of the tribe of Naphtali, clan by clan.

⁴⁰The seventh lot came out for the tribe of Dan, clan by clan. ⁴¹The territory of their inheritance included:

Zorah, Eshtaol, Ir Shemesh, ⁴²Shaalabbin, Aijalon, Ithlah, ⁴³Elon, Timnah, Ekron, ⁴⁴Eltekeh, Gibbethon,

Baalath, ⁴⁵Jehud, Bene Berak, Gath Rimmon, ⁴⁶Me Jarkon and Rakkon, with the area facing Joppa.

⁴⁷(But the Danites had difficulty taking possession of their territory, so they went up and attacked Leshem, took it, put it to the sword and occupied it. They settled in Leshem and named it Dan after their forefather.)

⁴⁸These towns and their villages were the inheritance of the tribe of Dan, clan by clan.

⁴⁹When they had finished dividing the land into its allotted portions, the Israelites gave Joshua son of Nun an inheritance among them, ⁵⁰as the LORD had commanded. They gave him the town he asked for—Timnath Serah in the hill country of Ephraim. And he built up the town and settled there.

⁵¹These are the territories that Eleazar the priest, Joshua son of Nun and the heads of the tribal clans of Israel assigned by lot at Shiloh in the presence of the LORD at the entrance to the Tent of Meeting. And so they finished dividing the land.

WITH THE WORDS "JOSHUA was old and well advanced in years," a new day for Israel dawns, even as signs of dusk settle over Joshua's life.[1] The years of war are gone, and a new part of the book of Joshua opens. In one sense, this is its most important part because it reports the fulfillment (finally!) of the promise to Abraham: "To your offspring I will give this land" (Gen. 12:7; cf. Josh. 11:23). Yahweh's command to Joshua initiates the settlement of Canaan (13:7), just as it did the conquest (cf. 1:2).[2]

Structurally, Joshua 13–19 has two main sections: Yahweh's commission of Joshua to distribute land west of the Jordan among nine-and-a-half tribes (ch. 13) and the detailed report that he does so (chs. 14–19). The latter, lengthy report itself comprises two subsections: (1) allotments made to Judah, Ephraim, and Manasseh by Eleazar the high priest and Joshua, perhaps at Gilgal (chs. 14–17); and (2) allotments made to the remaining seven tribes at an all-Israelite assembly in Shiloh (chs. 18–19).[3] The author

---

1. Syntactically, the opening, subject-first sentence structure (lit., "Now Joshua was old ...") both signals the opening of a new scene and the introduction of a new character, Joshua as an old man.

2. Technically, the settlement process per se comprises Josh. 13–22.

3. Joshua 19:51 indicates that Eleazar the high priest also presides over the Shiloh assembly along with Joshua and the tribal leaders.

pens at best a sketchy glimpse of the circumstances behind the first allocation to two-and-a-half tribes, whereas a full narrative with dialogue fleshes
out how the other seven come into land.[4] In short, Joshua 13 – 19 pictures
the distribution of land as a drawn-out, complex process rather than as the
simple outcome of a single event.[5] In essence, these chapters offer "the
creation story of the Israelite settlement."[6]

A casual glance through the material shows how much ground is covered—literally! Joshua 13 – 19 weaves together narratives (14:6 – 15; 15:13 – 19;
17:3 – 4, 14 – 18), lists of cities and towns (e.g., 15:20 – 63; 18:21 – 28), and
boundary descriptions (e.g., 16:1 – 8; 19:10 – 16).[7] It also incorporates two
special reports concerning the inheritance awarded the lone heroes of the
infamous spy mission under Moses (Num. 13 – 14), Caleb and Joshua. Fittingly, these reports bracket the entire land allocation narrative, Caleb the
first to receive an inheritance—the one promised him by Moses (14:6 – 14;
cf. 15:13 – 19)—and Joshua the last—the city he requested (19:49 – 50).

At the same time, however, the depth of treatment accorded each tribe
varies considerably. Judah has a detailed boundary description and list of
cities (15:1 – 12, 20 – 63), while Ephraim receives a brief boundary description report and no city list (16:5 – 10). The report concerning the seven
tribes awarded allotments at Shiloh uniformly follows a set pattern that
combines both boundary descriptions and lists of cities and/or towns for six
tribes (18:20 – 19:48). Only the first tribe of the seven, Benjamin, receives
an extensive boundary description (18:11 – 20), probably because of its
location "between the tribes of Judah and Joseph" (18:11).[8]

Why include all this dull administrative material? Certainly, one purpose is to sound the narrative's main theme, the fulfillment of Yahweh's
promise of land. That is what makes this section the very heart of Joshua:

---

4. Nelson (*Joshua*, 206 – 7) suggests that the large, important tribes (Judah, Ephraim, and
Manasseh) probably cast lots among themselves to determine their shares. The narrative in
18:1 – 10 clearly says that the other seven tribes divided the territory outside those already
assigned the dominant three, thereby receiving smaller portions.

5. The presence of two reports has earned considerable scholarly discussion, but Assis
has plausibly argued for their logical connection; see E. Assis, "'How Long Are You Slack
to Go to Possess the Land' (Jos. 18:3): Ideal and Reality in the Distribution Descriptions in
Joshua 13 – 19," *VT* 53 (2003): 1 – 25.

6. E. Ben Zvi, "The List of Levitical Cities," *JSOT* 54 (1992): 100, with reference to chs.
14 – 19.

7. Joshua 13 – 19 also teems with intriguing tribal tidbits of geography, topography, and
ethnography; cf. 13:19, 30; 14:15. For a convenient table of the land distribution sections,
see Howard, *Joshua*, 316, and the discussion of composition in the Introduction.

8. For discussion concerning the sources behind this narrative, see the section on composition in the Introduction.

the goal of the conquest of Canaan is to enable Israel to settle and possess the land and to pass it on as its "inheritance."[9] But repeated statements also sound two minor themes that anticipate the book's later parts: the inability of some tribes to destroy non-Israelite peoples within their allotments (13:13; 17:13);[10] and the fact that the tribe of Levi receives no territorial inheritance (13:14, 33; 14:3, 4; 18:7).[11] This latter theme anticipates the distribution of towns among the Levites (ch. 21; cf. 14:4).

Yahweh's Commission to Joshua (13:1–33)

THE COMMISSION PROPER (VV. 1–7). Joshua's advanced age leads Yahweh to raise an important matter.[12] What is to be done about the "very large areas of land [still] to be taken over" (v. 1)? Before Yahweh commissions Joshua to distribute Canaan among the tribes (vv. 6b–7), Yahweh surveys the land that remains to be conquered (vv. 2–6a). His concern is twofold (v. 6): Because of Joshua's old age, someone else will have to liberate the above lands later from possession by non-Israelites, and yet Joshua is to include those unconquered lands in the distribution.

After twice celebrating that "Joshua took the entire land" (11:16, 23), the book's mention of unconquered areas may strike some readers as a contradiction. The comment should not surprise us, however, since (as noted above) the existence of areas of Canaan still awaiting conquest is implicit both in the conquest narrative (Josh. 6–11) and in the celebratory list of kings (Josh. 12). Also, the celebratory claims probably reflect a touch of authorial hyperbole. The remaining land includes two large swaths along the Mediterranean coast (13:2–3, 4), one from the Egyptian border to

---

9. The introduction of the word "inheritance" (*naḥalah*) three times in 13:6–8 verbally sounds this theme. Cf. also Kitz, "Lot Casting in Joshua," 610 ("the retelling of the allocation of the land to all the tribes as a single unit was done to emphasize that they legally received their portions as inheritable property").

10. Caleb's destruction of the Anakim (15:14) marks the lone success story in this pattern. Most recent translations render *yaraš* hi. in Joshua as "drive out," following the tradition in the Jewish Targums. In my view, however, the root is best rendered "destroy"; cf. N. Lohfink, "יָרַשׁ," *TDOT*, 6:374–75, 382–83.

11. Instead, as their inheritance they receive the portions of offerings made to Yahweh by fire (13:14; cf. Deut. 18:1), both grain (Lev. 2:3, 10; 6:14–18; 10:12) and meat (7:31–34; cf. Num. 18:9); the privilege of priestly service (Josh. 18:7); and, more important, Yahweh himself (13:33; cf. Num. 18:20; Deut. 10:9; 18:2). The tithes that Yahweh receives from Israel also form part of the Levites' inheritances (Num. 18:24; Deut. 14:29).

12. Double phrases in both the report formula (i.e., the writer) and in Yahweh's speech doubly underscore Joshua's seniority: he is not only "old" (*zaqen*) but *"very old"* (lit. "entered the days")—like Abraham and David near life's end (Gen. 24:1; 1 Kings 1:1). Indeed, the same formula recurs in 23:1, thus casting Joshua 13–23 as Joshua's "Final Years."

Ekron (the Philistines, Geshurites, Avvites, Canaanites), the other through Phoenicia north of the plain of Acco or the Litani River (the Sidonians).[13] It also includes land east of the Sea of Galilee (the Gebalites).[14] The Sidonians, however, Yahweh promises to destroy (NIV "drive out") himself rather to leave the matter to Israel, so Joshua must include their territories in the distribution of inheritances (v. 6).[15]

In verse 7, Yahweh formally (lit., "And now ...") commissions Joshua to "apportion" (*ḥalaq* pi.) the entire land—that just described and the parts already within Israelite control—among the nine-and-a-half tribes. This command governs all the activity through 19:51. As we will see, the means of dividing them is to cast lots (lit., "throw it down"; NIV "allocate this land"). Theologically, Israel presumes that Yahweh invisibly guides the process of lot-casting that decides who gets what (e.g., 14:2; 18:11; 19:1). So, Israel accepts the results as Yahweh's will. But the question is, what about land for the other two-and-one-half tribes? That question occasions a glance backward.

Retrospective review (vv. 8 – 33). This section reviews Moses' prior land allocations east of the Jordan to two-and-a-half tribes (cf. Num. 32:33 – 42).[16] He did so on one condition—that they fight to win inheritances for the other tribes on the west side of the Jordan. As Israel prepared to cross the river, Joshua reminded them of their acceptance of that stipulation (Josh. 1:12 – 18; cf. 4:12). Now, for Joshua to launch his long land distribution report with the Transjordanian tribes makes chronological sense since they had received their land first. But it also makes the important point that every tribe—the entire nation—received its inheritance from either Moses or Joshua—and on both sides of the Jordan.

Thematically, this retrospective adds details to the description in 12:1–6 and anticipates Joshua's later dismissal of the east-bank tribes to their lands (ch. 22). The review begins by surveying the geographical sweep of all the land allotted in Transjordan. Two cities, Aroer on the rim of the Arnon River gorge and an unnamed one mid-river, mark its southern boundary (and its boundary with Moab to the south). To the north it extends across the Medeba plateau

---

13. Concerning the Geshurites (v. 2), cf. 1 Sam. 27:8; Nelson, *Joshua*, 162; Howard, *Joshua*, 298. The Shihor River (v. 3) is either the easternmost branch of the Nile (so A. Betz, "Shihor [Place]," *ABD*, 5:1212), or perhaps the Brook of Egypt (Wadi el-Arish), the traditional border between Egypt and Israel. The text of vv. 4–5 is difficult. The first word in v. 4 (Heb. *mitteman*) "from/in the south") and "all the land of the Canaanites" probably ends v. 3.

14. For convenient maps of the areas within and without Israel's control, see *CBA*, 59.

15. Heb. *raq* underscores this point (paraphrased): "The most important thing [*raq*] is to allocate *this* land, too ..."; cf. WO 39.3.5c (example #4; Deut. 28:33).

16. The transition between vv. 7 and 8 seems literarily abrupt (lit., "with it"). "With it" apparently refers to the other half of the tribe of Manasseh.

to the Ammonite border (i.e., the Jabbok River [Deut. 3:16; Josh. 12:2]).[17] It includes the city of Dibon a few miles away as well as the cities that King Sihon ruled from his capital at Heshbon twenty miles north (vv. 9–10).

It also incorporates land farther north—Gilead, the lands of the Geshurites and Maacathites, Mount Hermon, and Bashan as far east as Salecah (v. 11). The latter formerly belonged to King Og, another Trans-jordanian monarch who ruled from twin capitals, Ashtaroth and Edrei. Moses and Israel also destroyed him, laying claim by conquest to his terri-tory (v. 12; cf. Num. 32:33–35). But, stepping forward in history a moment, the author notes parenthetically that Israel failed to destroy Geshur and Maacah, so they still lived amid Israel in his own day (13:13). This marks the first mention of a theme soon to become prominent, the inability of some tribes to destroy peoples occupying Israel's lands (see Josh. 15:63; 16:10; 17:12). The author also comments that the tribe of Levi received no land east of the Jordan because their God-given inheritance comprised fire offerings (see comments above).

The retrospective next details the inheritance in Transjordan that Moses gave to Reuben (vv. 15–23), Gad (vv. 24–28), and East Manasseh (vv. 29–32).[18] Reuben's holdings run along the east bank of the Jordan from the Arnon River gorge past the city of Medeba to Heshbon, all territory in the Medeba plateau formerly in Sihon's kingdom.[19] It includes twelve towns dominated by the city-state of Heshbon. Zereth Shahar appears only here, while the rest find brief mention in itineraries in Numbers (chs. 21, 22, and 32) and Deuteronomy (chs. 2–4).[20] The town list may incorpo-rate an ancient source or the writer's own composition drawing on biblical materials just mentioned.[21]

---

17. The Arnon River flows westward, emptying into the Dead Sea. About fifty miles separate the Arnon and the Jabbok Rivers.

18. The opening "Moses gave …" (vv. 15, 24, 29; NIV "Moses had given …") and the concluding formula "this is the inheritance of tribe-X" (vv. 23, 28, 32) bracket each section. Technically, however, v. 32 summarizes the entire Mosaic distribution in Transjordan; cf. Nelson, *Joshua*, 171.

19. Verse 21 also lists five Midianite chiefs allied with Sihon and living in his realm, whom Moses also destroyed (cf. Num. 31:8). For more on the Midianites, see Howard, *Joshua*, 312. Compare the boundary description in Joshua 12:2–3.

20. "The slopes of Pisgah" sounds like a description of terrain but, in my view, contextu-ally makes better sense as a town, "Pisgah's Slopes"; cf. Boling, *Joshua*, 324, 443. For possible sites matching the present list, see Hess, *Joshua*, 222–25, 234–35. In my view, the sugges-tion of Nelson (*Joshua*, 171) and Fritz (*Josua*, 148) that a redactor (or redactors) drew on Deut. 3:8–14 in shaping Joshua 13:8–12 may account for the boundary descriptions but does not explain the origin of the city list.

21. The list of cities rebuilt by Reuben (Num. 32:37–38) mentions only three of the present twelve and might be one source for the list. Contrast Nelson (*Joshua*, 170), who

Perhaps reminded by Beth Peor (v. 20), the site near the Plains of Moab of a notorious episode of Israelite apostasy (Num. 25), the writer mentions another casualty of the conflict in Transjordan, the diviner Balaam (v. 22; cf. 31:16). Subtly, the reference reminds Israel of the dangers that non-Israelites pose to Israel's exclusive devotion to Yahweh, a theme that Joshua himself will sound (ch. 23). So, the writer concludes, the above constitutes the inheritance of Reuben, clan by clan, both towns and unwalled farming villages.

The opening formula "Moses had given to ..." (v. 24) and its concluding counterpart (v. 28) bracket the report of the inheritance Moses gave the tribe of Gad. In general, the report is briefer, less detailed, and less clear than that of Reuben. It combines boundary descriptions, a town list, and some general geographical references. Gad's inheritance included Jazer (v. 25), a town (and region) about ten miles north of Heshbon already taken by the Gadites (Num. 21:32; 32:35) and destined to become a levitical city (Josh. 21:39);[22] all the towns in southern Gilead south of the Jabbok and half of Ammonite territory as far as Aroer, a town just west of Rabbah (modern Amman, Jordan) that the Gadites also later built up (Num. 32:34); territory falling between two north-south axes—between Heshbon and two towns, Ramath Mizpah and Betonim (locations unknown; v. 26), and from Mahanaim (north bank of the Jabbok east of the Jordan)[23] to the territory of Debir (somewhere in eastern Gilead); four towns in the Jordan Valley, the best known of which are Succoth and Zaphon thought to be near where the Jabbok enters the Jordan; and, finally, the rest of Og's kingdom east of the Jordan and north to the Sea of Galilee (v. 27). Admittedly, the picture is murky, but Gad's land lay north of Reuben's, ran north along the Jordan Valley, and involved the Jabbok River as a boundary on the north and (perhaps) the east.[24] The concluding formula (v. 28) exactly matches that for Reuben (v. 24b), citing the towns and unwalled villages within Gad's terrain.

The inheritance of East Manasseh receives an even briefer, vaguer report than Gad's (vv. 29–31). Again, "Moses had given ..." opens it but, unlike those for Reuben and Gad, no concluding formula ends it. Its southern boundary is at Mahanaim (v. 30; cf. v. 26), but the description turns sweeping, general, and imprecise: It extends north to "all of Bashan" and "the entire realm of Og"—truly an imprecise end point. That realm includes sixty towns in Bashan associated with Jair along with half of Gilead (i.e., north

---

tries to relate them to Solomon's seventh and twelve districts—wrongly, in my view—and credits their inclusion to a post-DH redactor.

22. Jazer actually comprises both a town and a region (Num. 32:1, 3), presumably because of the city's influence on its surrounding countryside.

23. D. V. Edelman, "Mahanaim (Place)," *ABD*, 4:472.

24. For suggested locations of Gad's towns, see Hess, *Joshua*, 235–36.

of the Jabbok; v. 31a; cf. 12:2, 5),[25] and Og's two royal cities, Ashtaroth and Edrei (the latter, way east of the Jordan along the Yarmuk River). Jair may be the judge "Jair of Gilead" whose thirty sons, according to Judges, "controlled thirty towns in Gilead, which to this day are called Havvoth Jair" (Judg. 10:4).[26] Boling plausibly suggests that *ḥawwot yaʾir* (lit., "villages of Jair") may be an ancient name for the group of villages in Bashan conquered by the Manasseite Jair (Num. 32:41; Deut 3:13 – 14; cf. Josh. 17:1 – 6; 1 Chron. 2:22 – 23).[27] If so, despite its geographical imprecision, the term may preserve an early Manasseite memory of its ancestral holdings. In short, East Manasseh's inheritance belongs to half of the clan of Makir (v. 31b), undoubtedly a major clan descended from a prominent ancestor, the other half inheriting land west of the Jordan in West Manasseh.

Verse 32 sums up the entire retrospective ("this is the inheritance Moses had given . . ."). It anchors the historic moment at its historic site, "the plains of Moab across the Jordan east of Jericho" (Num. 22:1; 26:3). For the second time (cf. Josh. 13:14) the writer mentions that Moses gave no inheritance to the tribe of Levi (v. 33). The rationale this time, however, is that Yahweh himself is Levi's inheritance, just as Yahweh promised them (cf. 14:3 – 4). Set aside for Yahweh's service (Ex. 32:26 – 29), the tribe of Levi enjoyed the special blessing of ongoing contact with him and his personal provision of their financial needs (i.e., Israel's tithes and offerings). Levi formed the human bridge between holy Yahweh and unholy Israel that maintained their relationship. The theme of Levi's inheritance here will soon recur (Josh. 14:3 – 4; 18:7) and reach its culmination in ch. 21. In sum, chapter 13 affirms that Moses gave Israel's Transjordanian tribes their inheritances — and, thereby, the basis for their land claims — and reasserts that, despite the barrier of the Jordan, they help comprise larger Israel.

Joshua's Obedience: The First Allottment (14:1 – 17:18)

INTRODUCTION (14:1 – 5). From Transjordan the focus quickly shifts west of the Jordan to the land of Canaan. Comparable opening and closing formulae ("Now these are the areas/territories . . .") bracket the lengthy summary (chs. 14 – 19) of what lands the Israelites "received" as their inheritances (*naḥal* qal) in Cisjordan (v. 1; cf. 19:51). Indeed, the formulae stamp

---

25. It is not clear how "half of Gilead" relates to "all the towns of Gilead" assigned to Gad (v. 25).

26. In 1 Chron. 2:22 – 23, the number of Jair's towns was twenty-three, although v. 23 says that Havvoth Jair plus several other places total sixty towns; cf. Hess, *Joshua*, 236.

27. R. G. Boling, "Jair (Person)," *ABD*, 3:614. Nelson (*Joshua*, 174) compares the description to Solomon's sixth administrative district (1 Kings 4:13); cf. also Naʾaman, *Borders and Districts*, 168, 190.

the summary as primarily retrospective—a backward look at the results of the process, not necessarily a report of how it was done.

At the same time, the writer's summary report (vv. 2–5) does explain the distribution (*naḥal* pi. "to apportion as an inheritance"; NIV "to allot [land]") as the work of the high priest, Eleazar, Joshua, and the tribal leaders (in that order). This marks the debut in Joshua of Eleazar (cf. 19:51; 21:1), a debut undoubtedly driven by Yahweh's previous appointment (through Moses) of Eleazar and Joshua to allocate inheritances to the nine-and-one-half tribes (v. 1; Num. 32:28; 34:16–17).[28] The presence of the high priest and the use of lots per Yahweh's explicit command also mark the land distribution as specifically a *sacred* act (v. 2; cf. Num. 26:55; 33:54; 34:13; 36:2).[29] The main point of chapters 14–19, however, is to confirm that Joshua faithfully executes his commission to apportion Canaan among the nine-and-a-half tribes (13:7).

Lots (*goral*) were probably small stones or pieces of wood with markings keyed to the decision sought, which an authority placed in a receptacle, shook, and cast out on the ground to render it.[30] Whatever the matter at hand, Israel understood the lot to deliver "the final decision of Yahweh, against which there was no appeal."[31] Though humanly carried out, the distribution of land by lot marked the process and its results as Yahweh's own doing. In this case, land ownership by Israel as a whole is already a given; the process simply decides which Israelite gets which land as his inheritance.

Also, the writer underscores that instead of land, Levi received "only towns to live in, with pasturelands for their flocks and herds" (vv. 3–4). At first glance, the reason cited—that Joseph had become two tribes, Ephraim and Manasseh—seems a little odd. It presupposes an ideal number of twelve tribes and implies that the division of Joseph, so to speak, left Levi the odd-man-out—and, hence, ineligible for land. Probably, the missing piece

---

28. Rather than the high priest, the conquest narrative features nameless "priests" or "priests who are Levites" bearing the ark (e.g., 3:3; 4:10–11; 6:6). Interestingly, Eleazar and Joshua also share some history. The high priest presided over Joshua's commissioning by Moses as his successor (Num. 27:22), and Moses ordered the pair to hold the Transjordanian tribes accountable for their promise to aid their Cisjordanian kin before receiving their own inheritance (Num. 32:28).

29. The division of inheritances in the presence of gods was also typical of Old Babylonian practices; cf. Kitz, "Lot Casting in Joshua," 616–17.

30. Cf. A. M. Kitz, "The Hebrew Terminology of Lot Casting and Its Ancient Near Eastern Context," *CBQ* 62 (2000): 207–14, who cites both classical and biblical sources. According to Kitz (208, n.4), the root *garal* "has to do with stones or stoniness." For further discussion of lot-casting, see comments in the Original Meaning section concerning 7:14–15; Kitz, "Lot Casting in Joshua," 617–18; and 18:8–19:48.

31. W. Dommershausen, "גּוֹרָל," *TDOT*, 2:450–52 (quote 452), with reference to Joshua 18–20. But, in my view, the same principle applies to the entire land distribution section.

here is another biblical assumption—that Yahweh's choice of Levi to serve him exclusively removed him from the list of twelve and created the vacancy that the Josephite division filled.[32] (For other rationale, see 3:14, 33). In any case, the main point is that, with respect to the Cisjordanian tribes and Levi, the Israelites "apportioned the land" (Heb. *ḥalaq*) exactly as Yahweh had ordered (v. 5). Two long allotment reports (14:6–17:18; 18:1–19:51), each detailing distinct phases of distribution, confirm that claim.

A special allotment: Caleb (14:6–15). The first allotment phase probably takes place at Gilgal, Israel's home base near Jericho (14:6; cf. 4:19; 9:6; 10:43), and involves Judah, Ephraim, and West Manasseh.[33] It opens with a narrative concerning a special allotment for Caleb (14:6–15), then details the allotments to Judah (15:1–63) and the Josephites, Ephraim and Manasseh (16:1–17:13). It concludes with a supplementary allotment for the latter pair (17:14–18).

A Judahite visit with Joshua at Gilgal (14:6a) sets the context for a speech by Caleb, who presumably accompanies them there (14:6b–12). Caleb, of course, is the wilderness hero who represented Judah among the twelve spies and favored a bold Israelite attack into Canaan rather than a frightened retreat back to Egypt (Num. 13–14).[34] The sensitive reader imagines the poignant moment when Joshua and Caleb, two aging veterans of so much history, meet at Gilgal—itself, a site where powerful memories echo—surrounded by Judah's representatives. Caleb reminds Joshua, his only ally among the spies, of "what the LORD said to Moses ... about you and me" long ago at Kadesh Barnea (v. 6b). He refers to Numbers 14:30, where Yahweh declared that of the twelve, only Caleb and Joshua would enter and occupy the land. A brief review of his faithful spy service (vv. 7–8) leads Caleb to quote Moses' oath (v. 9 [actually Yahweh's]) promising him and his descendants an "inheritance ... forever" in the land he had traversed years ago as a spy (Deut. 1:36).

---

32. As Howard notes (*Joshua*, 316, n.56), the tribal arithmetic is actually more complex, since the division of Manasseh into eastern and western branches, in effect, adds an additional tribe. Also, Simeon receives only cities within Judah, not its own tribal land, because Judah did not need all its territory (19:1, 9), while Dan's inability to occupy its assigned territory drove it to settle elsewhere (19:47; Judg. 18:1).

33. So Howard, *Joshua*, 323; Seleznev, "The Origin of the Tribal Boundaries," 340–41; Assis, "Ideal and Reality in the Distribution Descriptions," 6. The supporting evidence for inferring Gilgal as the site are: (1) the mention of Gilgal in 14:6; (2) Gilgal's prominence in the prior narratives (Josh. 4–10); (3) Gilgal as the most likely site for this meeting. I admit, however, that the text does not underscore the fact, as it does Shiloh in chs. 18–19.

34. R. L. Hubbard Jr., "Caleb, Calebites," *DOTHB*, 120–22. The term "Kenizzite" reflects his descent either from a pre-Israelite people in southern Canaan (Gen. 15:19) or an important western Edomite clan (Gen. 36:11, 15, 42).

The promise rewards Caleb's one sterling trait: He "followed the LORD ...God wholeheartedly," a trait the context recalls verbatim three times (v. 9; cf. vv. 8, 14). In my view, the Hebrew phrase (lit., "to fill behind") is a short form of a longer idiom (lit. "to fill [one's] heart to walk behind").[35] As Snijders writes of the phrase, "The heart contains nothing against Yahweh: it is fully, completely for or [my addition: following] behind the Lord."[36] In other words, what Caleb did was wholeheartedly—i.e., resolutely, unswervingly, unhesitatingly—to obey God's will rather than his own or that of someone else. Therein lies what Yahweh himself calls the "different spirit" of Caleb that set him apart from his unfaithful comrades (Num. 14:24).

Caleb remarks (with apparent hyperbole) that God, as he promised, has kept him alive to age eighty-five—and just as vigorous and battle-ready as ever! (vv. 10 – 11). So, he asks to receive (lit.) "this hill country" Yahweh promised him long ago, and he promises to destroy (*yaraš* hi.; NIV "drive out") the Anakites despite their large, fortified cities (v. 12).[37] In reply, Joshua blesses his old friend and war buddy and gives him the city of Hebron as his inheritance. Caleb's family still possessed it at the time the writer lived (NIV "ever since" [lit., "to this day"]; vv. 13 – 14). For the third time, the writer singles out Caleb's signature act ("he followed the LORD ... wholeheartedly"; cf. vv. 8 – 9). Subtly, the repetition spotlights the old man's unwavering devotion to Yahweh against the dark background of his long-dead, rebellious contemporaries. The motif implicitly points the reader to the steps he followed in order to enjoy the divine blessings of long life and the retention of ancestral land.

A brief parenthesis notes that the ancient name for Hebron was Kiriath Arba ("city of Arba," named for the greatest Anakite hero, v. 15). If, as I suggest elsewhere, Caleb "represents a non-Israelite clan incorporated into the tribe of Judah and larger Israel,"[38] his settlement in southern Judah may have meant a return to his ancient, pre-Israelite ancestral land. Literarily, the comment pits the clans of two great heroes, the Anakite Arba and the Kenizzite Caleb, against each other for possession of a prized city and its surroundings, a battle whose outcome is soon to be told (cf. 15:13 – 19).

---

35. Num. 14:24; 32:11, 12; Deut. 1:36; Josh. 14:8, 9, 14; 1 Kings 11:6); cf. L. A. Snijders, "מָלֵא," *TDOT*, 8:300 – 301, who accepts "heart" as the direct object of "fill" but omits "walk" from (in my view) the implied idiom "to go after, to follow" (Heb. *leket ʾaḥarey*; e.g., Deut. 13:5; Jer. 2:2). It usage with Yahweh may intentionally contrast the use of the latter idiom with the names of other gods (Deut. 4:3; 1 Kings 11:5; 18:18; Jer. 2:23).

36. Ibid., 8:301.

37. The rendering of *yaraš* (hi.) as "destroy" rather than a "drive out" here and elsewhere in Joshua (so NIV) follows the persuasive case of Lohfink, "יָרַשׁ," 6:374 – 75.

38. Hubbard, "Caleb, Calebites," 120.

Finally, the narrator notes that "the land had rest from war," a verbatim echo of the conclusion of the conquest narrative (11:23). At first glance, the remark seems strange since chs. 13 – 14 neither report nor allude to any battles involving anyone, including Caleb. Probably, the writer repeats the line here as a literary cross reference to the prior, successful conquest that made possible the lengthy land distribution now to follow.[39] Thus, the scene is set: Peace prevails, and the long-anticipated settlement can proceed.[40]

Judah's allotment (15:1 – 63). The larger process begins with a long report of Judah's inheritance (15:1 – 63). The boundary description (vv. 1 – 12) traces in considerable detail its southern (vv. 2 – 4), eastern (v. 5a), northern (vv. 5b – 11), and western borders (v. 12).[41] The southern boundary description closely resembles the southern boundary of Canaan in Numbers 34:3 – 6. It heads south from the Dead Sea, turns southwest to below Kadesh Barnea and northwest to link up with the Wadi of Egypt (Wadi el-Arish) that empties into the Mediterranean. The eastern border runs north along the Dead Sea's western side to where the Jordan enters it (i.e., its "mouth"), and the Mediterranean marks Judah's western limit. The northern border description is strikingly detailed (most of the places well known), undoubtedly because it abuts the space reserved for Benjamin (Josh. 18:11 – 20) and also must exclude Jerusalem. That is why the border passes the city's south side through the semi-circular Hinnom Valley (v. 8). Its northeast and northwest sections—between the Jordan's mouth and Jerusalem, and from Jerusalem to the sea—may in fact have corresponded to ancient roads.[42]

Caleb returns on stage in a brief interlude (15:13 – 19) that also features his daughter, Acsah. The narrator recalls that Hebron (or Kiriath Arba) is Caleb's inheritance and lies within Judah's inheritance (v. 13). He also reports officially that Caleb destroyed (NIV "drove out") three descendants of Anak at Hebron (v. 14). The apparently easy defeat of Anak here smacks of poetic justice. The terror of confronting the Anakites had panicked Israel into its fateful rebellion in the wilderness (Num. 13:22, 28, 33), but Caleb here again displays his fearless faith in Yahweh (Num. 14:6 – 9).[43]

---

39. Nelson, *Joshua*, 179.

40. For a comparison of the treatment of Caleb in Josh. 14 – 15 and that in Judg. 1, see Hubbard, "Caleb, Calebites," 120 – 21.

41. Evocative names pop up occasionally (e.g., "Scorpion Pass" [v. 3], "the Stone of Bohan son of Reuben" [v. 6], "the gorge" [v. 7]), places no doubt familiar to ancient readers. For a convenient chart of the boundaries, see Hess, *Joshua*, 242 – 44.

42. Seleznev, "The Origin of the Tribal Boundaries," 353 – 56.

43. The conquest of Hebron here seems to conflict with the earlier claim that Joshua had annihilated them (11:21 – 22). But the fact that some Anakites fled and found refuge to the west (v. 22) leaves open the possibility that they or their descendants had somehow retaken Hebron in the interval.

Nor is old Caleb finished. He marches to Debir, fifteen miles southwest of Hebron, and offers his daughter, Acsah, in marriage to anyone who captures it. Caleb's nephew, Othniel, does so and claims the prize (15:15 – 17). At his new wife's urging, Othniel gets Caleb to grant them a field, and Acsah herself wins "a special favor" from her father—the area's upper and lower springs (vv. 18 – 19)—because the property lies in the "land of the Negev" (i.e., the desert). The wedding present permits them to irrigate land in the Negev's semiarid climate. This vignette implies that, besides Hebron, Caleb also held territory southwest of the city in the southern hill country of Judah and the Negev. The term "Negev of Caleb" (1 Sam. 30:14) may attest the presence of Calebites also in the northeastern Negev. Later, Israelite leaders will give Hebron to a priestly family but leave the farmland and villages around it to Caleb's descendants (Josh. 21:11 – 12; cf. 1 Chron. 6:41).[44]

The inheritance of Judah concludes with a lengthy list of Judah's towns (15:20 – 63) neatly organized by four geographical regions. Most scholars presume the four correspond to later royal administrative provinces, the town lists enabling monarchs to collect taxes and to draft troops (cf. 1 Kings 4:17 – 19).[45] Two regions (western foothills, hill country) also subdivide the data by four and five districts, respectively.

Careful readers may notice several oddities. The Negev roster lists thirty-six towns, but the final tally is only twenty-nine (v. 32).[46] The western foothills section ends (vv. 45 – 47) with an expanded description of three Philistine towns (Ekron, Ashdod, Gath). This is odd since Joshua 13:2 – 3 lists the Philistines (and presumably their lands) among Canaan's unconquered areas, and the Bible credits David with finally subduing the Philistines (2 Sam. 8:1). Apparently, their inclusion either voices an early ideal inheritance for Judah or reflects the situation later in the monarchy period. Also, nine of Judah's towns are among the eighteen towns listed for Simeon (19:2 – 9), undoubtedly because they fell within Judah's borders as Joshua 19 claims (19:1, 9). Two-thirds of the towns (83 of 122) appear only in lists (e.g., mainly Joshua, 1 Chronicles, Nehemiah), nearly half (58) never receive mention elsewhere in the Bible, and the locations of many remain unidentified.[47]

---

44. Hubbard, "Caleb, Calebites," 120 – 21.

45. Nelson, *Joshua,* 185 – 86 (with bibliography), who tentatively dates the lists to the reign of Josiah (as do other scholars). For details, see the chart in Hess (*Joshua,* 249 – 55) and the discussion in J. Svensson, *Towns and Toponyms in the Old Testament* (ConBOT 38; Stockholm: Almqvist & Wiksell, 1994), 29 – 59.

46. Scholars account for the discrepancy in several ways. Some attribute it to a copyist's error, others trace it to the fluidity of the list over time (i.e., names were added later but the prior total not adjusted), while others suggest that some listed towns may have been thought too insignificant to be counted; cf. Howard, *Joshua,* 341.

47. Howard, *Joshua,* 340.

The town list starts in the south, the Negev (vv. 20–32), then moves northwest to the western foothills, the low hills and small river valleys inland from the coastal plain (vv. 33–47). Nine southern Judean towns also make Simeon's list in the Negev (see above) and four lowland towns later assigned to Dan appear on Judah's list.[48] As is well known, however, Dan failed to possess them (19:47; Judg. 18), and later biblical evidence fails to confirm that Judah wrested all four from Philistine hands.[49] The three districts within the lowlands province all lie at least twenty-five miles southwest of Jerusalem. Fourteen towns comprise the most northern district (vv. 33–36), while sixteen lie to the southwest (vv. 37–41) and nine to the southeast (vv. 42–44). The three Philistine towns sat west of the other Judean lowland towns (vv. 45–47), and the fact that this list lacks a final tally perhaps signals the author's awareness of their back-and-forth history of possession.

From the lowlands Judah's list turns east to the hill country (vv. 48–60), the wide, mountainous, central spine that gradually slopes west to the low-lands and east to the Judean desert.[50] Five districts comprise this list of towns that basically runs north to south in direction.[51] The eleven towns and villages in the southernmost district lie southwest of Hebron in a nar-row, east-to-west band (vv. 48–51), while the band of nine lies to its imme-diate northeast and includes Hebron (vv. 52–54). The next list comprises ten towns and villages southeast and north of Hebron (vv. 55–57), while the last lists of six and two lie farther north, the latter west of Jerusalem (vv. 58–59, 60). The six-item list of towns in the barren, north-south strip along the Dead Sea ends the survey (vv. 61–62). The best-known is En Gedi, located just above and halfway down the Dead Sea.

---

48. Those on Simeon's list include: Moladah (15:26; 19:2), Hazar Shual (15:28; 19:3), Ezem (15:29; 19:3), Eltolad (15:30; 19:4), Hormah (15:30; 19:4), Ziklag (15:31; 19:5), Leb-aoth (15:32; 19:6), Ain (15:32; 19:7), and Rimmon (15:32; 19:7). The Danite cities also counted by Judah are: Eshtaol and Zorah (15:33; 19:41) and Ekron (a Philistine city) and Timnah (15:45, 47; 19:43).

49. Zorah apparently belonged to Judah in the late tenth century B.C. (2 Chron. 11:10) and Timnah in the mid–eighth century B.C. (2 Chron. 28:18), but the Philistines apparently controlled Zorah and Esthaol in the eleventh century B.C. The Bible consistently portrays Ekron as a Philistine city (1 Sam. 5:10; 6:16, 17; 17:52; 2 Kings 1:2, 3, 6, 16; Amos 1:8; Jer. 25:20), but there are indicators that Judah also possessed it at various times (Judg. 1:18; 1 Sam. 7:1; cf. Zech. 9:7).

50. Howard, *Joshua*, 341.

51. In v. 59 LXX has an additional fifth group of eleven towns: Tekoa, Ephrathah (i.e., Bethlehem), Peor, Etam, Culon, Tatam, Sores, Carem, Gallim, Baither, and Manach. They lie north of the fourth group centered around Bethlehem. Both this group and MT's fourth group end with "and their villages," so at some point a scribe may have accidentally skipped this section.

Now, many readers will find the Judah section—hands down, the largest in chs. 14−19—tediously detailed. But that is the point: Its sheer quantity underscores Judah's importance within Israel.[52] Canonically, this continues the biblical theme of Judah's destiny for leadership that first sounds subtly in the Joseph story (Gen. 43:3−10; 44:14−34), develops in Jacob's last words (Gen. 49:8−12), echoes in the book of Ruth (Ruth 4:17−22), finds full voice in David's emergence (1−2 Samuel), and reaches its climax in Jesus Christ (Matt. 1). It also firmly establishes Judah's tribal footprint in the land and founds Judah's claim to its land, whether centuries before the exile to Babylon (587 B.C.) or after its return (538 B.C.). Later history will confirm the importance of Judah's foothold in the land for it constituted the remnant of the twelve tribes that enabled Israel to continue its mission to the world.

For the first time, however, the book reports that a tribe did not destroy (*yaraš* hi., v. 63) indigenous people occupying its inheritance (see 16:10; 17:12). In this case, it is the Jebusites who live in Jerusalem, and the author adds that in his day they still (lit.) "live with the Judahites in Jerusalem." This comment is surprising because it assumes that Jerusalem belongs to Judah (or at least, is Judah's responsibility), whereas the border of Judah excludes it (15:8) and Joshua 18:28 assigns Jerusalem to the inheritance of Benjamin.[53] To belong to Benjamin rather than Judah makes both geographic and political sense. Wisdom would suggest that as the nation's capital, it should be politically independent of both northern (i.e., the Josephites) and southern (Judah) tribal behemoths. Belonging to Benjamin, whose territory essentially formed a buffer zone between them, would maintain that independence, at least symbolically.[54]

At the same time, by conquest (see 2 Sam 5) Jerusalem became David's personal city—"the city of David" (2 Sam. 5:2, 9), thereby associating it with Judah, David's tribe. The best explanation for Joshua 15:63 is to read it as reflecting the writer's Judahite perspective and probably a Davidic or post-Davidic time of writing.

The allotments of the Joseph tribes (16:1−17:18). The two tribes of Joseph now receive their inheritance (16:1−17:13), but Joshua turns down their request for a supplemental allotment (17:14−18). The Josephite southern border runs from east of Jericho to Bethel then southwesterly near Lower Beth Horon to Gezer and on to the Mediterranean. Interestingly,

---

52. The long list may also attest the author's Judean perspective and sources.

53. Cf. Judg. 1:21 which repeats Josh. 15:63 almost verbatim to report Benjamin's inability to handle the Jebusites.

54. Cf. Seleznev, "The Origin of the Tribal Boundaries," 348−49.

their southern boundary (16:1–4) does not directly abut Judah's northern border but instead leaves room for Benjamin in between them (18:11–28). The details of each tribe's inheritance now follow (16:5–17:13).

The boundary of Ephraim (16:5–10) apparently restates the southern boundary in simpler form (v. 6a), then traces Ephraim's northeastern boundary. It passes southeast from Micmethath (east of Shechem; cf. 17:7) past Taanath Shiloh to Janoah (or possibly east of it) through Jericho to the Jordan (vv. 6b–7). Its northwestern section goes southwest from Tappuah (ca. ten mi. south of Shechem) to the Kanah Ravine and on to the Mediterranean (v. 8). The author states that Ephraim also possesses all the towns and villages assigned it within West Manasseh but names none of them (v. 9).

Finally, as with Judah (15:63), the author again sounds the did-not-destroy (*yaraš* hi.) theme — in this case, the Canaanites of Gezer, who still live in Ephraim. Instead, the Ephraimites forced them to work (*mas* "forced labor") for the Israelites (v. 10). This seems to imply criticism of Ephraimite efforts in the matter, unless the force required to compel labor is less than that necessary to destroy the Canaanites. As Lohfink has observed, however, this pragmatic policy was not an inconsequential matter for Israel.[55] It kept at bay a potentially corrupting presence within Israel, a point that Joshua's later farewell speech attempts to drive home (see ch. 23).

The text clarifies that the inheritance of West Manasseh (17:1–13) concerns six clans of Manasseh (including the Hepherites) other than those of Makir or East Manasseh (vv. 1–2, 6b), already an inheritance recipient (13:28–31). Further, it briefly narrates a special appeal for land that Joshua grants the five daughters of Zelophehad, a Hepherite without male heirs, as Moses promised (Num. 27:3–6). West Manasseh receives ten sections of land in Cisjordan in order to accommodate them (17:5–6).

That clarification done, the boundary description (17:7–10) and a list of Manasseite towns within Issachar and Asher (v. 11) follow. The former is incomplete, detailing only the western section of the Ephraim-West Manasseh southern boundary. It runs from Asher (?) to Micmethath, then south to Tappuah, and west along the north rim of the Kanah Ravine (the south rim is Ephraim's) to its western border, the Mediterranean (vv. 9b–10). West Manasseh's northern and eastern boundaries are given in the most general of terms — Asher and Issachar, respectively (v. 10b). The references are, of course, anachronistic and retrospective, since the narrative has yet to assign territory to either tribe (cf. 19:17–23, 24–31).

---

55. Lohfink, "יָרַשׁ," 6:383.

The author's painstaking qualifications leave the impression that West Manasseh is something of a hodge-podge. It includes the land around Tappuah but not the town itself (it is Ephraimite; v. 8); it clarifies that Manasseh and Ephraim lie north and south of each other (v. 10a); it notes that Ephraim has towns within Manasseh (v. 9) and Manasseh has towns in both Issachar and Asher (v. 11).

Alas, the impressive list of towns written east to west suggests both good news and bad news. The good news is that it includes well-known towns and their surrounding settlements (lit., "daughters"): Beth Shean, Ibleam, Dor, Endor, Taanach, and Megiddo.[56] But the bad news surfaces in the recurrence of the did-not-destroy theme. Apparently, stubborn Canaanite determination to remain in the area stymied Manasseh's efforts to dispossess (*yaraš*) them of their towns (v. 12). Manasseh's lone success was to subject the Canaanites to forced labor (*mas*) once the Israelites gained the upper hand over them (v. 13; cf. 16:10). But, as the author's grammar underscores, the harsh fact remained: Manasseh did not destroy them.

Finally, an unexpected dialogue between the Josephites and Joshua closes both the Josephite allotment report and the larger first allotment section (17:14 – 18). The quick back-and-forth conversation abruptly begins with no setting of the scene, but we are probably to imagine its setting in Gilgal. Noticeably (and inexplicably) absent here is the high priest Eleazar, who had copresided over the first land distribution (14:1) and the land grant to the daughters of Zelophehad (17:4). The Josephites have come to protest, and, undeniably, the frustrating power struggle with Canaanites lies in the background.

Strikingly, the narrator phrases it in first person singular, as if the two tribes were speaking as a single individual (v. 14; but cf. NIV "our," "we"). This compares to other biblical references to Joseph as a single entity, sometimes called a "house" (18:11; Judg. 1:22, 35; Ps. 81:5; Am. 6:6). "I" demand to know, united Joseph asks, why "you" (Joshua) assigned "me" only "one lousy portion" (my paraphrase), despite the fact that, by Yahweh's abundant blessing, "I" am a very large people.[57] The implication is that Yahweh's blessing entitles "me" to land commensurate with "my" population size.

Joshua's reply turns the petitioner's premise ("I am a very large people") around. If the hill country of Ephraim (or, more narrowly, Mount Ephraim) lacks room (lit., "be too narrow"), he challenges Joseph to wield his large population as a powerful saw against the forest where the Perizzites and

---

56. For the obscure reference to Naphoth, see the commentaries.

57. The double wording ("one allotment and one portion") seems rhetorically emphatic ("one lousy portion") rather than a list of two items.

Rephaites live (v. 15).[58] It, too, comprises part of the basic territory assigned him—it merely needs development. So, Joshua orders, add more useable land within your allotment by clearing out the forest and its current inhabitants. In short, behind the difficulty lurks an opportunity.

Joseph's reply (now in plural "we"/"our") broadens their argument to say simply "our whole inheritance is unsuitable." They reiterate their original point (i.e., the hill country is too small for them) but with a new wrinkle. The military superiority of Canaanite iron chariots renders the areas allotted them in the plain, both at Beth Shean and in the Valley of Jezreel, similarly unsatisfactory.[59] Both geographical references recall the towns and settlements in verse 11 that proved to be a battleground for Manasseh (Ibleam, Endor, Taanach, and Megiddo all lie in or along the Valley of Jezreel). In short, Joseph's point is that neither the hill country nor the plain will do.

Contextually, of course, the Josephites apparently have a short memory and feeble faith. They have forgotten the decisive victory that Yahweh won against Canaanite chariotry at the Battle of Merom (ch. 11). The contrast with the bold and fearless eighty-year-old Caleb (chs. 14–15) is also stark and disappointing. That Caleb (14:6–12) and Zelophehad's daughters (17:4) appeal to God's prior promises of land likewise casts Joseph's approach in an arrogant, self-serving light. Worse, to challenge land assignments made by lot is, in effect, to challenge the wisdom and goodness of God himself, a mistake their ancestors made in the wilderness.[60]

Joshua's final ruling (vv. 17–18) parries both prongs of the Josephite argument. (1) He encourages them not to sell themselves short. "You [sing.] are numerous and very powerful" means that they already have the personnel and means to succeed. As in the wilderness (Num. 14:6–9), Joshua seeks to counter the growing Canaanite-ophobia before him with a positive word. (2) He turns their "one lousy portion" against them and reiterates his earlier challenge concerning the opportunities that the forest offers.[61] If they expand in that direction, there is no limit to how far beyond that one allotment they can extend their holdings through the larger hill country.

---

58. "Hill country of Ephraim" probably designates the more restricted area, Mount Ephraim (1 Kings 4:8); cf. Nelson, *Joshua*, 204. Perizzites are one of the seven indigenous peoples of Canaan named for annihilation (Deut. 20:17). Gen. 15:20 lists the Rephaites also as indigenous to Canaan (cf. 1 Chron. 20:4), although they were not on the list of seven. Apparently, this group differs from the Transjordan group(s) of the same name; cf. Deut. 2:11, 20; Josh. 12:4; 13:12. Cf. M. S. Smith, "Rephaim," *ABD*, 5:675–76.

59. Howard, *Joshua*, 357, hears in this despair before perceived Canaanite superiority an echo of the ten spies in the wilderness (Num. 13:26–33).

60. Cf. Howard, *Joshua*, 355–56.

61. For alternate interpretations of the terrain in view here, see Howard, *Joshua*, 356.

Above all, they will destroy the Canaanites and even expand into the problematic plain, Canaanite iron chariots notwithstanding.

Thus, the first allotment ends on a positive note. Granted, Canaanite enclaves still hold out against Israel's settling tribes, notably Gezer (16:10) and five Canaanite cities in the plain (17:12 – 13). The Jebusites also still occupy Jerusalem, a challenge for Judah. But occasionally Israel gets the upper hand—witness Manasseh (17:13)—and the pressing of Canaanites into laboring for Israel (16:10; 17:13) implies a shifting balance of power in Israel's favor. Echoes of Israel at its worst surface in the Josephite protest (17:14, 16), but Joshua's ruling and challenge (17:17 – 18) bode well for any subsequent tribe that follows it. Such, then, is the first allotment to the leading two-and-a-half tribes, Judah, Ephraim, and West Manasseh. Seven tribes still have yet to receive their inheritance, but their time comes next.

The Second Allottment: the Shiloh Assembly (18:1 – 19:51)

THE FIRST ALLOTMENT REPORTED the inheritances of Judah, Ephraim, and West Manasseh. The setting was apparently Gilgal (14:6), but the text did not detail the distribution procedure, other than implying the use of lots.[62] With the second allotment, however, opening and closing reports (18:1 – 3 and 19:51) set off the narrative that tells how land came to the remaining seven tribes (v. 2). The setting is a national assembly of all Israelite tribes at Shiloh, a town that now emerges as Israel's primary religious center prior to the temple in Jerusalem.[63]

Several features give the scene an especially solemn, momentous aura. (1) There the tribes have erected the Tent of Meeting, the portable place where Yahweh and Israel may meet (18:1; cf. Ex. 33:7; 1 Sam. 2:22; Ps. 78:60).[64] The tent symbolically implies Yahweh's presence (cf. vv. 6, 10 ["in the presence of the LORD"]), participation, and approval of the proceedings.[65]

---

62. Kitz ("Lot Casting in Joshua," 611 – 18) plausibly argues, however, that the process compares to the structure and terminology of an Old Babylonian text, the Imgua inheritance text. In the latter, however, birth order determines the order of distribution, whereas Kitz believes (615 – 16) that "a geographical agenda" is in play in Joshua 18 – 19. For more on the order of distribution, see below.

63. Josh. 21:2; 22:9, 12; Judg. 21:19; 1 Sam. 1:3, 9; 2:22; 3:21; Jer. 7:12, 14; cf. B. Halpern, "Shiloh (Place)," *ABD*, 5:1213.

64. With Howard (*Joshua*, 360), this assumes a distinction between the Tent of Meeting and the tabernacle. K. Koch, "אֹהֶל," *TDOT*, 1:123 – 30, reviews the higher critical discussion concerning the number and use of Israel's sacred tents.

65. Inheritance distributions in several Old Babylonian texts were similarly carried out in the presence of the gods; cf. Kitz, "Lot Casting in Joshua," 616 – 17.

(2) Further, the narrator comments that the land now is fully subdued "under their control" (v. 1b).[66] The latter echoes the phrase that Moses invokes as one condition for Reuben, Gad, and East Manasseh to receive their inheritances in Transjordan (Num. 32:22, 29). If the echo is intentional, the author signals that that condition has been met—that Israel now enters a decisively new phase. The previous legal barrier to the proper allocation of inheritances—the presence of squatters—is gone. The "take possession" part of Joshua's invasion order now begins for the seven tribes (Josh. 1:11), with the "subdued" land ripe for the taking.

(3) Finally, by detailing the inheritances of the last seven tribes, the narrative affirms Israel's national identity as a unified people living on divinely given land. This theme recurs in chapter 22 and, many centuries later, in the ideal, future land distribution of Ezekiel 47.[67]

Instructions and compliance (18:1 – 10). At first hearing, Joshua's opening statement ("How long will you wait …?") sounds like an accusation that faults the seven tribes for laziness (v. 3).[68] In reality, the seven have received no prior mandate to occupy land, so his seemingly blunt statement is merely motivational rhetoric to get them moving on his plan.[69] The plan (vv. 4–5, 8) calls for three men from each tribe—probably twenty-one in all—to survey the land still available outside the territory already occupied by Judah and Joseph.[70]

A wordplay cleverly captures their twofold mission.[71] "To survey" (*halak*, hithp., to "walk back and forth") pictures the group as thoroughly traversing the terrain on foot. They are also "to divide it" (*halaq* hithp.) into seven (presumably somewhat equal) parts and to make a written record of the

---

66. Heb. *kabaš* ("to subdue") is the same word in God's mandate to humans to "subdue" the earth (Gen. 1:28); cf. Num. 32:22, 29; 1 Chron. 22:18.

67. Cf. Nelson, *Joshua*, 209; Kitz, "Lot Casting in Joshua," 609–10, who suggests that the process dissolves the house of Israel in favor of independent tribal entities.

68. This is the view of Assis, "Ideal and Reality in the Distribution Descriptions," 7–8, who believes that 14:1–5 reports a convocation that distributed the land among the nine-and-a-half Cisjordanian tribes per the mandate of 13:2–7. Thus, in his view, in 18:3 Joshua criticizes seven tribes for failing to implement that distribution. In my view, however, 14:1–5 reports no such convocation but instead comprises a summary report that introduces two allotment reports (14:6–19:51).

69. Howard, *Joshua*, 360; Nelson, *Joshua*, 210 ("more motivational than accusatory"); cf. Ex. 16:28; Num. 14:11; Ps. 13:1–2 [2–3].

70. V. 7 implies the exclusion of the Levites (their priestly service is their inheritance), but it is unclear whether the surveyors include the remaining eleven tribes (i.e., thirty-three surveyors) or only the seven that would benefit from it (i.e., twenty-one surveyors). In my view, the latter seems most likely.

71. Nelson, *Joshua*, 210.

divisions.[72] Then the surveyors are to return to Joshua, who will cast lots before God and Israel to decide who gets what (vv. 6–7).

As Joshua dispatches the team (v. 8) one cannot help but recall two earlier scenes where Moses and Joshua, respectively, sent off small teams also to investigate Canaan and bring back a report. Granted, forty years separate those two spy missions from this episode, but the comparison reminds us that Canaan remains a land that requires careful study if one is to settle there (Num. 13; Josh 2). Some places are poor places to live, and it has other occupants to avoid or destroy. Like their predecessors, this survey team carries out the plan—minus the rebellion of their ancestors, of course (v. 9). There at Shiloh, the long-awaited drama begins: Joshua casts the lots under Yahweh's watchful eye ("before the LORD") and divides the seven land plots tribe by tribe (v. 10).

Tribal allotments (18:11 – 19:48). The text itself offers no explanation of the lot-casting procedure, but one plausible scenario commends itself.[73] One may imagine two containers, each with seven stones. The seven in one container somehow identify each of the seven land portions, while the seven in the other bear the name of a tribe eligible for land. Joshua then "cast" one stone on the ground from each container, either in sequence or simultaneously, to match a land portion with a tribe.[74] The next step—the subdivision of the seven tribal portions among the clans of each tribe—would require one vessel with land descriptors equal to the number of clans and a second vessel with the names of each clan.[75] The

---

72. To what extent the seven tribal allotments detailed below reflect or draw on this record, and whether it was stored over time at Shiloh, are matters of speculation. Interestingly, agreement among heirs as to the contents of an inheritance to be distributed and the portion due each one is attested in the Imgua inheritance text; cf. Kitz, "Lot Casting in Joshua," 616.

73. Kitz ("The Hebrew Terminology of Lot Casting," 111–12) persuasively argues that the idiom ʿalab goral le ("to come up for") pictures a process of lot-casting in which the officiant shakes and casts the lot from a receptable to the ground. This process would contrast the lot-drawing procedure of 7:14–15.

74. In my view, the idiom ʿalab goral le describes this first step, the selection of the tribe to receive the next allotment (cf. Lev. 16:9, 10), the following phrase ("clan by clan") a second one to subdivide the tribal allotment. The resulting order of selections, however, is striking and commends an alternative view: Benjamin (Rachel), Simeon, Zebulun (both Leah), Asher (Zilpah, Leah's maid), Naphtali, and Dan (both Bilhah, Rachel's maid). In this view, the idiom would describe only a single step, the allotment among clans. The order in which each tribe received its distribution was by assumed tribal rank based on birth mothers. I am grateful to Professor John Walton for calling this possibility to my attention.

75. The lone exception to this proposed process would be Simeon, who received by lot only towns within Judah because Judah had more territory that it needed (19:1, 9). For a variant, more nuanced scenario of lot-casting, see W. Dommershausen, "גּוֹרָל," *TDOT*, 2:452.

final step would apply the procedure to divide the clan portions among its families.

Benjamin (18:11–28). As with 7:14–15, this text assumes theologically that Yahweh selects the lots by causing them to "come up" from the container to fall to the ground.[76] The first "lot" identifies Benjamin (v. 11a), and his land (v. 11b) runs east-to-west between those of Judah and Joseph (v. 11b). As with Judah, his boundary description (vv. 11b–20) precedes the town list (vv. 21–28), the latter also being divided into districts of twelve (vv. 21–24) and fourteen (vv. 25–28a). Of the seven tribes, the treatment of Benjamin certainly shows the most detail, an indicator of the tribe's importance (it includes Jerusalem) and perhaps the writer's Judahite perspective. The descriptions of its northern and southern borders (vv. 12–13, 15–19) parallel their counterparts concerning Ephraim and Judah (16:1–3a; 15:5–9 [but in reverse direction]).[77] The description carefully includes Jerusalem (v. 16) and Jericho (cf. v. 21), and locates the northern border south of Luz (or Bethel) and Lower Beth Horon since both belong to Ephraim (cf. 16:2–3).

The western boundary runs south from a hill south of Beth Horon to Kiriath Baal (or Kiriath Jearim), a Judahite town (v. 14), while the Jordan marks its eastern end (v. 20).[78] By giving a western boundary, the description seems to leave room for Dan to the west, thus either reflecting an ideal of tribal locations or a source that preceded Dan's migration northward.[79]

The list of Benjamite towns—the third longest after those of Judah (ch. 15) and Levi (ch. 21)—now follows (18:21–28), subdivided into eastern (twelve towns) and western (fourteen towns) districts. The former (vv. 21–24), whose best-known towns are Jericho, Bethel, and Geba, basically lies east of the land's main north-south watershed. Inexplicably, Ophrah and Bethel seem to lie in Josephite territory (vv. 22, 23; cf. 16:1–3; Judg. 1:22–23), but the lack of a town list for Ephraim leaves the matter of tribal ownership uncertain. Beth Arabah (v. 22) also appears on Judah's list just inside the border (15:61), and the double listing may reflect lists of different dates and an occasional shifting of towns near the

---

76. Kitz, "The Hebrew Terminology of Lot Casting," 212, 214.

77. Concerning the identification and background on Beth Aven, see Nelson, *Joshua*, 213.

78. V. 28 lists Kiriath as a Benjaminite town, which distinguishes it from Kiriath Jearim (vv. 14–15); so Howard, *Joshua*, 365. But several LXX texts read the latter also in v. 28, suggesting the possibility that haplography led to the loss of Jearim in MT; cf. Nelson, *Joshua*, 212–13.

79. Cf. Howard, *Joshua*, 363; and Nelson, *Joshua*, 213, who interprets this phenomenon differently.

border.[80] The towns west of the watershed (vv. 25–28) lie north and west of Jerusalem—Gibeon, Ramah, and Gibeah (hometown of Saul) are best known—but more than half are of unknown location.[81]

Simeon (19:1–9). The second lot identifies the inheritance of Simeon. It consists exclusively of towns within Judah's territory. The writer explains that Simeon benefited from the fact that Judah's portion exceeded Judah's needs (v. 9). The phrase "more than" speaks of quantity, not size, so the reference must be to an excess number of Judahite towns, not to an excess of land. Simeon was a small tribe compared to Judah (1 Chron. 4:27), and that may account for its receipt of towns rather than territory. Canonically, another factor might be in play with Simeon (and also Levi). In his last words to his sons, Jacob declares that Simeon and Levi will be scattered among the other tribes (Gen. 49:5–7), perhaps as judgment for their unwarranted violence against the men of Shechem (34:24–30).[82]

Structurally, the list subdivides the towns into districts of thirteen (vv. 2–6) and four (vv. 7–8) along with their surrounding villages. The thirteen lie in southern Judah (e.g., Beersheba, Hormah, Ziklag), while the four include two in the Negev (Ain, Rimmon) and two in the western lowlands (Ether, Ashan). Baalath Beer (or Ramah in the Negev) marks either the southernmost village or the southern boundary within which they fall (v. 8a).[83] Two Egyptian texts and the ostraca from Arad mention Sharuhen in the southwestern Negev (v. 6), but twelve of the eighteen names listed are of unknown or disputed location.[84]

Zebulun (19:10–16). The third lot falls to Zebulun. Structurally, opening and closing formulae (vv. 10a, 16) bracket an extensive boundary description (vv. 10b–14) and a short town list (v. 15). Stylistically, the description adopts Sarid (probably Tel Shadud in the northern Jezreel Valley) as its starting and ending point, connecting border towns as if drawing a line between dots on a map.[85] From Sarid the southwestern border runs west to Maralah, north-northwest to Dabbesheth, and southwest to the ravine

---

80. For a more complex solution dating the list to Josiah's reign, see Nelson, *Joshua*, 214.

81. Hess, *Joshua*, 266–67. According to Howard (*Joshua*, 365), ten of Benjamin's twenty-six towns find no other mention in the Bible.

82. Cf. Howard, *Joshua*, 366.

83. A similar list forms part of the genealogy of Simeon (1 Chron. 4:28–33). For their locations, see the convenient map in *CBA*, no. 140 (p. 105).

84. Hess, *Joshua*, 268–69. For the Egyptian texts, see *ANET*, 233, 235; for the Arad ostraca, see Aharoni, *Arad Inscriptions*, 46–49. Cleverly, Nelson (*Joshua*, 219) dubs the towns in ch. 19 as "frontier towns."

85. R. Greenberg, "Sarid (Place)," *ABD*, 5:985. *CBA*, no. 72, provides a helpful detailed map.

near Jokneam, a town guarding a mountain pass along the Carmel Ridge (v. 11). Its southeastern border goes (lit., "turned") east from Sarid along the Nazareth Ridge to somewhere near Kisloth Tabor (probably Iksal, ca. 3 mi. west of Mount Tabor),[86] then to Daberath, and "up" (i.e., north) to Japhia (v. 12). The common identification of Japhia with Jafa (near modern Nazareth) is improbable because that would make the border senselessly backtrack westward. Instead, Japhia is probably "the town of Yapu" in the Amarna Letters located somewhere northeast of Nazareth (e.g., Mishad) or north of Mount Tabor (or perhaps the mountain itself).[87]

From there the territory continues (v. 13) north to Gath Hepher (NIV "eastward" refers to the direction the border faces) and Eth Kazin (perhaps near modern Lubiyeh), then to Rimmon (modern Rummaneh, ca. 6 mi. north of Nazareth), bending toward Neah (somewhere near the Beth Netophah Valley). Thereafter (v. 14) it turns toward Hannathon (making the border face north?) and ends at Iphtah El (perhaps modern Wadi el-Malik). In short, Zebulun is a small tribe set snugly between Asher (west), Naphtali (north and northeast), Issachar (southeast), and West Manasseh (southwest). The writer says that Zebulun's towns number twelve, plus their villages, but lists only five relatively obscure places (v. 15).[88]

Issachar (19:17–23). Issachar receives its inheritance with the fall of the fourth lot. As with Zebulun, opening and closing formulae (vv. 17, 23) set off the list of sixteen towns with villages (vv. 18–21), with possibly a terse description of its northern boundary ending at the Jordan (v. 22).[89] The locations of most of the sixteen towns are known, and the southern part of Issachar's allotment seems to overlap the northeastern part of Manasseh in the Beth Shean plain (11:16; 17:10–11).

Though its boundaries remain obscure, Issachar's territory lies east and south of Zebulun, north of West Manasseh, south of Naphtali, and west of the Jordan. Topographically, it occupies most of eastern Lower Galilee in three regions: the eastern end of the fertile Jezreel Valley (Jezreel, Kes-

---

86. Naʾaman, *Borders and Districts*, 134; R. Frankel, "Chisloth-Tabor (Place)," *ABD*, 1:910. Kisloth Tabor is probably a variant form of Kesulloth, a town belonging to Issachar (19:18). Probably, the present phrase ("the territory of ...") means simply "near...."

87. Boling, *Joshua*, 445, proposes the first option, Naʾaman, *Borders and Districts*, 134, the second; cf. D. M. Howard, Jr., "Japhia (Place)," *ABD*, 3:642. For a translation of the Amarna Letter (EA 365), cf. *ANET*, 485.

88. For the locations of the above towns or valleys, cf. P. M Arnold, "Rimmon (Place)," *ABD*, 5:773; Hess, *Joshua*, 269–70. For a more complete discussion on other biblical references to Zebulun's holdings, see Howard, *Joshua*, 369–70.

89. This counts Tabor as a village rather than as a mountain. Alternatively, one may divide Shahazumah into two names or add Beeroth, which the LXX lists. Cf. the convenient list and discussion in Hess, *Joshua*, 270–71; Howard, *Joshua*, 370–71.

ulloth, Shunem, Hapharaim), the basalt hills northeast of the valley (Shion, Anaharath, Rabbith [or Dabberah], Kishion, Ebez), and the edge of their northeast-facing cliffs (Remeth, Ein Gannim, En Haddah, Beth Pazzes).[90] Place names and the descriptions suggest that the allotments of Zebulun, Issachar, and Napthali all meet near Mount Tabor (i.e., Chisloth Tabor [v. 12], Tabor [v. 22], Aznoth Tabor [v. 34]).[91]

Asher (19:24 – 31). The fifth lot identifies Asher, and opening and closing formulae set off the report (vv. 24, 31). Literarily, it comprises what Nelson calls "a kaleidoscopic totality"—a boundary description interwoven with three sections of a town list. The tally of towns and villages totals twenty-two (v. 30b), a figure that apparently counts Rehob only once and omits Sidon and Tyre altogether.[92] The southwestern boundary connects Helkath with the Kishon River (NIV Shihor Libnath), which empties into the Bay of Acco north of and parallel to the Carmel Ridge (v. 26b). From Helkath, the southeastern boundary runs briefly to Zebulun's western border, then swings north past the Valley of Iphtah El (see v. 14).

Continuing north, the boundary passes west ("on the left") of Cabul and reaches somewhere north of the Litani River (vv. 27 – 28; for "Greater Sidon," see comments at 11:8). From there it backtracks southwest past (but not incorporating) Tyre on the coast, runs inland down the coast before veering west to the sea somewhere in the Plain of Acco (vv. 29 – 30).[93] In sum, Asher occupies a narrow swath of land east-to-west between the Mediterranean and Zebulun and south-to-north between the Kishon River and somewhere north of the Litani River. It does not include land along the coast between Tyre and the Plain of Acco. All the towns mentioned fall within those boundaries, and the data behind the inter-woven boundary description plus town lists may have originated as early as the era of Solomon (1 Kings 9:11 – 13) or David (2 Sam. 24:6 – 7). The text's unique combination of borders and town lists serves to support Israel's ancient territorial claim, based on God's will spoken through lots, and to keep hope alive for reclaiming it during periods when it falls into alien hands.[94]

---

90. Howard (*Joshua*, 371) groups the cities slightly differently: the first three (v. 18) follow a north-south line in Issachar's western side, while the next three (v. 19) follow a parallel line east of the first group. The next three towns are concentrated in the north near Mount Tabor (v. 20), the last four in eastern Issachar (v. 21).

91. Cf. Nelson, *Joshua*, 222 – 23; CBA, no. 72.

92. Cf. Howard, *Joshua*, 372.

93. Cf. CBA, no. 72; Howard, *Joshua*, 372 – 74; Nelson, *Joshua*, 222 – 23. For the locations of the towns listed, see conveniently Hess, *Joshua*, 272 – 73.

94. Nelson, *Joshua*, 223 – 24.

Naphtali (19:32 – 39). The sixth lot concerns Naphtali, and again opening and closing formulae (vv. 32, 39) set the section apart. Structurally, the author offers a boundary description (vv. 33 – 34) and a list of nineteen towns (vv. 35 – 38). The eastern leg of the southern border separating Naphtali from Issachar runs east from Heleph and an apparently well-known landmark ("the large tree in Zaanannim") past several towns to the Jordan, just south of where it leaves the Sea of Galilee (v. 33). Its western leg runs west through Aznoth Tabor (near Mount Tabor?), then arcs northwest around Zebulun's northeast corner to Hukkok. At the intersection of Zebulun (south) and Asher (west) it turns straight north just east of Cabul (v. 34).

Naphtali's northern border is not given, an omission that may reflect awareness both of Dan's original (and ideal) allotment (see below) and of its actual location north of Naphtali. Most of Naphtali's towns are identifiable and lie in the allotment's southern part.[95] The lack of northern towns poses an inexplicable curiosity, as does the disagreement of the final tally (nineteen) with the list of sixteen (v. 38).[96] Perhaps the original readers were expected to pick out three more towns from the border description, the discrepancy reflects the fluidity of such lists, or the sixteen included are simply representative of the nineteen total. In short, the territory of Naphtali occupies the eastern part of Lower Galilee and most of Upper Galilee west of Asher and east of the Sea of Galilee and the Jordan above it.[97]

Dan (19:40 – 49). Finally, the seventh lot falls on Dan. Again, opening and closing formulae (vv. 40, 48) enclose this report, the final section of the second allotment. The term "border" (*gebul*) actually introduces a list of the towns assigned to Dan (vv. 41 – 46), all of them west of Benjamin, south of Ephraim, or north of Judah (vv. 41 – 46).[98] As Nelson observes, however, "the towns ... do form a sort of framing pattern around Danite territory."[99] That several of the towns also appear in Solomon's second administrative district (1 Kings 4:9) has fueled scholarly speculation that the latter may be the source of the Danite list. The narrative omits a final tally of Dan's towns (Simeon is the only other tribe of the seven without

---

95. Naʾaman, *Borders and Districts*, 46 – 47. *CBA*, no. 72, offers a convenient map of Naphtali.

96. For the location of the towns, see conveniently Hess, *Joshua*, 274 – 75. Mysteriously, only this list calls them "fortified cities," although Naphtali was probably not the only tribe who had such. Textual corruption may explain the anomaly (so *BHS* editor).

97. For the possibility that the list predates David, see Hess, *Joshua*, 273.

98. Cf. the helpful map in *CBA*, no. 73. For the locations, see Hess, *Joshua*, 275 – 76.

99. Nelson, *Joshua*, 225.

one), a concession perhaps to the historical reality known to the original audience.

A parenthetical comment explains how Dan, unable to possess its allotment, militarily succeeds in settling way up north (v. 47). The comment (lit., "Dan's territory left them") seems to blame the land for skeedaddling rather than Dan for failing (cf. NIV "the Danites had difficulty taking possession"). The text implies sympathy — in modern terms, "it was just one of those things."[100] In short, the report strikingly combines the ideal (i.e., Dan's assigned location) and the real (Dan's actual settlement at Leshem) without apparent criticism or embarrassment. In my view, the roots of that balance lie in the author's intention through the long allotment narrative (chs. 13–19) to present the ideal of a united Israel as a hopeful antidote to despairing readers who may have experienced their own Danite-like historical displacements. At the same time, as Kitz suggests, the process also has important legal ramifications. It gives the tribes the right to occupy their assigned territory, including the subjugation of any remaining "squatters," and denies them the right to contest the boundaries of another tribe's territory.[101]

Joshua's Allotment (19:49–50). The allotment narrative opened with Joshua (13:1) and now fittingly returns to him (19:49). The tribes have received their allotments from Joshua, and now the collective body ("the Israelites") returns the favor, gifting him with his own inheritance. "Joshua son of Nun" sounds formal, a fitting tone for a special allotment for a lifetime of faithful service, and certainly Yahweh's command stands in the background (v. 50a).[102] But one almost hears affection in the phrase "an inheritance among them," as if by the gesture Israel aims to surround the aging leader with their collective loving care and protection in his declining years. They give him what he asks for, the town of Timnath Serah, in the middle of Ephraim, his own tribe (Num. 13:8).[103]

---

100. Cf. Howard, *Joshua*, 377, n.232 ("it slipped through their fingers, i.e., their enemies took it from them"). Other biblical texts attribute it to stubborn Amorite resistance (Judg. 1:34) or to apostasy (Judg. 18), but historians also factor in the presence of the Philistines along the coast.

101. Kitz, "Lot Casting in Joshua," 618.

102. The Bible nowhere reports this command, but the point is implicit in God's declaration that only Caleb and Joshua among the Exodus generation would enter the Promised Land (Num. 14:30).

103. Timnath Serah and Timnath Heres (Judg. 2:9) are probably the same place, s-r-h and h-r-s being simply the reverse of the other. For discussion of the name's significance, see H. R. Weeks, "Timnath-Heres (Place)," *ABD*, 6:557. The first name may be a wordplay ("portion of surplus") that aims to neutralize the pagan meaning of the second ("portion of the sun"); cf. Nelson, *Joshua*, 226.

Joshua makes the town liveable (NIV "built up") and settles in (v. 50b). (For this death and burial there, see 24:30). The absence of Timnath Serah from the list of Ephraimite towns suggests that it may have been Joshua's own personal possession—a special land grant to him from a grateful nation.[104] That highly unusual circumstance attests the stature that Israel and the biblical writer accord this wise, faithful leader.[105]

Summary (19:51). This concluding formula looks back over the proceedings of chapters 18–19 and draws them to a close. Its reintroduction of motifs from 18:1—Joshua, Shiloh, Yahweh's presence, the Tent of Meeting—forms a literary inclusio around the whole second allotment sequence. At the same time, the verbatim reappearance here of 14:1b ("Eleazar the priest, Joshua son of Nun and the heads of the tribal clans of Israel allotted ...") also literarily brackets the entire land distribution report (14:1–19:50). In short, verse 51 serves a double-duty function: It concludes both 18:1–19:50 and 14:1–19:50.[106]

The literary effect is to bring solemn closure to the giving (and receiving) of inheritances and to introduce a narrative pause in the book. As we will see in chapters 20–21, however, two more distributions await their moment before one may finally consider the settlement an actual reality.

THOUGH COMPLEX TERRAIN, JOSHUA 13–19 raises several subjects for further discussion in preparation for exploring their contemporary meaning. Additional background concerning Israel's understanding of inheritance will set the scene for treatment of the inheritance theme in the New Testament. In light of this history of violent conflict over the piece of land once called Canaan, the reader's most pressing question perhaps might concern who owns the land today.

The promised inheritance—at last! Earlier I commented that, however boring and irrelevant these chapters may strike modern readers, they actually comprise the heart of the book.[107] The reason is that they consummate a biblical theme that spans the Bible's first six books and

---

104. Nelson, *Joshua*, 226. Analogous situations concern Caleb, who receives Hebron from Joshua (14:14), and Othniel and Acsah, whom Caleb grants land and springs in the Negev (15:17–18). However, the Caleb analogy has its limits, since the Bible still reckons Hebron as a Judahite town (15:13, 54); cf. Howard, *Joshua*, 378.

105. Ibid., 378.

106. Cf. Nelson, *Joshua*, 226. For echoes in 19:51 of 18:1–10, see Howard, *Joshua*, 379.

107. Cf. Howard, *Joshua*, 322: "Despite their seeming impenetrability, the lists of Joshua will richly repay any time invested in understanding them. They are indeed the core of the Book of Joshua."

echoes in many others. Specifically, they give tangible—maybe all *too* tangible!—proof that Israel has finally received something God promised to give them long ago.

Recall that a single catalyst—the promise to Israel's ancestors of the land of Canaan—has driven the long, convoluted story of Israel. God first gave the promise to Abraham (12:7; 13:15, 17; 15:18; 17:8), then reiterated it to Isaac (26:3) and Jacob (28:13 – 15; 35:12; 48:4). Four centuries later in Egypt, Yahweh invoked anticipation of the land promised the patriarchs in establishing the Passover (Ex. 13:5, 11). At Mount Sinai he also guaranteed Israel long life there if they keep his command to honor their parents (Ex. 20:12). By then, Israel could only ponder that land as a far-off, enchanted, mythical Never-Never Land—a place to be sweetly savored with the imagination but not seen with the eyes. When Israel left Sinai, that land and its happy prospects were to be their immediate destination (Deut. 1:8). But, alas, it was entry into "the land I promised on oath to their forefathers" that the frightened rebels in the wilderness soon forfeited (Num. 14:23; Deut. 1:35).

Forty years later, on the Plains of Moab beside the Jordan, with the long-promised land clearly visible in the distance, Moses also invoked that phrase to motivate Israel to stay loyal to Yahweh (Deut. 6:18; 8:1). Thoughts of the land buttressed his exhortation to Joshua as his successor: To Joshua belonged the double privilege of going there with Israel and of later dividing it up (*naḥal* hi.) among them as their inheritance (Deut. 31:7; cf. Josh. 1:6). Finally, the theme of the Promised Land forms a literary envelope around Joshua 1 – 21. God exhorts Joshua to "be strong and courageous" since he is about to "lead these people to inherit [*naḥal*, hi.] the land I swore to their forefathers to give them" (1:6).

After assuming leadership of Israel, Joshua's first orders were for Israel to prepare to cross into the land to "take possession of the land the LORD your God is giving you" (1:11). Many battles and lot-castings later, the biblical narrator can write in retrospect, "So the LORD gave Israel all the land he had sworn to give their forefathers, and they took possession of it and settled there" (21:43). In short, the story of Israel from the patriarchs to Joshua 21 is about finally reaching and owning Never-Never Land after nearly seven centuries of waiting and imagining.

But what does it mean that Canaan is Israel's "inheritance"? The Hebrew verb *naḥal* ("to receive property") and its noun *naḥalah* ("inheritance") are basically legal terms that concern the passing of tangible property from an ancestor to succeeding heirs. It assumes that an estate is being divided among joint heirs, each of whom "receives" his or her rightful portion (an "inheritance"), not the whole estate.[108] This legal background illumines the distribution of land in Joshua 13 – 19.

It may be significant that these chapters refer to those receiving their inheritances (NIV "Israelites") as (lit.) "the children of Israel" (or Jacob). This might assume Jacob as the ancestor whose estate is being divided among his twelve children. If so, the roots of that assumption may go back to Abraham's visual survey of and walk through Canaan, gestures through which he symbolically claimed ownership of it (e.g., Gen. 13:13, 17).[109] More likely, however, the presumed owner is Yahweh himself, since the Bible universally acknowledges him as the land's "giver" (Deut. 32:49; Josh. 1:2, 11; 2:9, 14; 18:3). Indeed, Yahweh is the one who authorizes the apportioning to begin (14:2), further confirmation of his ownership of Canaan.

Nevertheless, while Yahweh gives the land, Israel still must actually "take possession" (*yaraš*) of it (Deut. 1:39; Josh. 1:15a; 21:43). Often paralleled with *nahal* and *nahalah*, *yaraš* merits a brief comment. In the context of military conquest (e.g., Joshua), the verb probably refers to "juridical seizure of enemy territory after battle."[110] To "take possession" explicitly or implicitly involves the military conquest of the current occupants of a place. Hence, the proper rendering of the verb is "to destroy," after which the legitimate assumption of legal ownership falls to the destroyer.[111] As Lohfink writes:

> The fact that the territory of nation A has been taken possession of by nation B (qal) is legitimated by the destruction of nation A by the god of nation B (hiphil), so that nation B can be the legal successor of nation A (qal).[112]

But what does Joshua mean when the text says that Yahweh "gives" something? The model that this compares most closely to is the ancient

---

108. Conveniently, Howard, *Joshua*, 302–4; cf. E. Lipiński, "נָחַל," *TDOT*, 9:319–35; C. J. H. Wright, "נָחַל," *NIDOTTE*, 3:77–81. The root (*nhl*) is also common among Northwest Semitic languages.

109. B. K. Waltke, *Genesis* (Grand Rapids: Zondervan, 2001), 222–23. If so, a further assumption might be that ownership claims originating with Abraham were passed down to his chosen heirs, Isaac and Jacob.

110. Lohfink, "יָרַשׁ," 6:378; cf. his larger discussion (383–85).

111. That the Bible nowhere indicates a destination for those ejected from their land or city further confirms this point.

112. Lohfink, "יָרַשׁ," 6:383. His comments technically concern "a late pre-Deuternomistic or early Deuternomistic stage" in the literary prehistory of Joshua and Judges and cite Judg. 11:21–24 as a representative example. For background from the ancient Near East and its application to biblical texts, see M. Weinfeld, *The Promise of the Land* (Berkeley: Univ. of California Press, 1993), 222–64 (esp. 261–62).

practice of the royal land grant.[113] The motif may assume one of two premises: a feudal principle that the king may give away title to lands he owns
in exchange for services rendered him (cf. 1 Sam. 8:14; 22:7; 27:6), or the
premise that the whole land is ultimately royal property. Whatever the
assumption (the texts are unclear), the Bible clearly understands Yahweh as
king (see comments in ch. 12) and, hence, ancient laws concerning kingship offer illuminating analogies for Joshua 13 – 19.

To be specific, as cosmic king, Yahweh rules over the nations as his
subjects and the lands as his territory, including agricultural land. His "giving" of land is, thus, a legal act of title transfer — in Israel's case, an action
to which he committed himself in advance. In this context, the verb *yaraš*
assumes that the "giving" (i.e., the legal title transfer by the king) has already
taken place and states that the new owner now "takes possession of" (i.e.,
exercises ownership over) the former royal land. Further, it clearly assumes
that the latter step takes place in a specific way, by military conquest.

The metaphor of royal land grant also applies to the lands granted to
Caleb and Joshua.[114] Each has rendered valuable service to Yahweh and
his program for Israel, and King Yahweh rewards each with an appropriate
royal land grant. Each receives a city — Hebron and its environs (Caleb)
and Timnath Serah (Joshua) — and in each case military conquest comprises
an integral part of the process of taking possession. Caleb must destroy the
Anakites from Hebron (Josh. 15:13 – 14), and Joshua (more generally) the
Canaanites from the land as a whole. That Caleb later grants Othniel and
Acsah title to portions of his allotment (15:18 – 19) confirms that Yahweh's
land grant endowed him with the full legal rights of ownership.

All the above examples of Yahweh's gift of land illustrate that *God is a promise keeper.* He promised Abraham that his descendants would inherit Canaan
and Joshua 13 – 19 confirms that they did. He promised Caleb and Joshua
inheritances in the Promised Land, and both received them. Theologically,
this mirrors one of God's attributes, his unwavering reliability. As Balaam
told King Balak, "God is not a human, that he should lie, not a human being,
that he should change his mind. Does he speak and then not act? Does he
promise and not fulfill?" (Num. 23:19 TNIV). The obvious answer is, "Absolutely not!" God is consummately reliable; he keeps his word.

---

113. So Lohfink, "יָרַשׁ," 6:385, who cites Ugaritic analogies. Hess argues that the ancient
royal land grant underlies the structure and content of the entire book of Joshua; cf. R.
S. Hess, "The Book of Joshua as a Land Grant," *Bib* 83 (2002): 493 – 506. Nelson (*Joshua*,
177 – 78) argues that the genre "land grant narrative" underlies the petitions for land by
Acsah (15:18 – 19), the daughters of Zelophehad (17:3 – 6), Joseph (17:14 – 18), and Levi
(21:1 – 3).

114. Cf. Weinfeld, *The Promise of the Land*, 261 – 62.

Joshua 13 illustrates another aspect of God's character worthy of comment. Recall that, in the context of Joshua's old age (v. 1), Yahweh surveys the areas within the land promised to Israel that remain unconquered (vv. 2−5). God voices no opinion as to what is to be done about them. In my view, his silence leaves the responsibility with Israel. But the Sidonians who live along the coast around Tyre and Sidon God himself promises to destroy (v. 6). This promise intrigues me because it underscores that God himself takes on the responsibility for doing this. In my view, the most likely reason is that, at the time, Israel was militarily stretched with taking over territory farther south, so God, as it were, applies his power to compensate for Israel's weakness.

The solemn covenant-sealing ceremony in Genesis 15 makes a similar point. God had reassured Abram of the promise of land and descendants and asked him to bring several kinds of animals to God. Abram cut each of them in half and set them across from each other and then, mysteriously, fell into a deep sleep overwhelmed by a "thick and dreadful darkness" (15:12). Then Abram watched as a smoking firepot and torch passed between the separated pieces. The animal pieces symbolized the deadly consequences of covenant breach by the parties, while the firepot pictured Yahweh's passing between them as Abram slept and watched. This symbolism underscored that, in this covenant, Yahweh himself took full responsibility for ensuring that the blessings of the covenant would happen. The assumption was that, without that divine commitment, the covenant would depend on fallible Abram and would certainly fail. Below we will pursue the implications of this aspect of God's character for Christian life today.

Land and identity. Though it may surprise some readers, the mind-numbing minutia in Joshua 13−19 actually serves two purposes. (1) It supports Israel's land claims on both sides of the Jordan. As Goldingay says:

> There might ... be other claimants to the land, but the king's grant guarantees the recipients secure possession over against other people's claims.... As the subjects of the King, the people can look to the future with confidence rather than fear.[115]

Concern for ownership of inherited land was more than just a theoretical or technical matter in ancient times. When the Ammonite king demanded that Jephthah return "my land" in Transjordan, Jephthah invoked history and theology to defend Israel's claim. He said that Yahweh had defeated Sihon and given Israel the land—and that Israel had already lived there for a long time (Judg. 11:13−27). More important, data like Joshua 13−19

---

115. Goldingay, *Old Testament Theology: Israel's Gospel,* 515.

would help individual clans preserve or restore their ownership — for example, to authorize the redemption process of inherited portions temporarily mortgaged because of financial hardships (e.g., Lev. 25:23 – 28, 41, 49). As Nelson astutely observes, this is the reason the allocation reports emphasize that the distribution involves subdivisions among clans.[116]

(2) The second purpose that Joshua 13 – 19 serves is to promote Israel's identity as a unified people.[117] In reality, the transition from the family-style existence of a single camp to the spread-out style of a settled people marked a major transition for Israel. To settle in towns and to meet the demands of daily life inevitably loosened larger familial ties, especially with enclaves of wary Canaanites still present. Village life meant that Israel had finally "come home," but it also fostered preoccupation with local rather than national concerns. But against that centrifugal momentum, Joshua 13 – 19 holds out the ancient ideal of "all Israel" — of Israel as a united people under Yahweh their God — as reflected in several subthemes.

(a) The first subtheme is that greater Israel comprises both Trans- and Cisjordan. That is why chapter 13 reviews the tribal holdings of the two-and-a-half tribes on the east bank. In chapter 22 we will learn that the Jordan proves a barrier to unity and the partial cause of inter-tribal suspicions. But the two allocation reports discussed above sound the theme that "Israel" includes all twelve tribes, regardless of their perceived distance from what became the west-bank heartland.[118]

(b) The second subtheme is that every town, however small, distant, or obscure, forms a constitutive part of Israel. To be sure, the order of the allocations and the depth of treatment accords special prominence to the towns in Judah, Joseph, and Benjamin. But the writer of Joshua 13 – 19 takes pains, within the limits of his source materials, to incorporate everyone — both heartland and periphery. As Seleznev says, "The vision of a unified 'Greater Israel,' with a balance of North and South, is dominant in this text."[119]

Further, it is important to remember that each town name — however unknown to modern geographers — was once home to real people who were born, grew up, married, had kids, raised them, and died there. Life for people in, say, Kabzeel in the semi-arid southern Negev (15:21) depended on wells and springs and an ongoing search for pastures to survive as sheepherders.[120] By contrast, residents of Ashnah (15:33), somewhere in the western foothills

---

116. Nelson, *Joshua*, 172 – 73; cf. Josh. 13:23; 15:1; 16:5; 17:2; 18:11; 19:10.
117. Ibid., 171; Howard, *Joshua*, 323.
118. Cf. Weinfeld, *The Promise of the Land*, 66 – 67.
119. Seleznev, "The Origin of the Tribal Boundaries," 345.
120. Some of what follows draws on *CBA*, no. 12.

near the Sorek River, had a steady, clean water supply and fertile valleys in which to farm and tend orchards of fig trees. Terrace farming of fruit trees in the steep slopes of the central hill country fed folks in obscure places like Giloh in Judah (15:51) or Helek in Ephraim (17:2). Springs and cisterns provided water but required manual delivery to the orchards. Farther north, the broad, fertile Jezreel Valley, watered by the Kishon River, offered people in the Zebulunite town of Maralah (19:11) Israel's lushest soil and access to international trade. The care of fruit trees probably preoccupied residents of Edrei in Naphtali (19:37), and they probably had more contact with the sea-faring Phoenicians of Sidon and Byblos.

The location of none of the above towns is known, but they made the lists of Joshua 13–19 because they had one thing in common: They were part of a tribe of Israel. They may have witnessed no historic events, produced no great leader, showed no great heroism, or earned no lasting fame. But each of them belonged to the people of Israel—to "all Israel."

(c) A third subtheme concerns the importance given to women as part of Israel. Supplementing the portrait of Caleb is that of his daughter, Acsah, whose apparent desirability drives Othniel to conquer Debir in order to claim her as his wife (Josh. 15:15–16; cf. Judg. 1:10–15). The brief narrative conveys a strong character typified by initiative, determination, and persuasive verbal skills (Josh. 15:17–19). The roles of her husband and father signal that patriarchal authority still prevails, but the freedom of women openly to press their case for consideration and even to own land is evident.[121]

The possession of land by women figures even more prominently with the daughters of Zelophehad (17:3–6). Indeed, in situation they parallel more Caleb than Acsah since both receive inheritances promised them long ago, and both by divine command (cf. Num. 27:1–11). Like Acsah, however, they present their personal case to the ruling authorities, much as the whole tribe will shortly (Josh. 17:14–18). Hawk rightly observes that the parallel listing of the names of the petitioning daughters (v. 3) and of Manasseh's sons (v. 2) implies a "social equivalency" between those sons and daughters. Further, three times the author says that the latter received an inheritance alongside the former. He rightly comments: "The daughters thus personify what Acsah [sic] anticipates, that 'Israel' cannot be identified fundamentally in male terms only."[122] Put differently, "If women possess land, women are Israelites in the most fundamental sense."[123]

---

121. Hawk, *Joshua*, 201–2. Nelson (*Joshua*, 177, 188–89) interprets her request as the genre land grant petition.

122. Hawk, *Joshua*, 208–9 ("patriarchy … does not constitute an essential element of Israelite national identity").

123. Ibid., 199; cf. Nelson, *Joshua*, 202.

(3) Finally, the linkage of land and identity plays a role in the vision of a future land distribution by the prophet Ezekiel (Ezek. 47–48). Like Joshua 13–19, his vision lays out the boundaries of Israel's restored land (47:15–20) and orders its division among the tribes (47:21–48:7). But in several startling ways Ezekiel 47–48 contrasts the allocation pattern in Joshua and, in so doing, lays some groundwork for the following discussion of contemporary meaning.[124]

(a) The first way is that Ezekiel speaks in a unique genre — what one scholar calls "theological geography." He wields geography as a metaphor to describe in concrete terms the spiritual reality of God's presence and the nature of the new Israel.[125] The highly symbolic, carefully contrived, and imaginative nature of the literature intends to convey a message rather than to announce the details of an actual, future historical resettlement.

(b) Rather than detail boundaries or list towns, Ezekiel 48 grants each tribe an east-west swath of land identical in north-south size but varying in width. Further, a division of seven northern and five southern tribes replaces the ancient pattern of ten northern and two southern tribes (see 1 Kings 11:31–36). Both the above provisions symbolize the future equality of the tribes and may even mark an attempt to remedy past inequities.[126]

(c) A third way in which Ezekiel 47–48 contrasts with Joshua is that, unlike Joshua 13–19, Ezekiel's distribution allots a "consecrated area" (vv. 48:8–22) between the northern and southern tribes. The temple and land portions for priests, Levites, the public, and someone called the "prince" (probably a messianic figure) occupy that special, sacred area. The description of the temple is clearly ideal, symbolic, and theological rather than a blueprint to be followed by later builders. Interestingly, the vision locates Benjamin and Judah closest to the consecrated area but in reversed locations (i.e., Benjamin to the south and Judah to the north).

---

124. For a detailed comparison of Joshua 13–19 and Ezekiel 47–48, see Hubbard, "Only a Distant Memory," 138–41.

125. The term is from G. C. Macholz, "Noch Einmal: Planungen für den Wiederaufbau nach der Katastrophe von 587," *VT* 19 (1969): 331; cf. K. R. Stevenson, *Vision of Transformation: The Territorial Rhetoric of Ezekiel 40–48* (Atlanta: Scholars Press, 1996), 143, 149–51, who prefers the term "territorial rhetoric" (i.e., the use of geography to convey Ezekiel's theological message).

126. W. Zimmerli, *Ezekiel 2* (Philadelphia: Fortress, 1983), 542 ("the rule of the just portion is to prevail"). Also, the east-west orientation of allotments more equitably distributes the desirable and undesirable lands among the tribes and avoids granting a monopoly to any tribe over the best areas; cf. M. Greenberg, "Idealism and Practicality in Numbers 35:4–5 and Ezekiel 48," *JAOS* 88 (1966): 63–66.

(d) Finally, Yahweh decrees that resident aliens with children born in Israel are to receive an inheritance among the tribe where they live just like native-born Israelites (Ezek. 47:22). As Levenson rightly observes, "This prescription is much more radical than anything else in all the legal corpora of the Hebrew Bible."[127] It certainly relaxes the much stricter policy toward aliens, which admitted only aliens from Edom and Egypt and only after three generations of residence in Israel (Deut. 23:2 – 9).[128] Thematically, Ezekiel's view parallels that of Isaiah 56:1 – 8, although the latter extends the welcome beyond resident aliens to any "foreigners who join themselves to the LORD" (vv. 6 – 7).[129] In my view, the important point is that Ezekiel's vision gives priority to theological (not territorial) concerns. It stresses as essential loyalty to Yahweh and Israel's unique, covenant-based identity regardless of whether the person is an ethnic Israelite or a resident alien permanently residing in the land. The land is still the place Israel dwells, but it is less the anchorage for their identity in Ezekiel's thinking than it is in Joshua 13 – 19. In short, as I observed elsewhere:

> Ezekiel's vision works out the logic of Israel's long experience with the person of Yahweh — his compassion toward all peoples, his eventual universal recognition by all peoples — and announces a new way for Israel to be Israel.[130]

Who owns the land today? At a recent college reunion, a classmate had the then-current Middle East crisis in mind when he asked me, "How do these events relate to biblical prophecy?" His quizzical silence over my answer suggested that he was unprepared for it, and the same may be true of some readers of this commentary. The question is: Does Joshua 13 – 19 imply anything for the present land dispute between Israelis and Palestinians over the ownership of the land? The most common answer among evangelical Christians is, "Yes, God gave the land to Israel, and that gift is still valid." This approach underlies the political support that Israel has traditionally enjoyed in North America, especially among evangelicals and fundamentalists.

---

127. J. D. Levenson, *Theology of the Program of Restoration of Ezekiel 40 – 48* (Missoula, Mont.: Scholars Press, 1976), 123. To be sure, it also assumes that the aliens will remain loyal to Yahweh alone and obey his covenant.

128. Zimmerli, *Ezekiel* 2, 532.

129. Obviously, they need receive no territorial inheritance since they already live outside the Promised Land.

130. Hubbard, "Only a Distant Memory," 140 – 41. Cf. Levenson, 124: "The central motivation of these reforms lies not in a doctrine of equality, but in a concern for the realization in social, even visible form of the relationships defined by *Heilsgeschichte*."

In my view, however, two weaknesses undermine such an approach. (1) It fails to reckon adequately with the implications of an idea that most Christians accept—progressive revelation. Progressive revelation affirms that God has chosen to reveal his truth through Bible writers over time, so that later biblical books may modify the ideas of earlier ones. This is most obvious in moving from Old Testament to New Testament, where Christians believe, for example, that the death of Jesus ended the need to follow the Israelite sacrificial system any longer.

(2) This leads me to mention the second weakness: It simply jumps from the Old Testament to today without reckoning with modifications the New Testament might have made on the subject. Did the New Testament reaffirm God's promise of land for Israel or in any way modify its understanding of it? In reply, a brief concordance search shows how little the New Testament says theologically about "land" compared to the Old Testament.[131] A few New Testament texts mention it in connection with past and present events (e.g., Matt. 2:20; Acts 7:3–5, 45; 13:19; James 5:17), but to my knowledge only Hebrews 11:9 interprets it theologically (see below). The New Testament seems to reflect an oft-overlooked phenomenon in the Old Testament highlighted by Chris Wright. Granted, the Old Testament accords great theological importance to land, it also shows awareness that Israel's relationship to God "did transcend that realm and was not permanently or exclusively bound to it."[132]

For example, according to Wright, that awareness underlies the motif of Israel as Yahweh's (firstborn) son. This motif actually predates the Exodus and (by implication) the gift of land (e.g., Ex. 4:22; Deut. 32:5, 6, 18, 19; Hos. 11:1), and it also anchors the later restoration when Israel is landless (i.e., in exile). The father-son motif explains why Israel can still affirm their relationship with Yahweh despite being away from their inherited land.[133] A second example, observes Wright, is an intriguing development in later Israelite prophecy. It evidences "a 'loosening' of—almost a dispensing with" the ancient connection of land with Israel's relationship with God. He sees this phenomenon in texts that anticipate the eschatological inclusion of types of people whose membership in Israel, if based on the traditional family-land connection, would otherwise be uncertain or unclear. These include unmarried, childless Israelite women (Isa. 54:1), foreigners and eunuchs (56:3–7), and resident aliens (Ezek. 47:22).

This same "loosening" also seems evident in the absence of the land-promise in the New Testament's interpretation of the Abrahamic promises.

131. Cf. J. G. Millar, "Land," *NDBT*, 623–27.
132. C. J. H. Wright, *God's People in God's Land*, 110.
133. Ibid., 15–16, 21–22.

Paul teaches that those who believe in Jesus, regardless of ethnic background, are all descendants of Abraham (Gal. 3:7) and that their faith fulfills the patriarchal theme of blessing to the nations (v. 8). Since Jesus is the "seed" of Abraham (Gal. 3:16), all who belong to Christ are also his "seed" and his "heirs according to the promise" (v. 29; cf. Eph. 3:3). Paul makes no mention of the patriarchal promise of land, apparently because it bears no relevance to his subject.

The land's reduced importance is even clearer in Hebrews 11. According to the writer, Abraham lived in tents in Canaan not to await the right moment to build houses but the arrival of "the [future] city with foundations, whose architect and builder is God" (vv. 9–10). In Hagner's words, Abraham "knew that what God ultimately had in store for his people transcended security and prosperity in a parcel of real estate on the eastern shore of the Mediterranean."[134] In short, the New Testament knows that the land of Israel remains the homeland of Jews, but its prime concerns lie elsewhere. Its preoccupation is with the Jews and Gentiles throughout the Roman world whose newfound faith in Jesus fulfills the Abrahamic promise.

At this point it is helpful to understand how the New Testament interprets the Old Testament. In a word, the New Testament interprets the Old Testament *typologically*. This interpretive approach assumes that since God's way of working in history never changes, one may rightly interpret correspondences between Old Testament redemptive events and New Testament ones. Thus, "NT persons consciously considered their experiences to match the patterns of God's redemptive history that began with Israel."[135] They assumed that a promise-fulfillment schema linked the Testaments together, so they read events in the Old Testament as "promise" and corresponding events in the New Testament as "fulfillment."

For example, the Gospels underscore that Jesus not only fulfills Old Testament messianic expectations, but also embodies Israel at its God-pleasing best.[136] Matthew 1–5 portrays Jesus as reenacting Israel's history (Matt. 2:15, 19–20; 3:13–17; 4:1–11; 5:1–2), but unlike Israel in the wilderness, he spurns the alluring temptations and stays loyal to God (4:1–11). John presents Jesus as the temple, the place (or person) to offer prayers to God and to deal with sin (e.g., John 2:19–32; 8:34–36; 16:23–24), and as the good shepherd (10:11–16), whose gathered sheep comprise a new Israel.

---

134. D. A. Hagner, *Hebrews* (Peabody, Mass.: Hendrickson, 1990), 190. Undoubtedly, the writer has the eschatological heavenly Jerusalem in mind (cf. 11:16; 12:22; 13:14; Rev. 21:2).

135. W. W. Klein, C. L. Blomberg, and R. L. Hubbard Jr., *Introduction to Biblical Interpretation* (Nashville: Nelson, 2004), 182–84 (quote 184).

136. S. Motyer, "Israel (Nation)," *NDBT*, 584–85.

Luke offers Jesus as Savior of both Jews and non-Jews (e.g., Luke 2:30 – 32; Acts 28:17 – 28).

Typology also underlies the foundational New Testament conviction that the church is the new Israel. As the community founded by the Messiah, "the Christian Church is the organic continuation of Israel. It is heir to the names and privileges of Israel, and therefore also falls under the same ethical responsibilities."[137] This is evident in the way apostolic writers apply to early Christian congregations, with both Jews and Gentiles, covenant concepts and terms previously associated with Israel. When Paul wishes "mercy and peace" on "the Israel of God" (Gal. 6:16), he probably refers to the church. Echoing Exodus 19:6 and Hosea 2:23, Peter writes:

> ... you are a chosen people, a royal priesthood, a holy nation, a people belonging to God. ... Once you were not a people, but now you are the people of God; once you had not received mercy, but now you have received mercy. (1 Peter 2:9 – 10; cf. Rom. 9:25 – 26)

According to Paul, churches are "the elect" (1 Thess. 1:4 – 5), the "redeemed" (Rom. 3:24; Eph. 1:7), and the "children of God" (Rom. 8:14; cf. Ex. 4:22). They may rightly appeal to God's covenant faithfulness for reassurance and security in the face of all dangers (Rom. 8:31 – 39) and expect the Lord to reward their wholehearted service with "an inheritance" (Col. 3:23 – 24; cf. 1:12).

In short, apostolic terminology assumes that the church, a mixture of Jews and Gentiles, is the new Israel—the ultimate offspring of Abraham by faith. It is international in scope, and its temple is not a building in Jerusalem but the collective body of Christian believers dispersed throughout the world—both Jews and Gentiles—in whom God's Spirit now lives (1 Cor. 3:16 – 17; cf. Eph. 2:21). Wherever located, the physical body of every believer is also a temple where the Spirit dwells (1 Cor. 6:19).[138] Indeed, in Acts it was the unexpected fall of the Holy Spirit on non-Jews after they believed in Jesus that forced the apostles to accept them as fellow believers without requiring them to join Israel first (Acts 11:15 – 18; 15:7 – 11).[139]

---

137. Wright, *God's People in God's Land*, xvii – xviii.

138. Cf. Millar, "Land," 623: "The context for obedience is no longer limited to one ethnic group in one place; it is now the new covenant community scattered throughout the earth."

139. Cf. Walton's comment that "the covenant continues on" in the sense that "Israel's election can be transferred from their revelatory role into the redefined people of God"; cf. J. H. Walton, *Covenant: God's Purpose, God's Plan* (Grand Rapids: Zondervan, 1994), 132. He distinguishes (123 – 25) between the purpose of God's covenant with Israel (their "revelatory role") and the purpose of the new covenant in Christ (its "soteric role"); cf. Gal. 6:15; Col. 2:11 – 12. Believing Jews remain the people of God, but under its new, soteriological definition.

This does not mean, of course, that God has rejected the Jews as the people of God and replaced them with the Gentiles. Nor does it mean that the Jews have stumbled so badly as to never recover (see Rom. 11:2, 11). Rather, through faith in Christ they become part of the new, redefined, and expanded people of God along with the Gentiles.[140] They may be "an identifiable subset within the people of God" and play a unique role within that newly redefined body, but they still form part of it.[141]

As for the land, the New Testament views it typologically (i.e., as fulfilled and continued in the church), not geographically (i.e., as a location of special importance). Paul offers a classic example of this understanding in Ephesians 2−3.[142] He masterfully melds two Old Testament motifs, sonship and inheritance, to expound the status of his Gentile audience. Invoking Old Testament language, he reminds them of their pre-Christian status—"excluded from citizenship in Israel and foreigners to the covenants of the promise" (Eph. 2:16). But, he continues, Christ's death has broken down the "wall of hostility" that separated Jews and Gentiles, made peace, and opened access for them to God (2:13−16). Now—and note the Old Testament terminology—they are "no longer foreigners and aliens, but fellow citizens with God's people and members of God's household" (2:19). In the Old Testament language of inheritance, Paul declares them to be "heirs together with Israel, members together of one body, and sharers together in the promise in Christ Jesus" (3:6).[143]

This fulfills the eschatological expectation of the prophets concerning the inclusion of the Gentiles within the people of God. They, too, are God's "son" entitled to their "inheritance" and full citizens of God's new Israel (cf. 1 Peter 1:3−5). In short, "the inheritance in Christ is no doubt different from the land received and lost by Israel, but it is greater, not less, than that land."[144]

Finally, what is Israel's status today? This remains a controversial matter, one to be treated carefully and humbly, ever mindful of subtle, sinister

---

140. For further discussion of Israel's place in God's plan according to the New Testament, see ibid., 123−33.

141. Ibid., 133. Unlike the present writer, however, Walton believes that the territorial and political promises made to Israel in their revelatory role did not transfer spiritually to the whole church under the new covenant.

142. Cf. Wright, *God's People in God's Land*, 111. For the suggestion that Jesus' command to "abide in me" and the vine-branches imagery of John 15 imply that Jesus himself fulfills the Old Testament motif of land, see G. M. Burge, "Territorial Religion, Johannine Christology, and the Vineyard of John 15," in J. B. Green and M. Turner, eds., *Jesus of Nazareth: Lord and Christ* (Grand Rapids: Eerdmans, 1994), 384−96.

143. Cf. Wright, *God's People in God's Land*, 111: "The inheritance language ... evokes the triangular pattern of relationships between God, Israel, and the land."

144. Millar, "Land," 627.

anti-Semitism.[145] Again, Paul in Romans 9−11 provides the classic exposition on the matter. (1) By "Israel" Paul means neither the physical land, nor a political state, nor Jews as an ethnic group. Instead, he argues that "not all who are descended from Israel are Israel," nor "because they are his descendants are they all Abraham's children" (Rom. 9:6−7). Instead, he has in mind the "children of promise" (v. 8)—the "remnant" (both Jews and Gentiles) who have received salvation by faith (9:23−27; 10:6−13).

(2) Paul denies that God has completely rejected Israel as a whole, thereby setting aside the idea argued by some Christians that God's covenant with Israel has ended (11:1). Rather, Paul cites himself—an Israelite but also a believer in Jesus—as evidence that God's sovereignty has preserved from Israel a "remnant chosen by grace" (vv. 1, 5).

To explain the big picture, the apostle invokes the metaphor of an olive tree, an Old Testament symbol of Israel (Jer. 11:16; Hos. 14:6). In rejecting the gospel, Israel (less the remnant, of course) became "hardened" (Rom. 11:7, 20, 25; cf. Isa. 6:9), and as a result, God pruned them as unsatisfactory branches from the root tree (vv. 17, 20).[146] This sad fact happily opened the way for Gentiles to be saved—that is, to be grafted into the original root (vv. 12, 15, 17). But, Paul says strongly, that boon gives absolutely no basis for any sense of Gentile spiritual superiority, thus (in modern terms) nipping anti-Semitism in the bud (vv. 17−20). Unlike the fine cultivated olive tree (Israel), the Gentiles are by nature "wild shoots"—not a compliment!—that God grafted into the superior root tree, an act in fact "contrary to nature" (vv. 17, 24). Gentile arrogance is completely without foundation: "You do not support the root, but the root supports you" (v. 18). And spiritually proud Gentiles themselves run the risk of being pruned by God just as Israel was (v. 21).

Ultimately, however—and as another one of God's mysteries (Rom. 11:25)—God will show Israel the same mercy as he has the Gentiles (vv. 31−32). Because of their election, covenant, and the patriarchal promises—all of them "irrevocable" (v. 29)—God will mysteriously save "all Israel" (vv. 26−28). In this case, "all Israel" does not refer to the church, nor does it likely assert that every individual Jewish person alive at the time will be saved regardless of his or her stance toward Jesus.[147] Rather, in Romans 11:26−27 the quotation from Isaiah 59:20−21 (LXX) clearly implies faith

---

145. For a select sample of alternative views, see Motyer, "Israel (Nation)," 586.

146. Contextually, the root tree probably symbolizes Israel's ancient faith, especially the covenant (v. 27) and the promise to the patriarchs (v. 26).

147. Klein, Blomberg, and Hubbard, *Introduction to Biblical Interpretation*, 497, with full bibliography.

in Jesus the Messiah as the condition for the prophecy to be fulfilled. Now, the existence of the modern state of Israel might anticipate that fulfillment, but nothing is said here (or elsewhere in the New Testament, for that matter) about the involvement of a "nation" of Israel in it. In my view, the reference is to some future recognition among Jews of Jesus as Messiah without reference to a political state presiding over national boundaries.[148]

In summary, the whole tenor of New Testament teaching points Christians away from a Holy Land-based perspective toward an international one—from Jerusalem to the uttermost parts of the earth. Its concern is with Jews *and* Gentiles worldwide—and this includes Palestinians—and not simply with modern Israel, itself a secular state. In my view, the demands of the gospel support a just, even-handed approach toward the question of the land rather than the decidedly pro-Israel leanings typical of many evangelicals.

WHAT REMAINS. JOSHUA 13–19 begins with Yahweh's conversation with aging Joshua concerning "the land that remains" (13:2). He surveys the terrain not yet in Israelite hands, leaving Israel to do its part and promising to drive out the Sidonians himself. An important contemporary theme emerges from this conversation: Given our human weakness, we always carry out God's tasks imperfectly, but God is strong and caring; he stands ready to aid our efforts rather than tolerate our compromise.

The first part of that theme reminds me of how imperfect is my execution of what God wants of me! The more I read Scripture and listen to the Holy Spirit, the more aware I become of areas of my person and my way of life not yet surrendered to the lordship of Christ. In my soul still lurk dark corners that I keep Jesus out of lest he discover the sin, self-centeredness, and rebellion hiding undisturbed there. (As if, of course, he did not know they were there!) Deep inside me are secret closets with big signs saying "Keep Out!" I have a hidden Sweet Revenge Closet, where I store my hurts, bitterness, anger, and juicy desire for revenge against people who have wronged me (or so I think). There I hide my secret files like "Slights

---

148. Against this view, Walton argues (*Covenant*, 136–44) that the New Testament's silence concerning the land of Israel does not invalidate the "eschatology of Israel," the so-called "aftermath oracles" in which the prophets treat Israel's future, including the land, after "the coming or present covenant crisis" (136). In his view, those oracles support the idea that "the believing remnant of Israel also continue to have a destiny of their own that is linked to their previous [i.e., revelatory] role" (142).

I'll Never Forget" and "Wish List of Disasters for You-Know-Who." With evil relish I often sneak into this closet to pore over the files and fantasize about scenarios that would vindicate me. Secretly, I admire the cleverness of Doc, a character in John Steinbeck's *Cannery Row*, who suggested a way to get revenge on a bank: "Rent a safety deposit box ... then deposit in it one whole fresh salmon and go away for six months."[149]

In my Self-Righteousness Closet I keep my file of "Speeches to Straighten Certain People Out." These are orations I keep for situations in which I somehow feel that my world—or, at least, the world as I want it to be—is threatened. They feign rhetoric to persuade people on whose decisions the tidiness of my world hangs, but in reality they are nothing but self-serving, passive-aggressive attempts at foot-dragging. The air in this closet reeks of fear and panic—and plain faithlessness. I suspect that my readers have dark, secret closets of their own where they shut out the searching light of Jesus, lest it expose the inner corruption and spiritual detritus stockpiled there.

Several years ago I had an episode of cardiac arrhythmia called atrial fibrillation (or "A-fib," for short). I noticed that my heart beat irregularly and that I lacked my usual "oomph" during exercise. After a few days of hemming and hawing, I finally visited my family physician who, alas, diagnosed the problem and sent me to the hospital. Four days later, the cardiologist released me, put me on various medications, and scheduled periodic follow-up visits to his office. During one such visit he advised me that the next step would be, so to speak, to hit the reset button on my heart. This means to shut down the heart with medication and then restart it with electric shock. "Now, doesn't that sound like fun?" I nervously laughed to myself.

Three months later during one of my daily heartbeat checks, I thought I heard the sweet sound of regular rhythm, and my wife confirmed it. One of my scheduled visits was a few days later, and I did not breathe a word of my suspicion as my cardiologist quietly listened to my heartbeat. "Well, Bob," he said when he was done, "you've saved us some electricity. Your heart has converted."

"Converted"? What an interesting word choice for a doctor! He meant, of course, the conversion of my heart from arrhythmia to regular rhythm. After learning the medical term, I joked to my wife, "I thought I'd done *that* a long time ago!" In Christian theology, conversion denotes a radical change of one's direction in life. It means to turn around from a trajectory *away* from Christ to one *toward* him. Granted, as an eight-year-old I was

149. Steinbeck, *Cannery Row*, 15.

"converted to Christ" in a genuine moment of personal commitment that launched my long life of discipleship. In reality, however, the more I learn about myself, the more I reckon myself among the partly converted. There is much about me that remains *un*converted. For my conversion to become more complete, I need to dismantle those hidden and forbidden closets deep down in my soul, thoroughly clean up the space, and toss their contents into the trash.

This is where the second part of this theme comes into play. God promised to give Israel the land, and Joshua 13–19 demonstrates that he did so. Similarly, God promises us his power to compensate for our imperfections and failures of Christians. As God's power compensated for Israel's military weakness against Sidon, so also his power offsets our spiritual weaknesses. God supplies this deficit in order to encourage us as we contend on his behalf against our spiritual Sidonians.

Recall Paul's classic encounter with God over a problem (2 Cor. 12:7–10). The apostle explains that, to keep him humble rather than boastful, he received a "thorn in the flesh," possibly an allusion to the cross of Christ.[150] If so, in citing the "thorn" Paul identifies his sufferings for the gospel with those of Jesus, as his later reference to "insults … hardships … persecutions … difficulties" (v. 10) indicates. God answers his persistent prayer for deliverance with a stunning declaration: "My grace is sufficient for you, for my power is made perfect in weakness" (v. 9). God assures Paul that his power is at its best when human weakness is at its worst — precisely Paul's own situation.

Weakness, therefore, is not a cause for despair but of boasting because of the paradox inherent in the gospel itself — that "the power of God is at work in weakness."[151] That paradox leads Paul to embrace and revel in his weakness — in the hardships, the opposition, the uphill battles, and so on. It leads him to voice his own paradox: "When I am weak, then I am strong" (v. 10). It also undergirds his affirmation in Philippians 4:13, "I can do everything through him who gives me strength."

Imagine what this means to us: When we feel the weakest, that is when we are the strongest! And one thing is certain: We never lack moments of personal or spiritual impotence. All of us have our temptations, whether it be addictions to food, alcohol, or drugs; whether it be personality traits

---

150. J. E. Powers, "A 'Thorn in the Flesh': The Appropriation of Textual Meaning," *Journal of Pentecostal Theology* 18 (2001): 93–97. Scholarly speculation has interpreted the "thorn" as either a physical ailment of some sort or an allusion to his opponents in Corinth. In the background lurks their questioning of Paul's apostolic authority, the issue that elicits Paul's lengthy defense (2 Cor. 10–13).

151. Ibid., 93.

that get us into trouble like jealousy, competitiveness, or a short temper; whether it be hard situations we cannot escape like painful memories from the past, a difficult marriage, or a job we hate but desperately need; or whether it be opposition to our Christian faith like the snide comments of coworkers, the cold distance kept by defensive neighbors, or the pressure to compromise by unbelieving relatives. Day after day and week after week we face the debilitating, strength-sapping forces around us.

Whatever our "thorn," the gospel paradox that Paul voices offers us encouragement: When I am weak — frustrated, beaten down, exhausted, at my wit's end — then I am strong. At that moment, the powerful grace of God comes into play. In a sense, it works like the engines in the hybrid cars of today: During acceleration to thirty miles per hours, the hybrid's electric engine quietly powers it, but above that speed — when more power is needed to sustain momentum — the gasoline engine kicks in. Similarly, our strength is like that electric motor. It can keep us going when things are not intense or hectic, but when they get hot and heavy — when we feel in over our head — that is when God's power is at its best. That was his promise to Joshua and Israel and to Paul — and that is his promise to us.

The trick, of course, is to relax and let that power take over. Here is what I suggest to surrender to God's power: Memorize Philippians 4:13, and when you feel yourself in need of God's power, simply say, "I can do everything through him who gives me strength." When you dread going to work: "I can do everything through him...." When you fail and need to repair a relationship: "I can do everything through him...." When you have no idea how to solve a problem, "I can do everything through him...." When you feel like you cannot live another day: "I can do everything through him...." You will experience the paradox of the gospel: It demonstrates its incredible power at the moment we feel at rock bottom.

The people of God today. Above, I pointed out how the seemingly endless, mind-numbing details of Joshua 13 – 19 symbolize the ideal of Greater Israel. I indulged in a short flight of fancy wandering among some of the obscure towns to bring them and their people a little more to life. Now, in my view, that picture of Greater Israel comprises a microcosm of God's people today, the Greater Church of Jesus Christ worldwide. As Greater Israel spread in various directions and in various concentrations across Canaan, God's people today are spread across the globe we call earth. But in what ways does Joshua 13 – 19 illumine our understanding of that Greater Church?

(1) It reminds us that there is no caste system or rank structure in it. Acsah and the daughters of Zelophehad anticipate the picture of the Gospels that the kingdom includes women of faith as well as men. As Acsah

sought Caleb's blessing, first-century women also navigated swarming crowds and reluctant disciples to connect personally with Jesus. Their perseverance brought them salvation, healing (in some cases), and the blessing of Jesus on them and their whole households.[152] Though Israel remained a patriarchal society, "Israelite faith was a woman's faith — cherished, defended and exemplified by women."[153] Their prominence in the Old Testament anticipates their prominence in the early church. On a broader scale, Acsah, Zelophehad's daughters, Rahab, and the Gibeonites prepare the way for Paul's two majestic declarations concerning status in the kingdom:

> There is neither Jew nor Greek, slave nor free, male nor female, for you are all one in Christ Jesus. (Gal. 3:28)

> Here there is no Greek or Jew, circumcised or uncircumcised, barbarian, Scythian, slave free, but Christ is all, and is in all. (Col. 3:11)

Among Christians, oneness in Christ, says Paul, has radically abolished the pecking orders of rank and status that may pertain outside the church. It has erased all the ugly, connotative labels with which we humans seek to prop up our feeling of superiority over others. Instead, each member of the church is just as important as any other. Per Paul's body analogy (1 Cor. 12:12 – 27), lesser body parts (e.g., the foot) are just as important as more honored ones (e.g., the hand), for each serves its God-given function within the larger body.

Charlie Brown's sister, Sally, once spoke about this truth in a *Peanuts* cartoon strip. As her brother watches television, Sally suddenly rushes in behind him, blurting out,

"Ha! You didn't think I could get mentioned, but I did!"

"What are you talking about?" Charlie asks.

"The School Play! The Program where everyone gets mentioned! See?" she says showing him the paper program. "They have the names of all the kids who were in the play and they have the names of all the adults who helped with scenery and food and things."

Charlie looks at the program. "Where do you come in?" he asks.

"Where do I come in? Just read that last line ... you'll see ..."

So Charlie reads: "'Space does not permit the listing of all those wonderful people who gave their time and effort when needed'."

---

152. Cf. Hess, *Joshua*, 246, citing Matt. 9:20 – 22; 15:21 – 28; 26:7 – 13; Mark 7:24 – 30; 14:3 – 9; Luke 2:36 – 38; 7:11 – 15, 36 – 50; 8:43 – 48; 13:10 – 17; 18:1 – 5.

153. P. A. Bird, "Women: Old Testament," *ABD*, 6:956.

Sally snatches the program from her brother and walks away, saying proudly, "By golly, don't tell me I'm not important enough to get mentioned!"

Yes, within the Christian community, everyone is important, but the challenge is to make sure that everyone feels that importance. We humans are all too prone to respond to first impressions, some that make us want to get to know people, others that lead us to avoid them. But, alas, in the Christian community Jesus has not given us the option of ignoring people within it because that violates its identity. If it welcomes attractive people and shuts out unattractive ones, it might as well go out of business. It has lost its true Christian identity and no longer has a reason to exist.

This might be a good moment to pause, close your eyes, and imagine yourself standing on the platform of your church on a Sunday. Let the eyes of your imagination pan across the audience. Visualize the individual faces before you. Observe which people you know by name and which are unfamiliar to you. Among the latter, observe whether they came in with or are seated among family or friends. Make a mental note of anyone who seems to be there alone. After your scan of the crowd ends, ask yourself, Who in my community is overlooked? Whom does the body keep on the periphery or deprive of attention? Resolve to approach one such person next Sunday simply to get to know them and to make them feel welcome.

(2) Joshua 13 – 19 reminds us the church is truly a worldwide church. The apostles have done their job well: The gospel message long ago moved out from Jerusalem through Samaria to the uttermost parts of the earth. I find great inspiration in pondering that I have sisters and brothers in all kinds of places with whom I have Jesus Christ in common. Indeed, that thought just confirms the power of the gospel for me—that it can transcend thousands of miles of geography, adapt its truths to all kinds of cultures, and transform lives. It confirms that the gospel is what it claims to be, "the power of God for the salvation to everyone who believes" (Rom. 1:16).

I have been privileged to see this firsthand in many places over the years.

- There is the compact, adobe Methodist church in Hipólito, a small railroad town in the barren, windswept desert of northeastern Mexico. As part of a youth gospel team, I preached my first sermon there, and the team supported a Mexican evangelist in holding several days of revival meetings in the town theater.
- During my military service in Vietnam, a Vietnamese friend took me to worship one Sunday evening at a small Christian church at Long

Xuyen. The music was very Asian, as was the Vietnamese language of which I knew barely a few words. But I sensed the presence of Christ there, the same Savior I worship, the one I was serving as a Navy chaplain.

- Then there is the small Pentecostal congregation at Kumah Dunyo, a small village in the lush, green mountains of Togo near the border with Ghana. Its church stood unfinished and unusable due to a lack of funds, so worship took place outdoors under a covering of tree branches. The pastor was a tall, gracious, and dignified man, who the day before had graciously visited the home where my family and I were staying. During worship I remember the fun of line dancing, Togolese style, to praise songs accompanied by a worship band with local, hand-made instruments.

These examples represent only a tiny sample of the small, obscure places of worship that dot the globe, places known only to the Lord in whose honor local peoples meet. Together they comprise that wonderful band, the Greater Church of Jesus Christ.

(3) Joshua 13 – 19 reminds us that our challenge is to make our worldwide unity work. Distances of culture and geography certainly divide us; they make it difficult for Christians in North America to keep aware of our international brothers and sisters. But there are several things we can do to live out our connection to the Greater Church. We can start with our Jerusalem by joining with other local Christian bodies to provide some practical service that this community needs. Such endeavors help dispel the popular impression that Christians are always bickering over doctrine or competing for importance.

For our Samaria, we may seek to support ongoing ministries, especially struggling ones, that serve a city or town nearby. For example, suburban congregations might band together to share their resources to assist nearby urban congregations. During my years in Denver, Colorado, I saw Mile High Ministries become one such innovative, suburban-urban cooperative venture. Today it sponsors Joshua Station, a holistic ministry to homeless families, and the Issachar Community, a leadership/discipleship community that mentors and trains young leaders from at-risk populations to do community development. Similar ministries are going on throughout North America and would gladly welcome new allies in their endeavors. Or God may lead churches into other creative ventures of Christian witness and advocacy.

(4) Finally, one good way to keep aware of fellow believers in the uttermost parts of the earth is to get to know people from there in our own

neighborhoods and towns. Granted, this requires some initiative on our part, but the recent waves of immigration have landed people from everywhere almost on our doorstep. International Students is an organization that befriends foreign students studying at colleges and universities in North America. The friendship of Christian families during their years of study opens up opportunity to sow the seeds of the gospel that may bear fruit in the distant lands to which they return.

In my city, World Relief enlists and advises local sponsors (e.g., churches, community organizations, etc.) on refugee resettlement. I can testify that my church's involvement with recent arrivals from Sudan has introduced me and my congregation to the needs of that country. Contacts with Christians working overseas or mission trips to other countries are two other ways to keep current on what God is doing elsewhere today.

I warn readers, however, that they will never be the same once they commit to involvement. But that is really the point of the gospel. It is not just fire insurance for eternity that lets us do whatever we want once we have it. It is not just a set of right beliefs (though it is that). Rather, "the land that remains" for Christians is a transformed people—a radically-changed, strikingly different kind of community—whose difference catches the eye of a cynical, watching world. As Philip Yancey writes:

> The kingdom of God will grow on earth as the church creates an alternative society demonstrating what the world is not, but one day will be: Barth's prescription of "a new sign which is radically dissimilar to [the world's] own manner and which contradicts it in a way which is full of promise." A society that welcomes people of all races and social classes, that is characterized by love and not polarization, that cares most for its weakest members, that stands for justice and righteousness in a world enamored with selfishness and decadence, a society in which members compete for the privilege of serving one another—this is what Jesus meant by the kingdom of God.[154]

We have an inheritance, too. Joshua 13–19 is about the inheritance of the tribes of Israel, a theme the New Testament picks up and applies to us today.[155] Obviously, the inheritance of Christians has nothing to do with actual physical property in Palestine. Rather, it builds on the understanding of the church noted above as the true descendants of Abraham who benefit from the fulfillment of the patriarchal promise in Christ, its true

---

154. Philip Yancey, *The Jesus I Never Knew* (Grand Rapids: Zondervan, 1995), 253.

155. J. Eichler, "Inheritance, Lot, Portion," *NIDNTT*, 2:295–303; P. L. Hammer, "Inheritance (NT)," *ABD*, 3:415–17.

heir (Gal. 3:29). The fulfillment of the land promise to Israel finds one historical fulfillment in Christ and a final fulfillment at the end of time.

Further, in the parable of the wicked tenants, Jesus uses the vineyard, an Old Testament symbol of Israel (see Isa. 5), to teach about the kingdom of God (Matt. 21:33–46; cf. 5:5, 10). The clear implication is that the themes of Israel and the Promised Land have expanded into Jesus' much broader theme of the kingdom of God. Ultimately, the kingdom is the form in which believers inherit in the future what was promised long ago in the past (Matt. 25:34; 1 Cor. 6:9; 15:50a; Gal. 5:21; Eph. 5:5; James 2:5). In a sense, the truth that both Jews and Gentiles receive inheritances through Christ represents a further extension of the inclusive vision of Ezekiel 47–48 (see above).

In the New Testament, the idea of inheritance and heirs has both soteriological and eschatological dimensions. It concerns, on the one hand, spiritual realities received from the past and experienced in the present, and, on the other, realities to be received and enjoyed in the future. It also has implications for how God desires his people to live today.

What are the *present realities* of our inheritance as Christians? (1) Through faith in Christ, the true heir of Abraham, we outsiders have been lovingly adopted into God's family (Eph. 1:5). Our spiritual adoption entitles us to be coheirs with Christ himself (Rom. 8:17; Gal. 3:29), with full rights to our promised inheritance. Imagine for a moment what this means. Before receiving salvation through Christ, we were nothing—poor, bedraggled beggars constantly scrounging for scraps to assuage our spiritual hunger. We were hopelessly lost and doomed to eternal oblivion as if we were living on some totally other, lifeless planet. Now, however, we live in Fat City! We have a loving, generous Father, who has graciously made us full members of his huge, caring family. He has added our names to the list in his will of legitimate heirs who will receive equal shares of inheritance. In spiritual status, we have risen from the outhouse to the penthouse. That is truly something about which to praise God!

(2) To reassure us that a full inheritance share really awaits us, our Father has even given us a deposit—the Holy Spirit in our hearts (2 Cor. 1:22; 5:5; Eph. 1:14). In ancient commercial transactions, "deposit" (Gk. *arrabon*) designated a down payment on a purchase. By paying part of the purchase price in advance, the buyer secured his legal claim to the item or made a contract valid and binding. He also accepted the obligation to make further payments or lose his deposit.[156] The same practice still prevails today. Anyone who buys a major purchase on credit—say, a house or car—knows the drill well. To hold the item while financing is arranged, the seller always

---

156. BDAG, 134.

requires a deposit. By accepting the deposit, the seller agrees not to raise the purchase price or sell the item to someone else. The buyer pays the deposit to confirm the seriousness of his interest and to promise to pay the full balance. The implication of the metaphor is that, by giving us the Holy Spirit now, God has obligated himself to pay us the full inheritance promised us. So, how do we know that we will get what is coming to us? We now have the Spirit—part of God himself—as a guarantee. I certainly cannot think of anything more reassuring to my faith than that!

Followers of Calvinist theology invoke the acronym TULIP to help them remember its main tenets.[157] A humorous description of the alternative Arminian theology is "daisy," meaning (with no acronymn implied) "he [God] loves me, he loves me not." At times we all struggle with doubts as to God's love, especially when dark days of suffering and despair envelope us in gloom. When the sky is dark and God himself seems silent and withdrawn, one wonders if God's promises are indeed true. At such moments, God certainly fails to meet our expectations. The temptation is to throw away our faith and to strike out on our own quest for certainty. Until, of course, we recall the guarantee in our hearts—the precious Holy Spirit of God. His is the soothing voice amid the chaos, the reassuring touch amid the hurts, the comforting presence amid the grief. His quiet, powerful presence reassures us that, despite the mystery of God's dealings in the moment, God's obligations to us remain sure. We can, so to speak, take them to the bank.

What are the *future realities* of our inheritance as Christians that the Spirit guarantees? Certainly, the special privilege of an eternal relationship with our heavenly Father and with Christ tops the lists. That was Jesus' promise to anyone who abandoned everything to follow him (Matt. 19:29–20:1; Mark 10:29–31; Luke 18:29–30; cf. Acts 20:32; Heb. 1:14). Through salvation we have become "heirs having the hope of eternal life" (Titus 3:7), the inheritance set aside for us from eternity (Matt. 25:34). It comprises unbelievable wealth (Eph. 1:18), and it marks the final reward for our faithful service for our Lord (Col. 3:24) and the moment we receive new bodies (1 Cor. 15:50a).

Several texts associate our inheritance with heaven. According to Peter, God keeps it safe and waiting for us in heaven, a guarantee that, unlike earthly legacies, it "can never perish, spoil or fade" (1 Peter 1:3–4). Like Abraham, the writer of Hebrews says, our inheritance includes life in the heavenly city "whose architect and builder is God" (Heb. 11:10; cf. Col. 1:12). Theologically, the ultimate roots of this concept go back to God

---

157. The letters represent an acronymn: Total depravity, Unconditional election, Limited atonement, Irresistible grace, and Perseverance of the saints.

himself—specifically, his deep desire to have a relationship with us. The inheritance theme captures something profoundly simple, God's loving desire to provide us a secure place to share with him forever.[158]

Inheritance as demand. The above discussion might create the impression that, since our inheritance is secure and its realization inevitable, we may live any way we wish. But that is a dangerous misperception. The Bible several times lists the kinds of people who will *not* inherit the kingdom of God: the sexually immoral, the greedy, idolaters, thieves, drunkards, slanderers, and swindlers (1 Cor. 6:9–10; cf. Gal. 5:19–21; Eph. 5:5).

The double-edged point of Jesus' parable of the good Samaritan is also worth remembering (Luke 10:25–37). He told the story to identify a neighbor for the Jewish law expert to "love as himself," as Leviticus 19:18 demanded. It critiques the disdain for Samaritans typical of the day and applauds the stunning compassion of the Samaritan, notwithstanding his status as an outcast. Jesus' conclusion answering the legal scholar before him also addresses us today: "Go and do likewise" (v. 37). He calls us to cross stupid, selfish barriers that divide, to stop slapping derogatory labels on victims, and to stop withholding compassion because we simply do not like some people. But I hasten to add that the above warnings in no way make our inheritance conditional. Paul's prohibition ("Do not be deceived" [1 Cor. 6:9]) simply aims to dispel any doubt that God tolerates such conduct (cf. Rev. 21:8). He rightly deems such behavior as unworthy of people whom God has graciously made coheirs with Christ.

By contrast, God commends good conduct to heirs waiting to receive their inheritance. In our secular employment, what pleases God is that we work not halfheartedly or lazily but wholeheartedly, as if the Lord himself, not a human, were our boss—which he, in fact, is! (Col. 3:23–24; cf. Heb. 6:12). When we confront daunting obstacles that test our faithfulness, we are to get the best of them, rather than let them buffalo us (Rev. 21:7).

Along this line, Caleb points us in the right direction. What set him apart from his panicked contemporaries was his optimistic trust in God ("a different spirit") that led him to "follow [God] wholeheartedly" (Num. 14:24; Josh 14:14). As we saw above, his stance earned him his promised inheritance, and a similar stance by us will similarly win us the approving "Well done, good and faithful servant" from our Lord Jesus (Matt. 25:21, 23; Luke 19:17). After all, as Yancey, writes, "the New Testament declares that the future of the cosmos is being determined by the church. Jesus played his part and then left. Now it is up to us."[159]

---

158. Cf. Eichler, "Inheritance, Lot, Portion," 2:295.
159. Yancey, *The Jesus I Never Knew*, 229.

Joshua 20:1–21:45

❦

THEN THE LORD said to Joshua: [2]"Tell the Israelites to designate the cities of refuge, as I instructed you through Moses, [3]so that anyone who kills a person accidentally and unintentionally may flee there and find protection from the avenger of blood.

[4]"When he flees to one of these cities, he is to stand in the entrance of the city gate and state his case before the elders of that city. Then they are to admit him into their city and give him a place to live with them. [5]If the avenger of blood pursues him, they must not surrender the one accused, because he killed his neighbor unintentionally and without malice aforethought. [6]He is to stay in that city until he has stood trial before the assembly and until the death of the high priest who is serving at that time. Then he may go back to his own home in the town from which he fled."

[7]So they set apart Kedesh in Galilee in the hill country of Naphtali, Shechem in the hill country of Ephraim, and Kiriath Arba (that is, Hebron) in the hill country of Judah. [8]On the east side of the Jordan of Jericho they designated Bezer in the desert on the plateau in the tribe of Reuben, Ramoth in Gilead in the tribe of Gad, and Golan in Bashan in the tribe of Manasseh. [9]Any of the Israelites or any alien living among them who killed someone accidentally could flee to these designated cities and not be killed by the avenger of blood prior to standing trial before the assembly.

[21:1]Now the family heads of the Levites approached Eleazar the priest, Joshua son of Nun, and the heads of the other tribal families of Israel [2]at Shiloh in Canaan and said to them, "The LORD commanded through Moses that you give us towns to live in, with pasturelands for our livestock." [3]So, as the LORD had commanded, the Israelites gave the Levites the following towns and pasturelands out of their own inheritance:

[4]The first lot came out for the Kohathites, clan by clan. The Levites who were descendants of Aaron the priest were allotted thirteen towns from the tribes of Judah, Simeon and Benjamin. [5]The rest of Kohath's descendants were allotted

ten towns from the clans of the tribes of Ephraim, Dan and half of Manasseh.

⁶The descendants of Gershon were allotted thirteen towns from the clans of the tribes of Issachar, Asher, Naphtali and the half-tribe of Manasseh in Bashan.

⁷The descendants of Merari, clan by clan, received twelve towns from the tribes of Reuben, Gad and Zebulun.

⁸So the Israelites allotted to the Levites these towns and their pasturelands, as the LORD had commanded through Moses.

⁹From the tribes of Judah and Simeon they allotted the following towns by name ¹⁰(these towns were assigned to the descendants of Aaron who were from the Kohathite clans of the Levites, because the first lot fell to them):

¹¹They gave them Kiriath Arba (that is, Hebron), with its surrounding pastureland, in the hill country of Judah. (Arba was the forefather of Anak.) ¹²But the fields and villages around the city they had given to Caleb son of Jephunneh as his possession.

¹³So to the descendants of Aaron the priest they gave Hebron (a city of refuge for one accused of murder), Libnah, ¹⁴Jattir, Eshtemoa, ¹⁵Holon, Debir, ¹⁶Ain, Juttah and Beth Shemesh, together with their pasturelands—nine towns from these two tribes.

¹⁷And from the tribe of Benjamin they gave them Gibeon, Geba, ¹⁸Anathoth and Almon, together with their pasturelands—four towns.

¹⁹All the towns for the priests, the descendants of Aaron, were thirteen, together with their pasturelands.

²⁰The rest of the Kohathite clans of the Levites were allotted towns from the tribe of Ephraim:

²¹In the hill country of Ephraim they were given Shechem (a city of refuge for one accused of murder) and Gezer, ²²Kibzaim and Beth Horon, together with their pasturelands—four towns.

²³Also from the tribe of Dan they received Eltekeh, Gibbethon, ²⁴Aijalon and Gath Rimmon, together with their pasturelands—four towns.

²⁵From half the tribe of Manasseh they received Taanach and Gath Rimmon, together with their pasturelands—two towns.

²⁶All these ten towns and their pasturelands were given to the rest of the Kohathite clans.

²⁷The Levite clans of the Gershonites were given:
from the half-tribe of Manasseh, Golan in Bashan (a city of refuge for one accused of murder) and Be Eshtarah, together with their pasturelands—two towns;

²⁸from the tribe of Issachar,
Kishion, Daberath, ²⁹Jarmuth and En Gannim, together with their pasturelands—four towns;

³⁰from the tribe of Asher,
Mishal, Abdon, ³¹Helkath and Rehob, together with their pasturelands—four towns;

³²from the tribe of Naphtali,
Kedesh in Galilee (a city of refuge for one accused of murder), Hammoth Dor and Kartan, together with their pasturelands—three towns.

³³All the towns of the Gershonite clans were thirteen, together with their pasturelands.

³⁴The Merarite clans (the rest of the Levites) were given:
from the tribe of Zebulun, Jokneam, Kartah, ³⁵Dimnah and Nahalal, together with their pasturelands—four towns;

³⁶from the tribe of Reuben,
Bezer, Jahaz, ³⁷Kedemoth and Mephaath, together with their pasturelands—four towns;

³⁸from the tribe of Gad,
Ramoth in Gilead (a city of refuge for one accused of murder), Mahanaim, ³⁹Heshbon and Jazer, together with their pasturelands—four towns in all.

⁴⁰All the towns allotted to the Merarite clans, who were the rest of the Levites, were twelve.

⁴¹The towns of the Levites in the territory held by the Israelites were forty-eight in all, together with their pasturelands. ⁴²Each of these towns had pasturelands surrounding it; this was true for all these towns.

⁴³So the LORD gave Israel all the land he had sworn to give their forefathers, and they took possession of it and settled there. ⁴⁴The LORD gave them rest on every side, just as he had sworn to their forefathers. Not one of their enemies withstood them; the LORD handed all their enemies over to them. ⁴⁵Not one of all the LORD's good promises to the house of Israel failed; every one was fulfilled.

CHAPTERS 13–19 SEEM to bring Israel's settlement in Canaan to completion, but chapters 20–21, in fact, tie up two leftover loose ends. (1) Yahweh himself (through Joshua) mandates and instructs Israel concerning the establishment of cities of refuge (ch. 20). Two things about Yahweh's instructions (vv. 1–6) are especially interesting. They mark the final time that Yahweh addresses anyone directly in the book—"The Last Words of Yahweh," as it were—and draw his involvement in it to a climactic close. Also, his command is that the Israelites (lit.) "give [these towns] for themselves" (v. 2)—that they surrender some of their own holdings but somehow receive benefit from the act.

(2) The Israelites as a whole honor the request of the Levites to have cities and pasturelands allotted them just as Yahweh had promised (ch. 21). Again, they "give" the town from their own inheritance, presumably out of gratitude to God and for the benefits that a local Levitical presence will offer.

Both provisions go back to Numbers 35, where Yahweh (through Moses) ordered the Israelites to set aside forty-eight cities for the Levites (vv. 1–8), of which six were to be cities of refuge, three on each side of the Jordan (v. 6a, 9–14; cf. Ex. 21:12–14).[1] Moses had already set aside three east of the Jordan—Bezer for the Reubenites, Ramoth Gilead for the Gadites, and Golan for East Manasseh (Deut. 4:41–43)—and also ordered Israel to designate three more west of the river once Israel settled there (Deut. 19:1–3). In Joshua 20, Israel completes this leftover task. The assignment of cities and of grazing grounds for the Levites (ch. 21) not only carries out Yahweh's command, but also draws to a close the literary theme in Joshua concerning the Levites' lack of inheritance (Josh. 14:3–4; 18:7). Finally, a retrospective summary closes the entire chapter (21:43–45).

Joshua 20 presupposes wide national boundaries, an observation that has caused scholarly speculation concerning the date of the institution of refuge cities. Suggestions include the early united monarchy, the territorially

---

1. For the possibility that Num. 35 might derive instead from Joshua 20, cf. Fritz, *Josua,* 203, 210; Nelson, *Joshua,* 229, 238.

expansionist era of Jeroboam II (eighth cent. B.C.; 2 Kings 14:25, 28), or the outward ambitions of Josiah (late seventh cent. B.C.).[2] By contrast, Nelson reads the text as simply a literary piece that conveys the book's view that "Israel" includes Transjordan, rather than a document with connections to a databale political program.[3] Whatever the case, the important point is that chapter 20 marks a turning point from matters of land distribution (chs. 13−19) to the central concern of chapters 22−24, "how life in the land is to be lived."[4]

The Cities of Refuge (20:1−9)

IT IS YAHWEH HIMSELF who raises the issue at hand by giving instructions for Israel through Joshua (vv. 1−6). The Israelites are to implement what he told Moses by setting aside cities of refuge (vv. 1−2). The term "cities of refuge" (*ʿarey hammiqlaṭ*) links Joshua 20 with the provision of Numbers 35:6 (cf. 1 Chron. 6:42, 52). But canonically, the provision of asylum ("a place I will designate") first appears in the Book of the Covenant in the context of wrongful deaths (Ex. 21:12−14). Its classic cases include those of Adonijah (1 Kings 1:50−53) and Joab (2:28−34), who find refuge from Solomon's political revenge at the altar in the tabernacle.[5]

The ancient custom of blood revenge—retaliation in kind against a killer by the victim's kin—stands in the background of Joshua 20. In Israel one duty of close male relatives was to avenge such deaths by killing the person thought responsible.[6] But a pattern of unrestrained retaliation poses a threat to the continuation of stable social order. Potentially, it may unleash an unending and possibly escalating cycle of tit-for-tat killings (see Lamech's boast in Gen. 4:23−24). The provision of cities of refuge seeks to break that cycle of blood revenge. It protects someone who has killed a fellow Israelite from the "restorer of blood" (*goʾel haddam*), a male relative of the victim (e.g., his son, brother, etc.) out to avenge the death.

---

2. For a convenient summary of possible options, see Butler, *Joshua*, 214−15.

3. Nelson, *Joshua*, 230.

4. Ibid., 230.

5. For general background on asylum, cf. P. Barmash, *Homicide in the Biblical World* (Cambridge: Cambridge Univ. Press, 2005), 71−93; for the relationship between Ex. 21 and Deut. 19, cf. J. Stackert, "Why Does Deuteronomy Legislate Cities of Refuge? Asylum in the Covenant Collection (Exodus 21:12−14) and Deuteronomy (19:1−13)," *JBL* 125 (2006): 23−49.

6. I prefer "restorer of blood" to NIV's "avenger of blood"; cf. S. D. Sperling, "Blood, Avenger of," *ABD*, 1:763. For background, cf. R. L. Hubbard Jr., "The Goʾel in Ancient Israel: Theological Reflections on an Israelite Institution," *BBR* 1 (1999): 3−19; idem, "גָּאַל," *NIDOTTE*, 1:791; H. Ringgren, "גָּאַל," *TDOT*, 2:352. For the phrase, see Num. 35:19, 21, 24, 25, 27; Deut. 19:6, 12; 2 Sam. 14:11.

But verse 3 clarifies that it only applies to accidental and unintentional killings, ones done "by mistake" or "inadvertently" (Num. 35:11–15) and "without [prior] knowledge or forethought" (Deut. 4:42; 19:4). Deuteronomy 19:5–6 offers an illuminating example of what constitutes an accidental killing: when two Israelites are felling trees in a forest and one man's axhead suddenly flies off, striking and killing his companion. In modern terms, the crime would equate to negligent homicide or manslaughter, not premeditated murder.[7]

The act of killing nevertheless incurs blood-guilt and legitimates retaliation by the aggrieved family. Thus, Yahweh outlines the procedure to be followed to obviate the latter (vv. 4–6). The text's phraseology echoes primarily Deuteronomy 19:1–8 but also Numbers 35.[8] If the killer desires refuge, he is to flee to the closest city of refuge and must argue his case at the city gate before the elders (v. 4). Since a full trial follows (v. 6), this process amounts to a preliminary hearing to determine whether his case qualifies for asylum—that his actions might have been, in fact, accidental and unintentional.[9] Once satisfied, the elders may admit (lit., "gather") him to the city and provide him a place to live during his long stay.

Poignantly, the Hebrew phrase (lit.) "gather him into the city to themselves" pictures the city and its people as protectively surrounding the asylum seeker. If a blood restorer tracks him there, the city's leaders may not hand the killer over since his actions seem to have been unintentional and not driven by anger (NIV "without malice aforethought"; v. 5). In other words, the city truly is his refuge against revenge. He may remain there, provided that a trial by a legal assembly in the city verifies his claim.[10] Presumably, an unverified claim would lead to his expulsion from the city and eventually land him in the hands of the restorer. If verified, the requirement to remain there rather than go free—in Koopmans' words, "house arrest in the city of refuge"—probably constitutes just punishment for his life-taking act.[11]

---

7. KB, 220, 1313; T. Seidl, "שָׁגַג/שָׁגָה," *TDOT*, 14:402 ("negligent homicide"). This lack of intention contrasts acts done "defiantly" (*beyad ramah*, lit., "with a high hand"), i.e., "with malice aforethought"; cf. Num. 15:30.

8. For details, see Nelson, *Joshua*, 230.

9. To read a preliminary hearing here eliminates the tension between the initial decision (vv. 4–5) and the trial (v. 6) that Nelson alleges (*Joshua*, 231). On the other hand, his suggestion that the text of Josh. 20 has been aligned with Num. 35 and Deut. 19—the latter deemed "canonical and scriptural"—merits consideration.

10. The "legal assembly" (Heb. *ʿedah*) apparently designates a legally authoritative local body drawn from the populace; cf. D. Levy and J. Milgrom, "עֵדָה," *TDOT*, 10:470–73.

11. W. T. Koopmans, "Vengeance and the Fair Trial Venue: A Sermon on Joshua 20," *CTJ* 37/1 (2002): 97.

Curiously, when the current high priest dies, the refugee receives an amnesty that permits his return home. Boling avers that the high priest's death apparently occasioned a "general amnesty," while for Nelson this provision reflects common postexilic practice, the high priest assuming the king's amnesty-granting authority.[12] More likely, however, the applicable laws view the high priest's death as somehow expiating the people's sins in general and, hence, mark the appropriate occasion to free those living in asylum.[13]

Dutifully, the Israelites carry out the instructions, setting aside three west-bank cities, all in the hill country (v. 7). The brief list moves from north to south and combines city names with geographical location: Kedesh (in Napthali) will serve northern Israel, Shechem (in Ephraim) the central heartland, and Kirath Arba (i.e., Hebron, in Judah) southern Israel. With the same combination of name and geography (but reading south to north), the Israelites also officially recognize the three east-bank cities authorized by Moses: Bezer serving the southern desert plateau of Reuben, Ramoth in Gilead serving central Transjordan including Gad, and Golan in Bashan serving East Manasseh (v. 8). All six enjoy a geographical distribution that ensures accessibility throughout the land.

Verse 9 reiterates the purpose of the institution—to provide one who has inadvertently taken a life a fair trial (i.e., mercy) rather than to abandon him (unjustly) to blood revenge. As does Numbers 35:15, the instruction extends the merciful protection also to aliens living permanently among the Israelites. This reflects the "inclusive vision" of the book, a vision that reckons aliens as part of Israel's covenant community (Josh. 8:33, 35) and also grants Rahab and the Gibeonites special status (chs. 2; 9).[14]

The Cities for the Levites (Joshua 21:1–42)

GENEALOGY AND GEOGRAPHY DRIVE this chapter's catalog of Levitical cities. It concerns the three clans who descend from Jacob's son Levi—Gershon, Kohath, and Merari—plus the priestly descendants of Aaron.[15] Its purpose is to explain how the priests and Levites, though technically denied "inheritance" (13:14, 33; 14:3; 18:7), still form an integral part of Greater Israel. It affirms that they, too, with their unique religious roles, have a place—indeed, actual locations—in the land.[16] Literarily, the very total

---

12. Boling, *Joshua*, 474; Nelson, *Joshua*, 231; cf. Fritz, *Josua*, 206.

13. See Butler, *Joshua*, 214–16; Howard, *Joshua*, 385–86, for details and bibliography.

14. Term comes from Howard, *Joshua*, 387.

15. Cf. Gen. 49:11; Ex. 6:16; Num. 3:17; 1 Chron. 6:1, 16; 23:6.

16. Nelson, *Joshua*, 236. The list also occurs in 1 Chron. 6:39–66, which is probably dependent on Joshua 21 rather than vice versa (so Nelson, *Joshua*, 237–38).

of forty-eight cities probably aims to reinforce that ideal since its constituent factors are four — the number of Levi's clans (Aaron, Kohath, Gershon, Merari) — and twelve (the number of Israel's tribes).[17]

The inclusion of Philistine cities never permanently held by Israel (e.g., Eltekeh, Gibbethon [v. 23]) or only later in Israelite hands (e.g., Gezer [v. 21]) implies that the list is more ideal than real.[18] The origin of the materials that compose the lists has been the subject of an ongoing scholarly discussion that need not detain us.[19] The lists (or, at least, their earliest sources) have been dated to the united monarchy (tenth cent. B.C.), the era of Josiah (seventh cent. B.C.), or to the postexilic period (after 538 B.C.). For further background on the Levites, see the Bridging Contexts section below.

Structurally, chapter 21 comprises a summary report of the allotment of towns to Levites (vv. 1–8) and a detailed, formulaic follow-up (vv. 9–42). Genealogy structures the treatment of towns assigned (in order) to the Aaronites (vv. 9–19), the remaining Kohathites (vv. 20–26), the Gershonites (vv. 27–33), and the Merarites (vv. 34–40).[20] Geography fleshes out the details, listing which towns each tribe supplied the four Levite families. A summary report (vv. 41–42) closes the chapter's central section.

In chapters 15–17, the historical importance of Judah and the Joseph tribes apparently accounts for their having received their inheritances first. Here, the religious importance of the priestly family of Aaron similarly explains why the report of their town allotments comes first (vv. 4, 9–19). Their location in Judah at Hebron and southward — the latter, the center of David's early reign (2 Sam. 2:4, 11; 5:1–3) — is also striking, an indication perhaps of longstanding ties, if not actual kinship, between the nation's religious and political leaders.[21] Their towns in Benjamin also position them near Israel's later religious capital, Jerusalem.

---

17. E. Ben Zvi, "The List of the Levitical Cities," *JSOT* 54 (1992): 86. Cf. also the wider historical-critical discussion of Josh. 20 and 21 in L. Schmidt, "Leviten- und Asylstädte in Num. xxxv und Jos. xx; xxi 1–42," *VT* 52/1 (2002): 103–21.

18. That the other two Danite cities (vv. 23–24) are located in that tribe's assigned territory west of Judah rather than its eventual northern settlement site also confirms the list's ideal nature. For further background, see the commentary at 19:40–49; Judg. 18.

19. Nelson, *Joshua*, 238–41, offers a convenient discussion of the issue with bibliography; cf. also Ben Zvi, "The List of the Levitical Cities," 77–106.

20. Genealogically, Aaron is the grandson of Kohath through his father, Amram (Ex. 6:18, 20; 1 Chron. 6:2–3; but cf. Num. 26:58–59).

21. Galil even plausibly argues that the marriage of Aaron and Elisheba, the sister of Judah's tribal leader, Nahshon (Ex. 6:23), actually linked Aaron's descendants with the tribe of Judah; cf. G. Galil, "The Sons of Judah and the Sons of Aaron in Biblical Historiography," *VT* 35/4 (1985): 488–95.

At the same time, discrepancies dog the list.[22] For example, verse 28 lists Daberah as from Issachar whereas in 19:12 this town forms part of Zebulun's boundary description. The fact that the tribes bordered each other, however, suggests several solutions — for example, that the town was a border town technically belonging to Issachar, or that at some point the town had somehow changed hands.

The summary report (vv. 1 – 8). Once again, an interested party proffers a petition before Eleazer, Joshua, and the tribal leaders at Shiloh (vv. 1 – 2a; cf. 14:1; 17:4; 19:51; 22:9). This time the petitioners are the heads of the three Levite families, and they ask for what Yahweh had promised them through Moses — "towns to live in" and "pasturelands for our livestock" (v. 2b; cf. Num. 35:1 – 8; Deut. 19:1 – 8). The specificity of NIV's "pasturelands" slightly misleads since *migraš* probably designates more generally a belt of land outside a city's walls over which the town exercised jurisdiction (cf. Num. 35:3 – 5).[23] Of course, the convenient land would allow Levite residents to graze cattle and sheep right outside their hometowns (Num. 35:3).

Again, echoing the theme of Israel's obedience, the people do so (v. 3), the first lot awarding towns to the Kohathites, descendants of Levi's second son (v. 4a). As in Joshua 14 – 19, the use of lots theologically presumes that their results convey Yahweh's will for the Levites and implicitly authorizes its implementation.[24] "Clan by clan" pictures a process of lot-casting involving all Kohathite subgroups, but the author immediately focuses on what the sons of Aaron (Kohath's grandson; Ex. 6:18, 20) receive (v. 4b) — thirteen towns from Judah, Simeon, and Benjamin.

The rest of the distribution ensues: The other Kohathites get ten towns from Ephraim, Dan, and West Manasseh (v. 5); the Gershonites get thirteen towns from Isssachar, Asher, Naphtali, and East Manasseh (v. 6); the Merarites get twelve towns from Reuben, Gad, and Zebulun (v. 7). Verse 8 again states that the Israelites obeyed Yahweh's command delivered by Moses; they allotted towns and pasturelands to the Levites. The total comes to the expected forty-eight, although the writer omits the figure (but cf. v. 41). Literarily, the summary report prepares the reader to understand the distribution that follows.

The allotment details (vv. 9 – 42). A simple, somewhat formulaic structure forms the skeleton of this long section. Grammatically, variations of

---

22. For full discussion, see Howard, *Joshua,* 389 – 91.

23. J. Barr, "*Migrash* in the Old Testament," *JSS* 29 (1984): 15 – 31; L. Jonker, "רָעָה," *NIDOTTE,* 3:1141.

24. For a suggested scenario by which lot-casting took place, see comments on chs. 13 – 19.

the phrase "give to ..." (*natan*) dominate (vv. 9, 11, 12, 13, 21) even where "give" is implicit (see below). Literarily, the verb repetition anticipates the statement "the LORD gave [to] Israel" (v. 43) that climactically closes chs. 13–21 and bestows proper theological credit. The writer precisely states that the land immediately surrounding a town (its *migraš*) went with it (vv. 11, 13–19, 21–39, 41–42). The underlying structure of verses 9–42 includes the following elements:

1. Introductory formula: "to family X [they gave] ..." (vv. 9, 11, 13, 20, 27, 34)
2. Tribal source formula: "from tribe X + town list + total number of towns" (vv. 9, 11, 13–16, 17–18, 28–29, 30–31, 32, 36–37)
3. Summary formula ("All the towns ...") with tally (vv. 19, 26, 33, 40)
4. Grand total tally for all Levites (v. 41)
5. Conclusion (v. 42)

The Aaronides (vv. 9–19). The paragraph on the Aaronides—Aaron's descendants who are priests—is the most detailed and complex one.[25] It especially underscores the priority of the Aaronides "because the first lot fell to them" (v. 10). Subtly, the statement suggests special divine favor because of the family's special calling as priests of Yahweh. The reader is perhaps surprised to learn up front (v. 11) that Kiriath Arba, formerly reckoned as Calebite (14:13–14; 15:13) and Judahite (15:54), is now Levite.[26] So the author clarifies that though Aaron receives the town of Kirath Arba (i.e., Hebron), Caleb still owns the land and villages surrounding the city (v. 12). This parenthetical reminder that Kirath Arba was a city of refuge (v. 13; cf. 20:7) might hint at an explanation—that for some reason a city of refuge should also be a priestly city—but the town's unexplained change of status still remains a mystery.

Judah and Simeon supply the Aaronides nine towns (vv. 13–16), most of them south of Hebron except for Libnah and Beth Shemesh (northwest). From Benjamin they receive four more (vv. 17–18), all a short distance north of Jerusalem, making a grand total of thirteen (v. 19), the total also for Gershon (v. 33). The towns of the other three clans are widely dispersed, but the Aaronide towns enjoy advantageous geographical clusters south of Hebron and north of Jerusalem.[27]

The Kohathites (vv. 20–26). Israel gives the non-priestly Kohathites ten towns and their land belts, four each from Ephraim, including Shechem

---

25. For all the cities of refuge and Levitical cities, see the convenient map in *CBA*, 108.
26. Hawk, *Joshua*, 222, who offers (223) an intriguing chiastic reading of vv. 11–12.
27. Ibid., 222.

(also a city of refuge [v. 21]) and Dan (see my comment above), as well as two from West Manasseh.[28] Most of their towns are geographically concentrated a good distance west of Jerusalem, but Taanach and Gath Rimmon sit near each other along the southern edge of the Jezreel Valley. As noted above, however, the Danite towns known to be Philistine at the time (Gezer, Eltekeh, Gibbethon) are occupied by Levites either much later or probably not at all.

The Gershonites (vv. 27–33). The Gershonites also receive thirteen cities, two from East Manasseh, including Golan (a city of refuge [v. 27]), four from Issachar and Asher, and three from Naphtali, including Kedesh (a city of refuge [v. 33]). Geographically, two of their towns lie way east of the Sea of Galilee, the rest spread north, south, and northwest of it.

The Merarites (vv. 34–40). Finally, the Merarites receive four towns from Zebulun, Reuben, and Gad (including Ramoth in Gilead, a city of refuge [v. 39]). The location of their towns seems the strangest one geographically (with the Kohathites a close second). They are, first, strewn north-to-south east of the Jordan (Reuben, Gad) and, second, concentrated in the western Jezreel Valley. This makes the Gershonites and Merarites the only Levitical clans with holdings in both Trans- and Cisjordan. All told, the narrator sums up, Israel gives the Levites forty-eight towns, each ringed by its land belt (*migraš*; vv. 41–42).[29]

Retrospective summary (vv. 43–45). The Joshua editor now steps forward personally to deliver a powerful closing comment. It marks one of the most important moments in the entire book. His simple words dramatically ring down the curtain on both the conquest of Canaan (chs. 1–12) and its settlement (chs. 13–21). He writes retrospectively, looking back on past events to underscore their significance. Quietly, he weaves together four unmistakable linguistic echoes from chapter 1 to form a thematic inclusio around chapters 1–21.

(1) He affirms that "the LORD gave Israel all the land"; that is, he kept his oath to their ancestors (v. 43a; cf. 1:6). In chapter 1, Yahweh's reference to "the land I am about to give to them" (1:2; cf. vv. 11, 15) sets in motion the dramatic events that culminate in this moment. Yahweh led the dramatic crossing of the Jordan (chs. 3–4) and the taking of the whole land (chs. 5–12). Through lots, he gave Israel its promised inheritance (chs. 13–21), so now the author can rightly claim that "the LORD gave Israel all the land."

---

28. Unable to dislodge the Canaanites in its assigned territory, Dan moved way north, conquered Leshem, and renamed the city Dan; cf. comments on 19:40–49; see also Judg. 18.

29. For an evaluation of the LXX's fascinating addition at v. 42, including the comment that Joshua took the flint circumcision knives (cf. 5:2–3) to his home in Timnath Serah, see Howard, *Joshua*, 395–97.

(2) The author affirms that Israel "took possession of it and settled there" (v. 43b). Again, he writes retrospectively; to "take possession" was what, on Joshua's orders, the officers told the people in order to motivate them in their preparations for the Jordan crossing (1:11; cf. 1:15). The entire allotment process, awarding permanent places to live both to the Levites and to the other eleven tribes, verifies that Joshua's word came true.

(3) The narrator recalls another fulfilled patriarchal promise—Yahweh's gift of "rest on every side" (v. 44a). Clearly, this "rest" that Yahweh accomplished (Heb. *nuaḥ* hi.) concerns his defeat (perhaps at times doubted by Israel!) of enemies opposing their settlement in Canaan.[30] Their defeat allows Israel now "to live in safety" (Deut. 12:10), unthreatened and unafraid. They can settle in comfortably and fully enjoy their long-awaited, safe arrival "home." The "rest" motif here also echoes and draws to a close a theme sounded in anticipation in Deuteronomy 3:20 and Joshua 1:13, 15. Preparing to cross the Jordan, Israel anticipated the "rest" soon to come (1:13, 15; cf. Deut. 3:20), a rest now realized at last (cf. 11:23). In between, Yahweh fought for Israel, as the book often avers, to bring it about (e.g., 6:2; 8:1, 7; 10:10–11, 14, 19; 11:8). In short, verse 44 joyously celebrates, "Mission accomplished!"

(4) The writer affirms that nothing Yahweh promised was left undone; it all came true (v. 45; cf. 23:14). Indeed, repetition of the word "all" punctuates verses 43–45 in a verbal drumbeat celebrating total victory: "*all* the land" (v. 43), "*all* their enemies" (v. 44), "*all* [God's promises] came true" (v. 45).[31] All credit goes to Yahweh, who swore the foundational oaths to "give" (Heb. *natan*) them land (vv. 43–44) and who "handed over" (*natan*) their enemies to them (v. 43). In Hawk's words, "the narrator powerfully attributes Israel's successes to YHWH and accentuates divine resolve in the face of national trepidation."[32]

All this both closes the heart of the book—the land distribution and settlement (chs. 13–21)—and sets the stage for what follows, namely, Joshua's dismissal of the Transjordanian tribes (22:4) and his farewell speech (ch. 23). Indeed, as his speech will reiterate, Israel has truly experienced the realization of all Yahweh's "good promises" (23:14, 15).[33]

---

30. Cf. H. D. Preuss, "נוח," *TDOT*, 9:280; cf. Deut. 12:10; 25:19; Josh. 23:1.

31. Cf. Mitchell's view (*Together in the Land*, 104) that a chiastic structure underlies vv. 43–45. As Nelson observes (*Joshua*, 243), the passage echoes earlier passages expectant of triumph (10:40–42; 11:16–20, 23; 12:7–24; 23:1) rather than those acknowledging unfinished business, especially the continuing presence of non-Israelite peoples (e.g., 13:2–6; 15:63; 16:10; 17:12–18; 23:4, 7, 12–13).

32. Hawk, *Joshua*, 225.

33. Cf. Nelson, *Joshua*, 243.

Bridging Contexts

SOMETHING DOESN'T JIBE. In moving from the ancient text to today, several leftover questions beckon for attention. The first may be the most nagging one, a question probably as troubling to some readers as it has been to many scholars. The problem is that the sweeping, upbeat claims of victory (11:16, 23; 21:43–45) seem to contradict earlier references to unfinished business—unconquered land and peoples (e.g., 13:2–6; 15:63; 16:10; 17:12–18; 23:4, 7, 12–13). As Hawk asks concerning 21:43–45, "What are we to make of commentary that seems to contradict all that we have just read?"[34] A related question is, What is the interpretive significance of comments that several tribes have failed to dislodge Canaanite inhabitants from their inheritances (i.e., 15:63; 16:10; 17:12–18; 23:7, 12–13)?

Some readers may well wonder how the book can frankly acknowledge such contrary views, yet still make coherent sense. The appeal by some scholars to the book's redactional history to explain the conflicts offers no real solution.[35] Whatever a biblical book's prehistory, readers rightly recognize the authority of its so-called "final form"—precisely the place where they confront the problem. In simple terms, they wonder which claim to believe—that God gave Israel the whole land just as he promised, or that his gift was incomplete and his promise only partially fulfilled.

An initial response to the problem is to suggest that the claims of verses 43–45 sound like hyperbole, a device invoked earlier in the book and well attested in ancient writings (cf. my comments at 11:16, 23). If so, a proper reading of them would be to take them as rhetorical flourishes made to celebrate a theme through exaggeration rather than a statement of precise historical claims. Hyperbole in such texts simply forms an expected, typical feature of their genre. In my view, this suggestion greatly relieves, if not eliminates, the sense of sharp contradiction within Joshua.

But other approaches are also possible. Older commentators like John Calvin and Keil and Delitzsch trace the conflict to failure on Israel's part.[36] They argue that God faithfully did his part (the whole-land claims) but that Israel simply reneged on its end (the still-present peoples). This is possible, but in my view, except possibly for 17:17–18, the book seems to report the latter motif matter-of-factly rather than critically. Even in his fervent farewell speech (Josh. 23), Joshua urges Israel simply to avoid intermarriage

---

34. Hawk, *Joshua*, 225; cf. Howard, *Joshua*, 400.

35. Cf. Nelson, *Joshua*, 242 ("this inconsistency is a function of the book's history of composition"). Nevertheless, he accepts the opposing views as compatible (see below).

36. Cited from Hess, *Joshua*, 284–85; cf. his excellent larger discussion (284–86).

and to minimize social contacts rather than at last to annihilate the Canaanites completely. In short, the book reports but never critiques Israel for the
continuing presence of non-Israelite peoples.

A second approach is to read the supposed conflicting statements as
compatible with other themes in the book. Nelson, for example, compares
them to the tension between the themes of "God's fidelity and human obedience (cf. 1:5 – 9)" — between what God does and what humans do. He
says that in 21:43 – 45 the author simply spotlights God's "total fidelity to
all oaths and promises ... and the provision of 'rest'" and leaves aside other
considerations.[37] This is no doubt true. Certainly, the point of verses 43 – 45
is that Yahweh has brought to pass everything the book anticipates earlier
(e.g., 1:2 – 6, 15). Also, these verses literarily anticipate things soon to follow — the dismissal of the east-bank tribes (22:4) and Joshua's sermonic line
about the "good things" Yahweh has done for Israel (23:14 – 15).[38]

Along a similar line, Mitchell observes that the portrait of other nations
in 13:1 – 21:42 differs from those in chapters 1 – 12 and after 21:42.[39] In
his view, the former chapters present the nations as isolated individuals
and groups still to be expelled, whereas the latter (chs. 1 – 12; post – 21:42)
portray them as a united force. If so, rather than contradict the reports of
continuing alien presence in Joshua 13 – 19, 21:43 – 45 affirms that Israel
had indeed experienced God's promised destruction of the nations. The
defeated enemies no longer posed the same threat as in chapters 1 – 12 (a
united army), but Israel's challenge remains to defend themselves and to rid
their land of the remaining hostile holdouts.

In my estimation, however, Polzin ultimately suggests the best solution
to the issue, one that fits well with the possible presence of hyperbole
noted above. He suggests that one read the "inflated claims" of 21:43 – 45 as
ironic, a rhetorical device to promote an ideal, not to claim what is real. Its
rhetorical purpose is not to condemn Israel's disobedience (so Calvin, Keil
and Delitzsch) but to uphold the ideal of the "legal limits" of Israel's God-
given land regardless of how real it is.[40] This is an important truth for Israel
to grasp, because through history the extent of Israel's territorial holdings
varies considerably. Thus, through a clever ironic touch, Joshua upholds
the ideal of true Israel — the full sweep of the land of promise — against
the vicissitudes facing any given generation.

---

37. Nelson, *Joshua,* 242 – 43.

38. Cf. Hawk, *Joshua,* 225 – 26, who compares the seeming contradictions to the book's
contrasting themes of "divine initiative and faithfulness" as the key to Israel's success and the
ever-present danger of "Israel's inconstancy," both prominent themes in chs. 22 – 24.

39. Mitchell, *Together in the Land,* 133 – 41.

40. Polzin, *Moses and the Deuteronomist,* 126 – 34 (quotes, 127, 128).

In conclusion, readers do well to recognize that the book intentionally portrays contrasting realities—the ideal and the real. The use of hyperbole serves to heighten the tension between them in order to speak ironically. The book does commend to readers of every generation an ideal Israel, the Israel that serves God's cosmic vision for the world. The realities of any given moment may conflict with that ideal, but they neither disprove nor discredit the ideal's ultimate success by God's power. At the same time, the book's ideal-real ironic tension puts the reader on notice that the other peoples present in Canaan potentially pose a dire threat to God's people (so chs. 22–24). Their presence must be treated seriously not casually. In sum, what seems contradictory in fact serves to convey the book's realistic worldview, an outlook that Christians share. In the face of contemporary reality, we cling in hope to the ideal that, as hymnwriter Isaac Watts wrote, "Jesus shall reign where'er the sun does his successive journeys run."

Blood revenge.[41] A second matter for follow-up concerns the background of the custom of blood revenge behind chapter 20. At first glance, readers may assume that the desire for simple revenge drives the "restorer of blood" to kill, but that is not the case. Instead, the ancient concept of tribal solidarity—a metaphysical idea that also undergirds biblical teachings on redemption—underlies it.[42] Ancient peoples thought of their clan or family collectively—that is, as an integrated, organic whole—not as simply a roster of individuals. Thus, they believed that the entire clan bore the loss suffered by an individual or family within it.

Such losses, as it were, disturbed an underlying sense of tribal wholeness or equilibrium, which required restoration for the tribe to enjoy well-being. The losses included financial setbacks (e.g., property mortgaged outside the clan, members in debt slavery) and blood lost to violence (the situation in Josh. 21). By avenging the killing of a relative, the restorer (lit., "redeemer") of blood redeems the blood of the deceased and restores the family's sense of equilibrium, wholeness, and well-being. As noted above, however, the blood revenge principle might produce an endless (and fruitless) blood feud between clans. Indeed, Lamech's boast illustrates (Gen. 4:23–24) that it might actually escalate the violence. If a family believes

---

41. Barmash (*Homicide in the Biblical World*, 23) prefers the term "blood feud" because, in her view, it conveys two essential, interrelated ideas inherent in the whole process: "It is local in nature, and it is rule-bound"; cf. her excellent discussion with ancient Near Eastern parallels (20–53).

42. Cf. Hubbard, "גאל," 1:790–91; idem, "Redemption," *NDBT*, 716–20. For biblical examples, see Lev. 25:25–34, 47–55. Sperling ("Blood, Avenger Of," 1:763) offers several illuminating ancient Near Eastern examples. The same idea underlies the punishment of Achan (see Bridging Contexts of ch. 7).

---

that the greatness of its lost kin requires more than one killing to offset its loss, it might carry out multiple killings to do so.

The provision of cities of refuge aims to restrict by law the reach of that ancient institution. It seeks to limit the practice to actual murders—premeditated acts whose just punishment may come at the hands of the restorer of blood. Theologically, such restrictions also accommodate the practice to the biblical idea that God holds absolute sway over all life, human and animal, and over the blood that embodies life.[43] By limiting the institution, God the Creator exercises his ownership over all life and his absolute right to regulate it. In my view, this marks an act of divine grace on behalf of people I would regard as the victims of circumstances beyond their control. It extends divine mercy toward people accidentally caught in unfortunate, life-threatening situations.

It may surprise some readers, but through many provisions of Old Testament law God often interposes his grace and mercy into situations of undeserved hardship. For example, the law graciously protects a daughter whose father, out of financial necessity, must sell her as a wife-slave (Ex. 21:7–11). The law protects her rights to food, clothing, and sexual relations, and to redemption under certain circumstances. It defines how her husband may or may not get rid of her should she no longer please him. The instruction may fall way short of modern sensibilities, but, read in its original context, the case of a wife-slave reveals divine grace at work.[44] In short, through such provisions God grants us a glimpse of his merciful side and models a character trait for us to emulate.

What about those Levites? A third leftover matter concerns the identity of the Levites in chapter 21. Scholars have long discussed the history and changing functions of the Levites during Israel's history, a discussion that need not detain us here.[45] But two points—one historical, the other terminological—need to be made at the outset. (1) Historically, the uniqueness of the Levites goes back to their special role in the redemption of all Israelite firstborn.[46] Yahweh owns all firstborn, including humans and animals, but in the wilderness he accepted the tribe of Levi in their place to redeem them (Num. 3:49, 51; cf. 8:15–18). This generous act of redemption forever allows all Israelite firstborn sons to remain with their families

---

43. Cf. Sperling, "Blood, Avenger Of," 1:763.

44. For this and other examples, see Hubbard, "Law Is Grace," 2–14.

45. The biblical picture suggests a prolonged, complicated process of reorganization and role changes involving the Levites but offers no explicit explanation or historical summary of the developments. For a thorough, judicious review of the scholarly discussion and biblical data, see M. D. Rehm, "Levites and Priests," *ABD*, 4:297–310.

46. Hubbard, "Redemption," 715–16.

and sets apart the tribe of Levi to serve Yahweh's wishes. That is why the descendants of Levi — the priestly Aaronides and the other groups of Levites — figure so prominently in the Bible, including Joshua 21.[47]

(2) (a) As for terminology, in the Bible the word "Levite" designates the tribe whom Yahweh redeemed, the descendants of Jacob's son, Levi, with its three clans (Gershon, Kohath, and Merari). This is the tribe from which Israel's priests came. Statements in Joshua that the "Levites" received no inheritance (14:3, 4; 18:7) invoke the tribal meaning noted above. "Levites" (members of the tribe of Levi) petition and receive towns and pasturelands throughout Israel (Josh. 21), their base of financial support in lieu of land inheritances (13:14, 33; 14:3–4; 18:7; ch. 21; cf. 1 Chron. 6; Deut. 18:1–5).

(b) "Levite" also denotes a person who, though still a priest, may serve a variety of functions, some temple-related and some not. In Jerusalem, the "Levites" made up three classes of temple personnel, each of whom served what seemed to be a long-established, distinct organizational function. Descended from Levi's firstborn son, the Gershonites comprised the altar priests, whereas the (second-born) Kohathites served as temple singers. The third group, the gatekeepers, descended both from Korah, son of Kohath's second son, Izhar (1 Chron. 9:19) and from Merari (9:14; 26:19). They monitored the sacred entrances and managed the temple's side chambers. They also administered its treasuries, collected yearly taxes, assessed special fees, and dispersed funds per the state's wishes (2 Chron. 24:6; 34:9–10). They assisted the sons of Aaron with items required for worship — furniture, utensils, and consumables like flour, wine, oil, incense, and spices (1 Chron. 9:26–32; 23:24–29). The singers provided vocal and instrumental accompaniment to services of sacrifice (1 Chron. 23:30–31; 2 Chron. 29:27–28).[48] Levites also served appointments as officers and judges, duties they carried out on visits throughout the land (1 Chron. 23:4; 26:29; 2 Chron. 19:8).

But what about the "Levites" who settled in the towns throughout Israel to which Joshua 21 assigns them? Since they had neither ark to carry nor temple tasks to tend, why did God disperse them around Israel? The Bible provides no systematic summary of their duties, but a mosaic of texts sketches a fairly clear picture of their work. Presumably, they performed

---

47. Cf. L. S. Fried, "Levites," *EDB*, 803–4, including in-depth treatment of the Levites in exilic and postexilic books (Ezekiel, Ezra and Nehemiah, and 1 and 2 Chronicles). For a nuanced discussion of the matter in light of redactional activity within Ezekiel, see L. C. Allen, *Ezekiel* 20–48 (WBC 29; Dallas: Word, 1990), 253–56.

48. The temple singers may have also had the task of interpreting, instructing, and copying the law itself. The reason is that worship songs may have incorporated the recitation of the law, thus necessitating the singers' intimate familiarity with it.

some of the same functions as their counterparts in Jerusalem. As "officials," some probably had charge of conscripting soldiers and laborers for royal missions as well as the collection of taxes and tithes (1 Chron. 26:23–30; cf. 2 Chron. 24:1–11; Neh. 10:37). As "judges," some probably rendered legal decisions, a duty consistent with their role as legal "scribes" in Jerusalem (2 Chron. 19:4–11; 34:13; 35:3; cf. Deut. 17:8–13).

Further, the Levites applied their knowledge of the Instruction of Moses by teaching it to Israelites in their local towns (1 Chron. 13:2; 2 Chron. 11:13; 35:3; Mal. 2:6–9; cf. 2 Chron. 17:9). They performed the same instructional function as they did on the dramatic day when Ezra read the "Book of the Law [Instruction] of God" to the returned exiles in Jerusalem (Neh. 8). During Ezra's dramatic reading, the Levites fanned out through the crowd to interpret what it meant — that is, to make sure that the people fully understood it (Neh. 8:8).

In short, with their towns as home bases, the Levites served as Yahweh's local representatives throughout the land. In Howard's words, "the Levites were to be 'salt and light' among their fellow Israelites, scattered as they were throughout the tribes."[49] As it were, they gave the invisible Yahweh a local incarnational presence — a flesh-and-blood person with whom to deal — in the towns and villages where people lived. As part of the tribe set aside for his service, they symbolically constituted the people closest to him, the ones who presumably knew him best, the ones who understood his mysterious ways, the ones to consult with in order to make wise decisions. Through their instruction, Yahweh addressed local Israelites in his own words, challenging and calming them in his own voice.

The Levites' judicial decisions maintained the social harmony — the *šalom* — of the local community so it might function amicably, if not actually flourish. Their more formal religious functions also mediated between God and his people, maintaining the precious, long-standing covenant connection between them. Their local presence among the tribes could serve to deter the construction of non-Yahwistic shrines or the development of syncretistic beliefs. Further, their civic duties linked local communities both with neighboring ones and with Israel's political and religious nerve center, Jerusalem. Finally, headquartered at Jerusalem and scattered throughout the land, the Levites symbolized the unity of Israel under Yahweh's lordship.[50] In my view, they anticipate something of the role that we as God's dispersed people may play in our own cities and towns.

---

49. Howard, *Joshua*, 387.

50. Cf. Hess, *Joshua*, 237 ("By scattering throughout the land, they would also represent the unity of the people who worshipped the God of Israel").

A final word about "rest." The Old Testament understands "rest" as the gracious gift of God to his people.[51] Against the background of a long journey and intense warfare (so ch. 21), it connotes a sense of relief from frightening threats, of safe, happy arrival, of realizing long-held dreams, of coming into unexpected wealth, of finally being "home." That is what Yahweh's faithfulness in settling Israel in its Promised Land means to Israel. But, rather than inactivity, "rest" also opens the door to unhindered creative activity—to making towns livable, to earning a livelihood, to raising a family, to savoring the good life.

A part of Israel's "rest" is its duty properly to maintain its relationship with the God of Israel. They connect to him at his own "resting place," the place where he himself settled in Canaan—the temple in Jerusalem (2 Sam. 7:1, 11; 1 Kings 5:3–5; 8:56; Ps. 132:14; 2 Chron. 6:41). Solomon's prayer of dedication (1 Kings 8) highlights the significance of Yahweh's "resting place" for each Israelite. To be near the temple, Yahweh's home, offers Israelites the spot of maximum intimacy with him. His eyes perpetually keep it in view, so it marks the one place on earth where one may surface on God's radar screen (8:29). Wherever an Israelite might be, to "pray toward this place" and confess sin would always secure a hearing and forgiveness (8:30). This is true after national defeats (8:33–34), droughts (8:35–36), and famines (8:37–39).

At the same time, Psalm 95 warns Israel not to squander their promised "rest." It recalls a famous episode when newly freed Israel, en route to Mount Sinai, loudly griped at Yahweh for providing no water (Ex. 17:1–7). Their thirst, they complained, proved Yahweh's absence from them. But God surprised them, producing water from an invisible source, from behind a desert rock. Over the centuries, Israel remembered the incident as a paradigm of faithlessness (see Deut. 6:16; 9:22; 33:8; Ps. 95:8). To hear the names of the site—Meribah ("quarreling") and Massah ("testing"; Ex. 17:7; Ps. 95:8)—evoked shame and sadness. The names recall the place where their ancestors, shamefully shortsighted and self-centered, made God angry, angry enough to decree, "They shall never enter my rest" (Ps. 95:11). The psalmist recalls the event to show how to avoid losing "my rest," the rest whose only source is Yahweh himself: "Today, if you hear his voice, do not harden your hearts" as Israel did that day (95:7b–8). To enjoy and keep the "rest" requires a soft heart—an eager, responsive, willingness to obey the Lord's voice whenever he calls.

---

51. Cf. J. C. Laansma, "Rest," NDBT, 729–30.

THE ISRAELITE INSTITUTIONS OF cities of refuge and Levitical towns seem a million miles from us. Today court-issued restraining orders and protective police custody eliminate the need for anyone in danger to flee to another town for safety. And most towns have more than one church where—or, so it seems—good teaching goes on all the time. What meaning, then, might Joshua 20–21 have for Christians living today?

In reply, three preliminary points merit mention. (1) Remember that both Israelite institutions are practices of the whole community, not just isolated individuals. Granted, an individual killer must hurry to the nearest official city of refuge to secure safety, and that city must agree to play its role. But the system works only because Israelite society as a whole embraces it.

(2) Understand that the foundations on which these institutions rest are several fundamental Israelite values, values not subject to question or debate. The reason such debate is out of bounds is, first, that Israelites accept those values as "givens," and, second, that those values are anchored in the very nature of God himself. Put differently, both practices put on public display the character of God. We can view them as ancient billboards advertising on God's behalf. They broadcast the character of the Israelite community—how Yahweh has shaped them—so the institutions mirror (or *should* mirror) his character.

(3) Finally, since the two institutions of cities of refuge and Levitical towns concern the whole community, their meaning today also will concern the whole Christian community, the church. Now, granted, that meaning directly relates to the attitudes and conduct of individual church members, but the proper application of a text about community must address the church, God's community of people today. As we will see, the key themes from Joshua 20–21 with contemporary meaning are the idea of refuge, representation, and rest.

The church: mercy and generosity. Two values that underlie both the cities of refuge and the Levitical towns are mercy and generosity. These also comprise two divine traits that God desires to cultivate in his people. To appreciate *mercy*, imagine yourself as the Israelite whose axhead had escaped its handle in mid-swing and killed his friend (Deut. 19:5). Instantly, you have become a killer—your hands tainted with blood, your soul black with guilt, your tidy life suddenly in tatters. The terrible damage has been done, and you face its terrible consequences. You stare at your bleeding, lifeless neighbor, and swirling panic yanks you back and forth. Your own grief pushes you toward him as if a simple hug will bring him back to life, but simultaneously a terrible dread pushes you to make a quick getaway. Instead, you calmly lift your friend over your shoulders and slowly walk toward town.

As you walk, you accept that there is no use in explaining, "It was an accident! I'm so, so sorry! I checked the tightness of the axhead but it just flew off as I chopped." You imagine how the news will devastate the dead man's family. You picture yourself facing his widow and children, your tearful apology and plea for forgiveness drowned out by the surging waves of their grief. You picture a shrouded body clutched by wailing women whose sorrow drives an erratic rocking motion. You imagine the mystical sense of loss—the ugly tear in the family psyche—and the quiet outrage and urge for justice building among the man's male relatives. You can expect revenge—family duty demands it. You curse God for letting it happen, but no reply comes. Inside boils a sinister stew of conflicting emotions—shame, guilt, self-doubt, dread, and above all, a desire to flee.

It is the kind of feeling that grips us when we, to use a current phrase, "screw up" badly in a way that affects someone else. I still remember the feelings that followed one of my screw-ups when I was only fifteen. My family was attending a denominational convention and staying in our travel trailer at a trailer park. That morning, Dad had left for the meetings and the rest of us were to do some sightseeing before meeting him that afternoon. I was a typical, hormone-driven male teenager, always itching to drive our pink '65 Rambler though I had no license to do so. In recent years Dad had ignored legal niceties and given my hormones a small outlet, at first, letting me start the car and rev it up in the driveway, then later letting me back it out and park it by the curb.[52]

So, on that bright summer morning in Colorado, I grabbed Mom's keys and executed my usual start-and-back-out routine. I turned the wheel to the right, looked over my right shoulder for oncoming vehicles, and briskly backed into the street. Wham! Ignoring the front end's swing to the left, I slammed into the front tongue of the mobile home next door. The collision left an ugly gash in the Rambler's left front fender and unnerved the neighbor inside. I dreaded having to tell my Dad, but to my surprise he showed me mercy. He even recalled the time in his youth when he had also scratched his father's car. Later, he paid the neighbor $75 to fix the damages I had done.

---

52. A true confession: One night during this informal training period I'd "started the car" in the church parking lot after a Sunday evening service. To my surprise, Dad got in the passenger's seat and told me to drive home, which I did—very carefully. I was only fourteen.

The Old Testament cities of refuge offered mercy for unfortunate Israelites. In my view, one aspect of their contemporary meaning is to challenge churches today to be "churches of refuge." By that I mean that they should be places to which people may flee from their misfortunes or screw-ups to find *mercy*. Mercy means, among other things, "a refraining from harming or punishing offenders, enemies, persons in one's power, etc.; kindness in excess of what may be expected or demanded by fairness."[53]

The word describes both what we do *not* do (i.e., get back at those who have wronged us or abuse those under our control) and what we *do* (show an unexpected level of kindness). Unfortunately, the world we live in too often runs short of mercy. It is too willing to seek revenge, too eager to lower the boom, too ready to get its pound of flesh. Victims of bossiness by others relish the chance to throw their own weight around when their underlings fail. The world thrives on competition between people, whether in the workplace or the playing field. In such a "game," someone's screw-up cedes a competitive edge to others eager to have it as they claw their way up the ladder of success. It is a game of "the survival of the fittest"—or the slyest, or the cleverest, or the luckiest, or the most conniving. People who fail often can expect to receive no mercy, not even from their family. Instead, the one foul-up is held against them and thrown in their face at every future misstep. Without mercy, the person is forever condemned to drag around the shame of that one mistake as a prisoner does a ball and chain.

What traits typify a "church of refuge"? (1) Its primary concern is with today and tomorrow, not yesterday. When people approach its front door, they sense they are entering a nonthreatening, safe place. They sense a place where their past will never get in the way of relationships or come back to haunt them. It is as if there is a sign posted outside saying, "Your past—good or bad—doesn't matter here. Welcome!" Once inside, the prime concern is, "How are you—the *real* you—doing today? What are your hopes and dreams—and how can we help?" Whether talk of the past is important is left up to the individual. He or she is free to bring it up if doing so meets a need.

(2) A safe church keeps its rules on file for emergencies rather than impose them every time they apply. It is a place where, in the words of James 2:13, "Mercy triumphs over judgment!" Yes, churches have rules—biblical standards of conduct and expectations—but refuge churches apply them only when necesary, and then gently and sorrowfully. They let people be who they are—warts and all!—and leave the transformation business to God. He is a lot better at it than they are, anyway.

---

53. *Webster's New World Dictionary*, 3rd college edition (New York: Simon & Shuster, 1991), 849.

(3) A safe church grows members well aware of their own warts. Its rank structure is—well, it has none. People may serve different organizational functions within it, but they enjoy the same status: They are all forgiven sinners, nothing more, nothing less.

(4) Finally, a safe church gives people the God-treatment. It treats people the same way God has treated them—with mercy and compassion. It works hard to live out Jesus' teaching that among his people the "greatest" is the "slave" who serves everyone else first (Matt. 20:26; Mark 10:4; Luke 22:26).

But our churches should also be known for their *generosity*. Their reputation should be as places that give failure-prone people both breaks (mercy) and tangible helps (generosity). Here the interpretive key comes in two especially timely uses of the word "to give" (*natan*) in Joshua 20–21. In Joshua 20:2, Yahweh orders Joshua to tell the Israelites "to designate the cities of refuge" (NIV; cf. v. 8). Actually, instead of the infinitive (NIV), the Hebrew literally quotes what Joshua is to say: "Give for yourselves [*tenu lakem*] the cities of refuge" (i.e., a plural imperative). In short, the Israelites are to "give" the cities "to themselves"—as it were, as a kind of present.

Similarly, in 21:2 the Levites remind Joshua that Yahweh had commanded Moses (lit.) "to give to us [*natan lanu*] towns to live in." They request the gift that Yahweh had long ago provided them, and the Israelites "give" (*natan*) it "out of their own inheritance" (v. 3; cf. vv. 8, 9, 11, 12, 13, 21). Now, understand that each gift carries a price tag. To serve as a city of refuge commits a town to certain responsibilities. It has to maintain its outer walls and gates in secure condition. Its leaders must be ready to hold trials on short notice and must make sure they know what they are doing. Its citizens have to set aside lodging for asylum-seekers, to integrate them into town life, and not to treat them as intruders or suspects. In short, it commits a town to sacrifice its own wishes in order to serve the common good.

To serve as a city of refuge demands that towns make available the life-sparing gift of refuge to people who need it, including their own citizens who may be involved in a killing. Similarly, Israelites who give up their towns to the Levites pay an even higher price. They have to surrender town ownership to the Levites. They also either have to move over—to leave space for their new Levite neighbors—or to move on—to find another place to live. Again, they have to sacrifice their own preferences—remember, Caleb gave up Hebron!—to serve Israel's common good. In short, they "give" so Israel might "receive" the benefits of refuge and local access to Levitical expertise. But all that Israel had, it had received from Yahweh's generosity. So the demands for towns of refuge and towns for Levites both provide Israel an opportunity to tell him, "Thanks for all you've done."

Recall one of Jesus' final instructions as he sent his disciples out on their first solo ministry tours: "Freely [i.e., without cost] you have received, freely give" (Matt. 10:8). Jesus tells his followers to follow God's example with what they have: "You've received everything free of charge, so give it away free of charge." That they have received everything they have from God implies that it does not really belong to them; they are merely its managers on God's behalf. It also means that the world, not they, is its intended final destination; they are simply the means to get it there.

In today's world so bent on accumulating more and keeping what it gets, Jesus charges his church with the same generosity it has received from God. He asks the church, his family, to join the family business, Giveaway, Inc., Father and Son, Proprietors. My observation is that church budgets typically tend to serve internal needs for the most part — staff salaries, building upkeep, Sunday school supplies, youth group activities, and the like. Jesus' call, however, asks churches to budget significantly for external needs — for mission to the world around it. John 3:16 says that "God so loved the world" — not just the church — "that he gave his one and only Son" to save it. That model of generosity calls for generous churches, ones ready to pay any price and bear any burden to reach the world.

A letter in the recent novel *Gilead*, by Marilynne Robinson, illustrates this priority. In it, a Methodist minister, retired after decades of ministry in small, rural Midwestern towns, writes to his son in the late 1940s. The letter recounts the lives of his father and grandfather (i.e., the son's grand- and great-grandfather). In one striking paragraph the letter writer recalls a kind of "holy poverty" that typified his grandfather:

> My grandfather never kept anything that was worth giving away, or let us keep it, either, so my mother said. He would take the laundry right off the line. She said he was worse than any thief, worse than a house fire. She said she could probably go to any town in the Middle West and see some pair of pants she'd patched walking by in the street. I believe he was a saint of some kind. When someone remarked in his hearing that he had lost an eye in the Civil War, he said, "I prefer to remember that I have kept one." My mother said it was good to know there was anything he could keep....
>
> When he left us, we all felt his absence bitterly. But he did make things difficult. It was an innocence in him. He lacked patience for anything but the plainest interpretation of the starkest commandments, "To him who asks, give," in particular.[54]

---

54. M. Robinson, *Gilead* (New York: Farrar, Straus and Giroux, 2004), 31. I am grateful to my friend and colleague the Rev. Helen Cepero for sharing this book with me.

The church: a safe place. The Old Testament cities of refuge offer places where someone whose negligence or bad luck had ended a life could find safety. No doubt, to arrive there required a nerve-wracking, draining, and at times even harrowing ordeal. The fear of being found by the restorer of blood would be unrelenting. Imagine making a journey on high alert round-the-clock, with ceaseless surveillance in all directions, to spot and elude the pursuer. Imagine days without sleep, first, because to stop would let the pursuer gain ground, and, second, because sleep would be too fitful to be truly restful.

Picture the joy of spotting the city of refuge on the horizon for the first time, the sheer relief of finally reaching its gates, and the physical and emotional collapse that would follow admission. Feel your gratitude for those huge city walls, for the simple joy of being around people rather than alone, for tokens of hospitality received, for the new friendships made. Consider the restless wait for your trial to begin and conclude — and the thrill of a favorable verdict. Imagine the ecstasy of finally feeling "safe." This is the experience of those who found refuge in the cities of refuge.

Joshua 20 displays the heart of a kind and merciful God who desires to provide safe places for disenfranchised people. He has designed the church to provide such a *safe place*. By that I mean, they should be places where people — the weary and worn, the bruised and broken, the unlovely and unloved — can find refuge. A refuge is a place of protection, a place that keeps out threats, a place where enemies cannot intrude, a place where people feel secure. That security frees them to relax worry-free, to drop their guard, to be at ease, even to feel at home. It also frees them to open up and reach out for relationships with others who have likewise found refuge.

Phrases from the theme song of the classic television show *Cheers* capture the essence of a safe church. It offers people exhausted from navigating today's world a "break from all [their] worries," somewhere to go to "get away." It is also a place where "everybody knows your name" — not your title, your position, your resumé, or your past. It marks a place where friends John, Joan, and Justin meet to enjoy being together. It is a place where strangers stop being strangers — where the friendly, trusting exchange of names with other strangers forges personal connections. It is a place where people are "always glad you came" — where everybody is genuinely glad to see you. It is an especially encouraging place because honest conversations happen. They reveal that "our troubles are all the same," so no one need feel alone, ashamed, or fatally singled out for doom.

A church that is a safe place is a *welcoming place*. Joshua 20 says that an arriving refugee is not left to sleep in the street but is provided a place to live (and presumably access to food, too). He is welcomed, given a "place" in the society, and incorporated in the community. The ill-fated journey of the Levite and his concubine in Judges 19 gives us a glimpse of what the welcoming I have in mind looks like. Picture them as someone who shows up unannounced at your church some Sunday morning. The couple and their servant start out in Bethlehem and head north toward their home in the hill country of Ephraim. (Theirs is a long journey that requires stops for rest en route.) As night begins to fall, they bypass an overnight in Jebus (Jerusalem) — a non-Israelite city — and press on to lodge with fellow Israelites at Gibeah a few miles north. (They are seeking other people like them, people with whom they can connect.) Ironically, "their own kind" gives the weary travelers the cold shoulder. They sit down in the town square in plain view, but no one invites them home for a meal and a night's rest. (Alas, I recall once visiting a church in which I entered, worshiped, and exited without one person speaking to me or even shaking my hand. I fear that this happens all too often, even when visitors pay a church return visits.)

But an Ephraimite man living in Benjamite Gibeah notices that they are strangers and talks with them. (Visitors often link up with other newcomers because that is easier than breaking into existing groups. A safe church plans to make that happen rather than leave it totally to chance.) The strangers introduce themselves and report that they have everything they need. (Visitors enjoy being friendly but, as guests, do not yet feel free to share the depths of their needs.) The man, however, welcomes them into his home, meets their needs, and feeds them. They spend an enjoyable evening together, perhaps reminiscing about Ephraim, but at least truly connecting. (May God grant every church a few such genuinely hospitable people!) Alas, a horrible, violent series of tragic and shameless events ensues — they earn an "X" rating from me — that end in tragedy for the visitors and shame for Gibeah. (As outsiders, newcomers may suddenly find themselves drawn into ongoing internal conflicts, even enlisted to support one side.)

Nevertheless, Judges 19 suggests several traits of the welcoming church. Such a church understands that visitors are people on a long, demanding journey — sometimes fleeing dangers and past hurts. The journey is their life, and it requires frequent rest stops and the companionship of other travelers to get through it. That is why they show up at church: They are looking for renewal and friendship for the trip. They want genuine hospitality — a warm welcome, sincere interest in who they are, and some new connections with which, in time, to do in-depth sharing. The unwelcoming church will ignore them, retreat behind closed doors, treat them as outsiders (read: "intruders"!), or abuse them by enlisting their support in internal squabbles. It will not offer them refuge; it will leave them to the thugs and avengers prowling the world outside. It will break the heart of God.

The church: scattered on purpose. Thus far, my discussion has been about the refuge needy people should find in the church. It concerns what some theologians call God's "gathered people"—the body of Christ assembled for worship. Now, however, the institution of Levitical cities (ch. 21) illumines our understanding about God's "scattered people"—the body of Christ spread throughout the community throughout the week.

To begin, let me pose these questions: Why is it that Christians do not live together in the same neighborhood or apartment building? Why is it that, when someone decides to follow Christ, they still live in the same place and hold the same job? My answer is that God wants them to be Levites in their local community. God wanted the Levites living all over the land rather than in Jerusalem because he had special things for them to do for the scattered Israelites. Similarly, God wants Christians spread around because he has important things for them to do. As Levites in their neighborhoods, they serve God by serving their local communities on his behalf. What do they bring there?

(1) They know God personally. They are, in fact, adopted members of God's own family, with all the requisite rights and privileges. They have an "in" with him—high-level, heavenly connections, indeed! Not everyone would dare call him "Daddy" (see Rom. 8:15; Gal. 4:6; cf. Mark 14:36), but they do regularly, and without embarrassment. As family, they enjoy ongoing conversation with him on a daily basis. He is their Father, after all, so they tell him what is going on in their lives: their day-to-day activities, great things they did, weighty things on their minds, heavy burdens on their hearts, decisions about which they need his advice, problems with which they need his help.

But the conversation is truly two-way, so they listen as he speaks to them, too. Sometimes, he speaks to them in writing—what the whole family calls "his Word." Other times, they hear his voice speaking inside them—what the family calls "his Spirit." Unfortunately, sometimes they get too busy or preoccupied to read his writing or to hear his voice in the moment. But they maintain a conversation nonetheless.

I hasten to underscore how unusual this is. Most people have some ideas about God, but not everyone would claim to know him personally. Many people report that they talk to God and hope he hears them, but they are not always sure. Certainly, they are curious about him—and not a little frightened, I might add. Their problem is how to get to know him better. That is one reason why God has scattered us, his Levites, around. He wants us available so that, when he comes up in conversation, we can speak about him from personal experience. Also, the Levites' family connection with God also means that they talk about him as they would any other family member. They are part of his family, after all, and that is what kids often do when they are around other people: They talk about their Daddy. Those comments also help people to come to know God personally. As we know from life in general, to get things done it never hurts to know someone who knows someone.

(2) Christian Levites bring knowledge about God to their neighborhoods. When my wife and I travel to a new place, one of the first places we visit is the Visitor Information Center. Most towns that attract regular visitors have them, and they offer crucial information—like where the nearest restrooms are! One time we wanted to rent bicycles for an afternoon, and the local office told us where to do so. Another time, we wanted to attend a local theater performance, and they helped us get tickets.

Now, Levites today are God's Visitor Information Center. There are a lot of rumors and opinions floating around about God, but not much knowledge about what he thinks. That is the information gap the Levites help to fill. Through "his Word," they have access to the best information. Whether sharing informally or teaching formally, today's Levites are the people from whom people outside the family can get information about the Father and his Son, Jesus. They are the people to consult with about God and to get answers to questions about him. Now, not every Levite feels they know enough to do so effectively. Few Levites can answer every question. But however long someone may have been a Christian Levite, he or she at least knows a little more than the questioner. And they have access to "his Word," too.

(3) Finally, they know how to contact God on behalf of others. The Levites were experts in Israel's religious practices—its prayers, hymns, sacrifices, and holy days. The same is true of Christian Levites. Earlier in this book I mentioned my past service as a Navy chaplain. Wherever I served, at the end of a conversation in which I sensed it appropriate, I would ask the person if they wanted me to pray for them. I still follow that practice, and no one has ever turned me down. Whatever their religious connection (or lack of it), people highly value prayer. They understand it as a way to get in touch with God, they respect someone who practices it, and they are grateful to be prayed for.

One thing a Levite can do for a neighborhood is to be available to pray for others or, at least, to assure them of ongoing prayers. In my view, an openness to pray is an attractive, inoffensive way to bring Jesus into the lives of neighborhood people. It is a simple but tangible way to be "salt and light" — to testify that Jesus is alive and at work right now. In my view, that is another reason why God scatters his people throughout communities. He wants people available to pray to the Father on behalf of needy people outside the family.

It is at this point, however, that I sense that the church itself may pose a threat to the work of the Levites. In a recent book, church leader Reggie McNeal insightfully argues that recent technological and cultural changes have rendered "church culture" (the way most churches operate) less relevant to the culture at large than it was a generation ago.[55] In church culture, for example, an outreach strategy typically asks, "How do we get people to come to our church?" But, according to McNeal, that approach simply no longer works because church culture no longer interests nonchurch people.

Part of the problem, says McNeal, is that most evangelical churches resemble exclusive clubs. They sponsor all kinds of age- and interest-group activities for members (notice that pregnant word!), and their leaders are preoccupied with keeping the club going efficiently. Club dues (read: "offerings") mainly go to support club ventures rather than, say, endeavors in the larger community. There is a clubby reluctance to give God's money away to people outside the church. Creative attempts to increase club membership most often involve some new club activity or event to draw outsiders into the church building. Instead, McNeal proposes that today churches must find ways to go out to where the people are: "Churches that understand the realities of the present future are shifting the target of ministry efforts from church activity to community transformation."[56]

To earn a hearing for the gospel, he suggests, churches need to make it a priority to invest their resources in ways that benefit the community at large, not just the church itself. In Jesus' words, their identity is to "serve" rather than to "be served" (Matt. 20:28; Mark 10:45). Rather than being huddled comfortably in cozy clubs, churches need to be "out there" where people are: "We need a church in every mall, every Wal-Mart supercenter, every Barnes and Noble."[57] According to McNeal, practical service in making the community a better place for everyone — that is, community transformation — must be the church's first priority. After all, ultimately God wants communities to thrive and to be places where his blessings flourish for everyone's benefit.

---

55. R. McNeal, *The Present Future: Six Tough Questions for the Church* (San Francisco: Jossey-Bass, 2003).

56. Ibid., 26.

57. Ibid., 35.

And when people ask why Christians are doing this—the change will truly get the culture's attention!—McNeal suggests the answer that Pastor Cho in South Korea teaches his people to give: "I am a disciple of Jesus. I am serving him by serving you, because that's what he came to do."[58] Now, McNeal's criticism of church culture is painful to hear and his vision for the church is indeed radical. But in my view, his conviction that evangelical churches need to reorient themselves from inward to outward is correct. In my terms, churches need to act more like the Levites!

Centennial, a novel by James Michener, has an intriguing scene set in Mexico during the early days of the Mexican revolution. Its purpose is to explain the dire circumstances that drove some Mexicans to immigrate to Colorado to find work. Poverty in Mexico, the novel recounts, left the poor no choice but to work in the silver mines owned by the ruthless, wealthy General Terrazas. In the scene in question, the local parish priest, Father Grávez, was pressuring a young man with the derogatory name "Capitan" Frijoles ("Beans") not to agitate for better working conditions. The priest told him:

> "God gives each of us our work to do, Capitan, and your work is to bring silver out of the earth. God watches what you do. He knows your excellence and one day He will reward you. Also, General Terrazas needs the silver for the good works he does in Chihuahua."

Michener's narrative continues:

> This line of reasoning impressed Frijoles at the moment, but later when he tried to recall one good thing General Terrazas had ever done for the people of Chihuahua, he could think of nothing. The general spent his money on big houses and bigger ranches and automobiles for his many children and trips to Europe and the entertainment of European businessmen and the paying of bribes to politicians in Mexico City. "Perhaps," Frijoles told his fellow workers, "when he's finished with all that, one of these days he'll get around to us." The miners suspected, from past experience, that this might take a long time.[59]

Similarly, the world is waiting for the church to abandon its holy huddle as a club, spending its resources on its own agendas, and to "get around to us." It needs to recover its identity and mission as God's "scattered (not huddled) people." As Christians, we need to see ourselves not as members

---

58. Ibid., 38.
59. J. Michener, *Centennial* (New York: Fawcett Crest, 1974), 823–24.

of a religious club but as Levites, people dispersed to serve sacrificially and lovingly wherever God places us. Our motto is: "I am a Levite whom Jesus has placed in my neighborhood. I serve my Lord by serving my community in his name. That is what he has commanded me to do." Such obedient service will entitle us to the "Sabbath rest" for our labors when Jesus returns (Heb. 4:9, 11).

Joshua 22:1–34

❦

THEN JOSHUA SUMMONED the Reubenites, the Gadites and the half-tribe of Manasseh ²and said to them, "You have done all that Moses the servant of the LORD commanded, and you have obeyed me in everything I commanded. ³For a long time now—to this very day—you have not deserted your brothers but have carried out the mission the LORD your God gave you. ⁴Now that the LORD your God has given your brothers rest as he promised, return to your homes in the land that Moses the servant of the LORD gave you on the other side of the Jordan. ⁵But be very careful to keep the commandment and the law that Moses the servant of the LORD gave you: to love the LORD your God, to walk in all his ways, to obey his commands, to hold fast to him and to serve him with all your heart and all your soul."

⁶Then Joshua blessed them and sent them away, and they went to their homes. ⁷(To the half-tribe of Manasseh Moses had given land in Bashan, and to the other half of the tribe Joshua gave land on the west side of the Jordan with their brothers.) When Joshua sent them home, he blessed them, ⁸saying, "Return to your homes with your great wealth—with large herds of livestock, with silver, gold, bronze and iron, and a great quantity of clothing—and divide with your brothers the plunder from your enemies."

⁹So the Reubenites, the Gadites and the half-tribe of Manasseh left the Israelites at Shiloh in Canaan to return to Gilead, their own land, which they had acquired in accordance with the command of the LORD through Moses.

¹⁰When they came to Geliloth near the Jordan in the land of Canaan, the Reubenites, the Gadites and the half-tribe of Manasseh built an imposing altar there by the Jordan. ¹¹And when the Israelites heard that they had built the altar on the border of Canaan at Geliloth near the Jordan on the Israelite side, ¹²the whole assembly of Israel gathered at Shiloh to go to war against them.

¹³So the Israelites sent Phinehas son of Eleazar, the priest, to the land of Gilead—to Reuben, Gad and the half-tribe of Manasseh. ¹⁴With him they sent ten of the chief men, one for

each of the tribes of Israel, each the head of a family division among the Israelite clans.

¹⁵When they went to Gilead—to Reuben, Gad and the half-tribe of Manasseh—they said to them: ¹⁶"The whole assembly of the LORD says: 'How could you break faith with the God of Israel like this? How could you turn away from the LORD and build yourselves an altar in rebellion against him now? ¹⁷Was not the sin of Peor enough for us? Up to this very day we have not cleansed ourselves from that sin, even though a plague fell on the community of the LORD! ¹⁸And are you now turning away from the LORD?

"'If you rebel against the LORD today, tomorrow he will be angry with the whole community of Israel. ¹⁹If the land you possess is defiled, come over to the LORD's land, where the LORD's tabernacle stands, and share the land with us. But do not rebel against the LORD or against us by building an altar for yourselves, other than the altar of the LORD our God. ²⁰When Achan son of Zerah acted unfaithfully regarding the devoted things, did not wrath come upon the whole community of Israel? He was not the only one who died for his sin.'"

²¹Then Reuben, Gad and the half-tribe of Manasseh replied to the heads of the clans of Israel: ²²"The Mighty One, God, the LORD! The Mighty One, God, the LORD! He knows! And let Israel know! If this has been in rebellion or disobedience to the LORD, do not spare us this day. ²³If we have built our own altar to turn away from the LORD and to offer burnt offerings and grain offerings, or to sacrifice fellowship offerings on it, may the LORD himself call us to account.

²⁴"No! We did it for fear that some day your descendants might say to ours, 'What do you have to do with the LORD, the God of Israel? ²⁵The LORD has made the Jordan a boundary between us and you—you Reubenites and Gadites! You have no share in the LORD.' So your descendants might cause ours to stop fearing the LORD.

²⁶"That is why we said, 'Let us get ready and build an altar—but not for burnt offerings or sacrifices.' ²⁷On the contrary, it is to be a witness between us and you and the generations that follow, that we will worship the LORD at his sanctuary with our burnt offerings, sacrifices and fellowship offerings. Then in the future your descendants will not be able to say to ours, 'You have no share in the LORD.'

²⁸"And we said, 'If they ever say this to us, or to our descendants, we will answer: Look at the replica of the LORD's altar, which our fathers built, not for burnt offerings and sacrifices, but as a witness between us and you.'

²⁹"Far be it from us to rebel against the LORD and turn away from him today by building an altar for burnt offerings, grain offerings and sacrifices, other than the altar of the LORD our God that stands before his tabernacle."

³⁰When Phinehas the priest and the leaders of the community—the heads of the clans of the Israelites—heard what Reuben, Gad and Manasseh had to say, they were pleased. ³¹And Phinehas son of Eleazar, the priest, said to Reuben, Gad and Manasseh, "Today we know that the LORD is with us, because you have not acted unfaithfully toward the LORD in this matter. Now you have rescued the Israelites from the LORD's hand."

³²Then Phinehas son of Eleazar, the priest, and the leaders returned to Canaan from their meeting with the Reubenites and Gadites in Gilead and reported to the Israelites. ³³They were glad to hear the report and praised God. And they talked no more about going to war against them to devastate the country where the Reubenites and the Gadites lived.

³⁴And the Reubenites and the Gadites gave the altar this name: A Witness Between Us that the LORD is God.

THE BOOK OF JOSHUA now leads the reader into the post-settlement period (chs. 22–24). Reports of Joshua's farewell speech (ch. 23), the covenant renewal ceremony (24:1–28), and three burial notices (24:29–33) conclude the book. But this period also begins with a long, speech-filled narrative about a controversy between the east- and west-bank tribes (ch. 22).[1] Indeed, chapter 22 surfaces something of the subtle, centrifugal force of geography that threatens to undermine the unity of Greater Israel. The issue of whether or not tribes living east of the Jordan enjoy full inclusion in Israel—whether their fears of exclusion are real—drives the plot. Further, memories of past apostasy still haunt

---

1. Parts of this chapter derive from my Kairos Lecture, "Suspicious Stones That Divide," given at First Evangelical Covenant Church, Oakland, California. It is a pleasure to express my gratitude to the church and its pastoral staff for the warm welcome and wonderful hospitality accorded me on that occasion.

Israel and sow suspicions in a later generation (vv. 20b, 31; cf. Num. 25; Josh. 7). As with the land distribution, a leading priestly figure—in this case, the crusading Phinehas, son of Eleazar (cf. Num. 25:7–13)—figures prominently. This may point to a priestly author or source for the chapter, but that is not certain.[2]

Structurally, the text features three main scenes: at Shiloh, Joshua's dismissal of the Transjordanian tribes to their inheritances (vv. 1–8); the discovery and investigation (in Transjordan) of their alleged scandalous action (vv. 9–31); and at Shiloh, the report of the investigation team (vv. 32–34). Literarily, long speeches dominate the chapter and prepare the reader to hear Joshua's speech in the next chapter. If a chiastic structure underlies the narrative (so several scholars claim), the text's spotlight falls on the Transjordanian rebuttal of the Cisjordanian accusations (vv. 21–30).[3]

The chapter sounds a new, important theme—the absolute demand that geographical distance never shake exclusive devotion to Yahweh alone (vv. 22, 34). The chapter also consummates the outsider theme heard earlier in the stories of Rahab, the Gibeonites, and Caleb.[4] In the end, the tribal conflict that the chapter narrates ends amicably, with the tribes rejoicing that all have been spared Yahweh's wrath (v. 31). The problematic action proves to be not apostasy but a witness to loyalty to Yahweh and to his worship at the tabernacle.

Scene 1 (Shiloh): "Troops, Dismissed!" (22:1–8)

JOSHUA'S REMARKS (VV. 1–6). With the fighting done and west-bank land secure, Joshua summons the Transjordanian tribes (Reuben, Gad, East Manasseh) to a private meeting (v. 1). Its location is unstated but is probably Shiloh, since in recent chapters Shiloh has replaced Gilgal as Israel's gathering place (see vv. 9, 12; cf. 18:1; 19:51; 21:2).[5] The initial "then" (lit., "at that time") introduces the occasion as a past event loosely connected chronologically to the context (cf. 8:30; 10:33; 20:6).[6] Its content, however, presupposes at least the completion of the military conquest west of the Jordan (ch. 11).

---

2. For literary-critical discussion of Josh. 22, see J. S. Kloppenberg, "Joshua 22: The Priestly Editing of An Ancient Tradition," *Bib* 62/3 (1981): 347–71.

3. Scholars who read the narrative chiastically include Hess, *Joshua*, 288; Nelson, *Joshua*, 251; and E. Assis, "'For It Shall Be A Witness Between Us': A Literary Reading of Josh 22," *SJOT* 18/2 (2004): 227.

4. Polzin, *Moses and the Deuteronomist*, 134 ("First the outsiders inside the land [Rahab, Gibeonites, Caleb], then the insiders outside the land"); cf his full discussion (134–41).

5. By contrast, the two covenant ceremonies are held at Shechem (8:30–35 [Mount Ebal]; 24:1).

6. WO §31.6.3; 39.3.4f.

Literarily, the scene forms a nice inclusio with Joshua's meeting with the same tribes in chapter 1 (Josh. 1:12 – 18) and signals that something important is about to come to an end. But unlike the first meeting on the eve of the Jordan crossing, at this miniceremony Joshua does all the talking (vv. 2 – 8). He recalls that long ago Moses had granted their requested inheritances in Transjordan on one condition — that they not occupy them until they and the other tribes had together conquered Cisjordan (Num. 35). He also recalls that at the Jordan they had committed themselves to obey Joshua (Josh. 1:16 – 18). Thus, Joshua affirms that they have fully met both obligations, obeying both Moses and himself (v. 2).

Specifically, they did not abandon their brothers, although the hardships implicit in the conquest narrative (chs. 1 – 12) gave them many reasons to bail out (v. 3). The treks into the mountains from Israel's home base at Gilgal to battle sites inland were long and arduous. Injury or death in battle — and for land not their own — stalked them constantly. An additional likely hardship was the long separation from their wives and children left at home east of the Jordan. So also was the sheer length of the endeavor ("a long time now" [v. 3]). Through it all, Joshua notes, they have remained loyal to their brothers. The prophet Obadiah would later critique Esau (Edom) for leaving Jacob (Judah, Jerusalem) to be sacked by invaders (Obad. 10 – 11), but Reuben, Gad, and East Manasseh have loyally stuck it out to the end.

Most importantly, Joshua affirms that, ultimately, their service was not to fellow Israelites but to Yahweh himself. "The LORD your God" had assigned them their mission, so their faithful execution of it lived out their faithfulness to God. But now that the job is done — God has given their west-bank kin "rest" (cf. comments at 21:44) — Joshua orders them (v. 4) to turn and head home (lit., to their "tents"). Their "land" (NIV) is specifically *ʾaḥuzzah* (cf. 21:12, 41) — the "property they own" in Transjordan that Moses gave them as their inheritance, land they have yet fully to enjoy. The Hebrew term bears one important implication relevant to the controversy soon to follow: Their land fulfills the promise to Abraham and, hence, forms part of the Promised Land (Gen. 17:8). A contrary view of them and of their land, however, will soon become apparent.[7]

In brief detail Joshua makes sure the returnees remember what is ultimately most important (v. 5). They must stay on their guard ("be very careful") to scrupulously observe everything Moses taught them ("the commandment and the law" means "Moses from A to Z").[8] Clarification comes

---

7. Assis, "A Witness Between Us," 210.

8. The phrase "the commandment" (*hammiṣwah*) and "the law [instruction]" (*hattorah*) stresses the comprehensiveness of the material to be lived out. For the pairing in the same

in the series of phrases that follow: "to love the LORD" (emotional devotion), "to walk in his ways" (i.e., live as he wants), "to hold fast to him" (i.e., stick to him like glue), and "to serve [perhaps 'worship'] him" wholeheartedly. The wording echoes the unique vocabulary of Moses' farewell speeches in Deuteronomy (e.g., Deut. 10:12−13; 11:22; 19:8−9; 30:20) and anticipates Joshua's own final address in ch. 23 (Josh. 23:6, 8, 11, 14). As Assis observes, the Mosaic language

> casts Joshua as Moses and the Transjordanian tribes as Israelites standing before Moses prior to the entrance to the land. The depiction of the ceremony in such a light is meant to reinforce the legitimacy of the departure of the Transjordanian tribes ... to settle in Transjordan, just as Moses' speeches precede the entrance of the people to the Land of Israel.[9]

Implicitly, the initial "be very careful" (lit., "watch, stay alert") warns them that constant threats besiege such devotion and that momentary inattention imperils it. With so much at stake and so many threats all around, one cannot be too careful.

Finally, Joshua pronounces a blessing over them, another echo of Moses whose final speech is a blessing of the tribes (Deut. 33). The implication of Joshua's Mosaic-like vocabulary and blessing is that Joshua regards the east-bank tribes as an integral part of Israel despite their distant settlement location. The blessing further legitimizes their settlement there, a view soon to come into question.[10] Cleverly, the narrator wields these words to set the scene for those subsequent events. At last, Joshua formally issues them their honorable discharge, and they head out (v. 6).

An authorial comment (v. 7). An awkward, parenthetical remark explains the special situation of Manasseh with branches on both sides of the Jordan. The remark traces the odd circumstance to the simple fact that Moses gave Bashan east of the Jordan to one tribal half, while Joshua gave the other half land west of it (v. 7a). It also stresses that Joshua's dismissal and blessing also apply to East Manasseh (v. 7b).[11] The reason for including such comments is unclear, but it is striking that Joshua 22 also omits

---

order, cf. only Ex. 16:28; Prov. 6:20, 23; 7:2. The reverse order is more common; cf. Ex. 24:12; 2 Kings 17:34, 37; 2 Chron. 14:4; 31:21; Prov. 3:1.

9. Assis, "A Witness Between Us," 211; cf. his discussion of the linguistic echoes of Moses (210−12).

10. Ibid., 214. Assis proposes (213−14) that a chiastic structure underlies Josh. 22:1−6, whose premeditated design serves further to legitimize their settlement with the force of law.

11. Cf. Howard, *Joshua*, 404−5, who interprets v. 8 as addressed to all the Transjordanian tribes. By the use of parentheses in v. 7a, the NIV seems to take the same approach.

Manasseh from three lists of eastern tribes (vv. 25, 32, and 33 [but not in LXX]). Also curious is the fact that in Numbers 32 it is Reuben and Gad who convince Moses to allot them land in Transjordan. But, out of the blue, his pronouncement of the land distribution inexplicably includes half of Manasseh in it (Num. 32:33; cf. Deut. 3:13; 29:8). Perhaps the best one can say is that behind these inconsistencies lies some special history unknown to us through which Manasseh received land in Transjordan. In any case, with one foot on each side of the Jordan, Manasseh comprises a "bridge people," a tribe whose very geography symbolizes Israel's unity. They also embody the chapter's central dilemma—the tension between geographical separation and religious solidarity.[12]

Joshua's charge (v. 8). Joshua's concluding charge (v. 8) also fits this understanding: "Very wealthy (in goods) go home" (lit.; the word order is emphatic). An inventory of their loot—all plundered or bartered in Canaan—includes great herds of livestock, silver, gold, bronze, iron, and lots of clothes (cf. Num. 31:22, 28).[13] Not a bad haul for one-time desert nomads to take home with them! Yahweh has truly showered his richest blessing on his people in their new land!

The last sentence urges East Manasseh to reciprocate their gains in Canaan by sharing future plundered goods from the east bank with their Cisjordanian brothers. The Mosaic Instruction mandates that Israelites split the spoils of war with battle participants, the community, Yahweh, and the Levites (Num. 31:27–30). But soldiers sometimes resented sharing them with noncombatants, an attitude David overruled on one occasion (1 Sam. 30:21–25). Joshua's point anticipates and concurs with David's later ruling: "The share of the man who stayed with the supplies is to be the same as that of him who went down to the battle. All will share alike" (30:24). If observed, such sharing would go a long way toward maintaining unity between east- and west-bank tribes. The command may even intend to promote generosity among those whom one regards as "kin."[14]

In sum, Joshua offers a grateful military commander's final, "job-well-done" farewell speech to some of his loyal, departing troops. They have finished a unique, tough assignment of shared hardships with their western brothers. But his charge warns them not to let distance from the Israelite heartland create distance between them and God. And so an era ends, as the two-and-a half tribes break camp at Shiloh and head east for a happy reunion with their families, who have awaited their safe return for so long.

---

12. Cf. Nelson, *Joshua*, 247; Assis, "A Witness between Us," 214; Woudstra, *Joshua*, 318.
13. Presumably, the metals are in the form of tangible objects.
14. Nelson, *Joshua*, 251.

Before long, however, events will transpire that will lead some Israelite quarters to call into question the picture of them here as obedient and loyal.

Scene 2 (Transjordan): What's Going On? (22:9–31)

REPORT: THE ALTAR BUILDING (vv. 9–10). The narrator follows the troops bound for home (and so do we). The two-and-a-half tribes leave Shiloh in Canaan and proceed to the land of Gilead, where they own land by God's command through Moses (v. 9).[15] Besides authorization from Joshua, they have Moses' authority to settle there and to assume that they remain part of Israel in doing so. The narrator, however, invokes terminology that noticeably contrasts the east and west-bank areas. It seems to represent a Cisjordanian perspective: "Shiloh in the land of Canaan" versus "the land of Gilead"; (lit.) "children of Reuben, Gad, and half-Manasseh" versus "the children of Israel."

This contrast raises a question: If Canaan is the true land of promise and the Israelites its recipients, what is the status of these two-and-a-half tribes outside it? The reader may rightly wonder how soon such sensitivity concerning their status might surface among those tribes. In any case, the travelers reach the area along the Jordan's west bank, presumably at a major crossing point, where they build an altar (v. 10).[16]

Ancient altars were made of packed earth (Ex. 20:24), piled field stones (20:25), wood (27:1–8), or large unhewn stones (Judg. 6:11–24). But the author here provides neither details about nor rationale for its construction. He says nothing about what, if any, religious ceremonies took place during or after the project. Instead, the lone comment is that the altar is "imposing" (lit., "big to seeing")—in modern terms, "so big you couldn't miss it."[17] The terse report leaves the reader to wonder what it symbolizes—human

---

15. According to Num. 32, Gilead was the region that Moses assigned primarily to the Reubenites and Gadites (vv. 1, 26, 29), although part (a few cities, perhaps) belonged to East Manasseh (vv. 39–40).

16. Heb. *gelilot* may designate a place (NIV "Geliloth") or an area (13:2; 18:17), in this case near the Jordan. Its west bank location is disputed but may be at Gilgal; cf. the persuasive case of N. H. Snaith, "The Altar at Gilgal: Joshua 22:23–29," *VT* 28/3 (1978): 330–35; contrast, B. E. Organ, "Pursuing Phinehas: A Synchronic Reading," *CBQ* 63 (2001): 213; Assis, "A Witness between Us," 217, who provides thorough discussion. For additional background on altars, cf. R. E. Averbeck, "מִזְבֵּחַ," *NIDOTTE*, 2:888–908; C. Dohmen, "מִזְבֵּחַ," *TDOT*, 8:209–25.

17. KB, 596 ("visible from afar"); DCH, 475 ("large, conspicuous"). The only other place where "big" and "appearance" occur together is in Moses' reaction to seeing the burning bush ("this great sight" [Ex. 3:3]).

---

arrogance like the Tower of Babel (Gen. 11), idolatry like Canaanite examples, or simple remembrance of something important like patriarchal altars (Gen. 12:7; 26:23–25; 35:1–8).[18] And what is its function—other than to attract attention? The narrative silence thus far is deafening.

A delegation to Transjordan (vv. 11–14). A report (or rumor?) concerning this striking structure beside the Jordan soon reaches the Israelites (v. 11). The NIV obscures the fact that the author quotes it but leaves its source anonymous: (paraphrased) "Look! The east-bank tribes [names spelled out] have built an altar by the Jordan on the Israelite side of the river!" This is a startling statement: "Israelite side" (v. 11) defines "Israel" as territory west of the Jordan, assumes Transjordan to be the *non*-Israelite side," and further characterizes east-bank residents as less than full Israelites.[19]

The report about the unsettling discovery conveys shocked urgency, as if the altar were scandalous and posed a serious threat to west-bank well-being. Apparently, no one bothers to ask why the returning troops have placed the altar there on the west bank—an inconvenient spot for Transjordanian access!—rather than (more conveniently) on their side of the river. Instead, the news sparks a rush of the "whole community of Israel" to an emergency pow-wow at Shiloh (v. 12). The same words ("the whole assembly ... gathered") open the earlier scene where the last tribal allotments are made (Josh. 18:1), but here Israel meets to prepare for war against the two-and-a-half tribes.[20]

Presumably, the war in mind is "holy war"—defense of the proper worship of Yahweh against apostasy. That the crowd thinks in terms of "us" versus "them" makes that normally unthinkable option acceptable. "They" (the altar builders) are no longer truly "Israelites." At the same time, to wage holy war also assumes some sense of collective oneness with and responsibility for the east-bank tribes. The thought is that, when grievously wrong, even second-class Israelites merit accountability.[21]

---

18. The LXX may read it negatively, since elsewhere the Greek word *bomos* usually designates pagan altars; cf. Ex. 34:14; Deut. 7:5; 12:3; 2 Chron. 31:1.

19. Cf. Nelson, *Joshua*, 251; Assis, "A Witness between Us," 215, 216, 218; Organ, "Pursuing Phinehas," 213. For a similar "in-out" attitude, see Judg. 20:1.

20. The "whole congregation of Israel" probably comprised an Israelite democratic institution accessible to all male adults whose portfolio included the waging of war, the hearing of legal cases, the meting out of punishment in some cases, and the attesting of important national events; cf. D. Levy and J. Milgrom, "עֵדָה," *TDOT*, 10:479 (cf. the entire discussion, 468–80). For the exact phrase, cf. Ex. 16:1; 17:1; Lev. 19:2; Num. 8:9; 35:1.

21. Assis, "A Witness between Us," 218, rightly points out that an isolationist stance would not have driven the nine-and-a-half tribes to action; only a collective sense of responsibility would.

But the assembly does not seek Yahweh's guidance on the matter through an oracle (i.e., a prophet or the Urim and Thummim), although Israel often did so before war (cf. 9:14).[22] And the reader wonders about the disonnect between two perceptions: Can the people whose obedience Joshua has praised so highly (vv. 1–8) really be the same people behind this scandal? Can they really have violated his parting injunctions so soon after their departure? First, however, the Israelites dispatch a delegation to the Transjordanian tribes (again, names spelled out) in Gilead with a priest, Phinehas son of Eleazar, as its head (vv. 13–14)—the only member explicitly named. To put a priest in charge assumes the issue to be a religious one, and this particular priest has an interesting past history.

The Bible knows Phinehas above all as a heroic "defender of the faith," especially of the proper way to worship Yahweh.[23] He is best known for his decisive, violent action at Baal Peor that ended a devastating plague in Israel's camp and won him special praise from Yahweh (Num. 25; cf. Ex. 6:25; Num. 31:6; Judg. 20:27–28). If the situation demands a ruling on altars or bold, daring initiative, Phinehas is certainly the right man for the job.

But the rest of the delegates are no slouches, either. They clearly comprise the highest level of leadership in Israel, the Israelite equivalent of a presidential cabinet. The NIV simplifies four Hebrew phrases into three, thus obscuring the narrator's piling up of phrases to portray them as political heavyweights (cf. the short version in v. 30). The group consists of ten "chief men" (*nasiʾ*, "chief, prince"), one from each tribe, each one head of a family unit within a clan among all Israel's clans. In the Old Testament, they occupy the same leadership level as Moses, Joshua, and high priests (Num. 4:46; 27:2; 36:11; Josh. 9:15). They represent the tribes in many decisions affecting the whole nation—for example, the ratification of Joshua's treaty with the Gibeonites (Josh. 9:15–21)—and present offerings at the tabernacle on behalf of the tribes (Num. 7:11; cf. Ex. 35:27).[24]

The west-bank view (vv. 15–20). Phinehas and the ten VIPs reach Gilead and, at an unnamed site, at length address the gathered Transjordanian tribes (again, spelled out by name; vv. 15–20). The opening messenger formula ("Thus says the whole community of the LORD") presents the speech as spoken, not by a single individual like Phinehas, but by the

---

22. Organ, "Pursuing Phinehas," 214. To seek Yahweh's will was to "inquire" of him, and the standard formula was to ask, "Shall we go up to battle against X?" (Judg. 20:23, 28; 1 Sam. 22:10, 15; 2 Sam. 5:19, 23; 1 Kings 22:15).

23. Organ, "Pursuing Phinehas," 209–10; cf. her larger discussion of the biblical portrait of Phinehas (203–18).

24. K. T. Aitken, "נָשִׂיא," *NIDOTTE*, 3:171; H. Niehr, "נָשִׂיא," *TDOT*, 10:44–53 (in-depth discussion).

community of Yahweh as a whole (v. 16).[25] Subtly, it also implies some serious problem with the standing of the east-bank tribes in the eyes of Yahweh and Israel.

The dignitaries' first question levels a blunt, strongly worded accusation: "How could you break faith with ... God like this?" "Break faith" (*ma'al*) echoes the report of Achan's secret perfidy (7:1)—the severest of crimes against God, one that imperiled all Israel—and immediately tars the audience with the same slimy brush.[26] The word implies rank hypocrisy: Publicly they act the part of Yahweh's faithful, but in secret they connive evil against him. "Today" (twice in the verse) they have turned and walked away from Yahweh by building an altar to revolt (*marad*) against him. The delegation assumes that, since Yahweh has authorized only one altar—the one in Canaan (cf. v. 19)—the new altar must honor another god. Therein lies the Transjordanian revolt, the visitors argue; it is apostasy, plain and simple.

The setting of *marad* ("to revolt, rebel") is the arena of international relations where an asymmetrical power relationship binds powerful kings with lesser kings and subordinates.[27] Political, economic, or military weakness forces the vassal king or royal subordinate willingly or unwillingly to swear political loyalty to the stronger king. *Marad* designates the attempt by the former to escape through revolt his burdensome bonds of dependence on the latter.[28]

Theologically, *marad* assumes a similar asymmetrical relationship between Yahweh and Israel and paints Israel's attempts to escape its commitment of loyalty to Yahweh as revolts (cf. v. 18; Num. 14:9; Neh. 9:26; Ezek. 2:3; Dan. 9:5, 9). In short, in the present case the visitors accuse their Transjordanian kin of two of the severest of crimes against Yahweh, treachery (breach of trust) and rebellion (breach of promise).

With a second question ("Was not the sin of Peor enough for us?"), the speech moves from blunt accusation to an appeal to spare everyone terrible consequences (vv. 17–20). For added rhetorical firepower, it invokes mem-

---

25. Contrast Organ, "Pursuing Phinehas," 214, who wrongly assumes Phinehas to be the spokesman and then (in my view) mischaracterizes him as "a bureaucrat rather than a fiery warrior."

26. For the meaning and use of *ma'al*, see the commentary at 7:1. Repetition of both nouns and verbs from the root in ch. 22 is a striking literary feature (vv. 16, 20, 22, 31).

27. L. Schwienhorst, "מָרַד," *TDOT*, 9:1–5; R. Knierim, "מָרַד," *THAT*, 1:925–28. The combination of *ma'al* and *marad* clarifies that the treachery alleged concerns the breaking of a covenant oath, not the poaching of Yahweh's property as was the case with Achan (cf. Milgrom, *Cult and Conscience*, 21).

28. E.g., rebellions by Hezekiah against Sennacherib (2 Kings 18:7, 20), Jehoiakim against Nebuchadnezzar (24:1, 20), Jeroboam against Solomon (2 Chron. 13:6), and the Jews against the Persian king (Neh. 2:19; 6:6).

ories of two recent, shameful episodes in which all present had sorrowfully shared. "Peor" recalls the place just east of the Jordan where Yahweh sent a terrible plague to punish Israel for worshiping an idol, the Baal of Peor—"the sin [ʿawon] of Peor" in Numbers 25. The plague took 24,000 lives, but the speakers stress that Israel still has not "cleansed [itself] from that sin" (v. 17). Here as elsewhere, ʿawon refers both to the original act (idolatry) and to the resulting "guilt" from which Israel (they claim) needs cleansing.

Behind the present argument stands the Old Testament's view that ʿawon-guilt is more than a simple black mark in Israel's account book with God. It actually constitutes a "trigger for disaster" (i.e., disaster inevitably follows it), disaster that cleansing seeks to ward off.[29] So, the speakers rhetorically juxtapose the Transjordanians' action "today" with the consequences to follow "tomorrow." Their point is: To add "today" more "disaster-causing guilt" ("now turning away from the LORD") to the already primed "trigger" of Peor really risks setting off Yahweh's fury against everyone "tomorrow" (v. 18).

To avert this disaster, the visitors propose that the two-and-a-half tribes leave "defiled" (ṭameʾ ["unclean"]) Transjordan and settle among the other tribes in Canaan, "in the LORD's land," near the tabernacle (v. 19). This comment shares the same Israel/non-Israel distinction seen earlier. It assumes—perhaps hyperbolically for sake of argument—that Transjordan is not "the LORD's land" but land belonging to some other deity. It voices the Cisjordanian perspective that east-bank land is not "holy" as Canaan is. It implies that the distance of the Transjordanians from Yahweh's center of gravity leaves them vulnerable to the gravitational pull of local defiling forces. More important, as Polzin notes, it seems to imply that

> their land is not Israel [they have not "crossed over" (Heb. ʿabar) into "Israel"; cf. Josh. 3:1–4:15], that they are not "Israel" in the full sense, and that they have not yet entered into the LORD's possession.[30]

The second shameful episode (v. 20) is the more recent one, the horrid treachery (maʿal) of Achan (ch. 7).[31] If the scandal at Peor marks the classic case of apostasy, Achan denotes the classic case of "treachery." He secretly kept for himself goods captured at Jericho (ḥerem) that, in fact, belonged to Yahweh. But the delegation's concern is not with the act of altar-building itself but with its consequences. Their climactic (perhaps

---

29. The phrase is that of K. Koch, "אָוֹן," *TDOT*, 10:552. In this context, one might render ʿawon as "the guilt that causes disaster." For the worldview behind the word, cf. R. Knierim, "אָוֹן," *THAT*, 2:243–50. The Bridging Contexts section provides further discussion.

30. Polzin, *Moses and the Deuteronomist*, 138.

31. Interestingly, this marks the only other biblical reference to Achan outside of Joshua 7; cf. Boling, *Joshua*, 515.

even melodramatic!) cry that "[Achan] was not the only one who died for his sin" (v. 20) powerfully drives home their message. The dignitaries remind their audience that, while Achan acted alone, divine wrath struck the entire community. That pattern, they argue, now seems likely to recur: The altar-building by a few tribes now threatens to bring down God's wrath on all twelve tribes of Israel, not just on the Transjordanians.[32] With that, the message of the west-bank tribes ends.

The east-bank view (vv. 21 – 29). The east-bank reply to the visiting VIPs is equally blunt and passionate — and (perhaps of necessity) longer (vv. 21 – 29). As noted above, structurally (and perhaps thematically) it probably comprises the key section of the entire chapter. Twice it references past internal deliberations ("We said ..."; vv. 26, 28), a hint that a solid tribal consensus supports their actions. That they speak as a group, not through a spokesperson, also reinforces the impression of tribal solidarity. Their sophisticated rebuttal effectively weaves in language from the original accusation (e.g., *maʿal* and *marad*).[33]

The opening rhetorical flourish, a string of orthodox names for Israel's God ("Mighty One, God, the LORD ...") aims immediately to dispel the visitors' doubts about their orthodoxy (v. 22).[34] There is, they claim, another side to this story. They strongly affirm that Israel's God understands the real situation ("He knows!") and voice the passionate wish that Israel (and especially the present delegation!) might, too. To prove their innocence, they make their visitors a bold offer phrased as a kind of self-curse. If the accusations of "rebellion" (*mered*) and "disobedience" (*maʿal*) against Yahweh be true, they ask Phinehas not to hold back proper punishment.[35] If their altar announces rejection of Yahweh (and, by implication, his altar in Canaan) and pledges loyalty to another god through sacrifices, they ask Yahweh himself to "call us to account" (v. 23). Thus, they deny the accusations; they claim to have nothing to hide. They share the visitors' conviction that Israel performs sacrifices to Yahweh only at Shiloh.

But now comes a surprising revelation. The Cisjordanians assume that an altar serves only one purpose, as a place for sacrificing. But the Transjordanians reveal something new — that fear, not rebellion, drove them to act

---

32. Organ, "Pursuing Phinehas," 213. Thus, their main aim is actually not to level an accusation but to establish the principle of the mutual responsibility of the tribes. Ironically, they will soon realize that this principle also applies to them in this case; cf. Assis, "A Witness between Us," 220–21.

33. For details, see Assis, "A Witness between Us," 225–27.

34. Cf. ibid., 223 ("to give an impression of credibility").

35. "Spare" is a second person (masc.) singular, and if addressed to Phinehas, might subtly allude to his decisive action at Peor (Num. 25:7–8) as a model to repeat against them.

as they did. They fear that future descendants of the present accusers will deny their own descendants to have access to Yahweh (v. 24a). They worry that descendants of the delegation will invoke the Jordan as a God-given boundary—an ancient Rio Grande—to bar east-bank descendants from the community worship (vv. 24, 28). They also quote a possible objection that future Cisjordanians might raise to exclude their descendants (vv. 24b–25a). In modern paraphrase it says:

> You are foreigners from Transjordan, this is Canaan. You have no legitimate relationship with Yahweh, the God of Israel. The Jordan River proves it: Yahweh made it to keep you out, you Gadites and Reubenites! You've got no connection with him.[36]

This statement clearly implies that the Cisjordanian tribes do not truly recognize their east-bank relatives as full members of God's people. But what really makes them shudder—their worst fear—is the frightening result of their exclusion: The Transjordanians' descendants will "stop fearing the LORD."

Now, if Assis is right, the highly structured rebuttal by the east-bank tribes implies that the altar-building was more than just something done on the spur-of-the-moment. Quite the contrary, Assis plausibly proposes that the returning soldiers preplanned the event for a purpose—to provoke a harsh response from the west bank in order to surface the thorny, underlying issue.[37] That assumption helps explain their claim that they built the altar in question not for sacrifices—that would imply disloyalty to Yahweh—but as "a witness" (Heb. ʿed) of the connection between all tribes astride the Jordan. The altar offers tangible testimony of the Transjordanian commitment to sacrifice only at Yahweh's west-bank sanctuary, not to fall into rebellion and apostasy.

This perspective rules out of bounds any west-bank attempt to deny them access to their "share in the LORD" in Canaan (vv. 26–27).[38] Coming generations of Transjordanian pilgrims can point to it, "a replica of the LORD's altar," as silent evidence of their connection to Yahweh at his official site, not at the riverside one (v. 28).[39] As a final, dramatic gesture, the Transjordanians voice a negative oath: "Far be it from us" to "rebel" (*marad*)

---

36. Inexplicably, v. 25 omits East Manasseh, as do vv. 32 and 34. Nelson (*Joshua*, 251) sees this as evidence that Manasseh was added to the story later.

37. Assis, "A Witness between Us," 225; cf. his detailed analysis of their speech, including the use of chiasm (224–26).

38. Cf. H. Simian-Yofre, "עֵד," *TDOT*, 10:506–7. For a parallel example, cf. the stone pile and pillar that "witness" the covenant between Jacob and Laban (Gen. 31:44–53).

39. "Replica" is Heb. *tabnit* ("copy, reproduction"); Gk. *homoioma* "(something) similar."

against Yahweh by sacrificing at any spot other than at the altar in front of the tabernacle.[40]

In short, the two-and-a-half tribes deny the delegation's accusation of apostasy, explain their actions, and strongly affirm their loyalty to Yahweh. They surface their deep fears and implicitly indict the west-bank tribes for the way the latter have dealt with them. They have in mind the Cisjordanians' not-so-subtle superior attitude, their shabby treatment of them as second-class Israelites, and their thinking the worst (rather than the best) of them. They betray great awareness of the dangers of distance from the Israelite heartland: fear of treatment as second-class Israelite citizens, if not outright outcasts. What worries them most is not rebellion by their descendants but the dampening of their devotion to Yahweh by west-bank exclusionary policy. The altar, thus, marks a symbolic preemptive strike against exclusion—a witness that binds Israelites on both banks to loyal devotion to Yahweh alone and to his tabernacle. Against appearances, the altar aims to attest their unwavering devotion, not their apostasy.[41]

Resolution (vv. 30–31). Suddenly, the Cisjordanians find the tables turned on them; the would-be accusers now find themselves the accused![42] The fact that the Transjordanians mount a defense longer than the original accusation implies that the sympathies of the biblical author also lie with them.[43] The scene concludes somewhat formally with lists of the names of the two-and-a-half tribes (twice in vv. 30–31!) and of Phinehas and his important companions (an abbreviation of vv. 13b–14). The lengthy explanation by the Transjordanians pleases (lit., "was good in the eyes of") the entire delegation (v. 30).

It falls to Phinehas the priest, the delegation's leader, to respond officially on their behalf (v. 31). (1) He acknowledges the rhetorical success of the Transjordanian statement: They had wished, "Let Israel know!" (v. 22), and he says, "Today we know...." The visitors know that "the LORD is with [lit., amidst] us"—as opposed to being *against* us in anger—since the alleged "breach of trust" (*ma'al*) against Yahweh has proven to be untrue. The easterners have given him no reason to abandon Israel, and here Phinehas may have past history in mind. Remember that Achan's secret sin caused Yahweh secretly to abandon Israel, a fact later revealed by Israel's catastrophic defeat at Ai. The alleged apostasy in Joshua 22 threatened a

---

40. On the grammatical form ("Far be it ..."), cf. WO §40.2.2c; cf. Josh. 24:16; Gen. 44:7, 17; 1 Sam. 12:23.
41. Cf. Butler, *Joshua*, 249 ("The Jordan is a symbol of separation. The altar is a symbol of unity").
42. Assis, "A Witness between Us," 228.
43. Ibid., 227.

painful replay of that catastrophe. But Israel need not worry: There has been no crime and, hence, no reason for Yahweh to abandon Israel. The key word in his statement, however, may be "us." It implies that Phinehas accepts the heart of the Transjordanian concern—they are full members of Israel.[44]

(2) Phinehas acknowledges emphatically that "now"—because of your persuasive explanation—the east-bank tribes "have rescued the Israelites from the LORD's hand." A nice Hebrew sound play knits together both of Phinehas's acknowledgments: instead of "breaking faith" (me͑altem) with Yahweh, the Transjordanians have in fact "rescued" (hiṣṣaltem) the Israelites from his hand. At first glance, the remark seems to highlight the happy result of their nontreachery—that, unlike the case of Achan, no angry divine judgment will befall all twelve tribes (cf. vv. 18, 20). In my view, however, the claim of rescue probably describes the result, not of the eastern tribes' nontreachery, but of their persuasive answer.

Remember that at Peor it was Phinehas's killing of an apostate couple that satisfied Yahweh and ended the horrible plague. In Joshua 22, Phinehas may mean that Transjordanian cooperation has headed off a doubly tragic Cisjordanian mistake. It has prevented an unjustified military attack that would have decimated the two-and-a- half tribes and possibly earned harsh divine retribution (i.e., "the LORD's hand") against the other nine-and-a-half. It has averted a disastrous civil war not unlike the near-annihilation of the Benjaminites a generation or so later (Judg. 19–21). And with that, Phinehas's reply ends.

It is important, however, to underscore the implications of the decision his delegation made. It both acquits the Transjordanian tribes of the charge of violating the Instruction of Moses (e.g., Josh. 22:29) and asserts their right "to be considered full-fledged members of the community of Israel."[45] At least for the time being.

Scene 3 (Shiloh): No Problem! (22:32–34)

THE GOOD REPORT (VV. 32–33). The report concerning the return trip of Phinehas and the other leaders from Transjordan marks the transition to the brief third scene (v. 32a). The narrator's style turns from expansive speeches to terse reports of facts without details (e.g., "[they] reported to the Israelites" [v. 32b]), a hint that the narrative's end approaches. Literarily, the repetition of the same phrase ("the word pleased So-and-So") connects the Israelites' satisfaction with the delegation's report (v. 33a) with the latter's

---

44. Ibid., 228; Polzin, *Moses and the Deuteronomist*, 137.

45. Polzin, *Moses and the Deuteronomist*, 137.

satisfaction with the Transjordanian explanation (v. 30b).[46] Both leaders and people meeting at Shiloh accept and approve the report.

Indeed, the centrality of the hero, Phinehas the priest, in the narrative fully legitimates the altar.[47] At least, nothing is said about tearing it down. And no doubt the crowd also feels a welcome sense of relief, since they immediately "praise (lit., 'bless') God" and say nothing more about going to war (v. 33b). Unlike verse 12, here the narrator mentions the mission of that now-unnecessary war — "to devastate (*šaḥet*) the country where [the Transjordanian tribes] lived." *Šaḥet* pi. ("to devastate") describes an action of almost unimaginable horror — complete, violent annihilation or decimation at the hands of other humans (Judg. 6:5; Isa. 14:20; Ezek. 30:11).[48] The writer probably invokes a word so evocative of terror, horror, and despair to highlight the holocaust the tribes have just avoided.

But the language of verses 32 − 33 also maintains the distinctions of geography ("Canaan" vs. "Gilead") and ethnic status ("children of Israel" vs. "children of Reuben and Gad") seen earlier. This implies that, despite having heard east-bank concerns, west-bank Israel remains isolationist and separatist.[49] If so, the reader wonders whether anything significant has changed after all — whether, in the end, a Cisjordanian perspective still prevails.

The altar's name (v. 34). Presumably, those assembled at Shiloh leave to resume daily life in their new home areas. The narrator, however, takes the reader back to Transjordan, back to the altar that, though built so innocently, nearly sparked a terrible civil war. In so doing, he hints that his own sympathies lie with — and the narrative promotes — the Transjordanian view.[50] No one tears the altar down. Instead, Reuben and Gad (plus in LXX East Manasseh) give it an appropriate sentence name: "A Witness Between Us that the LORD [and absolutely no one else] is God" (v. 34; cf. v. 22). Implicit also is the unspoken tagline, "and on both sides of the river, too!"

---

46. In my view, NIV's 'They were glad to hear the report" wrongly reads the formula as referring to the fact of having received a report rather to its contents ("The report pleased them").

47. Organ, "Pursuing Phinehas," 214.

48. J. Conrad, "שָׁחַת," *TDOT*, 14:584−85.

49. Assis, "A Witness between Us," 229−30. In his view, the contrast between Phinehas's inclusive statement (v. 31) and more exclusive language of vv. 32−33 suggests that only Phinehas (but not his companions) has moved beyond the isolationism and separatism with which the story began. As noted earlier, MT inexplicably lacks "the half tribe of Manasseh" in vv. 32 and 34 (so also v. 25), although LXX has it.

50. Nelson, *Joshua*, 253. Assis ("A Witness between Us," 230, n.51) summarizes alternative scholarly opinions and concludes (230−31): 'The Cisjordanian tribes act as a group loyal to God maintaining a concept of a united Israel. It appears, however, that the perfect concept of the unity of Israel is possessed only by the Transjordanian tribes."

Silently, that imposing structure reminds every Israelite who passes, whether traveling east or west, that "the LORD is God" over all Israelites, wherever located. Set on the west bank but built by east-bank hands, it symbolizes the bond that unites settlers along both banks as one people—their devotion to Yahweh as their only God.[51] That is a bond that even the mighty Jordan cannot sever. But one last point needs mention. Within the book of Joshua, the east-bank tribes enjoy what Polzin calls "typological status"—they dramatize the twin themes of

> the continuing unworthiness of Israel and her lack of right to the land she is herein described as occupying. Like the other "aliens"—Rahab, the Gibeonites, Caleb, the Levites and dependants ... all of them representative versions of the same typology—the Transjordanian tribes are a permanent representation of the obedience to God's law that never quite makes it.[52]

The plot, thus, ends in ironic reversal: The Cisjordanian fear of nationwide divine punishment proves a misperception while Transjordanian fear of exclusion proves true. The persistence of the Transjordanians-As-Semiobedient theme that Polzin observes shows that mainstream (i.e., west-bank) Israel apparently never fully embraces them.[53]

GEOGRAPHICAL PERSPECTIVE. TO CROSS the bridge from Joshua 22 to today requires additional comment concerning four topics. The first concerns the geographical perspective of Joshua 22. As noted above, for Cisjordanians the land of Israel lies only west of the Jordan in Canaan, not in Gilead to its east. Readers familiar with the wide, all-Israel perspective of the land and town distributions (chs. 13–21) find that perspective strange. But there is much biblical data to support it. It was Canaan that Yahweh promised Abraham (Gen. 17:8; Ex. 6:4) and to which Moses led the Israelites (Deut. 32:49). Consider, further, the symbolic significance of manna, Israel's special food supply in the wilderness. Biblical tradition says that Israel ate manna for forty years "until they reached the border of Canaan" (Ex. 16:35). It also records that the first year after Israel crossed the Jordan the manna stopped and Israel

---

51. Cf. Organ, "Pursuing Phinehas," 214 ("One God, one cult, one people").

52. Polzin, *Moses and the Deuteronomist*, 140–41, citing their repeated appearances throughout the book (1:12–18; 4:12–13; 6:7; 14:3; 18:7) and Phinehas's dramatic declaration in 22:31.

53. Similarly, Assis, "A Witness between Us," 227.

ate "the produce of Canaan" (Josh. 5:12). Clearly, these texts mentally map a world with two main geographical regions—the wilderness east of the Jordan and Canaan west of it.

Consider, also, the boundary description of Numbers 34. According to Moses, the eastern boundary of Canaan below the Sea of Kinnereth (i.e., Lower Jordan) runs along the Jordan and ends at the Dead Sea (Num. 34:12; cf. Ezek. 47:18). At the same time, the chapter also knows that tribes will occupy both sides of the river—nine-and-a-half to the west and two-and-a-half to the east—as their "inheritance" (Num. 34:13–15). Thus, whatever differences of status may apply elsewhere, Numbers 34 recognizes both locations as "inheritance," a word associated with Yahweh's land promise (e.g., Deut. 4:37–38).

Besides location, two apparent differences distinguish the two groups. Yahweh himself assigns the larger group to Cisjordan, and they will receive their individual portions "by lot"—presumably by Yahweh's hidden guidance (Num. 34:13). The smaller group, by contrast, has simply to "receive" their inheritance (vv. 14–15), but nothing is said about from whom. Numbers 34 concludes with a list of the men whom Yahweh appoints to divide up the land (vv. 16–29). Interestingly, the list contains only men from west-bank tribes. Neither Yahweh nor Moses makes any provision as to how the distribution in Transjordan is to be done. (But see below).

One final observation concerns what strikes me as a telling distinction in the way the book of Joshua talks about the allotments of eastern versus western land. Consider the implications of this text: "Now that the LORD your God has given your brothers rest as he promised, return to your homes in the land that Moses the servant of the LORD gave you on the other side of the Jordan" (22:4). It clearly contrasts tribal lands in Canaan as the fulfillment of Yahweh's promise with lands in Transjordan as a gift of Moses.

This is not the place to pursue the matter in depth, but a brief survey of language in the book of Joshua confirms the association of Yahweh with Canaan and of Moses with Transjordan. For example, Yahweh directly orders the distribution of land in Canaan, albeit originally through Moses and later through Joshua (e.g., 13:2–7; 14:2, 5). The case of Caleb, who received land in Cisjordan, conforms to this same pattern. The authority for his special inheritance derives from Yahweh's promise through Moses (14:6, 10, 12) and Joshua (15:13) in response to his (and Joshua's) unwavering loyalty to Yahweh (vv. 8, 9).[54] Further, as noted above, the mandated

---

54. See the commentary concerning the Caleb episode in ch. 14. Yahweh's command through Moses also marks the authority granting the special allotment to the daughters of Zelophehad (17:4) and the Levites (21:2, 8).

means for the distribution (by casting lots) also assumes Yahweh's indirect participation in the process. By contrast, the authority backing tribal allotments in Transjordan is Moses—e.g., "Moses the servant of the LORD gave it to them" (18:7; cf. 13:8, 15; 14:3; cf. Num. 32:33). In fact, he is the one who actually assigns each tribe its portion, and with no apparent recourse to lots or direct consultation with Yahweh (Josh. 13:15, 24, 29, 32).[55]

In short, the texts do not portray Yahweh as a direct participant in land distributions in Transjordan in the same way as he is with those in Cisjordan. Now, one might object that Moses' title ("the servant of the LORD") implies Yahweh's presence or his delegation of responsibility to Moses to act on his behalf. These views are certainly possible. In my view, the texts do not imply that the Mosaic distribution was unauthorized by Yahweh or displeasing to him. But the pattern of the language used in each case strikes me as requiring some explanation. For the present, my suggestion is that behind the language lies a view that Canaan marks Yahweh's priority, but that Gilead retains its own importance. Certainly, the primacy of Canaan, based on the tabernacle's presence there, reflects the perspective of Phinehas and his companions and drives the conflict in Joshua 22. How widely that view prevailed is a matter of speculation.

Several conclusions follow from the above discussion. Yahweh's direct involvement in west-bank distribution betrays a subtle, greater divine identification with Canaan. This would make sense, since that land had been his target for conquest and settlement from the time of Abraham. It also seems fair to say that his subsequent involvement with Israel certainly centers there as well. Further, from a human perspective, the scenario by which the Transjordanian tribes came into their inheritance may have forever saddled them with suspicion in the minds of their Cisjordanian kin. Joshua 22 reflects both their awareness of prejudice against them and the ready bent of west-bank tribes to suspect them of evil. Did the other tribes read their initiative in petitioning Moses for an inheritance in Transjordan as selfishness? What did they make of the Transjordanians' plea, "Don't make us cross the Jordan" (Num. 32:5)? Were the other tribes jealous of the huge holdings of livestock that made the east-bank region so attractive to them (32:1, 4)? What about the fact that they filed their request with Moses rather through Moses to Yahweh (v. 5)? Did the tribes read that as dishonoring to God—a symptom of weak covenant loyalty?

Moses clearly heard in their petition an echo of the ten rebellious spies and angrily railed at them as a "brood of sinners" (Num. 32:6−15; cf. chs.

---

55. As far as I can find, only one text evidences awareness of divine involvement, the answer by the Transjordanian tribes, "Your servants will do what the LORD has said" (Num. 32:31).

13–14). It struck him as a similar act of rebellion that could cause Yahweh also to destroy the present generation. Now, eventually Reuben and Gad agreed to Moses' conditions (vv. 16–32, esp. vv. 25, 31), and Moses granted their petition (v. 33).[56] But among some tribes their agreement may not have shaken the suspicion that the whole affair was masking a problematic streak of tribal independence. Indeed, Budd believes the deuteronomistic editors of Number 32:5–15

> saw in the request of Gad and Reuben the seeds of the old unwillingness to take possession of the land God had given. Investigation of the factors which had led to the loss of land was always uppermost in [their] minds ... and a lack of a serious commitment to Yahweh and his gift was often a major feature of their analysis.[57]

In short, the biblical text denies us full knowledge of how the tribes regarded each other, but this discussion helpfully suggests some of the real human dynamics behind both the events in Joshua 22 and the present written report about them. This recognition of very human intertribal dynamics in ancient Israel sets the scene for the discussion below of some of the interpersonal dynamics within our church life today.

The Jordan River. A second follow-up comment concerns the motif of the Jordan River as a natural boundary. The fear in Transjordan is that future Cisjordanians will deny their descendants any "share in the LORD" because Yahweh "made the Jordan a boundary" (v. 25). How real is this fear? As an obvious, indisputable landmark, the river clearly demarcates Cisjordan from Transjordan (Num. 32; cf. Deut. 1:4) and also provides the eastern boundary for various tribes (Josh. 15:5; 16:7; 18:2; 19:22, 33–34).[58] The question is, besides being a "boundary," is the Jordan also a "barrier"? How easy is it to cross?

Apparently, it was easy enough to permit Old Testament judges, kings, and their enemies to cross to do battle or make their escapes (e.g., Judg. 6:33; 8:4; 1 Sam. 13:5–7; 2 Sam. 10:17). Ancient east-west travel, of course, required knowledge of the Jordan's crossing points, much as we who live along rivers know where the bridges are. A letter by an Egyptian royal official named Hori (late thirteenth cent. B.C.) satirically asks his unknown correspondent, "The stream of Jordan, how is it crossed?"[59]

---

56. Their promise ("Your servants will do what the LORD has said" [v. 31]) even seems to accept Moses' ruling as a word from Yahweh—but, of course, only at the end.

57. P. J. Budd, *Numbers* (WBC 5; Waco, Tex.: Word, 1984), 346.

58. H. O. Thompson, "Jordan River," *ABD*, 3:953–58.

59. *ANET*, 477.

Fords offer the best crossing points, except when the spring runoff significantly increased the Jordan's depth and made it less passable, if not impassable.

Fords formed when silt deposited by tributaries shaped sandbars shallow enough to permit safe foot traffic across.[60] Fords, however, are also vulnerable to closure by force. Given this phenomenon, the fears voiced in Transjordan make good sense. Groups with sufficient force (e.g., armies, bandits, etc.) can control fords for their own purposes — such as to exact tolls, shut down all traffic, prevent escapes, and the like. For example, the judge Eglon and some armed Ephraimites seized the fords that led across to Moab and trapped and killed thousands of retreating Moabite soldiers (Judg. 3:28). In another example, the judge Jephthah and men from Gilead seized the Jordan fords on the east side to prevent their enemy, the Ephraimites, from escaping to the west (Judg. 12:1−6). Anyone who denied being an Ephraimite was asked to say "Shibboleth" ("flowing stream"), since Ephraimites pronounced the word as "Sibboleth." The clever screening snagged thousands of Ephraimites and cost them their lives.

Though occurring later than the pow-wow in Transjordan, these examples show that Transjordanian fears have some basis in reality. How much of a "basis" would depend on the good will of future Cisjordanians, and the second example illustrates a further complication — tribal jealousies. Theologically, Israel may be one people, but from time to time its tribes and clans might still squabble, compete, and promote their own interests.[61] For our purposes, the point is that, to be important, fears do not have to be real, only partially so — or thought to be. I will return to discuss the contemporary significance of this in the next section.

Before leaving this topic, mention should be made of the echoes of the Jordan River in Christian hymnody.[62] The crossing of the Jordan often appears as a metaphor for the transition from death to life or from the present world to heaven. For example, the chorus of the African-American song, "Roll, Jordan, Roll," says:

> Roll, Jordan, roll,
> Roll, Jordon, roll;

---

60. *CBA*, 10, has four crossing points between the Dead Sea and the Sea of Kinnereth, whereas Dorsey has four between the Dead Sea and biblical Adam (Josh. 3:16) and three more between Adam and Beth Shean; cf. D. A. Dorsey, *The Roads and Highways of Ancient Israel* (Baltimore; London: Johns Hopkins Univ. Press, 1991), Maps 7 and 12. For more on fords, cf. Thompson, "Jordan River," 3:957.

61. As noted above, a telling case in point is the near annihilation of the tribe of Benjamin by the other tribes because of the outrage at Gibeah (Judg. 17−20).

62. Thompson, "Jordan River," 3:957−58.

I want to go to heaven when I die,
To hear sweet Jordan roll.

Or note Samuel Stennet's eighteenth-century hymn "On Jordan's Stormy Banks," where the worshiper imagines himself as a Christian pilgrim gazing across in hopeful wonder at Canaan (i.e., heaven):

On Jordan's stormy banks I stand
And cast a wishful eye,
To Canaan's fair and happy land,
Where my possessions lie.
I am bound for the promised land,
I am bound for the promised land;
Oh who will come and go with me?
I am bound for the promised land.

This usage of the biblical image reflects a good reading of biblical texts. They understand Canaan to be the true Promised Land — Israel's long-expected final destination and place of final rest. In that sense, they represent the view of Cisjordanian primacy espoused by Phinehas and his delegation. By implication, they also accord Transjordan secondary status as a place to escape rather than to stay, a perspective similar to that of some Old Testament texts discussed above. They further confirm that the fears in Transjordan are not completely unfounded.

Corporate guilt and shared disaster. Another subject is the theme of corporate guilt and shared disaster. Although the theme received some treatment in chapter 7 (see comments), it bears additional comment here. The topic is so biblically important yet seems so strange to our modern, individualistic mindset. In Joshua 22, the idea surfaces in the citation of the Peor and Achan incidents (22:17–18, 20; cf. Num. 25; Josh. 7). The former symbolizes the increased risk for divine judgment caused by the alleged Transjordanian apostasy. The latter symbolizes that, though only two-and-a-half tribes committed the sin, the resulting judgment may strike all twelve. Both assume Israel to be a corporate entity in which the actions of subparts benefit or imperil everyone.

Totality-thinking, a key principle undergirding the Old Testament's understanding of reality, stands behind this.[63] Totality-thinking describes Israel's perception of individual persons or actions always as part of larger wholes. The family, clan, tribe, and nation comprise the larger whole for

---

63. Cf. R. L. Hubbard, Jr., "Ganzheitsdenken in the Book of Ruth," in *Problems in Biblical Theology*, ed. T. C. Sun and K. Eades (Grand Rapids: Eerdmans, 1997), 192–209.

persons, while individual actions form part of larger processes. That wholeness even extends over generations, as Joshua's comment at Gilgal about the Exodus shows:

> For the LORD your God dried up the Jordan before you until you had crossed over. The LORD your God did to the Jordan just what he had done to the Red Sea when he dried it up before *us* until *we* had crossed over. (Josh. 4:23, my italics).

Few in his audience had in fact been alive at the time of the Exodus, but "us" and "we" imply that his whole audience actually participated in it. Joshua's statement reveals his understanding that Israel constitutes a corporate whole that also transcends time.

In totality-thinking, the ideal reality is a state of wholeness or completeness (Heb. *šalom*) in which no essential part is missing or nothing essential is left incomplete. That sense of wholeness/completeness, for example, is what drives the restorer of blood to kill the person thought responsible for killing his kinsman (Josh. 20). The loss leaves the clan metaphysically incomplete, but the death of the killer restores its wholeness.

Totality-thinking also undergirds the Old Testament's view of reward and punishment. According to Boaz, Ruth's remarkable loyalty to Naomi had earned the Moabitess proper payment. So, twice invoking the root *šalem* ("to be complete, whole"), Boaz wishes that her deeds become "complete"—that she be paid in full (Ruth 2:11−12).

Sin, likewise, comprises part of a larger whole, as the Cisjordanian use of *ʿawon* above indicates (Josh. 22:17, 20). It designates both the original "sin" (idolatry) and the resulting "guilt" from which Israel needs cleansing. In Joshua 22, *ʿawon* does not mean "punishment"; contextually the idea of punishment as the expected result of *ʿawon* as "guilt" is clear (cf. Gen. 4:13; Ezek. 21:30, 34). Thus, the word *ʿawon* offers a microcosm of totality-thinking: Its framework is a whole process, the sequence of sinful act, guilt, and either forgiveness (Heb. to "carry *ʿawon* away") or punishment (Heb. "to impose *ʿawon*," Num. 14:18).

Tribal interaction. Finally, in light of the above, a retrospective debrief of the tribal interaction in Joshua 22 will lay helpful groundwork for the next section. In a word, there is plenty of praise and blame for both sides. The poor communication between east and west obviously creates a dangerous situation, given their differing perspectives and passionate feelings. Scholars tend to view the altar building as provocative in intent, but why did they resort to provocation rather than direct communication? They could have spared everyone the confrontation had they done so. Did a sense of social or spiritual inferiority lead them to avoid a confrontation, or were they just too eager to get home after their long absence?

Or, if provocation was not their intent, did they assume that their western kin would deduce that the altar's massive size excluded its use for sacrifice, an assumption some scholars make? In other words, in their minds, the altar's design made it obvious that it served no sacrificial purpose. Further, it probably never occurred to them that, after proving their loyalty to the other tribes in battle, anyone would suspect them of apostasy.

As for the western tribes, the text simply says that "they heard" and quotes the report about the altar (v. 11, cf. v. 12). But how did they know their eastern kin had built it? And, if one believes the later Transjordanian explanation, then why did the Cisjordanians (or their source) not notice that the altar showed no signs of sacrificial use (e.g., blood stains, ashes, blackened surfaces, etc.)? Why, instead, did they immediately think the worst of their fellow Israelites? Did blind fear of Yahweh's anger cloud their judgment and unleash their suspicions of apostasy? Or, did prior prejudices against the east-bank tribes predispose them to presume the worst?

To my knowledge the two-and-a-half tribes had no track record of apostasy. After all, the notorious Peor and Achan episodes each involved west-bank people, a Simeonite (Num. 25:14) and a Judahite (Josh. 7:1). Further, if the Transjordanians truly intended rebellion, why build the altar on the west bank rather than closer to home? In sum, whatever the roots of their reaction (fear, prejudice, superiority), they obviously overlooked questions or evidence that would have spared them their misunderstanding. At the same time, the entire incident has much to teach us about church life today, teaching to which we now turn.

WHAT BEGAN AS AN ordinary day suddenly changed as Betty cheerfully bore her grocery bags in from the car. When she entered the kitchen, she found her husband, Jerry, his back turned, writhing, and gyrating almost out of control. Then her eyes saw the electric wire dangling from him.

"Oh, my gosh!" she exclaimed. "It's that wire — he's being electrocuted!"

Now her only thought was to find a piece of wood to separate her husband from the wire. Quickly she tossed her bags aside, raced to the pantry, grabbed a broom, returned to her still-quivering husband, and swatted him as hard as she could on the arm.

"Hey, what're you doing?" Jerry protested, turning around.

It was then that Betty saw that the "wire" was connected to something metal in Jerry's hands. It ran up his body, split in two, one wire going to this left ear and the other to his right. He wasn't a victim of electric shock—he'd simply been listening to music on his Walkman.

Things are not always what they seem. That was true of the altar controversy, and it is often true of church life today. Indeed, to look closely at Joshua 22 is to look into a mirror at life in our churches. Though reporting an event long ago, it has very contemporary meaning. The central theme of Joshua 22 is "the unity of the people despite geographical separation."[64] Christianity also treasures that as a central conviction, so once again an Israelite experience can show us what Christ-like conduct in our church communities might look like. The Jordan River was the geographical symbol of theological tensions that could have divided Israel. It provides an appropriate metaphor to guide the following discussion of theological and nontheological differences within our churches. Wielded by misguided or overly-zealous members, they have the potential to cause divisons.

Beware the little Jordans. The Transjordanians feared that the Jordan River would be used to exclude them from worship. At that moment, what ably served as a natural boundary marker would become a barrier to keep them out. One group within Israel would use its geography to divide Israel into parts labeled "Us" and "Them." In my view, little Jordans, capable at least of eroding, if not dividing, Christian unity, flow quietly through every local Christian congregation.

Imagine the complex make-up of your own church, a complexity whose small Jordans might quickly reach a floodstage of divisive conflict. It has people of different ages (from newborns to senior citizens) and different genders (males and females). In some congregations, the old are in charge and hold the younger generation at bay, while in others the opposite situation prevails. Congregations define the roles that women may play in church life differently, including whether they may teach adults or serve as pastor or elder. Some gifted, mature women feel excluded from leadership, although the issue never surfaces. Others are perfectly content with the ministry opportunities that their church affords them. These days a congregation probably has people from various ethnic and cultural backgrounds, including recently arrived immigrants from other countries. Whether a Jordan rivulet separates them from settling in comfortably will depend on their facility in English and the warmth of the welcome they receive.

Some churches contain a mix of people with various denominational backgrounds and others without any religious upbringing at all. They may

64. Assis, "A Witness between Us," 231.

each be surprised — and at times irritated — at what the other regards as a "big deal" at church. A variety of religious experiences may also populate a congregation, with intellectuals, mystics, contemplatives, skeptics, charismatics, evangelists, and easy-goers in the mix. Such differing experiences raise divisive questions about what the church should be doing — evangelism, spiritual formation, worship, social service, and "all of the above." They also often cause divisions about how the church should worship — formal, informal, or blended worship style?

In recent decades, congregations have become more aware — and at times, divided — by political affiliation, too. In my experience, a congregation evenly divided between Republicans, Democrats, and independents is a rarity. Usually, one of the first two dominates, with the remaining two a minority. The challenge is to avoid criticizing or denigrating fellow believers for their political beliefs. Political passions often run hotter than theological ones! Of course, congregations differ as to how politically visible or partisan they choose to be. Sadly, in my view, the larger church seems divided over how to relate to another category, the rich and poor among us. The fact is that, while no (or perhaps few) churches turn away the rich, some congregations are more welcoming of the poor than others.

Finally, other possible little Jordans include the length of time attending a congregation (i.e., "newcomers" versus "oldtimers") and the visibility or invisibility of someone in church life. Visible people lead worship, serve on committees and boards, teach Sunday school, give announcements or make reports in church, and offer special music. Visible people tend to see themselves as part of the church's central core — its stakeholders, so to speak — whereas invisible people feel themselves more on the periphery. Visible people are more likely to attend church business meetings and to speak their mind than invisible people.

Now, I admit that the above picture involves oversimplification, if not distortion. Many congregations with multiple kinds of diversity function amicably. In mature congregations, an awareness of differences and a positive spirit toward them prevails. Everyone accepts the little Jordans as nothing more than an accepted part of the ongoing rhythm of congregational life. But the altar episode suggests that during a congregational crisis (or something perceived to be so) some little Jordans may quickly reach floodstage. The trick is for leadership to build understanding and trust across the streams through ongoing conversation. To alter the metaphor slightly, a truly, healthy, united congregation is one in which differences flow to the surface quickly to be dealt with openly rather than lurk menacingly beneath the surface of church life.

In Joshua 22, the west-bank group regarded itself as superior to their east-bank kin. For us, the question is, what barriers divide our congregations – or, to put it differently, how inclusive of diversity are we? Do our churches unconsciously think in terms of "castes" or "classes" — for example, the "truly committed," the "semi-committed," and the "pew-warmers"? Through misunderstandings, subtle prejudices can develop between the groups.

And what about visitors? How welcoming are we to people unlike us who make us uncomfortable? What about someone who wanders in off the street, who dresses, speaks, or acts inappropriately (by our standards)? How do we react to those who do not speak Churchese or who do not know the rules? Do we see them as an opportunity or an intrusion? Our constant challenge — indeed, a truly joyous task — is to keep the little Jordans flowing and enriching our church life but always below floodstage. That challenge applies to everyone who worships with us — members, regular attenders, seekers, and droppers-in.

Lucy Van Pelt in a recent "Peanuts" cartoon illustrates the cluelessness to be avoided:

> "The way I see it, Charlie Brown," she says, "your faults simply outweigh your virtues!" After a moment of thought, she adds, "I wish there were some way to demonstrate what I mean...."
>
> "I have it!" she brightens up. "I think I can give you a graphic presentation which will help you to see yourself as you really are!" She leads Charlie over to a fallen log and picks up a board just right for an impromptu teeter-totter.
>
> "This board will represent an evenly balanced personality," she explains. "Now, on one side I'll place this pebble which represents all of your virtues.... On the other side I'll place this boulder which represents your countless faults.... Now, watch what happens....
>
> Lucy drops the boulder on one end, and it quickly drives the board to the ground with a "Wump!" At the same instant the other end pops up with a "Boing!" flipping the pebble past the two of them. As Charlie Brown leaves sadly, Lucy speaks after him: "Don't you think you're lucky to have me around to point up these things in such a graphic manner?"[65]

The dangers of distance. Implicit in the Cisjordanians' argument is an assumption: Geographical proximity to Israel's central sanctuary made them theologically superior to their east-bank kin. As a result, distance

---

65. *The Chicago Tribune,* "Sunday Comics," December 23, 2006.

from Shiloh and the tabernacle posed a serious practical problem for the tribes living in Transjordan. It poses no less serious a threat to the vitality of our congregations.

Here I have in mind "distance" in two senses. The first sense—*geographical distance*—compares to the Transjordanian problem. By geographical distance I mean the distance, measured either in miles/kilometers or in time required to arrive—that separates our home from our place of worship. Now, at the risking of slaughtering a sacred cow, let me make full disclosure upfront: If given a choice, I think it better to associate with a truly "local" church (one a short distance from home), over a commuter-style one. I concede that there are often good reasons for selecting a more distant church over a closer one—e.g., a church's theological stance, spiritual vibrancy, programs for youth and children, public reputation, connections with family, and so on. The congregations near our homes may simply not be acceptable compared to ones farther away. I also freely confess that I myself have had church memberships in the past that required significant commutes, and so I am in no position to pontificate on the matter.

But permit me humbly to voice the main concern that drives my comments on geographical distance. It goes back to my comments in the last chapter, specifically, that I share the vision of people like Reggie McNeal, who says that to be effective today, churches need to engage their communities in order to transform them. In his view, that is the only way the church can live out its mission to impact society spiritually today.

In my view, a church congregation has two main goals: to bind its worshipers into a close, caring community and to maintain close connections with its surrounding community. The former aims to build up the people of God so they may love and serve Christ, the latter to provide the many avenues in which that service may take place. My concern, thus, is that church life at a distance may get in the way of reaching both goals. It may make it difficult for us to stay connected both with fellow worshipers and our neighborhoods. But, given that distance may separate our home and our church, how can we overcome these disadvantages (and perhaps even make them work for the kingdom)?

One good way is to find other Christians who live nearby and with them form a small group—a kind of local mini-congregation—for prayer, encouragement, accountability, and community service. Some larger churches intentionally facilitate the formation of such neighborhood subgroups, a strategy I affirm, but one may have to find a group of fellow believers nearby that is not from our church. Another good way is to maintain neighborhood connections through involvement in local community organizations such as schools, service clubs, professional societies, sports teams, and neighborhood interest groups. In short, the problem of distance in Joshua 22 reveals that geographical distance in our church life has its downsides, notwithstanding how common commuting to church is today. Through whatever means, the point is to minimize, if not overcome or utilize, those downsides for the advance of the kingdom.

The second sense—*emotional distance*—is a more uniquely modern problem. By "emotional distance" I mean the tendency to be standoffish or unengaged personally in relationships with others. It is the antithesis of the intimacy and transparency in which I share with someone else my true feelings about something important to me. I bridge emotional distance also when I listen empathetically to someone sharing their feelings. Emotionally distant people guard their emotions to prevent revealing them. They have trouble making a genuine personal connection with another human being.

Now, levels of emotional distance or intimacy vary from person to person. I have friends, for example, who weep or show anger easily, and others who rarely show either. In the latter case, the language they use in conversation is symptomatic. They initiate personal sharing with "I think" (i.e., my intellectual analysis of things) rather than "I feel" (i.e., my emotional response to them). In the climactic scene of *A Few Good Men*, Marine Colonel Nathan Jessup (Jack Nicholson) maintains emotional distance despite intense cross examination from Navy Lieutenant Daniel Kaffee (Tom Cruise). But when Kaffee cries, "I want the truth!" Jessup openly unloads his heretofore hidden anger, replying, "You can't handle the truth!" A few lines later, pushed emotionally to the edge, the visibly outraged Colonel blurts out testimony that, alas, amounts to self-incrimination and leads to his incarceration. In that moment he is emotionally close rather than distant.

People also keep emotional distance from God. I have known people who find God hard to talk about. When they speak of him, my gut feeling is that they have invisible hands stuck out to keep God at arm's length. People who have been emotionally hurt by unfortunate, negative church experiences are particularly standoffish. Though a Christian for many years, I sympathize with their desire for distance. (I have suffered some negative church experiences myself.) To them God is a mysterious, unpredictable, threatening, and spooky unknown with whom they have no way of dealing. That is true—until, of course, you get to know him.

In the previous chapter, we emphasized that church communities should be safe places. By that I mean places where people feel comfortable over time to drop their guard and open up. Only such churches create spiritual hothouses where, like lovingly tended plants, people can thrive and loving, healthy relationships bloom. Those relationships will grow both horizontally—with other people—and vertically—with God. The Cisjordanians in Joshua 22 pursued an approach that created distance between themselves and the Transjordanians. They opened the conversation with a frank, serious accusation and brought up past history to back it up. The charge of idolatry and allusions to Peor and Achan put the east-bank tribes on notice—and on the defensive, too. I would not advise that approach in day-to-day conversations at church!

But, occasionally some frank-spoken sisters and brothers plunge ahead nonetheless. Once at a graduation reception I encountered a man whom I knew casually and who knew me because of my position. After shaking hands and exchanging greetings, he abruptly threw me a hand grenade—a direct question on a matter of great controversy. Now, after several decades as an educator, I am quite used to being asked Bible or theological questions at any moment. But, quite frankly, my sense was that he, like Phinehas and company, was trying to "nail" me, and inside I felt resentment for his abruptness. A reception for graduates hardly seemed the occasion to probe what somebody believes on a hot topic. Thankfully, my mind framed a judicious answer that was both true to my convictions and satisfactory to him.

My general approach to bridging emotional distance is to draw people out by asking, first, nonthreatening questions, and, later, more personal ones. This go-slow approach puts strangers at ease and makes a personal connection. Whatever approach one takes, the point is to connect and launch an ongoing relationship. The focus should also be on the present and future, not the past. It is best to let the "past" be the "past"—long ago and far away and forgotten. This kind of relationship sets the stage for the Holy Spirit to work on narrowing emotional distance horizontally and vertically.

Many years ago, I watched a narrowing of emotional distance take place in someone. Out of friendship, Charlie (not his real name) had generously driven a close friend to a Christian group of which I was a part. He had never attended any of the group's twice-yearly meetings before, and the friend would have had difficulty attending without his kindness. Several of us introduced ourselves and learned a little about Charlie. For several years, Charlie would drop his friend off but stay outside in his vehicle during the meeting. He was keeping a safe distance, but he was also carefully watching. We always greeted him by name but never pressured him to come inside.

Then, several years later, at one meeting he unexpectedly came inside on his own, sat in the very back, and stayed the whole time. Several more years of watching from the back followed. Over time, he inched his way closer to the front and began to converse with others attending. Soon, he began actually to participate in the group, and he and I became friends. Gradually, he began to tell me bits and pieces of his life story and I came to understand his wariness. He also began to ask me hard questions about God and his love. He did not quite believe that God could really love him, but eventually he asked me to get him a Bible. In time, he became a regular member of the group and entered a new relationship with Jesus. It took a while, but the Holy Spirit patiently coaxed him closer, eventually closing his emotional distance with God and with others. And God desires to replicate that same process over and over again in our churches.

Hanging together. An African proverb says, "If you have enough friends, you can carry an elephant into the house." The east-bank tribes in Joshua 22 had been good friends to their west-bank kinfolk, and the result—the conquest of Canaan—was as amazing as carrying an elephant into the house. They rightly received their honorable discharge from Joshua, and their commitment to Israel's success reminds us of a foundational theme for Christians. At heart, we are a people of shared hardship. Paul summed up our motto with powerful simplicity: "When one [body] member suffers, all suffer together with it. Now you are the body of Christ, and each one of you is a part of it" (1 Cor. 12:26–27).

The metaphor of the human body underlies his words. When we stub a toe, the head feels the pain, the shoulders may shudder, and the stomach become tense. The body is not a loose collection of independent organs but an integrated whole. The same is true of the church of Jesus Christ. Granted, we do not all play the same role in the kingdom. Some of us get to be up front and to do the talking—and some readers are glad it is not them! Others preach even more eloquent sermons with their skilled hands, their organizational expertise, and their compassionate presence. Whatever our role, we Christians are a tight-knit family that mutually shares the ups and downs of life. We weep together, bear each other's burdens, lift each other up, hold each other accountable, and walk through shadowy death valleys together.

How wonderful that, when our duties are done, a commendation likewise awaits us—not from Joshua but from his namesake, Jesus: "Well done, good and faithful servant.... Come and share your master's happiness" (Matt. 25:23). Or, in Paul's words, "Now there is in store for me the crown of righteousness, which the Lord, the righteous Judge, will award to me on that day—and not only to me, but also to all who have longed for his appearing" (2 Tim. 4:8). Great joy awaits us!

In the present, however, one primary shared suffering consumes us. We are all engaged in obeying what Jesus taught:

> Whoever wants to be my disciple must deny themselves and take up
> their cross daily and follow me. For whoever wants to save their life
> will lose it, but whoever loses their life for me will save it. What good
> is it for you to gain the whole world, and yet lose or forfeit your very
> self? (Luke 9:23−24 TNIV; cf. Matt. 16:24−25; Mark 8:34−35)

Every day we all share the same hardship, the demand for self-denial and
for cross-bearing. As we all know, self-denial is no easy task. Self-preoccupation with our needs, wants, and agendas comes naturally to us.

We are all like the seagulls in the movie *Finding Nemo*. With great effort
Nemo has managed to escape both the aquarium in the dentist's office and
the clutches of his dentist's niece, Darla, the one with the mouth filled with
sparkling silver braces. Nemo has reached the open sea but, alas, right in
front of a row of hungry seagulls perched high above. They erupt into a
chorus of "Mine! Mine! Mine!" They are all eager to swallow little Nemo
to assuage their hunger. Similarly, how much more readily "Mine!" escapes
our lips than "It's all yours!" Our culture applauds and admires self-assertion,
especially if it leads to great wealth or celebrity.

Our culture is, well, full of itself. It perverts normal hungers—the need
to belong, to feel important, to be who I really am—into exaggerated, rav-
enous appetites. Only self-centeredness and self-preoccupation can satisfy
these appetites. But Jesus calls us not just to have our self-assertion take a
back seat. He expects us to crucify it and get rid of it! We must "lose" it
completely!

But that is not the end. After the crucifixion, Jesus also calls us to carry
our cross around every day as we follow him. That habit daily reminds us
not to resurrect the old selfishness again. That is the heavy price we pay
every day to follow Jesus. Life is a constant struggle to keep the old self
dead and buried. It is an especially ever-present struggle because the world
around us keeps tempting us to resuscitate it. That way, we will be like them
and fit in better.

The grip of selfishness on us is illustrated in a parable told in the The
Brothers Karamazov by Dostoyevsky. There was a wicked peasant woman
who died without having done a single good deed. As the devils plunged
her into the lake of fire, her guardian angel tried to remember a good deed
of hers to tell God. Finally, he said, "She once pulled up an onion in her
garden ... and gave it to a beggar woman."

God answered with this instruction: "You take that onion then, hold
it out to her in the lake, and let her take hold and be pulled out. And if
you can pull her out of the lake, let her come to Paradise, but if the onion
breaks, then the woman must stay where she is."

The angel ran to her and held out the onion to her. "Come, catch hold," he urged, "and I'll pull you out." Carefully, he began to drag her out and was about to succeed when the other sinners in the lake grabbed the woman in hopes of being pulled out with her. But the woman began kicking them, saying, "I'm to be pulled out, not you. It's my onion, not yours." At that moment the onion broke and the woman fell back into the lake, and the angel wept and left.[66] Similarly, the same instinct toward selfishness afflicts us all, and our daily challenge is to not breathe new life into it.

At the same time, the life of self-denial is crucial to maintaining credibility with the very world that seeks to trip us up. As Dr. Martin Luther King Jr. once warned, "If today's church does not recapture the sacrificial spirit of the early church, it will lose its authenticity, forfeit the loyalty of millions, and be dismissed as an irrelevant social club with no meaning for the twentieth century."[67]

Further, only as we follow in Jesus' footsteps, embracing our crosses as he did his, do we truly experience the power of our heavenly Father. Only on those days can we exult with Phinehas the priest, "Today we know that the LORD is with us" (Josh. 22:31). The cross-bearing becomes for us not only the place of our daily death to self, but also of our daily resurrection as our new selves. The only way the Transjordanians could enjoy their future home was to bear their cross—to proceed into battle beside their Cisjordanian brothers. For them there was no alternate route home except via the hard road of sacrifice. By the same token, no alternate route—and surely, no escape route!—permits us to bypass the narrow street called the Way of the Cross. That tight way is the only direct route to experiencing God's power in us conquering our selfishness. As Benner writes:

> The Christian life is filled with little deaths and little resurrections, little Good Fridays and little Easter Sundays. Each embrace of my cross is a further step into the kingdom of God, a kingdom we can reach only on the other side of the death of our kingdoms and queendoms of self-sufficiency and self-determination.[68]

Trust and loyalty. One implication of the episode in Joshua 22 is that ultimately we Christians should trust each other and give each other the benefit of the doubt. Imagine this: The nine-plus western tribes were ready to go to war against the two-plus eastern ones because of a misinterpreta-

---

66. F. Dostoyevsky, *The Brothers Karamazov* (New York: Penguin, 1957 [1880]), 425.

67. Martin Luther King Jr., "Letter from a Birmingham Jail," quoted in Stephen B. Oates, *Let the Trumpet Sound* (New York: Mentor, 1982), 221.

68. Benner, *Desiring God's Will*, 99.

tion. A horrible, unjust slaughter could have resulted. In the church, we do not treat each other violently, but we sometimes do treat each other with similar suspicion and distrust. But think of it this way: The care of the church and its people really belongs to Christ, and he is fully capable of doing so.

Therefore, rather than confront each other over every little thing, there are times simply to let things pass because we trust each other—and we trust the unseen work of the Holy Spirit. After all, unlike us, the Spirit sees the whole situation and truly knows what is best for all concerned. As the Transjordanian shout, "The LORD! He knows!" (Josh. 22:22). I cannot say this loud enough: The church suffers when we fail to give each other room, fail to trust each other, or fail simply to ignore minor mistakes. This means, further, that we need to beware that our knowledge of past history may mislead us. From a distance, much behavior is simply ambiguous. As an onlooker, I have interpreted scenes one way, only to discover that they were in reality about something very different.

It is too easy—out of pure motives and passion for Christ—to misread each other's actions or to attribute wrong motives to each other. We do not need churches where we eye each other warily across the pews because of misunderstandings. So, Joshua 22 warns us to be wary of our own eyes, lest we jump to the wrong conclusions about each other. Instead, rather than do what the Israelites did, it calls us to think the best of each other and to deal with each other directly. The best vaccination against misunderstandings is frequent contact with each other and direct, candid communication.

Joshua 22 also positively reaffirms the principle that we are mutually accountable to each other. I affirm the need in church life for a Christian sister or brother discretely to approach a fellow Christian and give feedback concerning ambiguous behavior. I have both given and received it—thankfully, not very often—and when I receive it I interpret it gratefully. I do not take it as spiritual one-upmanship, but as the sincere concern of a loving friend for my spiritual welfare and for the health of the body.

When a déjà vu moment occurs, the temptation is to read the past into the present: "Oh, here we go again! I should have expected this, given your history!" Frankly, some of us by temperament are pessimists and some of us are optimists. We are like the two people who died and found themselves in the afterlife locked in a room ceiling-high with manure. The pessimist wrung his hands crying, "Oh, this is terrible! We'll never get out of here!" while the optimist had grabbed a shovel nearby and started digging. "Relax, man!" he shouted cheerfully. "There's got to be a horse in here somewhere!" By temperament, some of us are more suspicious or paranoid than others and, hence, more inclined to compare present ambiguous conduct with someone's past track record. I remind us all, however, that Jesus forgives and forgets all confessed sin (including our own)—and so should we.

I also remind us that Jesus is in the business of transforming people and that there is no one better at it than he. The Bible and church history teem with examples of impossible, incorrigible, irredeemable people whom God marvelously changed, much to the surprise of their neighbors, family, and friends. I venture to guess that some of those transformed people sit next to you every Sunday—or you are one of them. In short, when we suspect bad things about a fellow Christian, I call us to set aside the past and treat the person on the basis of the present and the future.

Several North American restaurants have recently been experimenting with an intriguing new service called "dark dining."[69] In dark dining, customers enjoy the usual multicourse meal, but they dine blindfolded or seated in a completely dark room, and blind or visually impaired waiters serve them. Removal of the usual visual stimuli heightens the diner's awareness of and dependence on other senses.

"It's a mind-opening thing, like meditation would be," explains Benjamin Uphues, whose company, Opaque-Dining in the Dark, stages weekend dinners for fifty at one California hotel. The menus feature dishes with especially sensuous aromas, textures, and tastes (though soup is excluded for obvious reasons). In Greenwich Village, New York, sighted waiters serve up the dark-dining experience, which also includes audio artists—a bass player or Irish percussive dancer—and a surprise light neck massage.

"The most deeply satisfying thing that happens," says event hostess Dana Salisbury, "is that everybody becomes very open and drops their defenses and becomes incredibly wonderful to watch. People do soften in an extremely wonderful way."

Talk about a clever new idea for church worship! Seriously, imagine wearing mental blindfolds to church. A similar positive effect might occur. Removal of our usual observations would heighten our awareness of new aspects of people. It would certainly screen out our misperceptions of them and dispense with our misjudgments. Also, imagine the changed perspectives on life that might result from the experience of being temporarily blind or visually impaired. The experience would open us up to each other, level away all hierarchy, lead us to depend more on each other, and "soften" our spirits. The watching world might sit up and take notice of us—a truly unique people who hang together, give each other space, forget the past, and treat each other with trust and loyalty. That day, they might shout, "Now we know that the LORD is with us!" (Josh. 22:31).

---

69. "Who Moved My Cheese? And My Soup?" *USA Today*, Friday July 13, 2007, p. 8D.

Joshua 23:1–16

❧

AFTER A LONG time had passed and the LORD had given Israel rest from all their enemies around them, Joshua, by then old and well advanced in years, ²summoned all Israel—their elders, leaders, judges and officials—and said to them: "I am old and well advanced in years. ³You yourselves have seen everything the LORD your God has done to all these nations for your sake; it was the LORD your God who fought for you. ⁴Remember how I have allotted as an inheritance for your tribes all the land of the nations that remain—the nations I conquered—between the Jordan and the Great Sea in the west. ⁵The LORD your God himself will drive them out of your way. He will push them out before you, and you will take possession of their land, as the LORD your God promised you.

⁶"Be very strong; be careful to obey all that is written in the Book of the Law of Moses, without turning aside to the right or to the left. ⁷Do not associate with these nations that remain among you; do not invoke the names of their gods or swear by them. You must not serve them or bow down to them. ⁸But you are to hold fast to the LORD your God, as you have until now.

⁹"The LORD has driven out before you great and powerful nations; to this day no one has been able to withstand you. ¹⁰One of you routs a thousand, because the LORD your God fights for you, just as he promised. ¹¹So be very careful to love the LORD your God.

¹²"But if you turn away and ally yourselves with the survivors of these nations that remain among you and if you intermarry with them and associate with them, ¹³then you may be sure that the LORD your God will no longer drive out these nations before you. Instead, they will become snares and traps for you, whips on your backs and thorns in your eyes, until you perish from this good land, which the LORD your God has given you.

¹⁴"Now I am about to go the way of all the earth. You know with all your heart and soul that not one of all the good promises the LORD your God gave you has failed. Every

promise has been fulfilled; not one has failed. [15]But just as every good promise of the LORD your God has come true, so the LORD will bring on you all the evil he has threatened, until he has destroyed you from this good land he has given you. [16]If you violate the covenant of the LORD your God, which he commanded you, and go and serve other gods and bow down to them, the LORD's anger will burn against you, and you will quickly perish from the good land he has given you."

THE AUTHOR NOW LEADS readers through the book's closing section, two national assemblies convened by Joshua toward the end of his life (chs. 23–24). Together they mark the last days of Joshua, key moments in which Joshua prepares the people for a future without him.

By now, readers of this book are used to hearing Joshua speak. They have heard him giving instructions (1:13–15; 3:9–13; 17:17–18), relaying Yahweh's orders (4:5–7, 17), interpreting a victory (4:21–24), lamenting a defeat (7:7–9), praying (10:12), and encouraging military commanders (10:25). This chapter features his farewell speech, a kind of last testament that he gives Israel—his "ethical will" about what Israel should do when he is gone.[1]

Indeed, the inclusion of similar farewell speeches at key junctures is a unique literary feature of the DH (e.g., Deuteronomy; 1 Sam. 12; 1 Kings 2:1–9; cf. 1 Kings 8:1–2, 12–53). Like those speeches, Joshua's oration reviews the "good things" Yahweh has done in the past and urges Israel to firm, unswerving loyalty to him in the future. He warns Israel that if they fail to do so, they run the risk of losing the land so long awaited. The speech marks one of those dramatic moments when a landmark biblical narrative pauses at crucial turning points in history to voice major biblical themes and to connect them to Israel's larger story.[2]

Chapter 23 also continues the theme of Joshua's growth in stature as the worthy successor to Moses (cf. 3:7–8; 4:14; 6:27; 11:15, 23). At the end of his life, Moses had convened Israel to prepare them for their future (Deut. 5:1; 29:1; 31:7), and Joshua follows his example.

Further, in two ways Joshua's speech clearly echoes Moses' rhetoric in Deuteronomy: He speaks in the style of paraenesis—an impassioned,

---

1. For further discussion on this genre farewell speech, see Bridging Contexts section.
2. Cf. the useful study of P. R. House, "Examining the Narratives of the Old Testament Narrative: An Exploration in Biblical Theology," *WTJ* 67 (2005): 229–45.

personal appeal to his audience to choose — and he weaves in deutero-nomic vocabulary.[3] Joshua will urge Israel to not "turn aside to the right or to the left" (v. 6; cf. 1:7; Deut. 17:20; 28:14), to "hold fast" to Yahweh alone (23:8; cf. v. 12; 22:5; Deut. 10:20; 30:20), and to "love the LORD" (23:11; cf. 22:5; Deut. 6:5; 30:16, 20). The terms "great and powerful nation" (23:9) and "good land" (23:13, 15) also reflect the language of Deuter-onomy (Deut. 4:21; 11:23; 26:5). Finally, the stern warnings Moses issued in the plains of Moab significantly shape Joshua's warnings here (cf. Deut. 8:19–20; 11:16–17; 30:17–18). One might say that the speaking voice here is Joshua's, but the vocabulary comes from Moses.

Scholarly opinions and Bible translation layouts reflect various under-standings of the chapter's structure.[4] It has two parts: the introduction with its twofold time reference (v. 1) and the report of Joshua's farewell speech (vv. 2–16). The main sections of the speech are less obvious, but my read-ing finds two sections of remembrance and exhortation (vv. 2–8, 9–13) that culminate in a concluding warning (vv. 14–16).

Within the text there certainly is "a clear escalation in the severity of the rhetoric," as Nelson observes.[5] The first exhortation simply urges Israel to stay away from the nations and their gods (vv. 6–8), while the sec-ond actually warns of potential disaster (vv. 12–13). The final warning (vv. 14–16) turns up the rhetorical heat even higher: If Israel disobeys, Joshua stresses, their future will be as "bad" as the past was "good." In short, Joshua's message prepares Israel for a future without a designated succes-sor, an era fraught with new possibilities or new disasters, all contingent on Israel's fateful choice.

Remembrance and Exhortation, Part 1 (23:1–8)

THE NARRATIVE OPENING LOCATES what follows in time — a "long time" (lit., "many days") after Yahweh had given Israel "rest" from their enemies. The reference is to the memorable, watershed moment when hostilities in Canaan ended and peaceful settlement began (cf. 21:44; 22:4). The twofold formula that follows underscores that Joshua is not just "old" but "very old" (cf. v. 14; Gen 24:1; 1 Kings 1:1). It echoes 13:1, where both the narrator and Yahweh also invoke it, so the context implies that Joshua is now even older than when the long land distribution process began.[6]

---

3. Nelson, *Joshua*, 255; cf. P. R. House, "The God Who Gives Rest in the Land: Joshua," *SBJT* 2 (1998): 29, who also traces echoes in ch. 23 of Josh. 1:1–18.

4. For the details, see Howard, *Joshua*, 418.

5. Nelson, *Joshua*, 256.

6. According to 24:29, he lived to be 110 years old. From that figure, Howard (*Joshua*, 419) suggests that twenty-five years have elapsed between the land distribution (chs. 13–21)

The very fact that Joshua gives a farewell speech signals his awareness of the creeping sunset of mortality steadily falling over him.[7] Nightfall will soon usher Israel into a new context, an era without Joshua or any designated successor. The opening reminder of Joshua's advancing age casts a dark shadow over the scene and makes his speech all the more urgent.

Driven by the urgency of age, Joshua summons all Israel, including its major officials (cf. the same list in 24:1b; cf. 8:33), to hear his farewell address (v. 2a). The inclusion of a full roster of the leaders clarifies that the address applies to everyone in Israel, both leaders and people. Inexplicably, the narrative cites no location for the gathering, although Shiloh seems likely (18:1, 8; 19:51; 21:2; 22:9; cf. 24:1 [Shechem]).[8]

We should imagine a dramatic scene. All of Israel's key leaders sit up front facing Joshua, thousands of Israelites behind them.[9] Everyone has arrived from all over Canaan to hear the very man who allotted each of them their inheritances. A hush falls across the crowd as Joshua, white-haired, slightly stooped, and assisted by an aide, ascends a temporary platform or large stone to be seen and heard. All eyes are on him, all ears ready to hear what the grand old man, the one to whom they owe so much, has to say.

He begins with the obvious—his age (v. 2b)—invoking the two-part formula with which the narrator began (v. 1b; cf. 1 Sam. 12:2). The words immediately explain the reason for the assembly, evoke memories of his long career, and draw the crowd together to hear him as if for the last time. But Joshua quickly turns to remembrance (vv. 2–5), shifting the focus from himself to the audience and what (lit.) "you yourselves [emphatic pronoun] have seen [ra'ab]" (v. 3; cf. Deut. 29:2[1]). They have personally witnessed "all that Yahweh did" on their behalf to "these nations" by fighting for Israel.[10]

"These nations" may refer to the enemies Yahweh defeated east and west of the Jordan or only to those in Canaan (more likely). "Fought for you"

---

and ch. 23. If Joshua and Caleb were of comparable age, Joshua would have been eighty-five when the land distribution began (cf. 14:10).

7. Polzin, *Moses and the Deuteronomist*, 141; cf. Hawk, *Joshua*, 248, who observes that the opening references to Joshua's age and the land at rest show the completion of Joshua's God-given mission.

8. Nelson, *Joshua*, 260.

9. The exclusion of the priests from the list is noteworthy. The text may view Israel's non-priestly leadership as responsible for guarding Israel's obedience to the covenant, including during the imminent post-Joshua era; cf. Butler, 254; Hess, *Joshua*, 295; Deut. 29:10.

10. Interestingly, Joshua's words ("You yourselves [emphatic] have seen") closely resemble ones addressed to him by Moses (Deut. 3:21). The phrase commonly introduces a look backward at Yahweh's past victories, whether spoken by Yahweh (Ex. 19:4; 20:22; Jer. 44:2) or Moses (Ex. 18:8; Deut. 29:2[1]).

echoes the theme of Yahweh war in which Yahweh decisively defeated his (and Israel's) enemies (10:14, 25, 42; cf. Ex. 14:14, 25; Deut. 3:22). The promise of victory marks one of the promises that Yahweh fulfilled ("did") during the Conquest (Deut. 1:30; 20:4).

"See, here!" (*ra'ah*; NIV "Remember") puns on the earlier word "seen" and shifts attention to what Joshua did — his inclusion of the land of "the nations that remain" within their tribal inheritances (v. 4a; cf. vv. 3, 7, 9, 12, 13).[11] They still reside within Canaan (Josh. 15:63; 16:10; 17:12–13, 18; 19:47), but their land has been assigned among the tribes. Verse 4b is grammatically awkward, but "the nations I conquered" probably refers to peoples defeated (lit., "cut off") under Joshua's leadership (so NLT, NRSV, TNK; against NIV).[12] They live between the Jordan and the Mediterranean. As for their future fate, Joshua affirms that Yahweh will drive out and destroy them (v. 5), at that time finally fulfilling his promises (Deut. 6:19; 9:3–5).[13] Playing two senses of the same root, Joshua avers that their destruction (*yaras* hi.) will enable Israel to "possess" (*yaras* hi.) their abandoned property just as he promised (Deut. 31:3).[14]

Meanwhile, their continuing presence poses a serious threat to Israel that drives Joshua to his first exhortation, especially given his imminent death (vv. 6–8). He resorts to what Nelson calls a "democratization of obedience."[15] Joshua redirects to the people as a whole commands that Yahweh originally addressed only to himself in 1:6–9 (v. 6). Joshua commands them, "Be very strong!" as had Moses before his death (Deut. 31:23) and Yahweh at Joshua's commissioning (Josh. 1:6, 7, 9; cf. v. 18; Deut. 31:6, 7).[16]

Up to now, Joshua's calm, steely resolve has kept Israel close to Yahweh, but his death will leave the nation to maintain that closeness on its

---

11. "Nations" (*haggoyim*) normally designates foreign, pagan groups, but here preconquest Canaanite peoples are in mind (cf. Deut. 7:1, 17; 9:4–5; 11:22–23). "I allotted" is Heb. *napal* hi. ("to cast [the lot]"), an allusion to the process of land distribution (14:2; 15:1; chs. 18, 19, and 21).

12. The *BHS* editor reads "the nations I conquered" as a possible later textual addition. For discussion of the textual problems and solutions, see Boling, *Joshua*, 521; Butler, *Joshua*, 252. Joshua 11:21 provides a possible precedent for this unique use of *karat* with Joshua as its subject; cf. Howard, *Joshua*, 421.

13. Cf. 1 Kings 9:20–21, which reports that Solomon conscripted the Amorites, Hittites, Perizzites, Hivites and Jebusites for slave labor on royal construction projects.

14. This verse confirms the assumption that "to take possession" (*yaras* hi.) usually assumes a prior, violent conquest (*yaras* hi. "to destroy"). For further discussion, see Bridging Contexts in chs. 13–19.

15. Nelson, *Joshua*, 261.

16. In reality, in all cases "Be strong!" is paired with "Be courageous!" See comments on ch. 1.

own. They will need to muster Joshua-like strong, unwavering devotion to stick with Yahweh. Like Joshua, on their own they must also "be careful to obey"—to "be constantly on their guard, be vigilant" (*šamar* qal)—to continue to do what Yahweh commands (1:7; cf. 22:5). Their guidebook will be what Joshua followed, "the Book of the Law of Moses" (cf. 1:7–8; for the exact same phrase, see 8:31; 2 Kings 14:6; Neh. 8:1). Like Joshua, they are not to "turn aside [from the Law] to the right or to the left" (23:6; cf. 1:7; Deut. 17:20; 28:14). In short, they are not to stray in any direction from the path of blessing that Yahweh has laid out for them.

Specifically, Joshua cites things to avoid: to associate or intermingle with (lit., "come with") the remaining nations and to take an oath on the name of their gods or swear by them (v. 7).[17] The former probably refers to day-to-day contacts that might tempt the Israelites to become like the Canaanites just to get along and, thus, to lose their unique identity.[18] The latter specifies one common, ordinary transaction, the agreements two parties seal with an oath. To "take an oath" with a non-Israelite could require the Israelite party to speak the name of a god other than Yahweh aloud in public, tacitly accepting its power and authority. From that tacit recognition, it then becomes a small step to "worship" (NIV "serve") other gods and "bow down" prostate before their images, a violation of the third commandment (Ex. 20:5; Deut. 5:9).[19] To lie face down—to be completely prostrate on the ground—dramatically acts out a symbolic total surrender to and trust in the other god(s) rather than in Yahweh alone.

Instead, Joshua invokes two emphatic words (*ki ʾim*) to exhort Israel to do the opposite of what verse 7 prohibits. They are to stay the course pursued until now—"to hold fast" (*dabaq*) to Yahweh alone (v. 8; cf. v. 12; 22:5), a command that echoes Deuteronomy (Deut. 10:20; 11:22; 13:5; 30:20; cf. 2 Kings 18:6; Ps. 63:8[9]). Elsewhere, *dabaq* ("to cling") describes the tight clinging of a couple in sexual relations (Gen. 2:24) and Ruth's firm, loyal embrace of Naomi (Ruth 1:14).[20] To cling firmly to Yahweh is to embrace him so tightly—to observe such exclusive loyalty to him—as to leave not even the smallest crack for other gods between the two of you.

---

17. To "associate with" (lit., "to go into") may outlaw sexual contact since elsewhere the same phrase describes sexual intercourse; cf. Nelson, *Joshua*, 261. For "take an oath on the name of," cf. W. F. Smelik, "The Use of *hazkir bešem* in Classical Hebrew," *JBL* 118 (1999): 323–26.

18. Fritz, *Josua*, 230.

19. For the formulaic pairing of "worship" and "bow down," cf. Deut. 8:19; 11:16; 17:3; 29:25.

20. Cf. also the noun *debeq* that designates the "welding" of metals (Isa. 41:7); cf. Howard, *Joshua*, 422.

In short, to avoid association with non-Israelites means not to take the first step toward loosening Israel's embrace of Yahweh.[21]

Remembrance and Exhortation, Part 2 (23:9–13)

FROM EXHORTATION JOSHUA RETURNS again to the past deeds of Yahweh that they themselves have seen (vv. 9–10). He reminds them that Yahweh "destroyed" (*yaraš*; NIV "has driven out") once "great and powerful nations"[22] on their behalf. The words recall Joshua's assurance of the people just before the Jordan crossing (3:10), itself an echo of Yahweh's promise in Deuteronomy to destroy "[nations] greater and more powerful than you [Israel]" (Deut. 4:38; 9:1; 11:23). As part of the patriarchal promise, the words here imply that with the enemies' defeat, Israel has become the "great and powerful nation" God promised (Gen. 18:18; Deut. 26:5). That fact heightens the urgency of Joshua's speech all the more.

But Joshua repeats a phrase heard earlier in the book to highlight what Israel saw because Yahweh fought for them. Just as he promised, they were so unstoppable (see 10:8; 21:44; Est. 9:2) that one solitary Israelite could rout a thousand Canaanites (vv. 9b–10)![23] That was Israel's experience "to this day," but for that invincibility under Yahweh to continue, Israel must "be very careful [*šamar* ni.] to love the LORD your God" (v. 11). The imperative is strong language—lit., "Protect yourselves!"—as if Joshua were sounding an urgent alarm concerning a terrible, imminent disaster.

"To love the LORD" is a central demand in Deuteronomy that the DH also promotes (Josh. 22:5; 1 Kings 3:3).[24] This "love" reciprocates God's prior initiatives of love already shown to Israel (Deut. 7:8). It includes feelings of genuine affection toward God (Deut. 10:15) as well as a lifestyle of loyalty, fidelity, and devotion to him.[25] To live that lifestyle is to do what God commands and teaches through Moses—in Joshua 23, to avoid entanglements with the nations and their gods.

---

21. For further discussion of the problems of Israelite-Canaanite associations and intermarriage, see Bridging Contexts section.

22. "Destroyed" again follows Lohfink, "שׁרַיָ," 6:375. Here Heb. *mippenekem* means "for your sake," as in v. 3.

23. Elsewhere, the hyperbolic, almost proverbial expression "one routs a thousand" describes Israel's powerlessness before enemies once their rebellion against Yahweh leads him to abandon them (Deut. 32:30; Isa. 30:17).

24. Deut. 6:5; 10:12; 11:1, 13–14, 22–23; 19:9; 30:16, 20; cf. 13:4; cf. G. Wallis, "אָהַב," *TDOT*, 1:114–16.

25. This understanding of reciprocal "love" may have its roots in Yahweh's covenant with Israel. In ancient treaties, the suzerain king is said to "love" his vassal and the vassal his suzerain; cf. A. O. Haldar, "אָהַב," *TDOT*, 1:101.

But why should Israelites "protect themselves"? The threatening influence in verses 6–8 will derive from Israel's simply hanging around and doing business with Canaanites. But in the long conditional warning (vv. 12–13), the threatening influence is actual intermarriage with them in violation of Deuteronomy 7:1–5. It is the people, not their god(s), who pose the threat to Israel.[26] The underlying concern is not with racial or ethnic purity (a relatively modern idea) but with the complex bonds of legal and social relationships that marriages forge between families (see the case of Dinah in Gen. 34).[27]

For example, such kinship connections might entail acceptance of legal demands according to Canaanite standards and protected by Canaanite gods. That acceptance would be tantamount to recognizing the existence and authority of the latter. The stipulation Joshua lays down aims to preserve the people as a legal and cultic community related to Yahweh alone. Otherwise, if Israel "turns" from Yahweh and "clings" to Canaanites—that is, intermarries with them (v. 12; cf. 1 Kings 11:2, 11)—Israel should fully grasp the disastrous consequences they are risking (v. 13).[28] Rather than destroy the nations, Yahweh will leave them be (cf. Judg. 2:3) to become "snares and traps" for Israel.

The trapping metaphor colors the coming disaster as a complete surprise (i.e., an unintended consequence), inescapable and ultimately fatal (cf. Job 18:9–10; Ex. 23:33; Num. 33:55; Deut. 7:16). As a bird's entry triggers the trap, so intermarriage seals Israel's tragic fate. The paired metaphors of "whips" and "thorns" picture the punishment's ongoing petty irritation and electric agony (cf. Judg. 2:10–19). Inevitably, as a trapped bird is killed and eaten, Israel will "perish" from the "good land" Yahweh has given (cf. Josh. 23:16). The sad irony is that a foolish pragmatism on Israel's part will cost future generations the very land of promise for which past generations have so earnestly longed.[29] But it should come as no surprise. Nothing so hurts and infuriates God as when his people leave him and take up with other "lovers" (Ezek. 16:32–42; 23:22; Hos. 2:13). And Moses had long

---

26. Fritz, *Josua*, 230–31.

27. Nelson, *Joshua*, 261; Fritz, *Josua*, 231. For more on the Dinah episode, see Bridging Contexts section.

28. The verb "to intermarry" (Heb. *ḥatan* hithp., "to become related by marriage") derives from the noun *ḥatan* ("son-in-law"). Hence, intermarriage occurs when an Israel "son" marries the daughter of a Canaanite (i.e., becomes her father's "son-in-law") or a Canaanite "son" marries an Israelite daughter (i.e., becomes the son-in-law of an Israelite father); cf. E. Kutsch, "חתן," *TDOT*, 5:274.

29. "Good land" is a favorite Deuteronomic phrase for Canaan; cf. Deut. 1:25, 35; 3:25; 4:21, 22; 1 Kings 14:15.

ago warned them of that tragic truth in terms that shaped Joshua 23 (cf. Deut. 8:19–20; 11:16–17; 30:17–18).

Final Warning (23:14–16)

TO CLOSE, JOSHUA SOUNDS almost like a prophet voicing a dire warning of imminent danger (cf. Deut. 32).[30] He returns to where he began—with his age (v. 14a). The syntax of verse 14 (lit., "Look, today I am going ...") and language ("way of all the earth") betray an awareness that he could die any day now (so also David [1 Kings 2:2]). Rhetorically, he plays on their sympathy and appeals to their affection to persuade them to act on his words now. He also appeals to what they "know with all [their] heart and soul," the same prepositional phrase Joshua invoked in exhorting the departing Transjordanian tribes (v. 14b; cf. 22:5; Deut. 11:13; 13:4). In other words, they know without a shadow of doubt from personal experience that what he is about to say is true. For emphasis, he sandwiches a positive claim between two parallel negative ones. The words echo the summary conclusion by the DH in 21:45 (cf. 1 Kings 8:56):

> Negative: "... not one of all the good promises the LORD your God gave you has failed [lit., 'fallen down']"
> Positive: "every promise has been fulfilled [*bo*ʾ]"
> Negative: "not one has failed"

Clearly, the point is that Yahweh has kept every promise made to Israel.

The threefold affirmation of verse 14 forms the basis for a comparison ("just as ...") to drive home Joshua's final warning ("so ...") in verse 15. The comparison puns on the phrase "to come upon" (*bo*ʾ *ʿal*). As "all the good Yahweh spoke concerning you [lit.] came upon you" (*bo*ʾ *ʿaleykem*), so will Yahweh (lit.) "bring upon you [*bo*ʾ hi. *ʿaleykem*] all the bad" (v. 15).[31] "The bad" (*haraʿ*) describes the "disasters" Yahweh will send over time (e.g., the covenant curses in Deut. 28:16–68) until he achieves his purpose for Israel. That purpose is to "destroy" (*šamad* hi.) them "from this good land" they currently occupy (cf. Deut. 28:63).

The blunt juxtaposition of "good" and "bad" recalls the climactic appeal of Moses that Israel choose between them (Deut. 30:15), but unlike Moses, here Joshua simply warns them of danger. His appeal for a decisive choice will come in 24:15. Implicit, however, is the crucial question for Israel: Will Israel reciprocate Yahweh's "good word" in kind?

---

30. Cf. Polzin, *Moses and the Deuteronomist*, 141 ("a harsh prophecy of the future that awaits Israel").

31. In both grammar and content, v. 15 compares to Deut. 8:20 and 28:63 (the latter with *šamad* hi. "to destroy").

In verse 16, Joshua clarifies what a "bad word" would look like. Grammatically, the initial temporal clause ("when you …") describes it (v. 16a) and the concluding statement ("the LORD's anger …") declares its disastrous consequence (v. 16b). A clever, three-part sound play (ʿabar ["violate"], ʿabad ["worship"], ʾabad ["perish"]) knits both parts together. In essence, the "bad" would be to "violate the covenant" that Yahweh commanded by turning from him to idolatry.[32] This apostasy represents the final, fatal step along the path that begins with day-to-day association with non-Israelites (v. 7) and leads to intermarriage with them (vv. 12 – 13). Moses forbad intermarriage as risky; a non-Israelite spouse might influence an Israelite partner to turn away from Yahweh (Deut. 7:3 – 4; cf. 1 Kings 11:2). The three-step formula of apostasy ("go, worship [ʿabad] other gods, bow down to them") is common in the DH.[33] It describes the disastrous result of spousal influence — a voluntary swerve into open idolatry.

Verse 16 marks the first mention of the "covenant" concept in chapter 23, and its debut signals that idolatry is no casual matter.[34] On the contrary, idolatry strikes savagely at the heart of Israel's relationship with Yahweh by rejecting his central demand of them — exclusive loyalty. It also so waters down their identity as to make them useless and unable to carry out God's purposes. They lose their very reason for being and, hence, can readily be discarded.

"To violate the covenant" also recalls Yahweh's charge against Israel in the Achan episode (7:11, 15). The allusion spotlights the extreme seriousness of the breach and the extreme horror of the consequence to follow. Simply put, pursuit of idolatry marks a rejection of Yahweh that ignites his personal outrage ("the LORD's anger will burn") against them (cf. 7:1). Inevitably, that aroused fury will spill across Israel, and they will "quickly perish" (ʾabad) from the "good land" he gave them (cf. Deut. 7:3 – 4; 8:20). Under the covenant, possession of land and loyalty to Yahweh are inextricably linked. Loss of the latter inevitably leads to loss of the former. Worse, covenant breach puts at risk Israel's entire existence as a people.[35]

In short, Joshua's concluding warning brings his farewell speech to a rhetorical climax. He dispels any illusions Israel might have about "getting along" with both Canaanites and Yahweh. Such attempts at accommodation are foolhardy and futile, the risks grave. Joshua has lived long enough

---

32. For "violate the covenant," cf. Deut. 17:2; Josh. 7:11, 15; Judg. 2:20; 2 Kings 18:12; Jer. 34:18; Hos. 6:7; 8:1. In Deut. 29:11, ʿabar beberit means "to enter into a covenant."

33. Cf. Deut. 8:19; 17:3; 29:25; Judg. 2:19; 1 Kings 9:6 = 2 Chron. 7:19; cf. Jer. 13:10; 16:11; 25:6. Josh. 23: 7 combines "worship" and "bow down," as does 2 Kings 17:35.

34. Fritz, *Josua*, 232.

35. Ibid., 232.

to know that such well-intended experiments are doomed to failure; he knows where in the wilderness the bodies of Israel's ancestors are buried. For a people to "perish" is to vanish from history—and, in Israel's case, to trash centuries of postponed hope endured by their patient, longsuffering ancestors. Joshua's point is that for Israel idolatry is nothing but stupid. Alas, notwithstanding Joshua's warnings, a disastrous period of Canaanization—Israel's defection from Yahweh and adoption of Canaanite culture—will characterize the early post-Joshua period (see Judg. 2:11–13).

CLEARLY, JOSHUA WARNS HIS audience against both simple associations and intermarriage because of their adverse influence on Israelites. Brief expansion on the comments made earlier will help flesh out the picture and anticipate part of the Contemporary Significance of Joshua 23.

Problems the Canaanites pose. Why is Joshua so concerned about the Canaanites? Modern readers might be tempted to adopt a live-and-let-live stance toward them. One must remember that, unlike Israel, the Canaanites worshiped a pantheon of gods.[36] The head of the pantheon was the elderly patriarch El, the "father of humanity" and "creator of the earth," whose consort was Athirat, "creatress of the gods" and mother of Baal. The seventy gods that comprise the heavenly council are all called "sons" of El.

Canaanite religion also featured two other goddesses, Ashtarte, consort of the sea god, Yam, and ʿAnat, a childless young maiden, sister of Baal and patroness of kings. At Ugarit and in the Bible, the most prominent Canaanite god was the storm god, Baal, who shows a variety of forms tied to local places (e.g., Baal Peor, Baal Zaphon, Baal Shamen, etc.). The kingship of Baal is the main subject of the Baal Cycle from Ugarit (fourteenth cent. B.C.).[37] This, then, is the general religious landscape in which Israel settled in Canaan.

How would it adversely influence Israel in their day-to-day associations with Canaanites? Granted, what follows is somewhat speculative, but brief biblical glimpses of ancient daily life further flesh out the several situations of influence suggested above. Consider, for example, the common occasions on which one invokes the name of a god. When Boaz arrived at his

---

36. K. van der Toorn, "Theology, Priests, and Worship in Canaan and Ancient Israel," *CANE*, 2046–47.

37. M. S. Smith, "Myth and Mythmaking in Canaan and Ancient Israel," *CANE*, 2031–33; cf. S. B. Parker, "The Literatures of Canaan, Ancient Israel, and Phoenician: An Overview," *CANE*, 2404–6.

harvest field near Bethlehem, he greeted the workers with "The LORD be with you!" to which they responded, "The LORD bless you!" (Ruth 2:4). So, what god (or gods) would be invoked when a Canaanite greeted or said goodbye to an Israelite (or vice versa) somewhere in Canaan? Would each invoke his own god(s), or would they strike some compromise? The same situation would arise should they wish to seal a business transaction with an oath, since parties typically called on deities to enforce oaths.

Now the problem with such ordinary greetings, goodbyes, and oaths is that if the Canaanite invoked his god(s), the occasion would require religious accommodation of the Israelite. To accept a Canaanite's invocation of his god(s) would implicitly recognize their existence and authority and deny Yahweh's exclusive claim to sovereignty. This would be true even if the Israelite invoked only Yahweh's name in his participation. But the temptation to be courteous toward a Canaanite neighbor by also invoking god(s) other than Yahweh presented itself, and the Israelite had only a few seconds to decide. And once he did so, he had set a precedent that now bound him to do it again.

The presence of Canaanite worship sites near the Israelites also would pose a threat to their religious integrity. This would be particularly true in towns where no Levite was present to teach and encourage faithfulness. According to the Old Testament, Canaanite worship included fertility rites involving sexual relations between a worshiper and a cult prostitute (Deut. 23:17 – 18; Hos. 4:12 – 14).[38] The theory was that intercourse symbolically encouraged the god(s) to inseminate the land with abundant fertility. Thus, Canaanite worship may have had two attractions for Israelites. (1) As a fertility religion with the storm god Baal at its center, it would have immediate relevance to Israelites since they were farmers. Probably, the temptation would be to worship both Yahweh and Baal—to avail oneself of the strengths of each, so to speak. (2) The very sensuality of Canaanite fertility rituals also probably attracted Israelites. The twin appeals to relevance and to sexual pleasure tempted them to participate even if they never formally renounced loyalty to Yahweh.

The implications of intermarriage for Israel's exclusive relationship with Yahweh were even worse. Consider the incident involving Jacob's daughter, Dinah, and the Hivites at Shechem (Gen. 34).[39] It illustrates the potential

---

38. Cf. K. van der Toorn, "Prostitution," *ABD*, 5:512, who believes that Canaanite sanctuaries received the income of prostitutes associated with them but denies that Canaanite worship included sexual fertility rites.

39. The Hivites are among the seven peoples of Canaan that fall under the ban (*ḥerem*). I term them "Canaanites" because they inhabited the land of Canaan and were among the "nations that remain" (Josh. 23:4, 12).

tensions and maneuvering that might dog attempts at intermarriage with Canaanites. One day, Dinah went "to visit the women of the land"—a simple but unwise social association—but she was raped en route by Shechem, son of the local ruler (34:1–2). That he could do so with impunity hints at the marginal social status and vulnerability of the Israelites at the time. But Shechem actually loved Dinah, sought to woo her (v. 3), and asked his father Hamor to arrange their marriage (v. 4).

Meanwhile, the rape enraged Dinah's brothers, who called it "a disgraceful thing . . . that should not be done" (v. 7; cf. Josh. 7:15; Gen. 29:26; 2 Sam. 13:12). Unaware of their outrage, Hamor proposed not only a Shechem-Dinah marriage but intermarriage more broadly between Hivites and Israelites as a new general practice (Gen. 34:8–9). In essence, the Hivites and Israelites would become "one people" (vv. 16, 22). For Jacob's entourage that would mark a significant move from the margins of society to its center, while for the Hivites an expansion in clan size would enhance its regional power and prestige. The Hivites welcomed the Israelites to settle down permanently and acquire property. They granted them permission freely to trade anywhere (v. 10).

Now, notice the three-directional double-dealing going on here. The Israelites insisted that the Hivites receive circumcision before Shechem could marry Dinah. It was a trick, in that it would allow several of Jacob's sons to slaughter the Hivite males, all defenseless while recovering from the painful procedure. To win approval from the city fathers of the "one people" plan, Hamor hid the role his son's sexual misconduct played in the deal (v. 21) and played up its financial benefits (v. 23).[40] Likewise, he hid from Jacob and his family its true motive, a Hivite takeover of Israel's sizeable livestock holdings.

Several implications flow from this narrative. (1) Israelite-Canaanite relations were complex matters driven by competing interests and mistrust. This was particularly true when one or the other party felt itself at a disadvantage. (2) The two parties did not necessarily share the same ethical values. Apparently, Hamor did not find his son's conduct objectionable, especially since he saw a way to work it to his financial and political advantage. Dinah's brothers, however, read the rape as an outrageous violation of their clan's ethic. In short, Hivites and Israelites operated by different ethical standards; what Hivites considered acceptable the Israelites considered shameful. (3) Attempts to live in harmony with Canaanites might strain relations within Israel—such as between a slow-reacting father and his hot-headed sons.

---

40. Waltke, *Genesis*, 466.

But suppose Dinah had married Shechem? What consequences would have followed for Israel's identity? Given ancient sociology, Dinah would have left the sanctuary of her father's household and fallen under the authority of her Canaanite husband and father-in-law. She would have become financially dependent on them, and they would have had veto power over her choices, including her choice of god(s). More important, Jacob and his family would have compromised their unique sense of divine destiny. Their marginal status portrays them as comparatively small in number compared to the Hivites. If so, through intermarriage they likely would have been absorbed as just another clan within the tribal structure of the Hivites. They might have maintained some of their own laws and ethical standards, but they would also have been obligated to follow the laws, ethics, and religious practices of the "one people."

In this regard, the example of Ruth's integration into Israel may shed some additional, helpful light. In declaring her loyalty to Naomi, Ruth renounced her ties to her Moabite family and god and embraced Naomi's people and God (Ruth 1:16 – 17; cf. 2:11). How typical such declarations were is difficult to say. But it seems reasonable to assume that the merging of clans would certainly require all parties to affirm some level of loyalty to the larger people about to form. It also seems reasonable that some affirmation of loyalty to god(s) would also figure in the transaction. Since polytheism dominated the ancient world, the common tendency probably was for uniting clans to incorporate each other's god(s) in their worship life.

All this would, of course, realize the worst fears voiced by Joshua's passionate speech. Both religiously and sociologically, Israel would cease to belong to Yahweh alone as his unique people. The realization of the ancient patriarchal promise would be in doubt, to be saved only by divine intervention. In short, at stake in Joshua's speech is nothing less than the survival of Israel's reason for existence—their unique identity defined by the covenant with Yahweh.

The farewell speech genre. Finally, a word concerning the genre of "farewell speech" is in order. Farewell speeches play a prominent role in the Old Testament, as the number of examples attests.[41] Most concern addresses given to Israel assembled together. Moses, for example, gives two passionate farewell speeches to Israel on the plains of Moab shortly before his death (Deut. 31 – 33). They include a lengthy song (ch. 32), a final blessing of the tribes (ch. 33), and personal remarks to him by Yahweh

---

41. I distinguish a farewell speech from the well-known patriarchal blessings (e.g., Gen. 27:25 – 29; 48; 49).

(31:14–21; 32:48–52). It is apparent that Israel's rebellious spirit and inclination toward idolatry trouble both Yahweh and Moses.

One also usually reckons 1 Samuel 12 as Samuel's farewell speech to assembled Israel, although he continues his prophetic ministry (1 Sam. 13; 15; 16; 19:18–22; 25:1). On his mind is concern for Israel's continuing commitment to Yahweh under their newly appointed king, Saul. But the audience for David's farewell address, also given shortly before his passing, is only his son, Solomon (1 Kings 2:1–10). It concludes with an intriguing section in which David reviews with his royal successor the scores to be settled and kindnesses to be shown, all according to Solomon's wise discretion (vv. 5–9).

Scholars have also identified several farewell speeches in the New Testament.[42] According to Kurz and others, Luke's report of the Last Supper meal comprises one example and reflects the influence of the Old Testament models noted above (Luke 22:14–38).[43] Among its purposes are: to instruct early Christians on the Eucharist and on authority in the church, and to present the transfer of authority over his followers from Jesus himself to the twelve disciples.

John 13–17 also offers a farewell speech that aims to prepare the disciples for Jesus' imminent departure and their life as a community after it.[44] A central theme is love—Jesus' love for his father and his disciples, and his mandate that the disciples love each other. Its climax is Jesus' wonderful high-priestly prayer that his Father will especially care for his disciples after he has left them to return to heaven.

Finally, in Acts Luke incorporates his report of Paul's farewell speech to the elders of the church in Ephesus who have joined him at Miletus (Acts 20:17–38).[45] Paul is headed to Jerusalem and an uncertain fate and acknowledges the sad reality that they will never see him again (v. 25). He charges them to protect themselves and their flock from wolves—leaders within the community who will distort the truth and lead believers astray (vv. 28–31).

Ultimately, the biblical roots of farewell speeches go back to Israel's wisdom tradition.[46] It is typical for an authority figure to instruct his pupils (his

---

42. For examples in the Apocrypha, see the farewell speeches to their sons by Mattahias (1 Macc. 2:49–70) and Tobit (Tob. 14:3–11).

43. William S. Kurz, "Luke 22:14–38 and Greco-Roman and Biblical Farewell Addresses," *JBL* 104/2 (1985): 251–68.

44. Cf. F. F. Segovia, *The Farewell of the Word: The Johannine Call to Abide* (Minneapolis: Fortress, 1991), who, however, limits the speech to John 13:31–16:31.

45. Kurz ("Luke 22:14–38 and Greco-Roman and Biblical Farewell Addresses," 257) suggests that "Luke's plan to have a farewell address by Paul in Acts 20 may have inspired him to insert a parallel one by Jesus" in Luke 22.

46. Ibid., 264.

"sons") on the basics of how to avoid disasters and to achieve a happy life (e.g., Prov. 1−7). But farewell speeches are not set in the classroom of wisdom instruction nor are their speakers wisdom teachers. The different settings and different speakers have shaped in them certain common motifs.[47]

(1) The speakers are all leaders responsible for God's people: the lawgiver Moses, his successor Joshua, the priest-prophet Samuel, King David, Jesus the Messiah, and Paul the apostle.

(2) The approaching end of the speaker's life occasions the speech. The speakers themselves voice awareness of their old age (Deut. 31:2; Josh. 23:2; 1 Sam 12:2) or impending death (Josh. 23:14; 1 Kings 2:2; Luke 22:15−16, 18; John 13:33; 16:19−23; 17:11, 13; cf. 13:1, 3; Acts 20:25, 38).

(3) The speeches share the common purpose of preparing God's people for the transition to a new era without their being present. So, for example, Moses' preoccupation is that, in crossing the Jordan without him, Israel remain "strong and courageous" in the face of Canaanite opposition (Deut. 31:1−6). Joshua worries about intermarriage and its resultant apostasy once the Israelites settle in Canaan (Josh. 23:12, 16), while rebellion against Yahweh's law during the monarchy trouble Samuel and David (1 Sam. 12:14−15; 1 Kings 2:3−4).[48]

At the Last Supper, Jesus decrees a model of servant leadership in the kingdom over which the disciples are soon to preside and prepares Peter to survive his impending denial of Christ (Luke 22:25−27, 31−34; John 13:1−17).[49] In the Johannine account, Jesus recalls the figure of Moses, invokes the latter's "love" language, and applies it to the new era about to dawn. As Moses called Israel to "love the LORD your God" by obeying his commands, Jesus commands his disciples to "love" him through obedience, too (John 14:15; 15:9−10). More important, he issues a new commandment for the new kingdom: Besides loving the Father and the Son, the disciples are to "love each other" (John 13:34, 35; 15:12, 17). Finally, Paul prepares the elders of Ephesus for his absence by citing his example of faithful hard work amid great hardships (Acts 20:19, 31, 35). In short, each speech sought to enable its hearers to enter the new era well-prepared for its challenges.

(4) The speeches serve to legitimize the addressee(s) as the speaker's chosen successor.[50] This is obviously true of the relationships between Moses and Joshua (Deut. 31:7−8), David and Solomon (1 Kings 2:2−4),

---

47. Cf. ibid., 255−56.
48. For full treatment of 1 Kings 2:1−10, cf. ibid., 260−61.
49. For the Lucan texts, cf. ibid., 256−58.
50. Ibid., 264−65.

Jesus and the disciples (Luke 22; John 13–17), and possibly of Paul and the Ephesian elders (Acts 20). In 1 Samuel 12, the successor seems to be all Israel and its king, but what about in Joshua 23? In my view, the book of Joshua implies that the Instruction of Moses (and perhaps its dispersed Levite teachers) is Joshua's successor (23:6; cf. 1:7–8; 8:31–32; ch. 21; 22:5). That may explain why Joshua applies the personal charge Yahweh gave him ("Be strong!" [1:6, 7, 9; cf. v. 18) to the people as a whole (23:6, 11) just as he had to his military leaders (10:25).[51] The people are expected to follow Moses' teachings as if he and Joshua were still present to hold them accountable. By implication, the intended audience of the legitimization is not the successor-designate (e.g., Joshua, Solomon, the Twelve), but his followers (i.e., Israel and Christian believers). It passes on the authority of the predecessor and implicitly asks the Israelites and Christians to recognize and obey it.

(5) Finally, the speeches typically recall past history to support exhortations for the present and future.[52] So, Moses recalls the defeat of the Amorite kings, Sihon and Og, so Israel will remain "strong and courageous" (Deut. 31:4, 6). He also reviews "the days of old" to warn them to avoid the disasters that befell their ancestors for their idolatry (32:7–42). Samuel goes over the history from Jacob to the judges to exhort Israel not to abandon Yahweh, now that they have a king (1 Sam. 12:8–15). David reminds Solomon of what Joab, Barzillai of Gilead, and Shimei the Benjaminite did in the past to guide his treatment of them in the future (1 Kings 2:5–9). Similarly, both Jesus and Paul base their urgings on their own ministry history with the disciples and early churches, respectively (John 13:31–16:33; Acts 20:18–22, 34–35). Likewise, Joshua here asks the Israelites to recall their own memories of Yahweh's victories (Josh. 23:3, 9) as examples of what he will do to them for their apostasy (vv. 15–16).

In short, the past, both Israelite and Christian, offers the audience both reassurance of divine favor and warning of divine wrath as they move into the future. Acceptance of the message of the farewell speech will earn them the former, rejection of it the latter.

The genre of farewell speech implies two important things. (1) It assumes that older people have crucial things to teach younger ones. Few readers would object to that assumption initially, although some perceive their teaching as "quaint" rather than "with it." But Joshua 23 presumes that life

---

51. Cf. Nelson, *Joshua*, 258.

52. For full discussion of the elements of farewell speeches, cf. the convenient chart and commentary in Kurz, "Luke 22:14–38 and Greco-Roman and Biblical Farewell Addresses," 262–68.

is like a road on which one enters at birth and travels until death. However long or short the journey, every stage is a whole new experience because one travels this road only once and only in one direction — forward. The inexorable advance of aging ensures that. A young traveler can only imagine what the road is like at age forty or seventy because he or she has never traveled that part of it before. The only way to learn about what the road ahead is like is to listen to travelers who have passed there.

Thus, what Joshua 23 gives is the wisdom of someone who knows the road ahead — its rough spots and unexpected turns, its demands and dangers, its pains and pleasures not to be missed. Joshua speaks to the ignorant on how fully to enjoy the trip ahead, a message only the seasoned life traveler can give. That is why only old people give farewell speeches; only they know the road ahead. And that is why we should always listen to them.

(2) The genre of farewell speech reminds readers that God's plan outlives all of us. It was in full swing long before we were born and will remain so long after we are gone. It outlived Abraham, Moses, Joshua, Deborah, David, Elijah, Ezra, Esther, Mary, Peter, Paul, John, Irenaeus, Augustine, Aquinas, Luther, Jonathan Edwards, D. L. Moody, Mary Slessor, Mother Teresa, and Martin Luther King Jr. This blunt reality is both humbling and liberating. It humbles by reminding us that, however large a swath we cut through history, the kingdom advances without us — and, at times, in spite of us. It liberates us by reminding us that ultimately its success does not depend on our efforts — that we do not have to get everything done in our lifetime. Rather, we sow seeds whose harvest others will gather, lay foundations on which others will build, and open doors that others will enter. We are among the cast of players in the drama of history, but the entire company is huge. And, of course, the starring roles ultimately belong to God — Father, Son, and Holy Spirit.

CELEBRATING GOD'S AMAZING FEATS. From the pages of Scripture, Joshua's ancient farewell speech echoes across the ages. It still deserves a hearing because its themes are timeless and enduring. Heard properly, it speaks with the same power and relevance it had the day it was first delivered. It calls us to celebrate what God has done in the past with joy and gratitude. This is true for the church as a whole and for each believer personally. Though not present in Joshua 23, the wonderful Hebrew word *nipla'ot* ("amazing feats") captures the things that Israel "had seen" Yahweh do (v. 3; cf. 3:5). *Nipla'ot* mark events so astounding that they defy human explanation and description even by those who see them (e.g., Job 5:9; 37:14; Ps. 98:1; 106:22; 136:4; Mic. 7:15).[53] What great deeds has God done for his people in the past? The list of landmarks is lengthy—how much time do you have?

Psalm 136 offers a convenient catalog and provides the appropriate congregational response to each item ("His love endures forever"). The psalmist begins in the beginning with the "amazing feat" of creation. Yahweh wielded his awesome understanding to "[make] the heavens" and "spread the earth upon the waters" (vv. 5–6). Other psalms celebrate how he set the earth on its sturdy, firm foundations, then sent the waters retreating behind the boundaries of lakes and riverbeds never to overflow the earth again (Ps. 104:5–9). Today we reap the benefits of the stable, immovable earth ("it can never be moved") that God established in the past. And that stability reminds us that God is still the same powerful God today, a God always ready for relationship with his people, whatever historical era their lives occupy (cf. Ps. 102:25–28).

Next, echoing Genesis 1, Psalm 136 recalls God's creation of "the great lights"—"the sun to govern the day" and "the moon and stars to govern the night" (Ps. 136:7–9). The regularity of their rotation reminds us that the earth is governed 24/7—that it knows no moments of chaos outside their dominion. Given the "amazing feat" of creation, it is no wonder that Psalm 148 rallies a creation chorus of singers from heaven and earth to praise the Lord. From heaven the psalmist recruits angels, stars, sun, moon, and deep space; and from earth he summons sea creatures, ocean depths, lightning, hail, snow, storm winds, mountains, fruit and cedar trees, all kinds of livestock, creepy crawlers, birds, human kings and princes, young and old, males and females (vv. 1–12). To their chorus we each add our voice in celebration of God's "amazing feats" of creation, in the words of Robert Robinson:

> Mighty God, while angels bless Thee,
> May a mortal lisp Thy name?
> Lord of men, as well as angels,
> Thou art ev'ry creature's theme.
> Lord of ev'ry land and nation,
> Ancient of eternal days,
> Sounded thro' the wide creation
> Be Thy just and endless praise.

The Exodus from Egypt is the next item in the catalog of Yahweh's mighty deeds in Psalm 136. The psalmist recalls what Yahweh did in this great act of salvation (vv. 10–15): He struck down the Egyptian firstborn,

---

53. J. Conrad, "פֶּלֶא," *TDOT*, 11:540–43.

led Israel out by his overwhelming power, parted the Red Sea, led Israel across it, and swept Pharaoh and his army into it. As Moses told Israel, Yahweh did so because "the LORD loved you and kept his oath to your ancestors" (Deut. 7:8). Israel was, after all, the people whom Yahweh had singled out from all peoples "to be his people, his treasured possession"; only Israel was the object of his "affection" (7:6 – 7). To Psalm 136 Moses adds his own voice, exulting in the implications of the exodus from Egypt for Israel:

> Blessed are you, O Israel!
>> Who is like you,
>> a people saved by the LORD?
> He is your shield and helper
>> and your glorious sword.
> Your enemies will cower before you,
>> and you will trample down their high places. (Deut. 33:29)

Remembering the wilderness journey, the conquest, and the settlement comes next in Psalm 136: Yahweh led Israel through the desert (136:16) and struck down great and mighty kings (vv. 17 – 18) — Sihon and Og, for example (vv. 17 – 20) — and gave their land to Israel as an inheritance (vv. 21 – 23). As we have seen, the book of Joshua knows this story well and celebrates it as an "amazing feat," too. Its events demonstrate what is humanly unfathomable: the awesome power, deep affection, firm commitment that God has toward his special people. They confirm his unwavering commitment to their salvation, defense, and well-being.

Christians also celebrate "amazing feats" of God done through Christ. Concerning the gospel, for both Paul and Luke what was "of first importance" was that Jesus died for our sins, was buried, was raised from the dead, and appeared alive to his disciples (Acts 1:3; 1 Cor. 15:3 – 9). The amazing thing is that the riches-to-rags story of Christ's incarnation and self-sacrifice makes possible the rags-to-riches story of every believer. He left the wealth of heaven for the poverty of earth so that spiritually we might leave our poverty on earth for the wealth of heaven (2 Cor. 8:9). The salvation Jesus won on the cross lifts us from our degraded state as paupers to our exalted state as heirs to heaven's riches as God's own adopted children (Eph. 1:5).

The resurrection also marks an amazing feat of God with crucial implications for Christians. By raising Jesus, God confirms his acceptance of Jesus' sacrifice as payment in full for all our sins. As someone has said, in the resurrection of Jesus, God shouts "Amen!" to Jesus' cry on the cross, "It is finished!" Christians also celebrate the resurrection because it opens the way for them to enjoy their own resurrected life after death. Paul rightly teaches that the validity of the Christian faith hangs on the bodily resurrection of

Jesus. Had Christ not been raised, he argues, our faith would be worthless because without the resurrection we would be doomed to futility. Our only hope would be for meaning in this life, a prospect that Ecclesiastes long ago decried as "Meaningless!" (1 Cor. 15:17, 19; Eccl. 1:2). But Jesus rose—that is a fact! And, Paul continues, he marks the "firstfruits" of a huge future harvest that includes all believers, living and dead (1 Cor. 15:20, 23). Because he rose, so will we! More important, in the oft-sung words of André Crouch, "because He lives, I can face tomorrow." We experience the power of his resurrection today at work in our lives!

These are the big-picture "amazing feats." But every Christian has his or her own story to tell of something amazing God did for them. I remember mine every November 11 because it happened on that day in 1971, the day my ministry as a circuit-riding Navy chaplain took me to Kien An, a small Navy base in far western South Vietnam. It stood on the northern edge of the U Minh Forest, a place that a popular rumor said was so safe that the Viet Cong went there for rest and recreation. That made Kien An a place so dangerous that everyone slept in bunkers in case of mortar attacks. As I chatted with a young sailor that morning, I heard an explosion outside to my right and felt something hit my right foot. "We'd better get to a bunker, Chaplain," the young man said, so I rushed behind him out the back door.

As it turned out, a claymore mine planted in the ground outside had accidently detonated, spewing small ball bearings in a deadly arc. One had passed right through my right foot, another had lodged near the ankle. A corpsman gave me first aid, and a medevac helicopter soon took me to an Army field hospital for treatment. Months later, however, I learned of God's "amazing feat" on that day from a friend. A refrigerator along the wall between me and the mine apparently had absorbed most of the blast, thus sparing my life. That is why every November 11 my family and I do something to celebrate it and to express gratitude to God for the gift of the rich years of life since then.

Some of my friends (not their real names) have experienced their own *nipla'ot* from God.

- Charlie praises God for years of sobriety after decades of slavery to alcohol.
- Marian and John revel in the antics of the three small children God gave them after painful years of infertility.
- God helped Annette to overcome awkwardness and insecurity around people so she could pursue her personal dreams.
- Candice praises God for providing an employer willing to retrain and employ her after several hard, frustrating years of unemployment.

- Bernie and Tanya thank God for the inner healing that enabled their marriage to survive and to thrive despite some rocky years.
- Charlotte is still amazed that the frightening tumor surgeons removed a decade ago was benign and has not returned.
- George still thanks God for a timely medical exam that gave surgeons the chance to avert a life-ending disaster none too soon.

These examples represent only a small sample of the stories to be heard in a circle of Christian friends or within a local church.

They all represent personal crises, but some of God's feats involve more ordinary moments. Sometimes Jesus just lifts our spirits, gives us new insight into ourselves or others, or heals simple sicknesses. Other times his loving rebuke steers us around pitfalls, or his gentle nudge gets us past our reluctance to do the right thing. These, too, are "amazing feats," albeit on a smaller scale, and rightly lead us to celebrate with gratitude and joy over what God has done. In Joshua's words, we "know with all [our] heart and soul that not one of all the good promises the LORD [our] God gave [us] has failed" (Josh. 23:14). Such persuasive, personal knowledge leads us to sing with the psalmist:

> I will extol the LORD at all time;
>> His praise will always be on my lips.
> My soul will boast in the LORD;
>> let the afflicted hear and rejoice.
> Glorify the LORD with me;
>> let us exalt his name together. (Ps. 34:1 – 3[2 – 4])[54]

Warnings against harmful associations. Joshua's farewell speech warns us against harmful associations. His prime concern for Israel revolves around the faith-corrupting influences of Canaanites in daily dealings and in intermarriages. He knows such associations will exert influence, even when its participants are unaware of it. This raises a question as to what associations might somehow harm a Christian's commitment to Christ today. A common scriptural axiom today says that Christians are to be "*in* the world but not *of* the world." It acknowledges the delicate dance demanded of Christians. Their mission for Christ requires them to live amid pagan cultures while at the same retaining their unique Christian identity.

At first glance, the daily dance demanded to strike that delicate balance seems to involve easy, clear-cut steps. Believers are to continue their

---

54. For a contemporary expression of praise I commend Richard K. Carlson's "Come, Celebrate the Presence of the Lord," available in *The Covenant Hymnal: A Worshipbook* (Chicago: Covenant Publications, 1996), 512.

worship practices, maintain genuine piety, adhere to high standards of ethics and personal morality, and seek for a positive reputation in the community. My guess is that many Christians give little thought to their day-to-day associations, except when the latter bump up against something that obviously conflicts with their Christian faith. They also realize the necessity of avoiding associations that appeal to their weaknesses. For an alcoholic to go with friends to a bar obviously courts disaster, as do situations likely to light the fuse of someone with a hot, uncontrollable temper.

But more subtle influences preoccupy other biblical writers besides the author of Joshua. For example, Paul urged the Corinthians not to be "yoked together with unbelievers" because they simply have nothing in common (2 Cor. 6:14 – 16). His concluding exhortation suggests the reason for that sweeping statement: "Let us purify ourselves from everything that contaminates body and spirit, perfecting holiness out of reverence for God" (7:1). Apparently, too cozy associations with unbelievers "contaminates" a Christian's whole being ("body and spirit"), while more distant associations promote purity, holiness, and reverence for God. Consider, further, Romans 12:2 in *The Message*:

> Don't become so well-adjusted to your culture that you fit into it without even thinking. Instead, fix your attention on God. You'll be changed from the inside out. Readily recognize what he wants from you, and quickly respond to it. Unlike the culture around you, always dragging you down to its level of immaturity, God brings the best out of you, develops well-formed maturity in you.

Be wary of the world's influence. Many biblical passages similarly warn us to be wary of the world's influence. They assume that a subtle battle rages between God and rebellious cultures over our inner maturity in Christ. The culture promotes its vision of inner maturity, a vision that in reality amounts to immaturity. Unconsciously, we are caught in the crossfire between God's inner work and the culture's desire for conquest. Alas, as unimportant as we may think we are, we are in fact Ground Zero of the cosmic struggle of the forces of evil against God.

A story that author Max Lucado tells throws some light on this matter.[55] One night two prowlers made a crazy visit to a department store long after it had closed. They came, did their business, and left unnoticed.

---

55. M. Lucado, *No Wonder They Call Him the Savior* (Nashville: W Publishing Group, 2004), 13 – 14. I am grateful to my colleague Dr. Max Lee, who called my attention to this example.

Surprisingly, rather than rob, they simply pulled off an ingenious prank: They swapped the price tags of items in the store. They took the $395.00 sticker from an expensive camera and stuck it on a $5.00 box of ordinary stationery. A $5.95 tag from a paperback book now stuck to $500 outboard motor. The secret price-tag switch revalued every item of merchandise in the store. Even crazier, the next morning the store did four hours of business before anyone noticed the switched prices! Whoever bought the outboard motor got an incredible bargain, but the stationery purchaser got taken royally. The pranksters had assigned items values totally out of whack with their actual value.

Lucado points that out a similar, crazy, distorted system of values bombards us every day: "We see the most valuable things in our lives peddled for pennies and we see the cheapest smut go for millions."[56] In his view, the two things that fetch the highest prices today are performance and appearance. The culture highly values people who act and look the way it thinks is impressive. Celebrities such as famous athletes, successful business leaders, rising politicians, and entertainment stars carry hefty price tags. People who look athletic or who ooze sex appeal — people who draw paparazzi like flies to honey — fetch similar inflated prices. It is this distortion of price tags — and its preoccupation with superficial externals — that subtly interfere with God's work of reshaping Christians inside. The temptation is for ordinary folks, Christians included, to envy people bearing such hefty cultural price tags and to seek to be like them. The danger is that such preoccupations slow, if not stop, God's invisible inner work of transformation. His priority is powerfully to change people from the inside out — their character, attitudes, worldview, and values.

An exchange between Yahweh and the prophet Jeremiah illustrates this battle for priorities (Jer. 15:15–21). The prophet has obviously preached publicly and been jeered by the crowd for his message of judgment. That is why he asks Yahweh to "avenge me on my persecutors" in light of the "reproach [I suffer] for your sake" (15:15). To support his plea, Jeremiah affirms his faithfulness as a prophet — his delighted devouring of Yahweh's word and his solitary lifestyle away from the revelers around him (vv. 16–17). But he also complains. Why, he asks, has the reward for his devotion been "pain unending" and a "wound grievous and incurable" (v. 18a)? Finally, he levels a blunt accusation against Yahweh (v. 18b): "Will you be to me like a deceptive brook, like a spring that fails?" In other words, is Yahweh going to play with him, feigning genuine care for a time only to dump him in the end?

---

56. Ibid., 14.

Mighty powerful words! But deep hurt lies behind them. The rejection by his peers of his message has soured Jeremiah's attitude toward Yahweh. The jeering peers have disillusioned Jeremiah and embittered him against God. He does not truly "love the LORD [his] God" anymore. In reply, Yahweh makes two very telling statements featuring the word šub ("turn around, return"). First, he lays down a condition (Jer. 15:19a). To continue as prophet (šub hi. "I will restore"), Jeremiah must stop (šub "turn from") saying stupid things like his "deceptive brook" remark. Second (and even more telling), he says, "Let this people turn [šub] to you, but you must not turn [šub] to them" (v. 19b).

I have highlighted the use of šub here because it creates a picture of Jeremiah's situation. The prophet stands in the middle between Israel and Yahweh and can move ("turn") in either direction. Yahweh's call for him to "repent" (šub) implies that he has "turned" from Yahweh toward the people and needs to reverse his course. The point of being a prophet, Yahweh implies, is to get the people to "turn" toward Jeremiah (and Yahweh), not for Jeremiah to "turn" the other way. Apparently, the influence of the crowd is taking its toll on Jeremiah, compromising his standing with Yahweh as a prophet.

Today, the same crowd influence sinisterly seeks to get us to "turn" its way—to orient our lives around its values—rather than to get our bearings from God. That is why Joshua's ancient warning bears repeating: Be wary of the world's influences. The call is for us to audit our inventory of associations—our friendships, business associates, coworkers, club memberships, social networks, and the like—in order to assess their influence. Picture yourself in the middle of a street facing Jesus on one curb with a given association on the other. Be honest with yourself (and perhaps seek the advice of a wise outsider); has that connection drawn you away from Jesus or has it had no effect? (Ideally, it would draw non-Christians to join you in the middle, facing Jesus). Does it stir up ethical or moral qualms? Has it affected your attitudes or infected your vocabulary? Is your motivation to honor and represent God through it, or does it feed common but not necessarily Christ-like desires?

Guarding our unique identity. Finally, Joshua's farewell address calls us to guard our unique identity as God's people. Three commands summarize how we are to do that. (1) We are to obey God's word unswervingly (v. 6). In Joshua's day, God's Word was the "Book of the Law of Moses," but today it constitutes the entire Bible. Notice that the phrase "turn aside to the right or to the left" evokes a particular metaphor for God's Word, the picture of a path that one chooses for a trip.

When my kids were young, we periodically took car trips to visit family in two other states, each more than a thousand miles away. The idea of choosing the "right path" was important to us. The long distances required careful planning since no direct routes connected us with our destinations. We consulted maps to select the most direct, least mountainous, route and to estimate the time required to arrive. In two cases, both northern and southern routes were available, so we had to calculate which of the two took the shortest time. Once we had decided the route, we had to determine how long each day's drive would be and where to stop for meals and lodging. Guidebooks gave us options on the latter and also informed us of the kinds of weather we might face. Several trips demanded that we cross deserts. Since our early vehicles lacked air conditioning, we had to find out where the A&W Root Beer stands were!

With the Bible, the terrain to traverse is life, a long and important journey. Now, one might think that it is a given that Christians obey the Bible and that to stress this idea is simply to point out the obvious. But one recent signal undermines that assumption — the rise in biblical illiteracy among Christians. According to one recent survey, only twenty percent of Americans could identify the person who preached the Sermon on the Mount. (Most credited it to Billy Graham!). When Jay Leno asked his *Tonight Show* audience to name one of the twelve apostles, no one could. A recent Gallup Poll found that fewer Americans are reading the Bible than two decades ago. In the 1980s 79 percent of respondents reported reading it occasionally, but only 59 percent do so today. Among Christians, only 16 percent of those polled report reading it daily. When David Eikenberry, a youth pastor in Michigan, gave a simple quiz on Bible knowledge in his church, the average score was 40 percent. "We live in an America where we have Bibles everywhere, and yet we're too busy to read them," he commented.[57] Frankly, it is hard to obey God's Word if one does not read it much.

A further problem is that the path God's Word lays out is by no means the only path available to us. Our culture offers routes through life with wider roadways, less demanding terrains, more comfortable weather, and more attractions along the way. It even promotes shortcuts and fast lanes that promise to get us where we aspire to go quicker and easier. Joshua, however, challenges us to stick unswervingly to the only truly reliable path for life, the one in God's Word. The path courses through "the world," so it passes all the splashy billboards and flashing neon signs that our culture posts to entice us off the path, if only temporarily. The crossroads,

57. Clayton Hardiman, "Bible Literacy Slipping, Expert Says," from Religion News Service. Cited from http://home.snu.edu/~hculbert.fs/literacy.htm.

off-ramps, and detours to alternate routes mark many media offerings, and their tempting messages are cleverly persuasive.

But recall the twice-repeated warning from Proverbs: "There is a way that appears to be right, but in the end it leads to death" (Prov. 14:12; 16:25 TNIV). The glitz and glitter of the world's superhighways cannot hide that they end as a Dead End at the corner of Heartbreak Alley and Disaster Street. The only alternative is the path of the Word of God. It is imperative that churches and believers raise their level of biblical literacy. And by "biblical literacy" I mean learning Bible facts as well as feeling the grip of the Bible's vision of human life and destiny on our outlook and actions. Its vision and values point to the path of obedience—the only route to preserve our unique Christian identity.

(2) A second command is "to hold fast to the LORD your God" (23:8). "Hold fast" (or "cling to, stick with") creates a visual image of someone tightly clutching or sticking close to someone else. It reminds me of scenes in the park when my children were little. As my wife and I sat off to the side, they would frolic freely on every swing set or slide in sight. A small, shallow creek ran through our park, so when they tired of swinging, sliding, and climbing, they would wander off there to romp happily in the water. Occasionally, we would hear the heavy "Splash!" of a rock heaved in the creek. But when a dark afternoon storm threatened, the first clap of thunder would send them running to us. Fear drove them to cling to us for safety.

Love also drives people to cling to each other. Pairs of lovers of all ages strolled arm-in-arm through our park, too. Holding each other acted out their committed relationship and devotion to each other. Occasionally, holding would give way to a full embrace. If a couple walked widely separated, that signaled a distant, perhaps strained relationship. Friendship also led small groups to stick together as they walked the trails through our park, often enjoying lively conversation. In short, to "cling to" or "stick to" the Lord implies an ongoing relationship and closeness. The psalmist models that passion for closeness when he cries, "My soul clings to you; your right hand upholds me" (Ps. 63:8).

What does it mean to "cling to" our Lord? It means to stay close to him—to not let anything come between us. That implies that we do our best to confess sin as soon as we recognize it. That demands that when we are angry with him over some disappointment, we pray a psalm of complaint to give words to our turbulent feelings. We must work hard to carve out time for prayer, meditation, and worship to make contact with him. At such times, a healthy relationship with Jesus grows by the disciplined use of both speaking to God and of listening for his voice. That means that we affirm daily, "Lord, may all I do today please you greatly!" That means that we leave uncluttered spaces in our lives to do practical things for others in his name.

Further, "to hold fast" to Jesus means to depend on him alone for safety and security. One current, highly valued cultural theme is the personal trait of rugged independence. From John Wayne to Indiana Jones, our culture admires can-do people, people able to overcome incredible odds or surmount insurmountable barriers by their own pluck or cleverness. Not so with followers of Jesus. He wants us to rely on him every moment—to cling tightly to him as my children did to us when the thunder roared above them. He desires that we depend on his strength rather than our weakness—that we let his resurrection power flow through us. Whatever our need—danger, doubt, indecision, downheartedness—his name should be the first to come to mind or to be spoken. He is even more important than 9–1–1!

Each December, opinion researcher George Barna reviews what he deems the important themes that emerged in his religious surveys that year. Among the list for 2006 were two that bear on the subject under discussion. (1) He observed that

> people do not have an accurate view of themselves when it comes to spirituality. American Christians are not as devoted to their faith as they like to believe. They have positive feelings about the importance of faith, but their faith is rarely the focal point of their life or a critical factor in their decision-making.[58]

In Barna's view, most people neither set up benchmarks or measures by which to assess the progress (or regress) of their spiritual journey, nor do they pause for time to assess it. As a result, they think their faith is more important and more pure than it actually is.

(2) Barna also observed that, judged by biblical standards of how Christianity is to be practiced, Americans are spiritually lukewarm. Their efforts at spiritual growth are limited to church attendance, where they occasionally pick up a few ideas about it. Thus, most spiritual growth is "accidental"—it just sort of happens. This is because few people have both a clear understanding of what they aspire to become as followers of Christ and a well-thought-out plan to reach it. The numerous distractions that dominate the lives of most people simply crowd out such serious spiritual reflection.

If Barna is right, most of us live with Jesus at arm's length—unintentionally, of course. Our challenge is intentionally to move closer to God. This may require us to simplify our lives, to slow down a little, perhaps even to

---

58. G. Barna, *The Barna Update*, December 20, 2006. Cited from www.barna.org/FlexPage. aspx?Page=BarnaUpdate&BarnaUpdateID=252.

sit down quietly every so often. To carve out quiet moments will demand that we rid our lives of some of the distractions that shut Jesus out. And we will need to devote those quiet spaces to studying Scripture and prayer. The topic for study, reflection, and prayer concerns what Jesus expects of us, his followers. Over time, the Holy Spirit will give us a new sense of direction for our spiritual journey and help us plan the path to take to pursue it. In the process, we will rediscover what it means truly to "hold fast" to Jesus.

(3) The final command of Joshua is "to love the LORD your God" (23:11) — the greatest commandment, according to Jesus (Matt. 22:36 – 38). Here Jesus quotes Moses, especially the Shema (Deut. 6:5; cf. 11:1, 13, 22; 19:9; 30:16, 20), and reaffirms the validity of that ancient truth. But what does it mean to "love God"? In contemporary culture, "love" seems to connote something passive and sentimental. Lovers "fall in love," we say, as if they somehow caught love by accident like one catches a cold or the flu. Also, "love" has taken on so many uses that the word can mean almost anything. "I love your cooking," a well-satisfied guest might say to a host. In that case, "love" has the sense of "appreciate" or "enjoy," so by "love God" Jesus simply might mean to "appreciate" him. A fan might say to a hero, "I really love the way you (play the violin/carry yourself/run pass patterns, etc.)." In this context, "love" means to "think highly of" or "admire," so to "love God" might mean to admire him greatly.

But by quoting Moses' full statement, Jesus himself supplies one clue about the love of God — that it requires concerted effort. It is done right only, he says, "with all your heart and with all your soul and with all your mind." In biblical thought, the phrase "heart, soul, and mind" describes the totality of a person's inner self. The three terms share some semantic overlap, but in this context each suggests a specific sense. The "heart" marks primarily the center of the will and emotions, the "soul" the person's spiritual dimensions (i.e., awareness of and desire for God), and the "mind" the seat of thinking or self-awareness. In contemporary terms, Jesus commands us to love God "with everything we've got."

Jesus' final conversation with Peter (John 21:14 – 23) further illumines what love for God entails — that it requires self-giving to people about whom he cares. Jesus has just finished eating a meal during his third post-resurrection visit with his disciples. Suddenly, referring to the others, he asks Peter, "Do you truly love me more than these?" (v. 15). What a tough question! By "more than these" does Jesus want Peter to say that he loves Jesus more than they do? Or, is he asking whether Peter loves Jesus more than he loves his friends? Whatever the case, Peter answers, "Yes, Lord, you know that I love you," so Jesus commands him, "Feed my lambs." "Lambs" that belong to Jesus probably refers to young, vulnerable followers in need of Peter's nurture and guidance.

A second exchange follows the same script, but this time Jesus' command is: "Take care of my sheep" (John 21:16). "Sheep" probably designates Jesus' other, more mature disciples, and "take care" (lit., "tend, shepherd") tasks Peter with their care, especially instruction and leadership, on Jesus' behalf.

Finally, when Jesus asks the same question a third time, Peter feels hurt (John 21:17). He appeals to Jesus' omniscience ("you know all things") to convince Jesus that he does love him. Jesus replies, "Feed my sheep," a command that combines the imperative from the first exchange with the direct object of the second. Literarily, it knits both together to say, "Peter, feed my whole flock."

Why does Jesus put Peter on the spot? Because he knows that Peter is going to die a violent death at the hands of others, glorifying God in the process (John 21:18−19). Indeed, Jesus' final command is "Follow me!"—an indicator that Peter's death would be like his own. Jesus is testing the depths of Peter's love: Is he willing to die for Jesus?

From this conversation we learn that to love Jesus requires the engagement of every ounce of our being and focuses on the care of people about whom Jesus cares—the Christian community. In my view, Jesus also has in mind prospective community members, people who will later follow Jesus because of Christian witness. Further, to love Jesus may require the ultimate self-sacrifice from some of us (notice: in Peter's case, but not in John's [John 21:21−23]). To love Jesus truly means to be willing even to surrender one's life in his service and on behalf of the Christian community. That is the love that Jesus modeled and that he commanded of his disciples (15:12). He said, "Greater love has no one than this: to lay down one's life for one's friends" (15:13 TNIV). In short, to "love God" is as all-consuming and all-demanding as to love one's spouse, family, and friends.

This brings me back to one more observation by Barna. His radar screen shows an intriguing but generally unnoticed blip that, in his view, is already reshaping American religious faith. He calls it "the Revolutionary community," his collective term for diverse groups of like-minded people whose faith truly marks the driving force of their lives. He foresees the gap between the revolutionaries and other Christians widening in the future: "The difference will become strikingly evident between those who make faith the core of their life and those who simply attach a religious component on to an already mature lifestyle."[59]

---

59. Ibid.

Barna may be on to something here. I myself have observed that many sincere Christians seem to treat Jesus as an add-on to an already full life rather than as its center. To them he is like a spiritual Norton System Works: He operates in the background to ease their fears, keep their lives running smoothly, and to protect them from disasters and crashes. But background Jesus does not match the biblical Jesus, who demands to be the motherboard, the nerve-center running the whole show. In his words, he want to be nothing less than "Lord." He is quite clear on this:

> No servant can serve two masters. Either you will hate the one and love the other, or you will be devoted to the one and despise the other. You cannot serve both God and Money (Luke 16:13; Matt. 6:24 TNIV).

For us, the questions are: Is Jesus simply a background add-on or the absolute sovereign of our lives? Do we really love him "with all [our] heart and with all [our] soul and with all [our] mind"? Are we among Jesus' true "Revolutionary community," or simply a sincere, well-meaning member of the weekly crowd that gathers to hear him preach? Hopefully, we can sing, with hymnwriter Timothy Dudley-Smith ("As Water to the Thirsty"), that our living Lord is to us like refreshing water, renewed strength, beauty worth beholding, a soothing calm amid chaos, and the happy home to which we return after a long trip.

Joshua 24:1–28

❦

THEN JOSHUA ASSEMBLED all the tribes of Israel at Shechem. He summoned the elders, leaders, judges and officials of Israel, and they presented themselves before God.

²Joshua said to all the people, "This is what the LORD, the God of Israel, says: 'Long ago your forefathers, including Terah the father of Abraham and Nahor, lived beyond the River and worshiped other gods. ³But I took your father Abraham from the land beyond the River and led him throughout Canaan and gave him many descendants. I gave him Isaac, ⁴and to Isaac I gave Jacob and Esau. I assigned the hill country of Seir to Esau, but Jacob and his sons went down to Egypt.

⁵"'Then I sent Moses and Aaron, and I afflicted the Egyptians by what I did there, and I brought you out. ⁶When I brought your fathers out of Egypt, you came to the sea, and the Egyptians pursued them with chariots and horsemen as far as the Red Sea. ⁷But they cried to the LORD for help, and he put darkness between you and the Egyptians; he brought the sea over them and covered them. You saw with your own eyes what I did to the Egyptians. Then you lived in the desert for a long time.

⁸"'I brought you to the land of the Amorites who lived east of the Jordan. They fought against you, but I gave them into your hands. I destroyed them from before you, and you took possession of their land. ⁹When Balak son of Zippor, the king of Moab, prepared to fight against Israel, he sent for Balaam son of Beor to put a curse on you. ¹⁰But I would not listen to Balaam, so he blessed you again and again, and I delivered you out of his hand.

¹¹"'Then you crossed the Jordan and came to Jericho. The citizens of Jericho fought against you, as did also the Amorites, Perizzites, Canaanites, Hittites, Girgashites, Hivites and Jebusites, but I gave them into your hands. ¹²I sent the hornet ahead of you, which drove them out before you—also the two Amorite kings. You did not do it with your own sword and bow. ¹³So I gave you a land on which you did not

toil and cities you did not build; and you live in them and eat from vineyards and olive groves that you did not plant.'

[14]"Now fear the LORD and serve him with all faithfulness. Throw away the gods your forefathers worshiped beyond the River and in Egypt, and serve the LORD. [15]But if serving the LORD seems undesirable to you, then choose for yourselves this day whom you will serve, whether the gods your forefathers served beyond the River, or the gods of the Amorites, in whose land you are living. But as for me and my household, we will serve the LORD."

[16]Then the people answered, "Far be it from us to forsake the LORD to serve other gods! [17]It was the LORD our God himself who brought us and our fathers up out of Egypt, from that land of slavery, and performed those great signs before our eyes. He protected us on our entire journey and among all the nations through which we traveled. [18]And the LORD drove out before us all the nations, including the Amorites, who lived in the land. We too will serve the LORD, because he is our God."

[19]Joshua said to the people, "You are not able to serve the LORD. He is a holy God; he is a jealous God. He will not forgive your rebellion and your sins. [20]If you forsake the LORD and serve foreign gods, he will turn and bring disaster on you and make an end of you, after he has been good to you."

[21]But the people said to Joshua, "No! We will serve the LORD."

[22]Then Joshua said, "You are witnesses against yourselves that you have chosen to serve the LORD."

"Yes, we are witnesses," they replied.

[23]"Now then," said Joshua, "throw away the foreign gods that are among you and yield your hearts to the LORD, the God of Israel."

[24]And the people said to Joshua, "We will serve the LORD our God and obey him."

[25]On that day Joshua made a covenant for the people, and there at Shechem he drew up for them decrees and laws. [26]And Joshua recorded these things in the Book of the Law of God. Then he took a large stone and set it up there under the oak near the holy place of the LORD.

[27]"See!" he said to all the people. "This stone will be a witness against us. It has heard all the words the LORD has

said to us. It will be a witness against you if you are untrue to your God."

28Then Joshua sent the people away, each to his own inheritance.

IN A BOOK FULL of dramatic moments, the ceremony about to unfold marks its literary climax. The scene features the final appearance of Joshua, the man whose persona has dominated the book from the beginning (1:1). Once again, his initiative creates the event in which Israel will make a covenant (24:25). The author offers no explicit occasion or motivation for this gathering, but contextually Joshua's advancing age probably plays a role (cf. 13:1; 23:1 – 2).

The literary placement of this final appearance at the end of the book marks the ceremony as the capstone of Joshua's career. It supports the later claim that "Israel served the LORD throughout the lifetime of Joshua and of the elders who outlived him" (24:31; cf. 4:14).[1] At a crucial transition point in Israel's history, it proclaims the necessity for Israel to choose to worship Yahweh rather than other gods.

The scholarly discussion of Joshua 24 has been lengthy and lively but has not yielded a consensus on a range of issues.[2] But several intriguing observations that emerge from the discussion bear mentioning. Concern for the exclusive worship of Yahweh alone emerges here, replacing the book's earlier preoccupation with the Promised Land and its distribution.[3] The chapter also reflects several traditions unknown elsewhere: that in Mesopotamia and Egypt Israel's ancestors worshiped other gods (vv. 2, 14) and that "the citizens of Jericho fought against you" (v. 11).[4] Further,

---

1. As Brekelmans observes, Joshua 24 also looks backward into the Pentateuch and forward through Judges to Samuel's speech in 1 Samuel 12. Joshua 24 also forms an inclusio with 1 Samuel 12, the latter's historical summary updating that of the former; cf. C. Brekelmans, "Joshua 24: Its Place and Function," in *Congress Volume: Leuven, 1989*, ed. J. A. Emerton (Leiden: Brill, 1991), 1 – 9.

2. Cf. Nelson, *Joshua*, 265. For a digest of the scholarly discussion, see W. T. Koopmans, *Joshua 24 as Poetic Narrative* (JSOTSup 93; Sheffield: Sheffield Academic Press, 1990), 1 – 95, 469 – 88 (bibliography).

3. Brekelmans, "Joshua 24," 1 – 2, 7 ("will Israel, remembering all the great deeds of God, worship him, and him alone?" [2]).

4. Deut. 29:16 – 17 hints that Israel lived differently in Egypt and personally observed (but did not practice) the idolatry of the nations through which they passed en route to Canaan. The Jericho reference apparently refers either to a preemptive attack on Israel or resistance from the city's citizenry when Israel entered it.

Yahweh's historical review (vv. 2 – 13) surprisingly moves from the Red Sea to Transjordan without passing through Mount Sinai (vv. 6 – 8).[5] It omits the giving of the law and associates Moses and Aaron only with the plagues in Egypt (v. 5).

Structurally, the text features an introduction to set the scene (vv. 1 – 2a) and the report of the ceremony (vv. 2b – 28). In the latter, Yahweh's review of history (vv. 2b – 13) leads to Joshua's call for decision (vv. 14 – 15), the ritual dialogue (vv. 16 – 24), two ceremonial acts to enact the covenant (vv. 25 – 27), and Joshua's dismissal of the Israelites (v. 28). But what kind of ceremony is it? Many scholars read it as a ritual that renews the Sinai covenant between Yahweh and Israel.[6] Yahweh's long historical summary (vv. 2 – 13) suggests that genre since it resembles the historical prologues of suzerain-vassal treaties, the ancient analogy for such covenants.

But several observations point away from renewal of a suzerain-vassal treaty here.[7] Joshua 24 lacks any mention of the Instruction (*torah*) of Moses — the stipulations of ancient treaties — so prominent elsewhere in Joshua (e.g., 1:7, 8; 8:31 – 32; 22:5; 23:6). Indeed, the focus falls on Yahweh's faithful actions on Israel's behalf over centuries rather than on covenant stipulations. It also lacks other typical treaty elements (e.g., an oath, stipulations, blessings and curses). Further, its genre is a report of a covenant that Joshua made for Israel rather than a transcript of a two-party treaty or covenant.[8] The text's primary thematic word (*ʿabad* "to serve, worship") casts the spotlight on one central issue: Will Israel "serve the LORD" (vv. 14, 15, 18, 19, 21, 22, 24)?[9] In other words, will Israel truly obey the first commandment of the Decalogue — to have "no other gods before me" (Ex. 20:3; Deut. 5:7)?

In my view, the ceremony enacts a unique covenant, one between the Israelites themselves rather than a two-party covenant between them and Yahweh.[10] Israel responds to Yahweh's past deeds by taking on itself a sol-

---

5. This observation goes back to G. von Rad, "The Form-Critical Problem of the Hexateuch," in *From Genesis to Chronicles: Explorations in Old Testament Theology*, ed. K. C. Hanson (Minneapolis: Fortress, 2005), 1 – 58. Canonically, it skips over Ex. 16 to Num. 21.

6. Howard, *Joshua*, 426 – 28; Hess, *Joshua*, 300; Boling, *Joshua*, 543 – 44 (only the final editor); cf. Woudstra, *Joshua*, 340 – 41 ("a narrative adaptation of a treaty").

7. Butler, *Joshua*, 268. For what follows, cf. Nelson, *Joshua*, 266 – 67.

8. In my view, Nelson's claim (*Joshua*, 267) that vv. 15 and 19a undercut a reading of the text as a liturgy is not persuasive. Concerning possible parallels of Josh. 24 with ancient Near Eastern treaty forms, see Hess, *Joshua*, 298 – 308; Howard, *Joshua*, 426 – 28.

9. Moses first sounds this theme (Deut. 10:12; cf. 28:47), and it echoes in Samuel's farewell speech (1 Sam. 12:20) and in the later calls for religious reform by Kings Hezekiah, Manasseh, and Josiah (2 Chron. 30:8; 33:16; 34:33; cf. 35:3).

10. So also Nelson, *Joshua*, 277; Butler, *Joshua*, 268; Hawk, *Joshua*, 277.

emn, national pledge of exclusive loyalty to "serve the LORD" (vv. 18, 21, 24) — in Nelson's words, "a formal act of communal assent to the elemental substance of Yahwism."[11]

A Look Backward and Call for Decision (24:1 – 15)

THE SETTING (V. 1). The text opens with a report that Joshua assembled all the tribes of Israel and their leaders for a meeting at Shechem.[12] The initial verb is in the narrative past, and the language of verse 1b virtually repeats 23:2a. One might read the episodes as close in narrative sequence, perhaps as two sessions of a single meeting. But the specification of Shechem as the location of chapter 24 and the absence of a place in chapter 23 suggest that the present gathering is separate from that of chapter 23, although the two have the same attendees.

Specifically, the assembled Israelites "presented themselves before God," a formula whose usage elsewhere leads the reader to expect that God himself will speak in response (cf. Ex. 9:43; 1 Sam. 10:14). The formula hints that this is to be a momentous occasion for Israel.[13] Shechem held many ancestral memories for Israel. Patriarchal narratives picture it as a kind of "port of entry" into Canaan known especially for its landmark, "the great tree of Moreh" (Gen. 12:6; 33:18). Jacob purchased the site of his erstwhile campsite near the city from the sons of Hamor and built an altar there (Gen. 33:19 – 20). Later, this positive step turned ugly with the rape of Dinah and the shameful revenge her foolish brothers took on the city (Gen. 34).

Associations with important events involving Israel's patriarchs, however, may account for the selection of Shechem for the assembly. As if to welcome Abram to his new neighborhood, Yahweh chose Shechem as the first place in Canaan to appear to him (Gen. 12:7). Even more telling, when Jacob returned there after his years in Haran, Shechem was the site where he and his entourage renounced other gods, burying their idols and idolatrous jewelry under the landmark oak (35:4). Those memories made Shechem the ideal place for a later generation, the first one actually to occupy Canaan in fulfillment of the patriarchal promise, formally to renounce its allegiance to other gods and to pledge loyalty to Yahweh alone.[14]

---

11. Nelson, *Joshua*, 277.

12. Chapter 18 also reports a national assembly at Shiloh to allot lands to seven at-the-time landless tribes. Although Joshua addresses the crowd (vv. 3 – 8), the text omits mention of who initiated the gathering.

13. According to Hess (*Joshua*, 300), the usage of this phrase elsewhere creates two expectations, that a covenant ceremony is to follow and that Joshua is about to step down as leader.

14. Cf. Nelson, *Joshua*, 269; Deut. 27:4 – 26; Josh. 8:30 – 35; Judg. 8:33; 9:4, 46.

Certainly, the episode marks the only one in Joshua to take place at Shechem proper, although the city sits in the valley between Mounts Ebal and Gerizim, sites of the earlier altar ceremony (8:30–35).[15] Shechem does find mention as a territorial boundary marker (17:2, 7), as a city of refuge (20:7), and as a holding in Ephraim of the Kohathite clan of Levites (21:21). But the book of Joshua mysteriously never accounts for how Israel came to possess it.[16] A "holy place of Yahweh" is present near a prominent oak tree (v. 26), perhaps the one that other texts mention.[17] Nevertheless, besides its patriarchal associations, the city's location offered an ideal place for Israel to convene. It sits in central Canaan with excellent accessibility by road, and its surrounding valley could easily accommodate such a large gathering.[18]

Yahweh's speech (24:2–13). Joshua launches the proceedings by addressing the assembled crowd. His first words are the so-called messenger formula ("Thus says X"), the standard phrase invoked to introduce a verbatim message from a third party (e.g., Gen. 32:5; 45:9; Num. 20:14; Judg. 11:15; Isa 36:4). In this case, the formula is (lit.) "Thus says the LORD," the typical preface to oracles by prophets (e.g., Judg. 6:8; 2 Sam. 12:7; Isa. 29:22; Jer. 2:5). It clearly signals that the sound the assembly hears may be Joshua's but the voice speaking is in fact that of Yahweh. Indeed, this marks Yahweh's lone, personal, direct address to assembled Israel in the book.

Literarily, the effect is to portray God not as an aloof commander-in-chief speaking from offsite through his field commander, but as a personal participant in the proceedings. On this occasion, God himself personally engages his people "on the ground" and in their midst, a party to the relationship at stake in the present proceedings. He speaks as the "God of Israel"—the God with a long-standing, unique relationship with the people he is addressing. He speaks as someone who wants that long history of relationship to continue and to thrive.

---

15. The report concerning the ritual on Mount Ebal never mentions Shechem, so one could argue that technically the present gathering marks the *only* time that Shechem hosts such an assembly. The only other all-Israelite meeting at Shechem concerns the acceptance of Rehoboam as king after Solomon's death (1 Kings 12:1 = 2 Chron. 10:1; cf. Judg. 9:6).

16. Cf. Hawk, *Joshua*, 266, who wonders whether Israel had achieved "some sort of rapprochement" with Shechem's inhabitants. Archaeological evidence shows that Canaanite Shechem started to decline about 1300 B.C. and ended in massive destruction about 1100 B.C. Its "Israelite" occupation began about 975–929 B.C.; cf. *AEHL*, 460.

17. Cf. Gen. 12:6; 35:4; Judg. 9:6, 37. Other sanctuaries in Joshua include the "Tent of Meeting" (Josh. 18:1; 19:51) and "the tabernacle" (22:19, 29).

18. According to Seger, the present meeting of Israel best fits the archaeological picture of Shechem ca. 1200–1150 B.C.; cf. J. D. Seger, "Shechem," *OEANE*, 5:22.

The address reviews Israel's ancestral history beginning with Abraham (vv. 2 – 4).[19] The initial words ("beyond the River") transport the listeners from Canaan west of the Jordan to Mesopotamia east of the Euphrates. The combination of "long ago" and the name Terah, father of Abraham and Nahor, recalls Israel's ancestral past (Gen. 11:26 – 27). The people know the story well: It marks the beginning of Yahweh's connection with them as a people. The debut of the chapter's key word, however, surfaces its key issue: According to Yahweh, what typifies those ancestors is that they "served [*ʿabad*] other gods" (Josh. 24:2b). The driving theme of the speech concerns Israel's exclusive devotion to Yahweh alone.

The change of subject from "they" (v. 2) to "I" (v. 3) colors what follows as Yahweh's personal testimony, a highly-selective thumbnail sketch of Genesis 12 to Joshua 22. The relationship began when "I took" Abraham across the Euphrates (Terah died in Haran [Gen. 11:32]) and "led" him throughout Canaan (v. 3a). There "I gave" him many descendants — Isaac, Jacob, and Esau — and "I" settled Esau in Mount Seir (i.e., Edom) while Jacob and his children (third person) went down to Egypt (vv. 3b – 4). Though second-born, Jacob receives first mention since his descendants, not Esau's, stand before Yahweh on this occasion as his own people.

In Egypt "I sent" Moses and Aaron and "I [lit.] struck Egypt," an allusion either to the whole plague narrative (Ex. 5 – 12) or more specifically to the death of the firstborn, the decisive event that finally broke Pharaoh's will (v. 5; cf. Ex. 12:13, 23, 27).[20] Then "I" led their ancestors out of Egypt, and they (lit. "you" [pl.]) came to the shore of the Red Sea, chased by Egyptian chariots and horsemen (v. 6; cf. Ex. 14).[21] For Israel this marked a moment of crisis and hopeless despair. The unarmed former slaves now stood helplessly trapped with no way out. Ahead lay the sea, as impenetrable as any thick stone wall, while behind came the Egyptian army in hot pursuit.

In desperation and distress, Israel cried out to Yahweh (cf. Ex. 14:10), and he (third person) interposed darkness between them (lit., "you" [pl.]) and the Egyptians (v. 7a).[22] The latter apparently alludes to what Exodus

---

19. Brekelmans ("Joshua 24," 5) observes that neither the Pentateuch nor Joshua has such a detailed review of salvation history, especially by Yahweh. For briefer testimonies by Yahweh in the prophets, see Jer. 2:1 – 13; Hos. 11:1 – 11; Amos 4; Mic. 6:3 – 5.

20. In the plague narratives, the phrase "strike Egypt" occurs only in Ex. 12:23, 27.

21. Vv. 6 – 7 offer "a compact paraphrase of Exodus 14" (*Boling*, Joshua, 535).

22. Heb. *maʾapel* ("darkness") only occurs here. If, as some suggest, the initial "m" results from dittography (the preceding word ends in "m"), the original word might have been *ʾopel* ("darkness"; cf. BDB, 66; Ps. 91:6).

14:19–20 describes in more detail.[23] Militarily, the sudden onset of darkness probably sought to terrify the pursuing Egyptians and to blind them to Israel's whereabouts. Even worse, the speaker adds, Yahweh caused the sea to swamp and "cover" the pursuers, the latter verb a prominent one in the Exodus accounts (Ex. 14:28; 15:5, 10; cf. Ps. 78:53).

As if to drive the point home, Yahweh appeals to their own experience ("your eyes saw what I did . . ."), an echo of a common phrase of Moses in Deuteronomy. There it recalls Israel's witness of Yahweh's victories over the Amorite kings Sihon and Og (Deut. 3:21; cf. Num. 21), the god Baal of Peor (Deut. 4:3; cf. Num. 25), the rebels Dathan and Abiram (Deut. 11:6; cf. Num. 16), Pharaoh in Egypt, and the Egyptian army at the Red Sea (Deut. 11:3–4; 29:2; cf. 1 Sam. 12:17). In Israelite memory, these kinds of events epitomized Yahweh's awesome and overwhelming miraculous power. Here they rhetorically display Yahweh's unquestioned superiority over both mighty earthly kings and would-be rival deities, all in support of the central appeal to Israel that soon follows.

Compared to the text's parallels (cf. Deut. 26; 1 Sam. 12), it is striking that only Joshua 24 highlights details of the Red Sea crossing. Their special inclusion may sound a thematic echo of the continuity emphasized earlier between the Red Sea and Jordan River crossings (cf. 4:21–24). Further, the broad statement "you lived in the desert a long time" quickly summarizes that forty-year period (24:7b). A full treatment would have remembered the disastrous spies' report (Num. 13–14) and Moses' exclusion from the land (20:1–13). But rather than rehash Israel's shame, in the first person Yahweh skips ahead to the end of that era—how "I brought you [pl.]" into Transjordan, home of the Amorites (v. 8; cf. Num. 21). His focus remains on the good he has done for Israel—grammatically, the indicative mood—to tap into their reservoir of gratitude and win a favorable response (the imperative mood).

The Amorites "fought with you [pl.]" (*laḥam* ni.), Yahweh says, but "I" gave Israel victory, utterly sweeping them from "your" (pl.) path, so that "you" (pl.) took possession of their land (cf. Num. 32). The plural "you" here actually fits, since some of the attendees at Shechem had actually participated back then and settled in Transjordan after aiding in the conquest of Canaan (Josh. 22:1–9; cf. 12:1–6; 13:8–33).

One memorable event in Transjordan—how Moab's king Balak tried to get the seer Balaam to curse Israel—receives full treatment next (vv. 9–10;

---

23. Cf. Butler, *Joshua*, 271, who suggests that the substitution of a term akin to one in the plague narrative (Ex. 10:22) for the regular term for darkness (cf. Ex. 14:20) serves "to intensify the aura of divine action and power."

cf. Num. 22–24).[24] Yahweh says that "I" refused to listen to him (v. 10), so the seer actually blessed Israel instead—that is, "I" rescued (*naṣal* hi.) "you" (pl.) from Balaam's power.[25] In similar contexts, that key verb has the sense "to extricate" or "to separate" (someone) from grave danger, much as helicopters extract soldiers surrounded by enemy fire or people from burning buildings.[26] Again, many in the listening audience would remember this famous episode from personal experience. The theme of divine rescue marks one of the speech's key themes, another of a string of divine deliverances from hostile enemies over the centuries (Ex. 18:8–10; Judg. 8:34; 1 Sam. 17:37). The implication is that had Yahweh not intervened, there would be no Israel for him to address on this or any other occasion. Enemies would have overwhelmed them long ago.

But the story then moves closer to home, to the events of Joshua 3–12: the Jordan crossing, Jericho, and the defeat of Canaan's seven peoples (v. 11). For a third time (cf. vv. 8–9), Yahweh recalls that Israel's enemies "fought" against Israel but again "I gave" them to "you" (pl.) in defeat. By listing the nations (cf. 3:10), Yahweh highlights how widespread was enemy resistance to Israel—and how sweeping the victory. Like the two Amorite kings, all seven fell to "the hornet," a kind of advanced guard that "I" sent to drive them out before Israel arrived.

The term "hornet" (v. 12; Heb. *ṣirʿah*) probably designates either an actual plague of wasps (LXX *sphēkia* "wasp nest") or a panic-inducing terror.[27] The latter seems more likely since, on the one hand, it accords with a prominent theme in Joshua (cf. 2:10–11, 24; 5:1; 6:27; cf. Ex. 15:14–16; 23:27) and, on the other hand, evidence for the use of insects in warfare in the ancient Near East and in the Old Testament is lacking.[28] In dispatching "the hornet," Yahweh kept the earlier promises given to Israel long before

---

24. For "curse," the Balaam narrative features not *qalal* pi. as here but its synonyms *ʾarar* (Num. 22:6, 12; 23:7; 24:9) and *qabab* (23:11, 25). Since elsewhere *qalal* means "to put down," "to belittle," or "to revile," to "curse" here denotes "to initiate destructive events" against Israel with implied connotations of denigration or insult; cf. J. Scharbert, "קָלַל," *TDOT*, 13:39. The verb *ʾarar* designates the removal of something from God's favor or protection (God is almost always its grammatical subject). By contrast, *qalal* (with people as its grammatical subject) invokes words that seek to adversely affect someone; cf. J. H. Walton, *Genesis* (NIVAC; Grand Rapids: Zondervan, 2001), 229, 280–81.

25. Cf. the parenthetical comment in Deut. 23:5 ("Yet the LORD your God refused to heed Balaam; the LORD your God turned the curse into a blessing for you ...").

26. F. L. Hossfeld and B. Kalthoff, "נָצַל," *TDOT* 9:535–37.

27. E. Carpenter and M. A. Grisanti, "צִרְעָה," *NIDOTTE*, 3:847. The term occurs only two other times in the Old Testament (Ex. 23:28; Deut. 7:20).

28. Howard, *Joshua*, 432–33; Hess, *Joshua*, 304; Butler, *Joshua*, 264.

they crossed the Jordan (Ex. 23:28; Deut. 7:20).[29] The decisive role of "the hornet" supports the main point: Yahweh, not Israel's military ("not . . . with your own sword and bow"; v. 12b), swept out the land's occupants.

That means that Israel's possession of the land is God's gift, pure and simple ("I gave you [pl.]")—the fifth and final such gift in Yahweh's testimony (cf. vv. 3, 4 [2x], 8, 11). Israel had a hand neither in the land's conquest nor in its construction (v. 13). Yahweh generously handed over to Israel ready-made fields, vineyards, and olive groves to feed themselves, and ready-made cities in which to live (cf. Deut. 6:11). In short, the defeat of Canaan and the land gift are all Yahweh's doing. They mark the capstone of the stunning saga of salvation that he has singlehandedly orchestrated for Israel's benefit since the call of Abram.

The highpoints of that saga presented here attest his long, gracious, generous, and steadfast commitment to Israel through thick and thin. The "I-you" direct address speaks volumes of the profoundly personal connection that Yahweh feels toward his people. The bottom line of the speech: No one hearing his voice at Shechem that day would be there had Yahweh not been true to his covenant promise, "I will be your God, and you shall be my people." Yahweh's words argue that he has, indeed, always been there for them as Israel's faithful God.

Joshua's closing exhortation (vv. 14 – 15). A subtle, seamless shift from the divine "I" to the third person signals that Joshua speaks from here on. Syntactically, "now" shows that Joshua will draw out the logical implications of Yahweh's historical review. A shift from indicative to imperative mood also occurs: Two pairs of imperatives confront Israel with a decision to make in response (v. 14). The first pair echoes the pleas of Moses (Deut. 6:13; 10:20; cf. 10:12; 13:4) and even more closely anticipates that of Samuel (1 Sam. 12:24).[30] Israel must both "revere" (*yareʾ* NIV "fear") Yahweh (i.e., to treat him with the highest respect) and "serve" (*ʿabad*) him (i.e., to carry out his wishes as would an honest, loyal servant).

In the second imperative pair, the command to "put away" the gods their ancestors "served" in Mesopotamia and Egypt precedes the command again

---

29. The reference to the "two kings of the Amorites" seems out of place here since the phrase elsewhere only refers to the Transjordanian kings whose defeat v. 8 narrates (Deut. 3:8; 4:47; 31:4). LXX ("twelve kings") offers no good solution since Joshua features no such numerical royal grouping. More likely, "two kings" here designates Adoni-Zedek and Jabin, heads of the southern and northern coalitions, respectively, that opposed Israel (10:1,3; 11:1). Cf. Howard, *Joshua*, 433 ("a flashback to victories east of the Jordan to go along with those west of the Jordan").

30. It also anticipates the Deuteronomist's indictment of Israel's religious schizophrenia—i.e., it "revered" him but "served" other gods (2 Kings 17:33, 41).

to "serve" (cf. v. 23). "Put away (other gods)" is a stock phrase meaning radically to renounce loyalty to other deities and exclusively to embrace Yahweh. Jacob demanded it of his entourage upon his return to Canaan from Haran (Gen. 35:2), and Samuel will do so as well, as evidence of later Israel's repentance (1 Sam. 7:3; cf. Judg. 10:16; 1 Chron. 33:15).

Verse 14 mentions two places where Israel or their ancestors had lived long enough to put down roots, Mesopotamia ("beyond the River" [the Euphrates]) and "in Egypt." Since polytheism (the worship of many gods) dominates both, Israel's ancestors were polytheists, adding gods to their worship roster wherever they went. But with Yahweh, Joshua says, the logic of exclusivity applies: Israel may serve Yahweh or their ancestors' gods, but not both; polytheism is no longer an option.

So Joshua urges his hearers "this day" to make a choice one way or the other (v. 15): If they see service for Yahweh as "bad" (NIV "undesirable"), then choose the god they are willing to serve — for example, the Mesopotamian gods of their ancestors or those of their Amorite neighbors. Joshua's transition ("but as for me") draws a firm line between his household and the alternatives: "We will serve the LORD." In one sense, this announcement is no surprise; Joshua has a sterling track record behind him — a lifetime of devoted, unswerving, and faithful service for Yahweh. To do otherwise here would truly be a shock. The issue is whether other Israelite households will join his or whether his alone will serve Yahweh.

Given Joshua's expected death (cf. 23:1, 2, 14), at stake is whether the exclusive devotion to Yahweh — the kind typified by Joshua and Moses — will continue into the next generation. In demanding a choice, Joshua mirrors the pattern of Moses, who made a similar passionate plea before Israel entered Canaan (e.g., Deut. 30:19−20; cf. Josh. 23). Here Joshua asks for commitment from the present generation, the first one in Israel's history to occupy the Promised Land. But his words also confront readers today with a similar choice: Is Jesus your Lord or not?

The Ritual Dialogue: Loyalty Reaffirmed (24:16−24)

AT LAST, THE PEOPLE themselves speak in response to Joshua's call to decision (v. 16). The narrator portrays a collective voice ("the people answered ..."), a narrative device attested elsewhere (cf. 22:15; 1 Sam. 11:12; 14:45; 2 Sam. 18:3). But here it may specifically serve the ritual back-and-forth that now ensues between Joshua and the people. His speech done, literarily Yahweh now stands off-scene, apparently leaving the moment of decision for Joshua and Israel to handle through the ritual dialogue that follows.

The decision phase of the process (vv. 16—21) opens with the people's opening line, "Far be it from us ..." (in modern terms, "No way!"). They emphatically renounce any thought of abandoning Yahweh for the service of other gods. The Transjordanian tribes had invoked the same phrase to deny alleged rebellion against Yahweh (22:29), and it undergirds Samuel's promise to pray for Israel (1 Sam. 12:23).[31] To "forsake [*ʿazab*] the LORD" for other gods is to break the covenant with him and to risk the resulting terrible consequences, a certainty that Joshua himself will shortly reaffirm (Josh. 24:20).[32] Covenant breach is the ultimate outrage against God, so their emphatic denial of that possibility is not surprising.

They state their rationale just as Yahweh did, in their own historical review, their own testimony of what—and this is the main point—Yahweh "our God" (not other gods) has done for "us" (vv. 17—18a). Their review is briefer and less dramatic than Yahweh's, focusing on his miraculous rescue from Egyptian slavery, his protection amid hostile nations, and his expulsion of Canaan's residents including the Amorites.[33] By a subtle sound play, the people show keen awareness of what constitutes covenant breach: to abandon (*ʿazab*) Yahweh and "serve [*ʿabad*] other gods" (v. 16; cf. 23:16; Deut. 7:4). To "serve Yahweh," by contrast, is to "put away" (*sur* hi.) foreign gods (cf. vv. 14, 23), "incline" (*hiṭṭah*) one's heart to Yahweh, and obey (*šamaʿ*) his voice (vv. 23—24). Their decision lays the foundation for the covenant they will soon make (v. 25).[34]

The people also know who Yahweh is to them. He is the one who brought them and their ancestors out of Egypt, here remembered poignantly as (lit.) "the house of slaves" (cf. Ex. 20:2//Deut. 5:6; 8:14; 13:5, 10; Jer. 34:13), and who performed "those great signs" during that historic escape (v. 17).[35] Also, it was Yahweh who "protected us" during the subse-

---

31. For Samuel, to not do so would amount to sinning against Yahweh. The phrase common to these three texts comprises *ḥalilah le* ("far be it ...") + pronominal suffix + *min* + infinitive absolute. The preposition of separation (*min*) underscores the mental distance of the action envisioned (i.e., "Nothing could be farther from the truth!").

32. Both the DH (Judg. 10:9—10; 1 Kings 9:9; 2 Kings 17:16) and Jeremiah (Jer. 5:19; 16:11; 22:9) underscore the direct connection between covenant breach through apostasy and Israel's historical misfortunes.

33. Compared to Yahweh's speech, the people omit the patriarchs (vv. 2—4), the Red Sea and Jordan crossings (vv. 6—7a, 11), Balaam (vv. 9—10), and the conquest of Transjordan (v. 8).

34. H. Ringgren, "עָבַד," *TDOT*, 10:386—87.

35. In v. 17, "signs" (*ʾotot*) designates Yahweh's miracles and wonders associated with the Exodus (e.g., the plagues); cf. F. J. Helfmeyer, "אוֹת," *TDOT*, 1:178. Since most of the present generation was born in the wilderness, not in Egypt, the references to "us and our ancestors" (TNIV) and to the signs done "before our eyes" in connection with the Exodus presumes a corporate solidarity between the Exodus generation and the present wilderness-born one. For more on this fundamental concept, see the Bridging Contexts sections in chs. 7 and 22.

quent journey, including Israel's passage through other nations. The latter refers broadly to the period between the Exodus and Israel's stay in the plains of Moab along the Jordan's east bank. They remember that period as one in which Yahweh warded off attacks by various hostile peoples through whose territories Israel passed.[36] The omission of the momentous two years at Mount Sinai seems striking but is explained by the people's focus on Yahweh the warrior, the one whose decisive victories has brought them to this moment. Here the ongoing covenant relationship is simply presupposed. Finally, their historical review ends with the most recent period, the decisive events of the Conquest (chs. 1–12), where Yahweh "drove out before us" the land's former inhabitants (v. 18a; cf. v. 12).[37]

The people's response to Yahweh's mighty deeds is that "we too will serve the LORD" (v. 18b). Literally, it corresponds to Joshua's "we will serve the LORD" (v. 15b), affirming that they side with him. Their reason for doing so—namely, that "he is our God" (cf. "the LORD our God" [v. 17]; the liturgical echo in Ps. 95:7)—affirms that they also side with Yahweh against the alternative gods. Orally, the phrase may have sounded emphatic like this: "for *he* (not ancestral, Egyptian, or Amorite gods) is our God."

At first glance, Joshua's reply ("You cannot serve the LORD") sounds like an irritated rebuttal (v. 19; in modern terms, "In your dreams!").[38] But his seeming rejoinder in fact dispenses to theologically naive Israel a strong dose of divine reality in order to dispel a dangerous delusion. Probably Joshua senses in Israel's response (vv. 16–18) a mistakenly narrow preoccupation with Yahweh's ability to protect.[39] The danger is that they fail to reckon fully with Yahweh's unique character compared to the gods they have known. His audience viewed the latter as so easy to please that they

---

36. The Pentateuch records the following examples: the Amalekite attack at Rephidim (Ex. 17:8–16); Edom's refusal of safe passage (Num. 20:14–21); attacks by the Amorite king Sihon (21:21–24) and by Og king of Bashan (21:33–35); the attempt by Balak king of Moab to have Israel cursed (Num. 22–24); and the Midianite sex industry and resulting apostasy (25; 31).

37. The NIV's "all the nations, including the Amorites" reads (lit.) "the Amorite" (*haʾemori*), at first glance a reference to only one of the seven peoples in Canaan (e.g., 12:8; 24:11). But elsewhere the book designates Canaan's residents collectively (and especially those in the central hill country) as "the Amorites" (e.g., 5:1; 7:7; 10:5, 6; 24:12). So a better rendering would be "the peoples, the Amorites"; cf. Hess, *Joshua*, 231.

38. Butler (*Joshua*, 274) calls it "perhaps the most shocking statement in the OT." What follows draws on his insightful discussion (274). Joshua's remark is often interpreted as evidence of a later author or editor at work, but cf. Nelson's affirmation (*Joshua*, 276) of the paradoxical verse's clarity, "power and theological sophistication." Hess (*Joshua*, 306) reads a simple four-line chiasm in vv. 19–20.

39. Hess (*Joshua*, 309) thinks it indicative of Israel's eventual apostasy (Judg. 2:11–13) that the people's response omits any mention of other gods.

could serve several of them at the same time. They would, thus, assume they could easily get along with Yahweh in a mutual back-scratching relationship: They protect Yahweh and he protects them. Rhetorically, Joshua's reply underscores that two unique character traits of Yahweh—his holiness and his jealousy—make serving him all-demanding. Those traits also make the present moment a deadly serious transaction, not a simple, casual formality to be endured and then ignored.

(1) He is a "holy [*qedošim*] God."[40] To be "holy" means that he is one of a kind, not just any old "god," a truth that Hannah's memorable words reflect: "There is no one holy like the LORD; there is no one besides you" (1 Sam. 2:2; cf. Ps. 89:6–7[7–8]; Isa. 40:25). This poses a problem for humans since, when they approach him, his holiness explosively collides with their sinfulness. In other words, Yahweh is not as easy to get along with as Israel's quick, sincere reply might suggest. Humans may only come near him on his own terms, as Israel learned the first day they met at Mount Sinai (cf. Ex. 19:10–13, 21–24). Later, when seventy Israelites died for innocently peeking inside the ark of the covenant, the people of Beth Shemesh lamented, "Who can stand in the presence of the LORD, this holy God?" (1 Sam. 6:20). Humans must always reckon with the ever-present threat that Yahweh might "break out against" those who fail to honor his holiness (Ex. 19:22, 24; 1 Sam. 5–6).

(2) He is a "jealous God" (*ʾel qannoʾ*). He does not tolerate deviations from his policy. Instead, in defense of his honor he angrily lashes out at those who slight his sovereignty or oppose his plans (Nah. 1:2).[41] That is why, rather than forgive their "transgressions" and "sins," he will hold Israel accountable for them (v. 19b). It is simply out of character for him to let such conduct slide. In short, what Reuter calls "an intolerant demand for exclusivity" comprises his demand to be Israel's only God and not to share his claim for their worship and love with any other deity.[42] Yahweh is passionately possessive of his prerogatives.

This leads Joshua to issue a stern conditional warning (v. 20). If Israel does, indeed, break its solemn word—i.e., to "forsake [*ʿazab*] the LORD and serve foreign gods" (cf. v. 16)—"disaster" will surely follow. He will "turn (around)," bring terrible "disaster" on Israel, and even "make an end" (*killah*, "consume, finish off, exterminate") them—all this "after he has been good" to them. Joshua disabuses Israel of the misperception that Yahweh's good-

---

40. Cf. H. Ringgren, "קדש," *TDOT*, 12:531–32; Howard, *Joshua*, 437–38.

41. Usage of the parallel term *ʾel qannaʾ* clarifies that the worship of other gods is clearly the spark that ignites divine fury (Ex. 20:5//Deut. 5:9; Ex. 34:14; Deut. 6:15).

42. E. Reuter, "קנא," *TDOT*, 13:54; cf. G. von Rad, *Old Testament Theology* (New York: Harper & Row, 1962), 1:208.

ness toward them will continue no matter what. On the contrary, Joshua says, make no mistake: The "[very] bad" (NIV "disaster") will replace the "good" should Israel drop Yahweh and take up with foreign gods.[43] That coming "bad" will meet the same high standard of quality as the "good" (cf. 23:15; Deut. 28:63).

But Joshua's stern warning does not deter the people, who again commit themselves to serve Yahweh (cf. v. 18b). Their word choice and word order are emphatic: (lit.) "No! To the contrary, the LORD we'll serve!" (cf. 5:4; 1 Sam. 12:12; 2 Sam. 12:18).

Joshua's tone now softens, and the confirmation phase of covenant-making follows (vv. 22–24). In the absence of written records, ancient Israel relied on witnesses to legal transactions to verify their validity (Jer. 32:10) or to voice public acceptance of the outcome (Ruth 4:9–11). But here Joshua declares that the assembled crowd—the only ones taking on the covenant—are witnesses against each other in the present matter. That "witnesses" is plural implies that their testimony is individual, not corporate. Each person attests the participation of the others in the covenant, and each is responsible to hold the others accountable for keeping it.

What they witness is that they have "chosen" Yahweh as the one they will serve, a choice that also implies the rejection of other gods. The word choice implies an action of reciprocity: As Yahweh has "chosen" Israel as his treasured possession (e.g., Deut. 7:6; 14:2; Jer. 33:24), so Israel now properly has again "chosen" him as their God. With one voice, the people affirm, "Yes, we are witnesses," formally accepting their obligation to serve Yahweh exclusively.

Almost abruptly, as if dramatically setting off the moment, verse 23 opens with Joshua's command rather than the expected "And Joshua said...." (it is added in NIV). He commands Israel to evidence its commitment by a twofold step: to "throw away the foreign gods" from their midst (a simplified reiteration of v. 14) and to "yield your hearts" (*naṭab* hi., "tilt, bend [their] hearts") to Israel's God, Yahweh.[44] In Hebrew, the "heart" connotes emotional feelings, rational thinking, and chosen resolve, so Joshua orders the Israelites to surrender themselves totally to Yahweh. To be ambivalent, double-minded, or wishy-washy, or to divide their efforts among several gods, is no longer an option.

The people's response (v. 24) reiterates their twice-voiced earlier promise (vv. 18, 21) to "serve the LORD" (vv. 18, 21), again affirming him as "our

---

43. For the phrase "foreign gods" (*ʾelohey nekar*) elsewhere, see Gen. 35:2, 3; Deut. 31:16; Jer. 5:19.

44. For the first phrase (*sur ʾelohey nekar*), see Judg. 10:16; 1 Sam. 7:3; 2 Chron. 33:15. For "tilt your hearts" elsewhere, see 2 Sam. 19:14; 1 Kings 8:58; 11:2, 9.

God" (v. 18) and adding the commitment to "obey" him (cf. Deut. 13:8).[45] That the crowd three times affirms "we will serve the LORD" (vv. 18, 21, 24) "impels the reader to go along with assembled Israel and to concur with the text's agenda."[46] Israel's promise to serve and obey Yahweh exclusively brings the ritual dialogue part of the ceremony to a close.

The Ceremony: The Book and the Stone (24:25 – 28)

THE VOICES OF JOSHUA and the people fade and the narrator—unheard since v. 1—steps forward to present the ritual's final phase. He looks back on "that [momentous] day" in that place ("at Shechem") and reports tersely that Joshua "made [lit., 'cut'] a covenant for the people" (v. 25). At first glance, the action seems to renew the Sinai covenant, but despite Yahweh's earlier address (vv. 2 – 13), the text omits mention of him as a party. Instead, the covenant Joshua makes simply formalizes the people's prior verbal commitment (vv. 21, 24) as a self-imposed mandate or obligation.

This covenant most closely resembles two other transactions, the covenant David made with the northern tribes to submit to him as king (2 Sam. 5:3//1 Chron. 11:3) and the one Jehoiada made with the Carites to protect six-year-old Joash (2 Kings 11:4).[47] The following phrase confirms the transaction as an "obligation covenant." Joshua institutes "decrees and laws," a phrase that elsewhere suggests a hendiadys ("decree-and-law" as a single idea) summarizing a legally binding, standing policy (Ex. 15:25; 1 Sam 30:25; Ezra 7:10).[48] In short, the people take on themselves the "covenant" here enacted as a permanent, official, self-imposed public policy that Israel will serve Yahweh alone.

Two subsequent actions further confirm the covenant (v. 26). (1) Joshua writes down "these things"—"for the record," so to speak—in (lit.) "a book of God's instruction."[49] Apparently, this was a special document penned by Joshua here and separate from the Pentateuch (usually called "the law of Moses" or "the law of the LORD"). We know nothing further about this book since the term's only other appearance designates either a similar sacred

---

45. The object-first word order adds special rhetorical emphasis to the statement: *"The LORD our God we will serve, and him we will obey"* (my translation).

46. Nelson, *Joshua*, 268. As Howard rightly observes (*Joshua*, 440), the self-obligation also entailed obedience to the Instruction, the only explanation of *how* to serve Yahweh.

47. They share a common formula (lit., "X made a covenant for Y"), in which X imposes an obligation on Y, not on himself/herself or on Yahweh.

48. Alternatively, NIV's "decrees and laws" reads the Hebrew singulars as collective words; cf. H. Ringgren, "חֹק," *TDOT*, 5:143.

49. Cf. Howard, *Joshua*, 440. Presumably, "these things" comprise the words of the people's covenant-promise plus perhaps a detailed report of the entire ceremony.

writing or (more likely) the Pentateuch (Neh. 8:8, 18).[50] Its written form, of course, bespeaks its ongoing authority and accessibility for reading or consultation if needed.[51]

(2) Joshua erects a large stone under the oak tree at Shechem either "in" (NRSV) or "near" (NIV) "the holy place of the LORD," a reference either to the tabernacle (cf. Num. 19:20) or to space around the tree familiar to the readers as a sacred place.[52] The oak tree at Shechem had been a sacred landmark since the patriarchs. As noted above, it marked the first place in Canaan at which God appeared to Abram after his arrival (Gen. 12:6; cf. Deut. 11:30). It also may have been the site where Jacob later buried the foreign gods of his entourage (Gen. 35:4).[53]

The custom of raising a stone (or stone pile) to memorialize memorable events or people is well attested in the Old Testament, especially in Joshua. Joshua set up twelve stones in the Jordan's dry riverbed and at Gilgal to ensure that future generations remembered Israel's miraculous crossing (4:9, 20). Also, still-visible heaps of stones recalled the trouble Achan caused (7:26) and the execution of the king of Ai (8:29).[54] Jacob especially favored the custom, erecting a stone pillar at Bethel where God first appeared to him (Gen. 28:18, 22; 31:13; cf. 35:14) and a stone pile to attest his agreement with Laban (31:44−52).[55]

According to Joshua, the present stone pillar is to serve as a "witness" (*ʿedah*)—i.e., tangible evidence like a modern contract, sworn statement, or verbatim report—against him and the people concerning the transaction (v. 27; cf. Gen. 21:30; 31:52). The reason is that the stone, like any human witness, has "heard" Yahweh's speech (vv. 2−13)—metaphorically, of course—and, hence, amounts to a symbolic transcript of what he said that day. It offers irrefutable, unambiguous proof of Israel's pro-Yahweh choice.

---

50. The former would seem more likely, if the text distinguishes between the "Book of the Law of Moses" that Ezra read (Neh. 8:1−6) and the "Book of the Law of God" that the Levites used to instruct the people further (vv. 7−8; cf. v. 18). Alternatively, the book may have contained parts of ch. 24 or "something similar" (Hess, *Joshua*, 308).

51. Hess, *Joshua*, 308; Nelson, *Joshua*, 277.

52. The LXX lacks the MT's reference to the tabernacle. Hess (*Joshua*, 308) speculates that Israel kept the document at "the holy place" that v. 26 mentions as "part of a larger, older work."

53. Hess, *Joshua*, 309. For other landmark trees, see Judg. 4:5; 6:11, 19; 1 Sam. 10:3.

54. Cf. Hubbard, "Stones," 25−49.

55. Cf. also Moses' raising of twelve pillars at the foot of Mount Sinai to honor the covenant enacted there (Ex. 24:4), and Absalom's erection of a stone monument to perpetuate his memory (2 Sam. 18:18). For further discussion, cf. C. F. Graesser, "Standing Stones in Ancient Palestine," *Biblical Archaeologist Reader* 4 (Garden City: Doubleday, 1983), 293−321.

It protects against any future Israelite attempt to deny that fact by being "untrue to God" through apostasy (cf. Isa. 59:13; Jer. 5:12).[56] In short, the "book" and the "stone" guarantee indisputable condemnation should Israel seek to fudge, finagle a compromise, or worm out of their obligation.[57]

Finally, the narrator reports that Joshua dismisses the assembly, each participant returning "to his own inheritance" (v. 28; cf. Judg. 2:6). The conclusion leaves the impression that all is well with Israel: They possess the long-awaited promise of land, and their commitment to Yahweh stands firm. According to Judges 2:7, that commitment redounds to the glory of the leadership that Joshua and his generation provided. Later, the DH will show it did not last long.

THIS PASSAGE MARKS AN important leadership transition in Israel's history — indeed, the second of two great transitions that the generation gathered at Shechem had seen. The first was the long-anticipated leadership change from Moses to Joshua in the plains of Moab (cf. Deut. 34:5−9; Josh. 1:1−2). That change occasioned the crossing of the Jordan, the conquest of Canaan, and the settlement there under Joshua's two decades of leadership (Josh. 1:1). The second transition is the one soon to occur — Israel's transition to settled life in Canaan without either Joshua or a designated successor to convene similar assemblies at Shechem.

In my view, that imminent leadership vacuum forms part of the background of Joshua 24. Joshua apparently gathers the people in order to ensure their allegiance to the leader on whose behalf he led Israel during his tenure, Yahweh himself. With no designated human leader, Israel must now directly follow the guidance of God himself.[58] As with any leadership change, the issue for Israel concerns their unswerving loyalty to him — whether or not they will "serve" him.

Idolatry and polytheism. At the same time, the persistence of polytheism in Israel that this passage presupposes may surprise some readers. We usually think that Abraham introduced Israel to monotheism and that as a

---

56. M.A. Klopfenstein, "כָּחַשׁ pi.," *THAT*, 1:827; cf. Nelson, *Joshua*, 277 ("the stone as a reminder of Yahweh's saving deeds would accuse them").

57. Interestingly, the same oak and pillar apparently mark the site for Abimelech's ill-fated coronation as king (Judg. 9:6).

58. Cf. Hess, *Joshua*, 300, who regards the "representatives of the people" as Joshua's successor. In my view, Israel is to follow Yahweh's leadership by obeying the Instruction of Moses, so in a sense the latter also serves as Joshua's successor.

result, polytheism either died out or became a minority practice. But that assumption conflicts with the implication of Joshua's call that Israel throw away other gods that remain "in your midst" (v. 23). Apparently, many centuries after Abram, the practice of polytheism persists among God's covenant people. Israel's long relationship with God, including their personal experiences of his mighty power in action, have not weaned them from some connection with the gods of Mesopotamia, Egypt, and Canaan.

The Israelites have not followed the example of their ancestor, Jacob, who took the foreign gods that his household members had with them and buried them under the oak (Gen. 35:1 – 4). His actions mark the "first [biblical] instance of disposing of other gods" and make a statement concerning the importance of the matter.[59] They prepared his family for the altar-building and sacrifices at Bethel in honor of Yahweh, the God who had safely brought him back to Canaan as he had promised (Gen. 28). By persisting in idolatry, Israel also confirms Yahweh's word to Moses shortly before the latter's death (Deut. 31:14 – 22). Israel is encamped in the plains of Moab along the east bank of the Jordan River, the place from which they will soon launch their invasion of Canaan. Yahweh summons Moses and Joshua to meet him at the tabernacle (31:14), and there he informs Moses:

> You are going to rest with your fathers, and these people will soon prostitute themselves to the foreign gods of the land they are entering. They will forsake me and break the covenant I made with them. (31:16).

This is a startling statement given all that Israel has seen Yahweh do during the desert period. One would think that Israel's arrival at the Promised Land would solidify their commitment to him, but Yahweh tells Moses that that will not be the case. Their expected defection from Yahweh to worship "foreign gods" attests the continuing grip of polytheism on them. In fact, polytheism was the dominant form of religion in the ancient world, and that dominance persisted long after Israel entered its exclusive covenant with Yahweh (Ex. 24).[60]

These examples bring into sharp relief what really is at stake in Joshua 24. Put simply, Israel faces a decisive choice between irreconcilable options

---

59. Walton, *Genesis*, 631. These gods were probably brought by his household from Mesopotamia, but it is also possible that they were simply plunder taken by Jacob's sons during their sacking of Shechem (Gen. 34:27 – 29). The reason for also burying the earrings of his entourage is uncertain. The action may somehow relate to idolatry or, if the rings were plunder from Shechem, to impurity incurred through that violent episode.

60. For full discussion, see J. H. Walton, *Ancient Near Eastern Thought and the Old Testament* (Grand Rapids: Baker, 2006), 87 – 112; cf. also K. van der Toorn, "God (I)," *DDD*, 355.

with no safe "middle ground" in between. Israel must either continue to worship whatever gods they choose, or agree to Yahweh's "intolerant demand for exclusivity" (Reuter's term). Their ancestors may have added gods along their migrations like theological postcards kept to honor the places they had visited. But from now on it is either Yahweh or the highway. If they choose the "other gods" option, Yahweh will be gone, but to choose him means to throw the other gods away for good. Earlier Moses demanded the same decision of Israel encamped on the plains of Moab (Deut. 30:19 – 20). And centuries later Elijah would demand the same choice from wavering Israelites on Mount Carmel—either Yahweh or Baal, but not both (1 Kings 18:21).

Now, many readers will regard this point as obvious, but it bears underscoring as a bridge to our discussion below. Consideration of two other questions will also prepare us for that discussion. (1) What were these "other gods" like and how were they worshiped? Interestingly, they functioned not as individuals but as a group in Mesopotamia and at Ugarit (but not in Egypt). Just as the people of the ancient world found their own identity in community (rather than individualism), so they thought that the gods also found their identity in community—each god with tasks and roles.[61] The gods comprised the "assembly of the gods," the body that supervised the cosmos and decreed destinies both in the divine and human worlds. They competed with each other for power, with success or failure in such contests contingent on the success or failure of their human clients.

Further, as Walton observes, "the gods were viewed as having all of the same qualities, good and bad, as humans but without as many limitations."[62] They were presented anthropomorphically (i.e., in human terms), including sexual activity and procreation, and they also functioned within families. They experienced a humanlike existence: the full range of negative and positive human emotions, needs and desires, and daily routines (e.g., meals, sleeping, wake-up calls, jobs). Their temples constituted the geographical and geopolitical homebase from which they, like ancient kings, extended their influence to other territories. They operated within (not outside) the cosmos, each responsible for specific cosmic phenomena (e.g., the sun, moon, storms, fertility, etc.).[63]

The deity's image—the tangible sign of its presence—formed the center around which public ceremonial worship revolved. Through the image,

---

61. For what follows, cf. Walton, *Ancient Near Eastern Thought*, 92 – 111. The discussion concerns the state-sponsored religion as opposed to the worship of family and ancestral gods, e.g., the "God of your fathers" (Ex. 3:6).

62. Ibid., 103; cf. his full discussion (103 – 5).

63. Their specific divine attributes include justice, wisdom, goodness, faithfulness, and holiness; cf. ibid., 105 – 11.

devotees cared for the god's many needs in worship (and they had many needs). The god "was awakened in the morning, washed, clothed, fed two sumptuous meals each day (while music was played in its presence), and put to bed at night."[64] They received the deference and luxurious treatment fit for a king. Several beliefs underlie the rich care provided them by their human worshipers: the belief that the gods wielded more power than humans; that the gods were easily offended and subject to whimsy; that their anger brought all kinds of disasters; and that their anger needed appeasing.[65]

Their perceived ability to control frightening natural phenomena—thunderstorms, floods, agricultural plagues, extreme heat and extreme cold, sudden death, and so on—enhanced their reputations and retained worshipers. Baal's reputation as a storm god and dispenser of lightning probably led spectators on Mount Carmel to expect a dramatic display from Baal (1 Kings 18). The divine bent toward whimsy made people's relationship with the gods "a fragile symbiosis."[66] The deities offered humans protection and the prospect of success, but an accidental misstep by a devotee could cause divine desertion and leave the worshiper vulnerable to misfortunes.

Popular perception traced severe crises back to divine anger, so appropriate rituals—those commanded by the gods—sought from them the healing of deadly diseases or the defeat of dreadful enemies. No doubt, that is why King Ahaziah sent messengers to Ekron, a Philistine city, to ask Baal-Zebub whether or not the king would recover from his injuries (2 Kings 1). Further, the gods' possession of wisdom and knowledge distinguished them from humans and fostered human dependency on them. That is why the ancients, both public officials and private citizens, often sought their guidance on important decisions. No sense shooting in the dark when a knowledgeable god could reduce the risk!

In general, people thought that Mesopotamian gods had some human traits but also regarded them as superhuman. As van der Toorn remarks, "They surpass humans in size, beauty, knowledge, happiness, longevity—briefly: in all things that were positively valued."[67] In other words, they personified the ideals and perfections toward which their human worshipers also aspired, and so promised a possible resource for humans to improve their lot. At the same time, the national god and state-sponsored

64. Ibid., 136 (cf. the full discussion, 136–45).

65. Ibid., 136–42; Van der Toorn, "God (I)," 354.

66. For the phrase and discussion of the "whims of the gods" that drove ancient prayer and piety, see Walton, *Ancient Near Eastern Thought*, 138–49 (quote 144).

67. Van der Toorn, "God (I)," 357. For discussion of the role of ethics and morality in polytheism, see Walton, *Ancient Near Eastern Thought*, 149–61.

religion typically had little place in the day-by-day worship of the common people. They tended to rely more on family and ancestral gods than on the great gods, at times even asking the former to intercede with the latter.

Walton proposes a further plausible explanation for why Israel found the transition from the polytheism in which they grew up to the exclusive commitment to Yahweh difficult.[68] The priority in ancient Near Eastern religion was the maintenance of order in the cosmos and in human society. Satisfactory religious rituals upheld the former, acceptable ethical conduct sustained the latter, and together they earned the favor of the gods. Violations of cosmic or societal order earned the opposite — divine disfavor and dire punishments.

Absent from this system, however, is a theology of morality with its abstract notions of right and wrong, a theology rooted in the character of God rather than in the expectations of the cosmos and society. Through revelation from God, says Walton, Israel came to understand what God was like, what sin and guilt were, and the prime importance of imitating God's character in order to avoid both. In the process, an internal sense of right and wrong and also of "disinterested righteousness" (e.g., Job) came to shape Israel's conscience.[69] In short, the move from polytheism to Yahwism required divine revelation (the Instruction) to shape in Israel an internal ethical sense and to inform their conscience of Yahweh's expectations.

(2) The second question is: Since Joshua 24 only mentions "foreign gods" rather than specific names, who were some of these "gods"?[70] The god El is especially important since El typically comprises part of the names for God in the patriarchal narratives.[71] El is the proper name of a deity best known in texts from Ugarit, a Canaanite city (second millennium B.C.) along the present southern Lebanese coast. Those texts present him as "king" — that is, the senior-ranking member of the Ugaritic pantheon and, hence, the one with ultimate authority.[72] Ugaritic texts often call him "the benevolent, good-natured El" — probably a reflection of popular affection for him — and he is also known for his great wisdom, strength, and dignity.

---

68. Cf. Walton, *Ancient Near Eastern Thought*, 154–61.

69. Ibid., 154–55, 160 (quote 160).

70. In my view, Joshua 24 probably intentionally avoids naming names in order to include all possible divine candidates.

71. Exodus 6:3 says that the patriarchs knew God as El Shaddai (NIV "God Almighty"; cf. Gen. 17:1; 28:3; 35:11; 43:14; 48:3; 49:25), not Yahweh. Other early names include El-Olam ("Eternal God"; Gen. 21:33) and El-Elyon ("God Most High"; Gen. 14:18–22; Ps. 78:35).

72. For what follows, cf. W. Hermann, "El," *DDD*, 274–80. For more details, see F. M. Cross, "אל," *TDOT*, 1:242–61.

Some Israelite place names with the suffix *-el* (i.e., his name) still probably retained the ancient Canaanite name (e.g., Bethel ["El's house"], Carmel ["El's vineyard"], etc.).

A thorny question is whether or not the patriarchs actually worshiped El. The altar name El Elohe Israel (lit., "El, God of Israel"; Gen. 33:20) and the phrase (lit.) "El, God of your father" Gen. 46:3 [NIV "God, God of your father"]) might imply that, although we cannot be certain. If so, El may have been one of the "other gods" the patriarchs worshiped that Joshua summons the people to renounce (Josh. 24:2, 14, 23). Alternatively, once in Canaan, they may have borrowed local terminology (El) to name the God who revealed himself to them. At first, they may have associated him with the land but later came to identify him as Yahweh through his revelations (cf. Ex. 6:3).

Of course, the Bible's best-known "other god" is probably Baal, a god attested in lists as early as the third millennium B.C. and worshiped in Egypt, Ammon, and Syro-Palestine.[73] Biblical references to "the Baals" (e.g., Judg. 2:11; 1 Sam. 12:10) and "the names of the Baals" (Hos. 2:17) allude to his worship by various names and in widespread places.[74] Ugaritic texts frequently celebrate him as "victorious Baal" or "mightiest of the heroes," and another title ("Baal Zaphon") reflects popular belief that his palace stood on Mount Zaphon (northern Syria).

Baal is supremely a weather god—in Ugaritic texts the one presiding over clouds, storms, and lightning. He lifts a booming voice in thunderclaps and dispenses dew, rain, and snow. The son of the grain god Dagan, Baal is also a fertility god. He ensures the annual renewal of vegetation on earth by, first, descending to the underworld (i.e., vegetation decay) and, second, reviving in autumn (i.e., fresh vegetation). Finally, in his running battle with Yam (god of the sea), Baal is the god on whom seafarers depend for protection. In his conflict with Mot (god of death) Baal carries the epithet "healer" (cf. Baal Zebub in 2 Kings 1) and holds sway over the realm of death.

In short, Baal represents a major Canaanite god (he is often called "king") that offered practical help to ancient farmers, seafaring merchants, and the sick and dying. Thus, it is no surprise that Israelites apparently worshiped both Baal and Yahweh until the mid-ninth century B.C.[75] At that time, Ahab

---

73. For what follows, cf. W. Hermann, "Baal," *DDD*, 132–39; M. J. Mulder, "בַּעַל," *TDOT*, 2:181–200. Cf. also the in-depth study of M. S. Smith, *The Early History of God: Yahweh and the Other Deities in Ancient Israel*, 2nd ed. (BRS; Grand Rapids: Eerdmans, 2002), 65–91.

74. E.g., Baal Zephon (Ex. 14:2, 9); Baal of Peor (Num. 25:3); Baal Gad (Josh. 11:17); Kiriath Baal (Josh. 15:60); Baal Perazim (2 Sam. 5:20); et al.

75. Smith, *The Early History of God*, 43–47.

and Jezebel changed the royal policy in the northern kingdom to give Baal primacy, especially in the royal court. The Elijah-Elisha narratives reflect the prophetic reaction to that policy change. They attest the battle that begins between Baal and Yahweh over which god actually dispenses rain for agricultural fertility. Some scholars even suggest that the Elijah and Elisha protest mirrors a larger popular response, a "Yahweh-alone Movement," whose earliest written expression may be in the prophet Hosea.[76] If this is so, for more than two centuries, this movement promoted the exclusive worship of Yahweh as Israel's national God.

Other biblical texts strongly promote a Zero-Tolerance Policy toward idolatry. Early on, Moses forbids the Israelites from pursuing any relationship (not even "idol curiosity"!) with the gods of Canaan (Deut. 12:29−32). Specific Canaanite practices forbidden as "detestable" include child sacrifice, divination or sorcery, witchcraft, the interpretation of omens, the casting of spells, and communication with the dead by "a medium or spiritist" (Deut. 18:10−11). The DH blames the fall of the northern kingdom on the persistence of the "sin of Jeroboam"—his two golden calves and non-Levitical priesthood (1 Kings 12:28−30; 13:34; 2 Kings 17:22−23). In short, Yahweh sees idolatry as a detestable, intolerable insult to his lordship; as a result, when he returns his people from exile, he will simply leave idolaters behind (Isa. 42:17).

What about idolatry attracts people? (1) By nature people typically prefer the tangible and visible over the intangible and invisible. That is especially true of deities. Recall the child who, after bedtime prayers, asks her mother to stay until she falls asleep. When her mother assures her that God is right here with her, the child replies, "But I want somebody with skin."[77] When it comes to gods, people like ones that take on physical form to be located, seen, smelled, touched, carried, bowed down to, and served offerings "in person," as it were. People prefer gods with images. They perceive a greater sense of closeness to and connection with gods they can see than to ones they cannot.

(2) In my view, idols subtly (and perhaps deceptively) enhance the impression that the gods are subject to human influence. They assume that relationships with deities compare to relationships they enjoy with other

---

76. Smith (ibid., 65−79) theorizes about how the Ahab-Jezebel policy change played out. For the "Yahweh Alone Movement," cf. B. Lang, "Die Jahwe-allein-Bewegung," in *Der Einzige Gott: Die Geburt des biblischen Monotheismus*, ed. B. Lang (München: Kösel Verlag, 1981), 47−83; E. K. Holt, *Prophesying the Past: The Use of Israel's History in the Book of Hosea* (JSOTSup 194; Sheffield: Sheffield Academic Press, 1995), 113−15.

77. For further comments on the importance of God's presence, see the Contemporary Significance section of 8:30−35.

humans. Given a choice, most people would rather present an important request in person than through some intermediary (e.g., a representative, a written document, etc.). They assume that it is harder for a recipient to decline the request of a real, live person than one through an intermediary. The very presence of the person carries some, if not great, weight. Similarly, they may imagine that the same principle also governs prayer. Prayers done in person before an idol, they hope, are more likely to win the deity's response than ones done elsewhere.

The biblical critique against these assumptions pulls no punches. (1) Ancient peoples usually made idols out of wood, stone, silver, and gold (Deut. 29:17; Isa. 30:22). So, the prophet Habakkuk asks, "Of what value is an idol that someone has carved?" (Hab. 2:18a TNIV). The first point of critique argues that, if idols are man-made (as all are!), they have no more power than their human maker. They certainly have nothing approaching the power a *real* God has. If trouble ever comes, they are worthless because they can effect no rescue (Jer. 2:27−28).

(2) Several prophets point out the obvious as a second point of criticism: Idols are lifeless (Jer. 16:18; Hab. 2:19). They are carved or cast by some human, but their mortal creator cannot breathe life into them as God does into humans. Being lifeless, they also lack the basic capabilities typical of living things. Consider what one psalmist writes:

> Why do the nations say,
>   "Where is their God?"
> Our God is in heaven;
>   he does whatever pleases him.
> But their idols are silver and gold,
>   made by human hands.
> They have mouths, but cannot speak,
>   eyes, but they cannot see;
> they have ears, but cannot hear,
>   noses, but they cannot smell;
> they have hands, but cannot feel,
>   feet, but they cannot walk;
>   nor can they utter a sound with their throats.
> Those who make them will be like them,
>   and so will all who trust in them. (Ps. 115:2−7; cf. 135:15−18)

Idols, says the psalmist, "have ears, but cannot hear"—a big downside for people who pray! People expect their gods to hear what they have to say and to respond. Certainly, the psalmists expect that of Israel's God (Ps. 4:1; 17:6; 27:7; 55:2[3]; 86:1). A deaf idol is like a cell phone with a dead battery: The owner may speak into it loudly and with great passion, but not a syllable goes anywhere.

Further, idols have "eyes, but they cannot see"—an even worse divine deficit. Worshipers might tolerate a deaf idol as long as it could see or even recognize them. But, alas, the eyes of idols are simply artistic touches, not actual living organs of sight. The contrast to Yahweh is striking. His eyes "range throughout the earth to strengthen those whose hearts are fully committed to him" (2 Chron. 16:9). Yahweh not only *heard* the cry of the Israelites in Egypt but *saw* how the Egyptians were oppressing them (Ex. 3:9). He constantly watches the comings and goings of his people, never falling asleep (Ps. 121:3–4, 8).

Also, the psalmist points out that idols "have mouths, but cannot speak"—indeed, their throats can make no sound at all. This is a serious drawback for worshipers who expect to hear guidance from the gods in answer to their prayers (Hab. 2:19). It is a far cry from the many messages from Yahweh that the formula "Thus says the LORD" introduces. One sure thing about the God of the Bible—a feature certainly of Joshua 24—is that he *speaks!*

Idols also "have hands, but cannot feel, feet, but ... cannot walk." A worshiper may caress an idol's hands, but they feel nothing, and its lifeless feet can take it nowhere. Instead, as Jeremiah notes, a human has to secure it with hammer and nails so it does not jiggle or fall down, and it must be carried to go anywhere (Jer. 10:4–5; cf. Isa. 40:19). Yahweh, however, moves around freely on his own power. As Nahum says, "the clouds are the dust of his feet" as he roams about (Nah. 1:3).

(3) In short, idols are senseless, inanimate objects that create the impression of competence but that can in fact do nothing. Jeremiah compares them to a scarecrow in a melon patch (Jer. 10:5)—the illusion of a threatening person. The crow cannot distinguish a real human from a fake one and thus lives in a delusion, out of touch with reality. An idol operates similarly. It creates the illusion of grandeur and threatening power so worshipers treat it carefully. They live in fear of a lifeless, impotent object made of gold and silver and dressed in purple and blue (Jer. 10:9). They go to great lengths to placate it. But this is life in a crowlike delusion out of touch with reality. It is just plain lunacy, Jeremiah would say! "Do not fear them," he says, because "they can do no harm nor can they do any good." The implication is that idol worshipers are as crazy as crows. Or worse!

The delusion also blinds people to the true majesty and greatness of Yahweh. Unlike idols, the psalmist says, "our God is in heaven; he does whatever pleases him" (Ps. 115:2). Unlike the scarecrows, Jeremiah exults,

"No one is like you, O LORD; you are great, and your name is mighty in power" (Jer. 10:6). To this Habakkuk adds, "The LORD is in his holy temple; let all the earth be silent before him" (Hab. 2:20). These are statements by people who see clearly the glory of Israel's great and powerful God. One glimpse of what is really real—Yahweh's majesty and splendor—unmasks idolatry as foolish and futile. It also reveals idolatry for what it is—a terrible insult to God.

Recall the message Elijah gave King Ahaziah: "Is it because there is no God in Israel that you are sending men to consult Baal-Zebub, the god of Ekron?" (2 Kings 1:6; cf. vv. 3, 16). The question shames the king for turning his back on Yahweh, Israel's God, in favor of a god in a foreign country. Contrast that slight with the confession of the Syrian, Naaman, after his healing: "Now I know that there is no God in all the world except in Israel" (2 Kings 5:15). Which one is deluded and which sees reality clearly?

(4) Finally, idolatry renders its worshipers ritually unclean in Yahweh's eyes. According to Ezekiel, the making of idols defiles Israel, making her liable to divine judgment, including expulsion from the land (Ezek. 22:3–4; 33:25–29; cf. Deut. 4:25–28). Anyone who enters God's presence in a condition of ritual defilement puts his or her life at grave risk. The prophet's visionary experience in Ezekiel 8 suggests a metaphor that captures how offensive idolatry is to God. God's Spirit took Ezekiel from Babylon to the temple in Jerusalem, where he saw scenes of people practicing all kinds of idolatry. Now, the temple is Yahweh's house, and he generously hosts the worshipers as one might host human guests at home. But idolatry practiced in the temple compares to thoughtless guests who take over Yahweh's house without asking and banish him to a small part of it. They invite in all kinds of riff-raff and party days on end with their new-found "friends" at his expense and on his premises. Small wonder that Yahweh later announces that he will kick everyone out and abandon the house himself.

Now, this discussion of idolatry may strike some readers as overdone. They may feel a certain sense of superiority to the idolaters discussed above. But such a view is shortsighted, if not foolish. As we will see, forms of idolatry flourish today. In my view, those forms are just as much human creations as the objects of wood, stone, and precious metals in Israel's day. They also create the same illusion of power that deludes modern people into trusting in them. At first glance, they seem harmless and acceptable, simply cultural givens, but a closer look shows them to be close kin to the "other gods" Joshua called Israel to renounce. God's ancient Zero-Tolerance Policy concerning idolatry remains in effect.

THREE PRIMARY CONCERNS PREOCCUPY Joshua 24: to review Yahweh's mighty acts on Israel's behalf, the problem of other gods in Israel, and the demand that they renounce them and serve only Yahweh. The text's contemporary meaning revolves around the last two of those subjects framed as two questions: What (if any) false gods may tempt Christians today? And what does it mean for Christians to serve God today?[78]

What is a god? The great reformer Martin Luther once said that anything that one relies on and trusts in is a "god." Luther, of course, did not have in mind ways in which we exercise a normal, healthy trust or reliance on things. We rightly rely on and trust other people to advise, support, and help us with all kinds of things. We legitimately trust in a bank to guard the money we deposit there and in the school that our children attend to educate them well. We cannot live a normal life without relying on and trusting in institutions and people. Further, we properly value, lay out money, and devote time and energy to many worthy pursuits, some formal and others more casual, that no Christian would find offensive to God. Thus, the danger that Luther decried is that at times we rely on and trust institutions, people, and pursuits more than might be spiritually healthy. In his view, such times of unhealthy reliance amount to polytheism.

What makes something usually thought normal or healthy a "god"? It might be "god" if we willingly yield it excessive authority to direct our lives. For example, we may follow its advice or demands without even considering whether God has anything to say about the matter. It might be a "god" if it in any way plays a more significant, casual role in our lives than God does. That was what Israel did that so seriously offended Yahweh. They trusted other gods *instead of* Yahweh; they granted those deities a large role in their lives and ceded them authority over them rather than Yahweh. In short, the danger of polytheism is that we may be completely committed to the Lordship of Jesus Christ, yet still "rely on and trust in" other things with such a commitment and passion that makes them "other gods." We may "worship" (i.e., highly value) them, give them "offerings" (i.e., spend money on them), and "serve" them (i.e., devote time and energy).

Polytheism today. What (if any) false gods may tempt Christians today? In my view, the modern pantheon of "other gods" comprises a long list, but what follows suggests a few of the more popular "gods." (1) The *ideology of materialism* teaches that all human needs may be met by material means. It

---

78. For discussion of Yahweh's mighty acts, see Contemporary Significance of Joshua 23.

avers that happiness and satisfaction come through financial success, possession of material goods, and pleasure. "The more the merrier" states this
god's *torah* concerning money, possessions, and the good life. It promotes
leisure activities — travel, hobbies, recreation, sports, and the like — as spiritual retreats in its honor. The ideology of materialism is the consummate
televangelist. Its prime icon is the "media ad" aimed at convincing unbelievers to convert to consumerism. Chris Hedges has such media influence in
mind when he writes about our

> household gods, no longer made of clay, but all promising to fulfill
> us. Our computer, our television, our job, our wealth, our social sta-
> tus, along with the brands we wear and the cars we drive, promise us
> contentment and inform our identity. These household gods seem to
> offer well-being, health and success. But all these gods create cults.
> And all these cults circle back to us, to a dangerous self-worship fed
> by forces who seek to ensnare us in idolatry.[79]

Of course, there is nothing inherently wrong with owning a computer,
television, or nice car. I am writing this book on a computer; a TV set sits in
the other room, and a nice car is parked outside in the driveway! In my closet
hang clothes bearing brand names, and I enjoy a certain level of comparative
weath and social status. The problem arises when we really believe — and, I
mean, *really believe* — and act on the exaggerated claims that ads make about
the value and benefits of their products. They may create the same illusion
as the ancient gods did — that something material can satisfy people's basic
needs. They lead people to believe that they have the power that only God
has. I see three dangers in the view that this ideology propounds.

(a) Its claim to satisfy basic human needs promotes trust in a lie. At best,
material goods offer an escape or distraction from our worries, concerns,
fears, or pain. Like a ride at the amusement park, they help us temporarily
to forget them, but when the ride ends — they always do — the emptiness
returns. "Comfort food" may make us feel a little better, too, but it may also
leave behind the "discomfort" of an expanded waistline.

The song "Part of Your World" sung by the beautiful Ariel in *The Little
Mermaid* captures the emptiness of consumerism and the yearning for something more satisfying. Surveying her "stuff," she confesses a contradiction
in her life between appearance and reality. On the surface, she seems to be
the "girl who has ev'rything" — all the material things she could want — but

---

79. C. Hedges, *Losing Moses on the Freeway: The 10 Commandments in America* (New York:
Free Press, 2005), 41. I am grateful to my son and daughter-in-law, Matthew Hubbard and
Danielle Sandusky, for the gift of this interesting book.

she concedes that, at the end of the day, she in fact wants something more. "Stuff" or "activities" conveniently available simply cannot satisfy our basic human needs. Ariel eventually finds her satisfaction in love with a man, but I would argue that ultimately only Jesus can offer full satisfaction. Only he has the power truly to satisfy human longings.

(b) Finding our happiness-fix in things may reduce our dependence on God from total dependence to only partial dependence. We seek God to meet some needs, but also seek material pleasures and amusements to take care of others. Certainly, occasional enjoyment of fun things or interesting places is restorative in a healthy sense. The Bible is full of people feasting and celebrating and enjoying life's good things — but not every week, much less every day. The danger comes with unnatural dependence or addiction — when we need something or someone other than Jesus for a "fix"; I would compare this to polytheism. Spiritually, the god of materialism subtly aims to convert us to monotheism — to replace Jesus with hard goods as the true source of our comfort and well-being.

(c) Finally, undisciplined consumerism eats up financial resources that might otherwise be invested in the kingdom of God. A current facetious expression says, "You can tell the age of the boys by the price of the toys." But the harsh reality is that every dollar spent on something less than necessary ("toys") denies us the chance to invest it in the kingdom.

But how do we know when we have begun to worship the materialism god? In his book *The Agony of Affluence*, William Wells suggests a helpful standard by which to judge whether we have crossed that line into evil and idolatry. When career or the drive to accumulate adversely affects our relationship with our spouse, children, and local church, a mental red flag should wave. He writes:

> The Bible does not condemn the desire for worldly goods, but it does condemn perversions of that desire. Specifically, the Bible condemns desire that eclipses our love for God, our love for those around us, and our love for the weak and the poor. There are, therefore, limits on the pursuit of wealth. To transgress those limits is to be guilty of greed, covetousness, and oppression.[80]

(2) The close ally of the god of materialism is the *god of convenience*. Americans place a high value on convenience. The defining attributes of this god are omnipresence and omni-availability. No worshiper should have to travel any great distance to reach a sanctuary. And perish the thought that they should wait on this god because the nearest one is closed!

---

80. W. W. Wells, *The Agony of Affluence* (Grand Rapids: Zondervan, 1998), 72.

The prime icon of this god is the "convenience store," a local sanctuary where all manner of needs may be quickly met. Any telephone directory confirms the convenient ubiquity of stores belonging to the better-known "denominations." While they serve larger parishes than convenience stores, sanctuaries such as gas stations and supermarkets now offer services 24/7 in order to attract new believers and to increase the sanctuary's intake of offerings.

And lest the sanctuaries inconvenience any worshipers—for example, by requiring them to stand in line for service—many markets and gas stations now feature a special self-ministry option. Electronic, self-service altars permit worshipers to satisfy their needs without even consulting the clergy on duty. Above all, in a very impersonal world, the god of convenience makes people feel important or special. Its sanctuaries are open to serve *them*.

But why does "convenience" pose a spiritual problem? Certainly, there is nothing especially virtuous or spiritual about "*in*convenience." But worship of this god has three harmful side-effects. (a) It makes consumption more available and, hence, promotes the god of materialism. Its allure may lead believers to forget an important demand of Christian discipleship, the responsible stewardship of their God-given resources. Were the opportunities to buy less convenient, there would be less impulse-buying, more second thoughts given to it, and more resources left for kingdom use.

(b) It demands more of employees who staff places of convenience. Simply put, to remain open longer hours and more days requires staff to work them. Consider Christian employees whose employers are open on Sundays and ask them to work on the Lord's Day. In this case, the god of convenience may put the believers in a dilemma: They must choose between serving the convenience god on Sunday or risk unemployment by serving their own God.

(c) Also, consider employees whose employer is open evenings and asks them to work those hours. To do so means to sacrifice the time when family and friends are most available and when many church activities occur. The priority of convenience makes the priority of relationships take a back seat.

(3) Greek mythology tells the sad fate of a handsome young man named Narcissus. A beautiful nymph named Echo fell in love with him, but his good looks drew enough admirers so he sent her away into the woods. Later, Narcissus tried to find her, but he refused her invitation to come where she was and left the forest. All alone in the woods, Echo prayed, "May he who loves no one love himself." Meanwhile, Narcissus had gone to find water and was kneeling over a lake. Staring into the water, he saw

his reflection and realized how beautiful he was. In essence, he fell in love with himself. Echo's prayer had hit its target, but Narcissus also became aware of how much pain his beauty had caused his female suitors. He dove into the lake and took his own life. Later, when nymphs sought to find his body, instead they found a beautiful flower at the spot. They named the flower Narcissus after him.[81] From this name comes the common term for excessive admiration for or preoccupation with oneself—narcissism.

The consort of the gods of convenience and materialism is the *god "Me!"* This god preaches narcissism, the belief that every individual can be the center of his or her own world. Each person can be a kind of incarnation of "Me!"—the sun around which the entire surrounding galaxy spins. "Me!" inflates people's sense of importance through a unique kind of meditation—self-absorption. Worshipers of "Me!" are always preoccupied with their own needs and wants, and "I Gotta Be Me" is their favorite hymn. (If this sounds vaguely like a two-year old or early teen, you are getting the idea!)

In his book *The Culture of Narcissism*, sociologist Christopher Lasch illumines the theology of "Me!," the god of self-preoccupation.[82] Lasch argues that modern American society is self-absorbed (but not self-aware), greedy, and frivolous. Consumerism thoroughly dominates it, and its self-definition or identity depends completely on demographic analyses, opinion polls, and government policy. According to Lasch, you know you are a narcissist if you . . .

- are haunted by anxiety rather than guilt
- are seeking meaning in life
- are fiercely competitive for approval and acclaim but distrustful of competition
- secretly believe that normal rules and regulations do not apply to you
- give little thought to making provisions for the future
- love to acquire "stuff"
- find in "stuff" a sense of immediate gratification
- feel restless, your desires always unsatisfied[83]

The god of materialism says, "You *need* this," but the god "Me!" preaches, "You *deserve* this." The appeal is to the human ego and its deep desire "to be somebody." Like Narcissus, we love to look at ourselves—or better, to be seen as important by others. We have long honed clever ways to project

---

81. E. Hamilton, *Mythology* (Boston: Little, Brown, & Company, 1998), 113–15.

82. C. Lasch, *Culture of Narcissism: American Life in an Age of Diminished Expectations* (New York: Norton, 1979).

83. This list is my own, a distillation of the "new narcissist" described in Lasch, ibid., xvi.

importance. Name-dropping is one means ("Why, just this morning I was talking with [here fill in some VIP or celebrity name] ..."). Other strategies are to drive the right cars, wear the right clothes, attend the right meetings, and sit next to the right people. Worshipers of "Me!" need constantly to gratify their craving for importance. To do so, however, is to indulge in what Hedges calls "a dangerous self-worship fed by forces who seek to ensnare us in idolatry."[84]

The delusion of "Me!" is that our sense of importance depends on external things, not on who we really are inside. It draws on what other people think about us, not on what we think about ourselves. More important, while "Me!" welcomes the ego-stroking of others, it tends to shove the friendship of a loving God to the side. God requires the renunciation of the ego and its craving for importance and offers a transformation that changes us inside out. Only that inner transformation makes us comfortable with our true self in Christ.

A recent episode of the comic strip "Opus" offers a mirror reflecting something of ourselves. One night Opus the penguin and two young friends are staring up at the stars. Beside them stands another friend, the bespectacled African-American boy-genius Oliver Wendell Jones, peering through a telescope into space. "I love these summer evening reality checks from Oliver," Opus tells his two companions. Oliver opens the session by holding up to his rapt audience something tiny between his thumb and forefinger.

> "Hold out a speck of sand at arm's length," he says. "That's the portion of the night sky at which they pointed the Hubble telescope for a week. It was there—deep within that dot of dark nothingness ten billion light years distant—that they found the unexpected. All in the space of a single grain of sand on the vast beach of the cosmos," he says, pointing his three rapt listeners skyward.
>
> "Which nicely frames the question man has been asking for millennia," he adds, looking directly at the three.
>
> "What question?" one of them asks.
>
> Gazing quietly off into space, he answers, "What's the center of it all?"
>
> Immediately and simultaneously, two of them think to themselves, "Me."
>
> "Me, baby," Opus himself thinks contentedly.[85]

---

84. Hedges, *Losing Moses on the Freeway*, 41.

85. Berkeley Breathed, "Opus," *Chicago Tribune Comics*, Sunday August 5, 2007, Section 9, p. 2.

Opus and his friends are definitely devotees of the god "Me!" And they are not alone. Indeed, the god "Me!" may be the hardest for people to renounce in order to submit to Jesus as Lord.

(4) The final god in today's pantheon is the *god of nationalism*. The inclusion of this god on my list may come as a surprise, especially to readers who live in modern, Western democracies. But history shows that the influence of governments on their Christian citizens is often subtle and almost imperceptible—and not always healthy. This oft-overlooked god takes on as many forms as there are nations that demand loyalty from their peoples. By nationalism I mean the claims of a nation to being uniquely great and especially virtuous—that is, godlike—and hence to feel justified in demanding the unswerving loyalty of its people.

A successful nation may even come to think of itself so highly that it demands that other nations submit to its wishes because of that presumed greatness and virtue. It may even invoke religion or the Bible to support its claims. The loyalty sought from citizens is often called *patriotism*—a special pride in, love for, and devotion to one's own country. Now, nationalism or patriotism is different from what one might call "national, patriotic pride"—a healthy respect and affection for the history and cultural achievements of one's home country. That is a good, commendable spirit; it often produces united efforts in pursuit of the common good of people. Christians should always strive to be good citizens; they should support worthy causes and promote the common good of their fellow citizens.

The god nationalism emerges, however, when normal pride in one's country feeds a feeling of superiority that may lead a nation and its people, even from pure motives, to pressure other nations to do what it wants. Sometimes nationalism blurs the line between genuinely Christian virtues (what God expects of them) and genuinely patriotic ones (what their country expects of them). In reality, the two sets of values are not always the same; they often collide.[86] In times of crisis, a groundswell of popular pressure may urge citizens, including Christians, to rally in loyal support of some national policy. For believers, the danger is that such pressure may lead them to go along with the crowd and bypass the key step they normally take—to seek what the Bible says about things. At that moment, the nation has become a god—a competitor of the God of the Bible—because God's wishes for the world are probably different from the plans of any nation or world leader.

---

86. These and related issues find extensive and perhaps provocative treatment in G. A. Boyd, *The Myth of a Christian Nation* (Grand Rapids: Zondervan, 2005); S. Hauerwas, *After Christendom?* (Nashville: Abingdon, 1991); S. Hauerwas and W. H. Willimon, *Resident Aliens: Life in the Christian Colony* (Nashville: Abingdon, 1989).

In fact, to assess one's country from the Bible's perspective is always a necessary practice, whether in crisis or not. The priority of any nation is, after all, to look after its own interests, and those interests may or may not coincide with God's purposes for his larger world. The best way to avoid the sway of the god nationalism is to ask, Do my country's policies, lifestyle, values, and actions coincide or conflict with biblical teachings?

Joshua 24 demands that Christians today say "no" to other gods. So, even in today's humane, freedom-loving countries, it is worth taking what I might call "a reality check"—a review of what it means to be a Christian living as a citizen of our specific country. The crucial question for us is this: Does loyalty to a country, however biblical and noble its aims, compromise or detract from our exclusive commitment to the Lordship of Jesus? In this regard, missionary statesman Arthur Glasser states my standard of evaluation plainly: "There is but one acid test that should be applied to all activities that claim to represent obedience in mission. Do they or do they not produce disciples of Jesus Christ?"[87]

Put differently, if a nation achieves its political agenda, will more people have become Christians than would have otherwise? Will the kingdom of God and the gospel have been advanced or hindered? Throughout history, Christians have been tempted to help the gospel advance by allying themselves with political movements of all kinds, rather than through the power of the gospel message on its own. But here is a radical difference between genuine evangelism (sincere conversions of people by the Holy Spirit) and imperialism with a Christian veneer (conversions to a Christianized culture). In my view, to pair politics and evangelism is like being a polytheist—to rely on the power of Jesus as well as on the power of something (or someone) else. Paul is right: The gospel is "the power of God for the salvation of everyone who believes" (Rom. 1:16), not an alliance of various powers. Also, such ventures may ultimately end up harming God's work through us rather than advancing it. As Philip Yancey comments:

> A political movement by nature draws lines, makes distinctions, pronounces judgment; in contrast, Jesus' love cuts across lines, transcends distinctions, and dispenses grace. Regardless of the merits of a given issue—whether a pro-life lobby out of the Right or a peace-and-justice lobby out of the Left—political movements risk pulling onto themselves the mantle of power that smothers love. From Jesus I learn that, whatever activism I get involved in, it must

---

87. A. F. Glasser, "What Is 'Mission' Today? Two Views," in *Mission Trends No. 1*, ed. G. H. Anderson and T. F. Stransky (Grand Rapids: Eerdmans, 1974), 8.

not drive out love and humility, or otherwise I betray the kingdom of heaven.[88]

Joshua 24 calls us to renounce all other gods and to serve only Yahweh, and Jesus warns us that we cannot serve two masters (Matt. 6:24; Luke 16:13), one a god other than Jesus Christ. But to renounce our reliance on gods other than Jesus is one thing, to "serve him" as Joshua 24 commands is another. What follows explores what it means today to serve Jesus only.

Reclaiming our identity: to serve Christ. What does it mean to serve Christ? (1) The starting point, certainly, is to *affirm afresh Jesus' lordship* over our lives. Remember that we confess that "Jesus is Lord" (Rom. 10:9; 1 Cor. 12:3; cf. Heb. 13:15), a confession that not all people who believe in God make. Notice, first, that it is a confession specifically about Jesus, not God. Jesus (meaning essentially "Savior") is not a generic title but the personal name of the flesh-and-blood human person born in Bethlehem.[89] Observe, second, that the confession affirms Jesus as "Lord" (Gk. *kyrios*). The Greek term bespeaks his authority ("master, owner") and, more importantly, his divinity. In the LXX *kyrios* is the primary translation of the Hebrew Tetragrammaton *yhwh* ("Yahweh" or "the LORD"). Thus, to say that Jesus is *kyrios* is to identify him with the God of the Old Testament. The confession of Thomas ("My Lord [*ho kyrios*] and my God [*ho theos*]," John 20:28) makes the same identification. It applies to Jesus the language that the psalms use for Yahweh.[90] In short, Jesus is the personal name of the God-Man, the one to whom we surrender control over our lives as Master.

Let us be clear, also, that he differs radically from some popular images of God in American culture. He is not the vague, sentimental "Man Upstairs" or "the Good Lord," and "Somebody Bigger Than You and I" is not really a hymn about him. He is far, far more than the distant, impersonal "Nature's God" or "Divine Providence" of America's founding documents. This is clear from Scripture:

> For God so loved the world that he gave his one and only Son,
> that whoever believes in him shall not perish but have eternal life.
> For God did not send his Son into the world to condemn the world,
> but to save the world through him. Whoever believes in him is
> not condemned, but whoever does not believe stands condemned

---

88. Yancey, *The Jesus I Never Knew*, 245.

89. D. Zeller, "Jesus," *DDD*, 470, who observes that the name suggests "the concreteness of a historical person with a singular destiny."

90. D. Zeller, "Kyrios," *DDD*, 495. A related confession is to affirm that "Jesus Christ has come in the flesh" (1 John 4:2).

already because he has not believed in the name of God's one and only Son. (John 3:16–18)

He is God's one and only Son, and he did not come from heaven to earth on his own—God sent him. Jesus' mission was not to condemn the world but to save it. His unique role as Savior of the world implies that the world (and we) need saving—that it is not OK as it is. Divinely sent, his demands are absolute, not optional. One either believes in him or stands condemned. For us, the choice is simple: voluntarily to submit to him and verbally confess that "Jesus is Lord" now, or be compelled to do so at the end of history (Phil. 2:9–11; cf. Isa. 45:23). There is no escaping Jesus' divine-human nature and absolute lordship. To be truly Christian is to avow that "Jesus is Lord"—and no one else.

In his book *Everything You Always Wanted to Know about God (but Were Afraid to Ask)*, humorist Eric Metaxas clarifies the nature of the commitment that Jesus demands of us. It compares to the well-known song by Aretha Franklin in which a woman confronts her man with her sole demand to remain with him: "All I'm askin' is for a little respect when you come home (just a little bit) ... R-E-S-P-E-C-T, find out what it means to me." As Metaxas writes:

> If a guy is married and he tries to persuade his wife that he needs to have a few other women on the side, his wife will likely say, "Sorry, Romeo, but that's not going to fly. If you want to be married to me, you have to forego those other women. Period." It's just like that with God. He doesn't force us to pick him, but he does force us to choose between him and the others. We can't have both.[91]

The first step of service for Christ is to pay him R-E-S-P-E-C-T—to say "I have decided to follow Jesus—no turning back, no turning back."

(2) To serve Jesus also means to *do what he taught*. As Joshua obeyed the Instruction of Moses, so believers today are to do what Jesus taught. For example, he taught that "no one can serve two masters," especially "God and Money" (or the god of materialism). The reason is because each master has the right to demand exclusive devotion rather share their servants (Matt. 6:24; Luke 16:13). Jesus has no part-time servants. Certainly, Joshua understood that when he said that to serve the Lord was to "yield your hearts to the LORD" (24:23). "Yield" literally means "to turn, to guide" (*naṭab* hi.), and as I noted above, in Hebrew psychology the heart is the center of human thought, emotions, and will.

---

91. E. Metaxas, *Everything You Always Wanted to Know about God (but Were Afraid to Ask)* (Colorado Springs, Col.: WaterBrook, 2005), 139.

To "guide [one's] heart" toward Yahweh is to reorient one's whole self toward God and to let him call the shots. It means to dethrone the god "Me!" and to enthrone King Jesus in its place. Jesus also taught us to love fellow believers just like he loves us (John 13:34–35). The second of the two greatest commandments was "to love your neighbor as yourself" (Matt. 22:39; cf. Lev. 19:18; Gal. 5:14). Paul spread that attitude among early Christian churches, urging them to "be devoted to one another in love" and to "honor one another above yourselves (Rom. 12:10 TNIV; cf. 13:8; Gal. 5:13).[92] He encouraged early Christians to treat each other kindly, with humility and patience, freely cutting each other needed slack (Eph. 4:2). This is, of course, easier said than done, as this poetic quip admits:

> To live above with saints we love—
> Oh, that will be glory.
> To live below with saints we know—
> Well, that's another story.[93]

The Christians in Corinth certainly had trouble making it work. They had a competition going over who had been baptized by the more prestigious church leader (1 Cor. 1:12–13). Meanwhile, at Philippi two women had some sort of falling out (Phil. 4:2). Then there were those pesky promoters of circumcision setting the churches in Galatia at odds.

We are no different today. Jealousies and feuds occasionally flare up within church communities. It is not uncommon for fellow believers not to get along in other ways, or at least to regard each other warily. As someone once said, "The church is like Noah's ark. If it wasn't for the storm outside, you couldn't stand the smell inside." But Jesus' clear teaching—authoritative "Instruction" on par with that of Moses—is that we do more than just "get along." We must diligently transcend our dislikes, give each other the benefit of the doubt, treat others as if they were better than us, and maintain harmony and unity.

Further, Jesus commanded something that seems counterintuitive:

> Love your enemies, do good to those who hate you, bless those who curse you, pray for those who mistreat you. . . . If you love those who love you, what credit is that to you? Even "sinners" love those who love them. (Luke 6:27–28, 32)

---

92. This theme also dominates the first two letters of John (1 John 3:23; 4:7, 11–12; 2 John 5).

93. Slightly amended from R. A. Stedman, *Body Life* (Glendale, Calif: G/L Publications, 1977), 23.

Naturally, people react to enemies and abusers with outrage and a desire for revenge, and to friends and allies with affection and affiliation. But that is not the norm for Jesus' followers — and for one good reason. How they react to enemies measures the extent to which they remain "sinners" or have truly become "children" of their heavenly Father. Do they show his family traits — kindness and mercy to "the ungrateful and wicked" (Luke 6:35, 36) — and enhance his reputation? Do they resemble their Father in eschewing revenge or retaliation? If so, they demonstrate the inner transformation that Jesus offers and attract people to explore relationship with him. They prove themselves to be obedient followers of their Lord's example (cf. 1 Peter 2:21 – 23) and living proof that the kingdom wields incredible power.

On October 2, 2006 a milk deliveryman entered a one-room school-house for Amish children in rural Lancaster County, Pennsylvania. Heavily armed, he barricaded himself inside, apparently prepared for a long siege. By cell phone, he told his wife that he was seeking revenge for something that had happened twenty years earlier. Before state police could storm the building, the man killed five young girls and then took his own life. The tragedy devastated the tight-knit Amish community, a religious group known for its simple, rural lifestyle and pacifism.

But as the world watched, the story took two interesting twists. The first was the demonstration of forgiveness and compassion by the Amish toward the family of the man responsible. The grandfather of one of the victims went to the man's home to assure his wife that the Amish forgave him. The Amish community established a fund not only to help families of the victims but also the widow and children of the gunman. The second was the announcement by a pastor from the Midwest that he and his church would picket the girls' funerals, claiming that God had punished the Amish for alleged unorthodox beliefs. (Later, after a radio talk-show host offered him an hour of free air time, the pastor cancelled the demonstration.)

How strange the opposite reactions of two Christian groups to the same tragedy. Those devastated by it truly offered forgiveness to the offender's family. In my view, they obeyed Jesus while the church group sadly did not, ignoring Jesus' express command to extend mercy (Luke 6:37). But what about the rest of us who have not suffered so terribly?

My wife made an excellent point as we discussed the Amish tragedy. She pointed out that we rarely, if ever, pray for people with whom we disagree strongly — for example, public officials whom we oppose. She is right. I do not have enemies like the Roman soldiers who might have harassed Jesus and his disciples in biblical Palestine. But I do have enemies in one sense: Sometimes I have to deal with people with whom I strongly disagree. Convinced that I am right, I am tempted to feel myself smugly superior to them. Sadly, I confess I rarely pray for them, am quick to point out their faults, and am slow to extend them compassion. Subtly, I hate them and am disobedient to Jesus' commands. I do not show myself the true son of a merciful, forgiving heavenly Father. I am a poor imitation of Jesus Christ, the Lord whom I claim to serve.

Who are your enemies? Perhaps it is someone at work—perhaps your boss—who makes life tough for you. Perhaps it is someone competing with you for a promotion or pay raise. It may be a relative who quietly ridicules your commitment to Christ and his church. It may be a friend whose strong views on certain matters violently clash with your equally strong opposite views. It may be a cranky neighbor with whom it takes great effort to get along. If my experience is any guide, you may unconsciously feel a smug self-righteousness and superiority that (you think) exempts you from extending mercy or forgiveness. Unfortunately, Jesus does not let us off the hook on this one. I can hear his voice simply saying something like this (my own words):

> Someone slap you on the cheek? Give him the other one to hit. Someone steals your coat? Let her take your dress, too. Someone borrow something without returning it? Let it go. Forgive and forget. Not happy about that? Yes, I know. But you're a child of the heavenly Father. Just do it! Just like I did for you.

Finally, Jesus taught that the kingdom comes first (Matt. 6:24–34; cf. Luke 16:13). In his view, the kingdom is far more important that our typical, short-sighted preoccupation with houses, clothes, food, and drink. Jesus pointed out that pagans (and polytheists!) chase after such things, but we need not. Our heavenly Father faithfully feeds birds, beautifies fields with lilies, and clothes the ground with grass, so we need hardly fear destitution. He says, "Look, make kingdom work your first priority, and trust me for the rest." What is "kingdom work"? Jesus' own statement of his mission sums it up:

> The Spirit of the Lord is on me,
>   because he has anointed me
>   *to preach good news to the poor.*
> He has sent me *to proclaim freedom for the prisoners*
>   *and recovery of sight for the blind,*
> *to release the oppressed,*
>   *to proclaim the year of the Lord's favor.* (Luke 4:18–19, my italics).

We can recognize that kingdom work is being done by the evident anointing of God's Spirit on it and on those doing it. Kingdom work is present when God's people endeavor to make the lives of the poor better, to free prisoners wrongly held, to heal the blind, to seek the release of oppressed people, and to implement the equality provisions of the biblical year of Jubilee.[94] In short, kingdom work comprises the preaching and living out of a full-orbed understanding of the Gospel. It includes all efforts to get the word out about who Jesus is and his offer of salvation (cf. Rom. 1:9). It also includes all Christian efforts to counter societal values and priorities out of keeping with God's desires for his creation and his creatures. As James writes, what God regards as "pure and faultless" religious life is "to look after orphans and widows in their distress and to keep oneself from being polluted by the world" (James 1:27).

(3) To serve Jesus not only means to do what he taught but also to *do what he models.* Jesus' own life exemplifies the attitudes, priorities, and values he desires the Holy Spirit to cultivate in us. For example, in his message to the household of Cornelius, Peter remarked "how he [Jesus] went around doing good and healing all who were under the power of the devil ..." (Acts 10:38). He did so when, on the Sabbath, he healed the man with the withered hand—to the consternation of the Pharisees (Mark 3:4; Luke 6:9). He did so when he graciously accepted the expensive perfume a woman poured on him in Bethany—contrast the Pharisees' pious condemnation of the gesture as wasteful (Mark 14:3; John 12:3). He did so at Jericho when he answered the pained cry of blind Bartemaeus for healing (Mark 10:46–52). He did so near Tyre and Sidon when he healed the daughter of a Canaanite woman (Matt. 15:21–28).

In short, Jesus did a lot of good in the lives of ordinary people, and he blazes a trail for us to follow, too. There is a lot of good to be done today. There are hurting people in need of healing right in our neighborhoods or in our extended families. The list of possibilities is endless: kids that need tutoring, families barely making ends meet, lonely people needing friendship, and ignorant victims of oppression needing advocacy. The Hippocratic Oath to which physicians subscribe wisely counsels, "Do no harm." Jesus also wisely counsels us, "Do all kinds of good and dispense all kinds of healing."[95]

In his conversation with the woman at the well, Jesus exemplifies thinking outside the box for the sake of the gospel (John 4). First, he quietly breaks the mold of Jewish-Samaritan relations by simply asking a Samaritan (and a woman, too!) for a drink (v. 7). Normally, Jews would avoid travel

---

94. The "year of the Lord's favor" probably refers to the year of Jubilee (Lev. 25:10–24). For complete discussion of this Lukan text, see Evans, *Luke,* 70–71, 74–75.

95. For additional study of the theme of doing good, cf. Gal. 6:9–10; 1 Tim. 6:17–19; Heb. 10:24; 13:6; 1 Peter 2:11–17.

through Samaria, much less converse with a local woman of questionable morals. Jesus, by contrast, shows us that sometimes disciples must set aside personal scruples, religious traditions, and accepted norms for the gospel's sake. Sometimes they must cross from their comfort zones into dangerous territory in order to reach people there. Jesus also acknowledges the woman's checkered life but moves on to the key issue, whether she will believe in him as Messiah. Again, Jesus models a strategy of letting a person's sinful side speak for itself but not dwelling on it. Amazingly, from the conversation about living water a mini-revival breaks out among the Samaritans (vv. 39–42)—of all places!

In Vietnam, I once studied the military map of a helicopter pilot I met. With a grease pencil he had drawn boxes with crossed lines over certain places. In each box he had scribbled brief notations like "Beware: enemy turf" or "Avoid low altitude." They were his Samarias—dangerous places to be traversed with caution. All of us have Samarias and Samaritans on our mental maps of our own little world. They mark places or people thought "dangerous," "unpleasant," or "to be avoided." On some maps we label our own homes "off limits" to certain kinds of people we think undesirable or risky. A map identifies people I know whose chaotic lives threaten to consume my time or disrupt my routines. It blocks out places to avoid—nursing homes, AIDS clinics, hospital cancer wards, hospices, Muslim community centers, Mormon churches, certain ethnic neighborhoods.

Now, I am not arguing that we must go anywhere without concern for our safety or ordinary courtesy. I am suggesting that we expose our secret maps to the searching light of Jesus' example and the gospel mandate. I am asking that we face them and revise them, adopting a stance of openness to think outside the box. The worst thing would be to not go to places of great need because of personal scruples, religious traditions, or fear. Jesus came to messy old earth to filthy old us to bring us good news. How can we do less in return? To not do so is to worship the god "Me!" What Dr. Martin Luther King Jr. wrote in his famous "Letter from a Birmingham Jail" about the twentieth century church applies to the church in the present one:

> If today's church does not recapture the sacrificial spirit of the early church, it will lose its authenticity, forfeit the loyalty of millions, and be dismissed as an irrelevant social club with no meaning for the twentieth century.[96]

(4) Finally, to serve Jesus is to *share in his suffering*. This is the demanding side of being Jesus' disciple. It marks an extension of the theme of following

---

96. Oates, *Let the Trumpet Sound*, 221.

his example. By "suffering" I do not mean the hurts and pains that life's hard edges inflict on us. These are important, too, and Jesus certainly offers us healing and comfort for them. I refer specifically to the hurts and pains that result from our faithful obedience to Christ—difficulties we would avoid by holding back rather than stepping out in obedience. They comprise moments in which we pay a heavier than usual price simply for doing good in Jesus' name. In paying that price we follow Jesus' example and win God's commendation (1 Peter 2:20).

This is what Paul means when he embraces "the fellowship of sharing in [Christ's] suffering, becoming like him in his death" (Phil. 3:10). Far from being a shame or pity, Paul reckons suffering on behalf of Christ to be a special privilege on par with the gift of salvation (Phil. 1:29). Peter even calls Christians to rejoice over their participation in it (1 Peter 4:13). Early Christians experienced it through social ostracism and physical persecution. In 2 Corinthians 11:24–28 Paul tallied up the price he paid for serving Christ—truly an incredible inventory of physical, emotional, and spiritual hardships (cf. Acts 9:16).

Since most readers will not suffer outright persecution, in what ways may we share in Christ's sufferings? We participate in his sufferings every time we grieve over things that deeply moved him. At the tomb of Lazarus, Jesus wept both over the sad reality of human death and the hard reality of human unbelief (John 11:35). We share in that suffering when we comfort people grieving the loss of a loved one, especially an unbelieving one. At Jerusalem, Jesus bitterly lamented the city's rejection of his loving offer to protect its vulnerable citizens from the coming doom. We share that suffering every time someone spurns our gentle, genuine attempts to draw them to Christ. One reading used during communion at my church has this poignant line about Jesus: "For us he became poor, and knew the sadness in our days."[97]

To share Christ's suffering also is to share as he did in the world's great ongoing "sadness"—in the ordinary, everyday sufferings of a broken world. We share this sorrow when we cry with people who are physically and spiritually destitute. We share this grief when we stand with weak and confused friends helplessly trying to navigate huge, cold bureaucracies. We share this anguish when we grieve with people in places ravaged by floods, droughts, tornados, and mudslides. We share this suffering when we mourn with innocent people caught in the crossfire of political upheaval, social collapse, and bitter warfare. We share in Christ's suffering when we weep with parents whose children have been denied opportunity because

---

97. *The Covenant Hymnal: A Worshipbook* (Chicago: Covenant Publications, 1996), 943.

of prejudice. We share in his suffering when we agonize with families falling apart. We share in his suffering when we walk with people through the messes their own foolishness or stubbornness have created. To share in Christ's suffering is to live out in service his vision of his world.[98]

Conclusion. Joshua 24 has taken us a long way. It has challenged us to cast aside our modern false gods in favor of unwavering devotion to Jesus as Lord. It has sent us back to Jesus to hear afresh his words of command and again to glimpse him in action. At his ascension, Jesus left the work of his kingdom in the hands of his disciples, and they have passed it down to us (Acts 1:4–11). His final message was, "Once the Holy Spirit comes on you, go and be my witnesses everywhere." The "savior" called Joshua confronted Israel with a critical choice for their future (Josh. 24:15), and so does the "Savior" called Jesus. The question is, How will we respond?

In her book *Girl Meets God*, Lauren Winner tells a Talmudic story that suggests what a good response to Jesus' demand to serve him as our Lord might look like. The tale reports a conversation between Rabbi Yehoshua ben Levi and the prophet Elijah. The rabbi asks the prophet when the Messiah will come.

> "Go and ask the Messiah yourself," Elijah answers.
>
> "But where is he?" says the rabbi.
>
> "At the gate of Rome," answers Elijah.
>
> "How will I recognize him?" Rabbi Yehoshua asks.
>
> "He sits among the wretched ones with sores and wounds," Elijah says. "All the others uncover their wounds all at once and bind them up again all at once, but he uncovers and binds each one separately, for he thinks, 'Maybe I will be summoned today; I don't want to be detained.'"
>
> So the rabbi leaves Elijah, finds the Messiah, and greets him.
>
> "Peace be with you, Master and Teacher," he says.
>
> "Peace be with you," the Messiah responds.
>
> "When is the Master coming," the rabbi asks.
>
> "Today," says the Messiah.
>
> Disappointed and annoyed, Rabbi Yehoshua goes back to Elijah.
>
> "He lied to me," he tells the prophet. "He said he would come today, and he has not come."

---

98. For a hymn summarizing this vision I commend Bryan Jeffrey Leech's "Let Your Heart Be Broken," in *The Covenant Hymnal: A Worshipbook* (Chicago: Covenant Publications, 1996), 642.

But Elijah replies, "He meant 'today' if you would only listen to His voice."[99]

In essence, to serve Jesus is to "listen to His voice"—to shut out the voices of the other gods once and for all and to tune only to his. It means to obey what he taught and to pattern our lives after his model. It means daily to affirm "we will serve the LORD." It means to take to heart words often spoken in some congregations as a benediction at the end of morning worship: "So, reader, go from this place (or text) to love and serve the Lord."

99. L. F. Winner, *Girl Meets God* (Chapel Hill, N.C.: Algonquin, 2002), 295–96.

Joshua 24:29-33

A FTER THESE THINGS, Joshua son of Nun, the servant of the LORD, died at the age of a hundred and ten. ³⁰And they buried him in the land of his inheritance, at Timnath Serah in the hill country of Ephraim, north of Mount Gaash.

³¹Israel served the LORD throughout the lifetime of Joshua and of the elders who outlived him and who had experienced everything the LORD had done for Israel.

³²And Joseph's bones, which the Israelites had brought up from Egypt, were buried at Shechem in the tract of land that Jacob bought for a hundred pieces of silver from the sons of Hamor, the father of Shechem. This became the inheritance of Joseph's descendants.

³³And Eleazar son of Aaron died and was buried at Gibeah, which had been allotted to his son Phinehas in the hill country of Ephraim.

Original Meaning

THE EPIC STORY OF the book of Joshua has taken its namesake hero from a war camp east of the Jordan to the peaceful settlement of his fellow Israelites on their own lands. As it began "after" the death of the great Moses (1:1a), so it now ends "after these things," that is, sometime after the climactic covenant ceremony (vv. 1–28).[1] Two key words, "to die" (*mut*) and "to bury" (*qabar*), weave together three burial reports and sound the key themes of death and burial. Literarily, verses 29–33 compare to reports that signal the end of an important historical era (Gen. 35:28–29; Deut. 34:5). Within the DH they bring the curtain down on the era of conquest and settlement in Canaan and prepare the reader for the next phase (Judg. 2:10).

Two reports record the passing of Joshua and Eleazar, the two leaders who had guided Israel during the last two decades (vv. 29–30, 33). Their passing marks the end of the Exodus generation. The middle report features the fulfillment of a promise made at the death of Joseph that his bones be

---

1. "After these things" (Heb. ʾaḥarey haddebarim haʾelleh) typically signals an indefinite interval of time between events; cf. Gen 22:20; 48:1; 2 Chron. 31:21. Cf. our comments about the chronological relationship of Josh. 24:1–28 to its present context.

buried in the Promised Land (v. 32). His burial renders special honor to the hero responsible for Israel's survival and prosperity in Egypt during the centuries preceding the Exodus. His efforts kept Jacob's family from dying out from starvation in Canaan; without him, there would have been no Moses, no Joshua, and no Israel to fulfill the Abrahamic promise.

In remembering important gravesites, this short text compares to other Old Testament reports and reflects a common feature of Israel's religious life in Canaan.[2] By including the burial of Joseph, the book again thematically links the Exodus and settlement events, interpreting them as the bookends of a single grand plan (cf. 4:21–24). Each burial also links the deceased with his family's land, adding a sense of permanence to the theme of land inheritance.[3] Most important, the burial report of Joshua occasions a final authorial tribute to the great leader and, thus, draws to a fitting close one of the book's main themes—the effectiveness of Joshua's faithful leadership.[4]

Structurally, the verb that opens verse 31 ties it to the long preceding narrative of Joshua's life (i.e., 1:1–24:31), while the initial syntax in verses 32 and 33 marks those two reports as footnotes to the main storyline.[5] The book ends with the high priest Eleazar, thus bracketing 14:1–24:33 as a major structural subunit. The ending may also suggest that the narrator regards the high priestly line as the leadership thread responsible for Israel after Joshua's death. If so, that assumption probably rests on their key role as the teachers of Moses' Instruction (*torah*) and a cooperative relationship with the elders who survive Joshua. These possibilities would explain why neither Yahweh nor Joshua names some individual to lead the next generation.[6]

Joshua's death and burial (24:29–31). This small section reports the simple fact that "Joshua son of Nun ... died" (v. 29) and that "they buried him" (v. 30a). The Bible says nothing about Joshua having a wife or children, so the indefinite "they" probably refers to more distant relatives. Alternatively, it may designate a kind of "state funeral" at which all Israel

---

2. Nelson, *Joshua*, 279; Butler, *Joshua*, 282; cf. Gen. 35:8, 19–20; 1 Sam. 10:2; 2 Kings 13:20–21; 23:17–18.

3. Cf. Howard, *Joshua*, 442; Hawk, *Joshua*, 278–79.

4. Judg. 2:8–9 and 10b reprise this simple report of Joshua's death and burial verbatim, while Judg. 2:10b slightly rephrases Josh. 24:31a. Literarily, the repetition both links Joshua and Judges as part of a single narrative and delimits them as two subsections within it (cf. Howard, *Joshua*, 443; Hess, *Joshua*, 309–10).

5. Verse 31 opens with a verb of past narration, while verses 32 and 33 have, respectively, object-initial and subject-initial sentence structure.

6. Cf. Hess, *Joshua*, 311, who argues that Joshua's role was limited to his lifetime and that he never intended to appoint a successor. For discussion of the textual differences between MT and LXX, see Nelson, *Joshua*, 280–83; Howard, *Joshua*, 443.

publicly honored their heroic leader. The narrator carefully locates his final resting place "in the land [lit., border] of his inheritance." Specifically, Joshua's remains lie at the town of Timnath Serah just north of Mount Gaash (site unknown) in the hilly terrain of south central Ephraim.[7] At his request, the Israelites themselves had allotted him that land as the final act of the land distribution process (19:49–50). Joshua, thus, received a special inheritance portion in Ephraim just as his onetime spy partner, Caleb, did at Hebron (14:6–15).

Today a rock-hewn cave and half-oval stone just northwest of Ariel and near the Arab village of Kifl Hares purport to mark the gravesite of both Joshua and Caleb. Modern Israelis gather to pray at the spot on May 5, the date tradition assigns to Joshua's death. Besides recording the facts for posterity, the biblical report also lends the narrative the solemn formality and finality typical of burial reports.[8]

The contrast between Moses' unknown gravesite outside the land (Deut. 34:4–5) and Joshua's known gravesite inside it is striking. The difference highlights "the momentous changes in Israel's circumstances that Joshua has brought about."[9] Abraham had to buy from the Hittites a small burial site for Sarah (Gen. 23), and Jacob purchased the small land parcel on which his tent stood (Gen. 33:19; see below). But now the once-wandering, landless nation has land of their own in which to bury their dead and to live their lives.

A deft, subtle narrative touch also bestows on Joshua a telling posthumous award. His previous title had simply been "Moses' aide" (*mešaret mošeh;* Num. 11:28; Josh. 1:1), but here the writer honors him with the title "the servant of the LORD" (*ᶜebed yhwh*). This is the same posthumous title awarded Moses at his death (Deut. 34:5), and the honor shows the author's extremely high regard for Joshua. He and Moses are the only two leaders to ever receive the award.[10] As noted above, the remark also culminates the theme of Joshua's rise in popular stature as a worthy successor to Moses. To receive the same posthumous title ranks Joshua's eminence as on par with that of Moses—an incredible achievement indeed.

The writer also details that Joshua lived to be "a hundred and ten," the same age as Joseph but ten years younger than Moses (Gen. 50:26; Deut.

---

7. Nelson, *Joshua,* 279–80, suggests that Timnath Serah ("portion of surplus") represents an alteration of the site's original name, Timnath Heres ("portion of the sun"). If so, the change probably sought to remove the latter's pagan implication.

8. Cf. Gen 25:9–10 [Abraham]; 50:13 [Jacob]; Judg. 16:31 [Samson]; 2 Sam. 21:14 = 1 Chr. 10:12 [Saul].

9. Nelson, *Joshua,* 279.

10. Cf. Howard, *Joshua,* 443–44; Judg. 2:8; but cf. Ps. 18:1; 36:1 (David).

34:7). Finally, a brief narrative eulogy lauds Joshua for the fact that "Israel served the LORD" during his entire lifetime (v. 31). Through it the writer reasserts the connection made earlier in the chapter between Yahweh's acts and the demand to "serve" him (see comments on 24:1–28).[11] The comment further redounds to the glory of Joshua as a great leader.

To Joshua's credit also, Israel's faithful service continued under "the elders who outlived him and who had experienced everything the LORD had done for Israel" (i.e., the conquest and settlement; v. 31).[12] Indirectly, the comment also anticipates Israel's recurring disobedience in the post-Joshua era, the time of the judges.[13] As death takes the elders from the scene, memory of Yahweh's mighty deeds fade and Israel would lose one of its spiritual anchors. As noted above, neither God nor Joshua had named a successor, so the text may imply that the priests or elders succeeded Joshua in leadership. As I have noted elsewhere, the Instruction of Moses so prominent in the book may have filled that role (Josh. 1:7–8; 8:31, 34; 23:6; cf. 22:5). In any case, Joshua proves to be "the last of those foundational figures whose piety and significance are symbolized by extraordinary life spans."[14] With courage and conviction, he had lived up to Yahweh's opening demands (Josh. 1:7–8). He found Yahweh to be a keeper of promises: wherever he went, God had indeed been "with [him] as he was with Moses" (1:5; 3:7).[15]

The burial of Joseph (24:32). Above I mentioned that syntax sets this and the following report apart from the narrative flow of verses 29–31. Verse 32 details Israel's burial of the bones of Joseph, which the people had carried with them since leaving Egypt (v. 32; cf. Ex. 13:19). It bears no chronological indicator, but the incident probably took place earlier, when the tribes settled in their newly received land (21:43). The narrator purposely points out that Joseph's burial site was the very property outside Shechem that his father Jacob purchased from Hamor's sons (Gen. 33:19).[16] He even cites the original purchase price ("a hundred pieces of silver").

The explicit mention of both seller and price amounts to a kind of deed (cf. Gen. 23:15–16; 2 Sam. 24:24)—confirmation of land ownership

---

11. Hawk, *Joshua*, 279.

12. The phrase "everything the LORD had done for Israel" echoes Moses' review of God's marvelous deeds during the Exodus and in the wilderness (Deut. 11:7).

13. Nelson, *Joshua*, 279.

14. Nelson, *Joshua*, 279; Hess, *Joshua*, 310. In Nelson's view, Joshua's successful leadership also paves the way for the later influence—some good, some bad according to the DH—of Israel's kings.

15. Butler, *Joshua*, 284.

16. The reference to Hamor and sons repeats verbatim the same reference in Genesis 33:19.

through purchase.[17] In retrospect, the original land deal over a small parcel near Shechem proves to foreshadow Israel's possession of all of Canaan.[18] The safely settled Israelites fulfilled the promise of their ancestors to the man whose wise leadership had kept them alive in famine (Gen 50:24 – 25; cf. Heb 11:22).

The report's inclusion at the end of the book serves the narrator's thematic purposes, confirming, for example, the prior assignment of that terrain to the inheritance of Joseph's descendants (17:2, 7). Strikingly, through object-first word order the Hebrew throws the syntactical spotlight on the bones, not the burial. The generations between Jacob and the first settlers were buried either in Egypt or in the wilderness,[19] so to highlight the bones underscores their symbolic significance. They tangibly link the Israelite generation that realized the long-awaited promise of land with the patriarchal generations who first received it. The box of long-carried and now-buried bones tucked into the earth symbolizes the long epic journey from Genesis to Joshua. Implicitly, those bones echo the last sound of one of the book's central themes, God's fulfillment of his promise to the patriarchs.

The burial of Eleazar (24:33). Subject-first syntax sets this last report of death and burial apart from what precedes. It details the death and burial of Aaron's son, Eleazar, the high priest who presided (with Joshua and the elders) over the distribution of inheritance land among the Israelites (14:1; 17:4; 19:51; 21:1; 22:13, 31 – 32). The people buried him at (lit.) "the hill [*gib'at*] of Phinehas his son," apparently an Ephraimite town called "Gibeah of Phineas" to distinguish it from the better-known "Gibeah of Benjamin," the hometown of Saul (18:28; 1 Sam. 13:2, 14:16; cf. Judg. 19:14; 20:4).[20] As noted above, the work of priestly hands also evident earlier in the book may account for its inclusion here.

With Eleazar's burial, a generation of Israelite leadership — the two successors of Moses and Aaron, respectively — passes from the scene and the momentous book of Joshua ends. But even in death they share a piece of the inheritance allotted their family; they still reside in the warm bosom of their kin. The book remembers the enormous legacy they leave

---

17. Nelson, *Joshua*, 280. The traditional site of Joseph's tomb probably goes back at least to the early Byzantine period.

18. Hawk, *Joshua*, 279.

19. The notable exceptions, of course, are: Jacob, whom Joseph buried in the patriarchal gravesite near Hebron (Gen. 50:13); Caleb, presumably buried at Hebron (Josh. 15:13 – 14); Joshua; and Eleazar (v. 33).

20. There is also a Gibeah in the Judean hill country known only from a list of Judean cities and towns (Josh. 15:57).

behind—the conquest of Canaan and the assignment to the tribes of their precious inheritances.

For the narrator, the ending is not sad but satisfying. It provides an appropriate moment to draw one of the book's key themes to a close—the exemplary, successful leadership of Joshua (cf. 3:7; 4:14; 8:30–35; 10:14; 10:40–42; 11:22). More important, the burials mark the closing bookend of the long epic from a promise received in Genesis to a promise realized in Joshua.[21] Even gravesites celebrate the triumph of God's historic plan in the nation called Israel.

On the surface, the whole scene seems peaceful and serene compared to the earlier battles and Joshua's "grim admonitions" (chs. 6–12; 23).[22] But in reality a dark cloud of uncertainty now hangs ominously over Israel, a threatening portent of things soon to come.[23] The rest of the DH narrates the story of Israel's gradual, downward, spiritual spiral (Judges) that eventuates in the Babylonian exile (1–2 Kings). Eventually, of course, a new Joshua—also a "servant of Yahweh"—would come to fulfill God's plan for history and to inaugurate "a new kingdom unlimited by physical boundaries or human death."[24]

THE BRIDGE FROM THE burial reports to life today may seem difficult, but it starts with an understanding of the burial practices in ancient Israel.[25] Given the reality of physical decay that follows death, all cultures develop a way to dispose of the remains of their dead. Most also create ceremonial ways to honor them in doing so. Archaeological excavations in the ancient Near East commonly unearth a necropolis or cemetery area near cities, towns, or hamlets. Some, like the famous pyramids and rock-hewn tombs of ancient Egypt, attest the royal treatment that kings provided themselves in death, while others reveal the graves of less illustrious, mainly anonymous people across the social spectrum of

---

21. Cf. Hess, *Joshua*, 311.

22. I owe the expression to Hawk, *Joshua*, 279.

23. Cf. Howard, *Joshua*, 446 ("the calm before a great storm"). For more on ancient Israelite burials, see E. Bloch-Smith, *Judahite Burial Practices and Beliefs about the Dead* (JSOTSup 123; Sheffield: Sheffield Academic Press, 1992).

24. Butler, *Joshua*, 284.

25. Cf. K. Koch, "קָבַר," *TDOT*, 12:492–98; T. D. Alexander, "קָבַר," *NIDOTTE*, 3:865–68. For a recent study of the larger topic, beliefs about the afterlife, see K. Spronk, *Beatific Afterlife in Ancient Israel and in the Ancient Near East* (Neukirchen-Vluyn: Neukirchener Verlag, 1986); and B. Cripps, "Speaking on the Brink of Sheol: Form and Theology of Old Testament Death Narratives" (Ph.D. diss., the Southern Baptist Theological Seminary, 2007).

wealth and poverty, of obscurity and prominence. Surprisingly, the Bible's first recorded burial is Abraham's burial of Sarah near Hebron (Gen. 23:19), an incident recorded and remembered because of its great importance for Israel's history. It marks the first portion of the Promised Land owned by God's people.

What motivated burials in Israel? In the garden of Eden God told Adam that "dust you are and to dust you will return" (Gen. 3:19), the first biblical declaration that humans are mortal and destined for physical decay at death. It alludes to the fact that humans (*ha'adam*) are made from the ground (*ha'adamah*), but the comment seems more to declare a sad consequence of Adam and Eve's rebellion than to mandate that burials be done.

Instead, the association of corpses with ritual uncleanness apparently motivated Israel's practice of burial. The law declares those who touch them to be unclean for a week (Num. 19:11; cf. Hag. 2:13), a condition that prohibits their participation in Israel's public worship life. If they did, their presence would defile the sanctuary (v. 13; cf. Lev. 15:31) and render it temporarily unusable by everyone.[26] Unclean persons pose a pollution threat to the purity of the whole community since everything they touch becomes unclean until sunset on that day (Lev. 15:22). To restore the defiled to ritual purity, the law requires a week-long ritual process administered by someone in a state of ritual purity sprinkling specially prepared water. The procedure includes the ritual washing of the affected persons and their clothes (15:17–19). This is deadly serious business: Failure to remedy uncleanness results in the exclusion of the person from Israel's worship life. The risk they pose to the purity of the entire community must be dealt with (15:13, 20).

Archaeological evidence in Canaan shows that local terrain apparently dictated the specific mode of burial employed.[27] In major urban centers like Megiddo and Hazor remains were first placed in earthen jars and then interred in pits within the city limits. By contrast, in low-lying terrain along the coastal plain, burials in individual pits within a larger cemetery complex are the rule, a practice that presumes prior preparation of the site by gravediggers. Finally, in the central mountains and foothills, burial in caves predominates and for obvious reasons. Such tombs come ready-made, offer easy access to those living nearby, and can accommodate multiple burials.

---

26. H. Ringgren, "מָוֶת," *TDOT*, 5:333–34, 337. Israel also regarded graves as unclean places, especially those of the common people (2 Kings 23:6; Jer. 26:23).

27. G. Gilmour, "Foreign Burials in Late Bronze Age Palestine," *Near Eastern Archaeology* 65/2 (2002): 112–19. Cf. also R. Gonen, *Burial Patterns and Cultural Diversity in Late Bronze Age Canaan* (Winona Lake, Ind.: Eisenbrauns, 1992).

Since Timnath Serah, Joshua's final resting place, lay in the mountains of Ephraim, the Israelites probably buried him in such a cave. Certainly, modern Israeli pilgrims who occasionally visit the cave thought to be Joshua's gravesite assume so, although the Bible is silent on the matter.

The three burial reports share one feature that suggests another aspect of Israel's understanding of burial: Each locates the gravesite within the inheritance either of the individual or his tribe. Recall that in the Old Testament "inheritance" (Heb. *naḥalah*) is a technical word that designates land that Yahweh promised Israel, a promise whose final, happy fulfillment the book of Joshua narrates and in which every Israelite household shared (Josh. 13 – 19).[28] Ownership of family parcels was inalienable; the family was to own it in perpetuity down through the generations (Lev. 25:23). This rock-bottom principle explains the terrible punishment that Elijah decreed on Ahab and Jezebel for their malicious scheme to get the vineyard of Naboth (1 Kings 21). They not only unjustly took his life — in essence, murder — but they also violated his inheritance rights in disobedience of Moses' Instruction.

Joshua 24 takes pains to locate the burial of Joshua "in the land of his inheritance" (v. 30) and that of Joseph on land purchased by Jacob that came to belong to his descendants (v. 32). In place of tribal land, as a Levite Phinehas, Eleazar's son, receives a city and its pasturelands somewhere in the central mountains of Ephraim (Josh. 21:5, 20 – 22). Somewhere near there Israel also buried Eleazar.

More than mere geography may underlie the above three notices, however. As Alexander observes, "The existence of a family tomb appears to have indicated permanent ownership of the surrounding land."[29] In other words, a gravesite symbolically enhanced a family's claim to possession of property around it. This principle seems at work in the burial of Sarah by Abraham on land bought from Ephron the Hittite (Gen. 23). By selling the land for a burial place, the Hittites of Hebron apparently ceded its perpetual possession to Abraham and his descendants. If so, this may account for Jacob's insistence that his sons also bury him there: It reasserts his family's continuing ownership of the land and the rights of inheritance inherent in such ownership (Gen. 49:29, 31; 50:13).

In Genesis, that small parcel — at the time a mere toehold of possession in a vast land — thematically anticipated the full ownership that would fall to Israel when the divine promise came to realization. In the words of von Rad, "In death [the patriarchs] were heirs and no longer 'strangers.' A very

---

28. For details, see conveniently C. J. H. Wright, "נָחַל," *NIDOTTE*, 3:77 – 79.
29. Alexander, "קָבַר," 3:866.

small part of the Promised Land—the grave—belonged to them."[30] In short, the presence of ancestral graves apparently strengthened a family's claim to ownership of the land surrounding them. Potential claimants may have interpreted such land as "occupied" and, hence, already owned, as if by the dead themselves. Such a view would certainly have ensured continuity of possession even when the tragic vicissitudes of famine and war forced families to flee their ancestral lands for extended periods of time (cf. Ruth 1:1–2).

More important, several biblical comments suggest that Israel sensed a mystical connection between living and dead family members. The thought underlies the simple report about the Exodus in Joshua 24:6: "I [the LORD] brought your *ancestors* out of Egypt, and *you* [pl.] came to the sea ..." (my translation and italics). Now, only a few members of the audience in addition to Joshua and Caleb had experienced that event; their ancestors had all died in the wilderness, yet Yahweh says that "you came...." The statement implies that his audience somehow participated in that event—an indication of a mystical connection across generations living and dead.

In another example, Naomi wishes that Yahweh may treat her daughters-in-law, Ruth and Orpah, with the same "kindness" (Heb. *ḥesed*) they have shown toward the living and the dead (Ruth 1:8; cf. 2:20). The statement's precise sense defies firm definition, but it at least understands the dead as in some way recipients of the women's kindness as was Naomi. Similarly, Boaz underscores the twofold purpose for his redemption of the inheritance of Naomi's late husband, Elimelech: to "maintain the dead man's name on his inheritance" (4:5) and to prevent his being "cut off from his kindred and from the gate of his native place" (v. 10 NRSV). Again, the precise meaning is unclear, but these comments imply a continuing existence of the dead as well as a connection between the dead and their inheritance, surviving clan, and hometown.[31] Apparently, Israel thought that to have no heir possessing one's inheritance adversely affected the dead in some undefined way.

Similarly, in exile Nehemiah laments the ruins of Jerusalem, twice calling it "the city where my ancestors are buried" (Neh. 2:3, 5 NRSV). Interestingly, it is the connection of Jerusalem with those graves that drives his passion to rebuild the city, not a concern for the temple, as one might expect (v. 5).[32]

---

30. G. von Rad, *Genesis*, 2nd ed. (OTL; Philadelphia: Westminster, 1972), 250 (quoted from Koch, "קבר," 12:493).

31. Cf. Hubbard, *Ruth*, 244, 256–57; Num. 27:4.

32. Koch, "קבר," 12:494, who also observes a concern for royal ancestral graves in the Chronicler. For more on Israelite views of burial and ancestors, see K. van der Toorn, *Family Religion in Babylonia, Syria, and Israel* (Leiden: Brill, 1996), 48–52; H. C. Brichto, "Kin, Cult, Land and Afterlife—A Biblical Complex," *HUCA* 44 (1974): 1–52.

The above cultural background sheds light on the present case of Joseph's bones. Recall that Jacob chose burial with his ancestors (and wife, Leah), but Israel buried Joseph with his descendants. Since the latter had already received their inheritance, his burial implies less a concern for confirming inheritance rights than for a desire by his descendants to have him among them. The matter was of such importance to Joseph that he compelled his brothers to take an oath, promising to bring his bones from Egypt to Canaan with them. It was also of such importance to Moses that he took pains to execute the oath by bearing Joseph's bones with him as he left Egypt (Ex. 13:19). It was of such importance to Israel that they carried the bones through the forty-year wilderness wanderings and through the conquest of Canaan under Joshua. And it was of such importance to settled Israel that they ensured their burial within the tribal territory of Ephraim, Joseph's son.

In short, while a precise understanding of the details eludes us, the above texts suggest that Israel presumed an ongoing existence of the dead, in whatever form, that also connected them with their living family and their land. Indeed, the quality of existence they enjoyed in death seemed to depend on the quality of life enjoyed by their survivors.[33]

IN THE CLOSING ACT of *Our Town* by Thornton Wilder, the citizens of Grover's Corners, New Hampshire, huddle sadly under dripping umbrellas in the village's windswept, hilltop cemetery. They are there for the funeral of Emily Webb, who died in childbirth at age twenty-four. Nearby, unseen and unheard by the mourners, several of the dead stoically reminisce about familiar names on the markers and about happier times. Unexpectedly, Emily herself emerges from the mourners, an invisible attendee at her own funeral, and updates her mother-in-law, Mrs. Gibbs, on what she and her husband, George, have recently done to their farm. Suddenly, she pauses, looks directly at Mrs. Gibbs, and says: "Live people don't understand, do they?"

Her mother-in-law replies, "No, dear—not very much."[34]

---

33. The questions of Israel's view of the afterlife and whether Israel practiced or tolerated ancestral cults need not detain us. For this larger discussion, see P. S. Johnston, *Shades of Sheol: Death and Afterlife in the Old Testament* (Downers Grove, Ill.: InterVarsity, 2002); B. B. Schmidt, *Israel's Beneficent Dead: Ancestor Cult and Necromancy in Ancient Israelite Religion and Tradition* (Winona Lake, Ind.: Eisenbrauns, 1996).

34. Thorton Wilder, *Our Town. A Play in Three Acts* (New York: HarperCollins, 2003), 92–96.

This scene voices one major theme of *Our Town*, the transience of human life—how quickly time passes and how important it is to make the most of the present. The burial reports in Joshua 24, speaking in the context of death, likewise sound several key themes for us to understand today: the reality of death, the importance of having and being good models, and the power of the resurrection at work in us. Hebrews 12:1–3 provides a kind of a *midrash* on Joshua 24 to guide our study:[35]

> Therefore, since we are surrounded by such a great cloud of witnesses, let us throw off everything that hinders and the sin that so easily entangles, and let us run with perseverance the race marked out for us. Let us fix our eyes on Jesus, the author and perfecter of our faith, who for the joy set before him endured the cross, scorning its shame, and sat down at the right hand of the throne of God. Consider him who endured such opposition from sinful men, so that you will not grow weary and lose heart.

Death: face it! Death is a topic that most people avoid because, quite frankly, it comes too close to home. Death is, we think, something that happens to other people. Indeed, "denial" is how psychologists describe the prevalent modern attitude toward it. The only time one hears it discussed is either in academia (they discuss *everything*!) or at funerals, where its reality is inescapable. A well-known cemetery in California shows one ironic cultural attempt to keep the reality of death at a safe distance despite the tombstones everywhere. Its stately, manicured grounds incorporate museums of beautiful art and outdoor displays of classic statuary that actually intend to attract tourists. Someone once called it the "Disneyland of Death"—a place to go for fun at the expense of death.

Like the rest of the Bible, however, the three burial reports in Joshua 24 accept death as an inevitable reality, but they also suggest that death, though extremely saddening, does not divide the people of God. The text pictures the union of living and dead on ancestral land in Canaan, and Hebrews 12 also speaks of a similar mystical unity that binds Christians, living and dead. Both texts point us toward an often-overlooked Christian reality that trumps the reality of death, the unity that the Apostles' Creed calls "the communion of the saints."

Contextually, Hebrews 12 follows up the so-called "Hall of Faith" (Heb. 11), the lengthy retrospective on famous Old Testament characters of faith. The initial "therefore" signals that chapter 12 draws the implications of those exemplary lives for the lives of the readers, the "we" whom the writer

---

35. In Jewish tradition, a "midrash" is a commentary on a book of the Bible; cf. 2 Chron. 24:27.

addresses. The latter includes Christian readers in any generation; the Hebrews writer addresses "us," too.

Imagine the striking scene he surveys: an Olympic-like race course "marked out," a course apparently of great distance since it requires runners to run "with endurance" (my translation) and to abandon unneeded weight. But the startling insight concerns the spectators who "witness" the event; they comprise not a "crowd" lining the course but a "cloud" enveloping both course and runners.[36] They themselves are all former runners who know the course well, having completed it themselves. Also, they are completely nonpartisan: They cheer on *all* the runners, not just certain favorites.

At the end of the course, clearly visible to everyone, a solitary figure sits on the victor's throne of honor awaiting the racers' arrivals. During the grueling race, their eyes rivet on him, their hero and inspiration—the one in whose honor they devote themselves to run. The seated figure, of course, is Jesus, the greatest runner of all, conqueror of the cruelest race course ever run. To win the victory he endured jeering crowds and a shameful public crucifixion before rising again to occupy the honored victor's throne beside his heavenly Father.

This is the scene in which every Christian's life plays itself out today, much as Joshua, Joseph, and Eleazar did in theirs: We are all runners traversing a life course in honor of our Lord. But we are not alone: As Yahweh was with Joshua (Josh. 1:5; 3:7), so our beloved Lord Jesus is there watching us, as are all the ancient heroes who have finished their own races with great faith and endurance.

And they are not alone either. Elsewhere the New Testament informs us that another group—the "saints"—also comprises the witnessing crowd. "Saints" (*hoi hagioi*, lit., "the holy ones") is the New Testament's favorite term for Christian believers (e.g., Acts 9:13, 32; Rom. 8:27; 1 Cor. 14:33; Jude 3). The term implies that believers are "holy," meaning "set apart" for God alone (i.e., his elect people), and, unlike sinners, enjoy unique, ongoing, intimate access to him. That same access enabled Joshua to petition Yahweh for cosmic help at Gibeon (Josh. 10:12–14).[37] More important, the

---

36. Elsewhere, "witnesses" (*martyron*) designates those who give testimony in court. But as Ellingworth notes, "this sense is almost certainly excluded here, since the context requires the meaning of spectators in a stadium, watching an athletic contest"; cf. P. Ellingworth, *The Epistle to the Hebrews* (NIGTC; Grand Rapids: Eerdmans, 1993), 638; for an alternative view, see Hagner, *Hebrews*, 194–95.

37. Paul often addresses the recipients of his letters as "saints" (Rom. 1:7; 2 Cor. 1:1; Eph. 1:1; Phil. 1:1) and occasionally mediates exchanges of greetings between communities of "the saints" in different locales (2 Cor. 13:13; Phil. 4:21). In Revelation, John also addresses them in his appeals for perseverance in persecution (Rev. 13:10; 14:12).

term "saints" also includes Christians who have died and gone to be with Christ. Death does not disqualify them from the title "saints" or remove them from membership in the body of Christ.

On the contrary, they share in God's glorious inheritance along with living believers (Eph. 1:18; Col. 1:11–12) and are the "dead in Christ" who will accompany him at his return to earth (1 Thess. 3:13; 4:16; 2 Thess. 1:10). They are the martyrs whose firm faith in the face of death God will vindicate in future judgment on their executioners (Rev. 11:18–19; 16:5–6; 18:20, 24). Even in death they remain "in Christ" along with believers on earth. The Anglican Church's Christmas service of Nine Lessons and Carols rightly calls them

> those who rejoice with us, but upon another shore and in a greater light; that multitude which no man can number, whose hope was in the word made flesh, and with whom, in the Lord Jesus, we are one forevermore.

To speak more personally, these are Christians we know and love — dear family and close friends whose loss we grieve deeply and who now enjoy the very presence of our Lord Jesus. They comprise the so-called *church triumphant* — those who in death conquered death. We Christians on earth make up the *church militant* — those who still faithfully contend for the cause of Christ against oppression and injustice, against scoffing and ridicule, and in the face of ever-present temptations. It is that holy heavenly host of victorious runners that eagerly watches as we navigate our courses of discipleship in this life. In Christ we share a mysterious spiritual solidarity with all God's people, both living and dead. The body of Christ remains united.

Having a hero. Joshua 24 remembers Joshua, Joseph, and Eleazar as heroes of faith, much as Hebrews 11 does its list. What makes them all heroic is their perseverance over the long haul, an indispensable trait their lives commend to us. Life in Egypt was no picnic for Joseph — he certainly did not want to be there! But his faithfulness in hardship enabled Israel to survive famine, and his burial at Shechem rightly honors him.[38] Joshua similarly hung in with Yahweh through slavery in Egypt, the debacle in the wilderness, Israel's defeat at Ai I, and the long era of conquest and settlement.

Similarly, it is the endurance through the entire race course of life that gives the cheering crowd of witnesses in Hebrews 12 credibility. Their perseverance challenges us to do likewise, and their example inspires us,

---

38. Sadly, we know little of Eleazar's biography, but presumably his mention here has roots in the reality of his own long life of faith. Cf. conveniently, W. H. Propp, "Eleazar (Person)," *ABD*, 2:432–33.

too. At the same time, we should regard their heroism with a sober realism, lest we idolize them too highly and set for ourselves a standard impossible to meet. We need not think of them as super-Christians who achieved victory on their own. On the contrary, their races easily resemble ours: They sometimes strayed from the course marked out, stumbled, and fell. They sometimes sat down by the road in despair or shook angry, frustrated fists at God. (Remember Joshua's bitter lament in 7:6−9?) They sometimes lusted with relish or harbored cynical desires for cruel revenge. And they sometimes spoke words that hurt others or turned a deaf ear to pleas for mercy.

Like us, they gained the victory because God's grace worked to keep them persevering and because his mercy forgave all their sinful failures. Besides the trio in Joshua 24 stands Moses, who faithfully led Israel—but also grieved God enough to deny him entrance to Canaan. Among them stands David, who faithfully "served God's purpose in his generation" (Acts 10:36)—but also committed adultery and murder (2 Sam. 12). Among them stand people whom we know—fumbling, weak, proud, and self-deluded folks just like us for whom God's grace abounds.

But one clarification is necessary concerning the cloud of believers in Hebrews 12. According to the Bible they are merely encouraging witnesses, not advocates on our behalf. We need not venerate them, pray to them, or expect ongoing contacts or visitations. Nor can they intervene in our earthly affairs or in heaven with God on our behalf. Rather, in Christ we simply share, in the words of one hymn writer, "on earth ... union with God the Three in One // and mystic sweet communion with those whose rest is won." Instead, the Hebrews writer stresses that they are our inspiration for perseverance.

Jesus, however, is our supreme inspiration. His endurance of hateful opposition, the writer says, will help us "not grow weary and lose heart." We look to him, "the author and perfecter of our faith," and his example of perseverance driven by his unwavering focus on "the joy set before him." The demands of the Christian life are indeed often fatiguing and dispiriting, but the author suggests that moments of contemplation of Jesus will revive sagging spirits and renew flagging zeal.

At the same time, it is also beneficial to select an ordinary human hero—some lesser-known biblical character, revered family member, or famous Christian—whose devotion to Christ we highly admire and desire to emulate. Their exemplary life gives us a human model to follow, good human traits to cultivate in ourselves, and spiritual goals for which to aim. Each October around Halloween, the seminary where I teach celebrates "All Saints Day," a special chapel service to remember believers related to our extended community who have joined the church triumphant. The chapel displays pictures of loved ones warmly remembered by someone among our faculty, staff, and students. A prayer celebrating their lives and remaining influence invites those present to say aloud the names of "saints" for whom they have special gratitude.

The service marks a simple way to connect with the heavenly church and to draw encouragement from their victory over death for our ongoing race. To remember the saints is to grab hold afresh of Christ's triumph over death, as if to say, "I miss them, but what joy to know that in Christ we're still closely connected!" I personally find it deeply satisfying to say, "Mom," "Dad," "Uncle David," "Phil," or "Sid and Nicey"—a few of my own heroes.

The whole experience seems to leave two powerful after-effects. (1) It lifts my eyes above the all-too-frequent doldrums of preoccupation with that day's urgent demands so that I may see the race in eternal perspective. That helps me to sort out the really important from the less important. (2) My gratitude for them (and others) nudges me to live a life worthy of their memory, just as remembrance of our Lord Jesus does. So, who are your heroes of the faith? Besides Jesus and Joshua, to whom do you look for inspiration to persevere as you run your own course? Keep their memory before you at every turn in the long, difficult run.

Being a hero. Someone has said that most people spend their early years building up their resumé and their later years working on their obituary. As one passes the halfway point in life, it is, in fact, not uncommon for people to change their priorities from the pursuit of future success to the preparation of a legacy to leave behind. It finally dawns on them that they are soon to die and are running out of time if they want to leave one. They understand why Joshua in his old age summoned Israel twice to prepare them for the future (chs. 23, 24).

Having heroes also challenges us to be heroes to others watching us. By this I mean to live with an eye on leaving a legacy in the next generation—to prepare them for life with Christ after we are gone. Joshua 24:31 lauds Joshua for the fact that, during his lifetime, "Israel served the LORD," a legacy that also persisted during the years "of the elders who outlived him." He models what I am talking about. To be a hero would require us to make relationships with people a top priority—to follow the guiding principle that people are more important than anything else. But what would such a legacy look like? I suggest that a hero's life should center around several important themes.

(1) We would model *faithfulness* to God throughout our lifetime. Of course, such modeling does not require perfection. On the contrary, in my view, the evidence of occasional *imperfections*, if not failures—and

particularly how we handle them—enhances the impact our lives have on others. But the point is for our witnesses to see that we continue our walk with Jesus despite *all* that life may throw at us. It is crucial for them to see us persevere through adversity—unexpected unemployment, serious illness, great disappointment, severe loss, extreme fatigue.

(2) Another theme for our legacy would be *honesty and integrity*, both character traits in short supply these days. This means that we avoid underhanded or shady dealings of any kind. It means that we keep our word even when to do so may be inconvenient, undesirable, or costly. It also means that we treat people fairly, gently, and with low-key directness and transparency.

(3) A further theme would be a *reputation for doing good* for people. This, of course, was the reputation of Jesus (Acts 10:38) and also of the early Christian woman called Tabitha or Dorcas (Acts 9:36). The apostles often urged believers to make the doing of good a priority (Rom. 2:7; Gal. 6:9; Titus 2:7; 1 Peter 2:15). To do good is simply to treat people kindly, generously, and considerately. It means that we graciously give of our time, energy, and resources to help people in needs great and small. Also, doing good may require us, in a crisis or conflict, to stand up for what is right rather than to cave in to pragmatism. This means that when speaking, we always speak the truth, calling a spade a spade, albeit with gentleness. It also requires us to side with the weak against the strong, with the disadvantaged over the advantaged, and with the poor against the rich. In short, we model an appealing Christlikeness that represents Jesus well in our world and by example guides those watching us. Our tombstone epitaph would compare to that of the beloved, blind hymnwriter, Fanny Crosby (1820–1915): "She hath done what she could."[39]

Two clarifications need to be made here. (1) To qualify as a hero does not require one to do something heroic. A steady, consistent, and caring simple life will do, as a poignant scene in Anthony Trollope's novel *The Last Chronicle of Barset* illustrates. It offers a good summary of what it means to leave a legacy. The novelist narrates the burial of the Rev. Septimus Harding, a humble, relatively undistinguished clergyman associated with Trollope's fictional cathedral at Barchester. Although before his death no one would have said that Harding was popular,

> now that he was gone, men and women told each other how good he had been. They remembered the sweetness of his smile, and talked of

---

39. B. Ruffin, *Fanny Crosby* (Westwood, N.J.: Barbour, 1976), 240. Cf. E. L. Blumhofer, *Her Heart Can See: The Life and Hymns of Fanny J. Crosby* (Grand Rapids: Eerdmans, 2004).

loving little words which he had spoken to them, either years ago or the other day, for his words had always been loving.... And so they buried Mr. Septimus Harding, formerly Warden of Hiram's Hospital in the city of Barchester, of whom the chronicler may say that that city never knew a sweeter gentleman or a better Christian.[40]

(2) It is important to see our heroic efforts from God's perspective. Our ultimate goal—the motive that drives all the above heroic actions—is to honor God, to deepen our relationship with him, and to be used by him.

To pursue the traits of a hero is to please God, much as a child wants to make his or her parents proud. God highly values our honesty, kindness, generosity, and so on; they bring him great parental pleasure. To pursue the traits of a hero also serves to mirror the character traits of God himself so others may see him. Through us, God gives people brief glimpses of himself; that is one way that he draws people into relationship with himself. God uses people of godly character to bring the gospel and to advance the kingdom. As he valued and used the faithfulness of Joshua and Eleazar, so will he ours, too.

But such faithfulness is not an end in itself. Rather, the cultivation of godly character yields as its ultimate, lasting legacy a vibrant, wholesome relationship with God. For us it is not enough simply to follow the examples of biblical heroes, whatever their greatness. The lasting good that comes from that "following" is that, in so doing, we please and honor the God we love—that we enrich our relationship with him. As Joshua's example fostered the faithfulness of an Israelite generation, so will our example foster faithfulness among those who may regard us as a hero.

The resurrection shadow. The three burial reports that conclude Joshua demarcate the end of one era and the dawn of another. Similarly, the resurrection of Jesus marks the crucial turning point in human history. That event distinguishes Jesus—someone dead and powerfully resurrected—from his namesake, Joshua—someone dead and honorably remembered. Besides defeating death, our bitterest enemy, Jesus injects a new power—resurrection power—into our lives to strengthen us to finish the race. That power keeps us running even when we feel like quitting.

The hope of the resurrection also gives great comfort when we grieve our lost loved ones. For Christians it sets an upbeat tone quite different from the frustration that Emily Gibbs faces as *Our Town* closes. She accompanies her mother home, hoping to teach the living what only the dead know, but the two realms cannot meet. Her mother neither sees nor hears

40. A. Trollope, *The Last Chronicle of Barset* (London: Oxford Univ. Press, 1967 [1867]), 423–25.

her; the living simply do not "get it." So, in the end, she bids Grover's Corners goodbye and asks to return to the cemetery. At the last moment, she pauses and asks the stage manager, "Do any human beings ever realize life when they live it?—every, every minute?"

He replies, "No," but after a pause adds, "The saints and poets, maybe—they do some."[41]

Unlike Emily's living survivors, Christian saints realize the importance of living each moment for Christ. They understand that they are in a race—not a rat race, but a distance race demanding endurance. Their eyes seek inspiration from the face of the victor, Jesus Christ, who eagerly awaits their arrival. Granted, at any given moment some runners may find themselves exhausted and unable to continue because of wounds suffered or blows absorbed. Some may feel themselves barely staying in the race because age has sapped them of the strength they once had. Others may feel themselves hitting their stride, having just brought someone to faith in Christ or entered new depths of relationship with him or finally conquered some long-standing addiction.

Wherever one is on the course, the challenge of Joshua 24—indeed, of the book of Joshua as a whole—is to lift our eyes to Jesus who waits to award us the victor's crown and to present us the WDGFS Certificate ("Well Done, Good and Faithful Servant" [Matt. 25:21, 23]). The challenge today is to imagine the saints—our biblical and personal heroes—surrounding the course in spiritual solidarity with our faithful efforts. The task today is to feel the surge of resurrection power within us and to rededicate ourselves to continue the race, however slow our pace or unsteady our stride.

The race is on. The crowd of victorious saints watches and cheers. The victor's crown and the Savior's "Well done!" await us. Some of us are near the beginning, others somewhere along the course, and still others near its end. As we run, let us "fix our eyes on Jesus...." Imagine his smiling face animatedly beaming approval. Hear his voice shouting to us, "Keep your eyes on me—and keep going!"

---

41. Wilder, *Our Town*, 107–9 (quote, 109).

Scripture Index

32:7	92	1:18	272, 300, 518	6:26	27, 47, 288
32:18, 19	431	2:2–3	44, 376	6:27	55, 331
32:30	520	2:2, 3, 7	187	7:1	120, 502
32:35	317	2:9	53, 293, 424	7:2–3	113
32:44	26	2:10–11	191	7:2	363
32:49	424, 495	2:10	191, 361, 366	7:5	120
33	483, 527	2:14	53, 424	7:6–15	55
33:8	465	2:22	187	7:7	55
33:10	96	2:24	53, 187	7:10–15	76
33:11	340	3:1–4:15	489	7:10	76
33:27	290	3:2	84	7:11	120, 523
33:29	533	3:5	43, 198	7:12–13	55, 282
34	75	3:7	55, 75, 76, 331,	7:12	120, 191
34:4–5	592		593, 595, 601	7:13	120, 151
34:5–9	562	3:10	191, 362	7:15	120, 191, 523, 526
34:5	77, 590, 592	3:15	184	7:24	75
34:6	57	3:16	499	7:26	32
34:7	592, 593	3:17	75	8:1–29	252
34:8	77	4:1	76	8:1–2	253
34:9	26, 76	4:9	32	8:1	54, 76, 131, 300
34:10–12	296	4:10	46, 75, 202	8:2	363
Joshua		4:12	46, 75, 86, 202, 399	8:3	86, 187
				8:7	54
1:1–18	516	4:14	75, 595	8:8	198
1:1–9	26, 46, 201	4:15	76	8:9, 12	363
1:1–2	562	4:23–24	337	8:13	22
1:1	350, 562, 592	4:23	120, 501	8:18	76, 131, 297
1:2–9	340	4:24	338	8:26	22, 120, 198
1:2	53, 424	5:1–9	340	8:28–29	32
1:3	153	5:1	120, 191, 326	8:28	35, 198
1:4	53	5:2–9	260	8:30–35	40, 46, 100, 201, 202, 549, 595
1:5	55, 593, 601	5:6, 8	155	8:30–31	31
1:6	53, 272, 300, 423, 518	5:9	32, 76	8:31	75, 593
		5:10	159	8:33	55, 75, 84, 150, 245, 288, 453, 517
1:7–8	593	5:12	84, 496		
1:7	46, 159, 202, 272, 300, 518	5:13–15	55, 131	8:34	593
		5:13–14	23	8:35	75, 245, 288, 453
1:8	46, 202	6:2	54, 76, 86, 131, 231	9:1–2	44, 252
1:9	55, 272, 300, 518			9:1	84, 362
1:11	53, 184, 414, 423, 424	6:4	22, 35	9:3	363
		6:6	150	9:6	254
1:12–18	26, 159, 399, 482	6:16	54	9:9–10	225
		6:17	120	9:10	361, 366
1:13	31, 54	6:18	120, 335	9:14	113
1:14	187	6:19	47	9:15–21	487
1:15	54, 424	6:21	43, 120	9:15–20	262
1:16–18	482	6:23	113, 132, 335	9:15	487
1:17	46, 55, 202	6:25	32, 128, 132		

Subject Index

Subject Index

identity, 426–30; see
also the individual tribes
law, 82, 83, 90–91, 213,
246, 252–54, 256–57,
261, 262–63, 340,
425, 462, 483, 495,
527, 546, 560; Israel-
ite, 285; Mosaic, 60,
73, 75, 81, 88, 92,
158, 163, 193, 201,
225, 251, 270, 371,
378, 463, 464, 478,
482, 514, 519, 538,
548, 560, 561, 596;
Near Eastern 80, 425;
of asylum, 453, 462;
pharisaic, 105; Yah-
weh's 46, 90, 201, 202,
529
Lebanon, 27, 29, 73, 78,
277, 325, 326, 328,
333, 385; Valley of,
322, 331, 357, 361
Lebo Hamath, 324, 385
Levi (tribe), 386, 387,
398, 400, 402, 403,
416, 417, 425, 453; its
inheritance, 386, 387,
392, 398, 400, 402,
414, 450, 453, 454
Levite(s), 82, 145, 251,
258, 300; 387, 392,
403, 414, 429, 447,
448, 454, 466, 484,
495, 496, 568, 597;
as models, 469–70,
472–77, 525, 530;
background, 403–4,
417, 462–64; towns
and pastures, 24, 53,
59, 64, 69, 340, 387,
398, 401, 404, 447–49,
450, 454, 455–58,
469, 472, 550, 561; see
also church(es)
levitical cities, 365, 450,
453–58, 466, 473
Lewis, C. S., 343–44

Libnah, 280, 281, 301,
302, 303, 331, 358,
363, 389, 448, 456
liturgies (or readings),
171, 383–84
Lombardi, Vince, 94
*Lord of the Rings: The Return
of the King* (movie), 102
lot(s) (*goral*), 23, 24, 34,
58, 67, 80, 226–27,
243, 244, 387, 392–96,
399, 403, 412, 413,
415–21, 423, 447,
448, 455, 456, 457,
496, 497, 518
Luther, Martin, 214, 531,
572
Luz, 390, 393, 416

Maacathites, 400
Maccabees: First, 528;
Second, 93
Makkedah: cave of, 230,
280, 298, 302, 363;
city, 279, 280, 293,
298, 299, 301, 302,
303, 331, 358, 363,
389
Manasseh, 32, 387, 390,
396, 403, 404, 418,
428, 483, 484, 485
Manasseh, East, 24, 34,
73, 85, 95, 146, 159,
357, 361, 385, 386,
391, 392, 399–402,
410, 414, 447, 448,
449, 450, 453, 455,
457, 478, 479, 480,
481, 482, 483, 484,
485, 491, 494
Manasseh, West, 24, 34,
53, 57, 73, 340, 385,
391, 392, 402, 404,
404, 410–13, 418,
448, 449, 455, 457
Manasseh, King, 548
manna, 23, 70, 84,
176, 184, 205, 206,
495–96

Marron, Madon, 321, 323,
324, 325, 358, 362
Mary Magdelene, 345
Mary, 347, 378, 531
meditate (*hagah*), 73,
82–83, 101
Megiddo, 29, 30, 324,
358, 364, 365, 370,
391, 411, 412, 596
Merari, Merarite(s), 448,
449, 453, 454, 455,
457, 463
Merneptah Stele, 40, 42,
302
Merom: place, 321, 322,
323, 325, 326, 327,
328, 331, 412
Mesha Inscription,
198–99
Mesopotamia, Mesopo-
tamian, 70, 117, 196,
233, 547, 551; its gods,
554, 555, 562–66
Metaxas, Eric, 581
Midianites, 94, 400
mighty men, 86
Misrephoth Maim (place),
321, 328, 385
Moab, Moabites, Moabi-
tess, 46, 57, 122, 136,
138, 140, 198, 202,
264, 399, 499, 501,
527, 545, 552, 557
Moody, D. L., 531
Moses, 21, 22, 24, 25, 26,
31, 43, 46, 56, 57, 58,
59, 60, 67, 68, 73, 74,
75, 76, 77, 78, 79, 81,
82, 83, 85, 86, 87, 88,
89, 90, 92, 93, 94, 95,
96, 97, 98, 100, 101,
102, 112, 113, 121,
123, 127, 145, 146,
147, 149, 152, 159,
163, 166, 179, 186,
191, 194, 202, 206,
223, 224, 225, 234,
235, 251, 252, 253,

Author Index

Author Index

Hebrew Word Index

The index begins with *aleph* (ʾ) and *ayin* (ʿ), then follows the English alphabet, except for unique Hebrew letters, such as *het/he, sin/shin,* etc.

Hebrew Word Index

We want to hear from you. Please send your comments about this book to us in care of zreview@zondervan.com. Thank you.

ZONDERVAN.com/
AUTHORTRACKER
follow your favorite authors